THE PURITY OF KINGSHIP

DOCUMENTA ET MONUMENTA ORIENTIS ANTIQUI (DMOA)

STUDIES IN NEAR EASTERN ARCHAEOLOGY AND CIVILISATION

EDITED BY

P. M. M. G. AKKERMANS, C. H. J. DE GEUS, E. HAERINCK
TH. P. J. VAN DEN HOUT, M. STOL, D. VAN DER PLAS

VOLUME XXV

THE PURITY OF KINGSHIP

THE PURITY OF KINGSHIP

An Edition of CHT 569 *and Related Hittite Oracle Inquiries of Tutḫaliya* IV

BY

THEO VAN DEN HOUT

BRILL
LEIDEN · BOSTON · KÖLN
1998

This book is printed on acid-free paper.

Library of Congress Cataloging-in-Publication Data

Hout, Theo P. J. van den.
The purity of kingship : an edition of CHT 569 and related Hittite oracle inquiries of Tuthaliya IV / by Theo van den Hout.
p. cm. — (Documenta et monumenta Orientis antiqui, ISSN 0169-7943 ; v. 25)
Includes bibliographical references and index.
ISBN 9004109862 (cloth : alk. paper)
1. Hittite language—Texts. 2. Hittites—Kings and rulers--Religious aspects. 3. Oracles, Hittite. I. Title. II. Series.
P945.A2 1998
491'.998—dc21 98-22430
CIP

Deutsche Bibliothek – CIP-Einheitsaufnahme

Hout, Theo van den:
The purity of kingship : an edition of CTH 569 and related Hittite oracle inquiries of Tuthaliya IV./ by Theo van den Hout.
– Leiden ; Boston ; Köln : Brill, 1998
(Documenta et monumenta orientis antiqui ; Vol. 25)
ISBN 90-04-109862
NE: GT

ISSN 0169-7943
ISBN 90 04 10986 2

PRINTED IN THE NETHERLANDS

CONTENTS

PREFACE

"Il y a toujours eu des scandales dans le monde et les gazettes de l'Antiquité nous ont fait part de nombreux faits scabreux, dont les tablettes de Boghazkeui ont relatés quelques spécimens." With these 'spécimens' Alfred Boissier referred to the Hittite divinatory texts in his monograph on *Mantique Babylonienne et Mantique Hittite*.[1] Boissier thus early recognized the potential of such texts as a source for our reconstruction of Hittite history: "L'étude des pratiques divinatoires nous introduit dans les coulisses des ministères publics, dans les conciliabules de hauts dignitaires ecclésiastiques et militaires".[2] The feeling that oracle texts might thus preserve an unofficial but historically maybe more reliable version than the one we encounter in 'historical' texts, persists until today.[3] That this potential has nevertheless hardly ever been put into effect, has its reasons. The highly lapidary style of the oracle questions, the obscure terminology and the often poor state of preservation are not very inviting. By their very nature oracle recordings were not the sort of texts that were usually copied, so that one could regularly count on the help of duplicates. This ephemeral character also showed in the often low quality of clay and script as well as in the fact that the Hittites themselves may have dumped and destroyed many of the tablets after having stored them for maybe at the most two to three generations.[4] Finally, the irritated but also somewhat irritating and in fact unscholarly remarks of Ferdinand Sommer concerning this genre[5] will not have encouraged many students or scholars to devote themselves to these texts.

All the more admirable, therefore, are the efforts spent and results gained in this field of Hittite studies in recent decades. Special mention should be made of the invaluable work of Alfonso Archi in making available to us many of the texts[6], in clarifying to a large extent the different systems of divination[7] and thus enabling us to basically understand what is going on and to concentrate on the contents. One of the

[1] Paris 1935, 6.

[2] Ibid. 7.

[3] Cf. A. Ünal, THeth. 6, 12-13, and A. Archi, Ägypten-Vorderasien-Turfan 86.

[4] Cf. H.G. Güterbock, MDOG 72 (1933) 51-52, KBo XVIII, Inhaltsübersicht iii, and H. Otten, 30.CRRAI 185.

[5] Cf. the famous lines in KlF. 343 and, for instance, AU 275.

[6] See the volumes KUB XLIX, L and LII edited by Archi.

[7] See his seminal articles on cleromancy (KIN) in OA 13 (1974) 113-144, and on augury in SMEA 16 (1975) 119-180; see further his contributions in BBVO 1 (1982) 279-293, and Ägypten-Vorderasien-Turfan 85-90.

first and few exceptions in editing oracle texts for historical purposes is Ahmet Ünal's text edition of KUB XXII 70.[8] As a direct result of these works we may discern a growing tendency to use oracles as historical sources.[9] The present work is another such attempt to put and understand a major oracle inquiry in its proper historical setting.

The actual starting point for this text edition was footnote number seven in George C. Moore's 1981 article in the *Journal for Near Eastern Studies* on "^{GIŠ}TUKUL as 'Oracle Procedure' in Hittite Oracle Texts".[10] In this footnote he drew attention to CTH 569 which he proposed to expand and to retitle. Several Hittitologists including myself subsequently suggested various additions and modifications on Moore's proposal. During my work on KBo IV 10+ (CTH 106; ed. StBoT 38) and on a group of accession oracles[11] the texts in question gained more and more importance and I felt the need to evaluate the different proposals and to bring order into this CTH number which by then had become somewhat confused. The present edition is the result of that need. Apart from establishing which texts in my opinion belong to CTH 569 and which do not belong there and from giving an edition of the resulting text constitution, the main objectives of this book are to clarify the historical situation in which CTH 569 came into being, and to describe more in detail the various ways used by the Hittite chancellery to record oracle inquiries.

All this results in a completely renewed CTH 569 preserving the probably largest extant Hittite oracle inquiry (not including the texts presented here as having preceded CTH 569) after KUB V 1+ (CTH 561). Of an original number of six tablets having contained approximately some 1500 lines of text in all, almost 400 lines are more or less well preserved. Composed of fragments of the original comprehensive version as well as of several summaries these preserved lines allow us a fairly complete picture of the composition as a whole and thus enable us to use it as a source for Hittite history.

To many persons and institutions I am in various ways indebted. Most of the work on this book was carried out while working on a fellowship of the Royal Dutch Academy of Arts and Sciences (1993-1995). The Editors of the Chicago Hittite Dictionary, Profs. Harry Hoffner and Hans Güterbock twice (1994 and 1996) graciously allowed me the use of their files. On both occasions I enjoyed their warm hospitality as well as that of the Dictionary staff. Prof. Heinrich Otten of the Boğazköy-Archiv in Mainz kindly and generously supplied me with several unpublished

[8] THeth. 6 (1978).

[9] See, for instance, M. Hutter, AoF 18 (1991) 32-43, the work of Ph.H.J. Houwink ten Cate on CTH 568 in his contributions to FsGüterbock² 95-110, and FsOtten² 167-194, as well as his recent articles BiOr 51 (1994) 233-259, and AoF 23 (1996) 40-75, and my edition of KUB V 24+ in StBoT 38, 245-267 and the remarks ibid. 94-96, ZA 81 (1991) 274-300.

[10] JNES 40 (1981) 49-52.

[11] ZA 81 (1991), 274-300.

fragments. Dr. Silvin Košak and Dr. Silvia Alaura made available to me important information concerning findspots. Through its consecutive directors Dr. Evelyn Klengel-Brandt and Dr. Beate Salje as well as Prof. Horst Klengel the Vorderasiatische Museen in Berlin gave me the invaluable permission to see all the necessary photos and to reproduce some of them in this book. Mr. Ben van Gessel kindly let me use his collection of Hittite divine names before its publication. I also profited from the advice of Dr. Gary Beckman and Prof. Ali Dinçol. The Department of Humanities of the University of Amsterdam contributed to a grant which enabled me to travel to Chicago. Finally, I am grateful to Patricia Radder and Albert Hoffstädt of the Koninklijke Brill NV for the pleasant cooperation while this book was under way. I want to express my sincere feelings of gratitude to all these persons and institutions for their unrelenting help. A final and special word of thanks goes to my teachers Philo Houwink ten Cate and Erich Neu who both were so kind as to read an earlier draft of this book and through their comments and the interest they took in my work contributed in more than one way.

Theo van den Hout
February 1998.

ABBREVIATIONS

... /a, ... /b etc.	Inventory numbers of Boğazköy-tablets excavated 1931-1967
AA	Archäologischer Anzeiger, Berlin
AAA	Annals of Archaeology and Anthropology, Liverpool
ABoT	K. Balkan, *Ankara Arkeoloji Müzesinde Bulunan Boğazköy Tabletleri*, İstanbul 1948
ÄHK	see Edel, ÄHK
Ägypten-Vorderasien-Turfan	H. Klengel – W. Sundermann (edd.), *Ägypten-Vorderasien-Turfan. Probleme der Edition und Bearbeitung altorientalischer Handschriften*, Berlin 1991
AfO	Archiv für Orientforschung
AHw	W. von Soden, *Akkadisches Handwörterbuch*, Wiesbaden 1965-1981
AION	Annali dell'Istituto Universitario Orientale di Napoli, Napoli
AJA	American Journal of Archaeology, Bryn Mawr
Anatolia (Anadolu)	Revue annuelle d'archéologie de l'Université d'Ankara, Ankara
Anatolica	Anatolica. Annuaire International pour les Civilisations de l'Asie Antérieure. Institut historique et archéologique néerlandais à İstanbul, Leiden
Ancient Mesopotamia	see Oppenheim, Ancient Mesopotamia
ANET	J.B. Pritchard (ed.), *Ancient Near Eastern Texts Relating to the Old Testament*, Princeton 1969
AO	Der Alte Orient, Leipzig
AOAT	Alter Orient und Altes Testament; see Haas-Thiel, AOAT 31
AoF	Altorientalische Forschungen, Berlin
Archeologia dell'Inferno	see P. Xella
Arnaud, Emar VI	D. Arnaud, *Recherches au Pays d'Astata. Emar VI.1-3: Textes sumériens et accadiens*, Paris 1985-1986
AS	Assyriological Studies, Chicago
Aspetti	see Giorgieri-Mora, Aspetti
AT	D.J. Wiseman, *The Alalakh Tablets*, London 1953
AU	see Sommer, AU

Bauwerke	see Neve, Bauwerke
BBVO	Berliner Beiträge zum Vorderen Orient, Berlin
Beal	see THeth. 20
Beckman	see StBoT 29
Beran, BoHa 5	Th. Beran, *Die hethitische Glyptik von Boğazköy. I. Teil: Die Siegel und Siegelabdrükke der vor- und althethitischen Perioden und die Siegel der hethitischen Grosskönige*, Berlin 1967
Bin-Nun	see THeth. 5
BiOr	Bibliotheca Orientalis, Leiden
Bittel	see Boğ.
BMECCJ	Bulletin of the Middle Eastern Culture Center in Japan, Wiesbaden
Bo	Inventory numbers of Boğazköy tablets
Bo 68/... ff.	Inventory numbers of Boğazköy tablets excavated 1968ff.
Boğ.	K. Bittel, *Boğazköy I-VI. Funde aus den Grabungen*, Berlin 1935-1984
BoHa	Boğazköy-Ḫattuša. Ergebnisse der Ausgrabungen, Berlin; see Beran, BoHa 5
BoSt.	Boghazköi-Studien, Leipzig
BSL	Bulletin de la Société Linguistique de Paris, Paris
CAD	*The Assyrian Dictionary of the Oriental Institute of the University of Chicago*, Chicago
Catsanicos, Vocabulaire	J. Catsanicos, *Recherches sur le Vocabulaire de la Faute. Apports du Hittite à l'étude de la phraséologie indo-européenne*, Paris 1991
CHD	H.G. Güterbock - H.A. Hoffner (edd.), *The Hittite Dictionary of the Oriental Institute of the University of Chicago*, Chicago 1980ff.
ChS	Corpus der hurritischen Sprachdenkmäler, Roma
~ I/5	V. Haas - I. Wegner, *Die Rituale der Beschwörerinnen* ^{SAL}ŠU.GI, 1988
~ I/7	St. de Martino, *Die mantischen Texte*, 1992
CLL	see Melchert, CLL
Context	W.W. Hallo - K.L. Younger (edd.), *The Context of Scripture. Canonical Compositions from the Biblical World*, Leiden 1997
CRRAI	Compte rendu de la ... Rencontre Assyriologique Internationale
CTH	E. Laroche, *Catalogue des Textes Hittites*, Paris 1971
Edel, ÄHK	E. Edel, *Die ägyptisch-hethitische Korrespondenz aus Boghazköi in babylonischer und hethitischer Sprache, Band I: Umschriften und Über-*

	setzungen, Band II: Kommentar, Opladen 1994
Emar	see Arnaud, Emar VI
Eothen	Eothen. Collana di studi sulle civiltà dell' Oriente antico, Firenze
~ 1	see FsPugliese Carratelli
~ 7	M.-C. Trémouille, *^{d}Ḫebat. Une divinité syro-anatolienne*, 1997
Ertem, Flora	H. Ertem, *Boğazköy Metinlerine Göre Hititler Devri Anadolu'sunun Florası*, Ankara 1974
FHL	Fragments hittites du Louvre in *Mém. Atatürk* 73-107, Paris 1982
Flora	see Ertem, Flora
Forrer, Forsch.	E. Forrer, *Forschungen*, Berlin 1926-1929
FsAlp	E. Akurgal - H. Ertem - H. Otten - A. Süel (edd.), *Hittite and Other Anatolian and Near Eastern Studies in Honour of Sedat Alp*, Ankara 1992
FsDe Liagre Böhl	M.A. Beek et al. (edd.), *Symbolae Biblicae et Mesopotamicae F.M.Th. De Liagre Böhl Dedicatae*, Leiden 1973
FsGüterbock	K. Bittel et al. (edd.), *Anatolian Studies Presented to Hans Gustav Güterbock on the Occasion of his 65th Birthday*, İstanbul 1973
FsGüterbock^{2}	G.M. Beckman and H.A. Hoffner (edd.), *Kanišsuwar: A Tribute to Hans G. Güterbock on His Seventy-fifth Birthday May 27, 1983* (= AS 23), Chicago 1986
FsHallo	M. Cohen - D.C. Snell - D.B. Weisberg (edd.), *The Tablet and the Scroll. Near Eastern Studies in Honor of William W. Hallo*, Bethesda 1993
FsMeriggi^{2}	O. Carruba (ed.), *Studia Mediterranea Piero Meriggi dicata*, Pavia 1979
FsOtten^{2}	E. Neu, Chr. Rüster (edd.), *Documentum Asiae Minoris Antiquae. Festschrift für Heinrich Otten zum 75. Geburtstag*, Wiesbaden 1988
FsTÖzgüç	M.J. Mellink, E. Porada, T. Özgüç (edd.), *Anatolia and the Ancient Near East. Studies in Honor of Tahsin Özgüç*, Ankara 1989
FsPuhvel	D. Disterheft, M. Huld, J. Greppin (edd.), *Studies in Honor of Jaan Puhvel, Part One. Ancient Languages and Philology.* Journal of Indo-European Studies Monograph, No. 20, Washington 1997
FsPugliese Carratelli	F. Imparati (ed.), *Studi di storia e di filologia anatolica dedicati a Giovanni Pugliese Carratelli* (= Eothen 1), Firenze 1988
FsRix	G. Meiser et al. (edd.), *Indogermanica et*

	Italica. Festschrift für Helmut Rix zum 65. Geburtstag, Innsbruck 1993
Furniture	G. Herrmann (ed.), *The Furniture of Western Asia Ancient and Traditional*, Mainz 1996
Gesch.Syr.	see Klengel, Gesch.Syr.
van Gessel, OHP	B.H.L. van Gessel, *Onomasticon of the Hittite Pantheon, Part One and Two*, Leiden 1998
Giorgieri-Mora, Aspetti	M. Giorgieri - C. Mora, *Aspetti della Regalità Ittita nel XIII Secolo a.C.*, Como 1996
Götze, Ḫatt.	A. Götze, *Ḫattušiliš. Der Bericht über seine Thronbesteigung nebst den Paralleltexten*, Leipzig 1925
GsKronasser	E. Neu (ed.), *Investigationes Philologicae et Comparativae: Gedenkschrift für Heinz Kronasser*, Wiesbaden 1982
Güterbock	see CHD, SBo
Güterbock, – van den Hout, AS 24	H.G. Güterbock – Th.P.J. van den Hout, *The Hittite Instruction for the Royal Bodyguard* (= AS 24), Chicago 1991
Haas, GHR	V. Haas, *Geschichte der hethitischen Religion* (= HbOr I.Abt. Bd. 15), Leiden 1994
~, KN	~, *Der Kult von Nerik. Ein Beitrag zur hethitischen Religionsgeschichte*, Roma 1970
Haas-Thiel, AOAT 31	*Die Beschwörungsrituale der Allaituraḫ(ḫ)i und verwandte Texte*, Neukirchen-Vluyn 1978
Haas-Wegner	see ChS I/5
Haase, THR	*Texte zum hethitischen Recht: Eine Auswahl*, Wiesbaden 1984
Hagenbuchner	see THeth. 16
Ḫatt.	see Götze, Ḫatt.
Ḫattuša	see Neve, Ḫattuša
Hawkins, J.D.	see StBoT Bh. 3
Hazenbos, Diss.	J.J.M. Hazenbos, *The Organization of the Anatolian Local Cults During the 13th Century B.C. An appraisal of the Hittite cult inventories*, Amsterdam 1998
HbOr	Handbuch der Orientalistik, Leiden
HEG	J. Tischler, *Hethitisches etymologisches Glossar* (IBS), Innsbruck 1977ff.
Heinhold-Krahmer	see THeth. 8
Heth. Dienstanw.	see von Schuler, Heth. Dienstanw.
Hethitica	Hethitica, Louvain-la-Neuve 1972ff.
Hidden Futures	J.M. Bremer - Th.P.J. van den Hout - R. Peters, *Hidden Futures. Death and Immortality in Ancient Egypt, Anatolia, the Classical, Biblical and Arabic-Islamic World*, Amsterdam 1994

Hoffner	see CHD
van den Hout	see Güterbock-van den Hout, Hidden Futures and StBoT 38
HS	*Historische Sprachforschung (Historical Linguistics)*, Göttingen/Zürich
HT	Hittite Texts in the Cuneiform Character in the British Museum, London 1920
HTR	see Otten, HTR
(Das) Hurritische	see Neu, Das Hurritische
HW	J. Friedrich, *Hethitisches Wörterbuch*, Heidelberg 1952
HW 1., 2., 3.Erg.	~, *Hethitisches Wörterbuch 1.-3. Ergänzungsheft*, Heidelberg 1957-1966
HW^2	J. Friedrich - A. Kammenhuber, *Hethitisches Wörterbuch*, Heidelberg 1975ff.
Hymnes	see Lebrun, Hymnes
HZL	Chr. Rüster - E. Neu, *Hethitisches Zeichenlexikon. Inventar und Interpretation der Keilschriftzeichen aus den Boğazköy-Texten* (= *StBoT* Bh. 2), Wiesbaden 1989
IBoT	*Istanbul Arkeoloji Müzelerinde Bulunan Boğazköy Tabletleri* I-IV, İstanbul 1944, 1947, 1954, Ankara 1988
IF	Indogermanische Forschungen, Berlin-New York
JAOS	Journal of the American Oriental Society, New Haven
JCS	Journal of Cuneiform Studies, Baltimore
JNES	Journal of Near Eastern Studies, Chicago
Kammenhuber	see HW^2, THeth. 7
KBo	Keilschrifttexte aus Boghazköy, Berlin 1916ff.
Kellerman, Diss.	G. Kellerman, *Recherche sur les rituels de fondation hittites*, Paris 1980
Klengel, Gesch. Syr.	H. Klengel, *Die Geschichte Syriens im 2.Jahrtausend* I-III, Berlin 1965, 1969, 1970
~, Syria 3000 to 300 B.C.	~, *Syria. 3000 to 300 B.C. A Handbook of Political History*, Berlin 1992
KlF	Kleinasiatische Forschungen, Weimar 1930
Königssiegel der frühen Großreichszeit	see Otten, Königssiegel der frühen Großreichszeit
Košak	see StBoT 39, THeth. 10
KUB	Keilschrifturkunden aus Boghazköy, Berlin 1921ff.
Kühne	see StBoT 16
Kümmel	see StBoT 3
Kultobjekte	see Popko, Kultobjekte
Laroche, Rech.	E. Laroche, *Recherche sur les noms des dieux*

	hittites (= RHA VII/46), Paris 1959
Lebrun, Hymnes	R. Lebrun, *Hymnes et Prières Hittites*, Louvain-la-Neuve 1980
Linguistica	Linguistica, Ljubljana
Luv.	see Otten, Luv.
de Martino	see ChS I/7
MDOG	Mitteilungen der deutschen Orientgesellschaft, Berlin
Melchert, CLL	H.C. Melchert, *Cuneiform Luvian Lexicon*, Chapel Hill 1993
Mél.Mansel	*Mansel'e Armağan (Mélanges Mansel)*, Ankara 1974
del Monte, RGTC 6(/2)	G. del Monte - J. Tischler, *Répertoire Géographique des Textes Cunéiformes, Bd. 6* and *6/2: Die Orts- und Gewässernamen der hethitischen Texte*, Wiesbaden 1978 and 1992
Mora	see Giorgieri-Mora
Moyer, Diss.	J. Moyer, *The Concept of Ritual Purity among the Hittites,* Ann Arbor 1969
Natural Phenomena	D.J.W. Meijer (ed.), *Natural Phenomena. Their Meaning, Depiction and Description in the Ancient Near East*, Amsterdam/Oxford/ New York/Tokyo 1992
Neu, Das Hurritische	E. Neu, *Das Hurritische: Eine altorientalische Sprache in neuem Licht*, Mainz 1988
~,	see HZL, StBoT 5, 25, 32
Neufunden	see Otten, Neufunden
Neve, Bauwerke	P. Neve, *Büyükkale. Die Bauwerke. Grabungen 1954-1966*, Berlin 1982
~, Ḫattuša	~, *Ḫattuša – Stadt der Götter und Tempel. Neue Ausgrabungen in der Hauptstadt der Hethiter* (= Antike Welt, Sondernummer), Mainz 1992
OA	Oriens Antiquus, Roma
Oettinger, Stammbildung	N. Oettinger, *Die Stammbildung des hethitischen Verbums*, Nürnberg 1979
OLZ	Orientalistische Literaturzeitung, Berlin
Omentexte	see Riemschneider, Omentexte
Oppenheim, Ancient Mesopotamia	A.L. Oppenheim, *Ancient Mesopotamia. Portrait of a Dead Civilization*, Chicago 1964
Or.	Orientalia, Rom
Ortsadv.	see Zuntz, Ortsadv.
Ose, Sup.	F. Ose, *Supinum und Infinitiv im Hethitischen*, Leipzig 1944
Otten, HTR	H. Otten, *Hethitische Totenrituale*, Berlin 1958
~, Königssiegel der frühen Großreichszeit	~, *Die hethitischen Königssiegel der frühen Großreichszeit*, Mainz/Stuttgart 1995
~, Luv.	*Zur grammatikalischen und lexikalischen Bestim-*

	mung des Luvischen, Berlin 1953
~, Neufunden	~, *Zu einigen Neufunden hethitischer Königssiegel*, Mainz/Stuttgart 1993
~, Puduḫepa	~, *Puduḫepa. Eine hethitische Königin in ihren Textzeugnissen*, Mainz/Wiesbaden 1975
~	see StBoT 1, 16, 24
PIHANS	Publications de l'Institut historique-archéologique néerlandais de Stamboul, Leiden
Popko, Kultobjekte	M. Popko, *Kultobjekte in der hethitischen Religion (nach keilschriftlichen Quellen)*, Warsaw 1978
~, Religions	~, *Religions of Asia Minor*, Warsaw 1995
Puduḫepa	see Otten, Puduḫepa
RA	Revue d'Assyriologie et d'Archéologie orientale, Paris
Rech.	see Laroche, Rech.
RHA	Revue Hittite et Asianique, Paris
RIDA	Revue Internationale des Droits de l'Antiquité, Bruxelles
Riemschneider, Omentexte	K.K. Riemschneider, *Die hethitischen und akkadischen Omentexte aus Boğazköy* (unp. manuscript)
RlA	Reallexikon der Assyriologie und Vorderasiatischen Archäologie, Berlin/New York
de Roos, Diss.	J. de Roos, *Hettitische Geloften: Een teksteditie van Hettitische geloften met inleiding, vertaling en critische noten*, Amsterdam 1984
Rüster	see HZL
SBo	H.G. Güterbock, *Siegel aus Boğazköy* I-II (*AfO* Bh.5, 7), Berlin 1940, 1942
von Schuler, Heth. Dienstanw.	E. von Schuler, *Hethitische Dienstanweisungen für höhere Hof- und Staatsbeamte* (= AfO Bh.10), Graz 1957
Sefarad	Sefarad. Revista de Estudios Hebraicos, Sefardíes y de Oriente Próximo, Madrid
Singer, Muwatalli's Prayer	I. Singer, *Muwatalli's Prayer to the Assembly of Gods Through the Storm-God of Lightning (CTH 381)*, Atlanta 1996
SMEA	Studi Micenei ed Egeo-Anatolici, Roma
Sommer, AU	F. Sommer, *Die Aḫḫiyavā-Urkunden*, München 1932
Souček	see StBoT 1
Starke	see StBoT 30, 31
StBoT	Studien zu den Boğazköy-Texten, Wiesbaden
~ 1	H. Otten – V. Souček, *Das Gelübde der Königin Puduḫepa an die Göttin Lelwani*, 1965
~ 3	H.M. Kümmel, *Ersatzrituale für den hethitisch-*

	en König, 1967
~ 4	R. Werner, *Hethitische Gerichtsprotokolle*, 1967
~ 5	E. Neu, *Interpretation der hethitischen mediopassiven Verbalformen*, 1968
~ 16	C. Kühne - H. Otten, *Der Šaušgamuwa-Vertrag*, 1971
~ 24	H. Otten, *Die Apologie Hattusilis III. Das Bild der Überlieferung*, 1981
~ 25	E. Neu, *Althethitische Ritualtexte in Umschrift*, 1980
~ 29	G. Beckman, *Hittite Birth Rituals. Second Revised Edition*, 1983
~ 30	F. Starke, *Die keilschrift-luwischen Texte in Umschrift*, 1985
~ 31	F. Starke, *Untersuchung zur Stammbildung des keilschrift-luwischen Nomens*, 1990
~ 32	E. Neu, *Das hurritische Epos der Freilassung I. Untersuchungen zu einem hurritisch-hethitischen Textensemble aus Ḫattuša*, 1996
~ 38	Th. van den Hout, *Der Ulmitešub-Vertrag. Eine prosopographische Untersuchung*, 1995
~ 39	S. Košak, *Konkordanz der Keilschrifttafeln II. Die Texte der Grabung 1932*, 1995
~ Bh. 1	H. Otten, *Die Bronzetafel aus Boğazköy. Ein Staatsvertrag Tutḫalijas IV.*, 1988
~ Bh. 2	see HZL
~ Bh. 3	J.D. Hawkins, *The Hieroglyphic Inscription of the Sacred Pool Complex at Hattusa* (SÜDBURG). *With an Archaeological Introduction by Peter Neve*, 1995
Sup.	see Ose, Sup.
Syria	Syria, Paris
Syria 3000 to 300 B.C.	see Klengel, Syria 3000 to 300 B.C.
THeth.	Texte der Hethiter, Heidelberg
~ 3, 4	A. Ünal, *Ḫattušili III. I. Teil: Ḫattušili bis zu seiner Thronbesteigung, 1. Historischer Abriß , 2. Quellen*, 1973
~ 5	S. Bin-Nun, *The Tawananna in the Hittite Kingdom*, 1975
~ 6	A. Ünal, *Ein Orakeltext über die Intrigen am hethitischen Hof (KUB XXII 70 = Bo 2011)*, 1978
~ 7	A. Kammenhuber, *Orakelpraxis, Träume und Vorzeichenschau bei den Hethitern*, 1976
~ 8	S. Heinhold-Krahmer, *Arzawa: Untersuchungen zu seiner Geschichte nach den hethitischen Quellen*, 1977

~ 10	S. Košak, *Hittite Inventory Texts (CTH 241-250)*, 1982
~ 16	A. Hagenbuchner, *Die Korrespondenz der Hethiter. 2. Teil, Die Briefe mit Transkription, Übersetzung und Kommentar*, 1989
~ 20	R.H. Beal, *The Organisation of the Hittite Military*, 1992
THR	see Haase, THR
Tischler	see HEG, RGTC 6
Tjerkstra, Diss.	F.A. Tjerkstra, *Principles of the Relation between Local Adverb, Verb and Sentence Particle in Hittite*, Amsterdam 1996
Trémouille	see Eothen 7
TUAT	Texte aus der Umwelt des Alten Testaments, Gütersloh
Ünal	see THeth. 3, 4, 6
Ugaritica	Ugaritica, Paris
Weitenberg, U-Stämme	J.J.S. Weitenberg, *Die hethitischen U-Stämme*, Amsterdam 1984
Werner	see StBoT 4
WZKM	Wiener Zeitschrift für die Kunde des Morgenlandes, Wien
Xella, Archeologia dell'Inferno	P. Xella (ed.), *Archeologia dell'Inferno. L'Aldilà nel Mondo Antico Vicino Orientale e Classico*, Verona 1987
ZA	Zeitschrift für Assyriologie und verwandte Gebiete, Berlin/New York
ZABR	Zeitschrift für Altorientalische und Biblische Rechtsgeschichte, Wiesbaden 1995
Zuntz, Ortsadv.	L. Zuntz, *Die hethitischen Ortsadverbien arḫa, parā, piran als selbständige Adverbien und in ihrer Verbindung mit Nomina und Verba*, München 1936

* When referring to cuneiform editions of Hittite texts from Boğazköy (Boğazkale) the siglum "KUB" is left out.

** In text quotations bound transcription is used when the text is already available in a satisfactory modern edition, if not the text is transliterated.

Additional abbreviations

a/ ...	Stadtplanquadrat Ḫattuša Büyükkale
A/ ...	Stadtplanquadrat Ḫattuša Unterstadt
abbr.	abbreviation, abbreviated
abl.	ablative

abs.	absolute (case)
acc.	accusative
act.	active
add.	addit
adv.	adverb
Akkad.	Akkadian
all.	allative
Bh.	Beiheft
c	genus commune
C	consonant
Ch.	Chapter
col.	column
conj.	conjunction
dat.	dative
dem.	demonstrative
dep.	deponens
diss.	dissertation
dupl.	duplicate(s)
ed.	edition
encl.	enclitic
Erg.	Ergänzungsheft
gen.	genitive
Hitt.	Hittite
Hurr.	Hurrian
imp.	imperative
indef.	indefinite
inf.	infinitive
lit.	literature
loc.	locative
Luw.	Luwian
m.	masculine
MP	medio-passive
n.	genus neutrum
nom.	nominative
obl.	oblique
obv.	obverse
om.	omittit
p.	page
part.	particle
pers.	personal
pl.	plural
poss.	possessive
postpos.	postposition
prep.	preposition
pres.	present
pret.	preterite
prev.	preverb

pron.	pronoun
r.	right
refl.	reflexive
rel.	relative
rev.	reverse
Rs.	Rückseite
sg.	singular
st.constr.	status constructus
subordin.	subordinate
Sum.	Sumerian
sup.	supinum
unp.	unpublished
V	vowel
Vs.	Vorderseite
w.	with
//	indicates duplicates
+	indicates directly joining pieces of one tablet
(+)	indicates indirectly joining pieces of one tablet

CHAPTER ONE

INTRODUCTION AND TEXT CONSTITUTION

1. *Introduction*

The importance attached to both mental and physical purity in matters religious is probably near universal and was certainly of prime importance in the Hittite society of the second millennium BC. Because the influence of the gods was felt to be pervading practically every aspect of human existence, 'matters religious' in this context comes close to daily life. That is, at least daily life at the Hittite royal court. Anything disturbing the usual course of events could be explained as caused by divine wrath due to some kind of contamination. This is amply illustrated by the various rituals meant to free people through magic from witchcraft, illnesses or any other evil, and many rituals aim at restoring purity in general.[1] But it was not only the individual's purity which could be threatened: cities, armies, houses, temples and palaces could likewise be afflicted. Within the group of texts brought together in this study it is the institution of Kingship and its symbols as well as the Great King himself which were felt contaminated.

Many rituals specifically mention the king and queen as the object of magical acts.[2] The king's purity was of the utmost importance because the entire country's well-being was directly linked to his.[3] Moreover, as representative of the gods on earth and with his ultimately divine fate, the king was considered to be nearest to the gods. This importance attached to royal purity is well attested in other text genres besides rituals. The so-called festival texts are full of purification rites the king has to go through before he can participate or can continue to do so. Only too well-known is the example set in the Instruction for the Palace Personnel in XIII 3 (CTH 265[4]) where a man named Zuliya, responsible for the royal water supply, is

[1] See in particular J. Moyer, *The Concept of Ritual Purity among the Hittites* (diss. Brandeis University, Ann Arbor, Michigan 1969), further see V. Haas, GHR 876-911, and M. Popko, Religions 82-83, 104-108, both with extensive literature; see also below Ch. III.5.

[2] Cf. M. Hutter, AoF 18 (1991) 34, V. Haas, GHR 888.

[3] See J. Moyer, Diss. 79-93.

[4] See the translations by A. Goetze, ANET 207, E. von Schuler, TUAT 1.1, 124-125, and R. Haase, THR 63-64; for the term *gullakuu̯an* describing the effect of Zuliya's negligence as "harmful, defiled" cf. J. Puhvel, HS 109 (1996) 167. For IBoT IV 5 as the possible colophon to this text see ibid. Descriptive Catalogue xiii (Turkish) and xxv (English).

forced to undergo a water ordeal because the king found a hair in his wash basin. Similarly, we find the following stipulation in the loyalty oath imposed by the young king Tutḫaliya IV on his LÚ.MEŠSAG:

> [*našm*]*a=šmaš šumeš kuiēš* LÚ.MEŠSAG *ANA* LUGAL*=kan* / [NÍ.T]E-*i* *šuppai šalikiškitteni nu=šmaš šuppešni* / [IGI-*an*]*da tišḫanteš ēšten* *mānn=a=kan ANA* LÚSAG / [*kue*]*danikki* ḪUL-*luš maršaštarriš* / [*ap*]*āšš=a ANA* LUGAL NÍ.TE.MEŠ*=ŠU šaligai* GAM *MAMĪTI*

> [O]r you who (are) LÚ.MEŠSAG (and) regularly approach/ touch the king's sacred [bod]y, be aware of (that) sacredness! And if some LÚSAG (carries with him) an evil desecration and [h]e approaches/touches the king's body: (let that fall) under the oath![5]

The same functionaries are repeatedly made well aware of their important position vis-à-vis the bodily and mental welfare of the Great King; compare

> [*ŠA* dUTU-*ŠI=ma* N(Í.TE*=ŠU ḫūman*)] GIM-*an* / [o o *š*(*ummaš ANA* LÚ.MEŠSA)]G ŠU-*i*

> Since [His Majesty's b]ody [and soul(?)] (are) entirely in your hand, LÚ.MEŠ SAG, ...[6]

and

[5] XXVI 12+ XXI 42 iv 33-37 (CTH 255.1), ed. E. von Schuler, Heth. Dienstanw. 28-29, see also J. Tischler, HEG T, D/3, 382; for the first sentence cf. E. Neu, Linguistica 33 (1993 = FsÇop) 147. Because of the room available a restoration in line 34 to NÍ.T]E instead of *tu-ik-k*]*i-i* is preferred here. According to F. Starke, ZABR 2 (1996) 172, - within the framework of his specific interpretation of the function of the LÚ.MEŠSAG in the Hittite state and of the terms NÍ.TE, ZI and SAG.DU in texts involving them - the body of the king would stand not for his physical body but for the king as "body politic" ("der Staat als Gemeinwesen" ibid. 174). The closing sentences introduced by *mān=* , however, show that in all likelihood the physical body is meant here: *maršaštarri-* (cf. CHD L-N s.v.) often denotes a "sacrilege" resulting from a physical uncleanness of humans who have not washed themselves properly or of animals. The fact that in this connection the terms *šuppi-* "sacred, holy" and *šuppeššar* are used as opposed to *parkui-* "pure, clean" and its derivatives is not surprising, since the notions of body politic and body natural are in the case of a Hittite king very much intertwined if not inseparable: the king was the embodiment of the wellfare of country and state and his physical condition was seen by the Hittites as an expression of the gods' feelings towards that state. This is the basic and ever recurring thought which underlies the many oracle investigations and (resulting) rituals concerning illnesses of the king and/or queen.

[6] XXVI 1+ (CTH 255.2A) ii 10-11 with duplicates XXVI 8 (B) ii 3'-4' and XXXI 97 (C) obv. 7-8; ed. E. von Schuler, Heth.Dienstanw. 11.

> *ŠA* ^{d}UTU-*ŠI=ma kuit* NÍ.TE=*ŠU* ZI ^{d}UTU-*ŠI=i̯a / n=at=za parā lē kuiški / kuedanikki memai*
>
> Nobody, however, may pass on to anybody that which concerns His Majesty's body and His Majesty's soul![7]

Because of his position as well as the general awareness of and sensitivity to witchcraft the Great King was both vulnerable and a favorite target for his enemies.[8] A good example is furnished by the curses spoken by Mašḫuiluwa directed at the Hittite king through a statue somehow representing him witness the oracle inquiry V 6+XVIII 54 (CTH 570). The statue Mašḫuiluwa kept in his palace in Arzawa in western Anatolia, was the statue of *parnalliš* (...) ^{d}*Zawalliš ŠA* ^{d}UTU-*ŠI* "the Zawalli-deity of His Majesty's House". Although no doubt originally meant as an object of reverence and homage, he directed his curses at it, perhaps accompanied by certain magical acts. As a result both the Zawalli-deity and the king were bewitched. After the correctness of this reconstruction has been verified (iii 12-16), the investigation continues by inquiring into the possible ways to undo the curses (iii 17-37):

12 *ŠA* ^{m}PÉŠ.TUR-*u̯a ku-it* EME *A-NA PA-NI* DINGIR-*LIM ar-ḫa tar-nu-ma-an-zi* SIxSÁ-*at*
13 *nu pár-na-al-li-is ku-iš* ^{d}*Za-u̯a-al-li-i-iš ŠA* ^{d}UTU-*ŠI* ^{m}PÉŠ.TUR-*aš ku-in*
14 ^{URU}*Ar-za-u-u̯a ḫar-ta nu a-pé-e-da-ni pí-ra-an* EME-*an ar-ḫa tar-na-an ḫar-zi*
15 IGI-*zi* *TE*^{MEŠ} NU.SIG$_5$-*du*^{a} *ni* GAM *še-er-ma-aš-ši a-dam-ta-ḫi-iš* ZAG-*za an-ša-an* NU.SIG$_5$
16 EGIR-*zi* *TE*^{MEŠ} ^{b} *ni ši ta* GÙB-*la-za* RA^{IṢ} *zi* GAR-*ri* 12 ŠÀ DIR SIG$_5$ (erasure)

---

17 *nu* GAM *a-ri-iš-kir nu-za-kán ḫur-ta-uš me-eq-qa-uš tar-na-aš na-at IŠ-TU ṬUP-PÍ a-ni-i-ir*
18 *zi-la-aš-ma kal-la-re-*⸢*eš-kit*$_9$⸣*-ta-ri-pát* DINGIR-*LUM-ma-aš-ši al-u̯a-an-za-aḫ-ḫa-an-za a-pa-a-aš-ša*
19 *al-u̯a-an-za-aḫ-ḫa-an-za nu ki-iš-ša-an a-ri-i-*⸢*e*⸣*-er* ^{m}PÉŠ.TUR-*aš-u̯a I-NA* ^{URU}*Ku-u̯a-la-na*
20 *a-pa-ši-la pa-iz-zi Ú-NU-UT* LUGAL-*i̯a pé-e-da-an-zi na-at šu-up-pa-i̯a-za ḫar-kán-zi*
21 ^{m}PÉŠ.TUR-*aš-ma* ^{m}*Za-pár-ti*-ŠEŠ-*ša tu-u-u̯a-az a-ra-an-ta-ri Ú-NU-UT* ^{f}NÍG.GA.GUŠKIN-*i̯a*

[7] XXVI 1+ (CTH 255.2A) iii 23-25; ed. E. von Schuler, Heth.Dienstanw. 13.

[8] On the relation politics - magic/rituals see especially M. Hutter, AoF 18 (1991) 32-43.

22 *ḫar-ga-an-zi nu* DINGIR.MEŠ ^{f}*Zu-u̯a-ḫal-la-ti-iš* ^{f}*Ma-pí-li-iš-ša a-ni-i̯a-an-zi*
23 EGIR-*an-da*[c]*-ma Ú-NU-UT* LUGAL *a-ni-i̯a-an-zi nam-ma ar-ḫa da-a-li-i̯a-an-zi*
24 *ku-it-ma-an-kán* ^{m}PÉŠ.TUR-*aš* ^{m}*Za-pár-ti*-ŠEŠ-*ša IŠ-TU* SISKUR *a-ra-an-zi*
25 *ku-it-ma-an-ma-aš* SISKUR *ma-an-tal-li-i̯a* ^{URU}KÙ.BABBAR-*aš* ^{URU}*Ar-za-u̯a-aš-ša i-u̯a-ar*
26 *IT-TI* ⸢^{d}UTU-*ŠI*⸣ *i-i̯a-an-zi nu ú-u̯a-an-zi* DINGIR-*LUM* ^{d}UTU-*ŠI-i̯a da-a-an* EGIR-*pa a-ni-i̯a-an-zi*
27 *A-NA* ^{d}UTU-⸢*ŠI-i̯a-kán* DINGIR⸣-*LUM a-pí-i̯a tar-na-an-zi ar-ḫa-i̯a-za-an-kán*[e] *a-pí-i̯a šar-ri-i̯a-*⸢*zi*⸣
28 KI.MIN *nu TE*^{MEŠ} SIG_5-*ru ni ši ki ki-il*!?[d]*-ti-iš-kán* ZAG-*ni al-la-i-ti* SIG_5

---

29 *nu pa-i-u-e-ni ki-iš-ša-an-ma i-i̯a-u-*⸢*e*⸣*-ni I-NA* ^{URU}*Ku-u̯a-la-na* UN-*aš pa-iz-zi*
30 *ku-*⸢*iš*⸣?*-kán ŠA* DINGIR-*LIM a-ni-ú-ri kat-ta da-a-i nu-kán* DINGIR-*LUM* MÁŠ.GAL IZI-*i̯a iš-tar-na ar-ḫa*
31 *pé-e-da-an-zi nam-ma-*⸢*an*⸣ *a-ni-*⸢*i̯a*⸣*-an-zi* ^{m}*Maš-ḫu-u-i-lu-u̯a-ma* ^{m}*Za-pár-ti*-ŠEŠ-*ša*
32 *Ú-NU-UT* ^{f}⸢NÍG.GA-GUŠKIN⸣ *tu-u-u̯a-az ḫar-kán-zi nu* DINGIR-*LUM pí-di-ši pár-ku-nu-u̯a-an-za*
33 *nam-ma-an MA-ḪAR* ^{d}UTU-*ŠI ú-da-an-zi* ^{d}UTU-*ŠI-i̯a ka-a a-ni-i̯a-an-zi A-NA* ^{d}UTU-*ŠI-i̯a-*⸢*kán*⸣
34 *e-ni ut-tar* DÙ-*zi* MÁŠ.GAL-*i̯a-aš-ši še-er ap-*⸢*pa*⸣*[-a]n-zi nam-ma-aš-ši* DINGIR-*LUM še-er ḫal-za-a-i*
35 *nam-ma ar-ḫa da-a-li-i̯a-zi ku-it-ma-*⸢*an*⸣*[-kán* U]N?-*aš IŠ-TU* SISKUR *a-ri ku-it-ma-an-za*
36 [SISKU]R ⸢*ma*⸣*-al-*⸢*tal*?*-li*⸣?*-i̯a* ^{URU}KÙ.BABBAR-*aš* ^{URU}*Ar-za-u-u̯a-aš [i-u̯a-ar] IT-TI* ^{d}UTU-*ŠI* DÙ-*zi*
37 [ ] x x x[9] ⸢EGIR⸣-*pa a-ni-i̯a-an-zi* (text becomes too fragmentary)

[a] This verb is a later addition and written between the lines. [b] The expected result (SIG_5-*ru* or NU.SIG_5-*du*) is left out by the scribe. [c] For this reading see the "Verbesserungen" by A. Walther ad XVIII 54. [d] Compare the "Verbesserungen" by A. Walther ad XVIII 54. [e] Either *arḫai̯az*(*a*) is a form related to *arḫai̯a*/*arḫai̯an* (see HW^{2} A287b-289b) or the form is a mistake for **arḫai̯an=za=kan*.

As to the fact that the uttering of curses of Mašḫuiluwa in front of the deity was established, has Mašḫuiluwa uttered curses before that

[9] G. Beckman (personal communication) suggests: [*nu* DINGIR-]⸢*LUM* $^{d!}$UTU!⸣[-*ŠI-i̯*]*a*.

(Zawalli-deity) which (is) the Zawalli of the House of His Majesty which he kept in Arzawa? Then let the first exta be unfavorable. *Ni*(*pašuri*) below, an *adamtaḫi* on top of it, it is wiped on the right. Unfavorable. The later exta: *ni*(*pašuri*), *ši*(*ntaḫi*), *ta*(*nani*), damaged on the left, the *zi*(*zaḫi*) is lying, twelve coils. Favorable.
They kept continuing the inquiry. He has uttered many curses and they have recorded them on a tablet. But the (oracle) result remains unfavorable only. His (i.e. Mašḫuiluwa's Zawalli-) deity (is) bewitched and the other one (i.e. His Majesty) (is) bewitched.[10] They inquired thus: "Will Mašḫuiluwa himself go to the city of Kuwalana?" (Then) they will bring the regalia and keep them in a pure state. Mašḫuiluwa and Zaparti-ŠEŠ will stand far off holding the apparel of (the woman) NÍG.GA.GUŠKIN. Zuwaḫallati and Mapili will (ritually) treat the gods, subsequently they will treat the regalia. Then they will leave (them). Until Mašḫuiluwa and Zaparti-ŠEŠ come down from the ritual and until they perform *mantalli*-rituals in Hittite and Arzawa fashion together with His Majesty, they will come (and) treat the deity and His Majesty again for a second time. At that moment they will let the deity go to His Majesty and then he will separately? ... him, etc. Then let the exta be favorable: *ni*(*pašuri*), *ši*(*ntaḫi*), *ke*(*ldi*), *keldi* on the right, *allaiti*. Favorable.
Or will we go (and) do as follows? A man will go to Kuwalana, who will take down the deity's apparel. They will carry the deity right between a billy goat and fire (and) subsequently treat him (ritually). Mašḫuiluwa and Zaparti-ŠEŠ will hold the apparel of (the woman) NÍG.GA.GUŠKIN far off. The deity will be cleansed on its own premises. Then they will carry it in the presence of His Majesty and they will treat His Majesty here. For His Majesty he (i.e. the man who went to Kuwalana) will do that deed and they will hold a billy goat over him. Then he will invoke the deity for him. Then he will leave. Until [the ma]n? comes down from the ritual (and) until he performs *mantalli*-rituals [in] Hittite [and] Arzawa [fashion] together with His Majesty, they will treat [the deity? an]d [His Majesty?] again. ... [11]

The *mantalli*-ritual is a rite performed specifically in those cases where two parties are in antagonism and one of the two has taken recourse to magic and curses. Although this is by no means inherent to the *mantalli*-ritual,[12] it can be and often is conducted posthumously, that is, one of the

[10] The distinction here between -*ši* referring to the last mentioned subject (= Mašḫuiluwa) and *apāš* referring to the king I owe to P.M. Goedegebuure.

[11] On the Mašḫuiluwa affair and this oracle text in general see also below Ch. III.2.

[12] Contrary to A. Ünal, Anadolu/Anatolia 19 (1976-1976)[1980] 179-183; on the *mantalli*-ritual see further F. Ose, Sup. 37 with n. 1, HW^2 A 85b, CHD L-N 176b-179a (with lit.), M. Hutter, AoF 18 (1991) 38-39, and below Ch. III.5.

two parties or even both can be already deceased. In that case the ritual aims at pacifying the spirits of the dead.

It is a very similar situation that CTH 569 is dealing with. Considerable nervousness and uncertainty surrounded the accession of the 'new' Great King Tutḫaliya IV, son of Ḫattušili III.[13] In the not too recent past several persons had spoken curses against either ruling kings or persons who would become so. The memory of these was now somehow revived and the curses of the past were felt as possibly still effective and endangering Tutḫaliya's rule. Extensive oracle investigations were therefore undertaken in order to secure his accession, to identify the individuals responsible, and to ascertain the remedy to undo the curses. The inquiry preserved in CTH 569 falls into the last category.

2. *Status quaestionis*

In his *Catalogue des Textes Hittites* (Paris 1971) E. Laroche for the first time brought together KBo II 6+XVIII 51 and VIII 27 as partially "analogue" under a heading entitled "Oracles relatifs à Arma-ᵈU et Šaušgatti" and assigned it the number CTH 569. In earlier installments to his CTH both texts were still listed separately.[14] As early as 1932, however, F. Sommer, AU 119, had already recognized them as parallel; three years before he had seen a "gewisse Verwandtschaft" between KBo II 6 and XVI 32 in KlF. 343. Later, in 1974 it was A. Ünal, THeth. 3, 167, who for the first time explicitly mentioned VIII 27 as shorter in comparison to KBo II 6+. Meanwhile, A. Archi, SMEA 14 (1971) 213, and G. del Monte, AION 33 (1973) had given parts of KBo II 6+ in transliteration and translation. In the same study A. Ünal, THeth. 3, 102 n. 47, had included both texts in a useful listing of oracle texts concerning certain individuals, among whom Armatarḫunta and Šaušgatti. The common denominator of all these oracles is, according to Ünal, that the persons involved had fallen victim to injustice inflicted on them by family members. To ease the latter's conscience the oracle investigations were conducted in order to find out to what extent these acts of injustice in the past still influenced their lives in the present and, if so, what should be done about it. The texts are nevertheless quite diverse and not all individuals in Ünal's list (for instance both Katapaili and GAL-ᵈU /"Ura-datta" in XVI 32) necessarily belong to the category of victims. Although not referring to Ünal, G.C.

[13] See Th. van den Hout, ZA 81 (1991) 298-300, F. Starke, ZABR 1 (1995) 76-82.

[14] RHA 59 (1956) 102, 103: KBo II 6+ under nr. 221.2 (KUŠ, KIN et MUŠEN) and VIII 27 with a question mark under nr. 222 (Fragments divers). The question mark may have been prompted because of the omina recorded on the left edge of the tablet. The inclusion of these on the edge, whereas the remainder of the tablet contains an oracle investigation, must also have been the reason to publish this piece in KUB VIII among the astrological texts.

Moore, JNES 40 (1981) 49 n. 7 (and addendum on p. 52), somewhat restricted this list on the one hand and on the other proposed to bring more texts than just the two mentioned under the heading of CTH 569, which should then be retitled "'Oracles concerning Arma-^{d}U, Šaušgatti, Urhi-Teššub, Danuhepa, et al.' or, more succinctly, 'Oracles concerning Enemies of Hattušili III.'" The texts added by Moore (in the order given by Moore) are: XVI 32, XVI 41+7/v, XVI 58, XVI 77, XXII 35, XXXI 23, KBo IX 151 and L 6. Moore's suggestion was followed up by G. Beckman, BiOr 42 (1985) 141, who proposed to add LII 83 to CTH 569.[15] The same suggestion was made for LX 52 by the present author, BiOr. 51 (1994) 123. The latter, ibid. 126 and StBoT 38, 189-191, also supposed a connection of the fragments KBo XVIII 145 and LX 129 with this same group while proposing a date for the entire group during the reign of Tutḫaliya IV. Meanwhile, Ph.H.J. Houwink ten Cate, BiOr 51 (1994) 248-251, tried to fit this group of texts into a historical framework concentrating on Urḫiteššub's role in XVI 32+L 6. In order to "accommodate members of the still earlier generation of Mursilis II" he suggested broadening its title to "Oracles concerning Enmities within the Royal Family during the two Generations preceding Tudhaliyas IV."[16] At the same time he defined the purpose of these oracles as "to secure the purification of 'the Places of Kingship and the Thrones of Kingship' as well as of 'My Majesty' himself regarding his enthronement."

For a "Forschungsgeschichte" on the texts not originally included in CTH 569 by Laroche see the introductory remarks below to the text edition proper, Ch. V.1 and 3.

We must be cautious, however, not to let CTH 569 turn into a 'dustbin' for oracle texts containing names of certain individuals, mostly known from the later 14th and 13th century. Most of the texts originally brought together by Moore under CTH 569 as expanded and retitled by him have more in common than just the names of certain persons. It is the fact, as Houwink ten Cate rightly observed, that the purity of kingship is felt to be threatened by those persons or by events in the past involving them. It seems better, therefore, to redefine CTH 569 once more starting from KBo II 6+ and VIII 27 along the principles outlined in the next section, and to retitle it: "Oracles sur la purification du royauté (de Tutḫaliya IV)" or "Oracles concerning the purification of kingship (of Tutḫaliya IV)."[17]

[15] In the Inhaltsübersicht to KUB LII p. iv, A. Archi noted: "Nicht zu KBo II 6(+) und KUB VIII 27 gehörend." It is not entirely clear what Archi wanted to convey: did he deny a closer connection of LII 83 to the two texts mentioned or just the possibility of a join or duplicate?

[16] BiOr 51 (1994) 249.

[17] This is preferred to the possibility of including into CTH 569 the texts related to it as presented below in Ch. IV. The colophon to KBo II 6+ shows that the investigation into the purity of kingship was considered a separate series by itself. In a future revised edition of the CTH, in which the section B. "Pratique" of Chapter IX on "Divination" should be substantially changed, these texts might be

3. *Criteria for assigning texts to CTH 569*

The oracle texts brought together in this study all concern ritual purifications of the 'places of kingship' and of His Majesty himself. These purifications were considered in connection with curses uttered by former members of the Hittite ruling dynasty, most of whom were dead by the time the oracle investigations were performed. The exact nature of the defamations remains largely unknown, but related texts involving the same persons may shed some light on the historical background of the oracle investigations (see Ch. II and III).

The most important criterion for assigning texts to CTH 569 is the expression:

> EME PN *ANA* DINGIR.MEŠ LUGAL-*UTTI piran arḫa aniịanzi AŠRI*ḪI.A LUGAL-*UTTI* GIŠDAG.ḪI.A=*ịa parkunuụanzi* dUTU-*ŠI*=*ịa*=*za parkunuzzi*
>
> They will undo the curse of PN in front of the gods of kingship, they will cleanse the places of kingship and the thrones,[18] and His Majesty will cleanse himself.

With minor and major variations this expression is found in: KBo II 6+XVIII 51 (i 33'-34', iii 43-44), VIII 27(+)Bo 7787 (iv 2'-4'), XXII 35 (iii 3'-5'), L 6+XVI 41+7/v (ii 39-41, iii 4-5 and 48-50) and 10/v (2'-3'). The items mentioned are cleansed from the curses (EME) of certain individuals: Armatarḫunta (KBo II 6+), Šaušgatti (VIII 27+), Ḫalpaziti (XXII 35 iii), a *tawananna*, Danuḫepa and Urḫiteššub (all three L 6+). The variations predominantly concern the first sentence. Instead of being dependent on the syntagma *ANA* ... *piran arha aniịa-* "to undo in front of", the gods of kingship can be made object to the verb *parkunu-* "to cleanse" just as the places of kingship etc.; in this case the curse appears in the ablative: *IŠTU* EME PN DINGIR.MEŠ LUGAL-*UTTI AŠRI*ḪI.A LUGAL-*UTTI* GIŠDAG.ḪI.A=*ịa parkunuụanzi* dUTU-*ŠI*=*ịa*=*za parkunuzi* "From the curse of PN they will cleanse the gods of kingship, the places of kingship and the thrones of kingship and His Majesty will cleanse himself."[19]

After sometimes additional promises of compensation for the deceased there follows in the two largest texts (KBo II 6+ i 37'-40', iii 46-49 and 63-66, L 6+ ii 42'-46', iii 58-61) the phrase:

listed in a preceding entry under a title "Oracles concerning the enthronement of Tutḫaliya" vel sim.

[18] On this plural see the commentary Ch. VI ad L 6+ ii 40'. Although the translation "throne" is used throughout this study for GIŠDAG it may (also?) have had the character of a dais; cf. M. Popko, Kultobjekte 61-62, and F. Starke, ZA 69 (1979) 86-96.

[19] This variant is found in L 6+ iii 48-50 and probably in XXII 35 iii 2'-5'.

> *mān=ma=za* DINGIR-*LUM QATAMMA malān ḫarši* INIM PN=*naš=kan apēz meminaza laittari* DINGIR-*LUM=naš ANA* INIM PN *šer* TÚG*šeknun* EGIR-*pa UL namma kuitki* SUD-*i̯aši*
>
> If then you, o god, have thus approved (and) the affair[20] of PN will be solved for us through that deed (and) you, o god, will not pull back the robe at us anymore over the affair of PN (then let the oracle be favorable/ unfavorable).

In KBo II 6+ iii 46 the words *QATAMMA malān hark-*, in L 6+ iii 6 this entire expression is reduced to KI.MIN. In VIII 27(+), the summary of KBo II 6+, this second part is entirely left out. Only once does this part of the formula occur alone in KBo II 6+ iii 63-66 but the scribe was clearly elaborating upon an earlier oracle question and did not bother to repeat the first part. Of course, the introducing *mān* sentence can also be found in numerous other oracle texts, but the occurrence of the following two in combination with the first formula is restricted to this particular group. The last sentence is differently construed in L 6+ with among other, smaller variants the "matter of PN" as subject instead of the dat. + *šer* (ii 44-45: *zilatia=nnaš* INIM PN TÚG*šeknun* ḪUL-*uanni* EGIR-*pa UL namma* SUD-*i̯azi* "(and if) in the future the matter of PN will not anymore pull back the cloak on us in evil", cf. further iii 60-61: *ziladuu̯a=nnaš ŠA* PN ḪUL-*uanza* TÚG*šeknun* EGIR-*pa UL namma* SUD-*i̯azi*). The same phrase is found also in XVI 58 iii 3'-8' (*mān=ma=šmaš* DINGIR.MEŠ [*QATAMMA mal*]*ān ḫarteni aši=kan* INIM=*ša* [*apēz mem*]*iaz laittari* DINGIR-*LUM=naš* [*zilatii̯*]*a ANA* INIM ᵐ*Ḫalpa*-LÚ TÚG*šeknun* [*idal*]*auu̯anni UL namma kuitki* [...). The latter text also shares the name Ḫalpaziti who is the main character of XXII 35 iii, which contains the first part of the formula. XVI 58 may therefore be added to the group; on this see more in detail the Commentary (Ch. VI) ad LII 92 iv 18'ff. With XVI 32 added as duplicate to L 6+,[21] and XLIX 93 and LII 92 as duplicate and parallel respectively to XXII 35 as well as unp. 10/v as parallel to KBo II 6+, we come to the following texts as belonging together on the basis of the criteria just mentioned:

KBo II 6+XVIII 51
VIII 27(+)Bo 7787
XVI 58
XXII 35 // XLIX 93
L 6+XVI 41+7/v // XVI 32
LII 92
10/v.

[20] For the translation of INIM as "affair' throughout this book see the Commentary, Ch. VI, ad L 6+ ii 43'.

[21] See below the introduction to Ch. III.

To this list may be added KBo IX 151 and L 5 because of the close resemblance in wording and/or personal names to XXII 35 and L 6+ respectively; for more detail see the introductory remarks to Ch. III. With this, however, we have not yet reached the final text constitution. This depends on the specific relation of comprehensive version versus summary between the several texts.

4. *Comprehensive recordings versus summaries: general remarks*

Hittite oracle investigations normally make use of four divination techniques: augury (MUŠEN), extispicy (SU), the *ḪURRI*-bird and the lot- or KIN-oracle.[22] Of these the *ḪURRI*-bird oracle may be a form of extispicy. The techniques known as lecanomancy and clinomancy (or *šašt*-oracle) can be considered as special forms of the KIN-oracle and extispicy respectively. Although the termini technici used to describe the results of the observations made by the officiating priest are different for each method, the principles underlying any investigation are the same, regardless of the method or combination of methods used. That is, a question is posed, an expected result formulated, observations are made and the outcome described. The way of administering such investigations, however, differs. Most are recorded in what could be termed the comprehensive way, i.e. an oracle question is posed through one of the methods mentioned and subsequently checked and often counterchecked through others. In most cases the oracle process and its outcome as obtained by its particular priest are meticulously described including all the technical terms and abbreviations.

In other cases the oracle process is entirely left out, only the result is given, that is, the result of all techniques at once. This is done by saying either:

IŠTU ^{MUNUS}ŠU.GI ^{LU}ḪAL ^{LÚ}IGI.MUŠEN=*i̯a* (NU.)SIG$_5$

Through the 'Old Woman', the diviner and the augur: (un)favorable

or even shorter

IŠTU 3 ^{GIŠ}TUKUL (NU.)SIG$_5$

Through three ^{GIŠ}TUKUL-s: (un)favorable.

[22] For a general introduction and further literature on Hittite divination see A. Archi, Ägypten-Vorderasien-Turfan 85-90.

Both can be preceded by *zilaš* "outcome, result".[23] Only occasionally, it seems, we find the further variants

> *nu IŠTU TE*^{MEŠ} NU.SIG$_5$ KIN⸗*i̯a* NU.SIG$_5$ (V 6+ i 19')
>
> Through the exta unfavorable and (through) the KIN-oracle unfavorable

and

> *IŠTU* ^{MUNUS}ENSI MUŠEN *ḪURRI*⸗*i̯a* SIxSÁ-*at* (XXII 40 iii 13')
>
> Through the divination priestess and the *ḪURRI*-bird (oracle) it was ascertained.

The special meaning of ^{GIŠ}TUKUL in the second phrase and the summarizing function of the first two were recognized by G.C. Moore in his article on "^{GIŠ}TUKUL as 'Oracle Procedure' in Hittite Oracle Texts."[24] The question whether ^{GIŠ}TUKUL means "'type of oracle' or refers to the action of carrying out a single oracle process"[25] was left unanswered by Moore but might be decided in favor of the former. First of all, except for the second phrase, the other three refer to either the priest particular to a technique ("Through the 'Old Woman' etc."), the technique itself ("Through the exta etc.") or both ("Through the divination priestess and the *ḪURRI*-bird etc."). Moreover, the meaning "type of oracle" comes closest to the special use of Akkadian *kakku* "weapon, tool" as "sign (predicting certain events)" to which Moore already referred. It also has the advantage that when in fact four oracle procedures (SU, KIN, *ḪURRI*-bird and augury) were held, the phrase "Through three oracle types" is still justified if we assume that the *ḪURRI*-bird oracle was a special kind of extispicy as is more often suggested.[26] Therefore, the translation "oracle type" is preferred here.

The generally varying order in which the oracle priests are mentioned in this formula probably reflects the order of techniques used.[27] If not all

[23] Cf. L 6+ ii 33' and iii 39.

[24] JNES 40 (1981) 49-52.

[25] For the latter translation cf. M. Schuol, AoF 21 (1994) 272 ("Durchführung").

[26] On this see below sub 6. *Comprehensive investigations versus summaries within CTH 569*; for the *ḪURRI*-bird oracle as a kind of extispicy cf. A. Archi, SMEA 16 (1975) 139-140, and BBVO 1 (1982) 288.

[27] In most cases the order in CTH 569 is'Old Woman' - diviner - augur, but sometimes a different order is found like diviner - 'Old Woman' - augur (cf. L 6+ ii 33'-34'); in other summaries outside CTH 569 the order varies likewise. Instead of the 'Old Woman' the ^{MUNUS}ENSI can occur (e.g. XXII 40).

techniques have led to the same conclusion, this is stated as such, cf. for instance:

IŠTU ^{MUNUS}ŠU.GI ^{LÚ}IGI.MUŠEN=*ia* SIxSÁ-*at* *IŠTU* ^{LÚ}ḪAL NU.SIG$_5$

Through the 'Old Woman' and the augur it was ascertained; through the diviner: unfavorable (XXII 35 ii 8'-9'//XLIX 93, 14-16[28]).

This second way of administrating oracle procedures, therefore, can be seen as a summary or excerpt of comprehensive oracle recordings and composed on the basis thereof. Its most salient feature is that by way of the standard phrases several subsequent comprehensive paragraphs – i.e. the original question with check and countercheck(s) – can be reduced to a single one.

Oracle investigations thus summarized have to be distinguished from investigations which may also be considered to be 'shortened' inasmuch as the observations of the priest have been left out and only the result ("favorable/ unfavorable") is given. The middle-Hittite investigation KBo XVI 97 (CTH 571.2[29]) is an example of this type; it is shortened on its obv. 1-25 and rev. 1-3, 32, 43, but this text makes no use of checks or counterchecks.

Another type of summary, which may be seen as the ultimate form, is represented by texts like XVI 32, L 122 and large parts of CTH 568.[30] In these any reference whatsoever to oracle techniques seems to be lacking, in fact they offer a mere listing of what has been established. In this way such texts largely become narratives or edicts predominantly formulated in the present/future tense, with only an occasional formulaic SIxSÁ-*at* "it has been ascertained" to remind us of their mantic origin.[31] It cannot be ruled out, however, that such texts were part of a composition in which also the other summary type was used as will be demonstrated below to be the case in XVI 32. In between the two summary types there are finally some texts displaying a mixture of comprehensively styled paragraphs and summarized ones; some examples will be given below.

In the above mentioned article Moore offered a first listing of such oracle summaries which was later expanded by H. Berman.[32] To date the

[28] Cf. also L 6+ iii 45.

[29] See the edition by M. Schuol, AoF 21 (1994) 102-122.

[30] Cf. already K. Balkan in the Inhaltsübersicht (viii) to ABoT ad no. 14: "Vs. II und Rs. III 1-7 sowie Rs. IV 1'-5' in der bekannten Art der Wahrsagetexte, der Rest eher wie Festrituale abgefasst." For an edition of CTH 568 see R. Lebrun, Hethitica 12 (1994) 41-77, which should be supplemented by the remarks by M. Nakamura, AoF 22 (1995) 37-22.

[31] Cf. the remarks of G. del Monte, AION 35 (1975) 327 on XVI 32: "questo testo, più che una indagine oracolare, sembra essere una sorta di decreto, conseguente ad una indagine oracolare."

[32] JCS 34 (1982) 123.

following texts can be identified as oracle summaries on the basis of the formulae just mentioned:

KBo VIII 57	KBo IX 151,
V 6+ XVIII 54	V 8
VI 15	VIII 27(+)
XVIII 23	XVIII 36
XVIII 40	XVIII 67
XXII 12((+)13$^{?}$)	XXII 35
XXII 40[33]	XLIX 93
L 6+XVI 41+7/v	L 24
L 69	LII 14
LII 92	LX 26
250/f[34]	10/v;

from Alalaḫ the Hittite text AT 454 should be added.
As summaries of the 'ultimate' type might be considered:

KBo XXVII 203[35]	XVI 32	XLV 79+XLVII 89[36]
XLIX 47(?)	L122	LII 43
LX 100	LX 145	2275/c.[37]

To these one should also add parts of CTH 568. There may, however, be many more of them, especially smaller fragments, that have gone undetected hitherto, since they are not easily recognized.[38]

Of the first group, KBo IX 151, VIII 27(+), XVI 32, XXII 35, XLIX 93, L 6+, LII 92 and 10/v will be treated in this study as summaries of the comprehensive oracles KBo II 6+ and XVI 58 belonging to CTH 569. Of the remaining texts, XVIII 36 and XXII 12(+) belong to a larger group of oracle investigations concerning the accession date of Tutḫaliya IV, of

[33] XXII 40 has been listed under CTH 579 "KUŠ et MUŠEN": the KIN-oracle summarily referred to seems to have been overlooked.

[34] On this fragment see below in the commentary, Ch. VI ad LII 92 i 7'.

[35] Cf. V. Haas, AoF 23 (1996) 84-89.

[36] Cf. V. Haas, AoF 23 (1996) 84-89.

[37] On this fragment see below Ch. II.6.

[38] For XXI 33 (CTH 387) as a possible further example see Ph.H.J. Houwink ten Cate, BiOr 51 (1994) 241. Another interesting case is presented by the cult inventory XLII 100 (CTH 525 – ed. G. del Monte, OA 17 (1978) 178-192, J. Hazenbos, Diss. 12-22, cf. also ibid. 167-168) where at the end of a fragmentary paragraph (ii 23') suddenly an oracle result seems to be reported (*z*]*i*$^{?}$-*la-a*[*š*$^{?}$]NU.SIG$_5$ "outcome: unfavorable"). Does this mean the entire cult inventory was made the subject of an oracle investigation or just the paragraph ii 18'-23'? For a similar case compare the inventory text VBoT 83, 6' and 13' (see Ph.H.J. Houwink ten Cate, Natural Phenomena 142 n. 51, and J. Hazenbos, Diss. 167-168) Cf. also KBo XVIII 133: see H.G. Güterbock in the Inhaltsübersicht to KBo XVIII and HW^2 A 79b s.v. *annarumai* ("Orakelergebnis") and 303b s.v. *arkamman-* ("Orakel").

which VI 9+XVIII 59 (CTH 578), L 77+XLIX 73 (CTH 582) and XVI 20 (CTH 572) represent comprehensive versions.[39] Similarly, V 6+ (CTH 570) can be considered a summary versus the comprehensive texts XVIII 3 and XXII 8; for more detail see immediately below. In the remaining cases it is either difficult[40] or impossible to identify matching comprehensive versions.

To conclude, one could say that in a sense these summaries can be regarded as a special kind of duplicate, another rare phenomenon in the genre of oracle texts. H. Berman cited the following examples:[41] IBoT II 129//898/v+XVI 35(+?)KBo XXII 139,[42] XVIII 18//XVIII 19+L 107 and the various duplicates within CTH 568. G. Beckman added XXII 67//LII 72 rev.,[43] and the examples within CTH 569 complete the list for the time being. In spite of the generally poor state of preservation of oracle texts one cannot doubt that as a rule they were not meant to be kept for long in the Hittite archives nor were they regularly copied for the purpose of further use. Where we do have genuine duplicates or summaries, special circumstances must have required them. In the case of CTH 569 the political situation of the time will have been sufficient reason, whereas in the case of CTH 568 the implementation of the oracle results and their wide range of implications over several of the most important festivals may have justified the existence of more than one copy. All of these cases deserve and require further research. The genre of oracle texts thus turns out to be extremely complicated in terms of text tradition: besides the 'classic' comprehensive versions there existed copies in varying degrees of dependency, i.e. duplicates as well as summaries of various sorts. Moreover, the comprehensive recordings themselves bear evidence of different stages according to the frequent remarks that a certain topic still had to be investigated or had already been inquired into some other time. Finally, CTH 569 and related texts (see Ch. III.3 and VI) offer a good example for the fact that problems were seldom considered to have straightforward answers: often a long and complicated series of investigations was needed before a problem was solved.

[39] For this group see Th. van den Hout, ZA 81 (1991) 274-300, and below Ch. VI.

[40] For VI 15 A. Archi, KUB XLIX Inhaltsübersicht v, suggests a link with XLIX 94 because of the SISKUR *pupuu̯alanaš* mentioned in both texts (cf. VI 15 ii 13 SISKUR *pu-pu-u̯a-la-n*[*a*- and XLIX 94 ii 11' SISKUR *pu-*⌈*pu*⌉*-u̯a-la-an-*⌈*na*⌉*-aš*). A SISKUR *pupuu̯alannaš* is also attested in VBoT 25 i 4. Similarly, the texts XVIII 23 and LII 14 mentioning the *ḫii̯arra*-festival might be related to XVIII 18//19+L 107 (cf. A. Ünal, THeth. 6, 18); on the name *ḫii̯arra* see now M.-C. Trémouille, Eothen 7, 98-102, esp. 101. For a possible link between LX 26 (ed. H. Klengel, AoF 16 (1989) 185) and XXII 63 see my StBoT 38, 104-105.

[41] JCS 32 (1982) 123-124.

[42] Cf. H. Otten - Chr. Rüster, ZA 62 (1972) 106, and H. Berman, JCS 34 (1982) 95-96.

[43] Cf. G. Beckman, BiOr. 42 (1985) 140.

5. *Comprehensive recordings versus summaries: some examples*

As a first example of an oracle investigation of the comprehensive type versus the summarized version VI 9+XVIII 59 ii? (I.) and XVIII 36 (II. in small print) may serve respectively.[44] In order to show their parallelism they are given *in Partitur*:

I. 1 [*kuitman* M]U-*anni kēdani mēḫuni*
II. 7' [kuitman MU-a]nni kēdani mēḫ[uni
2 [*IN*]*A*? ITU.8.KAM *parā mān=ma ANA* ᵈUTU-*ŠI*
II.7' *INA*? ITU.8.KAM] (8') [parā mā]n?=ma *ANA* ᵈUTU-*ŠI*
3 [DINGIR.M]EŠ TI-*tar* GAM-*an šekteni* TI-*anzaš*
II. 8' DINGIR.MEŠ TI[-tar GAM-an šekteni] (9') [TI-anzaš]
4 [*A-N*]*A* SAG.DU ᵈUTU-*ŠI dapian dapiza* (erasure)
II. 9' *ANA* SAG.DU ᵈUTU-*ŠI* dapian [dapiza
5 [SIG_5-]*in nu* IGI-*ziš* UDU-*iš* SIG_5-*ru*
II. 9' SIG_5-in]
6 [EGIR=]*ma* NU.SIG_5-*du* IGI-*ziš* UDU-*iš*

(Room for ca.11 lines left open in I.)

If then, [until] the next [y]ear at this time [i]n the eighth month you, [o god]s, foresee life for His Majesty, (and) he will live, (and) everything in every way (will be) favorable for His Majesty's person, then let the first sheep be favorable, the following (one), however, unfavorable. The first sheep ...

The summary version XVIII 36, 7'-9' can technically be considered an exact duplicate of VI 9+ ii? 1-5, but then the two diverge. The latter starts in line 6 with a *šašt*-oracle which, however, was either never conducted or never recorded, since it continues after the blank space with a KIN-oracle:

I. 7 [*IŠTU* ᴹᵁᴺᵁˢŠ]U.GI IR-*TUM QĀTAMMA*[=*pat nu* KIN SIG_5-*ru*]
8 [*pankuš*=]*za* ZAG[-*tar ŠA* LUGAL=*i̯a ADAMMA* ME-*aš*]
9 [*n*=*at* DIN]GIR.MAḪ-*ni p*[*aiš INA* ŬD.2.KAM]
10 [*nu*=*kan* DINGI]R.MEŠ-*aš INA* UD.3.K[AM]
11 [ME-*aš nu*=*k*]*an* DINGIR.MEŠ-*aš* S[IG_5(?)]

---

[44] For a more detailed treatment of these two texts see Th. van den Hout, ZA 81 (1991)279-283, and below Ch. IV.3. Note that H. Berman, JCS 34 (1982) 124, had already linked these fragments as an example "of oracle questions or parts of oracle questions which occur in two different texts."

This matches the continuation in XVIII 36, 10' where only a KIN-oracle is mentioned:

II. 10' [*IŠT*]*U* ⌈^{MUNUS}⌉ŠU.GI [SIG$_5$(?)]

VI 9+ then continues as follows:

I. 12 [*A-NA* ^{d}UTU-*Š*]*I*=*kan kuit* LUGAL-*uiznani a*[*šātar*]
13 [*duuān*] *parā arḫa zalukišta*
14 [*mān*=*ma*=*z*]*a*=*kan kuitman* ^{d}UTU-*ŠI*
15 [LUGAL-*uiznan*]*i ešari kuitman*=*kan*
16 [*apiia*(?) EGI]R-*panda mān*=*ma* ^{d}UTU-*ŠI*
17 [*ḫadduliš*] *ANA* SAG.DU=*ŠU*=*ši UL kuit*[*ki* ḪUŠ-*ueni*]
18 [*nu* IGI-*zi*]*š* UDU-*iš* SIG$_5$-*ru* EGIR=*ma* NU.SIG$_5$-*d*[*u*]

(Room for ca.10 lines left open)

---

19 [*IŠTU* ^{MUNUS}ŠU.G]I IR-*TUM QĀTAMMA*=*pat n*[*u* KIN SIG$_5$-*ru*]
20 [DINGIR-*LUM*=*za*] *dapian* ZI-*an* T[I$^{?}$-*tarr*=*a* ME-*aš n*=*at* ... *paiš*$^{?}$]
21 [*INA* UD.2.KAM LUGAL$^{?}$-]*uš*=*za* ZAG-*tar* MU-*an* x[ME-*aš*]
22 [*n*=*at* DINGIR.MAḪ-*ni p*]*aiš INA* UD.3.KAM *ŠA*[DINGIR.MEŠ *minumar*$^{ḪI.A}$]
23 [ME-*aš nu*=*ka*]*n ANA* GIG.TUR [SIG$_5$/NU.SIG$_5$]

As to the fact that [for His Maje]sty the a[ccession] to kingship was further postponed, [if then], until His Majesty sits down [in kingshi]p (and) for as long as [(he will be) there afte]rwards, if then His Majesty [(will be) in good health (and) [we will have] nothi[ng to fear for] his person, [then let the fir]st sheep be favorable, but le[t] the following one be unfavorab[le]. (followed by check through KIN-oracle)

At this point XVIII 36, 11'ff. diverges from VI 9+ ii$^{?}$ 12ff. in the sense that it seems to leave out VI 9+ ii$^{?}$ 12-23 altogether and continues with a text possibly corresponding to line 24ff.:

I. 24 [ ]⌈^{d}⌉UTU-*ŠI* LUGAL-*uizn*[*ani*
II. 11 [kui]tman=za=kan ^{d}UTU-*ŠI* LUGAL-iznani ešar[i *ANA* ^{d}UTU-*ŠI*=kan(?)]
25 [*aš*]*atar ku-it* [
II. 12 [LUG]AL-iznani ašātar kuit za-lu-qa-nu-me-en
26 [ ] *mā*[*n*
II. 12 [n=at GAM-an] (13) [a]rḫa GAR-ru mān=ma=za=kan kuitman ^{d}[UTU-*ŠI*]
14 [LUGAL-i]znani ešari kuitman=kan *ANA* LU[GAL-iznani]
15 [EGI]R-pa anda mān=ma DINGIR.MEŠ *ANA* ^{d}UTU-*ŠI* x[

16 [GI]G GAM-an *UL* kuinki šekteni *ANA* ^{d}[UTU-*ŠI*=i̯a=kan(?)]
17 [LUGAL]-iznani ašātar UN-aš *IŠTU* MUD *U*[*L* arḫa]
18 [d]āi *IŠTU* ^{MUNUS}ŠU.GI *IŠTU* ^{LÚ}ḪAL=i̯a x[

> [Un]til His Majesty wi[ll] sit down in kingship, – that we have postponed [for His Majesty] the accession to [ki]ngship, let [that] be out of consideration now – if, until His M[ajesty] will sit down in [kings]hip, for as long as he will be in ki[ngship aft]erwards, if then, o gods, you do not foresee for His Majesty any [il]lness, [and (if)] from H[is Majesty] no man will [t]ake [away] with bloodshed the accession to [king]ship, through the 'Old Woman' and the diviner ... [...]

The scribe responsible for the excerpt XVIII 36 may also have deemed it expedient to combine the two paragraphs VI 9+ ii$^?$ 12-18 and 24ff. into one. For, if the lines XVIII 36, 11'ff. do indeed correspond to VI 9+ ii$^?$ 24ff., these two paragraphs amount to much the same thing. Note also that again the space left open for the clinomantic results announced after VI 9+ ii$^?$ 18 has not been filled out. Yet, XVIII 36, 18 this time does mention the officiating priest (^{LÚ}ḪAL). This means that either after the paragraph VI 9+ ii$^?$ 24ff. a *šašt*-oracle was actually conducted or that by the time XVIII 36 was written down they had started to do so for this part of the oracle. This example may show that at times summary and comprehensive version correspond closely to one another but that scribes also may have taken considerable liberties in rendering the comprehensive version into a shorter one.[45]

In his list Berman also included KBo II 2 (ii 20; CTH 577[46]) which was certainly justified in as far as the summarizing formula is found there too. Together with V 6+, however, KBo II 2 deviates from the summaries as represented in the group mentioned above: there the summarizing formulae are used throughout the text. KBo II 2 and V 6+ combine – each in a different way – comprehensive investigation recordings with summarizing parts. The investigation KBo II 2 tries in its entire first column (i 1-57) and in the first part of the second (ii 1-17) to determine the exact moment in which an illness (*tapašša-* "fever" vel sim.) will befall His Majesty. The techniques deployed are those of the diviner (*ḪURRI*-bird oracle and extispicy) and the 'Old Woman' (KIN-oracle). Then the text continues:

[45] If the series of questions which is asked here for the eighth month in VI 9+ ii$^?$ 2ff. was repeated for other months in a similar but still formulary way (compare the approval for an accession in the twelfth month in XVI 20, 11'), then the possibility cannot be excluded that XVIII 36 as a summary actually corresponds to questions about another of those months, which are not preserved. Note that in XVIII 36, 7' the section corresponding to "the eighth month" in VI 9+ ii 2 is broken away. As long as this cannot be verified or falsified, the correspondence as proposed here is maintained.

[46] For an edition of this text see below Ch. IV.4.

18 ≈*tapaššan ANA* ^{d}UTU-*ŠI*
19 DINGIR-*LUM kuiški i̯azi*
20 *IŠTU* ^{LÚ}ḪAL ^{MUNUS}ŠU.GI=*i̯a* SIxSÁ-*at*

---

21 DINGIR-*LIM-tar kuit* SIxSÁ-*at*
22 *katta* (erasure) *arii̯auen*
23 *nu* ^{d}UTU ^{URU}PÚ-*na* SIxSÁ-*at*
24 *zilaš* NU.SIG$_5$

Some deity will cause fever$^{?}$ for His Majesty. Through the diviner and the 'Old Woman' it was ascertained.
(To find out) which deity was ascertained, we continued the inquiry.
The Sungoddess of Arinna was ascertained. Outcome: unfavorable.

The lines ii 18-20 summarize the entire preceding investigation (i 1-ii 17). The next paragraph ii 21-24 forms the transition from the first part establishing fever for the king caused by a certain deity to the next part (ii 25-iii 9) where the exact variant of the Sungoddess of Arinna is ultimately determined (namely the Sungoddess DUMU-*annaš* "of Progeny"[47]). The remainder of the inquiry is devoted to the reason for her anger and the way to pacify her. It is likely that the transitional paragraph ii 21-24 itself summarizes an investigation (cf. the preterite *arii̯auen* "we investigated") of the nature of the deity causing the illness which resulted in the Sungoddess of Arinna as the angry one. The following paragraph ii 25-28 takes that investigation up at the point where the Sungoddess of Arinna had turned out to be the main cause but where it was asked whether she was the only one angry:

25 *nu dammaiš kuiški* DINGIR-*LUM kardimmii̯auanza*
26 *nu aši* INIM GIG *apāš i̯azi*
27 *nu TE*^{MEŠ} NU.SIG$_5$-*du zeḫilipšiman*
28 NU.SIG$_5$

(Is) some other deity angry and is that (deity) causing the aforementioned matter of the illness? Then let the exta be unfavorable. *Zeḫilipšiman*; unfavorable.

The remaining part of the investigation is, like this paragraph, again recorded in the comprehensive way, from now on using extispicy only. Therefore the formula (*IŠTU* ^{LÚ}ḪAL ^{MUNUS}ŠU.GI=*i̯a* SIxSÁ-*at*) is used only once in KBo II 2 ii 20 and cannot be directly compared to the same phrase in the summaries listed above. Here it summarizes the preceding investigation, leading up to a transitional paragraph which stands for what

47 For this term see Th. van den Hout, ZA 81 (1991) 291-292 with n. 30; for the translation cf. CHD P 153b.

must have been an entirely separate investigation. The transitional paragraph ii 21-24 is the actual one comparable to the group of summary texts: it summarizes something that is not recorded on this tablet. The summarized part, however, is so extensive that the two standard phrases did not suffice to express what was required here.

As far as its sometimes very fragmentary state of preservation allows us to judge, the large oracle investigation V 6+ XVIII 54 (CTH 570[48]), like KBo II 2, seems to deal mainly with an illness of His Majesty.[49] This problem is approached from many different angles, so much so that the tablet becomes somewhat of a *Sammeltafel*. Four techniques are mentioned as having been used (extispicy, augury and KIN-oracle; there is one mention of the *ḪURRI*-bird oracle[50]). The first column almost completely (i 6' till the end[51]) concerns the way (*ŠA* ᶠ*Mizzulla iu̯ar* "according to (the woman) Mizzulla"[52], *ŠA* (LÚ) ᵁᴿᵁ*Aštata iu̯ar* "according to (the man from the land) Aštata"[53] and ᵁᴿᵁKÙ.BABBAR-*aš iu̯ar* "according to Ḫattuša"[54]) in which certain festivals and rituals are to be celebrated in connection with His Majesty's illness (GIG ᵈUTU-*ŠI* i 42'). After a break of approximately 20 to 25 lines the text continues on column ii with the same topic (cf. ii 4' ᵁᴿᵁ*Aštata*) until the double paragraph after ii 12'. What remains of the second column (ii 13'-72b, end of column) and the beginning of the third (iii 1-38) deal with several Zawalli deities, again in connection with an illness of His Majesty.[55] It is here that penance has been established for His Majesty and a man by the name of Antarawa (or ᵈTarawa?). The Zawallis are those of the cities Zitḫara and Ankuwa and of His Majesty's house (*parnalliš* ... ᵈ*Zawalliš ŠA* ᵈUTU-*ŠI* iii 13), and deities of the geographical entities Aḫḫiyawa and Lazpa are mentioned. The last topic here is the curse of Mašḫuiluwa (iii 8 sqq.). It is not clear whether after a break of some 15 lines (iii 56'-82') the remainder of col. iii is still part of this same investigation but at least none of the elements of the preceding section seem to return. Instead, somebody's statue and a *tawananna*'s domain are mentioned (iii 64') as well as her(?) being "sent down from the palace" (*IŠTU* É.GAL-*LIM* GAM *uii̯au̯u̯aš* iii 74') and a *ḫegur* of ᵈLAMMA (iii 76'), the latter two strongly reminiscent of the last spouse

48 To the literature given in CTH 570 for this text can be added A. Archi, SMEA 22 (1980) 22-24, AoF 6 (1979) 87-89, Ph.H.J. Houwink ten Cate, JEOL 28 (1983-1984) 44 Anm. 26, F. Imparati, SMEA 18 (1977) 35-36, A. Ünal, THeth. 3, 168-169.

49 For a detailed analysis of its contents see F. Sommer, AU 275-288.

50 V 6+ iv 28.

51 The first preserved lines of the first column may have been concerned with again another aspect of His Majesty's illness because of the double paragraph line after i 5'. There seems to be a double paragraph line after i 1' as well.

52 V 6+ i 8'-9', 18', 23', 25'-26', 28', 34'.

53 V 6+ i 9' (*išḫiūl ŠA* ᵁᴿᵁ*Aštata*), 17', 20', 27'.

54 V 6+ i 36'.

55 V 6+ ii 38', 45', 65'; cf. also iii 5-6 *maḫḫan=ma* ᵈUTU-*ŠI* *ḫattulišzi* "if, however, His Majesty recovers, ..."

of Šuppiluliuma and *tawananna* under Muršili (on her see below Ch. II.2). Gold shoes play an important role (iii 75', 78', 80') there. Unfortunately, the fourth column is poorly preserved and it is not exactly clear what problems are dicussed. The left edge, finally, mentions oaths of the father and grandfather of His Majesty.[56]

This whole oracle investigation shows a mixture of comprehensive and summary paragraphs. The comprehensively styled paragraphs are all extispicies[57] in many cases checked and counterchecked through a KIN-oracle which is only given in summarized form; cf. i 15'-16' *IŠTU* MUNUSŠU.GI=*ma* KIN 3-*ŠU* SIG_5 "through the 'Old Woman' the KIN-oracle three times: favorable". Sometimes augury is added, cf. ii 5'-6':

> [... Š]À É.⌈DINGIR-*LIM*⌉ *A-NA* DINGIR-*LIM ši-ip-pa-an-du-wa-an-zi*
> [*IŠ-TU* LÚMUŠEN.]DÙ LÚ⌈AZU⌉ MUNUSŠU.GI-*i̯a* SIxSÁ-*at*
>
> [Through the aug]ur, the diviner and the 'Old Woman' it was ascertained to bring offerings [... i]n the temple to the deity.

Occasionally the experts had diverging opinions, cf. ii 8':

> *IŠ-TU* MUNUSŠU.GI SIG_5 *IŠ-TU* LÚAZU LÚMUŠEN.DÙ-*i̯a* NU.SIG_5
>
> Through the 'Old Woman' favorable, through the diviner and the augur unfavorable.

Often it is merely stated that the measures to be taken or a conclusion reached as laid down in a particular paragraph were "ascertained" (SIxSÁ-*at*) without mentioning any techniques at all.

That despite the several comprehensive paragraphs this tablet was a later compilation on the basis of completely comprehensive records is clear for two reasons. First of all, many paragraphs are concluded with a later comment on the situation, cf. i 34'-37':

> 34' *A-NA* DINGIR-*LIM ŠA* f*Mi-iz-zu-ul-la i-u̯a-ar kar-tim-mi-i̯a-ad-du-uš*
> 35' *še-er ar-ḫa da-an-zi nam-ma-kán* ⌈dUTU-*ŠI*⌉ *A-NA* DINGIR-*LIM* 1 GU_4 6 UDU-*i̯a*
> 36' URUKÙ.BABBAR-*aš i-u̯a-ar ši-ip-pa-an-ti* DINGIR-*LIM-za QA-TAM-MA ma-la-a-an ḫar-ti*

56 *ŠA ABI* dUTU-*ŠI*=*i̯a*=*za*=*kan U ŠA ABI ABI* dUTU-*ŠI MĀMĒTI*ḪI.A ŠÀ SISKUR.MEŠ? DÙ?-*zi* "and he (i.e. His Majesty) will make/treat the oaths of His Majesty's father and of His Majesty's grandfather in a ritual(?)."

57 Paragraphs containing comprehensively phrased extispicies: V 6+ i 2'-5', 6'-13', 14'-16', 27'-30', 34'-37', ii 42'-44', 45'-56', 57'-64', iii 8-11, 12-16, 17-28, 67'-70'(?), 76'-80'(?), iv 27-28(?).

37' *nu TE*^{MEŠ} SIG$_5$-*ru ni ši ta ke zi* GAR-*ri* 10 ŠÀ *DIR* SIG$_5$ *ka-ru-ú* SUM-*an*

Will they take away the anger from the deity according to Mizzulla? Will His Majesty, furthermore, offer to the deity one ox and six sheep according to (the custom of) Ḫattuša? If you, o god, have thus approved, then let the exta be favorable. *Ni(pašuri)*, *ši(ntaḫi)*, *ta(nani)*, *ke(ldi)*, a bladderworm lies (there), ten coils: favorable. Already given.

Other such short comments can be found in i 5' (*kar*]*ū parā* SUM-*ir* "They have already handed over"), ii 12' (*parā nāu̯i ari̯an* "Not yet further investigated") and iv 10 (*nāu̯i ari̯an* "Not yet investigated"); similar comments are also found after summarized oracle results or at the end of paragraphs without any reference whatsoever to oracular techniques, cf. ii 3' (*nu* ^{URU}*Urikina karū uiēr* "They have already sent to the city of Urikina"), 4' (*nu karū IŠPUR* "He has already sent"), iii 7 (^{LÚ}SANGA *nāu̯i zinnanza* "(The case of) the priest (is) not yet finished"), iv 2 (*nu antuḫš*[...] *uiēr* "They have sent a/the m[an/m[en"), 18 (*n*]=*an karū ari̯at* "He has investigated him already"). Longer comments can be found in ii 32'-35', 69', iii 73', 79'-80'. Because of the adverb *nāu̯i* "not yet" apparently a second phase of the inquiry had yet to come. From all this we can only conclude that the scribe in some cases faithfully copied his *Vorlage* and summarized it in others. Something of a system can be recognized in as far as he only extensively copied observations of the oracle priest, if it was the first technique used, but never the observations in checks and counterchecks.

Some texts can be identified as probably being fragments of comprehensive versions on the basis of which V 6+ might have been composed. This is, as was in a general way already seen by F. Sommer, AU 292-293, in his treatment of V 6+, undeniably the case with the fragments XXII 8 and XVIII 3.[58] In two of the five paragraphs preserved on the obv.? of XXII 8 the oracle technique can be identified as extispicy.[59] In four of those the *zankilatar ŠA* ^{d}UTU-*ŠI Ù ŠA* ^{m}*Antarau̯a* "the penance of His Majesty and of Antarawa" is mentioned five times.[60] This phrase matches the one in V 6+ ii 14'-15' and 48':

13' [^{d}*Za-u̯a-al-li*-]⌈*i*⌉-*iš ku-it* SIxSÁ-*at nu* ^{d}UTU-*ŠI ku-it A-NA* SISKUR EGIR-*an Ú-UL*

[58] The fragment XVIII 67 – a summary of the intermediate type – might be related to V 6+ as well. Its obv.? deals with one or more Zawalli-deities (obv.? 10) and curses which should be undone "according to (the custom of) the land Arzawa", thus recalling V 6+ iii 29ff. On the rev.? a "deity of the city of Ankuwa of His Majesty's father" is attested three times (2', 5', 7') which reminds of V 6+ ii 65ff.

[59] XXII 8 obv.? 4' and 10'.

[60] XXII 8 obv.? 2', 3', 5', 8' and 11' (all more or less fragmentary).

14’ [-*i*]*t nu a-pa-a-at* SIxSÁ-*at nu a-pád-da še-er ŠA* ^{d}UTU-*ŠI za-an-ki-la-tar*
15’ [*ŠA* ^{m}*An-ta-ra-u̯a-i̯*]*a za-an-ki-*⌈*la*⌉*-tar ma-aḫ-ḫa-an* SIxSÁ-*at na-at ka-ru-ú* SUM-*an*

As to the fact that [a Zawall]i-deity was ascertained: that for the offering His Majesty had not later [...], that was ascertained. The penance for His Majesty and penance [for Antarawa], as it was ascertained for that reason, (has) already (been) given.

(...)

45’ ^{d}*Za-wa-al-li-i-iš ku-it ŠA* ^{URU}*Zi-it-ḫa-ra A-NA* GIG ^{d}UTU-*ŠI še-er* [a] TUKU.TUKU-*at-ti* SIxSÁ-*at*
46’ *nu-kán* $^{MUNUS.MEŠ}$*dam-ma-ra-an-za I-NA* ^{URU}*Zi-it-ḫa-ra pa-ra-a ne-an-zi*
47’ *nu pa-a-an-zi* EME.MEŠ EGIR-*pa a-ni-i̯a-*⌈*an-zi*⌉ É.DINGIR-*LIM-*⌈*i̯a*⌉ *pár-ku-nu-u̯a-an-zi*
48’ *za-an-ki-la-tar*$^{HI.A}$*-i̯a ku-e ŠA* ^{d}UTU-*ŠI ŠA* ^{m}*An-ta-ra-u̯a*[*-i̯*]*a* SIxSÁ-*at*
49’ *na-at pí-an-zi* ...

[a] Both GIG and *šer* later added above the line, cf. already F. Sommer, AU 280 n. 3; somewhat differently (*A-NA* ^{d}UTU-*ŠI* GIG *še-er*) A. Archi, AoF 6 (1979) 88.

As to the fact that the Zawalli-deity of the city of Zitḫara was ascertained (to be) in anger in connection with the illness of His Majesty, will they send out *dammarā*-women to Zitḫara, will they go (and) undo the curses and purify the temple? And will they give the penances of His Majesty and of Antarawa which were established?

On XXII 8 rev.? we find again the GN Zitḫara (9’) and a temple (4’), which could link it to V 6+ 45’ff. or 70’ff., thus probably confirming the determination of the obverse and reverse side.

The fragment XVIII 3 seems to be related to V 6+ ii 21’-35’. It offers the right half or slightly more of a fourth? column with traces of the beginnings of some lines of a third? column. After two checks through extispicy (iv 1’-2’) and augury (iv 3’-5’) following a question now lost to us, the next paragraph (iv 6’-13’) contains a deposition about a ritual or offering in the palace involving *dammarā*-women (iv 7’). The question is answered through augury, although the result is surprisingly formulated as NU.SIG$_{5}$-*u̯a* “unfavorable” (iv 13’) instead of with the familiar *arḫa=u̯a peššii̯andu* vel sim. This result is subsequently checked and counter-checked by way of two other techniques of which only the twice “unfavorable” result is preserved (iv 14’ and 15’). The fragment ends with another longer deposition:

16' [ ]⌈*pu*⌉*-nu-uš-šir nu IQ-BI* ŠÀ É.GAL-*LIM-u̯a-kán*
17' [*I-N*]*A* ^{URU}*Ma-ra-aš-ša*[*-an-ti-i̯*]*a*$^{!}$*-u̯a-an-na-aš*
18' [ ]x *I-NA* ^{URU}⌈*Zi*⌉[*-it-ḫa-*]⌈*ra*⌉*-u̯a-an-na-aš*
19' [(-)*n*]*a-aš-za pí-ra-an* ⌈*ar-ḫa*⌉ *šu-u-u̯a-it*
20' [ ]x*-an-u̯a-an-na-aš I-NA* ^{URU}*Zi-it-ḫa-ra*
21' [ ]^{d}UTU-*ŠI* ^{f}*Ta-a-ti-u̯a-aš-ti-iš-ša* x[o]
22' [ ]*am-mu-uk-u̯a-za* ^{MUNUS}*dam-ma-ra-a ku-i*[*t*]
23' [ ]x*-aš za-aḫ-ta IŠ-*⌈*TU*⌉ SAG.DU-*i̯a*/*IA-u̯*[*a*]
24' [𒑱*ḫi-ru-ta-n*]*i-aḫ-ḫa* 𒑱*ti-u̯a-*⌈*ta*⌉*-ni-aḫ-ḫa*
25' [ ]x*-na-aš ma-al-lu-u̯a-an-zi*
26' [SIxSÁ-*at* DINGI]R-*LUM-u̯a-kán ku-u̯a-pí*
27' [ ]UD.3.KAM *pa-ra-a ú-u̯*[*a-*
28' [ ]x *pa-ra-a* ⌈*ú*⌉[-
29' [ ] x x [

16' [...] they interrogated and she[a] said: "In the palace
17' [... i]n the city of Marašša[ntiy]a (to/for?) us
18' [...] ... in the city of Zi[tḫa]ra (to/for?) us
19' [...] he chased away in front of [u]s?
20' [...] ... (to/for?) us in Zitḫara
21' [...] His Majesty and Tatiwašti ... [...]
22' [...] sin[ce] I am a *dammarā*-woman,
23' [...] ... she/he beat and with (my) head[b]
24' [...] I [swo]re, I cursed,
25' [...] ... to grind
26' [I? was/we were ascertained? ...]
27' [...] when [the dei]ty [...]."

[a] Because of line 22' it seems most likely that a *dammarā*-woman is speaking here. [b] Or *IŠ-*⌈*TU*⌉ SAG.DU-*IA-* "(and) with my head"?

Several of the key elements in the above passage (the GN Maraššantiya and Zitḫara, His Majesty and the PN Tatiwašti,[61] the *dammarā*-woman as well as the "milling/grinding") seem to recur in V 6+ ii 21'-29':

[61] Another possible occurrence of this name is attested in KBo XXXVI 111 ii 2 *DI-NU ŠA* ^{f}*Ta-a-*⌈*ti*⌉[-, cf. G. Wilhelm, KBo XXXVI Inhaltsübersicht vii.

21’ *nu-kán IŠ-TU* ^{MUNUS}ENSI *ŠA* x[o o o o o]⸢^{MUNUS}*dam*⸣-*ma-ra-*
⸢*a*⸣$^{?}$[o o o o] x x x x x [?]
22’ MUNUS ^{URU}*Iš-ki-i̯a-u̯a-za* NÍG.BA.ḪI.A x[ ] x [
23’ *nu-u̯a-ra-at A-NA* SISKUR *ŠA* ^{d}UTU-*ŠI* [
24’ ŠÀ É.DINGIR-*LIM-i̯a-u̯a-kán an-tu-uḫ-šu-u*[*š*
25’ *I-NA* ^{URU}*Ma-ra-aš–ša-an-ti-i̯a-u̯a*$^{!a}$*-za ku-u̯a-p*[*í*
26’ ^{f}*Ta-a-ti-u̯a-aš-ti-in-na* ^{MUNUS}*dam-ma-ra-*[*a*(-)
27’ UD.KAM-*ti-li ma-al-liš-kán-zi* ^{f}*Pa-az-*⸢*za*⸣[(-)
28’ *pa-ra-a tar-nu-ma-aš me-ḫur u̯a-aš-ta-nu-ir nu-u̯*[*a*
29’ *Ú-UL i-i̯a-at-ta-at* ...

a This emendation seems preferable to ^{URU}*Ma-ra-aš–ša-an-ti-i̯a-<u̯a-ra->aš-za* because it requires fewer changes, it leads, however, to a translation (see below) different from the one proposed by F. Sommer, AU 279: “al(s$^{?}$) sie/er in die/der Stadt Maraššantija [... ”.

21’ And by the divination priestess of ... [...] *dammarā*-
[woman/women ...] ...
22’ “The woman from the city of Iškiya gifts ... [
23’ and these for the offering of His Majesty [
24’ and in the temple people [
25’ Whe[n I$^{?}$ was] in Maraššantiya [
26’ Tatiwašti (and$^{?}$) the *dammarā*[-woman (obj.)
27’ daily they grind. Pazza[(-)
28’ the moment of setting free they made into a sin and [
29’ she$^{?}$ did not go ... ”

In line 40’ff. the city of Zitḫara is mentioned, where they will send *dammarā*-women. Although the parallelism between V 6+ on the one hand and XVIII 3 on the other is less exact than with XXII 8, there is a clear relation between the two. At this point the oracles XVI 16 and KBo XXIII 114 should be mentioned also: in these texts *dammara*-women figure in connection with the Zawalli-deity (of the temple) of Zithara (KBo XXIII 114) and the *parā tarnummaš*-festival (XVI 16) while certain impurities of a temple and cultic negligences seem to be at stake. If there exists a link between the latter two, XVIII 3 and XXII 8, as well as that section of V 6+ which deals with these *dammara*-women, this might plead for a late date for V 6+, since XVI 16 and KBo XXIII 114 may be part of the larger series of oracle inquiries of which CTH 569 constitutes only the last link.[62]

[62] For this see Ch. III.3; for an edition of XVI 16 and KBo XXIII 114 see Ch. IV.5.1.1-2. The date of V 6+ is disputed: whereas E. Forrer, MDOG 63 (1924) 14, merely characterized it as “ein Omentext, der Geschehnisse aus den ersten Jahren des Morsilis behandelt”, F. Sommer, AU 289-290, and H.G. Güterbock, AJA 87 (1983) 134 with n. 12, and of course Archi, loc.cit., opted for Muršili II, versus A. Kammenhuber, THeth. 7, 27-28 n. 51, F. Imparati, SMEA 18 (1977) 25 n. 26, and Th. van den Hout, StBoT 38, 242, who propose a date in the reign of his son

In conclusion we can say that 'pure' summaries like, for instance, XVIII 36 and fully comprehensive oracle investigations like VI 9+ represent only two extremes of more ways to record oracle investigations. The text V 6+ is an example illustrative of an intermediate form. Other representatives of this type are VIII 27+, as will be shown below, XVIII 67, XXII 40 and AT 454. Among the smaller summary fragments given above there may be others, but as long as they are not proven to be of the intermediary type by way of joins or duplicates they can best be treated as 'pure' summaries. At the end of this section an overview of those summaries is given where their correlating comprehensive versions may be identified:

'pure' summary	*'intermediate' version*	*comprehensive version*
Accession oracles:		
XVIII 36, XXII 12((+)13?)		VI 9+XVIII 59, XVI 20, L 77+XLIX 73[63] and possibly XLIX 2(+)?XVIII 6[64]
Illness of His Majesty:		
–	V 6+	XVIII 3, XXII 8
CTH 569:		
KBo IX 151, XVI 32, XXII 35, XLIX 93, L 6+, LII 92, 10/v	VIII 27(+)	KBo II 6+ XVI 58 L 5

By far the best illustration for the existence of different types of oracle recording as outlined in this section is supplied by the texts constituting CTH 569 to which we will turn now.

Ḫattušili III. A. Ünal, THeth. 3, 168-170, does not seem to commit himself. The terminus post quem of Mašḫuiluwa's death obtained by a definition of the *mantalli*-ritual according to which one of the two parties conducting such a ritual "was usually deceased" (CHD L-N 178b), is inconclusive (see above Ch. I.1). However that may be, F. Imparati, loc.cit., rightly remarks that the identification of the *tawananna* in V 6+ as Muršili's stepmother and a later date for this text are not mutually exclusive. The proposed link with XVI 16 and KBo XXIII 114 would even plead for a date in the reign of Tutḫaliya IV. The "grandfather of His Majesty" mentioned in V 6+ left edge 8 would then be Muršili II. and would at the same time support the fact that Tutḫaliya would have inquired into affairs from his days.

[63] The fragment XLIX 73 was not yet included in my article ZA 81 (1991) 274-300 as a direct join to L 77.

[64] For this text as probably part of the accession oracles see Ph.H.J. Houwink ten Cate, AoF 23 (1996) 71-72 with n. 56.

6. *Comprehensive recordings versus summaries within CTH 569*

The most obvious example of a summary within CTH 569 is to be found in VIII 27(+)Bo 7787, part of the investigation into the case of Armatarḫunta and Šaušgatti. Compare, for instance, rev. 1'-6':[65]

x+1 GAM *kišan a*[*ri̯i̯auen* EME ^{f}]$^{⸢\text{d}⸣}$*IŠTAR-atti kui*[*t*]
2' SIxSÁ-*at nu* EME [^{fd}*IŠTAR-atti*] *ANA* DINGIR.MEŠ LUGAL-*U*[*TTI*]
3' *pian arḫa ani*[*i̯anzi AŠR*]*I*$^{\text{ḪI.A}}$ LUGAL-*UTTI* [^{GIŠ}DAG.ḪI.A=*i̯a*]
4' *parkunuu̯anzi* ^{d}[UTU-*ŠI*=*i̯a*=*za*] *parku<n>uzzi*[GIDIM=*i̯a*]
5' UGU *ašeša*[*nu*]*anz*[*i šarni*]*kzell*[=*a* ME-*anzi*]
6' *n*=*at ANA* GIDIM [SUM-*anzi*] *ANA* DUMU.MEŠ=*ŠU*[ ]
7' *IŠTU* 3 ^{GIŠ}TUKUL[SIG$_5$]

This passage summarizes KBo II 6 iii 41-iv 23. Up to line 6' (*n*=*at ANA* GIDIM [SUM-*anzi*) it runs parallel to KBo II 6 iii 41-46:

41 GAM *kišan arii̯auen*
42 EME ^{fd}*IŠTAR-atti kuit* TI-*andaš* SIxSÁ-*at*
43 *nu kišan* DÙ-*anzi* EME ^{fd}*IŠTAR-atti ANA* DINGIR.MEŠ [LUGAL-*UTTI*]
44 *piran arḫa anii̯anzi* GIDIM=*i̯a šarā*
45 *ašešanuu̯anzi šarnikzell*=*a* ME-*anzi*
46 *n*=*at ANA* GIDIM SUM-*anzi mān*=*ma*=*za* DINGIR-*LUM* KI.MIN
47 *ŠA* INIM ^{fd}*IŠTAR-atti*=*naš*=*kan apēz m*[*e*]*minaza*
48 *laittari* DINGIR-*LUM*=*naš ANA* INIM ^{fd}*IŠTAR-atti*
49 ^{TÚG}*šeknun* EGIR-*pa UL kuitki* SUD-*i̯aši*

We continued the inquiry as follows: Because the curse of Šaušgatti, alive, has been ascertained, they will do as follows: the curse of Šaušgatti in front of the gods [of kingship] they will undo, and (an effigy of) the deceased they will set up and they will take the compensation and give it to the deceased. Now, if you, o god, etc., (if) the Šaušgatti affair is removed from us by that d[e]ed, (and if) you, o god, over the Šaušgatti affair will not pull back the robe at us in any way, ...

Note that the phrase *AŠRI*$^{\text{ḪI.A}}$ ... *parku<n>uzzi* (cf. VIII 27(+) rev. 3'-4') is left out in the comprehensive version, just as the same scribe substituted the formula *QATAMMA malān harši* for KI.MIN two lines later. This does not necessarily mean, that the summary VIII 27(+) cannot have been made on the basis of KBo II 6+ iii 41-46. It is conceivable that the scribe of KBo II 6+, if he wrote the preceding tablets as well, either forgot part of the formula or grew tired of repeating it over and over again, whereas the

[65] For an exact transliteration of the texts of CTH 569 see below Ch. V.

scribe who made the summary may have considered it of importance for a proper understanding of his text to write out the formulas in full.

The same question is then posed through a KIN-oracle (iii 46-51) and checked through a *ḪURRI*-bird oracle (iii 52-53) and a bird oracle (iii 54-59), i.e. all "three oracle types" mentioned in the last line of VIII 27+ rev. 7'. Then, KBo II 6 iii 60-62 continues by repeating the measures already set forth in iii 44-46 but extends it to Šaušgatti's children/sons followed by the usual question:

60 *nu kī=ma kišan* DÙ-*anzi*
61 GIDIM=*i̯a šarā ašešanzi šar*[*n*]*ikze*[*l* ME-*anzi*]
62 *n=at ANA* GIDIM SUM-*anzi ANA* DUMU[.MEŠ-*ŠU*]
63 *mān=ma=za* DINGIR-*LUM Q̣ATAMMA malān* [*ḫa*]*rši*
64 INIM ^{fd}*IŠTAR-atti=naš=kan apēz meminaza*
65 *laittari* DINGIR-*LUM=naš ANA* INIM ^{fd}*IŠTAR-atti*
66 ^{TÚG}*šeknun* EGIR-*pa UL namma kuitki* SUD-*i̯aši*

"Or will they do as follows: They will set up (an effigy of) the deceased, [they will take] co[mp]ensat[ion] and they will give it to the deceased. To [her] children [they will ...]. If you, o god, [h]ave thus approved, will the Šaušgatti affair be removed from us by that deed? Will you, o god, over the Šaušgatti affair not pull back the robe at us in any way anymore?"

This last question is investigated through a *ḪURRI*-bird oracle (iv 1-2) and checked by extispicy (iv 3-4), a lot oracle (iv 5-9) and a bird oracle (iv 10-16). Since the outcome of the last method performed by the augur Kurša-^{d}LAMMA seems to contradict the outcome of the first three, they ask for a second opinion. This countercheck conducted by the augur Armaziti (iv 17-23) finally yields the expected result. Then the tablet KBo II 6 ends. The whole passage KBo II 6+ iii 60-iv 23 is thus in a highly efficient way reduced to VIII 27(+) iv 6' *ANA* DUMU.MEŠ=*ŠU* [...] ! Phrased differently: over fifty lines of comprehensive version (KBo II 6+ iii 41-iv 23) have been reduced to seven lines of summary. The summarizing phrase *IŠTU* 3 ^{GIŠ}TUKUL in VIII 27+ rev. 7' applies, strictly taken, only to KBo II 6+ iii 41-59, where indeed three oracular techniques were deployed. In the continuation KBo II 6+ iii 60-iv 23 four techniques were used (of which one twice) but the scribe who excerpted this tablet must have deemed it of too little importance to dedicate a separate paragraph to this or counted the extispicy and the *ḪURRI*-bird oracle as one type of oracle.[66]

In spite of all this, however, VIII 27(+) is a summary of the 'intermediate' type, as was briefly mentioned earlier. Although highly

[66] On this see above sub 3. *Comprehensive investigations versus summaries.*

fragmentarily preserved, the two paragraphs formed by the lines VIII 27(+) obv. 10'-11' and 12':

---

10 *IŠ-T*[*U*
11 EGIR-*m*[*a*

---

12 *IŠ-T*[*U*

---

can only be explained, it seems, as check and countercheck in the comprehensive style (e.g. KBo II 6+ iii 52-53: *IŠTU* LÚḪAL IR-*TUM QATAMMA*=*pát nu* IGI-*ziš* MUŠEN *ḪURRI* SI[G$_5$-*ru*] EGIR=*ma* NU.SIG$_5$-*du* IGI-*ziš* MUŠEN *ḪURRI* NU.SIG$_5$ EGIR SI[G$_5$]). This same text has been described as a "Sammeltafel" by A. Kammenhuber[67] because of the omina written on the left edge. There may, however, be another explanation for this as we will see below (Ch. V.3).

More complicated is the situation in the investigation concerning a *tawananna*, Danuḫepa, Urḫiteššub and Ḫalpaziti. Unfortunately, the only parts of the comprehensive version which seem to have come down to us, are the small fragments L 5 and XVI 58. We do possess, however, several fragments of summaries. Their relation to one another is difficult to assess. There are two pairs of texts that duplicate each other as far as preserved: XXII 35//XLIX 93 (II.1A and B) and XVI 32//L 6+ (II.3A and B). Where these pairs run parallel (L 6+ iii 7-22 ~ XXII 35 ii//XLIX 93), the lines XLIX 93, 1-4 seem to give a shortened rendering of L 6+ iii 7-15 (§12), whereas XLIX 93, 5-20// XXII 35 ii 1'-17' offer an elaborated version of L 6+ iii 16-22 (§13). The text fragment LII 92 iv (II.4) in its turn is a slightly shorter version of XXII 35 iii. However, because the duplicates XXII 35//XLIX 93 are both longer and shorter compared to L 6+, we cannot be sure that LII 92 was on the whole shorter than XXII 35.

7. *XVI 32 and the structure of CTH 569*

As was briefly referred to above, XVI 32 is an example of an even shorter way of summarizing comprehensive oracle records, that is, by not referring to any techniques at all but simply by stating what was 'ascertained.' Where L 6+ takes over (ii 31'ff.), however, references to oracular techniques are mentioned again by way of the summarizing formulae. This is due to the fact that the whole text XVI 32//L 6+ describes two subsequent stages of the investigation. When XVI 32 starts *in medias res*, some of the results of the investigation of the 'affair of Danuḫepa' are given (§§1'-2'). They concern cities and their tribute. Then, after a

[67] THeth. 7, 84.

double paragraph line, the same is done concerning *mantalli*-offerings by His Majesty to the (*uliḫis* of the) gods of the city of Ḫalpa and the children/sons of Urḫiteššub and Armatarḫunta (§§3'-7'). As of this point, the familiar summarizing formulae start being used, first in two paragraphs about a *tawananna* (§§8'-9'). Then, the affairs of Danuḫepa (§§10'-14') and of the several *mantalli*-offerings involving (the children/sons of) Urḫiteššub (§§15'-19') are taken up again. Those of Danuḫepa and Urḫiteššub are introduced (§10', §16') by saying: "Concerning the matter of PN which was ascertained, we made further oracle investigations." The last paragraph (§14') of those devoted to Danuḫepa corresponds closely to the ones the text began with, mentioning cities and tribute. This implies that the first paragraphs devoted to Danuḫepa (§§1'-2'), continued in §14', were likely to be preceded by paragraphs continuing the topics referred to in §§10'-13'. These were in all likelihood preceded by paragraphs of which §§8'-9' about a *tawananna* form the continuation. The fragment XVI 32 being the lower part of a second column, we may thereby have reached the beginning of the tablet with the *tawananna* affair. Similarly, the paragraphs about Urḫiteššub (§§15'-19') again deal with the said *mantalli*-offerings of §§3'-4' and we may suspect the continuation of §§5'-7' concerning (the children/ sons of) Armatarḫunta after the break in L 6+ iii 65. The matching comprehensive version of this, of course, is preserved as KBo II 6+ i-ii 35 (§§1'-16"). Compare the following table:

'affairs of'	discussed in XVI 32 §§	resumed in L 6+ §§
tawananna	[ ]	8'-9'
Danuḫepa	1'-2'	10'-14'
deities of Ḫalpa	3'	15'
(sons of) Urḫiteššub	4'	16'-19'
(sons of) Armatarḫunta	5'-7'	(cf. KBo II 6+)

The summary XXII 35 ii, duplicated by XLIX 93, runs parallel to L 6+ iii 7-21(/22) (§§12'-13'), its third column concerns the Ḫalpaziti affair. Because, as will be shown, this Ḫalpaziti may be identified with his namesake, the king of Ḫalpa, one might theoretically suppose that, although his name is not mentioned there, XXII 35 iii would somehow be parallel to L 6+ iii 30-31 (§15'), which seems to refer back to XVI 32 ii 8'-13' (§3') where the gods of Ḫalpa and the founding of a priesthood there are discussed. However, this would leave only the paragraph L 6+ iii 23-29 (§14') to fill the gap between the second and third column of XXII 35. With XXII 35 ii belonging to the upper half of that tablet and, consequently, XXII 35 iii to the lower half, this gap amounts to approximately the length of an entire column. So, although the passage about the priesthood of Ḫalpa is likely to be connected with Ḫalpaziti, it seems much more probable that the gap was filled out with paragraphs corresponding to L 6+ iii 23'-65' (§§14'-19'). This implies that the Ḫalpaziti affair as preserved in XVI 58 and XXII 35 iii//XLIX 93 must have been inserted between the Urḫiteššub affair and that of Armatarḫunta at a later stage. This also explains why Ḫalpaziti is not himself mentioned in XVI 32. If the "taking up again" of the Šausgatti affair in KBo II 6+ ii 37 means this inquiry went through two stages also, the absence of her name in XVI 32 following Armatarḫunta may be explained by assuming that her affair was considered by the scribe of XVI 32 to be the same as that of her husband (for this see below Ch. II.7).

The summary XVI 32//L 6+ thus reflects the chronological sequence of the oracle process: the oldest part in the 'ultimate' summary type (= XVI 32), and the most recent investigation, continuing the former, but less radically excerpted (= L 6+). Whether the existence of two stages is also explicitly mentioned in the texts, when concerning the Tawananna and Danuḫepa it is said that "already earlier" (*karū*, L 6+ ii 36'-37' and iii 1-2) their curses have been undone in front of the Gods of Kingship as they will do now (*kinuna=*, ibid. ii 38' and iii 3), remains uncertain: this might also refer to times before Tutḫaliya IV. Compare the remark in L 6+ iii 19-20, where Tutḫaliya recalls the institution of a ritual for Danuḫepa's gods by his father. Similarly, according to KBo II 6+ ii 37, where the "affair of Šausgatti" is mentioned for the first time, this affair is "taken up again" by the deity. Only the Ḫalpaziti affair may have been restricted to the second stage, although the offering to the gods of Ḫalpa and the foundation of a priesthood there in XVI 32 probably are to be taken as a prelude to this. Although it cannot be proven at this time, it seems likely to assume that the ultimate summary XVI 32 was made on the basis of a summary using the standard formulae and not directly from a comprehensive version. If the latter were true, it is not clear why the scribe would have used the two ways of summarizing as he did.

Our text material, therefore, points at different stages of ever shorter versions, reflecting two subsequent phases of the oracle investigation. Besides this we have several parallel summaries of an investigation made by different scribes, existing next to one another while at the same time differing from each other. What the reasons for making more than one version and for the need of duplicates were, we can only guess. At least it seems to attest to the fact that the whole matter was considered to be of high importance. To date, this situation seems to be unique to CTH 569.

8. *The colophon, order and number of tablets, and final text constitution*

The only colophon preserved, at the end of the fourth column of KBo II 6+, states the following: *ŠA* ^{md}*SÎN*-^{d}U *Ù ŠA* ^{fd}*IŠTAR-atti ariịašešar* "Oracle investigation of Armatarḫunta and Šausgatti". After a blank of approximately ten lines DUB.5.KAM *UL QATI* "Fifth tablet; not finished" is added. As was already pointed out by G. del Monte,[68] it seems reasonable

[68] AION 33 (1973) 378.

to suppose that this is not to be taken in the sense that all four preceding tablets and the one or more that followed, dealt with the same couple. The fact that the phrases about the purification of the places of kingship typical to this composition are also found in the comprehensive recording XVI 58 and the several summary versions concerning other persons, supports this. The form of the colophon itself may also be taken into consideration: the separation by some ten lines of the actual topic of the tablet and the indication of the number of this tablet within the series seems to point in the same direction. This lay-out is in a way comparable to certain colophons found in the composition of the Hittite Royal Death Rituals (CTH 450): at the end of the two tablets describing the seventh and the twelfth/thirteenth day the colophon summarily refers to the particular 'theme' of the days described, followed by a number carved in the remaining blank space, indicating the next tablet number in the whole series.[69]

As will be shown below (Ch. V.3), we have reason to assume that the entire investigation comprised no more than six tablets. The two last ones, tablet number five KBo II 6+ and the missing final tablet number six, dealt with Armatarḫunta and Šaušgatti. The investigation into the affairs of a *tawananna*, Danuḫepa, Urḫiteššub and Ḫalpaziti thus preceded KBo II 6+ and may have taken up the first four tablets. Of these, the tablet of which XVI 58 dealing with Ḫalpaziti once was a part must have been the fourth one (see Ch. V.1). About the position of L 5 we can only make guesses. There is no evidence that other persons than the six mentioned here were part of the investigation as defined in this study. Assuming this series of six tablets was more or less uniformly written down, i.e. using a roughly similar tablet size throughout, the entire inquiry may on the basis of KBo II 6+ have amounted to some 1500 lines of text. If we are right (see above 7) in assuming that the summary version XVI 32 in its lost first column started out with the *tawananna*-affair, and the remaining preserved parts of XVI 32//L 6+ and its parallel versions further concerned the same affair and those of Danuḫepa, Urḫiteššub and Ḫalpaziti, followed by the investigation of Armatarḫunta and Šaušgatti as preserved in the summary VIII 27(+), then the summary reduced the comprehensive oracle investigation of six tablets to probably two tablets.

The recognition of the order of tablets and the order of treatment of the different affairs has important prosopographical and historical consequences. The sequence of a *tawananna* followed by Danuḫepa and Urḫiteššub is the same as in the prayer of Ḫattušili III and Puduḫepa, XXI 19+ (CTH 383). In this prayer the ordering of events is a clear

[69] See H. Otten, HTR 25; for the seventh day cf. XXXIV 68 and the photo in H. Otten, Das Altertum 1 (1955) 77, or in MDOG 88 (1955) 34, for the twelfth/thirteenth day cf. XXIX 8 iv after the colophon and the photo in H. Otten, Das Altertum 1 (1955) 78.

chronological one, as was already intimated by H.G. Güterbock[70] and explicitly stated by D. Sürenhagen.[71] This means, for instance, that the *tawananna* referred to was the stepmother of Muršili II, the Babylonian princess who was the last wife of Šuppiluliuma I (on this see further below).

If, in conclusion, we arrange the texts according to their topic, according to their being duplicates and/or summaries and in their proper order, we come to the following text constitution for a revised CTH 569:

I. *Comprehensive version (six tablets)*	II. *Summary (two tablets)*		*Topic*
I.1 L 5 (tablet no. 2 ?)	II.1A	XXII 35	*tawananna,*
2 XVI 58 (tablet no. 4)	B	XLIX 93	Danuḫepa,
	II.2	KBo IX 151	Urḫiteššub,
	II.3A	XVI 32	Ḫalpaziti
	B	L 6+ XVI 41+ 7/v	
	II.4	LII 92	
I. KBo II 6+ XVIII 51 (tablet no. 5)	II.5	VIII 27(+) Bo 7787	Armatarḫunta,
	II.6	10/v	Šaušgatti

For the tiny fragment FHL 111 as another possible candidate for CTH 569 see the commentary Ch. VI ad L 6+ iii 1-4. Because the passage L 6+ iii 7ff. (II.3B) is parallelled by both XLIX 93 (II.1B) and XXII 35 (II.1A), the summary must at least have existed in three versions. Although a number of theoretical join possibilities between some of the above fragments exists, not too many combinations seem to present themselves if we take into account such matters as sign forms and/or ductus (see below sub 10), column width or line height. Possibly, the fragment LII 92 (II.4) was once part of the otherwise lost first and fourth column respectively of L 6+ (II.3B). Similarly, 10/v might indirectly join VIII 27(+). These (indirect) joins can, however, only be verified at the original fragments themselves.

9. *Findspots*

There are three fragments within CTH 569 of which the findspot is known: KBo IX 151 (286/n), 7/v and 10/v. The latter two were both found in the *Stadtplanquadrat* L/19, i.e. to the east of the eastern storerooms of Temple I, "aus altem Grabungsschutt"; compare the usual gloss under the maps of Temple I in the KBo-volumes: "Dabei benennt K/19 bzw. L/19 Streufunde

[70] SBo 1, 15; see also Ph.H.J. Houwink ten Cate, FsGüterbock 126-127 and 133-134.

[71] AoF 8 (1981) 128.

aus den Ostmagazinen des Tempels I, insbesondere den Räumen 10-12". Because it does not seem likely that (L 6+XVI 41+)7/v and 10/v belonged to the same tablet (see below Ch. V.3) but that they are rather fragments of two subsequent summary tablets, this might indicate that at least one of the summary versions was kept in Temple I.[72]

KBo IX 151 is reported to have been found in the *Stadtplanquadrat* u/17, i.e. in the western half of room 1 of building H on Büyükkale or immediately adjacent to it. Unfortunately, no particulars are given. According to P. Neve building H itself does not seem to have contained any tablets.[73] This in contrast to building B which forms part of the complex B-C-H and where 24 (fragments of) tablets were unearthed in room 5.[74] We probably have to infer from this, that the tablet was not found *in situ*.[75] For the findspots of some of the fragments of texts related to CTH 569 see below Ch. IV.2, 3 and 5.

10. *Ductus and sign forms*

The sign forms of all manuscripts within CTH 569 are fully congruent with a dating of the composition in the (second half of the) thirteenth century BC. For details on the ductus and lay-out of the several manuscripts and some of their scribal particularities see the introductory remarks to Ch. V.

[72] For the possibility that one of the accession oracles (cf. ZA 81 (1991) 274-300) was found in this same area see below Ch. IV.3 n. 19.

[73] Cf. P. Neve, Bauwerke 116-118 with Beilage 38; R. Naumann, in K. Bittel et al., Boğ. 3, 15-16, does not mention any tablet finds in H either.

[74] P. Neve, Bauwerke 112b with Beilage 38; see also ibid. 139.

[75] It is somewhat surprising to find no remark whatsoever regarding tablet finds in or near building H in either R. Naumann apud K. Bittel et al., Boğ. 3, 15-16 or P. Neve, Bauwerke 116-118 and 139, although six fragments published in KBo IX are reported to have been found there (KBo IX 68, 88, 93, 98, 123, 151) as well as 377/n, which is part of KBo XV 10, and KBo XVIII 178, and more in the immediately adjacent quadrats. Because the majority of the fragments in question are paleographically young, i.e. dating from the thirteenth century (of the ones found within u/17 only KBo IX 93 and 123+XX 52 are older; for the former cf. F. Starke, StBoT 30, 303 and 320: "E. 14.Jh."), the chance, that they stem from Hittite dump for building purposes (cf. H.G. Güterbock, MDOG 72 (1933) 51-52, and in the preface to KBo XVIII), becomes relatively small, since the complex B-C-H is believed to be built by Tutḫaliya IV (cf. P. Neve, Bauwerke 104 and 111). The fact, that the join pieces to 377/n (see S. Košak, StBoT 39, 12 sub 101/b), which together constitute KBo XV 10+KBo XX 42 (CTH 443), were all found in Building A on Büyükkale, lends support to the suggestion that the fragments found in u/17 were not originally stored there. That their findspot probably is the result of later (Phrygian) building activities follows from the remarks kindly communicated to me by S. Košak, that 286/n (KBo IX 151) was found "an der phryg. Burgmauer", 377/n "in der phryg. Burgmauer"; the findspot of the other n-pieces is likewise related to this Phrygian wall.

Table I

	TAR (7) older / younger	IK (67) older / younger	AK (81) older / younger	URU (229) older / younger	LI (343) older / younger	ŠAR (353) older / younger
KBo II 6+						
KBo IX 151						
VIII 27						
XVI 32						
XVI 58						
XXII 35						
XLIX 93						
L 5						
L 6+						
LII 92						
10/v						

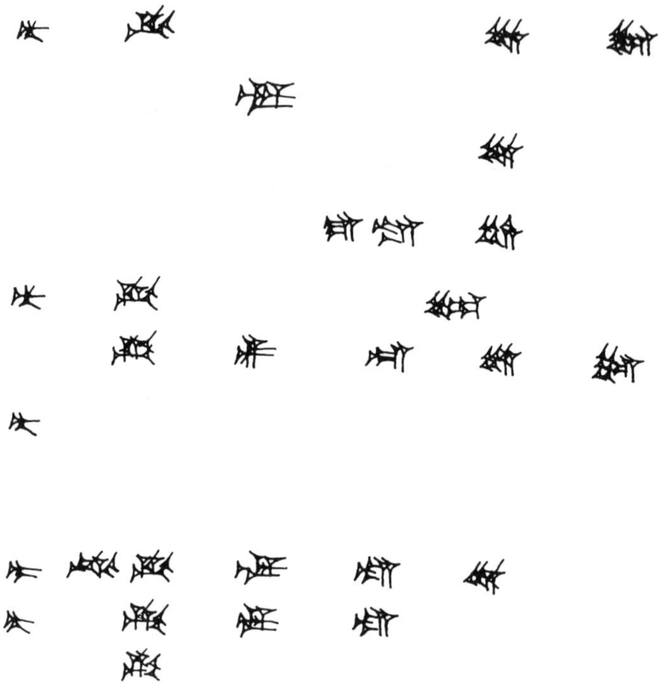

Table II

	QA (21) older / younger	EN (40) older / younger	UN (197) older / younger	ḪA (367) older / younger
KBo II 6+				i 32'
KBo IX 151				
VIII 27				
XVI 32				
XVI 58				
XXII 35				
XLIX 93				
L 5				
L 6+				
LII 92				
10/v				

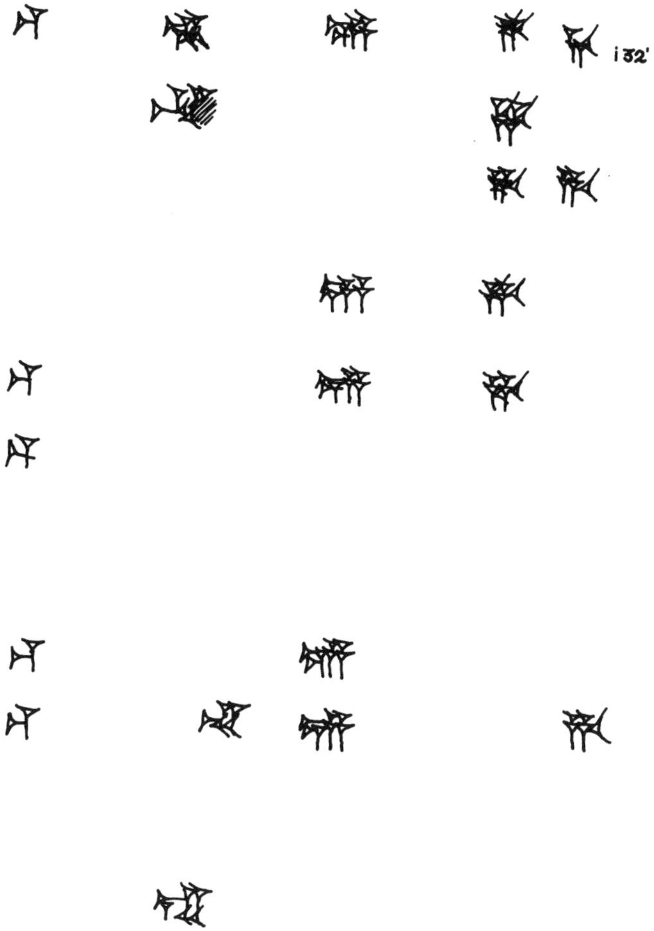

In Table I the most characteristic signs are listed according to their older or younger form; the numbers between brackets behind the signs refer to the numbers in Chr. Rüster - E. Neu, HZL. There are no older forms of the signs AK, ŠAR and TAR. Neither is the older form of the LI sign present except for in XVI 58 which has the younger form of the IK and TAR signs, however. The variant of the IK sign (HZL 67/3) closest to the older form can be seen once in L 6+ iii 38. The appearance of the older form of the URU sign (HZL 229/A) in XVI 32 is restricted to one ("hand a") of the two hands visible on that tablet; for more detail on this see below in Ch. V.1. As a special trait of the other hand ("hand b") of XVI 32 mention may be made of the DUMU sign (XVI 32 ii 14' and 19') with one inscribed vertical (HZL 237/11). The same is true of the LÚ sign in XLIX 93, 15 and 16 (HZL 78/12). Another peculiarity in the latter text is the strongly protruding lower horizontal of the UŠ sign with the Winkelhaken steeply slanting down, its foremost tip reaching under this lower horizontal as correctly drawn in the handcopy (compare HZL 132/5 although the protrusion is far more outspoken here). Both XXII 35 and L 6+ share the variant of the KI sign with the extra vertical instead of the second upper Winkelhaken (HZL 313/19ff.). Whereas XXII 35 displays only this variant, L 6+ has both (cf. e.g. ii 37' versus 38').
The four signs EN, ḪA, QA and UN with variants which (esp. in combination) may be considered characteristic for the second half of the thirteenth century,[76] are represented in Table II. The manuscript L 6+ is the only one with two out of the four younger variant forms. No serious conclusions therefore can be drawn from this.

11. *The date of CTH 569*

The fragment XVI 32 was already in 1940 ascribed to Tutḫaliya IV by H.G. Güterbock because of the "oath of His Majesty's father in connection with the affair of Urḫiteššub" (XVI 32 ii 27').[77] On the basis of this we may date the entire oracle inquiry CTH 569 as defined in this study in the reign of that same king. But the structure of the investigation as a whole as well as some of the personal names in the composition allow us to go beyond this general dating. As was shown above, we can distinguish two stages in the inquiry. The first stage is reflected in the 'ultimate' summary XVI 32. Where L 6+ takes over, the second and more recent stage begins. In XVI 32 ii 14'-18' (§4') and 19'-23' (§5') Tutḫaliya mentions "the man who did evil" to the sons of Urḫiteššub and Armatarḫunta respectively. In view of other oracle texts which point to an accession of Tutḫaliya during the life of his father Ḫattušili, it is evident that the latter is meant here.[78] The first stage of the inquiry, therefore, was conducted in the very first

[76] Cf. my StBoT 38, 297 ("IIIc") and 98 n. 125.
[77] SBo 1, 15.
[78] See my article ZA 81 (1991) 274-300, for XVI 32 cf. ibid. 294-297.

years of Tutḫaliya's reign, when his father still lived. The second stage, however, can only have been implemented much later. It is the death of Ḫalpaziti in XXII 35 iii and its parallel LII 92 iv which forms an important terminus post quem for this part of the inquiry. It will be argued below (Ch. II.5) that this Ḫalpaziti was in all likelihood identical to his namesake, the king of Ḫalap/Ḫalpa and that he may have been installed there by Tutḫaliya. We know from the Akkadian letter IBoT I 34 (CTH 179.1) that Ḫalpaziti still ruled in Ḫalap during Tutḫaliya's reign when Eḫlišarruma had succeeded Arišarruma as king in Išuwa.[79] In the Bronze Tablet iv 34 Eḫlišarruma merely appears as prince, whereas in KBo IV 10+ his father Arišarruma is still king of Išuwa. The second stage in the inquiry was therefore conducted after Eḫlišarruma had ascended the throne in Išuwa, an event which took place after the treaty KBo IV 10+ was concluded with Ulmiteššub of Tarḫuntašša. If the latter text is indeed to be ascribed to Tutḫaliya IV, this would mean that the last phase of the oracle investigation is to be dated after 1220.[80]

12. *Texts excluded from CTH 569*

In his article on ^{GIŠ}TUKUL as "oracle procedure" G.C. Moore[81] proposed to assign the oracle text XVI 77 (CTH 577) to CTH 569. This tablet deals with a "son of Arnuwanda", Pi(ya)ššili and Ḫaittili. Because of the "son of Arnuwanda" the present author[82] suggested, moreover, the possibility of an indirect join of XVI 77 with LX 52. The latter fragment mentions the cities Alalaḫ and Kiuta as well, which establishes a link with XVI 32 as pointed out by H. Klengel.[83] This impression is reinforced by the fact that, on the whole, XVI 77 and, to a lesser extent, LX 52 contain quite a few phrases which we also frequently encounter in CTH 569 (compare for XVI 77: DINGIR-*LUM*=*naš* ... ^{TÚG}*šeknun* EGIR-*pa UL namma kuitki* [SUD-*i̯aši*] ii 2-3, GIDIM *šarā*/UGU *ašeš*(*anu*)- ii 62, iii 10, 38; [*mān*=*k*]*an aši* INIM ... [*kē*]*z* INIM-*za lāittari* ii 64-65, iii 14-15; ^{d}UTU-*ŠI*=*za parkunuzi* iii 20-21, 40). In spite of this neither XVI 77 nor LX 52 display any of the criteria mentioned above and even fundamentally differ from CTH 569 in the sense, that at least Pi(ya)ššili and Ḫaittili seem to have been murdered; see also below Ch. III.2. In order to let the reader judge by him/herself the two texts are transliterated and translated in the Appendix.

The same criteria are likewise lacking in other oracle texts involving a *tawananna* or the personal names Armatarḫunta, Ḫalpaziti, Šaušgatti, Danuḫepa and/or Urḫiteššub, although they may be of importance in

79 Cf. H. Klengel, Or. 32 (1963) 280-291, and OA 7 (1968) 71; for Eḫlišarruma cf. my StBoT 38, 124-126.
80 On this see StBoT 38, 11-19 and 326.
81 JNES 40 (1981) 49 n. 7.
82 BiOr 51 (1994) 123.
83 KUB LX Inhaltsübersicht v.

reconstructing the general historical background of CTH 569. They will briefly be discussed here.

There are very few 13th century texts mentioning a *tawananna*. Apart from the attestations in CTH 569 there seem to be at least three oracle texts: V 6+ (CTH 570 - iii 68', on this text and its date see above note 62 and Ch. II.2: *Tawananna*), XXII 70 (CTH 566 - obv. 79; ed. A. Ünal, THeth. 6, for the date see my StBoT 38, 219-222) and the tiny fragment L 10 (CTH 573 - l. col. 6' ^{MUNUS}*ta-u̯a-an-na-an-na*(-$^{?}$)*iš*[84]). Paleogra-phically they cannot go back to the days of Muršili II nor do they seem to be directly related to CTH 569.

Two oracle texts mentioning Armatarḫunta are unp. 2275/c and LII 83 (CTH 570) where in both cases the É ^{md}*SÎN*-^{d}U "the estate of Armatarḫunta" occurs; on these texts see also below Ch. II.6: *Armatarḫunta*. Because of this name G. Beckman[85] considers assigning the latter fragment to CTH 569, A. Archi,[86] however, seems to deny any link or at least the possibility of a join or duplicate with KBo II 6+ and VIII 27. As far as preserved these fragments do not contain anything other than the name Armatarḫunta to suggest appurtenance to CTH 569. Finally, there is the apparently small one-column tablet KBo XXIII 105 with its text continuing over the lower edge. The name Armatarḫunta is attested twice (5'], 13'). Because of the combination ANŠE.KUR.RA-*aš u̯aštul* "lack/loss of horses/chariots", H. Otten and Chr. Rüster[87] indirectly refer to the *ḪIṬṬU* ANŠE.KUR.RA in V 3 (CTH 563), to which the vow LX 118+LVI 25 (CTH 590) might be added.[88] Nothing points to a link with CTH 569.

The only other oracle texts in which a Ḫalpaziti is attested, KBo XXIV 126 (CTH 577 - Vs. 23) and XVI 66 (CTH 577 - 27'), mention him as officiating augur, not as someone for or about whom the investigation is being carried out.[89]

Šaušgatti is possibly mentioned in XVI 69 (CTH 573) obv.$^{?}$ 4' (^{fd}]⌈*IŠTAR*⌉$^{?}$-*at-ti*). As far as preserved this oracle investigation makes use of augury only. Besides some technical terms and the name Šaušgatti nothing of the paragraph (obv. 4'-9'), in which this woman is mentioned, remains. In line 10' "[the ... o]f His Majesty's mother" is established. Both here and before ^{fd}]⌈*IŠTAR*⌉$^{?}$-*at-ti* (obv. 4') A. Archi[90] proposes to restore GIDIM "the spirit of ... " but one might also think of restoring ^{d}*Zawalli*. In the next paragraph (obv. 18'-26') someone speaking in the first person asks whether a SISKUR *parā tarnummaš* "a ritual of setting free" will be given to her(?), whether someone will set her(?) free and whether the speaker will pacify [her(?)] (obv. 19'-21'). On the even more

84 Cf. A. Archi, SMEA 22 (1980) 22.
85 BiOr 42 (1985) 141.
86 KUB LII Inhaltsübersicht iv.
87 KBo XXIII Inhaltsübersicht vi.
88 Cf. Th. van den Hout, BiOr 51 (1994) 125-126.
89 Cf. StBoT 38, 186, 188.
90 AoF 6 (1979) 83.

fragmentarily preserved rev.? we find again a mother (rev. 4', 8') and the rest of a name]-*ta*-^{d}LAMMA, which can only be restored to Kupanta-^{d}LAMMA. In the unpublished fragment 839/f of a bird oracle Šaušgatti is mentioned twice (obv. 6', 14'). It is asked whether "they will give as much compensation as the number of years [the festival(?) was left unce]lebrated" (obv. 15'-17').

In the oracle fragment XLIX 97 (CTH 582) Urḫiteššub occurs (2') together with Anuwanza (6', 7'), probably identical to the important thirteenth-century scribe. Nothing certain can be inferred from its contents.

All other oracle texts involving Šaušgatti, Danuḫepa and Urḫiteššub concern the Zawalli-deities of these persons: XVI 46 (CTH 573) and L 87 (CTH 578) (both Šaušgatti), as well as XVI 16 (CTH 570) and KBo XXIII 114 (CTH 570) (both Danuḫepa and Urḫiteššub). The latter two cannot have been the basis for L 6+ because they use extispicy exclusively and not the three techniques attested in L 6+. The same is true for XVI 46 since it uses augury only. None of the four mentioned, moreover, contain any of the criteria discussed above. They may, however, have been a link in the larger chain of oracle inquiries to which also CTH 569 belongs. These texts, therefore, are discussed below in Ch. III.3 and given in transliteration and translation in Ch. IV.5.

CHAPTER TWO

MATERIALS FOR THE HISTORICAL BACKGROUND

1. *Introduction*

The *dramatis personae* of the oracle inquiry into the purity of the kingship carried out by Tutḫaliya IV, as defined above, in the order in which they were treated are: a *tawananna,* Danuḫepa, Urḫiteššub, Ḫalpaziti, Armatarḫunta, and Šausgatti. In this order they will be discussed below in short prosopographical sketches. Brief remarks on the other persons occurring in CTH 569 conclude this chapter.

2. *Tawananna*

The identification of the *tawananna* in CTH 569 rests upon the combined evidence of the recognition of the chronological order of affairs dealt with in this oracle investigation and the same order of affairs in the prayer of Ḫattušili III and Puduḫepa to the Sungoddess of Arinna, XXI 19+ (CTH 383[1]). In the latter text the *tawananna* affair is described, after an introductory hymn (i 1-13) and after the applicants' names have been mentioned (i 14-15), as follows:

> *kuitman* / *ABU=IA* ^{m}*Muršiliš* TI-*anza ēšta* / *nu mān* DINGIR.MEŠ EN.MEŠ-*IA ABU-IA šalla*[*ka*]*rtaḫta* / *kuēzka memiianaz ammuk=ma=za=kan apēdani* / *ANA* INIM *ABI=IA UL kuitki an*[*da*] *ešun* / *nūua=za* TUR-*aš ešun mān=ma=kan* [Š]À É.L[UGAL] / *DĪNU ŠA* ^{MUNUS}*tawannanna* GEME=*KUNU kiša*[*t*] / *ABU=IA* GIM-*an* ^{MUNUS}*tawannan*[*n*]*an* MUNUS.LUGAL *tepnut* / *apāš=ma* GEME. DINGIR-*LIM kuit ēš*[*t*]*a* / [*n=at tuel ANA* Z]I DINGIR-*LIM* GAŠAN-*IA and*[*a ku*]*iš šakta*

"Whether, as long as my father Muršili lived, my father de[f]ied the Gods, my Lords, through whatever affair, I was in no way i[n]volved in that affair of my father: I was still a child. Because she w[a]s a servant of the god, you, o Goddess, my Lady, are the one, [wh]o knows i[n your he]art, how my father, when the court case against the

[1] See the edition by D. Sürenhagen, AoF 8 (1981) 83-168.

> *tawananna*, your servant, took place [i]n the pal[ace], humiliated the *tawanan*[*n*]*a*, the queen."[2]

In the following, very fragmentary lines, which can be restored with confidence after an identically phrased passage in the beginning of the second column, it is said that the person guilty in this affair "has already become a god (i.e. died) ... and has already paid with his head" (*n*=*a*]*t* *IŠTU* SAG.DU=*ŠÚ* [*karū parā šarnikta*]).[3] From this prayer passage it becomes clear that the *tawananna* of CTH 569 was also the Babylonian princess who became the last wife of Šuppiluliuma I and the stepmother of his successors Arnuwanda II and Muršili II.[4] Through a different and – in my opinion – less compelling argumentation, A. Archi had already come to the same conclusion.[5] The *tawananna* affair is mainly known because of the two highly personal and emotional appeals to the gods by Muršili II, CTH 70[6] and 71[7]; for possible references to her in the oracle V 6+ see above Ch. I.5. In the prayers Muršili almost desperately tries to justify the banishment of his stepmother from the court at Ḫattuša and her deposition from the office of *šiu̯anzanni*-priestess because – amongst other charges – of the death of his wife. Even after her removal from the capital, however, she continued cursing Muršili (*ḫurzakizzi* "she keeps cursing" KBo IV 8+ iii 16, 24). It may be these curses which according to Ḫattušili III and Puduḫepa were ultimately responsible for his death, and the same curses may be referred to by the EME ^{MUNUS}*tawananna* in L 6+ ii 32', 35', 36' and 41'.

In view of the appearance of the *tawananna* in connection with the Deities of Kingship in CTH 569, the immediate sequel to the famous passage in the fourth column of XIV 4 (CTH 70) about the solar eclipse may be of special interest:

> 24 [*ma-a-an I-NA* KUR *A*]*z-zi-ma i-i̯a-aḫ-ḫa-at nu* ^{d}UTU-*uš ša-ki-i̯a-aḫ-ta* MUNUS.LUGAL-*ma*
>
> 25 [*I-NA* KUR ^{URU}*Ḫa-at-t*]*i*^{a} *me-mi-iš-ki-it e-ni-u̯a ku-it* ^{d}UTU-*uš* ⌈*ša*⌉-*k*[*i-i̯*]*a-aḫ-ta*

[2] XXI 19+ i 15-24 (ed. D. Sürenhagen, op.cit. 88-89).

[3] XXI 19+ i 33-34 (ed. D. Sürenhagen, loc.cit.).

[4] For the seals on which this *tawananna* is attested see H. Otten, Königssiegel der frühen Großreichszeit 13-24 with literature.

[5] SMEA 22 (1980) 22, 25-29; initially, G. del Monte, AION 35 (1975) 327, had identified her as Danuḫepa, later (Archeologia dell'inferno 111) he retracted this in favor of Muršili's stepmother. Starting from a date of the oracle text V 6+ in the reign of Muršili II, Archi assigns XXII 70 to the same king. Subsequently he identifies any *tawananna* mentioned in other oracle texts with the same woman. The date of V 6+ is, however, disputed: see above Ch. I.5 n. 62.

[6] Unfortunately no complete up-to-date edition of this text exists, only the treatment by F. Cornelius, RIDA 22 (1975) 27-45; in the meantime two parallel fragments have been published in the form of KBo XIX 84 and 85.

[7] Ed. H.A. Hoffner, JAOS 103 (1983) 187-192.

26 [*i-ši-i̯*]*a-*⌈*aḫ-ta*⌉ *Ú-UL-u̯a ŠA* LUGAL-*pát*[b] *i-ši-i̯a-aḫ-ta nu-*⌈*u̯a*⌉ *ma-a-an*

27 [LÚ.]⌈MEŠ⌉ ^{URU}*Ḫa-at-ti-ma-u̯a-za AŠ-ŠUM BE-LU-UT-TI ta-ma-a-*[*i*]*n*

28 [*ku-in-ki i-la-li-i̯a-an-zi*[c] -]⌈*u̯a*⌉*-za* ^{f}*Am-mi-in-na-*⌈*i̯a-an*⌉ ŠA ^{f}*Am-mi-in-na-i̯a-i̯a*

29 [DUMU$^{?}$ *-i̯*]*a*$^{?}$*-an-zi* ^{d}UTU-*ŠI-ma-za I-NA* KUR ^{URU}*Ḫa-i̯a-ša*

30 [ ]x *tup-pí-az* EGIR-*an-da ḫa-at-ra-a-eš*

31 [*an-d*]*a u̯a-tar-na-aḫ-ta ma-a-an* ^{URU}*Ḫa-i̯a-ša-az-ma*

32 [ ]x *ḫu-u-da-a-ak Ú-UL me-mi-iš-ta*

33 [*ma-aḫ-*]⌈*ḫa*⌉*-an ku-u-*⌈*un*⌉ *me-mi-an iš-ta-ma-aš-ša-an-zi*

34 [*p*]*u-nu-uš-šu-un ku-u-un-u̯a ku-in*

35 [ ]x-*i̯a*/*IA Ú-UL ša-an-ni-eš-ta*

36 [ ]x-*ku*$^{?}$/*ma*$^{?}$*-i̯a* ⌈*me*⌉*-mi-iš-ta*

37 [ ] *m*[*e-m*]*i-iš-ta*

[When] I marched [to the land of A]zzi, the Sungod gave a sign. The queen, however, [in Ḫatt]i-land said[d]: "This sign which the Sungod gave, [what did it pred]ict? Did it not predict (something) about the king alone? And if [it predicted something about the king], will [the pe]ople of Ḫatti-land then [demand someone] else in power? Will they [...] Amminnaya and Amminnai̯a's [son$^{?}$?"] I, My Majesty, however, in Ḫayaša [...] " ... on a tablet you wrote back."$^{?}$ [and ...] ... she$^{?}$ gave orders. When, however, from Ḫayaša [...] ... she suddenly refused (saying$^{?}$) [" ... i]f they hear this word/matter [... " ...] I questioned: "[e]This (person$^{?}$) whom [...] ... you/he/she did not hide [...] ... said [...] said.

[a] F. Cornelius, RIDA 22 (1975) 39, restores *kiššan* but the sign trace after the break does not favor this. The statement in the lines 29-30 in which the queen(?) is said to "write back on a tablet" may, however, imply that she stayed in the capital. [b] H.A. Hoffner, FsGüterbock^{2} 90, reads (*ŠA*) LUGAL ÚŠ "the king's death/downfall" but there seems to be no word space between the two last signs. [c] For this restoration cf. for instance XXIII 1+ ii 13-14 (ed. H. Otten - C. Kühne, StBoT 16, 8-11) or with *šakk-/šekk-* XXVI 1+XXIII 112 i 13-14, cf. StBoT 38, 101-102. [d] The queen is the most likely subject for *memiškit* (so E. Forrer, Forsch. 2, 3, F. Cornelius, RIDA 22 (1975) 39 versus A. Götze, KlF. 406 with n. 1). [e] It is not clear where the direct speech ends.

In spite of the fragmentary state of this passage and the sometimes tentative restorations, with F. Cornelius we may in general conclude that it seems to emerge from the passage that, in real Babylonian fashion but quite unlike Hittite mantic practice, the queen took the solar omen as predicting the king's downfall. This is indeed the case in the solar omina originating from Mesopotamia and preserved in Boğazköy.[8] Upon hearing this, while already in Ḫayaša, a correspondence ensued and the king may have quickly returned from Ḫayaša to start an investigation. Unfortunately, nothing is known about the woman Amminnaya mentioned in iv 28 as well as in the related fragment KBo XIX 84, 7 (^f^*Am-mi-en-na-i̯a*). If, as is maintained by M. Salvini,[9] Malnigal was not the name of the Kassite princess Šuppiluliuma married, one might hypothesize Amminnaya was her name.[10] The lines iv 27-29 would then constitute the political climax of her schemes against her stepson. In view of these lines and the tentative restoration to [DUMU at the beginning of line 29, the listing of trials (*DĪNU*) in KBo XXXVI 111 ii is highly interesting: in ii 4-5 we read *DI-NU ŠA* MUNUS⌈*ta*⌉*-u̯a*[*-na-an-na*] / *Ù DI-NU ŠA* DUMU[.[11] It cannot be excluded, however, that this applied to Danuḫepa (see immediately below). Amminnaya may, finally, be attested in the small oracle fragment XVIII 42, 6' (^f^]*Am-mi-na-i̯a*) where certain persons are being questioned. They seem to talk about her in connection with a monthly festival(?). There is, however, nothing that explicitly points to a link with either CTH 70/71 or CTH 569.[12]

3. *Danuḫepa*

For a woman named Danuḫepa (NH 1244) we can adduce the following texts:

[8] See IV 63 ii 20'-iii 27 with its duplicates (ed. K.K. Riemschneider, Omentexte 69-85).

[9] Sefarad 50 (1990) 456-459; see also H. Otten, Königssiegel der frühen Großreichszeit 24. Note that already H.G. Güterbock, SBo 1, 18 n. 52, who was the first to mention the possibility of 'Malnigal' having been the *tawananna*'s name, pointed at the uncertainty of the reading 'Malnigal' itself.

[10] S.R. Bin-Nun, THeth. 5, 247 n. 118 suggested she might have been "the wife of Muršili's brother and predecessor Arnuwanda."

[11] Restoration to *tau̯a*[*nanna* by G. Wilhelm, KBo XXXVI Inhaltsübersicht vii. Note the possible attestation of (a trial of) ^f^*Tāti*[*u̯ašti* ibid. ii 2 (restoration again G. Wilhelm, loc.cit.) known from V 6+ ii 26' and XVIII 3 iv 21' (see above Ch. I.5).

[12] For the name Amminnaya we can refer to her namesake, the daughter-in-law of Itḫaya, probably king of Arrapḫa under the Mitannian king Šauštatar; see most recently G.N. Knoppers, JAOS 116 (1996) 686-687 n. 96 w. lit. Note that also Muršili made oracle investigations concerning his stepmother (cf. KBo IV 8+ ii 6-8 in the line count of Hoffner's edition, JAOS 103 (1983) 188). For three more oracle texts mentioning a *tawananna* see above Ch. I.12.

a. KBo IX 151, 5' (CTH 569 - Tutḫ. IV)
b. KBo XXIII 114 obv.? 17, 18 (CTH 570 - Tutḫ. IV)
c. XIV 7 i 16' (-*n*[*u*- / 17': MUNUSAMA.DINGIR-*LIM*), 17', 20' + XXI 19 ii 4, 11 (f]), 12, 16, 21 (CTH 383 - Ḫatt. III)
d. XV 5+XLVIII 122 i 7, iii 4, 9 (CTH 583 - Urḫiteššub/Muršili III[13])
e. XVI 16 rev. 1 (CTH 570 - Tutḫ. IV)
f. XVI 32 ii 1', 4' (-*ḫé*[-) (CTH 569 - Tutḫ. IV)
g. XXI 33, 19' (CTH 387 - Urḫiteššub/Muršili III[14])
h. XXII 35 i 4' (-]*pa-aš*) (CTH 569 - Tutḫ. IV)
i. XXXI 66(+)IBoT III 122 iii 15' (MUNUS.LUGAL) (CTH 297.6A[15] - Urḫiteššub/Muršili III[16])
j. XLVIII 120, 1 (CTH 582/584? - ?)
k. L 6+ ii 48', 56' (-*nu*[-), 57' (f[)

To these texts several bullae can be added:

l. P. Neve, Ḫattuša Abb. 157 (p. 58) (MAGNA.REGINA; Danuḫepa alone)
m. SBo 1.24-29 (MAGNA.REGINA together with a "Muršili")
n. SBo 1.42 ([MAGNA.REGINA] together with Muwatalli II)
o. P. Neve, Ḫattuša Abb. 158 (p. 58) (MAGNA.REGINA together with Muwatalli II; sealing possibly identical to SBo 1.42)
p. SBo 1.43-44 (MAGNA.REGINA together with Urḫiteššub[17]).
q. P. Neve, Ḫattuša Abb. 148 (p. 57) (MAGNA.REGINA together with Urḫiteššub; sealing possibly identical to SBo 1.44)
r. other bullae involving Danuḫepa, as yet unpublished but mentioned by P. Neve, Ḫattuša 87: "Muwatalli/UA-Szene (m. Urḫitešup/Danuḫepa)" and "Unbekannte Großkönige (davon 2 mit Danuḫepa)".

Orthography:

– cuneiform

f*Da-nu-ḫé-pa*	b c d e k
f*Ta-nu-ḫé-pa*	f i
f*Da-nu-ḫé-pa-aš* (nom.)	a d (iii 4)
f*Ta-nu-ḫé-pa-aš* (nom.)	g

13 On the date of this text see the discussion in J. de Roos, Diss. 55-62.

14 For literature on this text see C. Mora, SMEA 29 (1992) 127-148, to which now Ph.H.J. Houwink ten Cate, BiOr 51 (1994) 240-243, should be added.

15 The duplicate HT 7 is not relevant to the issue discussed here. As a further duplicate LII 93 can be considered: LII 93 i 3-12 = XXXI 66(+) i 6'-12'; for the related fragment XIX 21 see Ph.H.J. Houwink ten Cate, FsGüterbock 134.

16 On (the date of) this text see Ph.H.J. Houwink ten Cate, FsGüterbock 129-136, and again BiOr 51 (1994) 240-243, where all relevant literature is given.

17 For the preserved parts of a cuneiform ring on SBo 1 no. 44 (A/B) cf. H.G. Güterbock, SBo 1, 26.

^{f}*Da-nu-ḫé-pa-an*	c (XIV 7 i 17')
^{f}*Da-nu-*^{d}*Ḫé-pa-aš* (gen.?)	j
fragmentary	c f h k
– hieroglyphic	
*42-*nu-he-pa*	l-q

All of the above texts a-k date from the thirteenth century; all texts except for XLVIII 120 (j) can with certainty be ascribed to the queen Danuḫepa, who occurs on sealings together with a Muršili, Muwatalli II and Urḫiteššub. The tiny fragment XLVIII 120[18] is the remainder of a vow or oracle text starting out with the words Ù-*TUM* ^{f}⌈*Da-nu*⌉-^{d}*Ḫé-pa-aš* ["Dream of Danuḫepa." Because of the many dreams of queens recorded in such texts, it is reasonable to assume that this Danuḫepa, too, is the queen. The spelling of her name with the divine determinative preceding the second element *-ḫepa* is, however, unique. Not included in the list is KBo XIII 42, 7 (CTH 661.9): after the Akkadian preposition *ANA* one discerns the trace of a vertical wedge followed by a break of one sign. After the break there is a clear -]*nu-ḫé-pa*. Although a scribal mistake (^{m} instead of ^{f}) might have been made here and a restoration to, for instance, [*Aš*]*nuḫepa* still remains possible, male names ending in *-ḫeba*(*t*) are attested also.[19]

Danuḫepa is attested as queen on bullae next to Muwatalli (n, o, and possibly r) and Urḫiteššub (p, q, and possibly r). Although more indirectly, because neither Muwatalli nor Urḫiteššub are explicitly mentioned, one of the cuneiform sources, XXXI 66(+) (i) also attests to her status as queen, in all likelihood next to the same kings. Furthermore, she is said to have been a *šiu̯anzanni*-priestess in XIV 7 (c). The appearance of her name on bullae next to a Muršili (m), however, has caused some controversy. Initially, that is before the discovery of sealings unmistakably to be ascribed to Muršili II in Ras Shamra/Ugarit, all Boğazköy bullae (SBo 1.13-37) bearing the name Muršili were assigned to Urḫiteššub, whose name seemed to be written with the same hieroglyphs. Among them there were several with the name Danuḫepa on them (SBo 1.24-29). When after the finds at Ras Shamra/Ugarit it became clear that Urḫiteššub had chosen his grandfather's name Muršili (III) as his throne name,[20] confusion arose. E. Laroche now proposed to assign SBo 1.14-37 – including those with Danuḫepa – to Muršili II, leaving Urḫiteššub/Muršili III the only exemplar (SBo 1.13) of which he was the clear owner witness the cuneiform inscription with preserved genealogy on its rings.[21] This meant, that there

[18] Ed. J. de Roos, Diss. 301 and 440.

[19] For some examples (all from outside Boğazköy) cf. M.-C. Trémouille, Eothen 7, 19-20 and 25.

[20] Cf. H.G.Güterbock apud Cl.F.A. Schaeffer, Syria 29 (1952) 173, and H. Otten, MDOG 87 (1955) 19-22.

[21] Ugaritica 3 (1956) 104.

was now evidence for Danuḫepa as a queen next to three subsequent kings: Muršili II (SBo 1.24-29), Muwatalli (SBo 1.42) and Urḫiteššub (SBo 1. 43-44). On the latter two Urḫiteššub's name is spelled out as MAGNUS-*hí*-TEŠUB-*pa*. Laroche, thereupon, formulated three possibilities:[22] 1) there have been at least two Danuḫepas, one the last wife of Muršili II and another married to Muwatalli and reigning as *tawananna* under Urḫiteššub, or 2) there has been only one Danuḫepa, the last wife of Muršili II, reigning as *tawananna* under both Muwatalli and Urḫiteššub, or 3) there has been only one Danuḫepa, but the bullae SBo 1.24-29 belonged to Urḫiteššub/Muršili III rather than to Muršili II. The first of these options raised the problem that we know of no official queen next to Muwatalli, who, moreover, is said to have had no children of 'first rank.' The last possibility was seemingly falsified by Th. Beran,[23] who on purely stylistic grounds distinguished between joint Muršili/Danuḫepa sealings belonging to Muršili II (Beran 221-225 = SBo 1.24-28) and those belonging to Urḫiteššub/Muršili III (Beran 228 = SBo 1.29). These stylistic grounds were the form of the winged solar disk, the curved ("eigentümlich geschwungene") form of the 'dagger' sign *li* in the king's name, and whether the small vertical sign below the 'city' sign (URBS) was attached to it (= Muršili II) or not (= Muršili III). Besides this, Beran made the important discovery, that on sealings showing a king Muršili alone a neat distinction was made between Muršili II and Muršili III/Urḫiteššub by way of the direction in which the 'dagger' of the *li*-sign pointed.[24] Those pointing to the right (SBo 1.14, 15, 22, 23 = Beran 168, 172, 175, 174 respectively, and the additional 179) belonged to Muršili II, those pointing to the left (SBo 1.13 = Beran 180, and the additional 181) to Muršili III/Urḫiteššub.[25] Beran's division of the joint sealings was seen as a confirmation of Laroche's second option: one Danuḫepa next to three subsequent kings.[26] As Beran rightly observed, however, the criterion of the 'dagger' pointing to the right or left can be applied only to sealings bearing the name of a Muršili on his own with no queen present. So the 'evidence' for Danuḫepa as a queen ruling next to Muršili II completely depended on the above mentioned stylistic characteristics.

Although these characteristics worked out by Beran may be generally valid, caution is called for. Already in the material presented by him there seem to be contradictions. For instance, on the joint sealing of Danuḫepa

[22] Ugaritica 3 (1956) 105.

[23] BoHa 5, 74-75.

[24] BoHa 5, 74 n. 14.

[25] Th. Beran ascribes the bullae nos. 169-171, 173, 176-178 (= SBo 1.17-22) on the basis of the same criterion to Muršili II, although the 'dagger' is not preserved there. Similarly, he ascribes no. 182 (= SBo 1.16) to Muršili III/Urḫitešub, but again the 'dagger' is missing.

[26] Ph.H.J. Houwink ten Cate, FsGüterbock 124, A. Ünal, THeth. 3, 140; R. Stefanini, JAOS 84 (1964) 29 had already before Beran's book chosen for this option. S.R. Bin-Nun, THeth. 5, 169, must have misunderstood Beran, for she extends the 'dagger' criterion to joint seals.

and Muršili III/Urḫiteššub no. 228 (= SBo 1.29, compare the photo in SBo 1, Tafel I and Beran, Tafel 14) the vertical under the URBS-sign is clearly attached to it. The same can now be observed, it seems, on the more recently found Muršili III/Urḫiteššub sealing Bo 91/852.[27] Nevertheless, no. 228 is considered to be the most recent among the Urḫiteššub sealings on account of the form of the winged solar disk.[28] Conversely, H. Otten[29] notes that on the Ugarit sealing RS 17.382[30] of Muršili II the vertical does not seem to be attached to the URBS-sign. Furthermore, the form of the 'dagger' on the sealing Bo 90/266[31] comes very close to the "eigentümlich geschwungene Form" characteristic for Muršili II sealings. Finally, Beran concedes that at least on the sealings on which Muršili III calls himself Urḫiteššub (Beran 226-227 = SBo 1.43-44), the winged solar disk has "fast die gleiche graphische Form, die schon bei den Siegeln Muršilis II beschrieben wurde."[32] The evidence for Danuḫepa as the last wife of Muršili III, solely on the basis of the bullae, seems therefore weak and rather arbitrary.

It may be for these or similar reasons, that in his excavation reports[33] P. Neve ascribes all joint sealings of a Muršili and Danuḫepa to Muršili III/Urḫiteššub. Consequently, he explicitly calls Danuḫepa Muwatalli's wife and Urḫiteššub's mother. As was stated by Houwink ten Cate,[34] however, this runs counter to what emerges from the later sources dating from the reign of Ḫattušili according to which Muwatalli had no legitimate son and Urḫiteššub was the son of a concubine (cf. Apology iii 40'-42'). Moreover, there is one possible hint at Danuḫepa having been the last wife of Muršili II in the vow text XV 5+ i 7-17:[35]

> Ù-*TUM kuit memir* TÚG-*maịd*[*=ụa ANA*] ᶠ*Danuḫepa* / *piandu UMMA* ᶠ*Ḫepa*-SUM TÚG[-? *=ụa*]x / *ANA* DINGIR-*LIM* GAL *piandu nāụi* (§)

[27] See H. Otten, Neufunden 25 Abb. 20.

[28] BoHa 5, 75.

[29] Königssiegel der frühen Großreichszeit 26 n. 61.

[30] Cf. Ugaritica 3 (1956) 8-9 fig. 7 and 8, and Pl. II.

[31] See H. Otten, Neufunden 23 Abb. 16-17.

[32] BoHa 5, 75.

[33] See AA 1991, 328, AA 1992, 315, and Ḫattuša 54; cf. also V. Haas, OLZ 77 (1982) 253.

[34] BiOr 51 (1994) 239-240.

[35] Ed. J. de Roos, Diss. 203, 341-342; see also the comments by Ph.H.J. Houwink ten Cate, BiOr 51 (1994) 251-255. That Danuḫepa would have been the wife of Šarrikušuḫ/Piyaššili as S.R. Bin-Nun, Theth. 5, 281-298, tries to show, is highly speculative and ultimately based on two erroneous interpretations concerning XXI 33: first the assumption that the name ᵐᵈ*SÎN*-LUGAL (XXI 33, 3', 4') could be equated with ᵐLUGAL-ᵈ*SÎN*, and secondly that *memiaš*/*memini* in XXI 33, 3' and 6' respectively) would be identical with *memian* ibid. 20'.

> Ù-*TUM* EGIR-*an parā damaīš*[36] / *parā*=*ma* ^f*Arumuraš m[e]miškizzi* / *aši*=*ua*= *kan* AMA.AMA-*KA kuuat*=*pat* ḪUL-*lu tiian ḫarzi* / KASKAL-*ši*=*ma*=*uar*=*an* =*kan UL daitti* / *kinun*=*ma*=*ua*=*šši* ^{DUG}ÁBxA ZABAR *pāi* / *nu*=*uar*=*aš*=*za*= *kan anda [u]aršiiazi* / *UMMA* ^{f}*Ḫepa*-SUM $^{D[UG]}$ÁBxA ZABAR=*ua* / *ANA* DINGIR-*LIM* GAL *piianzi nāui*
>
> Dream: Concerning the fact that they said: "They must give the clothes [to] Danuḫepa." Thus (speaks) Ḫepapiya: "Let them give the clothes ... to the Great God." Not yet (done).
> Later on yet another dream: Arumura keeps further saying: "Why then has that grandmother of yours done evil? Won't you 'put her on the road'? Give her a/the bronze bowl now! It will be [p]acifying." Thus (says) Ḫepapiya: "They will give the bronze bowl to the Great God." Not yet (done).

The beginning of the second paragraph with *parā damaīš* "yet another" and the immediately following *parā*=*ma* suggest some link to the preceding one. If the two dreams recorded here are interrelated, the AMA.AMA-*KA* of i 12 might be identical to Danuḫepa in i 7, and thus be the (step)grandmother of the reigning king Urḫiteššub as was already assumed by Houwink ten Cate.[37] But this remains conjectural. All in all, we are left with a puzzling situation which cannot be solved, it seems, on the basis of the material now published.

Predominant in the texts in which Danuḫepa occurs, is a lawsuit against her. Again, the prayer of Ḫattušili and Puduḫepa, (XXI 19+) XIV 7 i (CTH 383) is the best source on the Danuḫepa affair:

> *mān*=*ma*=*kan uit* ŠÀ É.LUGAL *DĪNU ŠA* ^{f}*Dan[uḫepa]* / *ŠA* ^{MUNUS}AMA.DINGIR-*LIM*=*KA kišat* ^{f}*Danuḫepan* G[IM-*an tepnut nu*] / *QADU* DUMU.MEŠ-*ŠU* UN.MEŠ-*tarr*=*a ḫūman BĒLU*^{MEŠ}[=*ia*] / EGIR-*izziušš*=*a* UN.MEŠ-*tar kuuapi ḫarakta* / *ŠA* ^{f}*Danuḫepa*=*ma ḫargaš ANA* ^{d}UTU ^{URU}PÚ-*na* [GAŠAN=*IA*] / *mān* ZI-*anz[a] ēšta*
>
> When it happened that the lawsuit against Dan[uḫepa], your *šiuanzanni*-priestess, took place in the palace, h[ow he humiliated] Danuḫepa and whether, when along with her children/sons also (her) entire retinue, lords as well as lower (people), (that is her) retinue died, the downfall of Danuḫepa was your intention, o Sungoddess of Arinna, [my Lady], (you alone know).[38]

[36] Here I differ from J. de Roos, Diss. 203, who reads *da-a-i-iš*, and prefer to follow A. Kammenhuber, FsGüterbock 154. For the combination *parā tamai-* see CHD P 122b-123a.

[37] BiOr 51 (1994) 252.

[38] XIV 7 i 16'-21' (ed. D. Sürenhagen, AoF 8 (1981) 90-91). The fact that this trial must have taken place under Muwatalli and that Danuḫepa is still attested

The nature of this lawsuit is not specified but Danuḫepa seems to have dragged down with her, her children/sons and further entourage. Intriguing is Ḫattušili's subsequent remark (XXXI 19+ ii 4) about the "[...] of Danuḫepa's son." It is conceivable, that if Danuḫepa were indeed the last wife of Muršili II and if her children stemmed from this marriage, as A. Ünal suggested,[39] then she might have wanted one of these sons to succeed Muwatalli. Whether one of the "unbekannte Großkönige" mentioned by Neve[40] as occurring with Danuḫepa on two sealings, is identical to this son, can hopefully be determined once these bullae are published. Muwatalli, of course, will have preferred his own son for succession, which then led to a dynastic strife, possibly between one party in the former capital Ḫattuša and one in Tarḫuntašša. One of Danuḫepa's sons may have been temporarily in power but was soon ousted and somehow disposed of,[41] at the same time resulting in a political setback for Danuḫepa. Ḫattušili at any rate firmly denies in the prayer any involvement in putting an end to this affair. Instead, he again assures the goddess that the man who was responsible for all this, "already became a god, 'stepped off the road' and has already paid for it with [h]is hea[d]."[42] Because of the terminology used ("became a god"), the fact that Urḫiteššub still lived during Ḫattušili's reign (and longer), and that the next paragraph starts out with Muwatalli's death and Urḫiteššub's accession, this person can be none other than Muwatalli.[43] This is confirmed by the chronological ordering of events in the prayer, according to which the trial must have taken place during the latter's reign.

The trial is also attested in two texts that have been ascribed to Urḫiteššub: XXI 33 (g) and XXXI 66+ (i). In the latter text[44] it is Urḫiteššub who seems eager to shirk his responsibility in the matter:

> *ūqqa ⸗i̯a[⸗za UL me]miškinun / ABU ⸗IA⸗man⸗u̯a⸗ kan* MUNUS.LUGAL⸗*i̯a / lē ḫannetalu̯aniēš / ammuqq⸗ a⸗man⸗u̯a lē kuitki /* ḪUL-*uēšzi ammuk⸗man / apē* DI.ḪI.A *kuu̯at / ḫanneškinun / apāt ŠA* DINGIR-*LIM DĪNU ē[šzi] / nu mān ABU⸗IA ANA* MUNUS.LUG[AL] */ IŠTU DĪNI šarāzi[š UL] / kuitki ēšta ammuk⸗m[an⸗an] / ANA ᶠTanuḫepa* MUNUS.LUGAL *IŠTU DĪ[NI] / katteraḫḫeškinun / kūn memian ANA* ZI⸗*IA / šer ēššaḫḫun /*

as queen next to Urḫitešub, rules out the possibility, that her death would be described here, as S.R. Bin-Nun, THeth. 5, 277, maintains.

[39] THeth. 3, 143; also Ph.H.J. Houwink ten Cate, BiOr 51 (1994) 240 with n. 17.

[40] Ḫattuša 87.

[41] See Ph.H.J. Houwink ten Cate, BiOr 51 (1994) 240 with n. 16, and 242-243.

[42] XXI 19+ ii 13-15.

[43] Cf. Ph.H.J. Houwink ten Cate, BiOr 51 (1994) 243.

[44] Ed. Ph.H.J. Houwink ten Cate, FsGüterbock 129-137.

lē⸗man⸗u̯a⸗mu kuitki ḪUL-*uēšzi* / *ii̯anun⸗ma⸗at⸗kan damēdaz* / *IŠTU* KAxU *p*[*ar*]*ā*

"And I kept [ref]using: 'May my father and the queen not be opponents (in court) and may it in no way turn out bad for me!' Why would I have passed judgment on that trial? That i[s] a trial pertaining to a god! If my father had in no way been superior to the que[en] through the trial, w[ould] I have made [him] succumb to Danuḫepa, the queen, through the trial? This I said for (the benefit of) my own soul: 'May it in no way turn out bad for me!' I have done it, however, at someone else's behest."[45]

According to his last remark Urḫiteššub was, however reluctant, apparently forced to take sides in the matter but, unfortunately, it is not clear what exactly he did. The other text referring to the lawsuit, XXI 33 (g), and even more so the passage in which Danuḫepa (18'-22') occurs, is notoriously enigmatic:

x +18 [*ku-u̯*]*a-*⸢*pí*⸣ SISKUR.MEŠ *I-NA* ⸢^{URU}⸣*Pé-*⸢*e*⸣*-ra-na e-eš-ši-eš-ta*
19 [ ]x ^{f}*Ta-nu-ḫé-pa-aš-ša* SISKUR.MEŠ *ma-an-ta-al-li-i̯a*
20 [ ]x x x *in-na-ra-a-aš me-mi-an IŠ-TU* EME
21 [-]*i̯a*/*IA* *IŠ-TU DI-NI* (erasure)
22 [ ] (vacat).

The words in line 19' ^{f}*Tanuḫepašš⸗a* SISKUR.MEŠ *mantallii̯a* "and Danuḫepa *mantalli*-offerings" require another subject before Danuḫepa and the verb *išpant-*/BAL "to bring (offerings)" like in XXII 35 iii 9'-11' (*nu⸗za ABI* ^{d}UTU-*ŠI* ^{m}*Ḫalpa*-LÚ-*išš⸗a* 1-*aš* 1-*edani* IGI-*anda* SISKUR *mantali̯a* BAL-*anti*). The remaining trace of the sign before ^{f}*Tanuḫepašš⸗a* points to A or IA, thus suggesting the combination LUGAL.GAL EN⸗*IA* so frequently occurring in this text. The most likely candidates for the subject of the verb *eššešta* in 18' would seem to be Urḫiteššub/Muršili III or Danuḫepa but the space available at the beginning of that line just does not seem big enough to accomodate either [^{m}*Mur-ši*-DINGIR-*LIM-iš* or [^{f}*Ta-nu-ḫé-pa-aš ku-u̯*]*a-*⸢*pí*⸣. A possible solution is to restore something like [MUNUS.LUGAL-*ma-za ku-u̯*]*a-*⸢*pí*⸣ with MUNUS.LUGAL referring to Danuḫepa comparable to XXXI 66(+) iii 12' (MUNUS.LUGAL) and 15' (^{f}*Tanuḫepa* MUNUS.LUGAL). The combination *IŠTU* EME in 20' suggests a restoration with the verb *parkunu-* "to cleanse, purify" as in L 6+ ii 40'-41' and iii 48-50. Similarly, according to HW^2 Ḫ 155a-b *IŠTU DINI* in 21 is primarily attested with verbs derived from the adjectives *šarazzi-* "upper" and *kattera-* "lower" as, for instance, in XXXI 66(+) (i) just quoted. We may thus tentatively restore the above passage:

45 XXXI 66 iii 4'-21'.

x +18 [MUNUS.LUGAL-*ma-za ku-u̯*]*a*-⸢*pí*⸣ SISKUR.MEŠ *I-NA* ⸢^{URU}⸣*Pé*-⸢*e*⸣-*ra-na e-eš-ši-eš-ta*
19 [*nu-za* LUGAL.GAL EN-*I*]*A* ^{f}*Ta-nu-ḫé-pa-aš-ša* SISKUR.MEŠ *ma-an-ta-al-li-i̯a*
20 [BAL-*aš* ^{m}*Mur-ši*-DINGIR-*L*]*IM*?-⸢*iš-ma*⸣ *in-na-ra-a*<<-*aš*>>[45] *me-mi-an IŠ-TU* EME
21 [*pár-ku-nu-ut nu* LUGAL.GAL EN-]*IA* *IŠ-TU DI-NI* (erasure)
22 [*ša-ra-a-zi-i̯a-aḫ-ta*[46]/*kat-te-ra-aḫ-ta*] (vacat).

[Wh]en [the queen] performed offerings in the city of Perana, [the Great King, m]y [Lord] and Danuḫepa [brought] *mantalli*-offerings (to each other?). [Muršil]i, however, of his own accord, [cleansed] the affair from the curse [and he made the Great King,] my [Lord win/loose] through the lawsuit.

If so, this could mean that Danuḫepa, after a failed attempt to let her own son succeed her stepson Muwatalli and therefore perhaps exiled to Perana, a city otherwise unknown, tried to reconcile with the reigning king Urḫiteššub through a *mantalli*-ritual with the in the meantime deceased Muwatalli. This may – willingly or not – have been approved of by Urḫiteššub by way of an official disapproval of his father's measures against the queen. In this case the restoration required in line 22' would be *katteraḫta* "he made lose", which is in keeping with the tenor of the whole text: again Urḫiteššub reversed one of his father's original decisions. This would at least fit in with the fact that in spite of a possible temporary setback, Danuḫepa must have remained in or returned to power, because of the bullae on which she is attested together with Urḫiteššub.

A final but uncertain reference to Danuḫepa, her son and the trial may be contained in the small fragment KBo XXXVI 111 ii with a listing of trials, where it says in lines 4-5: *DI-NU ŠA* ^{MUNUS}⸢*ta*⸣-*u̯a*[-*na-an-na*] / *Ù DI-NU ŠA* DUMU[. If so, it would be the only instance where Danuḫepa is mentioned by the title of *tawananna*. It cannot, however, be excluded that this entry refers to the stepmother of Muršili II, the last wife of Šuppiluliuma I; see already above sub 2.

The possible coup attempt staged by Danuḫepa and her son most likely forms the background of her involvement in the oracle inquiry about the

[45] The text seems to be corrupt here; see on this problem already R. Stefanini, JAOS 84 (1964) 30. Even if *innarāš* were the first word of a sentence, a segmentation into *innarā* ⸗ *aš* – with ⸗ *aš* as either nom.sg.c. or acc.pl.c. of the enclitic pronoun – would still be impossible because a nom.sg. is only allowed with an intransitive verb (Watkins' rule, cf. A. Garrett, JCS 42 (1990) 227-242; excluded by *memian*) and in case of an intransitive verb we already have *memian* as object. There neither is any evidence for a noun **innara*-, cf. A. Kammenhuber, MSS 3^{2} (1956) 40.

[46] For the plene-spelling compare XXXI 66(+) iii 13' *ša-ra-a-zi*[-.

purity of kingship. From L 6+ iii 1-2 we learn, that a first "undoing of her curses in front of the gods of kingship" took place in the past. Whether the preterite *anniškir* (iii 2) refers to the first phase of this inquiry during the early years of Tutḫaliya's rule, remains uncertain. By this he may also mean the institution of a ritual or cult for her gods by his father Ḫattušili as mentioned later on in that same text iii 19-20, an act which can be linked to Ḫattušili's and Puduḫepa's prayer XXI 19+. According to XVI 32 ii 1'-7' (§§1'-2') Tutḫaliya initially decided to single out within each city, which formerly had apparently belonged to Danuḫepa, one household and assigned them to the cult of the deceased Danuḫepa. The "bringing back in" (XVI 32 ii 5' EGIR-*pa anda pedanzi*) of her gods suggests Tutḫalija is restoring an older situation here. The cities mentioned may have been given to her as her place of exile under Muwatalli or dedicated to her cult after her death by either Urḫiteššub or Ḫattušili. Moreover, the cities were to give a tribute to the deceased on a regular basis (XVI 32 ii 7' *arkamman* BAL-*eškiuu̯an ti*[*i̯anzi*). Over the years these promises do not seem to have been observed properly or were not even implemented at all, for according to the second phase of the inquiry as described in L 6+ ii 48'-iii 29 (§§10'-14') her estate is reported to have been "dispersed", her gods are "locked in" and, furthermore, her estate has been given to others. In this way an end was put to the cult of Danuḫepa's gods.[48] After the three charges have been set forth in §10' and the cleansing rite of the places and the thrones of kingship as well as of the King has been prescribed as a general cure, the individual charges are then dealt with one by one in §§12'-14'. Through these measures Tuthalija sought to remedy her posthumous anger.

4. *Urḫiteššub*

There are probably few persons in Hittite history about whom we are so well informed as Urḫiteššub/Muršili III. We do not need to list all the occurrences of his name in Hittite texts nor do we have to recount in detail the different stages of his life and career: his birth as son of a concubine to Muwatalli II, the upbringing by his father, his accession to the throne around 1274, the struggle and ultimate defeat against his uncle Ḫattušili III and his life's end at the Egyptian court of Ramses II. For all this and more the reader is referred to the treatises by Ph.H.J. Houwink ten Cate[49] and A. Ünal.[50] Yet, the circumstances around his accession – possibly involving the son of Danuḫepa – are still shrouded in mystery and it is probably this period in which we have to date the 'affair of Urḫiteššub'. The chronological ordering of affairs in CTH 569 and the fact that the one

[48] This may have been one of the reasons for the Sungoddess of Arinna "of Progeny" (DUMU-*annaš*) to accuse Tutḫaliya of *šallakartatar* (KBo II 2 iii 18ff., see Ch. III.3) against her.

[49] FsGüterbock 123-150, and BiOr 51 (1994) 233-259.

[50] THeth. 3, 108-175.

involving Armatarḫunta (and most probably Šaušgatti as well) certainly fell within in the reign of Muwatalli, while this seems likely for the Ḫalpaziti affair also, forces us to this assumption. At least one element in CTH 569 may support this. In XVI 32 ii 27'-30' (§7') an oath of Ḫattušili concerning Urḫiteššub is mentioned, which per Houwink ten Cate "is likely to have been administered either on the occasion of Urhi-Tessub's selection by Muwatallis II, or else at the solemnity of his enthronement."[51] Obviously, this oath of allegiance was broken by Ḫattušili which may have induced Urḫiteššub to utter the curses against his uncle which now form the topic of the sequel of the oracle inquiry in L 6+ iii 32-65 (§§16'-19'). However, the actual breaking of the oath took place years after the actual oath ceremony, but the general chronological sequence of affairs can only be upheld if we assume that Tutḫaliya took the pledge of allegiance by his father as his point of departure.

On the other hand, a comparison with the better known other affairs might suggest a different beginning. In the cases of the *tawananna*, Danuḫepa, and in the one of Armatarḫunta (and Šaušgatti?) to be dealt with below, it is each time that person wanting to depose either the reigning king (*tawananna* versus Muršili II, Danuḫepa versus Muwatalli) or a future king (Armatarḫunta versus Ḫattušili). In the further course of events that person is each time exposed and removed from court. The curses to be "undone" were certainly due to the use of sorcery in the cases of the *tawananna*, Armatarḫunta and Šaušgatti which they initially used to attain their goal. Sorcery is also attested for Ḫalpaziti, as we will see, possibly even in connection with Urḫiteššub. This same Ḫalpaziti is, again in the immediate context of sorcery (see below), linked to Šaušgatti. This could lead us to suspect that Urḫiteššub, prior to his own accession, was somehow involved in an intrigue against either his own father or his already powerful uncle Ḫattušili. There is, however, no positive evidence in our main sources on Urḫiteššub, to wit the Apology and related texts, to support such an assumption. If this were true, one would have expected Ḫattušili to say so, if not to emphasize it. We only have Ḫattušili's words in the Apology that when his brother Muwatalli died he "did not do anything (evil) out of regard for the love" for his brother (Apology iii 38'-39', StBoT 24, 21). According to the Apology it was only after his accession that Urḫiteššub started to thwart Ḫattušili. Since in accordance with the rules laid down by the old Hittite king Telipinu Urḫiteššub had every right to succeed his father, Ḫattušili's words are somewhat surprising and could be understood as a veiled hint that he felt fully justified to interfere but did not do so out of consideration for the memory of his brother. This finds some support in the introductory sentence to the final lawsuit against Armatarḫunta cum suis in the 'Apology' iii 14-15 (ed. H. Otten, StBoT 24, 18-19): [GIM(*-an=ma*)] *uit IŠTU* É.LUGAL DI-*eššar ku*[(*itki* EGIR-*pa ḫuitti*)]*iattat* "When it happened that the lawsuit was somehow reopened by the palace" (compare the first attempt in i 33ff.). If

[51] BiOr 51 (1994) 249-250, see also ibid. 254.

we are right in translating *appa ḫuittii̯a-* here and elsewhere (instead of "protract, prolong"; see below Ch. VI ad L 6+ ii 44') as "reopen, revive", court circles were indeed involved in attempts to get Ḫattušili out of the way.

Just as in the case of Danuḫepa, Ḫalpaziti, Armatarḫunta and Šausgatti (see below), Urḫiteššub's children probably suffered a fate similar to their parent(s) but were rehabilitated and remunerated by Tutḫaliya (see commentary to L 6+ iii 52).[52]

5. *Ḫalpaziti*

The different individuals bearing the name Ḫalpaziti have been discussed in StBoT 38, 186-193. There is evidence for an augur, a GAL $^{LÚ.MEŠ}$UKU.UŠ (ZAG-*naš*), a king of Ḫalpa, at least two scribes and a priest, all by the name of Ḫalpaziti or Ḫalwaziti. For convenience sake we will repeat here only those texts which are likely to belong to the Ḫalpaziti of CTH 569:

a. KBo XVIII 145, 1' (CTH 214/297? - ?; = Šaušgatti b)
b. XVI 58 iii 6' (CTH 569 - Tutḫ. IV)
c. XXII 35 iii 1' (*Ḫa*]*l*-), iii 9' (CTH 569 - Tutḫ. IV)
d. XXXI 23 obv.$^{!}$ 6' (-L[Ú) (CTH 832 - ?)
e. LII 92 iv 3' (-*p*]*a*-) (CTH 569 - Tutḫ. IV)
f. LX 129, 7' (^{LÚ}SANGA) (CTH 214/297? - ?; = Šaušgatti g)

Orthography

^{m}*Ḫal-pa*-LÚ	b c
^{m}*Ḫal-pa*-LÚ-*iš*	a e f
fragmentary	d

As opposed to the presentation in StBoT 38, the two pieces KBo XVIII 145 (a) and LX 129 (f) have been separated here because the possibility of an indirect join between them could not be verified through photo collation (for more detail on these two texts see below Šaušgatti b and g). Moreover, LII 92 (e) which was not yet recognized as containing the name Ḫalpaziti, can now be added.

Because of the "Gods of (the city of) Ḫalpa" mentioned in XXII 35 iii 13', who get compensated, A. Archi[53] suggested this Ḫalpaziti may have been identical to his namesake, the king of Ḫalpa, known from the

[52] The idea of E. Edel, ÄhK II 76, 101 and 118-119, on the basis of KBo I 15+ Rev. 13-21 (ed. ibid. I 62-63) that Ramses II at one time would have suggested to Ḫattušili III to install Urḫitešub on the throne in Ḫalpa is too speculative to be considered here.

[53] AoF 6 (1979) 82.

Akkadian letter IBoT I 34 (CTH 179.1 - Tutḫ. IV). Archi's suggestion was considered to be unlikely in StBoT 38, 189-190: it was argued that the fact that Ḫalpaziti is mentioned as already dead in XXII 35, was difficult to reconcile with the chronology of the texts in question: Ḫattušili is said to be still alive in XVI 32, the text which is important in dating the entire composition CTH 569, including XXII 35, to a relatively early phase in the reign of Tutḫaliya IV, whereas IBoT I 34 is securely dated to a late phase in his reign.[54] At this point the 'new' fragment LII 92 (e) forces us to reconsider Archi's proposal. In iv 7' the city of *Ḫal[pa* occurs once more in connection with Ḫalpaziti's children/sons and with some sort of a ritual laid down in that city. This evidence cannot be dismissed any longer, and Archi's suggestion seems inevitable. Fortunately, the better understanding of the different chronological layers of the inquiry CTH 569 as reflected in the two summary stages makes a reconciliation between the two options possible. It is now clear that the reference to Ḫattušili as being still among the living in XVI 32 appears in the so-called 'ultimate summary' part (see Ch. I.4), which summarized an earlier state of the investigation which must have been conducted in an early phase of Tutḫaliya's reign, when his father was still alive. Later in his reign, however, the investigation was taken up again and continued. The text XXII 35 is part of this later inquiry as shown by its col. ii which corresponds to the second stage in the discussion of the Danuḫepa affair. This renders it possible to date CTH 569 in its 'final' form to a late phase in Tutḫaliya's reign, that is, when not only his father Ḫattušili but also Ḫalpaziti had died, or in terms of texts, after IBoT I 34 when Eḫlišarruma had succeeded his father Arišarruma to the throne in Išuwa.[55] We should therefore now add to the above sources the one text which explicitly calls Ḫalpaziti "King of Ḫalpa":

g. IBoT I 34 obv. 8 (LUGAL ^{URU}*Ḫal-pa*) (CTH 179.1 - Tutḫ.)

Orthography: ^{m}*Ḫal-pa*-LÚ

According to XXII 35 (c) and LII 92 (e) Ḫalpaziti had children/sons who – just as the children of Šaušgatti – perhaps were involved too, since they are somehow appeased or remunerated.

An interesting consequence of this identification of the Ḫalpaziti in CTH 569 with the King of Ḫalpa is that witness LX 129 (f) he also bore the title "Priest." His earlier predecessor on the throne in Ḫalpa, Telipinu, Šuppiluliuma's son, is usually referred to as "Priest" as well. In the hieroglyphic ALEPPO 1 inscription of Telipinu's son and successor Talmišarruma he even figures as MAGNUS SACERDOS "high priest."[56] Although Telipinu seems to have been a priest already prior to his

[54] See StBoT 38, 192.

[55] Cf. StBoT 38, 124-126 (Eḫlišarruma) and 203-204 (Arišarruma).

[56] H. Klengel, Syria 3000 to 300 B.C. 129, erroneously ascribes this title to Talmišarruma himself.

appointment in Ḫalpa, the choice for a priest on this post was undoubtedly inspired by the importance of Ḫalpa as a cult center for the Stormgod.[57] Although Talmišarruma is never mentioned as "Priest" in our sources, the fact that this title is now attested for two kings of Ḫalpa could point to a certain tradition of priest-rulers there. There is no evidence for a genetic relation between Talmišarruma and Ḫalpaziti.[58] If they were related, Ḫalpaziti was his grandson rather than son since Talmišarruma was installed by Muršili II in his ninth year (1300-1299[59]) and Ḫalpaziti is attested as still living in a later phase of Tutḫaliya's reign. Moreover, the latest synchronism we have for Talmišarruma is the ALEPPO 1 inscription from the time of Muwatalli. A clue as to when Ḫalpaziti ascended the throne in Ḫalpa may be gained from CTH 569. In XVI 32 ii 8'-13' (§3'), reflecting the early or first stage of the oracle inquiry, we read:

> *kinuna=kan* GIM-*an ŠA* DINGIR.MEŠ ^{URU}*Ḫalpa uliḫiuš* UGU *u*[*da*(*nzi*)] / *nu=šmaš=za* ^{d}UTU-ŠI SISKUR *mantallii̯a* IGI-*anda arḫa* [BAL-*anti*] / GIM-*an=ma=kan* LUGAL KUR *Kargamiš* UGU *uizzi nu=šši=kan* ^{m}[*Kat*(*apa*-DINGIR-*LIM*-*in*)] / GAM-*an parā nei̯anzi nu* DINGIR-*LUM pidi=ši* GIM-*an a*[*nii̯*(*anzi*)] / *n=an=kan* KASKAL-*ši tii̯anzi* ^{LÚ}SANGA-*UTTA=i̯a apii̯*[*a t*(*ii̯anzi*)] / *kuiš* SIxSÁ-*ri*
>
> But now, when they c[arry] up the *uliḫis* of Ḫalpa's city gods, His Majesty [will] com[plete] the *mantalli*-rituals to them. When, then, the king of Kargamiš comes up (there),they will send Katapaili down out to him and when they celebrate the deity on its own premises, they will 'put him on the road' and found a priesthood the[re] (and install the one) who will be ascertained.

In view of the priesthood-rulership in Ḫalpa of Telipinu and Ḫalpaziti's priestly function, Tutḫaliya's remark about the "foundation of a priesthood" could very well be Ḫalpaziti's investiture as the local priest-king there.

What the affair of Ḫalpaziti consisted of is difficult to tell. It first of all depends on his relation to Šaušgatti and her relation to Armatarḫunta. If, as will be considered possible below, the last two formed a couple, Ḫalpaziti's appearance next to Šaušgatti in the two texts KBo XVIII 145 (a) and LX 129 (f) suggests he may have been part of the Armatarḫunta faction against Ḫattušili. Perhaps he was one of the "other people" mentioned in the Apology i 33-34 who joined Armatarḫunta in his first coup attempt (see below). In this case the Ḫalpaziti affair took place during Muwatalli's reign, which would be in keeping with the general chronological order of affairs. The sorcery, so prominent in those two

57 See H. Klengel, Gesch.Syr. 1, 197, and Syria 3000 to 300 B.C. 128.

58 See H. Klengel, Gesch.Syr. 1, 199, and more explicitly Syria 3000 to 300 B.C. 130. There is no evidence to assume that Ḫalpaziti was a son of Armatarḫunta, as A. Archi, SMEA 14 (1971) 213, says.

59 Cf. Th. van den Hout, ZA 84 (1994) 88.

fragments, is also attested in the fragment XXXI 23 (d).[60] As opposed to the handcopy of this text, the photo of the "Vs.$^{?}$" marks it as the reverse side and vice versa.[61] If this is correct, the obv.$^{!}$ and rev.$^{!}$ form a running text with perhaps only one line missing on the lower edge of the obv.$^{!}$. Neither the photo nor the text itself, however, seems to offer any clear evidence in favor of one of the two alternatives. Collation of the tablet itself might bring such evidence. For the time being indications on the photo are followed here. The fact that the (upper$^{!}$) edge is inscribed points to the text as a letter. It may thus somehow be linked to the fragments KBo XVIII 145 (a) and LX 129 (f).

Obv.$^{!}$
x+1 [ ] (traces) [
2 [ ] KUR$^{?}$ ⸢URU⸣[
3 *A-NA* DINGIR.MEŠ x[
4 *ma-a-an-ma-za* DINGIR.⸢MEŠ⸣[

(erasure)

---

5 *ke-e* INIM.ḪI.A *ku-e* ⸢*ŠA*/*ša*⸣[-
6 ^{m}*Úr-ḫi-*^{d}U-*ub* ^{m}*Ḫal-pa*-L[Ú
7 *ŠA* DUMU ^{m}*Ar-nu-u̯a*-⸢*an*⸣[-
8 *me-ek-ka*$_4$*-i̯a-aš-ša*[(-)
9 GIM-*an* SIxSÁ-⸢*ta*⸣[-*at*
10 [$^{URU?}$]KÙ.BABBAR[62]-*kán ú*[-[63]
11] x [
(possibly only one line lost till)

Rev.$^{!}$

1 x [ ] x [
2 *na*-x[*a*]*r*$^{?}$-⸢*ḫa*⸣$^{?}$[
3 *nu*-⸢*kán*⸣$^{?}$[ ]x x x[64] [
4 INIM UḪ$_7$-*i̯a ku-iš* SIxSÁ[-*at*
5 *nu ma-a-an* KAR-*u-e-ni ku*[-

[60] Cf. StBoT 38, 189 n. 349. The relevance of this small fragment for this text group was in fact first recognized in 1949 by W. Riedel in his "Bemerkungen zu den hethitischen Keilschrifttafeln aus Boghazköi", 15: "XXXI 23 wird wohl zu XVI 41 in Beziehung stehn."

[61] The height of the "Vs.$^{?}$" is 4.0 cm, its maximum width (line 9) is 5.0 cm. No photo of "Rs.$^{?}$" was available.

[62] Reading suggested by E. Neu.

[63] Possible also *Ú*[-*UL* (E. Neu).

[64] G. Beckman (personal communication) suggests *IT-TI* for the last two sign traces.

6 *nu-za* ^{d}UTU-*ŠI IŠ-TU* INIM [
7 *pár-ku-nu-zi ma-a-an-ma* (erasure)[
8 *ma-a-an-ma-kán* GAM *Ú-UL* x[
9 ⸢*A-NA* ^{d}⸣UTU-*ŠI-kán A-NA* x[
10 [ ]x x x x[

x+3 for/to the gods ... [
4 If you, o gods [

---

5 These affairs which ... [
6 Urḫiteššub [and$^{?}$] Ḫalpazi[ti
7 of Arnuwan[da]'s son [
8 and for$^{?}$ many [
9 as (it) was established [
(...)
Rev.
(...)
4 and the matter of sorcery which [was] established [
5 If we will find ... [
6 from the matter [of ...] His Majesty
7 will cleanse himself. If [
8 if, however, not ... [
9 for His Majesty, for ... [

Ḫalpaziti is mentioned here (obv.$^{!}$ 6') right next to Urḫiteššub. This could imply, that Urḫiteššub was a supporter of Armatarḫunta *cum suis* as well. Ḫalpaziti and his children may have suffered at the hand of Ḫattušili a fate similar to Armatarḫunta's family, that is, exile or at least some form of a political *negatio existentiae*. Ḫalpaziti's installation in the politically unimportant and subordinate city of Ḫalpa, could then be considered an effective measure of compensation and remuneration by Tutḫaliya. Later in his reign, that is before the second stage of the oracle inquiry Ḫalpaziti must have died witness the scene in XXII 35 iii where his GIDIM "death spirit" is mentioned. Chronologically, his death must have occurred after Eḫlišarruma's accession on the throne in Išuwa, which can be dated to 1220 or shortly afterwards (on this see Ch. I.11).[65]

[65] For the idea that Urḫitešub may have been a candidate for the throne in Ḫalpa see above n. 52.

6. *Armatarḫunta*

About Armatarḫunta we are relatively well, although somewhat one-sidedly informed. The following texts refer to somebody by this name (NH 138):[66]

a. Apology of Ḫattušili III, i 27 (A//B i 24//D i 3'), 33 (A//B i 29//D i 7'), ii 74 (A//B ii 54), iii 17 (F i 6), 23 (F i 14 -]^{d}IM-*an*), 28 (F i 24), 30 (B iii 1//F i 27 ^{m}*A*[*r-m*]*a*-), iv 3 (A//B iii 48//F ii 36), 66 (A), 71 (A), 72 (A)(CTH 81, ed. H. Otten, StBoT 24)
b. KBo II 6+ i 12', 31', 32', 38', iv 24 (CTH 569 - Tutḫ. IV)
c. KBo XXIII 105, 5' (^{md}*SÎ*]*N*-^{d}U-*aš*(-)), 13' (*SÎN*$^{!}$)(CTH 581? - ?)
d. XVI 32 ii 19' (CTH 569 - Tutḫ. IV)
e. XXI 17 i 3, 5, 7, 27, ii 3, 8, 9, 25 (^{md}*SÎN*-^{d}[), 34 (^{md}*SÎN*-^{d}[) (//XXXI 27, CTH 86.1 - Ḫatt. III)
f. XXXI 26, 3', 4' (CTH 86.2 - Ḫatt. III)
g. LII 83, 16 (CTH 582 - ?)
h. LV 27, 16' (CTH 670 - ?)
i. 2275/c, 8', 11'$^{?}$ (apud H. Otten, Luv. 95).[67]

One seal is known:

j. SBo 2, 22 (INFANS+REX).

Orthography:

– cuneiform

^{m}*Ar-ma*-^{d}U	a (iii 17, 30, iv 3)
^{m}*Ar-ma*-^{d}U-*aš*	a (iii 25
^{m}*Ar-ma*-^{d}IM	a (iii 28)
^{m}*Ar-ma*-^{d}IM-*an*	a (iii 23)
^{md}*SÎN*-^{d}U	a (iii 30 iv 3, 66, 71, 72) b c (13') d e (i 5, 27, ii 3, 8, 9, 25, 34) f g h i
^{md}*SÎN*-^{d}U-*aš*	a (i 27, 33, ii 74) c (5') e (i 3, 7)

– hieroglyphic

LUNA.TONITRUS	j

Palaeographically all published manuscripts can confidently be dated in the 13th century. Moreover, the Armatarḫunta of Ḫattušili's Apology and of the texts KBo II 6+ (b), XVI 32 (d), XXI 17 (e) and XXXI 26 (f) in all

[66] On Armatarḫunta and his relationship with Ḫattušili III see A. Ünal, THeth. 3, 92-107.

[67] Too uncertain to be used here is]⌈d⌉*SÎN*-^{d}U in L 114 rev. 9', which could also be read as]MEŠ ^{d}U. On its obv. a "deity of the road" (7', 12') is twice mentioned. The same holds true for the ^{md}*SÎN*-x[of LII 31 i 18".

probability refer to one and the same person, i.e. Armatarḫunta, son of Zida, the well-known adversary of Ḫattušili III. The mentioning of "Armatarḫunta's estate" in LII 83 (g) and 2275/c (i) renders it likely that the Armatarḫunta of these fragments too can be identified with the same person. The small oracle fragment KBo XXIII 105 (c; see Ch. I.12) and the festival-like text LV 27 (h) contain too little information to be of any real significance.

Being the son of Zida, a brother of the Great King Šuppiluliuma I, Armatarḫunta was one of many princes (cf. his seal j), a full cousin of Muršili II and thus directly related to the ruling dynasty.[68] On his relationship with Šaušgatti see below. During the reign of Muršili II he was in charge of the 'Upper Country' (KUR UGU-*TI*) but lost this position to Ḫattušili when Muwatalli II succeeded his father Muršili in 1295. This resulted in the first of several attempts by Armatarḫunta to betray Ḫattušili to Muwatalli. According to the Apology (a) i 33-34 Armatarḫunta was joined in the first coup he staged by "other people", whereas in XXI 17 (e) i 10-11 he is said to have enlisted the help of sorceresses, who cast their spells on Ḫattušili. This led to an investigation prompted by Muwatalli which, however, resulted in complete rehabilitation of Ḫattušili's name. Thereupon he was able to follow his brother to Northern Syria and to join him there in the battle of Qadeš, nominally still in command of the Upper Country. Ḫattušili's temporary absence from Anatolia was used by Armatarḫunta for a second attempt to oust him from power. This time his wife and son (singular DUMU-*ŠÚ*) are explicitly mentioned in the Apology (a) ii 77-78 as having been involved, although this later turned out not to have been his only son which we know by name, Šipaziti.[69] Again sorcery seems to have been their main weapon witness both the Apology (a) ii 77-79 and XXI 17 (e, cf. i 29 UḪ$_7$-*tar*). The city of Šamuḫa, an important cult center for the goddess Ištar, Ḫattušili's patron deity, was one of the prime targets. After Ḫattušili's marriage to Puduḫepa and his return to the province it came to a real trial. Armatarḫunta, his wife and his sons (Apology iii 17 plural DUMU.MEŠ-*ŠU*) were found guilty of practising sorcery and their fate was apparently laid in the hands of Ḫattušili. Muwatalli, however, intervened on behalf of Šipaziti, one of Armatarḫunta's sons, vouching for his innocence; later, however, after Muwatalli's death, Šipaziti would side with Urḫiteššub and was exiled by Ḫattušili. Because of his already advanced age and his being a relative, Ḫattušili released Armatarḫunta unharmed; his wife[70] and their other son,[71] however, he sent into exile on the isle of Alašiya.[72] Moreover, half

[68] See my StBoT 38, 237 and the genealogical chart ibid. 80-81.

[69] See my StBoT 38, 235-238, and F. Starke, ZABR 2 (1996) 158 n. 81.

[70] From the genealogical chart in StBoT 38, 80-81, it follows, that among court circles it was not at all uncommon for a man to marry a woman, who was a generation younger (cf. Nerikkaili, Arišarruma, Bentešina, Ammistamru; for Šaušgamuwa now see Ph.H.J. Houwink ten Cate, AoF 23 (1996) 53-54).

of Armatarḫunta's property and estates were confiscated by Ḫattušili and handed over to the cult of Ištar of Šamuḫa which seems to be the main topic of the edict XXI 17 (e). Although notoriously difficult to define as to its genre, one of the aims of the Apology likewise is the foundation of the cult of Ištar on the basis of the former possessions of Armatarḫunta, with Ḫattušili and his son Tutḫaliya IV as her principal priests.

The forfeiture of Armatarḫunta's domains seems to have been a major concern to Ḫattušili since three more sources as well as CTH 569 (cf. KBo II 6+ §9') refer to it. The text LII 83 (g) is a fragment of an oracle investigation into damaged temple inventory.[73] In the last preserved paragraph (i 14-17) a "matter of postponing" something is mentioned, possibly as a reason for divine anger (*zaluganumaš* INIM-*ni* [*šer*), as well as the "[... of the property? of ...] ... and of the property of Armatarḫunta" (]x *ŠA* É ^{md}*SÎN*-^{d}U=*i̯a* [). At present it seems unlikely that this is a matter of fact statement from the time of Armatarḫunta about the state of his possessions. Rather, the investigation may have played a role in Ḫattušili's decision to seize them or in a later justification of this act.

That Ḫattušili consulted the gods in this case and got their approval seems to emerge from 2275/c as well. This unpublished fragment, the knowledge of which I owe to Prof. Otten, was once part of a thick, one-column tablet with its reverse uninscribed; its surface is much weathered which makes reading very hard.[74] As far as preserved, it belongs to the category of oracle summaries. The only almost complete paragraph mentions the "downfall of the House of Armatarḫunta" (8' *ŠA* É ^{md}*SÎN*-^{d}U-*ma ku-it* ÚŠ ⌈SIxSÁ⌉??-*at*). In connection with this the killing of part of the personnel of Armatarḫunta's estate, freemen and slaves alike, seems to be questioned:

8' *ŠA* É ^{md}*SÎN*-^{d}U-*ma ku-it* ÚŠ ⌈SIxSÁ⌉??-*at nu a*-⌈*ri*⌉-*e*-⌈*er*⌉

[71] The change between the singular "son" and plural "sons" in the Apology ii 77 and iii 17 respectively may go back to historical reality in the sense that in ii 17 Ḫattušili describes what he knew to be true at the moment of writing down his text. In iii 17 he gives the verdict of the trial, according to which Armatarḫunta's "sons" were guilty, which was subsequently corrected into "son" after Muwatalli's intervention in favor of Šipaziti. This would imply that Armatarḫunta and his wife had two sons.

[72] According to A. Ünal, THeth. 3, 100-101, Ḫattušili sent Armatarḫunta in exile as well, but this does not follow from his account in the Apology iii 25-29, cf. H. Otten, StBoT 24, 19 note ad lines 27ff.

[73] Cf. A. Archi, KUB LII Inhaltsübersicht iv, and G. Beckman, BiOr 42 (1985) 141 and the remarks above in Ch. I.12.

[74] The fragment was found on Büyükkale, "Geb. E/Raum 4 (Südende des westl. oberen Mauerkastens)" and is now likely to have been part of the original inventory of this building as pointed out by S. Alaura, AoF forthcoming. This means it came to light in the vicinity of the oracle fragments KBo XVI 98 (2211/c from g/14) and KBo XXIII 114 (304/f+ from g/13), for which see below Ch. IV.2 and 5.

9’ *nu ŠA EL-LU-TI* ⌈SIxSÁ-*at*⌉[75]
10’ *ŠA* DUMU.MUNUS ^{m}AMAR.MUŠEN-*na* ⌈AMA⌉?[76] ^{m}AMAR.MUŠEN-*na EL-LU-TI-i̯a*
11’ *ku-i-e-eš nam-ma ŠA* ⌈É ^{md}*SÎN*-^{d}U⌉?[77] *ŠA* ARAD GÉME
12’ 𒑱!*ar-ra-aḫ-ḫa-ni-i̯a-aš* 𒑱*ti-u̯a*-⌈*ta*⌉!-[78]*-ni-i̯a-aš*
13’ ⌈UN⌉.MEŠ*-tar-ra-kán ku-it mar-ri ku-en-ni-eš*?[79]-⌈*kir*⌉

Concerning the fact that the downfall of the House of Armatarḫunta was ascertained, they have conducted an oracle investigation: (The affair) of the freemen was ascertained, of the daughter of AMAR.MUŠEN-*na*[80] (and of) the mother? of AMAR.MUŠEN-*na* and (of those) who (are) further freemen of the estate of Armatarḫunta?, (and) of the male (and) female slaves (who were people) of perjury?[81] (and) curse, that is, the people whom they have impetuously killed, ...

The third text in question is the small fragment XXXI 26[82] (f), 1’, possibly part of a deposition that was used in the trial mentioned earlier because of the direct speech quoted:

x+1 ⌈*kat-ta-an AD-DIN*⌉ *z*[*i-ik*[83]
2’ *Ú-UL ta-at-ti k*[*i*?-
3’ É ^{md}*SÎN*-^{d}U *da-a n*[*u*(-)[84]
4’ [UR]U.DIDLI.ḪI.A ^{md}*SÎN*-^{d}U *nu-u̯a-m*[*u*[85]
5’ [EGIR-]*an*[86] *da-a-i :šar-l*[*a-*
6’ [ ]x *i-i̯a* ^{d}UTU-*ŠI*-⌈*ma*⌉[

1 “I did [not] betray (or: Did I betray ?), y[ou
2 do not take an[d
3 the estate of Armatarḫunta take(-?)[

75 So after collation by E. Neu.
76 Thus read by E. Edel in a preliminary transliteration from the late thirties.
77 Reading with H. Otten, Luv. 95, although difficult to recognize in the provisional (“Rohkopie”) handcopy.
78 “eher -⌈*ša*⌉- als -⌈*ta*⌉-, daher eventuell -⌈*ta*⌉!- zu transliterieren” (E. Neu, letter).
79 So after collation by E. Neu.
80 For two instances of the name AMAR.MUŠEN-*na* (a scribe and a carpenter) see my StBoT 38, 204.
81 Cf. H. Otten, Luv. 95, who points to a certain parallellism with Luwian *ḫirutani-*; no specific meaning is suggested by F. Starke, StBoT 31, 254.
82 P. Meriggi, WZKM 58 (1962) 90-91.
83 This line is read as *kat-ta-an* x-*aḫ-zi* by A. Ünal, THeth. 4, 30.
84 So after collation by E. Neu.
85 So after collation by E. Neu.
86 So after collation by E. Neu.

4 [the cit]ies of Armatarḫunta ["

The expression used in the first line recurs in the description of the first betrayal by Armatarḫunta in XXI 17 (e) i 7-8 where Ḫattušili also used the syntagm *kattan pai-* (*=mu=za* ... GAM-*an peškiuu̯an dāiš* "he began to betray me").

In order to forego possible consequences of the curses of Armatarḫunta and his offspring, Tutḫalija in CTH 569 (KBo II 6+ i 11'-19' and 31'-41' = §§6" and 9") seeks the approval of the gods to compensate Armatarḫunta for his loss of property. Some of it is probably made into sacrosanct territory (KBo II 6+ i 35' *dammeli pidi tianzi*), some is directly assigned to the cult of the deceased. Moreover, he plans to rehabilitate his descendants in an as yet unspecified way (ibid. i 36'-37' *tamedaza kaniššanzi*).

7. *Šaušgatti*

For a woman named Šaušgatti (NH 1142, 1741b[87]) the following sources stand at our disposal:

a. KBo II 6+ ii 37, 38, 43, 50, iii 4, 17, 30, 32, 37, 42, 43, 47, 48, 64, 65, iv 24 (CTH 569 - Tutḫ. IV)
b. KBo XVIII 145, 2 (CTH 581/297[88] - ?)
c. VIII 27(+) iv 1' (^{f}]), 8' (CTH 569 - Tutḫ. IV)
d. XVI 46 iv 6, 13 (CTH 573 - ?)
e. XVI 69 obv.$^{?}$ 4' (^{fd}]) (CTH 573 - ?)
f. L 87 rev.$^{?}$ 4' (*IŠT*[*AR*-) (CTH 578 - ?)
g. LX 129, 4' (G[AŠAN-), 6', 9' (CTH 581/297[89] - ?)
h. unp. 839/f obv. 6' (^{f}]), 14'.

Orthography

^{fd}*IŠTAR-ti*	d
^{fd}*IŠTAR-at-ti*	a c e f h
^{fd}*IŠTAR-at-ti-iš*	a (iii 17, 30) c (iv 8')
^{fd}GAŠAN-*ti*	b g
fragmentary	f

All the texts listed show 13th century new script. They probably all refer to one and the same Šaušgatti. The deposition text XXXIV 45+KBo XVI 63

[87] Cf. E. Laroche, Hethitica 4 (1981) 53.
[88] Cf. StBoT 38, 191.
[89] Cf. StBoT 38, 191. The possibility of reading GAŠAN as Šaušga- here was raised by E. Laroche, Hethitica 4 (1981) 53; for GAŠAN in general as a means of writing the name Šaušga see id., Rech. 96.

shows an older script form[90] so that the Šaušgatti mentioned there (obv. 7' ^{f}*Ša-uš-ga-at-ti-iš*) will not have been the same as her younger namesake. The two women by the name of Šaušgatti in the "Gelübde der Königin Puduḫepa an die Göttin Lelwani"[91] are certainly not to be identified with the Šaušgatti concerned here. The vow only attests to the fact that this name was apparently not uncommon. The occurrence of this name in KBo XVIII 145 (b) was formerly read ^{fd}GAŠAN-*tiuni* (NH 1741b) which could be corrected after the publication of LX 129 (g).[92]

Two of the above texts refer to Šaušgatti in retrospect, that is, in KBo II 6+ (a) and VIII 27(+) (c) she is explicitly (cf. GIDIM in a ii 55, iii 6, 8 etc., and as a consequence in c) characterized as being deceased. If the oracle texts mentioning her Zawalli-deity are related to CTH 569, as considered above, then we may add XVI 46 (d) and L 87 (f); the unpublished text 839/f (h) may belong here as well. From KBo II 6+ (a) we learn, that she had children/sons who, along with their mother, were being accused of having uttered curses against His Majesty but were remunerated later on. Unfortunately, XVI 46, 69, L 87 and 839/f (d-f and h) provide no further information about the role of Šaušgatti in these oracles or about her life in general; for more detail on these texts see Ch. I.12. G. del Monte, however, rightly concluded from XVI 46, that she must at least have belonged to royal circles, since her Zawalli is a ^{d}*Zau̯alliš ŠA* É.LUGAL (XVI 46 i 10).[93]

The two fragments KBo XVIII 145 (b) and LX 129 (g) both show Šaušgatti in the company of Ḫalpaziti, the priest, and His Majesty, in connection with sorcery (cf. b 2 and g 6' UḪ$_7$-*tar*, b 5 *alu̯anzaḫḫeškit* "she bewitched") and defilement (g 2' and 10' *papraḫḫeške-* "to defile"). The height of KBo XVIII 145, the upper right hand portion of a tablet, is 4.0 cm (till upper edge), its maximum width is 4.5 cm (from left extremity to IŠ on right edge). The tablet is written in a clear, deep hand as opposed to LX 129 where the script looks superficial and is harder to read, the surface of the tablet, however, is worn as indicated in the handcopy. The possibility of an indirect join suggested on the basis of the handcopies[94] thus could not be verified through photo collation. The fragment LX 129 is 5.5 cm high and 6.2 cm at its widest point (line 9').

KBo XVIII 145 (b)

1 [ ]⌈*a*⌉-*uš-ta* ^{m}*Ḫal-pa*-LÚ-*iš* GIM-*an*$^{!}$
2 [ ]x É ^{fd}GAŠAN-*ti* UḪ$_7$
3 [(-)]⌈*e*⌉-*eš-ta nu-u̯a-kán* ^{d}UTU-*ŠI*

90 See my StBoT 38, 225, and S. Košak, StBoT 39, 59 n. 3 sub 661/b ("mh. Schrift").
91 Ed. H. Otten - V. Souček, StBoT 1 i 13, iv 8 (ms. O).
92 Cf. BiOr 51 (1994) 126.
93 AION 33 (1973) 381, cf. also A. Archi, AoF 6 (1979) 83-84.
94 BiOr 51 (1994) 126 and StBoT 38, 189.

4 [ ]x-*u̯a-ra-an* GIM-*an*
5 [-*u̯a*-]⌈*ra*⌉-*an al-u̯a-an-za-aḫ-ḫe-eš-ki-it*
6 [ ]x *me-mi-eš-kit*$_9$*-tén*
7 [ ]⌈*e*⌉-*eš-ḫar UL ku-it-ki* x[ ]x-*u̯a ku-u̯a-pí* DÙ-⌈*ri*⌉
8 [*al-u̯a-an-z*]*a*[95]*-aḫ-ḫu-u̯a*-⌈*an*⌉[-*zi*
9 [ ]x ⌈EGIR⌉[
(break)

1 [...] he/she saw. When Ḫalpaziti
2 [...] ... the house of Šaušgatti sorcery
3 [...] he/she did/was (or: he/she/it became) and His Majesty
4 [...] when him/her
5 [...] she kept bewitching him
6 [...] ... you (plur.) kept saying
7 [...] no blood(shed$^?$) ... [...] ... when (it$^?$) takes place
8 [... to bew]itch[...]
9 (no translation possible)

LX 129 (g)

x+1 [ ]-*kán Ú-UL* x[
2 [ ]x-*u̯a-ra-an pa-ap-ra-aḫ*[-
3 [-Ḫ]A]R$^?$-*u̯a-aš-ši-kán a-ar-aš* [96][
4 [-*u̯*]*a*$^?$*-za ar-ḫa ú-da-a-i* ^{fd}G[AŠAN-*ti*
5 [*e*-]⌈*ep*⌉-*zi nu-u̯a* x x$^?$-*za*$^?$ *ku-it an*$^?$[
6 [-*u̯*]*a-aš-ši-kán ŠA* ^{fd}GAŠAN-*ti* UḪ$_7$-*tar A-N*[*A*
7 [ ] x x -*a*-⌈*u̯a/ši*⌉ ^{m}*Ḫal-pa*-LÚ-*iš* ^{LÚ}SANGA x[
8 [ ] x x ^{d}UTU-*ŠI ar-ḫa* KIN-*u-an-zi e*[-*ep-*
9 [*pá*]*r-ku-iš-u̯a-za e-eš ŠA* ^{fd}GAŠAN-*ti* KAxU-*za*[
10 [-*i*]*t-u̯a-ta* NÍ.TE-*KA pa-ap-ra-aḫ-ḫe-eš-ki*[-
11 [ ]x-*u̯a-at-ta* ḪUL-*lu-un* MUŠEN-*i*[*n*
12 [ ]x-*pí-ip-pa* x x x[

x+2 [...] him [she] defil[ed
3 [...] ... for him/her has come [
4 [...] he/she will bring home. Š[aušgatti
5 [...] he/she will [t]ake and because/what ... [
6 [...] for him Šaušgatti's sorcery ... [
7 [...] ... Ḫalpaziti, the priest ... [
8 [...] ... His Majesty be[gin(s)]/be[gan] to undo [
9 [...] you shall be [c]leansed! At Šaušgatti's behest [
10 [... wi]th [...] your body [she] kep[t]/keep[s] defiling [

[95] So after collation by E. Neu.

[96] On the photo there are possible traces of a KI sign after *āraš*.

11 [...] for you an/the evil bir[d
12 [...] ... [

Whether or not both pieces were once part of the same tablet, it seems obvious that the two fragments are related. The use of the quotative particle throughout the texts reminds of depositions or letters and makes the identification of KBo XVIII 145 as "Orakelbericht auf Kleintafel"[97] seem less likely. Summarizing the information obtained from these sources, Šaušgatti and her children/sons were involved in sorcery which later after her death prompted Tutḫaliya in CTH 569 to pacify her spirit and to remunerate her children. Further accomplices seem to have been Armatarḫunta and Ḫalpaziti.

Her relation to Armatarḫunta, to whom she is linked only in KBo II 6+ and its shorter version VIII 27(+) (a and c), is, unfortunately, not explicitly given. Following a more general remark made by F. Sommer[98] on persons occurring together in oracle texts, G. del Monte[99] warns against assuming some sort of relationship on the basis of Armatarḫunta and Šaušgatti being mentioned and treated together in KBo II 6+. A. Ünal, however, assumed that her appearance in KBo II 6+ next to Armatarḫunta, must have had a special reason which led him to the question: "Könnte sie seine Frau sein?"[100] Although Del Monte's reluctance was methodically sound and understandable at the time, that is, prior to the recognition of Šaušgatti's name in KBo XVIII 145 and the publication of LX 129, the sorcery as prime topic in the latter two texts forces us to reconsider. Both Armatarḫunta and Šaušgatti along with their children now turn out to have been involved in sorcery according to the Apology and XXI 17 (= Armatarḫunta a and e) on the one hand, and to KBo XVIII 145 and LX 129 (= Šaušgatti b and g) on the other. Their linkage in KBo II 6+ may therefore be more than just two individuals who in the past fought a Hittite king by way of magic. Although it cannot be strictly proven, Ünal's suggestion that Šaušgatti was Armatarḫunta's wife, mentioned in the Apology (ii 77, iii 17 and 21), and that the DUMU.MEŠ of the Apology and KBo II 6+ refer to the same persons, is nowadays decidedly more attractive.

8. *Katapaili*

The following texts can be adduced for Katapaili (NH 543):

a. KBo II 2 iv 24, 28 (CTH 577 - Tutḫ.IV)

97 H.G. Güterbock, KBo XVIII vi.

98 AU 301 n. 1; cf. a similar remark by H.G. Güterbock, SBo 1, 15, on Danuḫepa and Urḫitešub occurring together in XVI 32.

99 AION 33 (1973) 378.

100 THeth. 3, 105.

b. KBo XVI 60 obv. 5 (CTH 295 - ?)
c. KBo XVIII 146, 1 (-⸢DINGIR-*LIM*⸣), 20 (-[*LI*]*M*) (CTH 581 - ?)
d. XV 11 iii 5' (-*ta*]-), 7' (-*t*[*a*-) (CTH 584 - Ḫatt. III/Tutḫ. IV)
e. XVI 32 ii 10' (^{m}[), 25' (CTH 569 - Tutḫ. IV)
f. L 6+ ii 11' (-*t*]*a*$^{?}$-) (CTH 569 - Tutḫ. IV)
g. LVII 113, 6, 12 (CTH 590 - Ḫatt. III/Tutḫ. IV)

Orthography:

^{m}*Ka-ta-pa*-DINGIR-*LIM*	a c
^{m}*Ka-ta-pa*-DINGIR-*LIM-iš*	e b
^{m}*Ka-ta-pa*-DINGIR-*LIM-in*	f
^{m}*Ka-ta-pa-i-li-iš*	g (6)
^{m}*Ka-ta-pa-i-liš*	g (12)
fragmentary	d e.

All texts stem from the 13th century and are likely to be assigned to one and the same person as is already assumed in the treatise by J. de Roos.[101] To the material collected by him can be added L 6+ (f) and LVII 113 (g), the latter still unpublished at the time.

De Roos rightly concluded that Katapaili must have been an important official during the reign of Ḫattušili III and/or Tutḫaliya IV. In most texts he seems attested as a special envoy of the Hittite King entrusted with the task of overseeing the implementation of certain measures taken by the latter, mostly as a result of oracle inquiries or related vows. We already saw that according to KBo II 2 (a) in combination with XVI 32 and L 6+ (e-f) he was in charge of the handing over of the city of Kiuta to the cult of the deceased Armatarḫunta as well as the foundation of a priesthood in Ḫalpa, most probably in favor of its priest-ruler Ḫalpaziti. In a similar function he appears at the end of two fragmentary paragraphs containing vows by a queen for the benefit of His Majesty's life in connection with the country of Kummanni in XV 11 rev. (d).[102] One vow is adressed to Išḫara, while the name of the other divine beneficiary is lost in the break. The vows preserved on the obv. concern Allani, to whom the queen promised several things "belonging to the temple of the Stormgod of Manuziya." Both the latter and the goddess Išḫara "of Kummanni" occur in what could also be a vow fragment, LVII 113 (g). In the first line the [Stormgod$^{?}$] of Manuziya is mentioned in connection with vows for which "Katapaili will bring gift (and) re[paration" (ll. 5-6), probably to Kummanni (l. 4). After a double paragraph line Išḫara of Kummanni appears concerning an illness for which Katapaili again will bring something. Shortly before the fragment breaks off altogether Ḫepat of Kummanni is mentioned (l. 13). The combination of the land Kummanni, the illness, the vow and Katapaili

101 Diss. 102-103, see also Anatolica 14 (1987) 102.
102 Ed. J. de Roos, Diss. 225-229 and 363-367.

not only recalls the vow XV 11 just mentioned (d)[103] but the oracles KBo XVI 98(+)$^{?}$XLIX 49 and KBo II 2 as well; for an edition of both texts see below Ch. IV.2 and 4. The date given above for XV 11 (d) and LVII 113 (g) as "Ḫatt. III/Tutḫ. IV" is not meant in the sense that the text cannot with certainty be dated either to the one or other but tries to indicate that this fragment may stem from the transitory period between the two kings when Tutḫaliya was travelling in the Kummanni region (see Ch. III.4). Of further importance and support for both the connection and this date is the restoration by J. de Roos of LUGAL-*u-i*[*z-nanni* on the obv. 22 of XV 11. In this paragraph (obv. 12-26) the queen promises to give to the goddess Allani 39 persons ("heads") as a propitiatory gift. Part of these she was supposed to have given earlier which, however, she confesses not to have done. Then she continues:

19 ... GIM-*ann⸗a⸗kan* ^{d}UTU-*ŠI laḫḫaz*
20 *šarā* SIG$_5$-*in uizzi dapianza⸗šši dapian*[-
21 *nu apii̯a⸗i̯a ANA* DINGIR-*LIM* 6 SA[G.DU.MEŠ *upp*]*aḫḫi*
22 1 GU$_4$.NIGA 6 UDU 1 ZI GUŠKIN LUGAL-*ui*[*znanni šer Ù*$^{?}$]
23 *ANA* TI ^{d}UTU-*ŠI šer upp*[*aḫḫi*
24 IGI-*ziaš* ANA SAG.DU.MEŠ *ú*[-
25 *INA* ^{URU}*Šuḫurii̯a* GISKIM[
26 *Ù ANA* KUR ^{URU}KÙ.BABBAR-*ti* x[

And if His Majesty will return from the mission safe and sound (and) the whole (mission will be) [a success] in every respect(?), then at that moment too I will [send] to the goddess six pe[rsons as a g]ift. One fat ox, six sheep (and) one golden soul [for the benefit of$^{?}$] kingsh[ip and$^{?}$] for the benefit of His Majesty's life [I will] send as a gift. [...$^{?}$] for the first ranking/ foremost$^{?}$ persons ... [...] in the city of Šuḫuriya an omen [...] and for Ḫatti-land ... [...]

Because on the rev. the land of Kummanni and a possible return from there are mentioned (rev. 2', 8'), the journey in question probably is the one to this country attested in KBo XVI 98(+)$^{?}$XLIX 49 in the year preceding the campaign into the Kaška region. Intriguing is the omen that allegedly occurred in Šuḫuriya situated in that same northern area[104]: it probably stands in some supposed relation to the kingship and His Majesty's life just mentioned.

The small oracle tablet KBo XVIII 146 (c; it belongs to the "Orakelberichte auf Kleintafeln"[105]) unfortunately remains largely

[103] Cf. Th. van den Hout, BiOr 47 (1990) 431.

[104] It does not seem necessary to conclude with G. del Monte, RGTC 6, 260, on the basis of this, that the temple of the Stormgod of the city of Manuziya located in the southern Kummanni, probably stood in Šuḫuriya.

[105] Cf. H.G. Güterbock, KBo XVIII Inhaltsübersicht vi.

obscure. Its topic seems to be the coming of the "Majesty" to a temple, the performing of a prayer there and whether the anonymous deity will oppose him or not. If in l. 5 a reading and restoration to *A-NA* É ^{d}[U] *Ma-n*[*u-zi*]-*kán* would be correct, the text might have to do with those just discussed. Of a purely administrative nature seems to be the very fragmentary KBo XVI 60 (b),[106] with which little can be done for our purpose.

9. *The other persons*

The other persons occurring in CTH 569 are Kurša-^{d}LAMMA, GAL-^{d}U and GE$_{6}$-^{d}LÚ (Armaziti). Both Kurša-^{d}LAMMA and GE$_{6}$-^{d}LÚ act as augurs: the former in both XVI 58 (ii 9, in either the Urḫiteššub or Ḫalpaziti affair, see below Ch. V.2)[107] and KBo II 6+ (iii 59 and iv 16 in Šaušgatti affair), the latter in KBo II 6+ (iv 17 and 23, Šaušgatti affair) only.

Kursa-^{d}LAMMA is known mainly as an augur in a number of Hittite texts from Boğazköy; see the listing by A. Archi, SMEA 16 (1975) 132. The only non-mantic text in which this name occurs seems to be the fragment of a letter concerning deportees:[108] KBo XVIII 82 rev. 9' (^{m}*Kùr-ša*-^{d}LAMMA). There is no way of telling whether we are dealing with the same person.

The augur Armaziti (GE$_{6}$-^{d}LÚ), however, may be connected with persons known otherwise. There are quite a few attestations of this name and the question of identity of the several bearers was addressed in detail by F. Imparati[109] which makes an extensive discussion here superfluous. She suggests that the augur may have been the same person as the Armaziti whom we know to have worked as a scribe, the Armaziti who was involved in the cult reorganization of Tuthaliya IV and the one who is known as a DUMU.LUGAL in Ugarit.[110] Whether he is also identical to the Armaziti mentioned in the fragmentary and difficult deposition text XXIII 91 (CTH 297.3[111]), cannot be ascertained. Important for Armaziti, the augur, may be the entry in the shelf list XXX 44+ r.col. 6'-7' (CTH

[106] Ed. R. Werner, StBoT 4, 48-49.

[107] The space available on the tablet pleads in favor of the restoration to *Kurša*-]^{d}LAMMA, so that this passage must be discarded as evidence for the augur ^{md}LAMMA (to be corrected in my StBoT 38, 82).

[108] Cf. H.G. Güterbock, KBo XVIII Inhaltübersicht v.

[109] FsPugliese Carratelli 79-94.

[110] It does not seem likely, however, to assign the attestations of the Armaziti mentioned in L 57 (5'$^{?}$, 10'), 58 (13', 15$^{?}$) and 59a (10') and 59b (8') to those of the augur Armaziti: in two cases (L 57, 5'$^{?}$ and 59b, 8'$^{?}$) he may have been part of the oracle question, in all the others he seems to function as one of the symbols within the KIN-oracle procedure, so that he is object of the inquiry rather than professionally involved in the divinatory practice. Nowhere in these fragments is there mention of a bird oracle.

[111] Cf. F. Imparati, FsPugliese Carratelli 81-83, and my StBoT 38, 167-168.

277.4B) with its parallel text XXX 51+45+ iii 18[112] (1 *ṬUPPU* INIM ^{md}*SÎN*-LÚ ^{LÚ}x[... (*mān* UN-*an daššuš lingaī*)*š* /] *ēpzi n=an* x["One tablet, text of Armaziti, the ... : 'If a serious (case of) perjury takes hold of a man and ... [...] him"). The phrasing of the entry ("One tablet, text of ... ") indicates Armaziti as the author of a ritual which, as Imparati rightly states, is not surprising in his profession. Whether the sign trace after ^{LÚ} can and should be read as D[UB.SAR "scribe", as Imparati wants,[113] is doubtful. The fact that in another shelflist (XXX 54 ii 8' - CTH 277.3, page 179) "Armaziti, the scribe" is mentioned, does not offer real support, because he figures there in the description of the contents of a tablet on the shelf. The identity between the scribe and the augur/author remains to be proven. Finally, it should be remarked, that the Armaziti occurring in KBo II 6+ is not the regular augur. He only appears at the very end after Kurša-^{d}LAMMA had threatened to annul a whole series of confirmations through a sudden and surprisingly unfavorable result. Armaziti is then asked for a second opinion and saves the inquiry by giving the expected confirmation. Was he of a higher authority or did he just happen to be around?

The numerous attestations and possible readings of the name sumerographically written as ^{m}GAL-^{d}U/IM have been discussed at some length in my StBoT 38, 157-164. There it was suggested – as V. Haas had done previously[114] – that the GAL-^{d}U mentioned in XVI 32 ii 24' may have been the king of Kargamiš known as Talmiteššub, the successor to Initeššub. Because of the early date within Tutḫaliya's reign of the results recorded in XVI 32 this must now be discarded as impossible, because at that moment Initeššub still ruled at Kargamiš. He may, however, have been the future king of that city in his previous function of GAL *KARTAPPI* mentioned three times,[115] with one attestation in Ugarit, a suggestion originally put forward by H. Klengel.[116]

112 See E. Laroche, CTH 277.4 and ibid. pages 157-161. Although technically ("A/B") listed as duplicates Laroche already hinted at the problematic relation of the two texts through his remark "avec quelques variantes". The differences between the two are not likely to be due to a scribe unfaithfully copying his original or deliberately deviating. Moreover, it would be the only case known so far of duplicates among the shelflists. It rather seems as if two scribes independently and unknowingly made an inventory of the same shelves; note that the script of B looks somewhat older than that of A. For these texts see also H.G. Güterbock, AfO 38-39 (1991-1992) 134, correcting Laroche on the findspot.

113 FsPugliese carratelli 80 n. 7.

114 OLZ 77 (1982) 254.

115 Cf. StBoT 38, 157.

116 Gesch.Syr. 1, 84, followed by me in StBoT 38, 162-163.

CHAPTER THREE

PURPOSE AND HISTORICAL BACKGROUND OF CTH 569

1. *The Gods of Kingship*

In the oracle inquiry recorded in CTH 569 the affairs of six individuals are the subject of investigation: the affairs of the Babylonian *tawananna*, who was Šuppiluliuma's last wife, and of Danuḫepa, Urḫiteššub, Ḫalpaziti, Armatarḫunta and Šaušgatti. A common denominator is in fact already given by the selection criterion for texts in this CTH number, i.e. the cleansing of the places of kingship, the thrones and of the Great King himself from curses in front of the Gods of Kingship. Before we embark on the question of how all six persons were apparently involved in acts resulting in this contamination and what their role in the inquiry is, something needs to be said about the DINGIR.MEŠ LUGAL-*UTTI* "the Gods of Kingship". This particular designation seems to be restricted to CTH 569.[1] It is not further specified nor does it probably need specification, since it is clear and will have been so to every Hittite that the Gods of Kingship *par excellence* were the Stormgod and the Sundeity, later the Sungoddess of Arinna. In the Hittite ideology of kingship as formulated in several mainly Old Hittite compositions, it was these deities who assigned the land and its population to the Labarna and installed him as governor in their name. In 13th century iconography we see this visualized in the identification of the king with both deities: the king as Sungod in his priestly dress and as Stormgod in military attire.[2] For two texts mentioning both deities together in relation to the king compare XXIX 1 (with dupls.) i 17-18 "But to me, the king, the gods, the Sundeity and the Stormgod, have entrusted the land and my house"[3] and XLI 23 ii 18'-21' continued by its

[1] I.e. with the plural DINGIR.MEŠ "gods". One example is known to me of the singular in the combination DINGIR-*LUM* GIBIL LUGAL-*UTTI* "the new god of kingship" occurring repeatedly in the oracle V 3+XVIII 52 (CTH 563.1; see B. van Gessel, OHP 973). This deity is held responsible for a plague(?) within the standing army while spending the winter in Ḫattuša. No mention is made of an accession to the throne or of anything else to suggest a closer link to CTH 569. The attribute "new" could mean "in addition to the usual gods of kingship, i.e. the Stormgod and the Sungoddess." For another reference to a possible plague in the standing army see KBo XVI 98(+?)XLIX 49 (cf. below in this Ch. section 3 and Ch. IV.2).

[2] On this see Th. van den Hout, BiOr. 52 (1995) 545-573.

[3] CTH 414, ed. G. Kellerman, Diss. 11.

dupl. LVII 86, 4'-7' "O Sundeity of the Gods, just as *marnuu̯an* and beer have mixed (and) your soul and innermost have become one, may here of the Sundeities of the Gods and the Labarna their soul and innermost become one! O Stormgod of the Gods, just as *u̯alḫi*, beer and wine have mixed (and) your soul and innermost have become one, may of the Stormgod of Heaven and the Labarna their soul and innermost become one!"[4] A third text expressing the same ideas but not hitherto mentioned in treatises on Hittite royal ideology is XXXVI 91(+)XLIII 68 (CTH 389) with its duplicates LX 156 (B), 871/z (C)[5] and 702/z (D).[6] Although the ductus of the published pieces shows the manuscripts A and B to be thirteenth century copies, the language of the text betrays the composition as undoubtedly older. In spite of its fragmentary state of preservation it can be described as a prayer by the king addressed to the Sundeity and the Stormgod, as is clear from the rev.$^{?}$ 4'-5' (line count after XLIII 68):

4' [(*nu* ^{d}U)]TU-*uš* ⌈^{d}⌉[(U-*aš-ša a-aš-šu* IGI.ḪI.A-*u̯a*) *ḫarten*] *na-aš-ta* LUGAL-*un* MUNUS.LUG[(AL-*an-na*)]
5' [(*an-d*)]*a* SIG$_5$-*an-te*-⌈*et*⌉[IGI.ḪI.A-*it* (*a-uš-tén nu-u*)]*š* TI-*an ḫar-te*$_9$-*en*

O Sundeity and Stormgod, [have$^{?}$] benevolent eyes and look upon the king and queen with benevolent [eyes] and keep them alive!

On the obv.$^{?}$ we read:

8'[7] ... [... *nu-mu A-BU-IA*] NU.GÁL *nu-mu* AMA-*IA* NU.⌈GÁL⌉
9' ⌈*nu-mu*⌉ *šu-meš* DINGIR.MEŠ-*iš A-BU* [AMA-*i̯a* EN.MEŠ$^{?}$-]*IA* ^{d}UTU-*ŠI šu-meš*
10' *ú-uk-ka*$_4$ ÌR.MEŠ-*KU-NU* [ ] *ú-uk*

11' *nu-mu šu-meš-pát* DINGIR.MEŠ LUGAL-*UT*[-*TA ki-iš-š*]*a-ri-mi da-a-iš-tén*

... [A father I] have not, a mother I have not: You, o Gods, (are) my father [and mother.] My Majesty's [lords] (are) you and I, your servant(!?) am I.
You alone, o Gods, have put kingsh[ip] in my [ha]nd.

[4] CTH 458.10A and B, ed. Th. van den Hout, BiOr. 52 (1995) 560.
[5] For the latter two texts see already H. Otten – Chr. Rüster, ZA 64 (1975) 243-244.
[6] Cf. S. Košak, ZA 84 (1994) 290.
[7] Line count after XLIII 68.

That this couple still functioned as the patrons of Kingship also at the end of the Empire period is illustrated by the Bronze Tablet, the treaty of Tutḫaliya IV and Kurunta as ruler of Tarḫuntašša, where a future Great King of Ḫatti-Land is warned not to undertake any evil against Kurunta's descendants or else

> *apēdani⸗ma⸗kan* ^{d}UTU ^{URU}*Arinna* ^{d}U ^{URU}*Ḫatti⸗i̯a ŠA* KUR ^{URU}*Ḫatti* LUGAL-*iznatar arḫa dandu*
>
> May the Sungoddess of Arinna and the Stormgod of Ḫatti take away from that (person) the Kingship over Ḫatti-Land![8]

2. *The role of the six individuals*

Returning to the six affairs we can state that all six individuals have certain characteristics in common which make it understandable why they were treated together in CTH 569 and why other persons were not included. First and foremost, all individuals can be proven or supposed to have belonged to the extended Royal Family. The *tawananna* and Danuḫepa were spouses to the Great Kings Šuppiluliuma I and Muršili II respectively, Urḫiteššub was the son and successor of Muwatalli II, while Armatarḫunta was a full cousin to Muršili II through his father Zida, the brother of Šuppiluliuma. Although no relationship can be established for Šaušgatti and Ḫalpaziti with such precision, the contexts in which they occur suggest they also formed part of the greater Royal Family; moreover, Šaušgatti may very well have been Armatarḫunta's wife as was suggested above (Ch. II.7: *Šaušgatti*).

In the cases of the *tawananna*, Danuḫepa and Armatarḫunta there is, moreover, explicit textual evidence outside CTH 569 for intrigues against either a reigning (*tawananna* versus Muršili II, Danuḫepa versus Muwatalli II) or a future king (Armatarḫunta versus Ḫattušili III). The same is true for Šaušgatti, who in turn is linked to Ḫalpaziti, if indeed she was Armatarḫunta's wife. Nothing positive, however, can be said in this respect about Urḫiteššub, at least not for the period under consideration.

Most probably just because of their position as members of the ruling dynasty, none of them were killed after their intrigues had been detected, but all were allowed to live, although sometimes in exile. The *tawananna* was banned from the palace in Ḫattusa and deposed from her position as *šiu̯anzanni*-priestess by Muršili. Although there is no explicit mention of banishment in the case of Danuḫepa, she must at least have suffered a temporary political setback following the trial under Muwatalli; temporary because several seals bear witness to her function of queen under Muwatalli's son and successor Urḫiteššub. The fate of Urḫiteššub is well-

[8] Ed. H. Otten, StBoT Bh. 1 iii 75-77 (kindly brought to my attention by S. Hutter-Braunsar).

known: after his final defeat at the hands of Ḫattušili and an initial stay in his place of exile Nuḫašše in Syria, where Ḫattušili had granted him some fortified cities, he spent the rest of his days at the court of Ramses II. For Ḫalpaziti there is reason to assume a similar measure by Tutḫaliya who seems to have installed him as priest-king in the politically unimportant Ḫalpa. Ḫattušili tells us in his Apology that he let Armatarḫunta live unharmed but sent his wife and son into exile to Alašiya. For Šaušgatti there is no evidence about the end of her life unless, again, she was Armatarḫunta's wife.

Likewise, there is evidence that all persons used magic spells and curses. Within CTH 569 this is mostly expressed by way of the sumerogram EME "curse"[9] (for the *tawananna* cf. L 6+ ii 35', Danuḫepa ibid. ii 49'ff., Urḫiteššub ibid. iii 48, Armatarḫunta KBo II 6+ i 8'ff., Šaušgatti ibid. ii 38ff.), in the case of Ḫalpaziti the Luwian word *tiu̯ataniịa-* is probably used (XXII 35 iii 2'). Outside of CTH 569 the *tawananna* is accused by Muršili of constantly uttering curses (*ḫurzakizzi*) in front of the gods (cf. XIV 4 ii [19'], iii 19, iv 22-23, KBo IV 8+ iii 12, 24) even after her removal from the court at Ḫattuša. The sumerogram EME is attested in connection with Danuḫepa in XXI 33, 20'.[10] Urḫiteššub and Ḫalpaziti occur together in XXXI 23 where there is also mention of an INIM $UḪ_7$ "matter of sorcery." Ḫalpaziti, moreover, is mentioned next to Šaušgatti twice (KBo XVIII 145 and LX 129), again in direct relation to sorcery ($UḪ_7$). Armatarḫunta, finally, used sorcery extensively in his struggle against Ḫattušili according to the Apology and XXI 17; here the verb *alu̯anzaḫḫ-* "to bewitch, cast spells on" and the abstracts $UḪ_7$-*tar* = *alu̯anzatar* and *alu̯anzeššar* are found. For more detail see above the prosopographical sketches in Ch. II.

A final element shared by all *dramatis personae* except for perhaps the *tawananna* is the presence and involvement of their children. The essence of the Danuḫepa affair may have been her attempt to promote her own son as Muwatalli's successor. Urḫiteššub had sons/children according to XVI 32//L 6+ ii 19', 28'-29' and iii 33ff., who receive some kind of remuneration and are destined to bring *mantalli*-offerings together with Tutḫaliya. Ḫalpaziti, too, had sons/children witness XXII 35 iii 15' (par. LII 92 iv 6') who likewise received a remuneration of sorts from Tutḫaliya. Armatarḫunta enlisted the help of his wife and sons/children in trying to thwart Ḫattušili on his way to power. For Šaušgatti children are attested in KBo II 6+ iii 6 and 62 (par. VIII 27(+) iv 6'): they get compensated too.

If we compare these persons to others appearing in Hittite oracle texts, they emerge as a very specific group indeed. On the whole, the number of individuals as topic in oracle inquiries – excluding the divination priests

[9] No doubt, Hitt. *lala-* is the reading behind the sumerogram EME, cf. HW 126 s.v. *lāla-* and 271 s.v. EME and CHD L-N s.v. *lala-*. It is interesting, however, that EME in V 6+ iii 9 ([m]PÉŠ.TUR-*aš PANI* DINGIR-*LIM* EME-*an arḫa tarnan harzi*), 12 and 14, is resumed by *ḫurtai-* in ibid. 17 (*ḫurtauš meqqauš tarnaš*).

[10] For this passage see Ch. II.3.

and priestesses as well as persons only marginally mentioned – is fairly limited, and A. Ünal's list[11] turns out to be reasonably complete. Counting out the persons mentioned in CTH 569 (including Katapaili and GAL-^{d}U listed by Ünal for XVI 32[12]) we are left with Antarawa, a son of Arnuwanda, Ḫaittili, Mašḫuiluwa, Pi(ya)ššili and Zaparti-ŠEŠ. Of these the son of Arnuwanda, Ḫaittili and Pi(ya)ššili occur together in XVI 77 (CTH 577; see Ch. I.12 and the Appendix). Whereas the affair concerning the latter two is clearly one and the same, there is no obvious link with the so-called son of Arnuwanda. Although this text comes very close to CTH 569 in wording, two points stand out: the several items and gods of kingship as well as kingship itself are nowhere mentioned, and the latter two were apparently killed, since the inquiry wants to know whether the deity "seeks compensation for [the blood] of Piyaššili and Ḫaittili" (XVI 77 iii 5-6, for the restoration cf. ibid. 8). In the case of the son of Arnuwanda there is only mention of the anger of the gods because of certain festivals that had been left uncelebrated. The exact identity of the three persons is difficult to establish. The son of Arnuwanda will probably have belonged to the Royal House because the name Arnuwanda almost certainly refers to one of the kings by that name. There is, however, no reason to assume, that Pi(ya)ššili is the same person as Šarrikušuḫ, the first Hittite king installed in Kargamiš by Šuppiluliuma around 1325. Muršili describes in his Annals Piyaššili/Šarrikušuḫ's death in his ninth year as due to an illness, so he does not seem to have died a violent death. Moreover, this Piyaššili/ Šarrikušuḫ is in no way linked to a person named Ḫaittili whose fate seems to have been so closely interwoven with that of the Pi(ya)ššili in XVI 77. The two other possible occurrences for someone by that name (XXXI 62 ii 15 $^{m?}$*Ḫa-i-t*[*i*-]*l*[*i*$^{?}$ - CTH 232.1, and KBo XVI 83+ ii 10' ^{m}*Ḫa-i-i*[*t*$^{?}$*-ti-li* - CTH 242.8[13]) seem to denote one or more persons of lower social status rather than someone directly related to the court at Ḫattuša. As a consequence, XVI 77 is difficult to date exactly.[14]

The other three persons, Antarawa, Mašḫuiluwa and Zaparti-ŠEŠ, are likewise attested in one text: V 6+XVIII 54 (CTH 570).[15] Again, this does not necessarily mean they are part of the same 'affair'. The case of Antarawa does not seem to have anything to do with that of the other two. Zaparti-ŠEŠ, however, only (iii 21, 24, 31) occurs in the immediate company of Mašḫuiluwa, both here and most probably in KBo XVIII 143 Rev. 4 (-*t*]*i*-ŠEŠ);[16] he is not otherwise attested. The affair of Mašḫuiluwa is, of course, well-known:[17] he was king in the local western land of Mira-

[11] THeth. 3, 102 n. 47; see also above Ch. I.2.

[12] For these and other persons occurring in CTH 569 without forming an 'affair' themselves see Ch. II.8 and 9.

[13] See S. Košak, THeth. 10, 88 for the restoration.

[14] On the date of this text see A. Kammenhuber, THeth. 7, 29.

[15] On this text see already above Ch. I.1 and 5.

[16] So with S. Heinhold-Krahmer, THeth. 8, 198 n. 289.

[17] See S. Heinhold-Krahmer, RlA 7, 446-447 with lit.

Kuwaliya during the reign of Muršili II and to strengthen the bonds between the two partners he received Muršili's sister Muwatti in marriage. After an attempt at revolt against the Hittite Great King he was forced to flee but extradited not long after and, finally, sent off into exile.[18] On the throne he was replaced by his adopted son Kupanta-LAMMA. The oracle V 6+ is, among other affairs, concerned with curses which Mašḫuiluwa allegedly uttered before the Zawalli-deity "of the House of His Majesty",[19] which he kept in Arzawa. As a result both the deity and the Hittite king himself were 'bewitched' (iii 18-19 *alu̯anzaḫḫanza*).[20] All this would have made Mašḫuiluwa quite a suitable candidate for CTH 569: through his wife Muwatti he had become a member of the Royal Family, he had used magic to plot against the ruling king Muršili II and had not been killed or executed, it seems, by way of punishment but was given a domain to stay. His adopted son Kupanta-LAMMA, however, apparently remained loyal to the dynasty in Ḫattuša. Moreover, Mašḫuiluwa is said to perform *mantalli*-offerings together with His Majesty just as in the case of the sons of Urḫiteššub and Armatarḫunta, of Ḫalpaziti and Šausgatti. Why he was not included in CTH 569 in spite of this, can only be surmised. It could simply be that a preliminary oracle inquiry showed that his affair was already sufficiently solved and taken care of in the past so that – from the Hittite point of view – it was not taken up again by the deity. Or it might be that the Mašḫuiluwa affair, in contrast to the ones concerned in CTH 569, for reasons unknown did not bother Tutḫaliya's conscience. In a more practical explanation, although by no means excluding the former two, one could again (see above Ch. I.8 and Ch. II.2) point to the Ḫattušili-Puduḫepa prayer to the Sungoddess of Arinna (XXI 19+, CTH 383) where the Mašḫuiluwa affair is not mentioned either. Just as Muršili II ordered a search in the archives in order to find the causes of the gods' anger made manifest in the ongoing epidemic, Tuthaliya may have consulted the archives as well. It is conceivable his scribes came up with the prayer of his parents in which the affairs of the *tawananna*, Danuḫepa and Urḫiteššub were mentioned and which he subsequently may have expanded with similar affairs involving people whom his father had dealt with (Armatarḫunta, Šausgatti and possibly Ḫalpaziti). Mašḫuiluwa, of course, was not among those.

[18] So with Ph.H.J. Houwink ten Cate, FsMeriggi² 274 with translation on 279-280, and 288-289.

[19] So CHD P 176b; cf. A. Archi, AoF 6 (1975) 87-88, paraphrasing the expression as "uno Zawalli della casa del re" but translating "quello Zawalli familiare della Maestà".

[20] See the passages quoted in Ch. I.1.

3. *CTH 569 and related oracle investigations*

In an earlier treatment of oracle texts concerning the accession of Tutḫaliya IV,[21] I argued that already during the lifetime of Ḫattušili and Puduḫepa, Tutḫaliya was raised to the status of Hittite king. The accession ritual, however, had to be postponed. According to these texts the young king was at the time engaged in activities in Kummanni to the south-east of the capital and in the northern Gašga territory near Nerik as well. A recurring item in connection with the accession ceremony in these oracle texts is an illness which at first is only feared[22] but later established as a certainty in the separate inquiry KBo II 2.[23] A direct link between the latter text and CTH 569 is given in the person of Katapaili. After the exact hypostasis of the Sungoddess of Arinna, namely the one of "Progeny",[24] and the reason for her anger in KBo II 2 have been determined, it is decided that penance for unfulfilled vows and promises will be done and offerings will be given. After an empty space of four lines (iv 18-21) the inquiry then ends in the following manner:

iv 22 *eni* INIM SUM-*annaš kuit* (erasure) SIxSÁ-*at*
23 *eni kuit* INIM SUM-*annaš*
24 ^{m}*Katapa*-DINGIR-*LIM IDE*
25 *nu TE*^{MEŠ} NU.SIG$_5$-*du zeḫilipšiman*
26 NU.SIG$_5$

27 *mān eni=pat* INIM SUM-*annaš*
28 ^{m}*Katapa*-DINGIR-*LIM kuin IDE*
29 *namma=ma* KI.MIN *nu TE*^{MEŠ} SIG$_5$-*ru*
30 *ni* ZAG-*za* GÙB-*za šer=ma=šmaš*
31 *ukturiš ši ta* ^{GIŠ}TUKUL ZAG-*za*
32 GÙB-*za* RA^{IŠ} *zi* GAR-*ri*
33 12 ŠÀ *DIR* SIG$_5$

34 *pānzi aši* INIM SUM-*annaš*

[21] Th. van den Hout, ZA 81 (1991)274-300.

[22] Cf. XVIII 36 and its summary VI 9+XVIII 59, L 77+XLIX 73, XVI 20, XXII 12(+)[?]13; for these texts see Ch. IV.3

[23] Cf. my ZA 81 (1991) 289-292 and Ch. IV.4. That the illness is at first only treated as a possibility may be caused by the fact that an illness had already broken out but not yet affected the king himself. This could be deducted from the small group of the two MUŠ oracles XLIX 1 and KBo XXIII 117 (CTH 575) and the extispicy oracle XLVI 37 (CTH 570) as brought together and interpreted by Ph.H.J. Houwink ten Cate, AoF 23 (1996) 65-72. In this case Tutḫaliya's wife would have fallen victim first, at which the king became alarmed about his own health and his planned accession ritual. For other oracle texts mentioning an illness of Tutḫaliya's wife see Houwink ten Cate, ibid. 64-65.

[24] Cf. ZA 81 (1991) 291-292 n. 30.

35 *kišan išḫiulaḫḫanzi*
36 *mān=ma=kan šakti*
37 *eni=naš=kan uttar laittari*
38 *nu TE*^{MEŠ} SIG$_5$-*ru* ZAG-*za* RA$^{\textit{IŠ}}$ NU.SIG$_5$
(blank space till end of column)

Concerning this affair of giving which was acertained, (is it) this affair of giving that Katapaili is overseeing/oversaw? Then let the exta be unfavorable. *Zeḫilipšiman*; unfavorable.
If (it is) only this affair of giving that Katapaili is overseeing/oversaw but furthermore etc., then let the exta be favorable. *Ni*(*pašuri*) right (and) left, on top of them *ukturi*, *ši*(*ntaḫi*), *ta*(*nani*), the weapon right, damaged on the left, *zi*(*zaḫi*) lies (there), twelve coils; favorable.
They will go and thus enjoin the affair of giving. If, then, you acknowledge (it), will this affair be solved for us? Then let the exta be favorable. Damaged on the right; unfavorable.

The dating of both KBo II 2 and of the first stage of the inquiry CTH 569 as documented in XVI 32 to the very beginning of Tutḫaliya's rule makes a connection of the "affair of giving that Katapaili is overseeing/oversaw" with the handing over of the city of Kiuta by Katapaili to a deceased in XVI 32, 24'-26' (§6') highly likely. Katapaili was likewise instructed to look after the foundation of the priest-rulership in Ḫalpa (XVI 32, 8'-13', §3') together with the King of Kargamiš. In view of the illness mentioned in the group of accession oracles and in KBo II 2 it is interesting, that an illness is also attested in CTH 569: in LII 92 i (II.4) 5', a fragment pertaining to an early part of the summary, GIG-*anza* is mentioned. Moreover, a "small or great" GIG turns up several times as a symbol in the KIN-oracles (KBo II 6+ ii 33, 41, iii 14, and 38). Through KBo II 2 the group of accession oracles listed earlier[25] – including the related oracle fragments KBo XVI 98(+)$^?$XLIX 49 – is thus historically linked to CTH 569. Summarizing the contents of these texts we come to the following general sequence of texts and events: The planning of the accession after a journey to Kummanni is attested in KBo XVI 98(+)$^?$XLIX 49. The accession oracles as listed all concern the postponement of the ceremony to the following year in connection with an illness of the young king which is dreaded. The next stage is represented by KBo II 2 inquiring into the divine causes of the illness which in the meantime has become a *fait accompli*. CTH 569 fits into this picture as the specification of the unfulfilled promises which ultimately were the cause of the goddess' wrath: the ultimate settling of the disputes with former members of the royal dynasty which was never fully carried out and which caused their curses to be still effective.[26]

[25] See above at the end of Ch. I.5.

[26] This chain of events (conspiration by dynasty members uttering curses - their punishment by removal from court and curtailing of their deities' cult - the latters'

What we miss, however, is an inquiry into the exact identity of the individuals whose affairs are treated. In CTH 569, as we have it, the anger and curses of the *tawananna*, Danuḫepa, Urḫiteššub, Ḫalpaziti, Armatarḫunta and Šaušgatti are already common knowledge and the investigation regards the measures to be taken to soothe their anger and to undo the curses. But there must have been oracles to determine that it was these persons and not others whose anger and curses were still causing trouble because certain vows to them and their offspring had not been fulfilled or had been neglected. It may be here that the oracle texts concerning the Zawalli-deities of Danuḫepa, Urḫiteššub and Šaušgatti, XVI 16 and KBo XXIII 114 as well as XVI 46 and L 87 (see already above Ch. I.12; for an edition see Ch. IV.5) find their proper place.

In the one-column extispicy oracle XVI 16 the obverse concentrates on the cultic negligence and impurity of *dammara*-women according to statements of the 'men of the palace.' Judging by the remark in the handcopy at the beginning of the obverse ("Es mögen etwa 7 Zeilen weggebrochen sein") only little is lost of this tablet. In establishing the anger of a certain deity the 'signs' of offerings for the Zawalli-deities of both Danuḫepa and Urḫiteššub are investigated each (rev. 1 and 23 respectively). In between there are again depositions by the 'men of the palace.' The same Zawalli-deities are the subject of the oracle investigation KBo XXIII 114.[27] This too is a one-column tablet containing extispicy only and might be a or the sequel to XVI 16.[28] The obverse is reasonably well preserved, of its reverse the beginnings of merely four lines remain. After the Zawalli of the temple in Zitḫara has been established (obv. 7-11), they ask whether it is the Zawalli of Urḫiteššub and only his (obv. 12-14). The answer must have been negative, since the investigation continues with the question whether it was the Zawalli of the 'mother of his Majesty as well' (obv. 15-16). This is denied.[29] The next question is whether it is Danuḫepa's (obv. 17). The answer to this most probably was negative as well, because they go on asking whether it was the Zawalli of both Urḫiteššub and Danuḫepa (obv. 18-20). This is confirmed and the remainder of the oracle as far as preserved deals with the possible anger of the Zawalli of Urḫiteššub because of 'the known

anger over this by reviving the curses manifest in an illness) is thus different from the one envisaged by M. Hutter, Behexung 115, for rituals combining references to illnesses and "tongues" where an illness of the king leads to rumors and intrigues.

[27] For a transliteration and translation of obv. 9-24 see A. Archi, AoF 6 (1979) 84-86. In the *Inhaltsübersicht* to KBo XXIII H. Otten and Chr. Rüster (p. vi) suggest some connection between the text numbers 111 and 114 and the former is also included among the "Orakeltexte". The fragment deals with (a group of?) *katra*-women and contains the beginning of a deposition by them in which Urḫitešub is mentioned (12'). It is, however, not certain that this fragment is indeed an oracle text.

[28] Note also in both texts the peculiar way of writing the nom.sg. with the LIŠ-sign: *ᵈZa-u̯a-al-li (l)iš* in XVI 16 rev. 23 and KBo XXIII 114 obv.? 14.

[29] So contrary to A. Archi, AoF 6 (1979) 85.

offenses'. In this connection the skipping, among other festivals, of those of 'the sixth year' is mentioned. On the whole, the motif of cultic negligence fits well into the picture resulting from CTH 569 itself.

The oracle XVI 46 uses bird oracles to ascertain, it seems, the anger of a particular Zawalli-deity. Officiating augurs are Zella (i 9', 18') and Piyammu (iv 5 and 12). After Zawalli deities in general have been established near the end of the first column (i 1'-3') as probably being the cause of something, it is asked whether only one among them is in anger:

> 4' *kēdaš=kan* ᵈ*Zau̯allii̯*[*aš*] 1-*aš kuišk*[*i*] ᵈ*Zau̯a*[*lliš*
> 5' *anda* TUKU.TU̯KU-*uanza nu* MUŠEN.ḪI.A *apāt šakii̯aḫḫir nu* MUŠEN.ḪI.A [SIxSÁ-*andu*]
>
> Among these Zawalli-deities (is there) an individual Zawa[lli-deity] angry and have the birds indicated that? Then [let them ascertain] the birds.

After this seems to have been confirmed, the inquiry starts out with a Zawalli of the Palace in i 10', and in iv 1 (?), 6 and 13 the Zawalli of Šaušgatti is established. In the last paragraph (iv 13-21) someone in the first person asks whether Šaušgatti's Zawalli-deity will be "undone" (*arḫa* KIN-*anzi*) by offering to her and by "dispatching", i.e. satisfying her. The outcome of the augury is not preserved. The very fragmentary L 87 contains extispicy (obv.) and lot oracles (rev.). On the obv. the anger of an anonymous deity is investigated in connection with smiths; on rev.? 4' the Zawalli of Šaušgatti is mentioned in context with the queen (rev.? 5'[30]).

If the Zawalli-deity, as Archi maintains, indicates the spirit or genius of a deceased, the death of the persons mentioned becomes an important terminus post quem for the oracle text KBo XXIII 114. Urḫiteššub still lived during Tutḫaliya's reign: in L 6+, part of the second stage of the inquiry to be dated around 1220, he seems to be spoken of as being still alive.[31] This means, that this text can stem from the reign of Tutḫaliya at the earliest. If, moreover, the "mother of His Majesty" were Tutḫaliya's (adoptive?-)mother Puduḫepa and her death would be taken as a terminus post quem, this would imply an even later date close to 1200 if she indeed corresponded with Niqmaddu III of Ugarit.[32] However, although in some cases "the Zawalli of PN" may refer to persons deceased, it does not seem necessary to assume in all cases that a person, whose Zawalli-deity is mentioned, must have been dead at the time. The "constant parallelism" between the terms Zawalli and GIDIM "(spirit of the) deceased", mentioned by Archi,[33] consists of one passage only in which the reading of

30 Possibly MUNUS.LUGAL.⌜GAL⌝?
31 Cf. Ph.H.J. Houwink ten Cate, BiOr 51 (1994) 250-251.
32 Cf. H. Otten, Puduḫepa 31.
33 AoF 6 (1979) 91.

the sumerogram GIDIM is an incorrect emendation.[34] Besides this, the existence of a Zawalli "of the palace", "of the house(-hold) of His Majesty" as well as of several cities (Ankuwa, Urikina, Zitḫara) suggests that a Zawalli-deity could belong to something or somebody contemporaneous.[35] A Zawalli-deity may thus be redefined as a kind of divine spirit or genius dwelling in people and places or institutions or somehow representing them. This spirit may have been considered embodying the essentials of an individual or place which could receive offerings[36] and could be angry if neglected but through which that individual or place could be "bewitched" as well.[37] This makes it possible to date these Zawalli-oracles earlier, that is during the lifetime of some of the persons mentioned and to hypothesize about a connection with CTH 569. It may not be sheer coincidence that, except for the Zawalli-deity of É.GAL-PAB,[38] of the mother of His Majesty,[39] and of a Muršili,[40] the only other persons in oracle texts having a Zawalli-deity are exactly those mentioned. These oracle texts would in that case fit in between the so-called accession oracles and KBo II 2.

The oracle inquiry CTH 569 can thus be seen as part of a larger group of similar investigations conducted in connection with the accession of Tutḫaliya IV.[41] Its importance is attested to in the presence of more than one summary made for future reference and of duplicates[42] to these summaries. Note that summaries existed also in the case of the accession

[34] In XVIII 2 ii 9'-10' Archi, AoF 6 (1979) 82, reads: *ŠA* AMA ^{d}UTU-*ŠI* ^{d}*Za-u̯a-al-li-iš* / *ŠA* DUMU.MUNUS GIDIM! *kar-ši-i̯a-an-du*; instead of GIDIM the handcopy shows ⌜A⌝.NA which is confirmed after collation by H. Klengel (see Archi loc.cit. n. 6). The correct reading, however, must be ⌜^{m}⌝*Na-kar-ši-i̯a-an-du*, the name occurring also in the oracle texts KBo XVI 99 i 26, 30, and KBo XXIV 124 obv. 7 and 13.

[35] This also solves the problem of the ^{d}*Zawallin*] NÍ.TE-*aš* LUGAL "Zawalli] of the person of the King" in XXII 40 ii 4' as convincingly restored by F. Sommer, AU 281 n. 4, but rejected by Archi, AoF 6 (1979) 91 n. 19.

[36] Compare KBo XIII 234+LI 69 (CTH 530, cf. H. Berman, FsGüterbock^{2} 35), where the Zawalli of Muršili is mentioned and its offerings are listed.

[37] Compare V 6+ iii 18'ff., quoted above Ch. I.1. For an overview of attestations of ^{d}Zawalli see B. van Gessel, OHP 577-580.

[38] XXII 67, 13 (ed. A. Archi, AoF 6 (1979) 86-87).

[39] XVIII 2 ii 9 (ed. A. Archi, AoF 6 (1979) 82), KBo XXIII 114 obv. 15 (see Ch. IV.5.1.2). In the view expressed above Ch. II.3, that Danuḫepa was the last wife of Muršili II, it is impossible to identify her as this "mother of His Majesty" as V. Haas, OLZ 77 (1982) 253, suggests.

[40] KBo XIII 234+LI 69 obv. 1, 11, and possibly also LII 89 ii? 5' (cf. A. Archi, KUB LII Inhaltsübersicht); theoretically, of course, this Muršili could be Urḫitešub/Muršili III.

[41] For the reason not to include these additional texts into CTH 569 see above Ch. I note 15.

[42] For the relatively rare phenomenon of duplicates within the genre of oracle texts see H. Berman, JCS 34 (1982) 123-124, and above Ch. I.4.

oracles. The several texts just mentioned may be chronologically arranged as follows:

Topics	*Texts*
First signs of anger of Sungoddess of Arinna: will His Majesty still ascend the throne in between his journeys to Kummanni and Nerik?	KBo XVI 98(+)?XLIX 49
After signs predicting an illness: will the illness not ultimately annul the accession?	VI 9+XVIII 59, XVI 20, XLIX 2(+)? XVIII 6(?), L 77+XLIX 73 (=comprehensive versions) XVIII 36, XXII 12(+)?13 (=summaries)
The Sungoddess of "Progeny" is angry because of disrespectful conduct of His Majesty and unfulfilled vows. As a result the illness will strike him both in Nerik and in Ḫattuša.	KBo II 2
These unfulfilled vows may be related to promises made in the past to the *tawananna*, Danuḫepa, Urḫiteššub, Ḫalpaziti, Armatarḫunta and Šaušgatti, because of which their Zawalli-deities are angry and their former curses are still effective.	XVI 16, KBo XXIII 114 (Danuḫepa and Urḫiteššub) XVI 46, L 87 (Šaušgatti)
Countermeasures will be taken to undo their curses by cleansing the places etc. and Gods of Kingship.	CTH 569 - first stage (as represented in XVI 32)
Again their curses will be undone by cleansing the places etc. and Gods of Kingship, penance will be done and remuneration given to those concerned.	CTH 569 - second stage.

For a detailed synopsis of the contents of CTH 569 see below Ch. V.4. Transliteration, translation and commentary of CTH 569 will follow in Chapters V and VI, the chronologically preceding texts will first be transliterated and translated in Chapter IV.

4. *CTH 569 and related inquiries: a historical reconstruction*

The edition of the "Hethitische Fragmente historischen Inhalts aus der Zeit Ḫattušilis III." by K.K. Riemschneider[43] and the surprising find of the Bronze Tablet[44] as well as of several seals[45] and a relief[46] attesting to Kurunta in the position of "Great King" have considerably contributed to our knowledge of the circumstances surrounding Ḫattušili's succession by his son Tutḫaliya IV. The fragments made it clear that Ḫattušili was very eager to promote his son and it induced Riemschneider to suspect a feeling of danger on Ḫattušili's side which at the time could not yet be substantiated. This was made possible by the combination of the Bronze Tablet and the seals. Whereas the former illustrates Tutḫaliya's policy – continuing that of his father – to bestow important concessions upon Kurunta in an attempt to keep him satisfied as king of Tarḫuntašša, the latter show the ultimate failure of that policy. Thus the coup d'état of 1267 by Ḫattušili still cast its shadow on Hittite inner politics decades afterwards. CTH 569 and related texts confirm this general picture and provide us with a unique opportunity to sketch the nervousness surrounding Tutḫaliya's accession in more detail.[47]

Even allowing for some time during which Tutḫaliya reigned during the life of his father, we will not be too far off if we date his accession somewhere in the period between 1245, i.e. the last secure date for Ḫattušili III, and ca. 1235, the first secure date for Tutḫaliya himself.[48] In trying to reconstruct the chain of events leading up to his official inauguration, it seems that Tutḫaliya IV on the eve of a mission to Kummanni suffered from repeated dreams (*tešḫaneškittari*) in which the Sungoddess of Arinna appeared:

> ^{d}UTU ^{URU}PÚ-*na kuit eneššan tešḫaneškittari* / *nu*=*kan* GIM-*an* ^{d}UTU-*ŠI IŠTU* KUR^{URU}*Kummanni* UGU *ārḫi* / *nu*=*za*=*kan* LUGAL-*iznanni ešḫaḫari namma*= *za* EZEN$_4$.MEŠ / DÙ-*mi* GIM-*an*=*ma*=*za*=*kan* EZEN$_4$.MEŠ *karpmi* / *nu INA* ^{URU}*Nerikka paimi nu ANA* DINGIR-*LIM*

[43] JCS 16 (1962) 110-121.

[44] Ed. H. Otten, StBoT Bh. 1.

[45] For a listing see Th. van den Hout, StBoT 38, 82.

[46] This is the relief found near Hatip south of Konya reported by Prof. A. Dinçol at the IIIrd International Hittitological Congress, Çorum, September 19, 1996.

[47] For references to Tuthaliya's accession outside CTH 569 see ZA 81 (1991) 275-276, to which now may be added Bo 87/5a iv (2-)4 apud H. Otten, FsTÖzgüç 365 n. 3.

[48] For these years as the termini post and ante quem respectively for Tutḫaliya's accession see RA 78 (1984) 90. Possibly the second marriage of a sister of Tutḫaliya with Ramses II based on the *insibja*-letter III 68 (cf. E. Edel, ÄHK II 266-267), which must accordingly have taken place between 1237 and 1223, was agreed upon in order to confirm the existing good relations after the change of power in Ḫattuša.

> SISKUR *peḫḫi* / *i̯i̯ami* = *ma UL kuitki parā* = *ma* MU.KAM-*anni* / *ANA* KASKAL [URU]*Nerikka* EGIR-*an* = *pat arḫaḫari*
>
> Concerning the fact that the Sungoddess of Arinna thus keeps appearing in my dreams: If I, My Majesty, will come up from the country of Kummanni, will I sit down in kingship and subsequently conduct the festivities? But if I end the festivities, go to the city of Nerik and bring an offering to the deity without doing anything (else), will I concern myself with a journey to Nerik next year? (KBo XVI 98(+) ii 10-16).

What the dreams were about, we are not told, but it is clear that the young king is worried about his accession ceremony and a journey to Nerik planned immediately afterwards as well as another one in the following year. Note that Tutḫaliya already styles himself [d]UTU-*ŠI* "My Majesty" although the official installation has yet to take place.

What the purpose of the missions to Kummanni and Nerik was, is not explicitly stated: Were they of a peaceful (KASKAL/*palša*- = "trip, mission") or military (KASKAL/*palša*- = "campaign") nature? In the case of Nerik there does not seem to be any real evidence for the latter. After Nerik had been brought back into the Hittite fold Ḫattušili restored it to its former status of important cult center and it was there that his son and successor Tutḫaliya IV was installed as Priest of the Stormgod of Nerik[49] which was probably identical to being named king of that area. This position may also have been one of the reasons to visit Nerik because of certain religious duties he had to fulfill there. Moreover, the fact that an additional trip to Nerik for the following year is already foreseen at this stage, does not point to a military campaign the outcome of which only will have dictated the necessity to return.[50]

The country of Kummanni (or Kizzuwatna) had been in the firm grip of Hittite rule since the reign of Šuppiluliuma I and on the whole seems to have remained so till the end of the Hittite empire. The oracle text just quoted, KBo XVI 98(+), itself refers (i 3-4) to a vow by a queen to Ḫepat of Kummanni and the Goddess of the Netherworld Lelwani in a paragraph concerning the ÉRIN.MEŠ *šarikui̯a* and the ÉRIN.MEŠ UKU.UŠ (i 1), who probably made up the Hittite standing army,[51] as well as the term ÚŠ-*an* (i 6). The latter could either be "downfall, death" or "plague". Taking it as "plague", Ph.H.J. Houwink ten Cate[52] linked this paragraph to offerings or rites to be performed by Tutḫaliya for his ailing wife's benefit in Kummanni as mentioned in the MUŠ-oracle texts XLIX 1 iv 6' and in KBo

[49] XXXVI 90 (CTH 386.1), ed. V. Haas, KN 175-183.

[50] Ph.H.J. Houwink ten Cate, however, draws my attention to the fact that, rather surprisingly, Nerik is not included among the holy cities mentioned in the Bronze tablet (iii 63).

[51] Cf. R.H. Beal, THeth. 20, 37-55.

[52] AoF 23 (1996) 70.

XXIII 117 rev. 12'. On the other hand, [*ḫu-u*]*l-la-at-te-*⌈*ni*⌉ "you (o gods) will [de]feat [...]" precedes ÚŠ-*an* in XVI 98 and might be taken to refer to a military expedition. Since, however, KBo XVI 98(+) seems to be a 'Sammeltafel' there is not necessarily a link between this paragraph about the army and the section ii 10ff. dealing with his accession. On the whole, therefore, it is very difficult to assess the situation in Kummanni at the time and what Tutḫaliya's reasons were for going there.[53] It is also conceivable that both trips stand in an immediate relation to the accession in the sense that the young king had to tour the most important centers of his empire in order to get all the necessary recognition and support.

Returning to our attempts at a general reconstruction, an inquiry was initially made whether it was indeed his accession which was at stake:

> [*nu*? *kī*] *kuit* LUGAL-*iznani ašātar* SIxSA-*at* [?] / [*mān* G]IG-*i̯a arii̯ašešnaz* SIxSÁ-*kittar*[*i*] / [*mān*=*m*]*a*(?) *ANA* ᵈUTU-*ŠI* LUGAL-*iznani ašā*[*tar*] / [*arḫa*(?)] *UL peššii̯azi*
>
> Concerning [this] fact that the accession to kingship was ascertained, if an illness also will be ascertained without, [how]ever, annulling for His Majesty the accession to kingship, ... (XXII 13(+?), 2-5)

From the other accession oracles it follows that the actual ceremony, scheduled between his return from Kummanni and the journey to Nerik, had to be postponed to the following year.

> [*kui*]*tman*=*za*=*kan* ᵈUTU-*ŠI* LUGAL-*iznani ešar*[*i ANA* ᵈUTU-*ŠI*=*kan*] / [LUG]AL-*iznani ašātar kuit zalukanumen* [*n*=*at* GAM-*an*] / [*a*]*rḫa* GAR-*ru mān*=*ma*=*za*=*kan kuitman* ᵈ[UTU-*ŠI*] / [LUGAL-*i*]*znani ešari kuitman*=*kan ANA* LU[GAL-*iznani*] / [EGI]R-*pa anda mān*=*ma* DINGIR.MEŠ *ANA* ᵈUTU-*ŠI* x[...] / [GI]G GAM-*an UL kuinki šekteni ANA*

[53] The vow texts XV 11 and LVII 113 (see Ch. II.8 *Katapaili*) may be related to these events as well and thus belong to the same period. Mention should be made here of another vow to Ḫepat of Kummanni is preserved in XV 29 (ed. J. de Roos, Diss. 262-263 and 400-401) in which a ᵐᵈ*IŠTAR*-LÚ appears whom we know to have been involved in an affair dealing with a royal son in Kummanni witness LIV 1 (CTH 297, ed. A. Archi - H. Klengel, AoF 12 (1985) 52-64). Unfortunately, the particulars of this affair remain in the dark; cf. my StBoT 38, 182-184. Besides this, there are some fragments, mostly only generally dating from the thirteenth century, that may contain hints that the situation there at times may have been temporarily less secure: sometimes Kummanni is mentioned in connection with Assur (KBo XXVIII 145/CTH 216, XVIII 43/CTH 572, XXXVI 125 /CTH 215); see also XVIII 46 - CTH 582 (cf. Kummanni in rev. 10' and ibid. 5' and 14' the phrase *taraluḫmi*=*z*=*šan* "will I win?"). Mention should be made, finally, of the small oracle fragment L 111 in which a KASKAL ᵁᴿᵁ*Kummanni* (5', cf. also *K*]*ummanni* ibid. 4'), an illness (GIG 6') and a reference to a following year (*parā* MU-*anni* 6') are attested. None of this, however, can be securely linked to the situation discussed here.

d[UTU-*ŠI*=*i̯a*=*kan*] / [LUGAL]-*iznani ašātar* UN-*aš IŠTU* MUD *U*[*L arḫa*] / [*d*]*āi*

Concerning the fact that we have postponed [for His Majesty] the accession to [ki]ngship [un]til His Majesty wi[ll] sit down on the throne: let [that] be out of consideration now. If, while His M[ajesty] will sit down in [kings]hip (and) for as long as he will be in ki[ngship aft]erwards, if then, o gods, you do not foresee for His Majesty [il]lness, [and (if)] nobody will [t]ake [away] with bloodshed from H[is Majesty] the accession to [king]ship, ... (XVIII 36, 11-18)

Both texts mention an illness which is still only dreaded. The combination of the dreams and the possible signs or symptoms foreshadowing an illness as mentioned above, was undoubtedly interpreted as a contamination of the institution of Kingship and thereby forbade the planned accession ritual which could only take place if the king's purity was guaranteed.[54] This contamination induced the king to conduct two kinds of inquiries. On the one hand he wanted to assure his accession after the postponement (= the group of accession oracles). On the other, he had to determine the cause of the presaged illness and the remedy to forestall it (= KBo II 2). In the latter text the illness is ascertained to befall the king both in Nerik and in the capital, and it is again the Sungoddess, i.e. her hypostasis "of Progeny", who is identified or confirmed as the cause of the dreaded disease. The reasons for her anger turn out to be certain unfulfilled vows and signs of disrespect (*šallakart*-[55]) by the king.[56] Since there is no mention of Kummanni anymore here, KBo II 2 has probably to be dated after the journey thither. Apart from doing penance and giving compensation for the king's disrespectful conduct, the remedy consisted of still fulfilling the vows, which we may see specified in the first stage of CTH 569 as summarized in XVI 32. According to this text certain cities and domains therein would be dedicated to the cult of Danuḫepa, Ḫalpaziti(?) would be installed in Ḫalpa as priest-king under the supervision of the king of Kargamiš, and the sons of Urḫiteššub and Armatarḫunta remunerated. What was decided upon for the erstwhile wife of Šuppiluliuma, the *tawananna*, is unfortunately lost. In view of the sons/children of Urḫiteššub and Armatarḫunta and the fact that the involvement of children seems to be

[54] See also the oracle texts brought together by Ph.H.J. Houwink ten Cate, AoF 23 (1996) 65-72, already referred to. In this context the letter KBo XVIII 79 (CTH 209; ed. A. Hagenbuchner, THeth. 16, 178-181) might be of interest: in line 3' an INIM GIG *BĒLU* is mentioned and in 12' [m*T*]*utḫali̯ann*=*a* appears at the beginning of a new paragraph where there is mention of an illness (GIG: 16', 17').

[55] Cf. *šallakartan ḫarkun* KBo II 2 iii 20, 27, iv 3.

[56] A case of anger of the Sungoddess of Arinna directed at Tutḫaliya IV is also attested in his prayer KBo XII 58+KBo XIII 162 (CTH 385.9) for which see Ph.H.J. Houwink ten Cate, FsGüterbock[2] 110 with literature, and Natural Phenomena 106-107.

one of the common denominators of the persons in CTH 569 the epithet DUMU-*annaš* "of Progeny" of the Sungoddess of Arinna in KBo II 2 passim can be seen as another confirmation of the relation of this text with CTH 569. It should be noted, by the way, that the tablet KBo II 2 is not a complete investigation by itself: apart from the fact that its lines ii 21-24 summarize a separate inquiry as was demonstrated above Ch. I.5, the negative outcome of the last paragraph iv 34-38 might imply a further sequel.

As we saw, however, CTH 569 reflects two stages: one which must be dated to the very first years of Tutḫaliya's reign around the period of his official inauguration to which the reconstruction just given applies, and a second one some twenty years later. In this part of the inquiry the six affairs are one by one evaluated and, at least in the case of the promises to Danuḫepa, the text makes it clear, that they were indeed not or only partially fulfilled or neglected after a while; see above Ch. II.3. Again, the central issue of the inquiry is the "cleansing of the places of kingship, the thrones and of His Majesty himself". It is tempting, therefore, to suppose some connection between the end of Kurunta's interregnum and the second stage of the inquiry implying some sort of a reinstatement of Tuthaliya on the throne: the chronologies of Kurunta's rule[57] and of the second phase of CTH 569, both established independently from each other, largely coincide. This assumption offers a satisfactory way to explain why the topic of the purity of kingship surfaced again after approximately two decades. We must always bear in mind that it is the person ordering the inquiry, who by searching his or her conscience, has to indicate in what direction the solution to a problem has to be sought. When confronted with the infamous epidemic, which had already demanded so many lives, Muršili II was very explicit on this point when he said in his first Plague Prayer:

> *mekki=i̯a* / *kuit* KUR [(^{URU}*Ḫat*)*ti*] *akkiškitta*[*ri nu ammu*]*k šer AWAT* / ^{m}*Dutḫa*[(*lii̯a* TU)]R-*RI ŠA* DUMU ^{m}*Dutḫali*[*i̯a*] *nakkiēšta IŠTU* DINGIR-*LIM-i̯a* / *arii̯a*[(*nun*) *nu=za*] *AWAT* ^{m}*Dutḫalii̯a* DUMU-*RI I*[*ŠT*]*U* DINGIR-*LIM-i̯a ḫandāittat*
>
> And since Ḫat[ti]-Land is dying in large numbers, the affair of Dutḫaliya the Younger, son of Dutḫali[ya] started to weigh on me and through the deity I conducted an oracle investigation and through the deity, too, the affair of Dutḫaliya the Younger was ascertained.[58]

Similarly, when reclaiming his throne Tutḫaliya may have been reminded of the troubles years ago when he first ascended the throne and probably assumed the same curses of the past were still haunting him.

[57] Cf. StBoT 38, 18-19.

[58] XIV 14+ i 9-12, ed. A. Götze, KlF. 164-165.

5. *Rituals of purification*

Since the oracle inquiry CTH 569 speaks of "undoing" (*arḫa anii̯a-*) the curses and of cleansing "the places of kingship, the thrones and His Majesty", the question should finally be addressed whether in the extensive Hittite ritual literature there are any texts which might be identified as such a ritual or such rituals. As stated at the outset of this study: many rituals are directed at the king or the royal couple, sometimes in connection with the throne.[59] However, there do not seem to be any rituals specifically mentioning "the places of kingship" and neither is the throne very often explicitly the object of purification. Only one text is mentioned[60] in connection with a cleansing of the throne, viz. the so-called *azūri(u)* ritual XLIII 58 with its duplicates XV 42 and FHL 158 (CTH 491.1[61]). Instead of the verb *parkunu-* "to cleanse, purify" or the adjective *parkui-* "clean, pure" this text uses the denominative verb *k/gangat/dai-* derived from *k/gangati-*^{SAR} denoting some kind of a plant or vegetable substance used for cleansing purposes.[62] The ritual aims at freeing a patient and his house from the influence of "evil words, perjury, curse, bloodshed, tears and everything" (XLIII 58 i 46-48, cf. also i 55-56); since later on the throne is mentioned, the patient is likely to have been a king. The latter passage which is preserved in the duplicates XV 42 (B) iii 17'-25' and FHL 158 rev. (C) only, reads (text according B):

17' *nam-ma-aš-ša-an A-NA* ⌈5⌉ NINDA.SIG *ku-e-da-aš kán-ga*[!a]*-ti ki-it-ta*
18' *na-aš-ta* ^{LU}AZU *A-NA* NINDA.SIG *kán-ga-ti te-pu túḫ-ša-i*
19' *na-at iš-ta-na-ni* EGIR*-pa pé-eš-ši-iz-zi nu* DINGIR.MEŠ
20' *kán*[b]*-ga-ta-iz-zi* EGIR-*ŠÚ-ma nam-ma-pát A-NA* NINDA.SIG *kán*[c]*-ga-ti-i̯a*
21' *te-pu túḫ-ša-i na-at-ša-an* ^{GIŠ}DAG*-ti pé-eš-ši-az-zi*[d]
22' *nu* ^{GIŠ}DAG*-ti-in ga-an-ga-ta-iz-zi* EGIR-*ŠÚ*[e]*-ma kán*[f]*-ga-ti*
23' *iš-tar-ni-i̯a-aš ku-ra-ak-ki da-a-i* EGIR-*ŠU-ma*
24' *ga-an-ga-ti A-NA* ^{GIŠ}ÙR.ḪI.A É*-ri iš-tar-na pí-di da-a-i*
25' EGIR-*ŠÚ-ma kán-ga-ti* É*-ri-pát iš-tar-na pí-di da-a-i*

[a] Handcopy has TA. [b] C rev. 4' *ga-an-*. [c] C rev. 5' *ga-an-*. [d] C rev. 6' *-ši-iz-z[i*. [e] C rev. 7' *-ŠU*. [f] C rev. 7' *g[a-*.

[59] Compare, for instance, the old Hittite ritual edited in StBoT 8 by H. Otten and V. Souček. Often the throne also appears in a sequence of places or objects (the hunting bag, the throne, the window, the door beam, the hearth) where libations or the like are made; cf. e.g. E. Neu, StBoT 25 nrs. 25, 30, 36, 46, 88.

[60] Cf. M. Popko, Kultobjekte 64 with n. 76 on p. 76, V. Haas, GHR 293.

[61] XLIII 58 is a clear middle Hittite contemporary copy, XV 42 is younger, probably dating from the 13th century; the fragment FHL 158 is too small to allow for a definite statement.

[62] Cf. H. Ertem, Flora 40-42, J. Tischler, HEG A-K 484-485.

On the five flat breads on which *kangati* is lying, the sorcerer then cuts a small piece of *kangati*, throws it back on the table and treats the gods with the *kangati*. Afterwards he once again cuts another small piece of *kangati* on the flat bread, throws it on the throne and treats the throne with the *kangati*. Afterwards he lays (the?) *kangati* at the center pillar?. Afterwards he lays (the?) *kangati* on the roof beams in the middle of the house. Afterwards he lays (the?) *kangati* in the middle of the house itself.

The priest then continues to lay down the substance in the hearth, on the door beam, beside the hearth and finally, it seems, in the most intimate quarters of the king, possibly the bedroom.[63] Then the text breaks off.

Another ritual, which is likewise directed against curses, does not explicitly mention any items of kingship but would seem to suit the occasion of CTH 569 and related texts to a certain extent: this is the well known ritual of the priestess Maštigga "gegen Familienzwist" (CTH 404).[64] It describes a rite in case of dissensions between father and son, man and wife, and brother and sister. In spite of these specific family relations which would not *stricto sensu* apply to the relations between the six individuals and their adversaries in CTH 569, we may take these relations as standing for familial strife in general. Of course, there are more rituals concerned with "tongues and defamations",[65] but only in this text, it seems, are those tongues called *mantallīēš* "venomous(?), rancorous(?)",[66] a term clearly related to the SISKUR *mantalli-*. After the purpose of the ritual has been stated (KBo XXXIX 8 i 1-4) and all the ingredients have been prepared (i 5-17), the 'Old Woman' brings in the two persons who have uttered curses against each other (i 18). She takes a thick bread, cheese and a jug of wine and holds them out to the 'patients' to lay their hands on them (i 19-21). By doing so they publicly declare, so to speak, their willingness to bring an end to their strife and the 'Old Woman' has induced them to bring their curses out into the open:[67]

22 *nu* 1 [NINDA.GU]R$_4$.RA G[A.K]IN.AG=*i̯a paršii̯a* GEŠTIN=*i̯*[*a*] *šipanti*
23 *nu kiššan tezzi* ^{d}UTU-*i išḫā*=*mi kāša*=*u̯a*=*tta*
24 *parā tit*[*t*]*anunun mantallīēš*

[63] XV 42 iii 29' É-*ŠU-ma kán-ga-ti A-NA* É.ŠÀ *ša-aš-ta-an*? x[. The alleged *šaštan* seems to be written over erasure.

[64] See the edition by L. (Jakob-)Rost, MIO 1 (1953) 345-379; the text constitution as given under CTH 404 has in the meantime changed considerably, see most recently the additional fragments and new copies in KBo XXXIX 8-10 and 35.

[65] Cf. M. Hutter, Behexung 113-115, and id., AoF 18 (1991) 34-39.

[66] Thus with the CHD L-N 176b.

[67] Ed. L. (Jakob-)Rost, MIO 1 (1953) 348-349 (lines "20'-24'"), but line count after KBo XXXIX 8 i.

25 EME.ḪI.A-*eš nu=u̯[a=]šmaš kāša kēdani* UD-*ti* ^{d}UTU-*i*
26 x[... [68]] EME$^{?}$.ḪI.A x[-*i̯*]*anzi*[69]

She breaks the one [thick bre]ad as well as the c[he]ese a[nd] libates the wine. Then she says: "Sungod, My Lord, just now I have brought to the fore for you, rancorous$^{?}$ tongues. Behold, on this day, O Sungod, they will [...] their tongues."

Then the ritual proper starts and through various ways the 'Old Woman' removes from them the "curses and defamations of the past" (cf. i 42 *apedaš* UD-*aš* EME.ḪI.A *ḫūrtāuš*). Although it is not explicitly called a *mantalli*-ritual, it certainly "serves this purpose"[70] and may for that matter be considered a *mantalli*-ritual. It would also be applicable, if needs be,[71] to dead persons, present in some form of an effigy, if the actions of both or one of the two individuals, which are restricted to laying hands on something, spitting in the mouth of an animal, killing and burying that animal, toppling *ḫuwaši*-stones and washing themselves, could be performed by others instead. They hardly speak a single word, however.

Whether the two kinds of rituals, the one cleansing the throne and the *mantalli*-ritual, each sufficed by itself to bring about the desired purification mentioned in CTH 569 or had to be performed both, remains unclear but they do give us an idea of the actions undertaken once the oracle investigation had been brought to an end.

[68] A restoration to, for instance, *Q*[*A-TAM-MA*] seems conceivable ("They will thus ... their tongues"), although the horizontal wedge of the first sign trace might be a little too high for the sign QA.

[69] L. (Jakob-)Rost, MIO 1 (1953) 348-349, apparently thought of a reading *ti̯anzi* because of the translation "werden sie legen". A reading/restoration ⌈*a*⌉[-*ni*-*i̯*]*a-an-zi* seems possible as well: "They will ... treat their tongues".

[70] Thus CHD L-N 176b, see also M. Hutter, AoF 18 (1991) 38.

[71] This is, however, not necessary for a *mantalli*-ritual; see already Ch. I.1.

CHAPTER FOUR

THE INQUIRIES PRECEDING CTH 569

1. *Introduction*

Before proceeding with the text of CTH 569 proper, in this Chapter the texts which were above in Chapter III.3 considered to have preceded CTH 569, are transliterated and translated in groups (§§2-5) in a tentative and approximate chronological ordering:

2.	KBo XVI 98(+$^?$)XLIX 49
3.1	XXII 12(+$^?$)13
3.2.1	I. VI 9+XVIII 59
	II. XVIII 36
3.2.2	L 77+XLIX 73
3.3	XLIX 2(+$^?$)XVIII 6
3.4	XVI 20
4.	KBo II 2
5.1	XVI 16 and KBo XXIII 114
5.2	XVI 46 and L 87.

For the order in which the texts are given see Chapter III.3 and 4 as well as below. All sections are preceded by short introductory remarks; some brief notes are given where deemed necessary or useful but no extensive commentary is given.

2. *KBo XVI 98(+$^?$)XLIX 49 (CTH 577)*

The indirect join between the fragments KBo XVI 98 and XLIX 49 was proposed in ZA 81 (1991) 293. The former has preserved remains of all four columns, the latter only a substantial part of col. ii and some scanty remains of col. iii. The script of both pieces is New Script. Starting from an average number of some sixty to seventy lines per column, the gap between the end of KBo XVI 98 i/ii (33 and 31 lines respectively) and the beginning of XLIX 49 ii (21 lines) may amount to approximately ten to twenty lines. An edition of KBo XVI 98 was offered by P. Cornil and R. Lebrun, Hethitica 1 (1972) 1-14, for a possible connection with several oracles concerning an illness of Tutḫaliya's young Babylonian spouse see Ph.H.J. Houwink ten Cate, AoF 23 (1996) 64-72; for further literature see my remarks in ZA 81 (1991) 292-294, to which M.-C. Trémouille, Eothen 7, 68, should now be added.

At least three subjects seem to be dealt with on this tablet. First (i 1ff.) there is the vow of a queen to Ḫebat of Kummanni, Lelwani and possibly one other deity in between, in connection with parts of the army; this recalls the vow XV 11 for which see above Chapter II.7. Then there is the matter of – so it seems – a campaign of His Majesty to Gaittana (ii 3-9)

KBo XVI 98 i

1 [ ]x ⸢ÉRIN.MEŠ⸣ *ša-ri-ku-ua* ⸢ÉRIN⸣.MEŠ UKU.UŠ [ ]x
2 [-]*at nu a-ri-ia-u-en nu* DINGIR-*LUM* EGIR[ ]x
3 [*nu-za-kán* M]UNUS.LUGAL *A-NA* ^{d}*Ḫé-pát* ^{URU}*Kum-ma-an-ni* x[o]x x
4 [^{d}*Le-*]⸢*el*⸣*-ua-ni IK-RU-UB ma-a-an-ua-mu* DINGIR.MEŠ[?]
5 [*iš-t*]*a-ma-aš-te-ni* GEŠTUG*-an-mu pa-ra-a e-ep-*⸢*te*⸣[*-ni*
6 [*ḫu-u*]*l-la-at-te-*⸢*ni*⸣ ÚŠ*-an Ú-UL* DÙ*-ri* [*nu* IGI*-zi*]
7 [*TE*^{MEŠ}] SIG$_5$*-ru* EGIR*-ma* NU.SIG$_5$*-du* IGI*-zi TE*^{M}[^{EŠ} KASKAL*-NU*]
8 [*iš-ki-*]*ša* GAM IGI*-zi*[1] *zi* GAR*-ri* 12 ŠÀ *DIR* S[IG$_5$ EGIR *TE*^{MEŠ}]
9 [^{GIŠ}ŠÚ.]⸢A⸣*-ḫi* GÙB*-an* NU.SIG$_5$

---

10 [ ]x x x x*-za*? ⸢*a*⸣*-ra-aḫ-za* SIxSÁ*-at* ⸢*nu-za-kán*⸣ *pa-*⸢*a-i-mi*⸣
11 [ ]x*-ši ku-e-da-*⸢*ni-ik*⸣*-ki*
12 [ ]x-⸢AḪ⸣*-ḫi* ⸢*ma-a*⸣*-an-ma a-ši*
13 [*-š/t*]*a-*⸢*ri*⸣ *nu* MUŠEN.ḪI.A SIxSÁ*-an-du*
14 [ ]x*-kán* EGIR UGU SIG$_5$*-za*
15 [E]GIR KASKAL*-NI* TI$_8$^{MUŠEN}*-kán*

[1] For the phrase KASKAL-*NU iškiša* GAM IGI-*zi* see P. Cornil-R. Lebrun, Hethitica 1 (1972) 10, and CHD P 76a.

and finally, the inquiry about the accession ceremony and the trips to Kummanni and Nerik (ii 10ff.). The three do not seem to be interconnected and are separated by double paragraph dividers (between ii 2 and 3 and ii 9 and 10), thus giving the impression of a 'Sammeltafel'.[2] As is typical of many oracle texts, KBo XVI 98 (2211/c) was found secondarily used as filling material "in Mauerkasten" on Büyükkale g/14, which seems to be the stretch of wall linking building F to building E.[3]

i

1 [Concerning the fact that? ...] ... the *šarikuu̯a*-troops (and) the heavily-armed troops [...] ...
2 [... was/were ascertain]ed?, we conducted an oracle inquiry and a/the deity [was] later [ascertaine]d.?
3 [The q]ueen made a vow to Ḫepat of Kummanni, ...
4 [(and) to L]elwani: "If you, o gods, [?]
5 [h]ear me, (if) yo[u] lend me (your) ear, (if) you [def]eat [the enemy?],
6 (and) no downfall occurs"[4], [then let the first]
7 [exta] be favorable but let the following (ones) be unfavorable. The first ext[a: ... the road]
8 [(is turned) backwa]rds down in front, a bladderworm lies (there), twelve coils; fa[vorable. The following exta:]
9 [the thr]one left; unfavorable.

---

10 [Concerning the fact that? ...] ... outside was ascertained: will I go[5]
11 [(and) ...] to some ... [...]
12 [...] will I [...]? If, however, that
13 will [...], then let them ascertain the birds.
14 [... a ...](bird) [came] above behind from favorable (direction),
15 [... be]hind the road: an eagle

[2] See Ph.H.J. Houwink ten Cate, AoF 23 (1996) 70.

[3] See now the forthcoming AoF-article by S. Alaura on the fragments found during the 1933 excavations (.../c) in and around Building E on Büyükkale; compare also below the remarks on the findspot of KBo XXIII 114 (5.1.2) found in g/13, and on 2275/c (above Ch. II.6) found within Building E.

[4] The quotative particle -*u̯a*(*r*-) is used only once in line 4 (*mān⸗u̯a⸗mu*), so it is difficult to determine where exactly the direct speech is supposed to end. Since the queen is said to have made a vow, not an oracle inquiry, and since it is conceivable that the condition of the vow was later made subject of such an inquiry by others, it seems most plausible to end the quotation here.

[5] The particles *⸗za⸗kan* suggest the possibility of a restoration to a form of Hittite *mald-* or Akkadian *karābu* "to make a vow". It might even be considered whether the]x-*aḫ-ḫi* in i 12 should be restored to *ma-al-t*]*a-aḫ-ḫi* and whether the beneficiary deity is expressed in i 11 as DINGI]R-*LIM* *kuedanikki*.

16 [*ar-ḫ*]*a pa-it*
17 [ ]EGIR UGU SIG$_5$-*za*
18 [*UM-MA* UGULA $^{LU.MEŠ}$]⸢IGI⸣.MUŠEN [6]SIxSÁ-*at-u̯a*

---

19 [EGI]R-*ma* NU.SIG$_5$-*du*
20 [ ]x
21 [N]U.SIG$_5$

---

22 [Ù-*TUM*$^?$-*u̯a*-]⸢*za*⸣-*kán u-uḫ-ḫu-un*
23 [-]*ti-ši*
24 [*me*-]*mi*$^?$-*iš-ki-mi*
25 [ ]x
26 [ ]
27 [ ]*ku-it*
28 [ ]x-*e*
29 [ ]
30 [S]IG$_5$

---

31 [ ]
32 [ ]*ú-it*
33 [ ]x
34 [ ]x

KBo XVI 98 ii

1 IGI-*zi T*[*E*^{MEŠ} o o o]x[7] GÙB-*za* RA^{IṢ} S[IG$_5$$^?$]
2 EGIR *TE*^{M}[^{EŠ} o o o N]U.SIG$_5$

(blank space of one line)

---

3 ^{d}UTU-*ŠI ku-it* ^{URU}⸢*Ga*⸣[-*i*]*t-ta-na pa-iz-zi*
4 *nu-za A-NA* ^{d}*Ša-ú*[-*ma-d*]*a-ri* ^{GIŠ}TUKUL-*an-za* BAL-*i*
5 MUNUS.LUGAL-*ma-kán tu-u-u̯*[*a-a*]*z* BAL-*i ma-a-an-ma-za* DINGIR-*LUM* KI.MIN
6 *nu* IGI-*zi TE*^{MEŠ} SIG$_5$[-*ru* E]GIR-*ma* NU.SIG$_5$-*du*
7 IGI-*zi TE*^{MEŠ} *ni ši* ^{GIŠ}[TUKUL Z]AG-*aš ŠA* ^{d}*Ḫé-pát* ^{GIŠ}TUKUL ZAG-*aš*
8 *še-lu-uš-ḫi-ta-aš-ši-iš* [GÙ]B-*za* RA^{IṢ} *zi* GAR-*ri* 12 ŠÀ *DIR* ⸢SIG$_5$⸣
9 EGIR *TE*^{MEŠ} *ir-liš* ZAG[-*za*] NU.SIG$_5$

---

[6] Cf. A. Archi, SMEA 16 (1975) 134.
[7] Could be *k*]*e* for *keldi* as in KBo II 6+ i 42' and iv 3; P. Cornil-R. Lebrun, Hethitica 1 (1972) 2, suggest *ir-li*]*š*.

16 [...]went [of]f,
17 [...] above behind from favorable (direction)
18 [... Thus the head of the a]ugurs: they were ascertained.

---

19 [That same question through the ... : let the first ... be favorable, but let the lat]er (one/ones) be unfavorable,
20-21 [... ; u]nfavorable.

---

22 [... a dream] I saw.
23-end (no translation feasible).

ii

1 The first e[xta: ...] ... on the left damaged; fa[vorable$^{?}$].
2 The later ext[a: ... u]nfavorable.

---

3 Concerning the fact that His Majesty will go to the city of Ga[i]ttana:
4 will he offer (his) weapons[8] to Šau[mad]ari,
5 while the queen will bring offerings from afar? If you, o god, etc.[9],
6 then [let] the first exta be favorable but let the [fo]llowing (ones) be unfavorable.
7 The first exta: *ni*(*pašuri*), *ši*(*ntaḫi*), the w[eapon (is) on the r]ight, Ḫepat's weapon (is) on the right,
8 the *šelušḫitašši*-[10] is damaged on the left, a bladderworm lies (there), twelve coils; favorable.
9 The following exta: *ir*(*kipel*)*liš* [on the] right; unfavorable.

---

[8] For ^{GIŠ}TUKUL-*anza* as a Luwian acc.pl.c. compare the same form in VBoT 25 i 5, 12, 17, for which see H.C. Melchert, CLL 296 s.v.

[9] The KI.MIN probably stands for a phrase like below line 17 *mān=ma=za* DINGIR.MEŠ *kūn* IR-*TAM* GAM-*an malān ḫarteni*.

[10] See F. Starke, StBoT 31, 252 n. 864.

(blank space of one line)

---

10 ^{d}UTU $^{⌈URU⌉}$PÚ-*na ku-it e-ni-eš-ša-an te-eš-ḫa-ni-eš-kit*$_{9}$*-ta-ri*
11 *nu-kán* GIM-*an* ^{d}UTU-*ŠI IŠ*-⌈*TU*⌉ KUR^{URU}*Kum-ma-an-ni* UGU *a-ar-ḫi*
12 *nu-za-kán* LUGAL-*iz-na-an-ni e*[*-e*]*š-ḫa-ḫa-ri nam-ma-za* EZEN$_{4}$.MEŠ
13 DÙ-*mi* GIM-*an-ma-za-kán* ⌈EZEN$_{4}$⌉.MEŠ *kar-ap*[11]*-mi*
14 *nu I-NA* ^{URU}*Ne-ri-ik-ka*$_{4}$ *pa-i-mi nu A-NA* DINGIR-*LIM* SISKUR *pé-eḫ-ḫi*
15 *i-i̯a-mi-ma Ú-UL ku-it-ki pa-ra-a-ma* MU.KAM-*an-ni*
16 *A-NA* KASKAL ^{URU}*Ne-ri-ik-ka*$_{4}$ EGIR-*an-pát ar-ḫa-ḫa-ri*
17 *ma-a-an-ma-za* DINGIR.MEŠ *ku-u-un* IR-*TAM* GAM-*an ma-la-a-an ḫar-te-ni*
18 *nu* MUŠEN.ḪI.A SIxSÁ-*an-du* TI$_{8}$^{MUŠEN}-*kán* ⌈EGIR⌉ UGU SIG$_{5}$-*za*
19 *na-aš tar-liš pa-an pa-it* 2 *mar-ša-na-aš-ši-iš-ma*-⌈*kán*⌉ *pí*[*-an* S]IG$_{5}$-*za*
20 *ú-e-er na-at-kán pí-an ar-ḫa* ⌈*pa-a-ir*⌉ x x x[
21 2 *kal-tar-ši-iš-kăn ta-pa-aš-ši-iš-š*[*a*
22 *na-at* 2-*an ar-ḫa pa-a-ir UM-MA* ^{m}x[

---

23 *nu* IGI-*an-da la-aḫ-la-aḫ-ḫi-ma-aš* MUŠEN.ḪI.A[
24 *pí-an ku-uš na-aš* 2-*an ar-ḫa* [
25 EGIR GAM *ku-uš na*-⌈*at*⌉ x[
26 *šu-lu-pé-eš-kán pí*-⌈*an*⌉[
27 *ku-u̯a-at-tar-ma-aš*[12][

---

28 *IŠ-TU* ^{MUNUS}ŠU.G[I
29 LUGAL-*uš-za* x[
30 ⌈*I*⌉-*NA* UD.2.K[AM
31 [ ] x [

(break of approximately ten to twenty lines)

XLIX 49 ii

x+1 [ ]x x
2 [*UM-MA* ^{m} ... *ar-ḫa-u̯a pé-eš-š*]*ir*

---

3 [IGI-*zi T*]*E*^{MEŠ} SIG$_{5}$-*ru* EGIR-*ma* NU.SIG$_{5}$-*du*
4 [ ]x GÙB-*za za-al-zi-ma-an*[13]
5 [*zi*] GAR-⌈*ri*⌉ 12 ŠÀ *DIR* SIG$_{5}$

[11] Last sign written over erasure.

[12] For this alleged hapax see J. Tischler, HEG A-K 700-701, and E. Neu, IF 89 (1984) 305. A designation of another species of oracle bird cannot be ruled out.

[13] For this extispicy term cf. H. Berman, JCS 34 (1982) 120, and G. Beckman, BiOr. 42 (1985) 141.

---

10 Concerning the fact that the Sungoddess of Arinna thus keeps appearing in my dreams:
11 If I, My Majesty, will come up from the country of Kummanni,
12 will I sit down in kingship and subsequently conduct the festivities?
13 But if I end the festivities,
14 go to the city of Nerik and bring an offering to the deity
15 without doing anything (else),
16 will I concern myself with a journey to Nerik next year?
17 If you, o gods, have further approved of this question,
18 then let them ascertain the birds. An eagle (came) above behind from favorable (direction),
19 and went across *tar*(*wiyal*)*liš*. Two *maršanašši*(-birds) came in fr[ont from fa]vorable (direction)
20 and passed in front. ... [...]
21 Two (birds), a *kaltarši*(-bird) and a *tapašši*(-bird) [...]
22 and they went off through the center (or: together). Thus ... [...].

---

23 As a countercheck [we observed] the birds of agony [...]
24 in front *kuš*(*tayati*) and off it [went] through the center. [...]
25 down behind *kuš*(*tayati*) and they [...]
26 a *šulupi*(-bird) in front [...]
27 ...

---

28 Through the 'Old Wom[an' that same question: let the *kin* be ...]
29 The king [took for himself] ... [...]
30 On the second day [...]

(ii)

2' [... Thus ...: "They have ca]st [away.]"

3' [... : let the first e]xta be favorable but let the following (ones) be unfavorable.
4' [The first exta: ...] ... on the left, ...
5' [... a bladderworm] lies (there), twelve coils; favorable.

6 [ ]x *ta-ú-ti-iš* NU.SIG$_5$

---

7 [*IŠ-TU* ^{MUNUS}ŠU.GI IR-*TU*]*M QA-TAM-MA-pát nu* KIN SIG$_5$-*ru*
8 [ ]x ⌈*da*⌉-*a-ir na-at pa-an-ga-u-i* SUM-*ir* NU.SIG$_5$

---

9 [-*kán*]x *pa-ra-a ne-eḫ-ḫi*
10 [ ]x SIG$_4$$^{?}$[14]-*i̯a* SUD-*an-zi*
11 [(-)]*ap-pa-an-zi* ^{d}UTU-*ŠI-ma-za*
12 [EZEN$_4$.MEŠ DÙ-*mi* G]I[M$^{?}$-*an-ma-z*]*a-kán* ^{d}UTU-*ŠI* EZEN$_4$.MEŠ *kar-ap-mi*
13 [*nu I-NA* ^{URU}*Ne-ri-i*]*k-ka*$_4$ *pa*[-*i-mi*] ⌈*A*⌉-*NA* DINGIR-*LIM* SISKUR *pé-eḫ-ḫi*
14 [*Ú-UL ku-it-ki i-i̯*]*a*$^{?}$-*am-*⌈*mi pa-ra*⌉-*a-ma* MU-*an-ni* (erasure)
15 [*A-NA* KASKAL ^{URU}*Ne-r*]*i-ik-ka*$_4$ EGIR-*an ar-ḫa-ḫa-ri ma-a-an-ma-za* DINGIR.MEŠ
16 [*ku-u-un* IR-*TAM* GAM-*an*] *ma-la-a-an ḫar-te-ni nu* MUŠEN.ḪI.A SIxSÁ-*an-du*
17 [-*kán* EGI]R UGU SIG$_5$-*za ú-it na-aš pa-an tar-liš pa*-[*i*]*t*
18 [-*kán* EGI]R UGU SIG$_5$-*za ú-it na-aš* 2-*an ar*[-*ḫa*] *pa-it*
19 [-*ká*]*n* EGIR UGU SIG$_5$-*za ú-it*
20 [*šal*-]*u̯i*$_5$-*ni-eš-ma-kán* EGIR UGU SIG$_5$[-*z*]*a*
21 [*ú-it* *ar-ḫ*]*a pa-a-ir* SIxSÁ-*at-u̯a* MUŠ-*kán* [*p*]*a-it*

(end of column)

XLIX 49 iii

1 [ ] x [o$^{?}$] *ḫu* [o$^{?}$] x [
2-3 (nothing preserved)
4 [-]*it*
5-6 (nothing preserved)
7 [ ]x-*i*
8 [ ]x-*ra*-⌈*an*⌉$^{?}$-*za* NU.SIG$_5$

9$^{?}$ (not preserved)
10' [ ]x-*ak*
11' [-]*am-mi*
12' [LUG]AL-*iz-na-an-ni*[15]

[14] See my remark ZA 81 (1991) 294 n. 37.
[15] For this reading cf. ZA 81 (1991) 293 n. 36.

6’ [The following exta: ...] ... *tautiš*; unfavorable.

7’ That same [questi]on [through the ‘Old Woman’]: let the *kin* be favorable.
8’ [...] ... they have taken and given it/them to the *panku*; unfavorable.

9’ [...] ... will I send forth?
10’ [...] ... will they pull/attract?
11’ [...] will they [...] while I, My Majesty,
12’ [will conduct the festivities? But if] I, My Majesty, end the festivities,
13’ g[o to the city of Neri]k and bring an offering to the deity
14’ [without d]oing [anything (else)],
15’ will I concern myself [with a journey to Ner]ik next year? If you, o gods,
16’ have [further] approved [of this question], then let them ascertain the birds.
17’ [A ... (-bird)] came above [behi]nd from favorable (direction) and we[n]t across *tar*(*wiyal*)*liš*.
18’ [A ... (-bird)] came above [behi]nd from favorable (direction), went o[ff] through the center
19’ [...] came above behind from favorable direction
20’ [and went .... X *šal*]*wini*(-birds) [came] above behind [f]rom favorable (direction)
21’ [and ... of]f they went. (Thus the augur:) “It was ascertained.” The snake has [g]one.[16]

iii

(no translation feasible)

[16] On this expression see the commentary Ch. V ad LII 92, 7’.

13’ [ ]x

(ca. two lines not preserved)

14” [-*r*]*u*
15” [ ]x
16” [ ]x NU.SIG$_5$

(break of unknown length)

KBo XVI 98 iii

x+1 [E]GIR$^?$-⸢*ma* NU.SIG$_5$⸣-[*du*$^?$]
2 [ ]SIG$_5$

3 [*k*]*u-iš-ki* TUKU.TUKU-*az*
4 [ ] (vacat)

5 [N]U.SIG$_5$-*du* SIG$_5$

6 [(NU.$^?$)S]IG$_5$-*du* SIG$_5$

7 ⸢*ma-a-an*⸣[-*za* *ma*]*r*$^?$-*ki-i̯a-an ḫar-ti*
8 *nu TE*^{MEŠ}[ ] (vacat)

9 *ma-a-an-za* [ ]*mar-ki-i̯a-an ḫar-ti*
10 *nam-ma-m*[*a*$^?$ KI.MIN *nu* IGI-*zi TE*^{MEŠ} SIG$_5$-*r*]*u* EGIR-*ma* NU.SIG$_5$-*du*
11 IGI-*zi T*[*E*^{MEŠ} SI]G$_5$ EGIR *TE*^{MEŠ} *ni-eš-kán*
12 ZAG-*na-a*[*š*] (vacat)

13 ^{d}UTU-*ŠI ku-u̯a-*⸢*pí*⸣ [-]*ma-na A-NA* ^{d}*Pí-ir-u̯a* ⸢SISKUR⸣ *pé-eš*-x[
14 *nu* ⸢SISKUR⸣-*aš TE*^{MEŠ}[ ]x *ma-a-an-za* DINGIR-*LUM* SISKUR *da-at-ta*[?]
15 *A-NA* ^{d}UTU-*ŠI-ká*[*n* IGI.ḪI.A-*u̯a a*]*n-da-an aš-šu-li ne-i̯a-at-ta*[-*ri*]
16 *nu* IGI-*zi TE*^{MEŠ} [SIG$_5$-*ru* E]GIR-*ma* NU.SIG$_5$-*du* IGI-*zi TE*^{MEŠ}
17 *ni ši* KASKAL 12 ⸢ŠÀ⸣[*DIR* SIG$_5$ E]GIR *TE*^{MEŠ} ^{GIŠ}ŠÚ.A-*ḫi* GÙB-*an* NU.⸢SIG$_5$⸣

(end of column)

13'-16'' (no translation feasible)

(iii)

1'-6' (no translation feasible)

7' If you, [o god,] have [di]sapproved [of ...]
8' then [let] the exta [be ...]

9' If you, [o god,] have disapproved [of ...]
10' b[ut] further [etc., then l]et [the first exta be favorable] but let the later (ones) be unfavorable.
11' The first e[xta: ... ; favora]ble. The later exta: *ni(pašuri)*
12' on the righ[t ...].

13' When [I$^{?}$,] My Majesty, [in the city$^{?}$ of ... -]mana g[ave$^{?}$] an offering to Pirwa,
14' and the offering's exta [...] ..., if you, o god, have accepted the offering,
15' [will] you then turn [(your) eyes to]wards My Majesty in benevolence?
16' Then [let] the first exta [be favorable] but let [the fol]lowing (ones) be unfavorable. The first exta:
17' *ni(pašuri)*, *ši(ntaḫi)*, the road, twelve co[ils; favorable. The fol]lowing exta: the throne on the left; unfavorable.

KBo XVI 98 iv

x+1 [ ]x *nu* MUŠEN[.ḪI.A SIxSÁ-*an-du*
2 [-*a*]*n*[17] *ku-uš* ⌈*ú-it*⌉[
3 [*ar-ḫ*]*a pa-it kal-tar-ši-i*[*š*(-)
4 [ ]x-*an IK-ŠU-UD kal-t*[*ar-ši-*
5 [ ]x *ú-it na-aš-ká*[*n*
6 [-*i*]*š-kán* EGIR GAM[
7 [*UM-MA* ^{m} *ar-ḫa-u̯a*] *pé-eš-šir*[

---

8 [*IŠ-TU* ... IR-*TUM QA-T*]*AM-MA-pát nu*[
9 [ ]x [

(break)

18" [*nu*] K[IN NU.S]IG$_5$-⌈*du*⌉ x[
19" [*I-NA* UD.2.]KAM DINGIR-⌈*LUM*⌉-*za da-pí-an* Z[I-*an da-a-aš na-an* DINGIR.MA]Ḫ-*ni pa-iš*
20" [*I-NA* UD].3$^{?!}$.KAM *pa-an-ku-uš-za* ZAG-*tar da-a-a*[*š*

21" [*ke-e*] *ku-i-e MA-ME-TE*^{MEŠ} ⌈*da*⌉-*pí-an-da* x x[
22" [EME$^{?}$ *Š*]*A* NÍ.TE ^{d}UTU-*ŠI ar-ḫa a-ni-i̯a-nu-un* ⌈*na-an/t*⌉(-)x[o o$^{?}$ *d*]*a*$^{?}$-*pí-an*
23" [ ]x-*at-ti* BAL-*an-zi ma-a-an-ma-za* DINGIR-*LUM* KI.MIN *nu* K[IN SI]G$_5$-*ru*
24" [*ŠA* DINGIR.]MEŠ *mi-nu-mar*$^{\text{ḪI.A}}$ *da-an-te-eš nu-kán an-da* SIG$_5$-*u-i* ⌈*I*⌉[-*N*]*A* UD.2.KAM
25" [LUGAL-*uš-z*]*a* ZAG-*tar da-a-aš nu-kán* DINGIR.MEŠ-*aš I-NA* UD.3.KAM DINGIR.MEŠ GUB-*aš* TI-*tar*
26" [ ] *nu-kán* EGIR-*pa* ^{GIŠ}DAG-*ti* SIG$_5$

(end of tablet)

[17] Either *zi-a*]*n* or *pí-a*]*n*, cf. Ch. VI, Commentary ad KBo II 6+ iii 56.

iv

1’ [...] ..., then [let them ascertain] the birds. [?]
2’ [...] ... *kuš*(*tayati*) it came [...]
3’ [... of]f it went. A *kaltarši*[(-bird) ...]
4’ [upon a ... (-bird)] ... it came. The *kalt*[*arši*(-bird) ...]
5’ [...] ... came and it [...]
6’ [... went. A ... (-bird)] down behind [...]
7’ [Thus ... :] “They have cast [away].”

8’ [Through the ... that s]ame [question:] then [...]
9’ [...] ... [...].

18” [...] ... let the *k*[*in* be unfa]vorable ... [...]
19” [On the second day] the DEITY[18] [took] for him/herself the S[OUL] entirely [and] gave [it to the MOTHERGODD]ESS.
20” [On the] third$^{?}$ day the *panku* too[k] itself RIGHTNESS [...].

21” [Concerning] all [these$^{?}$] oaths which ... [...]
22” [the curse$^{?}$ aga]inst His Majesty’s body I have undone. Will they ...
23” [...] ... offer? If then you, o god, etc., then let the *k*[*in* be favor]able.
24” [The GOD]S’ FAVORS have been taken and (they are) in FAVORABLE (position). On the second day
25” [the KING] took [for hims]elf RIGHTNESS and (it is) with the GODS. On the third day the GODS, standing/rising$^{?}$, LIFE
26” [...] and back on the THRONE (it is). Favorable.

[18] The ‘tokens’ used in the KIN-oracle procedure symbolizing the various items relevant to the investigation are here and elsewhere given in small capitals. The Sumerogram KIN which is left untranslated, therefore appears italicized.

3. *The accession oracles*

Under the general heading of "accession oracles" those oracles are grouped together which center around the postponement of the festive inauguration ceremony of Tutḫaliya IV as Great King of the Hittite empire:

3.1	XXII 12(+?)13 (CTH 582)
3.2.1	I. VI 9+XVIII 59 (CTH 578)
	II. XVIII 36 (CTH 582)
3.2.2	L 77+XLIX 73 (CTH 582)
3.3	XLIX 2(+?)XVIII 6 (CTH 575)
3.4	XVI 20 (CTH 572)

Except for the MUŠ-oracle XLIX 2(+?)XVIII 6 (3.3) which is added to this dossier by Ph.H.J. Houwink ten Cate, AoF 23 (1996) 71-72 n. 56 (for the proposed join see A. Archi, KUB XLIX Inhaltsübersicht), these fragments were already discussed in my article "Hethitische Thronbesteigungsorakel und die Inauguration Tudḫalijas IV." in ZA 81 (1991) 274-300. However, the exact relationship between VI 9+ and XVIII 36 (3.2.1.I and II) as comprehensive version and summary respectively was not yet recognized (see above Chapter I.5). Therefore the two are given below *in Partitur* to bring this out more clearly. Similarly, I had not yet found the join piece L 77 to XLIX 73 (3.2.2). Besides XVIII 36 (3.1.II), the two fragments XXII 12(+?)13 (3.1) also represent a summary version.

Put at the very beginning are the fragments XXII 12(+?)13 (3.1), apparently inquiring into the relationship between an illness and the accession ceremony. The possibility of the (indirect) join was already indicated in the handcopy by A. Walther. Judging by the indication "Spaltenstrich" in that same handcopy, XXII 12 probably was part of a right, that is either second or third column. The relative position of XXII 13 cannot be determined.

The two subsequent texts (3.2.1 and 2), VI 9+ – including its summary XVIII 36 – and L 77+, share the phrase *ANA* dUTU-*ŠI kuit* LUGAL-*uiznani ašātar duu̯ān parā arḫa zalukišta* "Concerning the fact that for His Majesty the accession to kingship was further postponed", they might even partly be considered duplicates: VI 9+ obv. 12-17 and 24-25 = L 77+ r. col. 4'-9' and 14'-15' respectively. Their precise relationship, however close, is unclear if not enigmatic. First of all, they are not likely to have formed parts of the same tablet (cf. the sign ḪA with two wedges in VI 9+ obv. 13 versus ḪA with one wedge in L 77+ r. col. 5' and 8'; *za-lu-ki-iš-ta* VI 9+ obv. 13 versus *za-lu-kiš-ta* L 77+ r. col. 5'; *INA* written with the AŠ sign in VI 9+ obv. 22 versus *I-NA* in L 77+ r. col. 11' and 12'). Neither is one a summary of the other, both being comprehensive versions as far as preserved. In VI 9+ obv. the oracle question is each time announced to be answered by means of a *šašt-* or clinomantic oracle but the technique was not used: instead there is a blank space. The check is each time made by way of a

KIN-oracle. The text L 77+, on the other hand, twice shows the latter technique in an unbroken sequence. Is L 77+ then a forerunner of VI 9+ obv. which was then copied unto VI 9+ with blanks for the results of the *šašt*-oracle, still to be filled in? In that case, one must object, the check in VI 9+ obv. 19-23 should have corresponded to the description of the KIN-oracle in L 77+ r. col. 10'-13' which it obviously does not. The latter description, surprisingly, does correspond, however, word for word to the previous KIN-oracle of VI 9+ obv. 8-11, in spite of its fragmentary state of preservation! Do we have to conclude that the scribe of VI 9+ copied a wrong oracle description? Both VI 9+ and L 77+ were parts of the right hand column of their original tablets. The handcopy of XVIII 36 offers no clues in this respect.

Although highly fragmentary in its historically relevant parts, the MUŠ-oracle XLIX 2(+$^{?}$) (3.3) might indeed belong in the vicinity of these texts. Parts of all four columns are preserved. After the best preserved column i, the tablet counted at least some sixty lines per column originally. The oracle fragment XVI 20 (3.4), finally, deals with the chronological details of the postponement. According to A. Walthers's remark ad KUB XVIII 59 this fragment looks very similar to VI 9+.

For none of these texts the findspot is known.[19] All pieces display characteristics typical of New Script.

[19] In his very first report of December 1907 in the MDOG 35, 17 Hugo Winckler, speaking of Šuppiluliuma I and the tablet finds of the excavations of 1906-1907, wrote: "Ein kleines Bruchstück ist vielleicht auf dessen Thronbesteigung zu deuten und spricht von Orakelmachenschaften, die dabei in Szene gesetzt wurden." Could he have referred to one of the above accession oracles? We know of no such text from the time of Šuppiluliuma I. That Winckler considered assigning the fragment to the latter king, may have to do with the find spot. On pp. 14-15 he had stated: "Subbiluliuma, von dem (...) die wichtigsten Urkunden nur hier gefunden worden sind", the "hier" referring to the store rooms of Temple I. This would be interesting in view of the possibility that one of the summary versions of CTH 569 was kept there; see above Chapter I.9.

3.1 XXII 12(+)$^{?}$ 13

a) XXII 12

x+1 *ku-it-ma-an-kán* ^{d}UTU-*ŠI* U[GU
2 *ku-it-ma-na-aš la-aḫ-ḫa-az* [*neiari*/EGIR-*pa uizzi*(?)]
3 *ma-a-an-ma A-NA* ^{d}UTU-*ŠI I*[*Š-TU*
4 *Ú-UL ku-it-ki* ḪUŠ-*u-e-n*[*i*
5 *IŠ-TU* ^{MUNUS}ŠU.GI ^{LÚ}ḪAL-*i̯*[*a*$^{?}$

(break)

b) XXII 13

x+1 [o o] x x [ ]-*az* ⌈SIG$_5$⌉

2 [*nu*$^{?}$ *ki-i*] *ku-it* LUGAL-*iz-na-ni* ⌈*a*⌉-*ša-a-tar* SIxSÁ-*at* [?]
3 [*ma-a-an* G]IG-*i̯a a-ri-i̯a*-⌈*še-eš*⌉-*na-az* SIxSÁ-*kit*$_9$-*ta-r*[*i*]
4 [*ma-a-an-m*]*a*(?) *A-NA* ^{d}UTU-⌈*ŠI*⌉ LUGAL-*iz-na-ni a-ša*-⌈*a*⌉[-*tar*]
5 [*ar-ḫa*(?)]⌈*Ú*⌉-*UL pé*-⌈*eš-ši*⌉-*i̯a-zi*
6 [*IŠ-TU* ^{MUNUS}Š]U.GI [NU$^{?}$.] SIG$_5$

7 [*ki-i ku-it I*]*Š-T*[*U*] ⌈^{LÚ}⌉ḪAL-*i̯a* NU.SIG$_5$
8 [*ŠA* ^{d}UTU ^{URU}PÚ-*na*$^{?}$ *t*]*a-pa-aš-ša še-er* DINGIR-*LIM-tar* SI[xSÁ-*at*]
9 [*kiš-an a-ri-i̯a*-]⌈*u*⌉-*en nu* ^{d}UTU ^{URU}PÚ-*na* SIxS[Á-*at*]

(break)

3.2.1 I. VI 9+XVIII 59 obv. ii$^{?}$
II. XVIII 36

II. x + 1 [(-)]na-aš[(-)
2 [ ]⌈ma⌉-a-a[n-
3 [^{d}UTU-*ŠI* LUGAL-iz-na-ni e-š]a-ri ku-i[t-ma-an
4 [ ]x ^{d}UTU-*ŠI* x[
5 [ ]⌈*Ú*⌉-*UL* ku-it-k[i
6 [*IŠ-TU* ^{MUNUS}ŠU.GI] [NU.SIG$_5$/SIG$_5$]

I. 1 [*ku-it-ma-an* M]U-*an*$^{!}$-*ni* ⌈*ke-e-da-ni*⌉ *me-e-ḫu-ni*
II. 7’ [ku-it-ma-an MU-a]n-ni ke-e-da-ni me-e-ḫ[u-ni]
2 [*I-N*]*A*$^{?}$ ⌈ITU.8⌉.KAM *pa-ra-a ma-a-an-ma A-NA* ^{d}UTU-*ŠI*

a)

---

x+1 As long as His Majesty (is$^{?}$) u[p in ...],
2 until he [returns] from (his) mission,
3 if then for His Majesty fr[om ...]
4 we [will] have nothing to fear [?]
5 Through the ‘Old Woman’ a[nd] the diviner: [(un)favorable].

---

b)

x+1 [...] ... favorable.

---

2 [Concerning this fact] that the accession to kingship was ascertained,
3 [if an il]lness also keep[s] being ascertained through the oracle inquiry,
4-5 [if, how]ever, it does not for His Majesty annul (his) access[ion] to kingship
6 [Through the ‘Ol]d Woman’: [un$^{?}$]favorable.

---

7 [Concerning this fact that t]hrou[gh] the diviner also it was unfavorable,
8 (and that) because of [the il]lness [of the Sungoddess of Arinna] the deity(‘s statue) was ascer[tained],
9 we [conduct]ed [the following inquiry] and the Sungoddess of Arinna was ascerta[ined].

II. x+2 [...] whe[n ...]
3 [His Majesty] will [si]t down [in kingship], un[til ...]
4 [...] ... His Majesty ... [...]
5 [...] nothing [...]
6 [Through the ‘Old Woman’ ... (un)favorable.]

---

1 If then, [until] the next [y]ear at this time
II. 7’ [I]f then, [until] the next [yea]r at this ti[me]
2 [i]n the eighth month you, [o god]s, foresee for His Majesty

II.7' *I-NA*$^{?}$ ITU.8.KAM] (8') [pa-ra-a ma-a-a]n$^{?}$-ma *A-NA* ^{d}UTU-*ŠI*

3 [DINGIR.M]EŠ TI-*tar* GAM-*an še-ek-te-ni* TI-*an-za-aš*

II. 8' DINGIR.MEŠ TI[-tar GAM-an še-ek-te-ni] (9') [TI-an-za-aš]

4 [*A-N*]*A* SAG.DU ^{d}UTU-*ŠI da-pí-an da-pí-za* (erasure)

II. 9' ⌜*A*⌝-*NA* SAG.DU ^{d}UTU-*ŠI* da-pí-an [da-pí-za]

5 [SIG$_5$-]*in nu* IGI-*zi-iš* UDU-*iš* SIG$_5$-*ru*

II. 9' SIG$_5$-in]

6 [EGIR-]*ma* NU.⌜SIG$_5$⌝-*du* IGI-*zi-iš* UDU-*iš*

(Room for ca.11 lines left open in I.)

I. 7 [*IŠ-TU* ^{MUNUS}Š]U.GI ⌜IR-*TUM QA-TAM-MA*⌝[-*pát nu* KIN SIG$_5$-*ru*]

8 [*pa-an-ku-uš-*]⌜*za* ZAG⌝[-*tar ŠA* LUGAL-*i̯a A-DAM-MA* ME-*aš*]

9 [*na-at* DIN]GIR.MAḪ-*ni p*[*a-iš INA* UD.2.KAM]

10 [*nu-kán* DINGI]R.MEŠ-*aš INA* UD.3.K[AM]

11 [ME-*aš nu-k*]*án* DINGIR.MEŠ-*aš* S[IG$_5$(?)]

II. 10' [*IŠ-T*]*U* ⌜^{MUNUS}⌝ŠU.GI [SIG$_5$(?)]

I. 12 [*A-NA* ^{d}UTU-*Š*]*I-kán ku-it* LUGAL-*u-iz-na-*⌜*ni a*⌝[-*ša-a-tar*]

13 [*du-u̯a-a-an*] *pa-ra-a ar-ḫa za-lu-ki-iš-ta*

14 [*ma-a-an-ma-z*]*a-kán ku-it-ma-an* ^{d}UTU-*ŠI*

15 [LUGAL-*u-iz-na-n*]*i e-ša-ri ku-it-ma-an-kán*

16 [*a-pí-i̯a*(?) EGI]R-*pa-an-da ma-a-an-ma* ^{d}UTU-*ŠI*

17 [*ḫa-ad-du-liš*] *A-NA* SAG.DU-*ŠU-ši Ú-UL ku-it*[-*ki* ḪUŠ-*u-e-ni*]

18 [*nu* IGI-*zi-i*]*š* UDU-*iš* SIG$_5$-*ru* EGIR-*ma* NU.SIG$_5$-*d*[*u*]

(Room for ca.10 lines left open)

---

19 [*IŠ-TU* ^{MUNUS}ŠU.G]I IR-*TUM QA-TAM-MA-pát n*[*u* KIN SIG$_5$-*ru*]

20 [DINGIR-*LUM-za*] ⌜*da*⌝-*pí-an* ZI-*an* T[I$^{?}$-*tar-ra* ME-*aš na-at* ... *pa-iš*$^{?}$]

21 [*INA* UD.2.KAM ... [20]-]⌜*uš*⌝-*za* ZAG-*tar* MU-*an* x[ME-*aš*]

22 [*na-at* DINGIR.MAḪ-*ni p*]*a-iš INA* UD.3.KAM ⌜*ŠA*⌝[DINGIR.MEŠ *mi-nu-mar*$^{ḪI.A}$]

23 [ME-*aš nu-ká*]*n A-NA* GIG.TUR [SIG$_5$/NU.SIG$_5$]

---

[20] A restoration to LUGAL- would seem to fit the space available whereas *pa-an-ku-* seems too long. All restorations in this paragraph are tentative.

II. 7' [in the eighth month] (8') you, o gods, [foresee] for His Majesty
3 life, (and) he will live,
II. 8' li[fe, (9') (and) he will live,]
4 (and) [fo]r His Majesty's person everything in every way (will be)
II. 9' (and) for His Majesty's person everything [in every way (will be)]
5 [favor]able, then let the first sheep be favorable,
II. 9' [favorable],
6 but let [the following (one)] be unfavorable. The first sheep:

---

7 [Through the 'Ol]d Woman' [that] same question. [Then let the *kin* be favorable.]
8 [The *panku* took] for itself RIGHT[NESS and the KING'S BLOOD]
9 [and] g[ave them to the MO]THERGODDESS. [On the second day ...]
10 [... (it is) with the GO]DS. On the third day [...]
11 [(s)he took and (it is)] with the GODS; fa[vorable].

II. 10' [Thro]ugh the 'Old Woman': [favorable].

---

12 As to the fact that [for His Maje]sty the a[ccession] to kingship
13 was further postponed,
14 [if then], until His Majesty
15 sits down [in kingshi]p (and) for as long as
16 [(he will be) there afte]rwards, if then His Majesty
17 [(will be) in good health] (and) [we will have] nothi[ng to fear for] his person,
18 [then let the fir]st sheep be favorable but le[t] the following be one unfavorable.

---

19 [Through the 'Old Woma]n' that same question. T[hen let the *kin* be favorable].
20 [The DEITY took for him/herself] the entire SOUL [and] L[IFE and gave it to ...].
21 [On the second day the KIN]G? [took] for himself RIGHTNESS, the YEAR (and) ... [...]
22 [and to the MOTHERGODDESS] he [g]ave [it/them]. On the third day [the GODS]' [FAVORS]
23 [he took and] (it is) with the SMALL ILLNESS; [(un)favorable].

---

24 [ ]⸢^{d}⸣UTU-*ŠI* LUGAL-*u-iz-n*[*a-ni*
II. 11 [ku-i]t-ma-an-za-kán ^{d}UTU-*ŠI* LUGAL-iz-na-ni e-ša-r[i *A-NA* ^{d}UTU-*ŠI*-kán(?)]

25 [*a-š*]*a*-⸢*tar*⸣? *ku-it* [
II. 12 [LUG]AL-iz-na-ni a-ša-a$^{!}$-tar ku-it za-lu-ka$_4$-nu-me-en

26 [ ] ⸢*ma*⸣?-*a*[-*an*
II. 12 [na-at GAM-an] (13) [a]r-ḫa GAR-ru ma-a-an-ma-za-kán ku-it-ma-an ⸢^{d}⸣[UTU-*ŠI*]
14 [LUGAL-i]z-na-ni e-ša-ri ku-it-ma-an-kán *A-NA* LU[GAL-iz-na-ni]
15 [EGI]R-pa-an-da ma-a-an-ma DINGIR.MEŠ *A-NA* ^{d}UTU-*ŠI* x[
16 [GI]G GAM-an *Ú-UL* ku-in-ki še-ek-te-ni *A-NA* ⸢^{d}⸣[UTU-*ŠI*-i̯a-kán(?)]
17 [LUGAL]-iz-na-ni a-ša-a-tar UN-aš *IŠ-TU* MUD *Ú-U*[*L* ar-ḫa]
18 [d]a-a-i *IŠ-TU* ^{MUNUS}ŠU.GI *IŠ-TU* ^{LÚ}ḪAL-i̯a x[

---

19 [ku-i]t-ma-an-kán *A-NA* EZEN$_4$ a-ša-an-na-aš EGIR-pa [
20 [ma-]⸢a⸣-an-ma ^{d}UTU-*ŠI* *A-NA* EZEN$_4$ a-ša-an-na-aš x[
21 [ma-a]-⸢an⸣ ar-ḫa *Ú-UL* ku-iš-ki u̯a-at-ku-nu-z[i
22 [*IŠ-TU*] ⸢^{MUNUS}ŠU.GI⸣ ^{LÚ}ḪAL-i̯a x x x x [

Rev. iii?

x+1[21] [ ]x x[
2 [ ]x x x[
3 [ ]*ne*?[
4 [ ]⸢GAM⸣-*an ar*-⸢*ḫa*⸣[
5 [ ]x x?[

(break of three lines)[22]

9[23] [ ]x? ⸢ITU⸣[
10 [*a-ri-i̯a-še*-?]⸢*eš*⸣-*na-aš* x[24][
11 [*nu* KIN]⸢SIG$_5$-*ru*⸣ LUGAL-*uš-za* ZAG-*t*[*ar* ME-*aš*]
12 [*na-a*]*t pa-an-ka$_4$-u-i pa-iš* ⸢*I-NA*⸣[UD.2.KAM
13 [ZA]G[25]-*tar* MU-*an-na* ME-*ir nu-kán* EGI[R
14 [*I-N*]*A* UD.3.KAM *a-aš-šu* ME-*an na-at* ⸢DINGIR⸣[
15 [SU]M-*an* SIG$_5$

(blank space until end of column)

[21] The position of the first five lines relative to VI 9 rev., i.e. the space to be assumed in the break on the left, is not clear.
[22] So according to the remarks by A. Walther in KUB XVIII ad 59.
[23] = VI 9 rev. 1' according to Walther, loc.cit.
[24] See the improved reading by Walther, loc.cit.
[25] See the improved reading by Walther, loc.cit.

24 [Until] His Majesty [will sit down] in kingsh[ip,] – that [
II. 11' [Un]til His Majesty wi[ll] sit down in kingship, – that [for His Majesty]
25 [we have postponed the acc]ession [to kingship,
II. 12' we have postponed the accession to [ki]ngship, let [that]
13' be out of consideration now – if, until His M[ajesty]
14' will sit down in [kings]hip, for as long as he will be in ki[ngship]
15' [aft]erwards, if then, o gods, you do not foresee for His Majesty
16' any [il]lness, [and (if)] from H[is Majesty]
17' no man will [t]ake [away] with bloodshed the accession to [king]ship,
18' through the 'Old Woman' and the diviner ... [...].

19' [U]ntil [he will] re[turn$^{?}$] for the festivity of the accession,
20' [i]f for the festivity of the accession His Majesty [...]
21' [(and) i]f no one [will] dispel (him), [?]
22' [through] the 'Old Woman' and the diviner ... [...].

iii$^{?}$

(no translation feasible)

10 [of the inqui]ry$^{?}$ ... [...]
11 [then] let [the *kin*] be favorable. The king [took] himself RIGHTN[ESS ...]
12 [and] gave [i]t (or: [th]em) to the *panku*. On [the second day ...]
13 [RIGH]TNESS and the YEAR they took and bac[k ...]
14 [O]n the third day GOOD (was) taken and [to] the DEITY [...] it
15 (was) [gi]ven; favorable.

3.2.2 L 77+XLIX 73 r. col.[26]

x+1 [ ]x-*ir*[
2 *nu-ká*[*n* EGIR-*pa* ^{d}]DAG-*ti INA* UD.3.K[AM
3 *kar-p*[*í-in* ME-*aš*] *nu-kán an-da* S[IG$_5$-*u-i* SIG$_5$(?)]

---

4 *A-NA* ^{d}[UTU-*ŠI-ká*]*n ku-it* LUGAL-*iz-na-ni* [*a-ša-a-tar*]
5 *du-u̯a-a-a*[*n pa-r*]*a-a ar-ḫa za-lu-kiš*[*-ta*]
6 *ma-a-an-ma-z*[*a-kán*] *ku-it-ma-an* ^{d}UTU[-*ŠI* LUGAL-*iz-na-ni*]
7 *e-ša-ri ku-*⌈*it*⌉*-ma-an-kán a-pí-i̯*[*a* EGIR-*pa-an-da*]
8 *ma-a-an-ma* ^{d}UTU-*ŠI ḫa-ad-du-liš* (Rasur) *A-NA* [SAG.DU-*ŠU Ú-UL*]
9 *ku-it-ki* ḪUŠ-*u-e-ni nu* ⌈KIN⌉ SIG$_5$-*r*[*u*
10 *pa-an-ku-uš-za* ZAG-*tar* [*Š*]*A* LUGAL-*i̯a A-D*[*AM-MA* ME-*aš*]
11 *na-at* DINGIR.MAḪ-*ni* ⌈*pa*⌉[-*i*]*š I-NA* U̯[D.2.KAM
12 *nu-kán* DINGIR.MEŠ-*aš I-N*[*A* UD.3.KAM
13 ME-*aš nu-kán* DINGIR.⌈MEŠ⌉[-*aš* SIG$_5$]

---

14 *ku-it-ma-an-za-ká*[*n*
15 [*n*]*u* LUGAL-*iz-na-n*[*i*
16 [o o]x x[

(break)

3.3 XLIX 2(+$^{?}$)XVIII 6[27]

XLIX 2 i

x+1 [ ] x [
2 [ ]x ITU x[
3 [*t*]*i-i̯a-z*[*i*
4 [ ] *QA-TAM-MA ti*[-
5 [*-kán* *-i̯*]*a pa-ra-a*
6 [*ar-ḫa Ú-UL z*]*a-*⌈*lu-ga*⌉*-nu-um-me-e-ni*
7 [*nu-kán*] x-x-⌈*š/ta*⌉[28]-*aš* DINGIR-*LUM* ḪUL-*u-i*
8 [*an-da-an*] *Ú-UL ne-i̯a-ši nu* ^{d}*Ḫi-iš-ḫu-ra-aš*
9 [SIxSÁ-*d*]*u*$^{?}$ MUŠ *ŠUM* LUGAL-*kán IŠ-TU* MU.KAM.ḪI.A GÍ[D.DA]
10 [*ú-it*] *na-aš-kán* GUNNI *pa-it*

[26] The fragment L 77 still preserves traces of a left (first of fourth) column in the intercolumnium next to r. col. line 8': -]*i-nu-ut*.

[27] Since according to the handcopy of XVIII 6 the surface of this piece of the tablet seems to be badly worn, not all damages are indicated by means of small brackets (⌈ ⌉).

[28] For this reading see Chapter V in the commentary ad LII 92, 7'.

x+2 and [(it is$^?$) back] with the THRONE[-DEITY].[29] On the third day [...]
3 [took] wra[th] and (it is) in fa[vorable (position); favorable].

---

4 As to the fact that for His [Majesty the accession] to kingship
5 was [furth]er postpon[ed],
6 if then, until His Majes[ty] sits down [in kingship]
7 (and) for as long as (he will be) the[re afterwards],
8 if then His Majesty (will be) in good health (and) for [his person] we will
9 have [no]thing to fear, then l[et] the *kin* be favorable. [...]
10 The *panku* [took] for itself RIGHTNESS, and the KING's BL[OOD]
11 and ga[v]e it to the MOTHERGODDESS. On the [second] da[y ...]
12 and (it is) with the GODS. O[n the third day ...]
13 (s)he took and (it is) [with] the GODS; [favorable].

---

14 Until [...]
15 [an]d to kingshi[p
16 [...] ... [...]

i

x+2 [..] ... month ... [...]
3 [... (s)he s]tep[s ...]
4 [...] likewise ... [...]
5 [If$^?$ ...] ... we will [not] further
6 postpone
7 [and] you, o god, will not in evil
8 turn [towards ...], then [le]t$^?$ Ḫišḫura
9 [ascertain$^?$]. The snake (called) NAME OF THE KING
10 [came] from LO[NG] YEARS and went to the HEARTH.

[29] Cf. above KBo II 6+ iii 27.

11 [*na-aš-ká*]*n ku-ra-ak-ki pa-it*
12 [*na-aš-za*]⌈*ku*⌉*-ra-ak-ki kar-ap-ta*
13 [ ]x *nu-kán* GUNNI KU$_6$*-un e-ep-*⌈*ta*⌉
14 [ ]x GUNNI-*pát* GAM 𒑱*pa-aš-ta*
15 [*na-aš-kán*] TI*-an-ni pa-it nu* KAxU*-iš* ⌈*ar*⌉*-ḫa*
16 [*e-ep-t*]*a nu* EGIR*-pa* BAL*-nu-ut*
17 [*nu-kán* T]A$^{??}$ GUNNI *ú-it nu nam-ma*
18 [KU$_6$*-un*] *e-ep-ta na-an* GAM 𒑱*pa-aš-ta*
19 [MUŠ]⌈*ŠUM*⌉$^?$ LUGAL*-ma-za a-ra-aš kar-ap-ta*
20 [MU]Š *a-ri-i̯a-*⌈*še*⌉[*-eš*]*-na-aš-ma-kán* GUNNI*-za ú-it*
21 [*nu*]⌈^{d}U ^{URU}⌉[*Ḫ*]*al-pa an*[*-d*]*a* KAR*-at*
22 [ ]x *pa-it na-aš-kán* GUNNI
23 [ ]x*-ta-ri na-aš-kán ku-ra-ak-ki*
24 [*pa-it nu-kán* Š]À É.LUGAL *pa-it*
25 [*-n*]*u-ut nu la-aḫ-la-ḫi-im-*⌈*ma-an*⌉
26 [ ]x *nu-za* EGIR*-pa* ME*-aš*
27 [ ]⌈*pa-it*⌉ *nu nam-ma* KU$_6$[*-un*$^?$]
28 [*e-ep-ta na-an*$^?$ *ku-r*]*a-ak-ki* [

(break of unknown length)

XVIII 6 i

x+1 [ ]x-⌈*i̯a*⌉ x x?
2 [ ]x? SIG$_5$

---

3 [*ma-a-an*$^?$(-) *u*]*d-da-ni-i-ma*
4 [*-z*]*i nu-kán ma-aḫ-ḫa-an*
5 [(-)*Š*]*UM*[30] LUGAL*-UT-TI*
6 [*-z*]*i nu-uš-ši-kán pa-ra-a*
7 [*-z*]*i nu* GIM*-an A-NA* ^{d}UTU*-ŠI*
8 ⌈*a-ri-i̯a-še*⌉*-eš-na-za* SIxSÁ*-ri*
9 *nu-za-kán a-pu-u-un pí-an ar-ḫa* (erasure)
10 *pé-eš-ši-i̯a-zi a-pa-a-aš-ma-za-kán*
11 *QA-TAM-MA e-ša-ri ma-a-an-ma-za* x x[31]
12 *QA-TAM-MA ma-la-a-an* ⌈*ḫar*⌉$^?$- x x x$^?$

[30] Instead of MUŠ *Š*]*UM* LUGAL*-UTTI* "the snake (called) NAME OF KINGSHIP" (cf. Ph.H.J. Houwink ten Cate, AoF 23 (1996) 72 n. 56) a restoration to *AŠ-Š*]*UM* LUGAL*-UTTI* "for (the sake of) kingship" is also possible and perhaps more likely since the description of the priest's observation of the animal's movements in the basin does not begin until line 17ff.

[31] At this point one expects either DINGIR*-LUM* "o god" or DINGIR.MEŠ "o gods" in this expression but both are equally difficult to read into the traces drawn in the handcopy.

11 [It] went to the PILLAR$^?$
12 [and it] lifted$^?$ [itself] at the PILLAR$^?$
13 [...] ... and it caught a fish at the HEARTH
14 [and] it swallowed [it] down ... right at the HEARTH.
15 [It] went to LIFE and the MOUTH[32]
16 i[t hel]d away and stirred up again.
17 [Fro]m$^?$ the HEARTH (it) came and again
18 caught [a fish] and swallowed it down.
19 [The snake (called)] NAME OF THE KING'S FRIEND$^?$ lifted$^?$ itself,
20 while [the sna]ke of the ORACLE came from the HEARTH
21 [and] encountered the STORMGOD OF ḪALPA[33]
22 [It ...] ... went and at the HEARTH it
23 [...] ... and to the PILLAR$^?$ it
24 [went and i]nto the PALACE it went
25 [and ca]used [to ...]. AGONY
26 [...] and it retreated.
27 [...] it went and again a fish
28 [it caught and ... at/to the PI]LLAR$^?$ [...]

(i)

x+2 [...] ... ; favorable.

---

3 [If ... over the m]atter, however,
4 [...] ... and just as$^?$
5 [... for the s]ake of$^?$ kingship
6 [...] ... and for/to him$^?$
7 [...] ... and just as for His Majesty
8 it will be ascertained through an oracle inquiry:
9 will he throw him/it$^?$ away (for himself$^?$)
10 but will he
11 likewise sit down (on the throne)? If then ...
12 [will] have thus approved [and]

[32] = (to) slander? Cf. HW^2 E 70, and G. Beckman, StBoT 29, 38.
[33] For the Stormgod of Ḫalpa in snake oracles compare IBoT I 33, 22, 43 and 44.

13 *A-NA* ^{d}UTU-*ŠI* ⌈UD.KAM.ḪI.A ITU.KAM.ḪI.A⌉[?[34]]
14 *ke-e-ez-za* ⌈INIM-*za Ú*⌉[*-UL*]
15 *ma-ni-in-ku-*⌈*u̯a*⌉- x x x x x x -*zi*?
16 *nu* ^{d} x x x illegible traces SIG$_5$ x-⌈*du*⌉?
17 MUŠ *ŠUM* LUGAL-*U*[*T-TI*?] illegible traces *a-ú-um-me-e*[*n*]
18 ⌈GAM? *ḫar*⌉-*a*[*k-ta*?] illegible traces *nu-kán* ^{d}UTU ^{d}x x
19 illegible traces *na-aš-kán ku-ra-ak-ki* x x
20 illegible traces *-aš*? *kar-ap-ta*
21 illegible traces MUŠ *A-NA* GUNNI
22 illegible traces *na-an a-pí-i̯a-pát*
23 illegible traces[35] MUŠ *a-ri-i̯a-še-eš-na-aš-ma-kán*
24 illegible traces ⌈*pa*?-*it*⌉ *nu* ^{d}U? *pí-ḫa-am-mi-in*
25 illegible traces *-e-ez-za-ma*
26 illegible traces MUŠ *an-da* KAR-*at*

(end of column)

XLIX 2 ii[36]

x+1 [o] x [
2 ⌈*nu*⌉ MUŠ[
3 *a-pa-a-aš-k*[*án*?
4 MUŠ *ku-*⌈*iš*⌉[
5 *ti-i̯a-an-za* x[
6 *a-ú-um-me-en*[
7 *pa-it nu* EGIR[
8 *na-aš-kán ti-a*[*n-*
9 *ḫa-da-an-ti* x[
10 MUŠ *ŠUM* LUGAL-*m*[*a*(-)
11 *nu-*⌈*kán*⌉ *a-pa-a*[*-aš*
12 *ar-ḫa* ⌈ME⌉?[-
13 *na-aš-*⌈*kán*⌉[
14 *na-aš-*⌈*kán*⌉[
15 *na-aš*[(-)
16 *na-a*[*š*(-)
17 x[

(break of unknown length)

[34] There is still room available for a restoration MU.KAM.ḪI.A "years", cf. the example for this sequence in combination with the verb *maninkuu̯aḫḫ-* "to shorten" in the CHD L-N 171a.

[35] Possibly GAM *ḫar-ak-ta*, cf. XVIII 6 iv 8-9.

[36] A translation of the beginnings of lines in XLIX 2 ii-iii and XVIII 6 ii-iii is not worthwhile.

13 for His Majesty, (his) days, months [?]
14 through this deed [will] n[ot]
15 short[en? (vel sim.)[37]],
16-26 (no translation feasible)

[37] There can be little doubt as to the general sense of this sentence, but the exact translation will differ according to the restoration of the practically illegible sign traces in this line. Whether one thinks of a form from *maninkuu̯aḫḫ-* "to shorten", *maninkuu̯ant-* "short", *maninkuu̯andaḫḫ-* "to make short" or *maninkuešš-* "to become short", they all are very difficult to reconcile with the traces drawn in the handcopy.

XVIII 6 ii

x+1 *nu-za* EGIR-*pa* ME-*aš*[
2 *na-aš-kán ku-ra-a*[*k-ki*
3 MUŠ *ŠUM* LUGAL-*ma*[
4 *na-aš-kán A-NA*[
5 *na-aš-kán A-NA*[
6 *na-aš-kán A-NA*[
7 x x x ⸢*lu*?-*lu*⸣?[-*t*°
8 *na-aš-k*[*án A-N*]*A*? [
9 x [ ]x[

(break of approximately ten lines with few illegible traces)

19" ⸢*nu*⸣[
20" *nu*[
21" *nu*-⸢*uš*⸣[
22" *nu*-⸢*uš*⸣[
23" MUŠ[
24" *nu-za*[
25" *na*[-
26" *na*[-
(end of column)

XVIII 6 iii

x+5? x[
6 *na*[-
7 x[
8 x[

(break of unknown length)

XLIX 2 iii

x+1 *na*[-
2 *na*-⸢*an*⸣[(-)
3 *nu-kán*[
4 *A-NA* dU[
5 *na-an-kán*[
6 *na-an A-N*[*A*
7 MUŠ *ŠUM* [LUGAL-?
8 *a-ú-um*[*-me-en*
9 *pa-it n*[*u*?
10 ⸢*na-an*⸣[(-)

(break of unknown length)

(For the remnants of the columns ii and iii no translation will be given.)

XVIII 6 iv

1 [G]IM-*an-kán lu-lu-ti pé-e-da-aš*
2 *a<-pé>*[38]*-e-ez-za-ma-aš-kán I-NA* EGIR.UD.KAM (erased: *pa-it*)
3 *pa-it na-aš-kán* TI-*an-ni pa-it*
4 *na-aš-kán A-NA* MU.KAM.ḪI.A GÍD.DA *pa-it*
5 MUŠ *ta-ma-a-iš-ma-kán A-NA* GUNNI
6 KU$_6$-*un e-ep-ta* (erasure)
7 *na-an-kán A-NA* ^{d}U ^{URU}*Tal-ma-li-i̯a*
8 *pé-e-da-aš na-an a-pí-i̯a* (erasure)
9 GAM *ḫar-ak-ta* MUŠ *ŠUM* LUGAL-*ma-kán*
10 ŠÀ É.LUGAL *pa-it* (erasure)
11 *na-an-za-an* MUŠ *a-ri-i̯a-še-eš-na-aš*
12 *kar-ap-ta* SIG$_5$

(remainder of column uninscribed)

3.4 XVI 20

x+1 [*u̯a-*]*aḫ-*⸢*nu*⸣*-um-m*[*e-en*
2 [*nu-za-kán*]⸢^{d}⸣UTU-*ŠI* LUGAL[*-u-iz-na-ni e-ša-ri ma-a-an-ma-za*]
3 [*A-NA* ^{d}]⸢UTU⸣-*ŠI I-NA* ITU.[x.KAM LUGAL-*iz-na-ni a-ša-a-tar*]
4 [*ma-la-a-a*]*n ḫar-te-ni* ⸢*A-NA* SAG.DU⸣[^{d}UTU-*ŠI*
5 [ ]x SIG$_5$-*in* KI.MIN *nu* KIN SIG$_5$-⸢*ru*⸣ x[
6 [o o NINDA.GUR$_4$.R]A *iš-pa-an-du-zi* ME-*ir nu*[*-uš-ma-aš* GÙB-*za*]
7 [GAR-*ri* DINGIR-*LU*]*M-za* EGIR-*an ar-ḫa kar-pí-i*[*n* ... ME-*aš*]
8 [*nu-kán A-NA*]⸢GIG⸣.TUR NU.SIG$_5$

(blank space - partly erased - of approximately 4 lines)

---

9 ⸢MU⸣[*ku*$^?$*-i*]*t*$^?$ *u̯a-aḫ-nu-um-me-en nu A-NA* MU-*ti ku*[*-it* ITU.12.KAM SIxSÁ-*at*$^?$]
10 *nu-*⸢*za-kán*⸣ ^{d}UTU-*ŠI* LUGAL-*u-iz-na-ni e-ša-ri m*[*a-a-an-ma-za*]
11 *A-NA* ^{d}UTU-*ŠI I-NA* ITU.12.KAM LUGAL-*iz-na-ni* [*a-ša-a-tar*]
12 *ma-la-a-an ḫar-te-ni A-NA* SAG.DU ^{d}UTU-*Š*[*I da-pí-an*]
13 SIG$_5$-*in* KI.MIN *nu* KIN SIG$_5$-*ru IŠ-TU* G[IG GAL]
14 ḪUL-*u-u̯a-zi-i̯a iš-tar-na ar-ḫa* ⸢*ú*⸣[*-it*]
15 *iš-pa-an-du-zi-i̯a* MU TI-*tar-ra* ME-*a*[*š*]
16 *I-NA* UD.2.KAM LUGAL-*uš-za* ZAG-*tar da-pí-an* [ME-*aš*]

[38] Since a reading A-*ēz*- does not seem to make any sense whether read sumerographically or Hittite, this emendation is proposed (one could also opt for *ke*$^!$*-e-ez-*) but the sequence x-*e-ez-za-ma* in XVIII 6 i 25, where the x does not seem to be either *a-pé-* or *ke-*, calls for caution.

iv

1 [W]hen it brought (something) to GOOD FORTUNE
2 it went from there to the FUTURE,
3 it went to LIFE
4 and it went to LONG YEARS.
5 A second snake at the HEARTH
6 caught a fish,
7 brought it to the STORMGOD OF THE CITY OF TALMALIYA
8 and there <it ... -ed>$^{?}$ it
9 (and) it died down. The snake (called) NAME OF THE KING, however,
10 went into the PALACE
11 and the snake of the ORACLE INQUIRY
12 lifted$^{?}$ it; favorable.

1 [... we c]hange[d ...],
2 [will] His Majesty [sit down in] kingship? [If then]
3 [for] His Majesty in the [...-th month] you have [approve]d [of (his) accession],
4 (and) for the person [of His Majesty everything]
5 [...] ... (will be) all right etc., then let the *kin* be favorable. ... [...]
6 [... THICK BREA]D (and) WINE RATION they took and [at their left]
7 [it lies. The deit]y [took] for her-/himself from behind WRAT[H ...]
8 [and (it is) at] the SMALL SICKNESS; unfavorable.

---

9 [Concerning the fact th]at we changed the year and th[at] in the year [the twelfth month was ascertained],
10 will His Majesty sit down in kingship? I[f then]
11 for His Majesty in the twelfth month you have approved of (his) acce[ssion]
12 (and) for the person of His Majest[y everything ...$^{?}$]
13 (will be) all right etc., then let the *kin* be favorable. From the [GREAT]
14 and EVIL IL[LNESS] (... $^{?}$) c[ame] through the middle
15 and too[k] WINE RATION, YEAR and LIFE.
16 On the second day the king [took] for himself RIGHTNESS entirely

17 ⸢*na*⸣-*an pa-an-ka*$_4$-*u-i pa-iš I-NA* UD.3.KAM [
18 ⸢ZÁLAG⸣.GA-*an mi-nu-mar-ra* ME-*aš* ⸢*nu-kán* DINGIR⸣[.MEŠ-*aš*

(break)

4. *KBo II 2 (CTH 577)*

This oracle inquiry is written on an almost completely preserved tablet containing four columns with an average number of 57 lines according to column i but the other columns contain fewer lines due to blank spaces. It probably was the first Hittite oracle text published in transliteration and

Obv. i

1 *ku-it-ma-an-kán* ^{d}UTU-*ŠI* ŠÀ ^{KUR}*Ne-ri-ik-ka*$_4$
2 *ku-it-ma-na-aš-kán ša-ra-a ú-iz-zi*
3 *ma-a-an-ma* ^{d}UTU-*ŠI* ⸗*ta-pa-aš-ša-aš an-da UL*
4 *ú-e-mi-i̯a-zi nu* SU.MEŠ SIG$_5$-*ru* NU.SIG$_5$

---

5 *ta-pa-aš-ša-aš ku-iš A-NA* ^{d}UTU-*ŠI* SIxSÁ-*at*
6 *ku-it-ma-na-aš a-pí-i̯a* ŠÀ KUR^{URU}*Ne-ri-ik-ka*$_4$
7 *na-an ta-pa-aš-ša-aš a-pí-i̯a* (erasure)
8 *ú-e-mi-i̯a-zi nu* MUŠEN *ḪUR-RI* NU.SIG$_5$-*du* NU.SIG$_5$

---

9 *IŠ-TU* ^{MUNUS}ŠU.GI IR-*TUM QA-TAM-MA-pát*
10 *nu* KIN NU.SIG$_5$-*du* GIG.TUR KUR-*TUM* MU.KAM-*na* ME-*aš*
11 *na-an pa-an-ga-u-u̯i*$_5$ *pa-iš* NU.SIG$_5$

---

12 *ma-a-an* ^{d}UTU-*ŠI* ⸗*ta-pa-aš-ša-aš*
13 ⸢*a*⸣-*pí-i̯a-pát* ŠÀ KUR^{URU}*Ne-ri-ik-ka*$_4$
14 *ú-e-mi-i̯a-zi ka-a-ma Ú*[39]-*UL*
15 *nu* IGI-*zi* MUŠEN *ḪUR-RI* SIG$_5$-*ru*
16 EGIR-*ma* NU.SIG$_5$-*du* IGI-*zi* MUŠEN *ḪUR-RI* NU.SIG$_5$
17 EGIR-*ma* SIG$_5$

---

18 *IŠ-TU* ^{MUNUS}ŠU.GI IR-*TUM QA-TAM-MA-pát*
19 *nu* KIN SIG$_5$-*ru* DINGIR-*LUM da-pí-an* ZI-*an* ME-*aš*

[39] Probably written over erasure.

17 and gave it?[40] to the *panku*. On the third day [...]
18 LIGHT and FAVOR (s)he took and (it is) [with] the GOD[S; ...].

---

translation with a commentary in BoSt. 3, 28-59 (1918) by B. Hrozný. J. Friedrich translated obv. i 1-33 and ii 18-28 in AO 25 (1925) 23-24. On the summarizing character of obv. ii 18-24 see above Chapter I.5, on the historical background see above Chapter III.3-4. KBo II 2 shows New Script.

i

1 As long as His Majesty (will be) within the country of Nerik
2 until he comes up (home),
3 if then fever?[41] will not befall His Majesty,
4 then let the exta be favorable; unfavorable.

---

5 Concerning the fever? which was ascertained for His Majesty:
6 As long as he (will be) there within the country of Nerik,
7 will the fever?
8 befall him there? Then let the *ḫurri*-bird be unfavorable; unfavorable.

---

9 Through the 'Old Woman' that same question:
10 Let the *kin* be unfavorable. The SMALL ILLNESS took COUNTRY and YEAR
11 and gave it to the *panku*; unfavorable.

---

12 If the fever? will befall His Majesty
13 right there within the country of Nerik
14 but not here,
15 then let the first *ḫurri*-bird be favorable
16 but the following one unfavorable. The first *ḫurri*-bird unfavorable,
17 the following one favorable.

---

18 Through the 'Old Woman' that same question:
19 Let the *kin* be favorable. The DEITY took the ENTIRE SOUL

[40] If the enclitic pronoun acc.c. *-an* refers to ZAG-*tar* in the previous line there is gender incongruence here. Or was ZAG-*tar* followed by another common gender noun in the break (e.g. *dapian*[*dan* ZI-an "(and) the entire SOUL")?

[41] On *tapašša-*, traditionally rendered as "fever" see J. Tischler, HEG T, D 121-123.

20 *na-an-za-an*<<*-kán*>> *kar-pí* ME-*iš* NU.SIG$_5$

---

21 *ki-i ku-it ku-u-uš* MUŠEN *ḪUR-RI* ⸢*kal*⸣*-la-ra-an-ni*
22 *ar-ḫa ap-pa-an-ta-at*
23 DINGIR-*LIM* 𒑱*ta-pa-aš-ša-an A-NA* ^{d}[U]TU-*ŠI*
24 ⸢*ka*⸣*-a-i̯a uš-ki-ši nu* MUŠEN *ḪUR-RI* NU.SIG$_5$-*du*![42]
25 NU.SIG$_5$

---

26 *IŠ-TU* ^{MUNUS}ŠU.GI IR-*TUM QA-TAM-MA-pát*
27 *nu* KIN NU.SIG$_5$-*du* DINGIR-*LUM-*⸢*za da*⸣*-pí-a*[*n*] ZI-*an*
28 *mi-nu-mar-ra* ME-*aš nu-kán A-NA* ⸢GIG⸣.TUR
29 NU.SIG$_5$

---

30 *ta-pa-aš-ša-aš ku-iš A-NA* ^{d}UTU-*ŠI* ⸢SIxSÁ*at*⸣
31 *pi-ra-an pa-ra-a ku-it-ma-an-za-aš*[43]*-kan*
32 LUGAL-*iz-na-an-ni na-a-u̯i*$_5$ *e-*⸢*ša*⸣*-ri*
33 *nu* MUŠEN *ḪUR-RI* NU.SIG$_5$-*du* NU.SIG$_5$

---

34 *IŠ-*⸢*TU*⸣ [^{MUNUS}ŠU.GI] IR-*TUM QA-TAM-MA-pát*
35 *nu* KI[N NU$^?$.SIG$_5$-*du* LUGAL-]⸢*uš*⸣*-za* ZAG-*tar* NINDA.GUR$_4$<.RA>-*i̯a* ME-*aš*
36 ⸢*nu*⸣[-]⸢*i*⸣?[44]
37 [*pa-iš*?]x-*da* SUD-*li*$_{12}$
38 [ ]
39 ⸢*kar-pí-in*⸣[45] ME[-*aš*] x x$^?$ x
40 SIG$_5$

---

41 *nu-kán* ^{d}UTU-*ŠI ḫup*<*-pí*>*-al-la-za-ma*
42 *ku-e-da-aš* UD.KAM.ḪI.A *u̯a-al-aḫ-ḫa-an-zi*
43 *pí-ra-an-kán ku-e-da-ni me-mi-i̯a-ni*
44 *la-aḫ-la-aḫ-ḫe-eš-ga-u-e-ni*
45 *na-an-kán* 𒑱*ta-pa-aš-ša-aš a-pí-i̯a*
46 *ku-iš-ki an-da ú-e-mi-i̯a-zi*
47 *nu* MUŠEN *ḪUR-RI* NU.SIG$_5$-*du* NU.SIG$_5$

---

48 *IŠ-TU* ^{MUNUS}ŠU.GI IR-*TUM QA-TAM-MA-pát*
49 *nu* KIN NU.SIG$_5$-*du* DINGIR.MEŠ *a-ra-e-er*
50 *ta-pa-aš-ša-an* ME-*ir na-an pa-an-ga-u-i* SUM-*ir*

[42] The tablet has TA which had already aroused B. Hrozný's suspicion: BoSt. 3, 34 n. 3.

[43] The order of the particle *-za* and the enclitic pers.pron. nom.sg.c. *-aš* is irregular (recte: *-aš-za-*); for a similar example see J. Friedrich, HE 1, 148 Anm. 1.

[44] A possible restoration would be *pa-an-ga-u-*]*i*.

[45] For this reading see already B. Hrozný, BoSt. 3, 36 n. 1.

20 and put it on WRATH; unfavorable.

---

21 Concerning this fact that these *ḫurri*-birds
22 were taken away in unfavorableness:
23 Do you, o god, see fever$^{?}$ for His Majesty
24 here too? Then let the *ḫurri*-bird be unfavorable.
25 Unfavorable.

---

26 Through the 'Old Woman' that same question:
27 Then let the *kin* be unfavorable. The DEITY took for him-/herself the ENTIRE SOUL
28 and FAVOR and (it is) in the SMALL ILLNESS;
29 unfavorable.

---

30 Concerning the fever$^{?}$ which was ascertained for His Majesty:
31 (Will it be) before he
32 will sit down in kingship?
33 Then let the *ḫurri*-bird be unfavorable. Unfavorable.

---

34 Through [the 'Old Woman'] that same question:
35 Let the *ki*[*n* be un$^{?}$favorable. The kin]g took himself RIGHTNESS and THICK BREAD
36 and [to ...] ...
37 [he gave. ...] ...
38 [...]
39 WRATH [(s)he] took. ... ;
40 favorable.

41-42 Or on the days on which His Majesty is (usually) beaten with the *ḫuppial*(*la*)[46]
43 – for which matter
44 we keep worrying –,
45 will some fever$^{?}$ at that moment
46 befall him?
47 Then let the *ḫurri*-bird be unfavorable. Unfavorable.

---

48 Through the 'Old Woman' that same question:
49 Let the *kin* be unfavorable. The gods arose,
50 they took FEVER$^{?}$ and gave it to the *panku*;

[46] To what particular (cultic?) event this sentence refers, remains unclear; for a form $^{\text{GAD/GIŠ}}$*ḫūppii̯alla*(=*i̯a*$^{?}$) cf. XXXI 77 ii 16 (ed. J. de Roos, Diss. 268 with n. 8 on p. 270, and 408).

51 NU.SIG$_5$

---

52 *ma-a-an* DINGIR-*LUM* ⸗*ta-pa-aš-ša-an*
53 *A-NA* ^{d}UTU-*ŠI* ŠÀ UD.KAM *ḫup-pí-al-la-aš-kán*[47]
54 *uš-ki-ši* ^{d}UTU-*ŠI* ⸗*ta-pa-aš-ša-aš*
55 *a-pé-e-da-aš-pát* UD.KAM-*aš an-da* KAR-*i̯a-zi*
56 *nam-ma-ma* KI.MIN *nu* MUŠEN *ḪUR-RI* SIG$_5$-*ru*
57 NU.SIG$_5$

(end of column)

Obv. ii

1 *IŠ-TU* ^{MUNUS}ŠU.GI$^{!}$ ⸢IR-*TUM*⸣ *QA*-[*T*]*AM-MA*[-*pát*]
2 *nu* KIN SIG$_5$-*ru*
3-6 (vacant)

---

7 *ma-a-an-kán pí-ra-an-*⸢*ma*⸣?
8 *la-aḫ-la-aḫ-ḫe-eš-ga-u*[-*e-*]*ni*
9 *nu e-ni ut-tar a-pí-i̯*[*a* o o]x-*ša-ni*[?][48]
10 *nam-ma-ma* DINGIR-*LUM A-NA* ^{d}UTU-*ŠI*
11 *dam-ma-in* ⸗*ta-pa-aš-ša-an*
12 *Ú-UL ku-in-ki uš-ki-ši*
13 *ku-it-ma-na-aš-kán INA* ^{URU}*Ḫat-ti še-*⸢*er*⸣
14 *nu TE*^{MEŠ} SIG$_5$-*ru* ^{GIŠ}ŠÚ$^{!}$[49].A-*ḫi* ⸢GÙB⸣-*an* NU.SIG$_5$

---

15 *IŠ-TU* ^{MUNUS}ŠU.GI IR-*TUM QA-TAM-MA-pát*
16 *nu* KIN SIG$_5$-*ru*
17 (vacat)

---

18 ⸗*ta-pa-aš-ša-an A-NA* ^{d}UTU-*ŠI*
19 DINGIR-*LUM ku-iš-ki i-i̯a-zi*
20 *IŠ-TU* ^{LÚ}ḪAL ^{MUNUS}ŠU.GI-*i̯a* SIxSÁ-*at*

---

21 DINGIR-*LIM-tar ku-it* SIxSÁ-*at*
22 *kat*[50]-*ta* (erasure) ⸢*a*⸣-*ri-i̯a-u-e-en*

[47] For other occurrences of the particle -*kan* in mid sentence cf. E. Neu, Linguistica 33 (1993, = FsÇop) 145-148.

[48] The CHD L-N 11a restores "⸗*tap*]*ašani*(?)". There is, however, no evidence for (⸗)*tapašša*- as an *n*-stem (cf. J. Tischler, HEG T,D 121-123) nor does the sign preceding -*šani* look like PA.

[49] This sign looks more like a repeated IZ/GIŠ.

[50] Cf. B. Hrozný, BoSt. 3, 40 n. 3: "Nach der Photographie scheint hier ein *kat*(?)-*ta* (...) vorzuliegen, während die Edition ein frageloses *an-ta* bietet. Eine Entscheidung könnte hier nur eine Besichtigung des Originals bringen."

51 unfavorable.

---

52 If you, o god, see fever$^{?}$
53 for His Majesty on the day of the *ḫuppialla*,
54 will fever$^{?}$ befall His Majesty
55 in those very days
56 but further etc.[51], then let the *ḫurri*-bird be favorable.
57 Unfavorable.

---

ii

1 Through the 'Old Woman' that s[am]e question:
2 Let the *kin* be favorable.
(3-6)

---

7 Since in advance
8 we keep worrying,
9 (will) that matter the[n/ther[e ...] ...
10 but do you further, o god, for His Majesty
11 do not see some
12 other fever$^{?}$
13 as long as he (will be) up in Ḫatti-land?
14 Then let the exta be favorable. The throne (is) on the left; unfavorable.

---

15 Through the 'Old Woman' that same question:
16 then let the *kin* be favorable.
17

18-19 Some deity will cause fever$^{?}$ for His Majesty.
20 Through the diviner and the 'Old Woman' it was ascertained.

---

21 (To find out) which deity was ascertained,
22 we continued the inquiry

[51] A sentence starting with *namma=ma* has not occurred yet in KBo II 2 but in all likelihood something like *namma=ma* DINGIR-*LUM ANA* ^{d}UTU-*ŠI dammain* :*tappaššan* UL *kuinki uškiši* (ii 10-12) is meant.

23 *nu* ^{d}UTU ^{URU}PÚ-*na* SIxSÁ-*at*
24 *zi-la-aš* NU.SIG$_5$

---

25 *nu dam-ma-iš ku-iš-ki* DINGIR-*LUM kar-dim*$_x$[52]-⸢*mi*⸣-*i̯a-u-an-za*
26 *nu a-ši* INIM GIG *a-pa-a-aš i-i̯a-zi*
27 *nu TE*$^{ME.EŠ}$ NU.SIG$_5$-*du zé-ḫi-li-ip-ši-ma-an*
28 NU.SIG$_5$

---

29 ^{d}UTU ^{URU}PÚ-*na ku-it A-NA* GIG ^{d}UTU-*ŠI*
30 *še-er* SIxSÁ-*at nu-za-kán pa-iz-zi* ^{d}UTU-*ŠI*
31 ^{d}UTU ^{URU}PÚ-*na* EGIR-*pa e-ep-z*[*i*]
32 *a-ri-i̯a-u-e-ni-ma nu ku-it* SIxSÁ[-*ta*]-*ri*
33 *nu A-NA* ^{d}UTU ^{URU}PÚ-*na a-*⸢*pa*⸣[-*a-at*]
34 SUM-*an-zi ma-a-an-ma-na-aš* ⸢^{d}⸣[UTU ^{URU}PÚ-*na*]
35 *iš-dam-ma-aš-ti a-ši*(-)*na*(-)x[[53] *Ú-UL*?]
36 *u̯a-aš-ta-nu-uz-zi* ⸢*nu*⸣ [*TE*$^{ME.EŠ}$ SIG$_5$-*ru*/NU.SIG$_5$-*du*]
37 ^{GIŠ}ŠÚ<.A>-*ḫi* GÙB-*an* x[ ]
38 *a-dam-ta-ḫi-iš*[ ]

---

39 ⸢*nam*⸣?<-*ma*> ⸢^{d}UTU ^{URU}PÚ-*na* ^{d}UTU-*ŠI máš-kán*⸣ *pa-a-i*
40 ⸢*ma*⸣-*al-ta-i-za-kán* KI.MIN
41 *nu TE*$^{ME.EŠ}$ SIG$_5$-*ru* 3-*ŠÚ Ú-UL ar-ḫa*
42 *ap-pa-at-ta-at*

---

43 *ma-a-an-za zi-ik-pát* ^{d}UTU ^{URU}PÚ-*na*
44 *kar-dim*$_x$-*mi-i̯a-u-u̯a-an-za*
45 *nu-ut-ták-kán a-ri-i̯a-še-eš-na-za*
46 2-*an na-a-u̯i*$_5$ *pa-a-i-u-e-ni*
47 *nam-ma-ma-ták-kán dam-ma-iš* DINGIR-*LUM*
48 *pa-ra-a Ú-UL ku-iš-ki a-ra-an-za*
49 *nu TE*$^{ME.EŠ}$ SIG$_5$-*ru* ZAG-*za* RA^{IṢ} NU.SIG$_5$

---

50 ^{d}UTU ^{URU}PÚ-*na ku-iš* SIxSÁ-*at*
51 ^{d}UTU ^{URU}PÚ-*na ŠA* ^{URU}PÚ-*na ku-iš*
52 ^{GIŠ}ZAG.GAR.RA *nu TE*$^{ME.EŠ}$ NU.SIG$_5$-*du*
53 *ni ši ke* 12 ŠÀ *DIR* SIG$_5$

[52] For the possible reading *dim*$_x$ (also below ii 44, iii 22, 25) of the sign DAM in this text see Chr. Rüster - E. Neu, HZL no. 298.

[53] Although a restoration to =*naš*(-) "us" seems attractive, this is not favored by the sign trace in the handcopy.

23 and the Sungoddess of Arinna was ascertained.
24 Outcome: unfavorable.

---

25 (Is) some other deity angry
26 and is that (deity) causing the aforementioned matter of the illness?
27 Then let the exta be unfavorable. *Zeḫi(-)lipšiman*[54];
28 unfavorable.

---

29 Concerning the fact that in connection with His Majesty's illness the
30 Sungoddess of Arinna was ascertained: His Majesty will go
31 (and) retreat to[55] the Sungoddess of Arinna.
32 We will then conduct an inquiry and what will be ascertain[e]d,
33 th[at] to the Sungoddess of Arinna
34 they will give. If you, o S[ungoddess of Arinna]
35 hear us and that (matter?) will [not?]
36 make u[s?] sin, then [let the exta be (un)favorable].
37 The throne on the left, ... [...]
38 *adamtaḫiš* [...].

---

39 Will His Majesty moreover give a gift to the Sungoddess of Arinna,
40 will he make a vow etc.?
41 Then let the exta be favorable. Thrice they were not
42 taken away?.[56]

---

43 If you alone, o Sungoddess of Arinna,
44 (are) angry
45 and through the inquiry
46 we have not yet gone to you a second time
47 but furthermore some deity other than you
48 has not come forward,[57]
49 then let the exta be favorable. On the right damage; unfavorable.

---

50 Concerning the Sungoddess of Arinna who was ascertained:
51 (Is) it the Sungoddess-of-Arinna of Arinna('s)
52 altar? Then let the exta be unfavorable.
53 *Ni(pašuri)*, *ši(ntaḫi)*, *ke(ldi)*, twelve coils; favorable.

[54] For this term see the discussion by M. Schuol, AoF 21 (1994) 260-261.

[55] Or: "take up again (the matter of)"? For this *appa(n) epp-* cf. HW^2 E 69a.

[56] Cf. above i 21-22 where *arha epp-* could be interpreted as a variant of SIxSÁ-*at/ḫandaittat* "were ascertained" (cf. similarly E. Neu, StBoT 5, 24 with n. 6); therefore here to be taken as "were (not) brought to conclusion/completed"?

[57] This translation is highly tentative. In view of what follows, it might be taken as if this paragraph inquires into the possibility whether an hypostasis of the goddess is involved. For the expression *parā ar-* see the commentary Ch. VI ad L 6+ ii 31'.

---

54 *nu* ^{d}UTU ^{URU}PÚ<-*na*> *ŠA* ^{URU}*Ḫat-ti-ma ku-iš*
55 *nu-kán e-da-ni me-mi-i̯a-ni zi-ik*
56 *pár-ri-an-ta ša-li-ik-ti*

Rev. iii

1 *nu TE*$^{ME.EŠ}$ SIG$_5$-*ru* ^{GIŠ}ŠÚ.⸢A⸣-*ḫi* GÙB-*an* NU.SIG$_5$

---

2 *nu* ^{d}UTU ^{URU}PÚ-*na* DUMU[58]-*an-na-aš-ma ku-iš*
3 *nu TE*$^{ME.EŠ}$ NU.SIG$_5$-*du* (erasure) GISKIM *ḫa-i-kal-li-ta*
4 NU.SIG$_5$

---

5 *ma-a-an-kán e-da-ni me-mi-i̯a-ni*
6 ^{d}UTU ^{URU}PÚ-*na* DUMU-*an-na-aš-pát*
7 *pí-ra-an ti-i̯a-zi*
8 *nu TE*$^{ME.EŠ}$ SIG$_5$-*ru ni ši ta ke*
9 *zi* GAR-*ri* 12 ŠÀ *DIR* SIG$_5$

---

10 ^{d}UTU ^{URU}PÚ-*na ku-it* DUMU-*an-na-aš* SIxSÁ-⸢*at*⸣!
11 *A-NA IK-RI-BI*$^{ḪI.A}$ *še-er*
12 *nu TE*$^{ME.EŠ}$ NU.SIG$_5$-*du* SAG.ME NU.SIG$_5$

---

13 *ma-a-an-za* ^{d}UTU ^{URU}PÚ-*na*
14 *zi-ik-pát* DUMU![59]-*an-na-aš*
15 *A-NA IK-RI-BI*$^{ḪI.A}$ *še-er kar<-dim*$_x$*-mi-i̯a>-u-u̯a-an-za*
16 *nam-ma-ma* KI.MIN *nu TE*$^{ME.EŠ}$ SIG$_5$-*ru*
17 ⸢*ni*⸣! *nu-kán* ZAG-*na-aš* KAxU-*i* NU.SIG$_5$

---

18 [*k*]*i-i ku-it zi-la-aš ki-ša-at*
19 [DIN]GIR-*LUM ku-it du-u̯a-an pa-ra-a*
20 [*š*]*al-la-kar-ta-an ḫar-ku-un*
21 *nu-*⸢*za*⸣ [DINGIR]-⸢*LUM*⸣! *a-pád-da-an še-er*
22 *kar-d*[*i*]*m*$_x$*-mi-i̯a-u-u̯a-an-za nu* ⸢*TE*$^{ME.EŠ}$ NU.SIG$_5$-*du*⸣
23 ^{GIŠ}ŠÚ.A!-*ḫi* GÙB-*an* NU.SIG$_5$

---

24 *ma-a-an-za* DINGIR-*LUM a-pád-da-an-pát še-*⸢*er*⸣
25 *kar-dim*$_x$*-mi-i̯a-u-u̯a-an-za*
26 *du-u̯a-an-ta ku-it pa-ra-a*
27 *šal-la-kar-ta-an ḫar-ku-un*
28 *nam-ma-ma* KI.MIN *nu TE*$^{ME.EŠ}$ SIG$_5$-*ru*

[58] Tablet has I.
[59] Tablet has I.

54 Or (is) it the Sungoddess of Arin<na> of Ḫatti-land,
55-56 and will you press on beyond that matter?

iii

1 Then let the exta be favorable. The throne on the left; unfavorable.

2 Or is it the Sungoddess of Arinna of Progeny?
3 Then let the exta be unfavorable. A sign towards the palace[60];
4 Unfavorable.

5 If in that matter
6 the Sungoddess of Arinna of Progeny indeed
7 steps forward,[61]
8 then let the exta be favorable. *Ni*(*pašuri*), *ši*(*ntaḫi*), *ta*(*nani*), *ke*(*ldi*),
9 a bladderworm lies, twelve coils; favorable.

10 Concerning the fact that the Sungoddess of Arinna of Progeny has been ascertained,
11 (is it) because of vows?
12 Then let the exta be unfavorable. SAG.ME; unfavorable.

13 If, o Sungoddess of Arinna,
14 it is only you of Progeny
15 (who are) angry because of vows
16 but further etc., then let the exta be favorable.
17 *ni*(*pašuri*) and in the mouth (it is) on the right[62]; unfavorable.

18 Concerning [th]is fact that as a result has come out
19 that I have until now
20 [o]ffended the [go]ddess,
21 (are) you, o [godd]ess, for that reason
22 angry? Then let the exta be unfavorable.
23 The throne on the left; unfavorable.

24 If you, o deity, (are) for that reason only
25 angry,
26 because until now
27 I have offended you
28 but further etc., then let the exta be favorable.

[60] For Hurrian *ḫaikalli* (or with article *ḫaikal*^{i}*ni*) "palace" see E. Neu, StBoT 32, 228-230, with literature.
[61] For this phrase see above Chapter V ad L 6+ ii 31'.
[62] Cf. M. Schuol, AoF 21 (1994) 255.

29 *TE*$^{\text{ME.EŠ}}$ *ši-i̯a-an* EGIR-*ŠU*!-*ma zi* SIG$_5$

(blank space of four lines)

---

30 *a-ši ku-iš*[63] ^{d}UTU ^{URU}PÚ-*na* DUMU-*an-na-aš*
31 *A-NA IK-RI-BI*$^{\text{ḪI.A}}$ *še-er* SIxSÁ-*at*
32 *nu* ^{d}UTU-*ŠI pu-nu-uš-ša-an-zi*
33 *ku-iš IK-RI-BU šar-ni-in-ku-u̯a-aš*[64]
34 *na-an šar-ni-in-kán-zi*
35 *Ú-UL-ma ku-iš šar-ni-*⌈*in*⌉[*-ku-u̯a-aš*]
36 *nu-uš-ši za-an-ki-*⌈*la*⌉[*-tar*
37 *ma-a-an-ma-za* DINGIR-*LUM m*[*a-*[65]]x x[
38 *nu TE*$^{\text{ME.EŠ}}$ SIG$_5$-*ru* NU.S[IG$_5$]

---

39 *nu IK-RI-BI*$^{\text{ḪI.A}}$*-ma* [*ku-i-e-eš Ú-UL*]
40 *šar-ni-in-ku-u-u̯a*[*-aš*[66]
41 *kat-ta-an-na za-*⌈*an-ki*⌉[*-la-tar* SUM-*an-zi*]
42 *IK-RI-BI*$^{\text{ḪI.A}}$[*-i̯a*? *šar-ni-in-kán-zi*]
43 DINGIR-*LUM-za* KI[.MIN
44 x[

---

45 *nu IK-RI-B*[*I*$^{\text{ḪI.A}}$ *ku-i-e-eš Ú-UL*?]
46 *šar-ni-in-*⌈*ku*⌉[*-u̯a-aš*

Rev. iv

1 *kat-ta-an-na za-an-ki-la-tar* ⌈SUM⌉*-an-zi*
2 DINGIR-*LUM-i̯a ku-it du-u̯a-an pa-ra-a*
3 *šal-la-kar-ta-an ḫar-ku*[67]*-un*
4 *nu a-pád-da-an-na še-er* SISKUR![68] SUM-*an-zi*
5 KI.MIN *nu TE*$^{\text{ME.EŠ}}$ SIG$_5$-*ru* (erasure)
6 *ke-eš-kán ne*!*-i̯a-at-ta-at* NU.SIG$_5$

---

7 *nu IK-RI-BI*$^{\text{ḪI.A}}$*-ma ku-i-e-eš*

[63] Last sign written over erasure.

[64] For this reading see A. Walther apud A. Götze, Ḫatt. 140.

[65] Probably some form of the verb *malai-* "to approve of" (e.g. *ma-la-a-ši* or *ma-la-a-an ḫar-ti*) has to be restored here; in view of the space available the addition of *kišan* "thus" seems less likely.

[66] Possibly the line ended here but one could also think of a restoration *nu-uš-ši* "and to her" for which compare above iii 36.

[67] Last sign written over erasure.

[68] The handcopy gives only two inscribed Winkelhaken.

29 The exta (are) pressed (together), behind it, however, (there is) a bladderworm; favorable.

---

30 Concerning that Sungoddess of Arinna of Progeny who
31 was ascertained because of vows:
32 they will ask His Majesty
33 which vow is to be fulfilled,
34 and that (one) they will fulfill.
35 The one, however, which [is] not [to be] fulfill[ed],
36 [they will not give] compensat[ion] (for) to her.
37 If then you, o goddess, [have (thus)] a[pproved$^{?}$],
38 then let the exta be favorable; unfa[vorable].

---

39 Or [concerning] the vows [that (are) not]
40 to [be] fulfilled, [?]
41 [will they give] later compensation
42 [as well as fulfill] the vows?
43 (Are) you, o goddess, e[tc.
44 ... [...].

---

45 [Concerning] the vows [which (are) not$^{?}$]
46 t[o be] fulfilled, [?]

iv

1 and [for which$^{?}$] later they will give compensation,
2 and concerning the fact that until now
3 I have offended the goddess,
4 will they for that reason too give an offering?
5 Etc. Then let the exta be favorable.
6 *Ke(ld)i* has turned; unfavorable.

---

7 The vows which

8 *šar-ni-in-ku-e-eš*[69] *na-aš šar-ni-in-kán-zi*
9 *kat-ta-an-na za-an-ki-la-tar* SUM-*an-zi*
10 *máš-kán-na-kán* BAL-*an-zi*
11 *A-NA* DINGIR-*LIM-i̯a-kán* ≈*ma-ta-aš-šu*
12 *Ú-UL* BAL-*an-za-kir*
13 *ki-nu-un-ma-kán* BAL-*an-za-ki-u-u̯a-an*
14 *ti-an-zi ma-a-an-ma-za* DINGIR-*LUM* KI.MIN
15 *nu TE*$^{\text{ME.EŠ}}$ SIG$_5$-*ru ni ši ta ke*
16 *en-tíš* GÙB-*aš zi* GAR-*ri*
17 12 ŠÀ *DIR* SIG$_5$ ⸢INIM SUM⸣-*a*[*n-na-aš*]

18-21 (vacant)

---

22 *e-ni* INIM SUM-*an-na-aš ku-it* (erasure) SIxSÁ-*at*
23 *e-ni ku-it* INIM SUM-*an-na-aš*
24 ^{m}*Ka-ta-pa*-DINGIR-*LIM I*-⸢*DE*⸣
25 *nu TE*$^{\text{ME.EŠ}}$ NU.SIG$_5$-*du zé-ḫi(-)li-ip-ši-ma-an*
26 NU.SIG$_5$

---

27 *ma-a-an e-ni-pát* INIM SUM-*an-na-aš*
28 ^{m}*Ka-ta-pa*-⸢DINGIR⸣-*LIM ku-in I*-⸢*DE*⸣
29 *nam-ma-ma* ⸢KI.MIN⸣ *nu TE*$^{\text{ME.EŠ}}$ SIG$_5$-*ru*
30 *ni* ZAG-*za* GÙB-⸢*za*⸣ *še-er-ma-aš-ma-aš*
31 *uk-tu-ri-iš ši ta* ^{GIŠ}TUKUL ZAG-⸢*za*⸣
32 GÙB-*za* RA^{IṢ} *zi* ⸢GAR⸣-*ri*
33 12 ŠÀ *DIR* SIG$_5$

---

34 *pa-a-an-zi a-ši* INIM SUM-*an-na-aš*
35 *kiš-an iš-ḫi-ú-la-aḫ-ḫa-an-zi*
36 *ma-a-an*-⸢*ma-kán*⸣ *ša-ak-ti*
37 *e-ni-na*[70]-*aš*-⸢*kán*⸣ *ut-tar la-it*-⸢*ta*⸣-*ri*
38 *nu TE*$^{\text{ME.EŠ}}$ SIG$_5$-*ru* ZAG-*za* RA^{IṢ} NU.SIG$_5$

(blank space till end of column)

5. *Oracles concerning Zawalli-deities*

The four texts grouped under this heading are given in pairs: the first two attesting to the Zawalli-deity of Danuḫepa and Urḫiteššub, the last two to those of Šausgatti. For remarks see above Chapter I.12 and II.3, for the possible link of the first two to the oracle V 6+ see Chapter I.5. The find-

[69] For this form see the discussion in E. Neu, GsKronasser 124-125.

8 are to be fulfilled, they will fulfill
9 and later they will give compensation
10 and they will offer a gift.
11-12 To the goddess they have neither offered a *mataššu*[71]
13 Now, however, they will start offering (it).
14 If then you, o goddess, etc.,
15 then let the signs be favorable. *Ni*(*pašuri*), *ši*(*ntaḫi*), *ta*(*nani*), *ke*(*ldi*),
16 *en*(-)*tiš* left, there lies a bladderworm,
17 twelve coils; favorable. The affair of givi[ng].

---

22 Concerning the fact that this affair of giving was ascertained,
23 (is it) this affair of giving which
24 Katapaili is overseeing/oversaw?
25 Then let the exta be unfavorable. *Zeḫi*(-)*lipšiman*;
26 unfavorable.

---

27 If (it is) indeed this affair of giving
28 which Katapaili is overseeing/oversaw
29 but further etc., then let the exta be favorable.
30 *Ni*(*pašuri*) on the right (and) left, on top of them
31 (it is?) normal, *ši*(*ntaḫi*), *ta*(*nani*), the weapon on the right,
32 damaged on the left, there lies a bladderworm,
33 twelve coils; favorable.

---

34 They will go (and)
35 thus enjoin the affair of giving.
36 If then you acknowledge (it),
37 will this affair be solved for us?
38 Then let the exta be favorable. Damaged on the right; unfavorable.

spot of KBo XXIII 114 (304/f (+4/m)) is known: g/13, which lies on Büyükkale in the angle formed by the western wall of building F and the stretch of wall connecting the buildings F and E. It was thereby found in the vicinity (g/14) of KBo XVI 98 (above 2.) and 2275/c the latter of which

70 Last sign written over erasure.
71 On this word cf. CHD L-N 211a.

seems to have been originally stored in Building E (see above Ch. II.6). Both KBo XVI 98 and KBo XXIII 114 having been found in the same area,

5.1.1 XVI 16 (CTH 570)

Obv.

x+1 [DI]NGIR$^?$-*L*[*UM*$^?$(-)[72]

---

2 *ma-a-an-za* x$^?$[
3 ^{GIŠ}ŠÚ.A-*ḫi* ⸢GÙB⸣[-

---

4 *nu A-NA* DINGIR-*LIM* ⸢É⸣[

---

5 *ma-a-an-za* DINGIR-*LUM ke-*⸢*e*⸣[*-da-ni me-mi-ni še-er* TUKU-*u-an-za*]
6 *nu* SU.MEŠ SIG$_5$-*ru n*[*i*

---

7 *ki-i-kán ku-it* (erasure) [
8 *UM-MA ŠU-NU-MA* LUGAL KU[R ^{U}]^{RU}⸢*I-šu*⸣-*ṷ*[*a*
9 1 DUG KA.GAG.A *A-NA* ⸢EZEN$_4$⸣ *la-la-at-*⸢*ta*⸣[*-aš*] x x x [
10 *ku-it-ṷa-ra-at kar-ša-an* DINGIR-*LUM-za k*[*e-e-da-n*]*i*$^?$ *me-mi-ni še-er* x[
11 *nu* SU.MEŠ NU.SIG$_5$-*du* ŠU-*TI* GÙB-*la-aš* NU.SIG$_5$

---

12 *ma-a-an ki-i-pát nam-ma-ma* KI.MIN ⸢*nu*⸣ SU.MEŠ SIG$_5$-*ru ir-liš* NU.SIG$_5$

---

13 *na-aš nam-ma pu-nu-uš-šu-u-en nu me-mi-ir* $^{\text{MUNUS.MEŠ}}$*dam-*⸢*ma*⸣*-ra-aš-ṷa* MUŠ *UL e-ep-*⸢*pir*⸣
14 *pa-ra-a tar-nu-um-ma-aš-ša-i̯a* EZEN$_4$ UDU *Ú-UL* GUL-*ḫi-ir* DINGIR-*LUM-za ke-*⸢*e-da*⸣*-ni*
15 *me-mi-ni še-er nu* SU.MEŠ NU.SIG$_5$-*du* ŠÀ DAB-*an* NU.SIG$_5$

---

16 *ma-a-an ki-i-pát nam-ma-i̯a* KI.MIN *nu* SU.⸢MEŠ⸣[SI]G$_5$-*ru* ZAG-*za* RA^{IŠ} NU.SIG$_5$

---

17 *na-aš nam-ma-ma pu-nu-uš-šu-u-en nu me*[*-mi-ir*]x*-e-aš-ṷa I-NA* MU.2.KAM *ku-it*
18 $^{\text{MUNUS.MEŠ}}$*dam-ma-ra-aš ḫal-ki-in Ú-UL* ⸢*ap*⸣[*-pa-an-z*]*i* GEŠTIN-*i̯a-ṷa* LÚ.MEŠ É.GAL.ḪI.A

[72] For this reading compare below rev. 2 and left edge 1.

this could imply that these pieces were too once part of the same lot of tablets housed in Building E. All texts have New Script.

Obv.

1 [(Are$^{?}$) you,] o deit[y, ...]

---

2 If you, [o deity (are) angry because of this affair ... then let the exta be ...]
3 The throne [on the] left[...].

---

4 To the deity the house/domain/te[mple$^{?}$

---

5 If you, o deity (are) [angry because of] th[is affair ...
6 then let the exta be favorable. *N*[*i*(*pašuri*), ...].

---

7 Concerning this fact that [...]
8 Thus they (said): "The king of Išuw[a ...]
9 one jug of ... -beer for the *lalatta*-festival[...]
10 since it was neglected." (Are) you, o deity, because of t[hi]s$^{?}$ matter a[ngry?]
11 Then let the exta be unfavorable. The hands[73] on the left; unfavorable.

---

12 If only this (is the case) but furthermore, etc., then let the exta be favorable. *Ir*(*kipel*)*liš*; unfavorable.

---

13 We further questioned them and they said: "The *dammara*-women have not caug[ht] a$^{?}$ snake [?]
14 and they have not slaughtered a sheep (of/for$^{?}$) the festival of releasing. (Are) you, o deity,
15 because of this matter <angry>? Then let the exta be favorable. The heart is taken; unfavorable.

---

16 If only this (is the case) and furthermore, etc., then let the exta be [favo]rable. On the right damaged; unfavorable.

---

17 We then further questioned them and [they] sa[id ...] ... since for two years
18 the *dammara*-women do not t[ake] grain and the personnel of the palaces (or: palace complex)

[73] For the "hand" in extispicy cf. M. Schuol, AoF 21 (1994) 265.

19 *UL* (erasure) *pí-iš-ki-ir nu-kán* UDU.ḪI.A ⸢*IŠ-TU*⸣ KAŠ x[74]-*ki-ir BI-IB-RI*$^{\text{ḪI.A}}$-*i̯a-u̯a-kán*
20 *IŠ-TU* KAŠ *šu-un-ni-eš-ki-ir* DINGIR-*LUM-za ke-e-da-ni me-mi-ni še-er* TUKU-*u-an-za*
21 *nu* (erasure) SU.MEŠ NU.SIG$_5$-*du* ⸢^{GIŠ}ŠÚ.⸣A-*ḫi* GÙB-*la-an* NU.SIG$_5$

---

22 *ma-a-an ki-i-pát nam-ma-ma* KI.MIN *nu* SU.MEŠ SIG$_5$-*ru*[75] *ki-eš-kán ne-i̯a-ad-da-at* NU.SIG$_5$

---

23 *na-aš nam-ma pu-nu-uš-šu-u-*⸢*en*⸣ *nu me-mi-ir* $^{\text{MUNUS.MEŠ}}$*dam-ma-ra-aš-u̯a ku-i-e-eš da-pí-an-te-eš*
24 *nu-u̯a-kán ma-a-an* DUMU.NITA ⸢*ku*⸣-*e-da-ni-ik-ki a-ki nu-u̯a-aš-ma-aš-kán* GIDIM$^{?}$[76]-*i da-pí-an-te-eš-pát*
25 *še-er ša-li-kiš-kán-*⸢*zi*⸣ NINDA-*i̯a-u̯a* KAŠ *ŠA* GIDIM *az-zi-ki-ir*
26 $^{\text{MUNUS.MEŠ}}$*dam-ma-*⸢*ra*⸣*-aš-ša-u̯a ku-i-e-eš da-pí-an-te-eš nu-u̯a-ra-at IT-TI* LÚ.MEŠ KUR *Ar-za-u-u̯a*
27 *še-eš-kiš-ke-eš-kán-zi*[77] EGIR-*pa-ma-u̯a-ra-at I-NA* É.DINGIR-*LIM an-da ú-e-ri-i̯a-an-te-eš*
28 *u̯a-ar-pa$^{!}$-an-zi-ma$^{!}$-u̯a-aš-ma-aš$^{!}$*[78] *Ú-UL* TÚG.ḪI.A-*i̯a-u̯a-aš-ma-aš-kán Ú-UL ar-ha ar-ra-an-zi*
29 *nu-u̯a-ra-at I-NA* É.DINGIR-*LIM an-da ú-e-ri-i̯a-an-te-eš* DINGIR-*LUM-za ke-e-da-ni*
30 *me-mi-ni$^{!}$ še-er* TUKU-*u-an-za nu* SU.MEŠ NU.SIG$_5$-*du ḫi-*⸢*ri*⸣*-ḫi-iš da-*⸢*li-in du-da-mi*⸣*-it-ta* NU.SIG$_5$

---

31 [*ma-*]⸢*a-an*⸣ *ki-i-pát nam-ma-ma* KI.MIN *nu* SU.MEŠ SIG$_5$-*ru* ZAG-*za* RA^{IṢ} NU.SIG$_5$

(blank space of approximately four lines till lower edge)

[74] The IŠ-sign is written over erasure ("they anointed")?

[75] Comparison with the lines 12', 16' and 31' as well as the phonetic complement *-ru* show the NU-sign before SIG$_5$ to be either a mistake or to have been erased; note the small question mark in the handcopy by A. Walther.

[76] Sign looks partly written over erasure; tentative reading with G. del Monte, AION 35 (1975) 342.

[77] The doubly characterized *-ške*-form might be colloquial and/or a sign of the speakers' emotional involvement.

[78] The signs followed by an exclamation mark look in the handcopy rather like GA, TÚG and ḪAL respectively.

19 has not given wine, they have ... the sheep with beer and filled the rhytons
20 with beer. (Are) you, o deity, angry because of this matter?
21 Then let the exta be unfavorable. The throne on the left; unfavorable.

---

22 If only this (is the case) but furthermore, etc., then let the exta be favorable. *Ke(ld)i* has turned; unfavorable.

---

23 We further questioned them and they said: "As far as all the *dammara*-women are concerned:
24 when somebody's son dies, they all together approach the deceased
25 and they have each eaten the deceased's bread (and) wine.
26 And as far as all the *dammara*-women are concerned, they constantly sleep with the men from Arzauwa
27 but later they (are) summoned into the temple
28 without, however, washing themselves, and without cleaning their clothes
29 they (are) summoned into the temple.[79] (Are) you, o deity, because of this
30 matter angry? Then let the exta be unfavorable. *Ḫiriḫiš dalin dudamitta*[80]; unfavorable.

---

31 [I]f only this (is the case) but furthermore, etc., then let the exta be favorable. On the right damaged; unfavorable.

[79] This translation assumes a chiastic structure for the sentences from 27' EGIR-*pa=ma=u̯ar=at* onwards. It is, however, also possible that the last sentence is to be understood as a sort of conclusion or climax: "and (thus) they are summoned into the temple!"

[80] For these terms cf. M. Schuol, AoF 21 (1994) 285.

Rev.

(blank space of approximately four lines from upper edge)

---

1 ⸢^{d}⸣*Za-u̯a-al-*⸢*li*⸣ ^{f}*Da-nu-ḫé-pa* SISKUR-*aš* SU.MEŠ IR-*u-en nu* SU.MEŠ SIG$_5$-*ru* NU.SIG$_5$

---

2 [DING]IR-*LUM-za* SISKUR ⸢*te*⸣-*pa-nu-u̯a-an ḫar-ti nu* SU.MEŠ (erasure) NU.SIG$_5$-*du* <<*nu*>> NU.SIG$_5$

---

3 [*n*]*u* LÚ.MEŠ É.DINGIR-*LIM pu-nu-uš-šu-u-en nu me-mi-ir* 1 *PA* 4 BÁN ½ BÁN 2 *UP-NI* BA.BA.ZA

4 7 ^{DUG}ḪAB.ḪAB GEŠTIN 4 BÁN ½ BÁN GA ½[81] BÁN 1 *u̯a-ak-šur* 1 *du-ud-du-uš* Ì.NUN

5 2 ^{DUG}*PUR-SÍ-TUM* LÀL *IŠ-TU A-BI* ^{d}UTU-*ŠI kar-ša-an* $^{LÚ.MEŠ}$ENGAR.MEŠ-*TIM-ma*

6 *ku-i-e-eš e-šir nu-kán a-pu-u-uš I-NA* LÚ.MEŠ ^{URU}*A-ra-u-un-na pa-ra*[*-a*]*n-da*

7 *pa-a-ir a-pu-u-uš-ma-kán I-NA* LÚ.MEŠ EN.NU.UN ḪUR.SAG-*i pár-ra-an-da pa-a-ir*

8 1-*aš-ma-u̯a-kán ku-i-e-eš e-eš-ta nu-u̯a te-pa-u-*⸢*u̯a*⸣*-za pé-eš-ki-it*

9 DINGIR-*LUM-za ke-e-da-ni me-mi-ni še-er* TUKU-*u-an-za nu* SU.MEŠ NU[82].SIG$_5$-*du ir-liš* NU.SIG$_5$

---

10 *ma-a-an ki-i-pát nam-ma-ma* KI.MIN *nu* SU.MEŠ SIG$_5$-*ru ke-*⸢*eš-kán*⸣ *ne-i̯a-ad-da-at* NU.SIG$_5$

---

11 *na-aš nam-ma pu-nu-uš-šu-u-en nu me-mi-ir* x x -⸢*le*⸣*-e-eš-u̯a ŠA* KÙ.BABBAR GUŠKIN

12 ⸢DINGIR⸣-*LUM ar-ḫa iš-ḫu-u-u̯a-an ḫar-zi A-NA* DINGIR-*LIM-u̯a* É.TU$_7$ *UL e-eš-zi*

13 ⸢*nu*⸣*-u̯a A-NA* DINGIR-*LIM IŠ*[83]*-TU* É ^{LÚ}MÁŠDA GU$_7$-*na pé-eš-ga-u-e-ni*

14 ^{GIŠ}BÚGIN-*i̯a-u̯a* ^{DUG}[84]⸢*iš*⸣*-nu-ri* GIR$_4$![85].ḪI.A *da-pí-an-da ŠA* ^{LÚ}MÁŠDA-*pát*

15 *da-aš-ga-u-e-ni nu-u̯a A-NA* DINGIR-*LIM* GU$_7$-*na u̯a-aš-ta-nu-u̯a-an-da-za pé-eš-ga-u-e-ni*

[81] Last sign written over erasure.
[82] Last sign written over erasure.
[83] Last sign written over erasure.
[84] Last sign written over erasure.
[85] Handcopy shows Ù.

---

1 Concerning the Zawalli of Danuḫepa we consulted the offering's exta. Let the exta be favorable. Unfavorable.

---

2 Have you, o [dei]ty, spurned the offering?[86] Then let the exta be unfavorable. Unfavorable.

---

3 We questioned the temple personnel and they said: "One *PARĪSU* plus four and a half BÁN plus two fistfuls of porridge[87],
4 seven jugs of wine, four and a half BÁN of milk, half a BÁN plus one *u̯akšur* plus one *duddu*[88] of butter,
5 (and) two bowls of honey (were) neglected by the father of His Majesty. But it was the cultivators
6 of whom some went across to the people of the town of Araunna
7 while others went across to the watchmen on the mountain.
8 The group that was (left$^{?}$) alone, however, kept giving in (too) small amount.
9 (Are) you, o deity, angry because of this matter? Then let the exta be unfavorable. *Ir*(*kipel*)*liš*; unfavorable.

---

10 If only this (is the case) but furthermore, etc., then let the exta be favorable. *Ke*(*ld*)*i* has turned; unfavorable.

---

11 We further questioned them and they said: "The ...-vessels of silver (and) gold
12 the deity has scattered (and) the deity has no kitchen
13 so that we usually give the deity to eat from the poor man's kitchen.
14 Also trough(s), kneading-bowl(s) (and) all (sorts of) ceramics from that same poor man
15 we keep taking so that we constantly give the deity to eat from sinful (things).

[86] Cf. J. Tischler, HEG T, D 316.
[87] This may amount to approximately 90 litres; cf. RlA VII 524.
[88] For this measure see RlA VII 525b.

16 DINGIR-*LUM-za ke-e-da-ni me-mi-ni še-er* TUKU-*u-an-za nu* SU.MEŠ NU.SIG$_5$-*du* ZAG-*za* RA^{IṢ} NU.SIG$_5$

---

17 *ma-a-an ki-i-pát nam-ma-ma* KI.MIN *nu* SU.MEŠ SIG$_5$-*ru* SAG.ME NU.SIG$_5$

---

18 *na-aš nam-ma pu-nu-uš-šu-u-en nu me-mi-ir* ⸢UR⸣.GI$_7$-*aš-u̯a-kán* ^{GIŠ}NÁ-*aš* UGU *pa-it*
19 ^{MUNUS}*dam-ma-ra-aš-ma-u̯a-kán še-eš-ki-iš-ki-it-pát* BAPPIR-*i̯a*-⸢*u̯a*⸣ *ŠA* ^{LÚ}MÁŠDA
20 *da-a-u-e-ni nu-u̯a-ra-at A-NA* DINGIR-*LIM* SUM-*u-en* DINGIR-*LUM-za* ⸢*ke-e*⸣-*da-ni me-mi-ni*
21 *še-er* TUKU-*u-an-za nu* SU.MEŠ NU.SIG$_5$-*du ir-liš* NU.⸢SIG$_5$⸣

---

22 *ma-a-an ki-i-pát nam-ma-ma* KI.MIN *nu* SU.MEŠ SI[G$_5$-*ru* o o o o o]x-⸢*an*⸣$^?$-*za* ⸢NU.SIG$_5$⸣

(blank space of one line)

---

23 ^{d}*Za-u̯a-al-li-(l)iš* ^{m}*Úr-ḫi*-^{d}U-*ub-ša-aš* SISKUR x[

---

24 *nu* LÚ.MEŠ ⸢É⸣[.DINGIR-*LIM*] ⸢*pu-nu*⸣-*u*[*š-šu-u-en nu me-mi-ir*
25 *pé-eš-ki-ir*$^!$ [
26 GEŠTIN-*i̯a-u̯*[*a*
27 DINGIR-*LUM-za*[

---

28 [*m*]*a-a-an* [*ki-i-pát nam-ma-ma* KI.MIN *nu* SU.MEŠ SIG$_5$-*ru*

---

29 x [

Left edge

1 DINGIR-*LUM-za ke-e-da-ni me-mi-i̯a-ni še-er* TUKU-*u-an-za nu* SU.MEŠ NU.SIG$_5$-*du*[89]
2 ŠU-*TI* GÙB-⸢*la*⸣-*aš* NU.SIG$_5$

---

3 *ma-a-an ki-i-pát nam-ma-ma* KI.MIN *nu* SU.MEŠ SIG$_5$-*ru ki-eš-kán ne-i̯a-ad-da-at* N[U.SIG$_5$]

[89] Followed by some illegible traces and break.

16 (Are) you, o deity, angry because of this matter? Then let the exta be unfavorable. On the right damaged; unfavorable.

---

17 If only this (is the case) but furthermore, etc., then let the exta be favorable. SAG.ME; unfavorable.

---

18 We further questioned them and they said: "A dog jumped on the bed
19 while a *dammara*-woman used to sleep (there)! And a poor man's wort
20 we take and gave it to the deity. (Are) you, o deity, because of this matter
21 angry? Then let the exta be unfavorable. *Ir*(*kipel*)*liš*; unfavorable.

---

22 If only this (is the case) but furthermore, etc., then let the exta be favo[rable. ...] ... ; unfavorable.

---

23 Concerning the Zawalli of Urḫiteššub [we consulted] the offering's e[xta? ...].

---

24 The te[mple] personnel [we] questi[oned and they said: " ...]
25 they gave [...]
26 and wine [... "].
27 (Are) you, o deity [angry because of this matter? Then let the exta be ...].

---

28 If [only this (is the case) but furthermore, etc., then let the exta be ...].

---

29 ... [...].

Left edge

1 (Are) you, o deity, angry because of this matter? Then let the exta be unfavorable. ... [...]
2 the hands on the left; unfavorable.

---

3 If only this (is the case) but furthermore, etc., then let the exta be favorable. *Ke*(*ld*)*i* has turned; u[nfavorable].

5.1.2 KBo XXIII 114 (CTH 570)

Obv.?

1 [-]*kán* ^{d}⸢*Za-u̯a*⸣-*a*[*l-li*(-)

2 [*n*]*u* SU.MEŠ NU.SIG$_5$-*d*[*u*

---

3 [ ]x *ku-i-e-eš nam-ma-ma*

4 [KI.MIN *nu* IGI-*zi* SU.MEŠ SIG$_5$-*ru* EGIR-*ma* NU.SIG$_5$-*d*]*u* IGI-*zi* SU.MEŠ *ni-eš t*[*a*?

5 [ ]x[*ar-ḫ*]*a-i̯a-an ši ke* GÙB-*za* [?]

6 [ ] x[o]x NU.SIG$_5$

---

7 [ ]x É.DINGIR-*LIM-aš ku-i*[-*e*?-*e*]*š* SIxSÁ-*ta-at ŠA* ^{URU}*Zi*-⸢*it-ḫa*⸣[-*ra*

8 [ ]⸢*ta*⸣-*ú-tíš* NU.SIG$_5$

---

9 [ ]x-*uš ŠA* ^{URU}*Zi-it-ḫa-ra nu nam-ma-ma* KI.MIN *nu* IGI-*zi* S[U.MEŠ

10 [EGIR-*ma* NU.SIG$_5$-*d*]*u* IGI-*zi* SU.MEŠ *ni ši ke* 12 ŠÀ *DIR* SIG$_5$ EGIR SU.MEŠ *zu*[-*ul-ki-iš*?

11 [ ] NU.SIG$_5$

---

12 [^{d}*Za-u̯a-al-li*-]⸢*iš*⸣ É.DINGIR-*LIM ŠA* ^{URU}*Zi-it-ḫa-ra ku-iš* SIxSÁ-*at* ⸢*ŠA*⸣ ^{m}*Úr-ḫé*-⸢^{d}⸣[U-*ub*

13 [*nu* SU.MEŠ NU?.SI]G$_5$-*du* x 8 ŠÀ *DIR* NU.⸢SIG$_5$⸣

---

14 [*nu* ^{d}*Za-u̯a-a*]*l-li-*(*l*)*iš ŠA* ^{m}*Úr-ḫi* ^{d}U-*ub-pát* KI.MIN *nu TE*^{MEŠ} SIG$_5$-*ru* x ^{GIŠ}ŠÚ.A-*ḫi* GÙ[B-*la*-

---

15 [*ki-i ku-it* NU.S]IG$_5$-*ta nu* ^{d}*Za-u̯a-al-li-iš ŠA* [A]MA ^{d}UTU-*ŠI-i̯a nu* SU.MEŠ NU.SIG$_5$-*du* x[

16 [ ]x EGIR-*ŠÚ zi* GAR-*ri* 11[90] ŠÀ *DIR* SIG$_5$

---

17 [*nu* ^{d}*Za-u̯a-l*]*i-iš*[91] *ŠA* ^{f}*Da*[92]-*nu-ḫé-pa-ma nu* SU.MEŠ NU.SIG$_5$-*du* ZAG-*za* RA^{IṢ} N[U.SIG$_5$]

[90] Number written over erasure.

[91] The available space and comparison with the next line forces to assume a spelling without *-al-* for which compare XLVIII 124 rev. 8 and LVI 1 iv 2.

[92] Last two signs written over erasure.

1 [...] ... the Zawa[lli-deity ...]
2 [... th]en le[t] the exta be unfavorable[...]

---

3 [...] ... who [...] but furthermore,
4 [etc., then let the first exta be favorable but le]t [the following (ones) be unfavorable]. The first exta: *ni(pašur)eš*, *t[a(nani)*?
5 [...] ... [... sep]arately *ši(ntaḫi) ke(ldi)* on the left [?]
6 [...] ... [...] ... ; unfavorable.

---

7 Concerning [the ...] ... of? the temple wh[o] were ascertained: Of the city of Zitḫ[ara ... ?]
8 [...] *tautiš*; unfavorable.

---

9 [Is it the ...] ... of the city of Zitḫara but furthermore, etc.? Then let the first e[xta be favorable]
10 [but le]t [the following (ones) be unfavorable]. The first exta: *ni(pašuri)*, *ši(ntaḫi)*, *ke(ldi)*, twelve coils; favorable. The following exta *zu[lkiš*? ...]
11 [...]; unfavorable.

---

12 [Concerning the Zawall]i-deity of the temple of Zitḫara which was ascertained: (is it the one) of Urḫi[teššub?]
13 [Then] let [the exta be unfavo]rable. Eight coils; unfavorable.

---

14 [(Is it) the Zawal]li-deity of Urḫiteššub only? Then let the exta be favorable. The throne on the lef[t; unfavorable.]

---

15 [Concerning this fact that it was unfa]vorable: (Is it) the Zawalli-deity of the [m]other and His Majesty? Then let the exta be unfavorable. [... ?]
16 [...] ... behind it there lies a bladderworm, eleven coils; favorable.

---

17 Or [(is it) the Zawa]lli-deity of Danuḫepa? Then let the exta be unfavorable. On the right damaged; u[nfavorable.]

---

18 [*nu* ^{d}*Za-u̯a-a*]*l-li-iš ŠA* ^{m}*Úr-ḫi-*^{d}U*-ub-pát ŠA* ^{f}*Da-nu-ḫé-pa-i̯a* KI.MIN
19 [*nu* IGI-*zi* SU.ME]Š SIG$_5$-*ru* EGIR-*ma* NU.SIG$_5$-*du* IGI-*zi* SU.MEŠ *ni ši ta*
^{GIŠ}TUKUL ZAG[
20 [Š]À *DIR* SIG$_5$ EGIR SU.MEŠ *zé- ḫi-li-ip-ši-ma- an*! NU.SIG$_5$

---

21 [ ]x *ŠA* ^{m}*Úr-ḫé-*^{d}U*-ub* ⸢SIxSÁ⸣?[93]-*at* DINGIR-*LUM-za še-ek-*
kán-du-uš u̯a-aš-ku-uš [
22 [ ] *ka-ru-ú ku-i-e-eš še-*⸢*ek*⸣*-ku-e-ni nu* SU.MEŠ NU.SIG$_5$-*du*
ZAG-*za* RA[*IṢ* NU.SIG$_5$]

---

23 [^{d}*Za-u̯a-a*]*l-li-iš* ^{m}*Úr-ḫé-*^{d}U-⸢*ub*⸣ *še-ek-kán-du-uš-pát u̯a-aš-ku-uš še-er*
TUKU.T[UKU-*u-an-za*
24 [*nu* SU.MEŠ S]IG$_5$-*ru ni ši ta ke* [G]ÙB-*za an-ša-an* 12 ŠÀ *DIR* SIG$_5$

---

25 [*ki-i*? *ŠA*] ^{m}*Úr-ḫé-*^{d}U*-ub ku-it še-ek-kán-du-uš u̯a-aš-ku-uš še-er* x[94][
26 [ ]x EZEN$_4$.MEŠ *ŠA* MU.⸢6?.KAM⸣ *kar-ša-an-te-eš*$_{17}$ *nu ŠA* 1-*EN*
MU.KAM EZ[EN$_4$
27 [E]ZEN$_4$.MEŠ *Ú-UL i-i̯*[*a-a*]*n-te-eš*$_{17}$ ZA.ḪUM 1-*EN* GÍN? ½ GÍN?-*i̯a*
(erasure)[DINGIR-*LUM-za*]
28 [*ke-e-da-aš*] *u̯a-aš-ku-u̯a-aš še-er* TUKU.TUKU-*u-an-za nu* SU.MEŠ
NU.SIG$_5$-*du* ŠU-*TI*[

---

29 [DINGIR-*LUM-za ke-*]⸢*e-da*⸣*-aš u̯a-aš-ku-u̯a*[*-a*]*š še-er* TUKU.TUKU-*u-*
an-za KI.MIN *nu* SU.MEŠ S[IG$_5$-*ru*

---

30 [(-)]*nu*? *e-ni-i̯a* [*k*]*u-*⸢*it*⸣ LÚ.MEŠ ⸢É.DINGIR-*LIM me-mi*⸣?*-ir*
É.DINGIR-*LIM-u̯*[*a*
31 [ ]x *Ú-UL* x [o]x MUNUS.MEŠ x[o o o]x-⸢*u̯a*⸣? *ḫar-kán-*
t[*e-*
32 [ ]x[ ]x x[ ]x x ŠÀ[*DIR*

---

33 [ ]x[

[93] Because of the *-za* behind DINGIR-*LUM* immediately following, the x-*at* in front of it must be the verb of the preceding sentence. Although the sign trace seems quite short, the proposed restoration seems to be the most plausible one.

[94] Parallel to line 23 one might expect TUKU.TUKU- but the sign trace does not favor such a reading. A reading SIxSÁ- also seems possible although one misses the lower horizontal.

---

18 [(Is it) the Zawa]lli-deity of Urḫiteššub indeed as well as of Danuḫepa etc.?

19 [Then] let [the first ext]a be favorable but let the following (ones) be unfavorable. The first exta: *ni(pašuri)*, *ši(ntaḫi)*, *ta(nani)*, the weapon [on the] right [...]

20 [... c]oils; favorable. The following (ones): *zeḫilipšiman*; unfavorable.

---

21 [Concerning this fact tha]t$^{?}$ (the Zawalli-deity) of Urḫiteššub was ascertained: (Are) you, o deity, [angry because of] known offenses,

22 [that is, the ones] we already know of? Then let the exta be unfavorable. On the right dama[ged; unfavorable.]

---

23 [(Is) the Zawa]lli-deity of Urḫiteššub ang[ry] because of those known offenses only?

24 [Then] let [the exta be fa]vorable. *Ni(pašuri)*, *ši(ntaḫi)*, *ta(nani)*, *ke(ldi)*, on the right wiped, twelve coils; favorable.

---

25 [Concerning this fact] that [the deity] because of the known offenses [against] Urḫiteššub [was] ascer[tained.$^{?}$

26 [(Is it because) ...] ... the festivals of the sixth year (were) neglected and the fest[ival] of the first$^{?}$ year [...]

27 [and the ... fe]stivals (were) not celebrated and the jug (of) $1\frac{1}{2}$ shekel$^{??}$ [... (Are) you, o deity,]

28 because of [these] offenses angry? Then let the exta be unfavorable. The hands [...]

---

29 [(Are) you, o deity,] because of [th]ese offenses angry etc.? Then [let] the exta be fa[vorable. ...].

---

30 [...] ... and concerning that fact that the temple personnel has said: "The temple[...]

31-33 (no translation feasible)

Rev.?

(blank space of approximately three lines)

x+1 GIM[-*an*
2 *na-a*[*š*?
3 ⌈*i*⌉-x[[95]
4 ⌈*tar*⌉?-x[

5.2.1 XVI 46 (CTH 573)

Obv. i

x+1 ⌈*ku*⌉-*u-uš-kán ku-i-e-eš* ^{d}⌈*Za*⌉-*u̯*[*a-al-li*(-)
2 [*š*]*e-er ú-te-er e-eš-zi a*[*n*-/⌈^{d}⌉[
3 ⌈^{d}⌉*Za-u̯a-al-li-iš a-ri-i*-x[o o o]x x x [
4 *ke-e-da-aš-kán* ^{d}Za-*u̯a-al-li-i̯*[*a*?-*aš*] 1-*aš ku*-⌈*iš*⌉[-*k*]*i* ^{d}*Za-u̯a-a*[*l-li*(-)
5 *an-da* TUKU.TUKU-*u-an-za nu* MUŠEN[96].ḪI.A *a-pa-a*-⌈*at*⌉ *ša-ki-i̯a-aḫ*-⌈*ḫi*⌉-*ir nu* MUŠEN.ḪI.A [
6 TI$_8$^{MUŠEN} *tar-li*$_{12}$*-an NI-MUR na-aš-kán pí-an* SIG$_5$-*za ú-it na-aš-kán* ⌈EGIR⌉ U[GU]
7 *ú-it* (erasure) *na-aš-kán pí-an ar-ḫa pa-it* EGIR KASKAL-*NI* 2 *pát-tar-pal-ḫi-iš* GUN-*liš*[[97]
8 *na-at-kán* EGIR UGU SIG$_5$-*za ú-e-er na-at-kán pí-an ar-ḫa pa-a-ir*
9 *UM-MA* ^{m}*Ze*-⌈*el-la*⌉ SIxSÁ-*at-u̯a*

10 ^{d}*Za-u̯a-al-li-iš ku-iš* SIxSÁ-*at* ^{d}*Za-u̯a-al-li-iš ŠA* É.LUGAL
11 *nu* MUŠEN.ḪI.A SIxSÁ-*an-du pát-tar-pal-ḫi*-⌈*in*⌉ GUN-*li*$_{12}$-*an NI-MUR* *n*[*a*-]*aš-kán* EGIR UGU SIG$_5$-*za*
12 *ú-it na-aš-kán pí-an ar-ḫa pa-it ḫal-u̯a-aš-ši-in*!-*ma* [G]UN-*li*$_{12}$-*an NI-MUR*
13 *na-aš-kán* EGIR UGU SIG$_5$-*za ú-it na-aš tar-liš* (erasure) *pa-an pa-it*
14 TI$_8$^{MUŠEN} *tar-li*$_{12}$*-an NI*-⌈*MUR*⌉ *na-aš-kán pí-an* SIG$_5$-*za ú-it na-aš-za* ⌈GUN-*li*$_{12}$⌉-*an* TUŠ-*at*
15 KAxU-*ŠÚ-ma-za-kán pí-an ar-ḫa na-a-iš na-aš a-ra-iš*
16 *na-aš* 2-*an ar-ḫa pa-it* EGIR KASKAL-*NI* 2 *a-ra-am-na-an-du-uš*
17 [G]UN-*li*$_{12}$-*an NI-MUR na-at-kán* EGIR UGU SIG$_5$-*za ú-e-er*
18 [*n*]*a*-⌈*at*⌉-*kán pí-an ar-ḫa pa-a-ir UM*[-*M*]*A* ^{m}⌈*Ze-el*⌉-*la* SIxSÁ-*at*-⌈*u̯a*⌉

(end of column)

[95] *I-NA*! ?
[96] Last sign written over erasure.
[97] Or GUN-*li*$_{12}$[-*an*.

Rev.?

(no translation feasible)

Obv. i

---

x+1 Those Zaw[alli-deities] who [...]
2 they carried up[98], is ... [... ?]
3 The Zawalli-deity ... [...]
4 Among these Zawalli-deities (is there) an individual Zawa[lli-deity ...?]
5 angry and have the birds indicated that? Then [let them ascertain] the birds.
6 An eagle *tar(wiyal)lian* we observed and it came in front from favorable (direction) and ab[ove] behind
7 it came and went past in front. Behind the road: two *pattarpalḫi*-birds [came?] GUN-*liš*/-*li*[*an*]
8 and they came above behind from favorable (direction) and went past in front.
9 Thus Zella: "It was ascertained."

---

10 Concerning the Zawalli-deity which was ascertained, (is it) a Zawalli-deity of the palace?
11 Then let them ascertain the birds. A *pattarpalḫi*-bird GUN-*lian* we observed: above behind from favorable (direction)
12 it came and went past in front. Then a *ḫalwašši*-bird GUN-*lian* we observed:
13 it came above behind from favorable (direction) and went across *tar(wiyal)lian*.
14 An eagle *tar(wiyal)lian* we observed: it came in front from favorable (direction) and sat down GUN-*lian*
15 while it turned its beak past in front. It rose
16 and went off through the center. Behind the road: two *aramnant*-birds
17 we observed [G]UN-*lian*: they came above behind from favorable (direction)
18 [a]nd went past in front. Thus Zella: "It was ascertained."

---

98 For the expression cf. above XVI 32, 8'.

Obv. ii

x+1 *u̯[a-*
2 *pa-a-i[*
3 *nu A-NA* DINGIR-*LIM[*
4 DINGIR-*LUM-za* KI.MIN x[
5 *na-aš-kán pí-an[*
6 *na-aš-kán* EGIR[
7 EGIR KASKAL-*NI* 2 x[
8 *ú-e-er* x[
9 *na-aš pa-an[*
10 *UM-MA* ^{m}Z[*e-el-la*

(end of column)

Rev. iii

1 SIxSÁ-*at* [

(blank space of three lines)

2 *pa-iz-zi[*
3 *ar-ḫa-i̯[a-an*
4 ZAG-*eš-z[i*
5 ⸢GUN⸣-*l[iš*?[99]

Rev. iv

1 [o o o -]⸢*iš*⸣ *ku-iš* ^{d}*Za-u̯a-al-li-iš* x x[100] *ŠA* ^{f}x[[101]
2 [*nu*] ⸢MUŠEN⸣.ḪI.A SIxSÁ-*an-du ta-pa-aš-ši-in tar-li*$_{12}$*-an NI-MUR na-aš-kán* EGI[R
3 [*n*]*a-aš* 2-*an ar-ḫa pa-it ḫa-aš-ta-pí-in-ma* GUN-*li*$_{12}$*-an NI-*⸢*MUR na-aš-kán*⸣ *pí-an ku-*⸢*uš*⸣ *ú-it*
4 *na-aš tar-liš*[102] *pa-an pa-it* EGIR KASKAL-*NI* TI$_{8}^{MUŠEN}$ GUN-*li*$_{12}$*-an NI-MUR na-aš-kán pí-an ku-uš ú-it*
5 *na-aš zi-an ku-uš pa-it UM-MA* ^{m}*Pí-i̯a-am-mu ar-ḫa-u̯a pé-eš-šir*

99 Or -*l[i*$_{12}$*-an*.

100 One expects a SIxSÁ-*at nu* at this point but the space available seems a little too short to allow of this restoration. Is the break at the beginning of the line to be restored with another *ku-*]*iš* ("And wha]tever Zawalli-deity was ascertained, (is it) the Zawalli of Š[aušgatti?") or could the alleged IŠ be the end of GIDIM with a preceding *ŠA* ("Concerning the Zawalli-deity [of the dece]ased which was ascertained, (is it) the Zawalli-deity of Š[aušgatti?")?

101 A restoration to ^{fd}[*IŠTAR-ti* is unlikely in view of the denial below in iv 5 and the next question in iv 6 ("(Or is it the Zawalli-deity) of Šaušgatti?").

102 Last sign written over erasure.

ii

2 (s)he will give[...]
3 to the deity[...]
4 (Are) you, o deity, etc. ... [...]
5 In front it [...]
6 and behind it [...]
7 Behind the road: two ... [...-birds ...]
8 came ... [...]
9 and across it [...]
10 Thus Z[ella: ...]

iii

1 It was ascertained.

---

2 (S)he will go [...]
3 outs[ide ...]
4 it/(s)he wi[ll] become right [...]

iv

1 The Zawalli-deity which [...] ..., (is it) [...]'s ?
2 Let them ascertain the [b]irds. A *tapaššši*-bird *tar*(*wiyal*)*lian* we observed: [above] beh[ind] it [came out of favorable (direction)]
3 [a]nd went off through the center. Then a *ḫaštapi*-bird GUN-*lian* we observed: it came in front *kuš*(*tayati*)
4 and went across *tar*(*wiyal*)*liš*. Behind the road: An eagle GUN-*lian* we observed: it came in front *kuš*(*tayati*)
5 and went *zi*(*law*)*an kuš*(*tayati*). Thus Piyammu: "They have cast away."

(blank space of three lines)

---

6 *nu ŠA* ^{fd}*IŠTAR-ti-ma nu* MUŠEN.ḪI.A SIxSÁ-*an-du a-ra-am-na-an-ta-an tar-li*$_{12}$*-an NI-MUR*

7 *na-aš-kán pí-an* SIG$_5$-*za ú-it nu* GUN-*li*$_{12}$*-an* MUŠEN *e-ep-ta na-an* 2-*an*

8 *ar-ha pé-e-da-as* TI$_8$^{MUŠEN} *tar-li*$_{12}$*-an NI-MUR na-aš-kán pí-an* SIG$_5$-*za ú-it*

9 *na-aš* 2-*an ar-ḫa pa-it* TI$_8$^{MUŠEN} GUN-*li*$_{12}$*-an NI-MUR na-aš-kán* EGIR UGU SIG$_5$-*za* ⸢*ú-it*⸣

10 *na-aš-kán pí-an ar-ha pa-it* EGIR KASKAL-*NI ta-pa-aš-ši-in* GUN-*li*$_{12}$*-an NI-MUR*

11 *na-aš* GUN-*liš* (erasure) *pa-an ú-it* TI$_8$^{MUŠEN}-*ma* GUN-*li*$_{12}$*-an NI-MUR na-aš-kán* EGIR UG[U]

12 *ú-it na-aš-kán pí-an ar-ḫa pa-it UM-MA* ^{m}*Pí-i̯a-am-mu* SIxSÁ-*at-u̯a*

---

13 ^{d}*Za-u̯a-al-li-iš ku-iš ŠA* ^{fd}*IŠTAR-ti* SIxSÁ-*at* [*n*]*a-an ar-ḫa* KIN-*an*-⸢*zi*⸣[

14 SISKUR-*ši pé-eḫ-ḫi nam-ma-an ar*-⸢*ḫa*⸣ KASKAL-*ši-aḫ-mi ma*-⸢*a-an-ma-za* KI⸣.MIN *nu* MUŠEN.ḪI.⸢A⸣[SIxSÁ-*an-du*]

15 2 *ta-pa-aš-ši-iš* GUN-*li*$_{12}$*-an NI-MUR na-at* GUN-*li*$_{12}$*-an* x[o] ⸢*ú-e*⸣*-er ḫa-aš-t*[*a-pí-in*]

16 *tar-li*$_{12}$*-an NI-MUR na-aš-kán* EGIR GAM *ku-uš ú-it na-aš* 2[-*an a*]*r-ḫa pa-it ta-pa-aš-ši-i*[*n*

17 [G]UN-*li*$_{12}$*-an NI-MUR na-aš-kán pí-an ku-uš ú-it* ⸢*na-aš*⸣*-kán* ⸢EGIR⸣[

18 [E]GIR KASKAL-*NI a-ra-am-na-an-ta-an tar-li*$_{12}$*-an NI-MUR na-aš-kán*[

19 [*n*]*a-aš* 2-*an ar-ḫa pa-it ḫal-u̯a-aš-si*-⸢*in-kán tar-li*$_{12}$*-an*⸣[

20 [*n*]*a-aš* 2-*an ar-ḫa pa-i*[*t*

21 (vacat) [

(break)

5.2.2 L 87

Obv.?

x+1 x [

---

2 *AN-NU*-⸢*Ú*⸣*-TI* ⸢LÚ.MEŠ⸣ ^{d}/*an*[

3 [DI]NGIR-*LUM-za-kán* ŠÀ É.DINGIR-*LIM ku-it-ki* TUKU.TUKU-*u*[-*u̯anza nu* SU.MEŠ NU.SIG$_5$-*du* ?]

4 *zé-ḫi-li-ip-ši-im-ma-an* NU.SIG$_5$

---

6 Or (is it the Zawalli-deity) of Šaušgatti? Then let them ascertain the birds. An *aramnant*-bird *tar*(*wiyal*)*lian* we observed:
7 it came in front from favorable (direction), caught a bird GUN-*lian* and through the center
8 carried it off. An eagle *tar*(*wiyal*)*lian* we observed: it came in front from favorable (direction)
9 and went off through the center. An eagle GUN-*lian* we observed: it came above behind from favorable (direction)
10 and went past in front. Behind the road: A *tapašši*-bird we observed:
11 it went across GUN-*lian*. Another eagle GUN-*lian* we observed: above behind it
12 came and went past in front. Thus Piyammu: "It was ascertained."

---

13 The Zawalli of Šaušgatti which was ascertained, will they undo her (influence)?
14 Will I give her an offering and then send her off? If then, etc., then [let them ascertain] the birds.
15 Two *tapašši*-birds GUN-*lian* we observed: GUN-*lian* they came .... A *ḫašt*[*api*-bird
16 *tar*(*wiyal*)*lian* we observed: below behind it came *kuš*(*tayati*) and went [o]ff through the cen[ter]. A *tapašši*-bird
17 GUN-*lian* we observed: it came in front *kuš*(*tayati*), and [above] beh[ind ...]
18 [Be]hind the road: An *aramnant*-bird *tar*(*wiyal*)*lian* we observed: it [...]
19 [a]nd it went off through the center. A *ḫalwašši*-bird *tar*(*wiyal*)*lia*[*n* we observed: ...]
20 [a]nd it wen[t] off through the center [...]

Obv.

---

2 These men ... [...]
3 (Are) you, o deity, angr[y] over something inside the temple? [Then let the exta be ...]
4 *zeḫi*(-)*lipšimman*; unfavorable.

---

5 [*m*]*a-a-an-za-*[*ká*]*n* DINGIR-*LUM* ŠÀ É.DINGIR-*LIM-pát*
TU[KU.TUKU-*uṷanza nam-ma-ma-za*]
6 *Ú-U*[*L k*]*u-it-ki* TUKU.TUKU-*u-ṷa-an-za nu* SU.ME[Š

---

7 [DI]NGIR$^{?}$.MEŠ$^{?}$ *ku-it IŠ-TU* $^{\text{LÚ.MEŠ}}$KÙ.DÍM x[
8 *nu a*[*-pá*]*d-da še-er* TUKU.TUKU-*at-ti* SIxSÁ-*at n*[*u*

---

9 [*n*]*u-kán ku-it* $^{\text{LÚ.MEŠ}}$KÙ.DÍM ⌈*ú*⌉-*e-* x x[
10 x x x DINGIR.MEŠ ZI-*an*[103] x[
11 x-*at nu* ⌈IGI-*zi*⌉[
12 [ ]x[

Rev.$^{?}$

x+1 [TA] ⌈^{MUNUS}ŠU⌉.G[I IR-*TUM QA-T*]*AM-MA-pát n*[*u* KIN
2 [*IN*]*A* UD.2.KAM *pa-an-ku-uš-za* ZAG-*tar* INIM$^{?}$[104] x[
3 [*I*]*NA* UD.3.KAM DINGIR.MAḪ GUB-*iš* ZAG-x[

---

4 ^{d}*Za-ṷa-al-li-iš ŠA* ^{fd}*IŠTAR*[-
5 *ki-nu-un ku-it* DINGIR-*LUM A-NA* MUNUS.LUGAL x x[
6 *nu A-NA* DINGIR-*LIM* SISKUR SUM-*an-zi ku-it-m*[*a-an*
7 *na-aš-mu a-ri-i̯a-še-eš-na-za* GIM-*an* SIxS[Á-*at*

---

8 DINGIR[-*LU*]*M*$^{?}$-*ma*$^{?}$ *pí-di-iš-ši I-NA* ^{URU}*Li-i*[*p-ra-aš-ša*$^{?}$[105]
9 *nu-kán an-ku* GIM$^{?}$-*an* $^{\text{MUNUS?}}$*u-ṷa-ar-ṷa-an-z*[*i*[106]
10 *na-an pí-di-eš-ši QA-TAM-MA ar-ḫa a-ni-i̯*[*a-an-zi*
11 *nu A-NA* DINGIR-*LIM* SISKUR SUM-*an-zi ku-it-ma-an*[
12 *na-aš-m*[*u*] *a-ri-i̯a-še-eš-na-za ma*<*-a*>*-an* SIxSÁ-*at na-a*[*n*
13 [*I*]*Š-TU* ^{MUNUS}ENSI SIxSÁ-*at*

---

14 (illegible traces)

(break of two lines, then end of column)

[103] Or *zi*-x?
[104] Or *ka*-?
[105] Thus following a suggestion by G. Beckman; cf. G. del Monte, RGTC 6/2, 95.
[106] Or *šal-u-ṷa-ar-ṷa-an-z*[*i*?

5 If you, o deity, (are) ang[ry] over (something) inside the temple only [but (if you are) further]
6 not angry over anything, then [let] the ext[a be ...]

---

7 Concerning the fact that the gods? by/from the smiths ... [...]
8 Has (s)he been ascertained (to be) in anger for that reason? Th[en let the exta be ...]

---

9 Concerning the fact that the smiths ... [...]

Rev.

1 [Through] the 'Old Wom[an'] that [s]ame [question]. Th[en let the *kin* be ...]
2 [O]n the second day the *panku* [took] for itself RIGHTNESS ... [...]
3 [O]n the third day the MOTHERGODDESS rose, RIGHTN[ESS? ...]

---

4 (Is it) the Zawalli-deity of Šauš[gatti? ...]
5 since now, o deity, for/to the queen ... [...]
6 and will they give an offering to the deity unt[il ...]
7 and just as she [has been] ascertai[ned] for me through the inquiry, [...]

---

8 The deity on his/her premises in the town of Li[praššа? ...]
9 and just as? completely ... [...]
10 [will they] thus undo him/her on his/her premises [...]
11 and give the deity an offering until [...]
12 and just as (s)he has been ascertained for m[e] through the inquiry, [will they? ...] he[r?]
13 Through the divination priestess it has been ascertained.

CHAPTER FIVE

CTH 569: TEXT AND TRANSLATION

1. *Text constitution: tablets one to four*

I.1	L 5 (?)
2	XVI 58
II.1A.	XXII 35
B.	XLIX 93
2.	KBo IX 151
3A.	XVI 32
B.	L 6+XVI 41+7/v
4.	LII 92.

Ad I. The comprehensive version

The fragment published as XVI 58 (Bo 1294, I.2) can be identified with certainty as having been part of the comprehensively recorded oracle investigation concerning the *tawananna*, Danuḫepa, Urḫiteššub and Ḫalpaziti as defined in Chapter I. It can be assigned to this group by the formula, rev. iii 3'-8' *mān*= *ma*=*šmaš* DINGIR.MEŠ [*QATAMMA mal*]*ān ḫarteni aši*=*kan* INIM-*ša̰* [*apēz mem*]*iaz laittari* DINGIR-*LUM*=*naš* [*zilatii̯*]*a ANA* INIM ᵐ*Ḫalpa*-LÚ ᵀᵁ́ᴳ*šeknun* [*idal*]*auu̯anni UL namma kuitki* [EGIR-*pa* SUD-*i̯aši*] "If you, o gods, have [thus appr]oved (and) that affair will be solved through [that de]ed (and) you, o god, will not [in futu]re [pull back] the robe at us anymore in evil over the affair of Ḫalpaziti."

XVI 58 is max. 5.5 cm high on the obverse, 6.0 cm on the reverse (including *Randleiste* till lower edge). The width is 5.7 cm for the obverse and 6.0 cm for the reverse. It constitutes the upper right corner of the second column and the lower right corner of the third column of a, most probably, originally two-column tablet. Because of the order in which the several affairs are treated and the fact that KBo II 6+ was the penultimate tablet of the series followed by one more concerning Šaušgatti, XVI 58 is likely to have been the fourth tablet in the entire series of six. For its relative position to the summary fragments see below 2.

Another fragment of the comprehensive version could be L 5 (Bo 9269, I.1). It is a small one-sidedly preserved piece with remains of two columns. Although it does not contain any of the parts of the distinctive formula, its right column 2'ff. runs closely enough to L 6+ 7ff. (§§12'-13') to consider it part of CTH 569. The left column merely shows traces of ends of two lines

(1' S]IG$_5$, and 3']x), which will not be given separately anymore below. Because six different affairs take up six tablets, the fragment L 5, if indeed dealing with the second affair (Danuḫepa), may possibly have been part of the second tablet.

Ad II. The summaries

The fragment XXII 35 (Bo 4863, II.1A) was first attributed to CTH 569 by G.C. Moore, JNES 40 (1981) 49 n. 7. Column iii has attracted scholarly attention quite often, see my StBoT 38, 190, to be supplemented by G. del Monte in P. Xella (ed.), Archeologia dell'Inferno 106-107; the lines ii 2'-12' were transliterated and translated by G. del Monte, AION 35 (1975) 335-336. The right hand edge of the obverse is 7.2 cm high, the column width is 6.8 cm, the intercolumnium 0.7 cm on the obverse, 0.5 cm on the reverse. This piece contains the ends of only four lines of column i, just one possible trace of a sign of column iv (next to iii 9'), but larger portions of the columns ii and iii over their entire width. Judging by the curve of the fragment the preserved part of the second column belonged to the upper half of the tablet, the preserved part of the third column to the lower half. The legible remains of column i (2' *-r*]*i-an*, 4' -]*pa-aš*) recall KBo IX 151 (286/n, II.2) with twice the Glossenkeilwort : *ša-ak-ku-ri-an* (lines 2' and 8') and the PN ^{f}*Da-nu-ḫé-pa-aš* (line 5). A transliteration of KBo IX 151, a small fragment of either a first or fourth column, is therefore tentatively included immediately following that of XXII 35 i. Theoretically, it could even be a duplicate of XXII 35 i.[1]

The fragment XLIX 93 (Bo 6860, II.1B) forms the upper left portion of a second column. This fragment was not yet recognized as belonging to CTH 569; H. Berman, JCS 34 (1982) 122, 123, included it, however, in his listing of oracle investigations where the description of the oracle procedure was "omitted". It measures 8.7 by 4.0 cms. Before the slightly indented first sign of line 2, two horizontal strokes are visible running over from the otherwise lost first column. The lines ii 6-19 duplicate XXII 35 ii 1'-12' while ii 1-10 constitute a parallel and slightly elaborated version of L 6+ iii 10-15 and 17-21. XLIX 93 thus shows that XXII 35 ii belongs to the investigation of Danuḫepa, and therefore links the investigation concerning Ḫalpaziti contained in XXII 35 iii to the one concerning Danuḫepa and Urḫiteššub of XVI 32//L 6+.

A join to the large fragment XVI 32 (Bo 2514, II.3A) was proposed by V. Haas apud A. Archi, SMEA 22 (1980) 25 (cf. there n. 15) with L 6 (Bo 10189, II.3B). Later Haas, OLZ 77 (1982) 253-254, suggested that KBo IX 151 might have belonged to the first column of the same tablet. To these

[1] Another possibility would be to suppose that KBo IX 151 is part of the inquiry into Danuḫepa's estate as announced in L 6+ iii 9-10 (GIDIM=*i̯a*=*kan* ŠÀ É *arii̯azi* "(They will call a man ...)and he will make the deceased at the estate subject of an oracle inquiry"). If this estate was located outside the capital, the text of that inquiry might not have been kept in Ḫattuša though.

pieces XVI 41 (Bo 2651, II.3B) was added by G. del Monte in P. Xella (ed.), Archeologia dell'Inferno 111 n. 23, which had previously been enlarged itself by unp. 7/v by H. Otten - Chr. Rüster, ZA 62 (1972) 106-107. Sections of XVI 32, XVI 41+7/v and/or L 6 were given in transliteration and translation by A. Archi, SMEA 14 (1971) 211-212 and 214, ibid. 22 (1980) 25-29, A. Ünal, THeth. 3, 173-174, and THeth. 4, 104-111 and 112. G. del Monte, AION 35 (1975) 327-328, gave a summary of XVI 32, which was later in Archeologia dell'Inferno 111-115, supplemented by a translation of the 'full' text XVI 32+L 6+XVI 41+7/v. Finally, a paraphrase of the sections concerning Urḫiteššub can be found in Ph.H.J. Houwink ten Cate, BiOr 51 (1994) 250-251.

Through this major join (KBo IX 151(+)?XVI 32+L 6+XVI 41+7/v) the almost complete second and third column of the original tablet seemed to have been regained with the small piece KBo IX 151 possibly pertaining to either the first or fourth column. However, photo collation has shown that XVI 32 cannot be part of L 6+XVI 41+7/v. As is immediately obvious from the photo but not from the handcopy, L 6+ (see Pl. I) is written in a deep, clear and generally more regular hand than XVI 32. The tablet XVI 32 itself shows two different hands (see Pl. II). The first seven lines are also fairly regularly written but the signs are slightly smaller than in L 6+. However, after the sloppily drawn double paragraph line preceding line 8', the writing suddenly becomes smaller and more superficial with a tendency for the horizontals to slant downwards to the right. As such it resembles the second hand on KBo II 6+ iii 38-40 (see below); compare, for instance, the NA signs in XVI 32, 8'ff. with the one in KBo II 6+ iii 40. Significant for the two hands on XVI 32 is further the shape of the URU sign: in lines 1'-7' it has four times the 'older' form with three equally long horizontals, whereas the middle horizontal in the lines 8'-30' is three times (8', 24', 29') very much protruding, lending the sign its specific late thirteenth century form. The size of the signs as well as the density with which they were written on the tablet also has its consequences on the amount of signs per line. In L 6+ most lines do not exceed the number of 15-16 signs in a line, whereas XVI 32, 1'-7' normally has 18-20 signs and 8'-30' mostly has more than 20. Moreover, the indication "Am Strich abgebrochen" on the lower end in the handcopy of XVI 32 seems to be a mistake: what we see, is the lower edge of the tablet. Finally, the two fragments are different in size, i.e. XVI 32, 1'-30' is 10.6 cm high, whereas L 6 ii 1'-30', which is supposed to join the former directly, is only 9.5 cm high. As far as concerns KBo IX 151, some slight differences in sign forms might suggest a different hand than the one of L 6.[2]

On the other hand, the pieces XVI 32 and L 6+XVI 41+7/v come back together again as duplicates. The restoration of the ends of the lines XVI 32, 14'-17' are securely based on the lines 19'-23' of the same text. The words ḪUL-*aḫḫun*, -]*el kuit* and -]*anzi* of L 6+ ii 16'-18' not only show that

[2] The exact size of KBo IX 151 cannot be given here because the measuring rod was not visible on the photo (BoFn 14358).

the two texts use similar wordings but if taken as duplicating the line ends of XVI 32, 15'-17' as restored after ibid. 20'-22', all line ends of L 6+ ii 1'-29' turn out to match exactly the restorations expected in XVI 32. There are, however, some slight discrepancies between the two copies. First of all, XVI 32 uses four lines for its last paragraph (27'-30'), whereas L 6+ ii (28'-30') seems to have three for the corresponding one. Moreover, whereas L 6 ii seems to have a double paragraph line between the lines 24' and 25', XVI 32 shows only one paragraph line between the corresponding lines 23'-24'. Note that, when the texts were considered as joining directly, the line count between the two fragments differed one line from L 6 ii 9' onwards because the double paragraph line between XVI 32, 7' and 8' corresponded to an empty space in L 6, which was counted as a line by Archi in his handcopy of L 6. Now that the texts are duplicates rather than belonging to one tablet, this may still be true. Finally, in view of the difficulties in restoring XVI 32, 3' and 6', L 6+ ii 1'-7' may have had a somewhat different wording here.

XVI 32 constitutes the lower part of the second column of a tablet. It is 10.6 cm high and 7.0 cm at its widest (line 7'). Of L 6 the columns ii and iii are almost in their entire length preserved (cf. the indication "oberer Rand nahe"), although we have only the very ends of lines of ii 1'-30'. Of col. i only the traces of two ends of lines remain visible near ii 44'-45' (x+1]x-*at*, 2']x). With the addition of the join piece XVI 41+7/v (see the join sketch) this leads to a column length of at least 70 lines. The length of the tablet L 6 as now preserved (57 lines for col. ii, 56 for col. iii) is 21.0 cm, the column width measures 7.5-8.0 cm. With the join piece XVI 41+7/v added, the total length becomes 24.5 cm. Only two signs remain of the first column and can be seen next to L 6 ii 44'-45' (-]x-*at*). The traces in lower left hand corner of the intercolumnium of XVI 41, accompanied by a question mark, are hardly discernible on the photo; if they are signs, they are much smaller than the other signs. Moreover, as drawn in the handcopy, they would be written upside down.

Finally, the small fragment LII 92 (Bo 6947, II.4) iv 2'-6' turns out to be a parallel, shorter version of XXII 35 iii 7'-16'. The obv. is 3.5 cm high, its longest line (7') 2.3 cm long; the rev. is 4.0 cm high, line 9' 1.8 cm long. The texts of column i cannot as yet be matched to any of the known fragments of this larger oracle investigation. Its fourth column correspon-ding to XXII 35 iii, the obv. i must get a place in the earlier parts of the investigation. It is here tentatively put at the very beginning, although, for instance, with a tablet format smaller than that of XXII 35, it might have followed XXII 35 i as well. Its exact position cannot be determined.

2. *The order of fragments in the tablets one to four*

First come the remains of the first column L 6 i and LII 92 i which may have concerned the *tawananna* affair. The further order in which the texts will be presented below is dictated by the two key fragments XXII 35 and

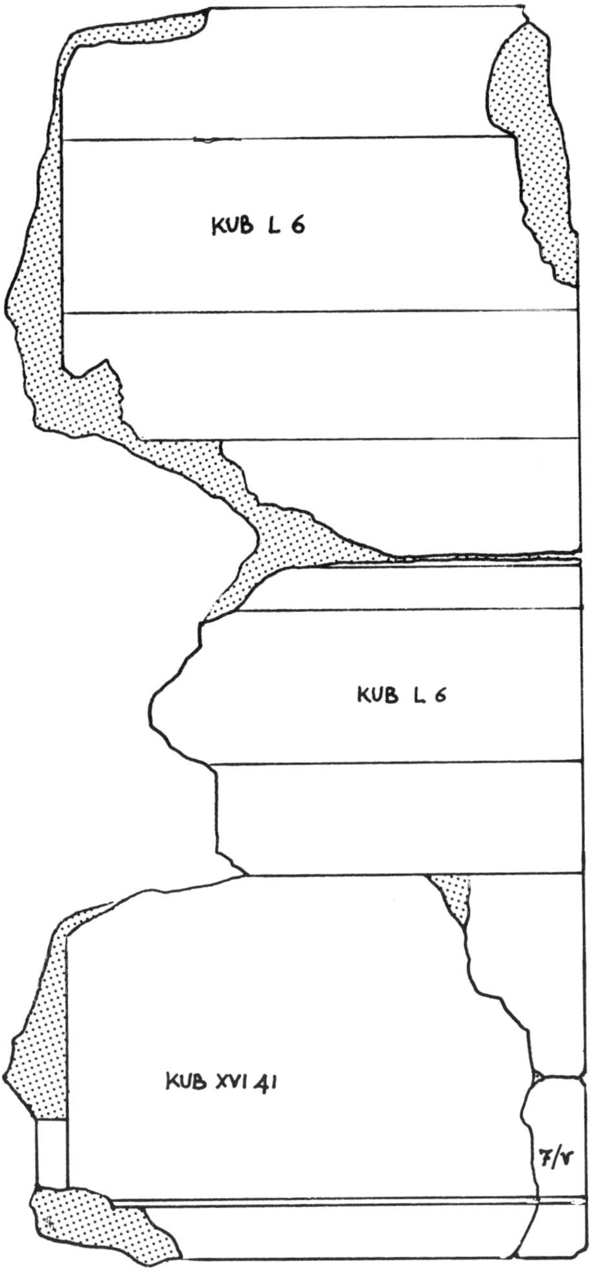

L 6+XVI 41+7/v rev.

XLIX 93 (II.1A and B). In general they show that after the *tawananna* affair those of Danuḫepa and Urḫiteššub were dealt with first, followed by that of Ḫalpaziti. Most problematic is the position of KBo IX 151. The fragments XXII 35 i and KBo IX 151 are kept together as remains of a part of the investigation preceding XVI 32. The similarity of KBo IX 151 to L 6+ ii 48ff. must in that case be considered due to the resuming of the same topic since, with XXII 35 ii//XLIX 93, 1-10 running parallel to the more or less immediately following passage L 6+ iii 10-21, this would leave hardly any text between the remains of the first and second column of XXII 35. The fact, that it is styled differently from XVI 32, that is not in the manner called 'ultimate', can be explained by the existence of more summary versions as is proven by XXII 35//XLIX 93 and XVI 32//L 6+.

Then follow XVI 32//L 6+ with XXII 35 ii//XLIX 93 *in Partitur*, where they are parallel. The small fragment of the comprehensive recording L 5 is inserted here at the point where it seems to correspond to the summary. Finally, the matter of Ḫalpaziti is dealt with in the summaries XXII 35 iii and LII 92 iv, again *in Partitur*. Due to a fortunate coincidence both XXII 35 iii and the comprehensive XVI 58 iii preserve different parts of the two standard phrases characteristic of CTH 569 and may therefore textually – not physically – touch on each other (see below in the Commentary, Ch. VI). As shown above (Introduction, Ch. I) the two always occur together sometimes only separated by additional promises of compensation and remuneration. Therefore, XVI 58 iii is placed directly after its summaries XXII 35 iii and LII 92 iv; this probably implies that XVI 58 ii should be inserted between XVI 32//L 6+ and XXII 35 iii and its parallel LII 92 iv. It will either have belonged to the end of the Urḫiteššub affair or the beginning of the Ḫalpaziti affair. This results in the following sequence:

a)	L 6 i	(*tawananna*?)
	LII 92 i	(*tawananna*?)
b)	XXII 35 i	Danuḫepa?
c)	KBo IX 151	Danuḫepa
d)	XXII 35 ii//XLIX 93	Danuḫepa
	XVI 32//L 6+	*tawananna*, Danuḫepa, Urḫiteššub
	L 5 r.col.	(inserted; Danuḫepa)
e)	XVI 58 ii	?
f)	XXII 35 iii	Ḫalpaziti
	LII 92 iv	Ḫalpaziti
g)	XVI 58 iii	Ḫalpaziti
h)	XXII 35 iv	?

3. *Text constitution: tablets five and six*

I.	KBo II 6+XVIII 51
II.1	VIII 27(+)Bo 7787
2	10/v.

Ad I. KBo II 6+, the comprehensive version

KBo II 6+ XVIII 51 (see the join sketch) is a large two-column tablet with ca. 70 lines per column (including blank spaces). Except for just the ends of the lines 1-2, the first ca. 32 lines of column i are missing. Correspondingly, a similar but somewhat smaller portion of the beginning of col. ii is broken away. The indication ("Lücke von mindestens 10 Zeilen") in the handcopy at the beginning of col. ii is somewhat inexact and therefore misleading. The gap between the sign trace in ii 5 and the first traces when KBo II 6 resumes again, extends over ca. 17 lines, or if we take the join piece XVIII 51 into account, ca. 15 lines. The consequently incorrect line count[3] of the handcopy has nevertheless been maintained here. Both pieces Bo 6 (KBo II 6) and Bo 6695 (XVIII 51) were already glued together when the photographs (BoFn. 866-869) were taken in Berlin. The tablet measures 27.5 cm high and 18 cm wide (ii 35). Important corrections to the handcopy by H. Figulla as given in KBo II were published by A. Walther as "Verbesserungen zu KBo II 6" in KUB XVIII p. 40 ad no. 51 (henceforth referred to as "Walther, Verbesserungen"). All have been confirmed by photo collation. The lines iii 38-40 occupy a space normally filled with 4 lines and are more superficially written in what looks like a different hand with the horizontals slanting downwards to the right, thus resembling the second hand on XVI 32 (cf. above 1. ad II). The beginnings of these lines are slightly more indented than the others in this column. Since it is not a case in which the oracle result was added later (the beginning of this starts already in iii 37), the reason for this remains unclear. Note, finally, that the tablet shows a considerable number of erasures and mistakes (see the notes to the transliteration and the commentary)

Parts of this text have already been given in transliteration and translation by A. Archi, SMEA 14 (1971) 213, G. del Monte, AION 33 (1973) 377-380, 382-383, and in P. Xella (ed.), Archeologia dell'Inferno 108-110, and by A. Ünal, THeth. 3, 103-106.

Ad II. The summaries

The obverse of VIII 27 (Bo 3042) is 9.3 cm high, its maximum width (lines 10'-11') is 1.0 cm. The height of the lines 1'-12' on the reverse is 5.0 cm.

[3] Because of the uncertainty about the exact number of lines missing at least a prime should have been added to the line numbers after line 5.

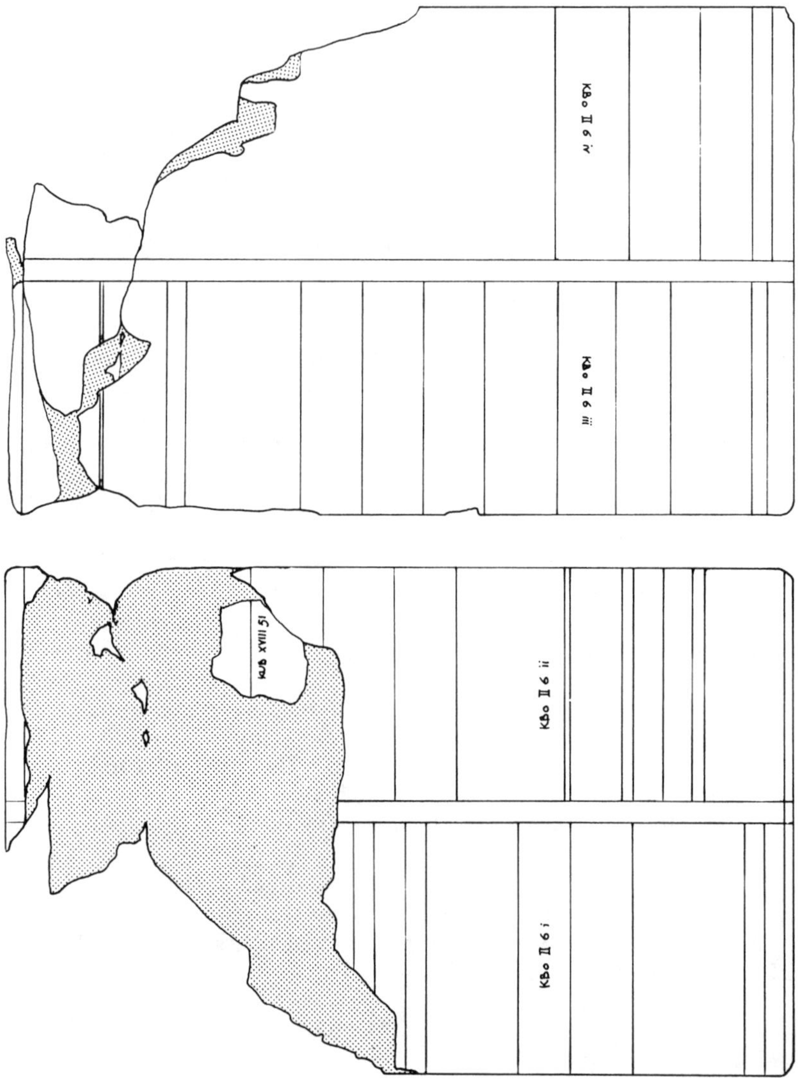

KBo II 6+XVIII 51 obv. and rev.

It joins on its rev. 1'-8' unp. Bo 7787 indirectly as shown in the transliteration below. This tiny fragment, of which only one side is preserved, is 3.5 cm high, its width varies from 2.4 cm (line 1) to 2.0 cm (line 6). Nothing of the second and third columns seems to be preserved.

The unpublished piece 10/v is a tiny fragment of 3.3x2.5 cm, one-sidedly preserved only. It summarizes KBo II 6+ i 31'-ii 3ff. (§§9"-12"). Theoretically it might indirectly join VIII 27(+) but this cannot be substantiated. It seems less likely to suppose it might still belong to the lost fourth column of L 6+, since this column will have contained the remaining parts of the Urḫiteššub and Ḫalpaziti affairs first.[4]

As has already been stated in the Introduction (Ch. I.6) VIII 27(+) may not have been a summary in all its (fragmentarily) preserved paragraphs. Nevertheless, its lines iv 1'-7' effectively summarize KBo II 6+ iii 41-iv 23. Although the following paragraph VIII 27(+) iv 8'-12' seems to match KBo II 6+ iii 17-22, that is, an *earlier* part of the full investigation, it seems illogical to suppose that the order of the paragraphs would have been reversed by the scribe drawing up the summary. Instead, we probably have to assume that these lines are a repetition of the earlier part of KBo II 6+ in the sense that this part of the oracle investigation is taken up again, just as in XVI 32//L 6+ the affairs of the *tawannanna*, Danuḫepa and Urḫiteššub were resumed. At this point it should be noted that the length of the lines in VIII 27 suggests, that compared to KBo II 6+ iii 17-22 an extra element was added to the question. This would imply that the lines in question form the summary of the beginning of the missing sixth tablet of this oracle series. The reverse ends with a blank space of about seven lines. Given the fact that there is a blank space of approximately five lines on the obv. between the lines 12' and 13' also, the text does not necessarily end here. Judging by the curve of the tablet, the reverse side belongs to the lower half of the tablet but there may have been room for some 15 lines until the lower edge would have been reached.

The appearance of the omina at the left edge of VIII 27(+)[5] suggests that the oracle investigation proper ended on its fourth column. As a consequence, the full investigation of which only KBo II 6+ seems to have come down to us, will have comprised no more than six tablets: even if VIII 27(+) iv contained more text, it is not likely to have summarized more than a whole extra tablet. The reason for the inclusion of omina at the left edge of the tablet can only be surmised. It may, however, be no coincidence that the protases preserved on the left edge b, refer to ^{d}*SÎN* (the Moongod) and ^{d}GAŠAN (a sumerographic way of rendering the name of the goddess Šauška). Especially, since in the entire Boğazköy omina literature the latter is attested only here. Possibly, the Hittites investigated this

[4] One could also point at the spellings *pár-ku-nu-an-zi* without the glide in L 6+ ii 40', iii 5, 49 as opposed to *pár-ku-nu-u̯a-*⸢*an*⸣[*-zi* in 10/v, 3' and *ka-ni-iš-ša-an-zi* in L 6+ iii 52 versus *ka-*]⸢*ni*⸣*-eš-ša-an-zi* in 10/v, 6'. On the other hand, VIII 27(+) has both *pár-ku-nu-u̯a-an-zi* in iv 4' and *ku-at-ta* in iv 8'.

[5] See K.K. Riemschneider, Omentexte 149-150.

obviously highly important matter from all possible angles, including even references to omina collections of Mesopotamian origin referring to those deities, who were onomastically closely related to Armatarḫunta (^{md}*SÎN*-^{d}U) and Šaušgatti (^{fd}GAŠAN-*ti*). If so, this would be a rare instance of practical use of such scholarly compendia.

4. *Synopsis*

Because of the break of unknown length between the tablets one to four on the one hand and five and six on the other this synopsis is likewise split in two parts with a separate numbering of paragraphs.

Tablets one to four: Since no real significant information can be distilled from the highly fragmentary pieces LII 92 i, XXII 35 i and KBo IX 151, which are to be placed at the very beginning, this synopsis starts with XVI 32//L 6+.

§§	Text	*Tawananna*	*Danuḫepa*	*Urḫiteššub*
		[lost paragraphs about the *tawananna*, *continued in §§8'-9'*]		
			[lost paragraphs about Danuḫepa?]	
§1'	XVI 32 ii 1'-5'		Out of each city given to Danuḫepa they will assign one household to her ancestor cult and they will bring back Danuḫepa's gods.	
§2'	XVI 32 ii 6'-7'		The cities will give tribute to the ancestor cult; *continued in §§10'-14'*.	
	double §§-line			
§3'	XVI 32 ii 8'-13'			The Majesty will complete the *mantalli*-ritual for the gods of Ḫalpa; Katapaili will appease the deity

			(in Ḫalpa?) together with the king of Kargamiš and they will found a priesthood there for the one destined by oracle.
§4’	XVI 32 ii 14’-18’		The Majesty does not have to complete the *mantalli*-ritual for the sons of Urḫiteššub.
§5’	XVI 32 ii 19’-23’		The Majesty does not have to complete the *mantalli*-ritual for the sons of Armatarḫunta.
§6’	XVI 32 ii 24’-26’		They will take the city of Kiuta from Talmitešub and give it to the deceased (= probably Armatarḫunta).
§7’	XVI 32 ii 27’-30’		To undo the oath of His Majesty’s father to Urḫiteššub they will give one city near? the city of Neya to the sons of Urḫiteššub; *continued in §§15’-19’.*
§8’	L 6+ ii 31’-34’	(continuation of the *tawananna*-affair) fragmentary: something about a curse [of the *tawananna*?]	
§9’	L 6+ ii 35’-47’	Like they regularly undid the curse of the *tawananna* before, they will undo it	

		now likewise once and for all.		
§10'	L 6+ ii 48'-55'		(continuation of the Danuḫepa affair) The curse of Danuḫepa is ascertained (–> §11'); her soul is angry because her estate was squandered (–> §12'); her deities were 'locked in' (–> §13'); her estate was given to others (–> §14').	
§11'	L 6+ ii 56'-iii 6		Like they regularly undid the curse of the Danuḫepa before, they will undo it now likewise once and for all.	
§12'	L 6+ iii 7-15 ~ XLIX 93, 1-4 (inserted L 5)		As to her estate: they will send somebody to inspect any cultic shortcomings and do penance.	
§13' / §13' a	L 6+ iii 16-22 ~ XLIX 93, 5-XXII 35 ii 12'		As to her 'deities': they will regularly give the offerings which were established by his Majesty's father.	
§14'	L 6+ iii 23-29		As to the cities given to Danuḫepa: fragmentary, something about tribute.	
§15'	L 6+ iii 30-31			(continuation of the §§3'-7') fragmentary: something about His Majesty and a

		mantalli-ritual [in Ḫalpa?]
§16'	L 6+ iii 32-39	In connection with the curse of Urḫiteššub it was established that his Majesty's father had promised something but not given it.
§17'	L 6+ iii 40-45	It is not recommended to send word to Urḫiteššub as it stands.
§18'	L 6+ iii 46-62	Therefore they have undone the curse of Urḫiteššub; they will recognize his sons and wives; they will conduct an oracle investigation about the *mantalli*-ritual for his sons and follow up its results; no envoy will be sent to Urḫiteššub.
	double §§-line	
§19'	L 6+ iii 63-65	The sons of Urḫiteššub and his Majesty will perform the *mantalli*-ritual.
	(inserted from comprehensive version: XVI 58 ii)	
	break of unknown length	

Ḫalpaziti

§20"	XXII 35 iii ~ LII 92 (and comprehensive version XVI 58 iii)	The Majesty will perform a *mantalli*-ritual for Ḫalpaziti; the father of His Majesty and Ḫalpaziti will perform a *mantalli*-ritual for each other; they will do penance to the gods of Ḫalpa and a ritual will be officially established there.

Tablets five and six: Since VIII 27(+) i is too fragmentary, the synopsis starts with KBo II 6+ i. As was pointed out in the Introduction (Chapter I), KBo II 6+ can be seen as the continuation of XVI 32, 19'-23' (§5') dealing with the *mantalli*-rituals to the sons/children of Armatarḫunta. Because of the break of unknown length between the tablets one to four and the beginning of tablet five and in order to avoid an excessive number of primes behind the paragraph numbers, a new numbering of paragraphs starts.

§1'	KBo II 6+ i 1-2 (break)	(fragmentary) someone is ang]ry?
§2"	i 1'-3'	(fragmentary, *ḫurri*-bird oracle, denial)
§3"	i 4'-5'	(confirmed through KIN-oracle)
§4"	i 6'-7'	[Armatarḫunta] has uttered curses (*ḫurri*-bird oracle)
§5"	i 9'-10'	(confirmed through KIN-oracle)
§6"	i 11'-19'	the deceased Armatarḫunta is angry, his gods have been 'scattered', his descendancy utters curses and his curse has been ignored(?) (SU-oracle)
§7"	i 20'-24'	(confirmed through KIN-oracle)
§8"	i 25'-30'	(confirmed through augury)
§9"	i 31'-41' ~ 10/v	the curse of Armatarḫunta having been established, they will cleanse the places of kingship and the thrones, His Majesty will cleanse himself, they will compensate for the 'house' and recognize his grandson (*ḫurri*-bird oracle)
§10"	i 42'-43'	(confirmed through SU-oracle)
§11"	i 44'- ii 2	(confirmed through KIN-oracle)
§12"	ii 3-5	([confirmed] through augury)
§13"'	ii 12-15	(fragmentary) something about festivals
§14"'	ii 16-22	(fragmentary) festivals have been left uncelebrated; they will make up for them (SU-oracle?)
§15"'	ii 23-29	(confirmed through SU-oracle)

§16'''	ii 30-35	(confirmed through KIN-oracle)
§17'''	ii 36	(blank followed by double §§)
§18'''	ii 37-41	the deity has taken up again the Šaušgatti affair because of the curse of Šaušgatti during her life (KIN-oracle)
§19'''	ii 42	(confirmed through *ḫurri*-bird oracle)
§20'''	ii 43-45	this has happened not only because of the curse of Šaušgatti during her life (*ḫurri*-bird oracle)
§21'''	ii 46-48	the deceased is angry because of something (else)(KIN-oracle)
§22'''	ii 49	(confirmed through *ḫurri*-bird oracle)
§23'''	ii 50-54	it is not only the curse of Šaušgatti during her life and the anger of the deceased (*ḫurri*-bird oracle)
§24'''	ii 55-iii 2	the deceased's children utter curses and stir up the deceased (KIN-oracle)
§25'''	iii 3	(confirmed through *ḫurri*-bird oracle)
§26'''	iii 4-10	it is the curse of Šaušgatti during her life, the anger of the deceased and because her children utter curses (*ḫurri*-bird oracle)
§27'''	iii 11-15	(confirmed through KIN-oracle)
§28'''	iii 16	(confirmation through augury but result is not given)
§29'''	iii 17-23	whatever the reasons of her anger, they will appease Šaušgatti; she demands, however, a *mantalli*-ritual (SU-oracle)
§30'''	iii 24-29	(confirmed through KIN-oracle)
§31'''	iii 30-35	both His Majesty and Šaušgatti will perform *mantalli*-rituals (*ḫurri*-bird oracle)
§32'''	iii 36-40	(confirmed through KIN-oracle)
§33'''	iii 41-51 ~ VIII 27(+) iv 1'-6'	undoing the curse of Šaušgatti by cleansing the places of kingship and His Majesty, by setting up the image of the deceased and by giving her compensation, is not approved of (KIN-oracle)
§34'''	iii 52-53	(confirmed through *ḫurri*-bird oracle)
§35'''	iii 54-59	(confirmed through augury)
§36'''	iii 60-iv 2 ~ VIII 27(+) iv 6'	they will set up the image of the deceased and give both her and her children compensation (*ḫurri*-bird oracle)
§37'''	iv 3-4	(confirmed through SU-oracle)
§38'''	iv 5-9	(confirmed through KIN-oracle)
§39'''	iv 10-16	(denied through augury)
§40'''	iv 17-23	(confirmed through counter-augury)

§41'''	VIII 27(+) iv 8'-12'	whatever the reasons of her anger, they will appease Šaušgatti; she might, however, demand a *mantalli*-ritual

CTH 569: TRANSLITERATION AND TRANSLATION

5. *The texts: transliteration and translation*

a) L 6+ i (II.3B)

x+1]x-*at*
2]x

LII 92 i (II.4)

x+1 [*IŠ*-]*TU* ^{MU}[^{NUS}ŠU.GI

---

2 [*A-N*]*A*$^{?}$ ^{d}*UTU-ŠI*[
3 [IG]I-*an-da-ma* x[
4 *nu-kán ma-a-a*[*n*
5 GIG-*an-za* GAM(-)x$^{?}$[
6 *IŠ-TU* $^{\text{MUNUS!}}$[6]Š[U.GI

---

7 ^{d}*Ḫi-iš-ḫu-ra-za*[
8 GAM-*ma a-ri-i̯*[*a-*
9 DINGIR-*LIM-tar*-⸢*ma*⸣[

(blank space of three lines until break)

b) XXII 35 i (II.1A)

x+1 [ ]x
2 [*ša-ak-ku*$^{?}$*-r*]*i-an*
3 [ ]x

---

4 [^{f}*Da-nu-ḫé*$^{?}$-]*pa-aš*

c) KBo IX 151 (II.2)

x+1 [ ]x *še-er* TUKU.TUKU-*u*<*-an*>*-za*
2 [*a*]*r*$^{??}$*-ḫa* 𒑱*ša-ak-ku-ri-an*
3 [SIxS]Á$^{?}$*-at*
4 [*IŠ-TU*] 3 ^{GIŠ}TUKUL SIG$_{5}$

---

5 [*a-ri-i̯a-*]*u-en* ^{f}*Da-nu-ḫé-pa-aš*
6 [EGI]R-*an* SIxSÁ-*at*
7 [É-]⸢*TI*⸣$^{?}$ *še-er*

[6] On the photo it looks as if the scribe had initially forgotten to write MUNUS and had started with the lower horizontal of ŠU. Having noticed his mistake he wrote MUNUS over what was already there.

a) L 6+ i

(no translation feasible)

LII 92 i

x+1 [Thr]ough the 'O[ld Woman' ...

---

2 [Fo]r$^{?}$ His Majesty[...
3 [agai]nst, however, ... [...
4 and i[f ...
5 illness ... [...
6 Through the 'Old Wo[man' ...]

---

7 Through (the deity) Ḫišḫura [
8 [we] continued the inq[uiry ...
9 the divinity, however, [...]

---

b) (no translation feasible)

c)

x+1 [...] (is/was) angry because of [...]
2 [...] dispersed
3 [... was ascer]tained
4 [... through] three oracle types: favorable.

---

5 [...] we [investigat]ed [through oracle]. Danuḫepa
6 [... la]ter was ascertained
7 [...] because of [the esta]te

8 [*ar-ḫ*]*a* 𒑱*ša-ak-ku-ri-*⸢*an*⸣
9 [*ú-*]⸢*e*⸣*-ri-i̯a-an-z*[*i*]
10 [ ]x-*nu-zi*
11 [ ]x-*an*(-)x[

d) – L 5 (I.1)
– A. XVI 32 (II.3A)
B. L 6+XVI 41+7/v (II.3B)
– A. XXII 35 ii (II.1A)
B. XLIX 93 (II.1B)

II.3A ii

§1' x+1 *ŠA* ^{f}*Ta-nu-ḫé-pa ku-i-e-eš* URU.DIDLI.ḪI.A *pa*$^{!?}$[*-ra-a* SUM*-an-z*(*i*)]
2 *nu-kán IŠ-TU* 1 URU*-LUM* 1 É*-TUM da-aš-*⸢*ki*⸣[*-u-an ti-i̯a-an-*(*zi*)]
3 *na-at A-NA* GIDIM *pí-an-zi nu-uš-ma-aš* 1 URU-[*LUM* (x x x[7])]
4 *na-an a-še-ša-an-zi nu-kán* DINGIR.MEŠ ^{f}*Ta-nu-*⸢*ḫé*⸣[*-pa*]
5 EGIR*-pa an-da pé-e-da-an-zi*

---

§2' 6 *nu* URU.DIDLI.ḪI.A*-ma ku-i-e-eš ḫar-kán-zi na-aš ar-kam-*⸢*ma*⸣[- (x*-ti*)]
7 *nu A-NA* GIDIM *ar-kam-ma-an* BAL*-eš-ki-u-u̯a-an* ⸢*ti*⸣[*-i̯a-an-z*(*i*)]

---

§3' 8 *ki-nu-na-kán* GIM*-an ŠA* DINGIR.MEŠ ^{URU}*Ḫal-pa ú-li-ḫi-uš* UGU ⸢*ú*⸣[*-da-a*(*n-zi*)]
9 *nu-uš-ma-aš-za* ^{d}UTU*-ŠI* SISKUR *ma-an-tal-li-i̯a* IGI$^{!}$[8]*-an-da ar-ḫa* [BAL*-an-ti*]
10 GIM*-an-ma-kán* LUGAL KUR *Kar-ga-miš* UGU *ú-iz-zi nu-uš-ši-kán* ⸢^{m}⸣[*Ka-t*(*a*$^{?}$*-pa-*DINGIR*-LIM-*⸢*in*⸣)]
11 GAM*-an pa-ra-a ne-i̯a-an-zi nu* DINGIR*-LUM pí-di-ši* GIM*-an a-*[*ni-i̯*(*a-an-zi*)]
12 *na-an-kán* KASKAL*-ši ti-i̯a-an-zi* ^{LÚ}SANGA*-UT-TA-i̯a a-pí-i̯*[*a t*(*i*$^{?}$*-*⸢*i̯a*⸣*-an-zi*)]
13 *ku-iš* SIxSÁ*-ri*

---

§4' 14 *A-NA* ^{d}UTU*-ŠI ku-it A-NA* DUMU.MEŠ ^{m}*Úr-ḫi-*^{d}U*-ub* 𒑱SISKUR *ma-an-ta*[*l-li-i̯*(*a*)]
15 IGI*-an-da ar-ḫa* BAL*-u-an-zi UL* SIxSÁ*-at UL-aš ku-it* [^{d}UTU*-Š*(*I* ḪUL*-*⸢*aḫ-ḫu*⸣*-un*)]

[7]]x x.MEŠ or]x-*eš*? L 6+ may have had a different wording here as well as in line 6'.

[8] There is one vertical too many.

8 [...] dispersed
9 [... a man] the[y] will [c]all,
10 [...] he will [...]
11 [...] ... [...].

d)

A ii

1 The cities of Tanuḫepa which [the]y [will hand] o[ver$^{?}$],
2 out of each city one estate they$^{?}$ [will start$^{?}$] taking
3 and they will give it to the deceased and the one city [which$^{?}$] to them [...] ...,
4 they will populate it and bring the gods of Tanuḫe[pa]
5 back in.

---

6 Or, what cities they have, those [they will make$^{?}$] trib[utar]y$^{?}$
7 and to the deceased they will start offering tribute.

---

8 But now, when they c[arry] up the *uliḫis* of Ḫalpa's city gods,
9 the Majesty [will] com[plete] the *mantalli*-rituals to them.
10 When, then, the king of Kargamiš comes up (there), they will send Katapaili
11 down out to him and when they c[eleb]rate the deity on its own premises,
12 they will 'put him on the road' (i.e. satisfy him) and found a priesthood the[re],
13 (and install) whoever will be ascertained.

---

14 Concerning the fact that it was not ascertained for My Majesty to complete the *manta*[*lli*]-rituals to the sons of Urḫiteššub,
15 because I, [M]y [Majesty], had not wronged them,

16 ḪUL-*aḫ-ta-aš ku-iš* UN-*aš na-aš nu-u-u̯a ku-it* TI-*za nu* ⌈*a*⌉[-*pé*-(*el ku-it*)]
17 ZI-*za UL u̯a-ar-ši-i̯a-an-za nu* SISKUR *ma-an-tal-li ar-ḫa*[9] B[AL-*u*-(*an-zi*)]
18 ⌈*a*⌉-*pé-ez UL* SIxSÁ-*at*

---

§5' 19 *A-NA* ^{d}UTU-*ŠI ku-it A-NA* DUMU.MEŠ ^{md}*SÎN*-^{d}U SISKUR *ma-an-tal-l*[*i-i̯*(*a*)]
20 IGI-*an-da ar-ḫa* BAL-*u-an-zi UL* SIxSÁ-*at UL-aš* ⌈*ku*⌉[(-*it* ^{d}UTU-*ŠI*)]
21 ḪUL-*aḫ-ḫu-un* ḪUL-*aḫ-ta-aš ku-iš* UN-*aš na-aš nu-u*-[(*u̯a*[10] *ku-it*)]
22 TI-*za nu a-pé-el ku-it* ZI *UL u̯a-ar-ši-i̯a-a*[(*n-za*)]
23 [*nu*] SISKUR *ma-an-tal-li-i̯a ar-ḫa* ⌈KIN⌉[11]-*an-zi a-pé-ez* [*UL* SIx(SÁ$^{?}$-*at*)][12]

---

§6' 24 [^{UR}]^{U}*Ki-i-ú-ta-an-kán* URU-*an A-NA* ^{m}GAL-^{d}U[13] *ar-ḫ*[(*a* ME-*an-zi*)]
25 [*n*]*a-an A-NA* GIDIM SUM-*an-zi* ^{m}*Ka-ta-pa*-DINGIR-*LIM-iš* [(*ka-ru-ú*)]
26 [*u̯*]*a-tar-na-aḫ-ḫa-an-za nu* GIDIM *a-pa-a-aš* 𒑱*ar-šu-l*[*a*-(*iz-zi*)]

---

§7' 27 *MA-ME-TUM ŠA A-BI* ^{d}UTU-*ŠI ku-it A-NA* INIM ^{m}*Úr-ḫi*-^{d}[(U-*ub še-er*)]
28 [SI]xSÁ-*at nu* GIM-*an MA-ME-TUM ar-ḫa* KIN-*an-zi nu A-N*[(*A* DUMU.MEŠ)]
29 [^{m}*Ú*]*r-ḫi*-^{d}U-*ub I-NA* ^{URU}*Ne-i-i̯a* 1 URU-*L*[*UM*
30 [*pa-ra*-]⌈*a*⌉ SUM-*an-zi*

(lower edge in A)

B ii

---

§8' 31 [^{MUNUS}*ta-u̯a-an-na-na*] *ku-it pí-ra-an ti-i̯a-an-na* SIxSÁ-*at*
32 [GAM *a-ri-i̯a-u-e*]*n na-aš A-NA* EME
33 [*še-er* SIxSÁ-*a*]*t zi-la-aš IŠ-TU* ^{LÚ}ḪAL
34 [^{MUNUS}Š]U.GI ^{LÚ}IGI.MUŠEN-*i̯a* ⌈SIG$_5$⌉

---

[9] Like all other ḪA signs in XVI 32 but contrary to the handcopy this one also has two Winkelhaken.

[10] So B ii 22′ after collation contrary to handcopy which gives ŠI.

[11] After collation.

[12] B may have had a double paragraph line after 24' as indicated in the handcopy.

[13] Erasure.

16 and (because) the person who did wrong them, is still alive and because h[i]s
17-18 soul (has) not (been) pacified, therefore, it was not ascertained to complete the *mantalli*-ritual<s>.

---

19 Concerning the fact that it was not ascertained for My Majesty to complete the *mantall*[*i*]-rituals to the sons of Armatarḫunta,
20 because I, My Majesty, had not
21 wronged them, and (because) the one who did wrong them, is still
22 alive and because his soul (has) not (been) pacified,
23 therefore, it was [not estab]lished to bring the *mantalli*-rituals to an end.

---

24 They shall take away Kiuta, the city, from Talmiteššub
25 and give it to the deceased. Katapaili (has) already
26 (been) given [o]rders and he will ... the deceased.

---

27 Concerning the oath of the father of His Majesty which was ascertained in connection with the Urḫiteššub affair,
28 if they will undo the oath, to the sons
29 of [U]rḫiteššub in Niya one settle[ment ... ?]
30 they will hand [ove]r.

B ii

---

31 As to the fact that [the *tawananna*] was ascertained to step forward,
32 w[e continue]d [the inquiry] and in connection with a curse she
33 [was ascertain]ed. Outcome: through the diviner,
34 [the 'O]ld Woman' and the augur: favorable.

---

§9’ 35 EME ^{MUNUS}*ta-u̯a-an-na-na ku-iš* SIxSÁ-*at*
36 *nu* EME ^{MUNUS}*ta-u̯a-an-na-na ka-ru-ú* GIM-*an*
37 [14]*pí-an ar-ḫa an-ni-iš-ki-ir*
38 *ki-nu-na-i̯a-an A-NA* DINGIR.MEŠ LUGAL-*UT-TI QA-TAM-MA*
39 *pí-an ar-ḫa a-ni-an-zi AŠ-RI*$^{\text{ḪI.A}}$ [LUG]AL-*UT-TI*
40 ^{GIŠ}DAG.ḪI.A-*i̯a pár-ku-nu-an-zi* ^{d}UTU-*ŠI*-[*i̯a*-]⸢*za*⸣[15]
41 *IŠ-TU* EME ^{MUNUS}*ta-u̯a-an-na-na pár-ku-*⸢*nu*⸣*-zi*
42 *ma-a-an-ma-za* DINGIR-*LUM QA-TAM-MA ma-la-a-an har-ti*
43 INIM ^{MUNUS}*ta-u̯a-an-na-na-kán a-pé-ez* INIM-*za* DUḪ-*ri*
44 *zi-la-ti-an-na-aš* INIM ^{MUNUS}*ta-u̯a-an-na-na*
45 ^{TÚG}*še-ek-nu-un* ḪUL-*u-an-ni* EGIR-*pa UL*
46 *nam-ma* SUD-*i̯a-zi IŠ-TU* ^{MUNUS}ŠU.GI
47 ^{LÚ}ḪAL ^{LÚ}IGI.MUŠEN-*i̯a* SIG$_5$

---

§10’ 48 INIM ^{f}*Da-nu-ḫé-pa ku-iš* SIxSÁ-*at*
49 GAM *a-ri-i̯a-u-en na-aš A-NA* EME TI
50 *še-er* SIxSÁ-*at* GIDIM-*i̯a* TUKU.TUKU-*ti* SIxSÁ-⸢*at*⸣
51 A-NA É-*TI-aš še-er* SIxSÁ-*at* É-*ir-ši* [*ku-it*?]
52 *ar-ḫa ša*!^{16}*-ak-ku-ri-an* DINGIR.MEŠ-*aš-ši-k*[*án*]
53 *ku*!^{17}*-it* EGIR-*pa iš-tap-pa-an-te-eš* É[*-ir-ma*]
54 *ku-it ta-me-e-da-aš pa-ra-a* ⸢SUM⸣[*-an*]
55 *na-aš a-pé-da-ni-i̯a* EGIR-*an* S[IxSÁ-*at*]

---

§11’ 56 GAM *a-ri-i̯a-u-en* INIM ^{f}*Da-nu*[*-ḫé-pa ku-iš A-NA*]
57 EME TI SIxSÁ-*at nu* INIM ^{f}[*Da-nu-ḫé-pa*]

(end of column ii)

Reverse iii

1 [*ka-ru-ú* GIM-]*an A-NA* DINGIR.MEŠ LUGAL-*U*[*T-TI*]
2 [*p*]*í-an* ⸢*ar*⸣*-ḫa an-ni-iš-ki-ir*
3 *ki-nu-na-i̯a-an QA-TAM-MA pí-*⸢*an*⸣ [*ar-ḫa*]
4 *a-ni-an-zi AŠ-RI*$^{\text{ḪI.A}}$ LUGAL-*UT-TI* [^{GIŠ}DAG.ḪI.A-*i̯a*]
5 *pár-ku-nu-an-zi* ^{d}UTU-*ŠI-i̯a pár*[*-ku-nu-zi*]
6 KI.MIN ⸢*IŠ-TU*⸣ ^{MUNUS}ŠU.GI ^{LÚ}ḪAL ^{L}[^{Ú}IGI.MUŠEN-*i̯a* SIG$_5$]

---

14 <*A-NA* DINGIR.MEŠ LUGAL-*UT-TI*>? Cf. below iii 1-2.

15 Both the length of the break on the photo after ŠI and the shape of the sign rest following it, suggest this restoration and reading.

16 The beginning of a small horizontal wedge is written immediately preceding ŠA; it does not look like one Glossenkeil.

17 Tablet has KI.

35 Concerning the curse of the *tawannana* which was ascertained,
36-37 just as they have at an earlier stage undone the curse of the *tawannana* in front <of the gods of kingship>,
38 will they now, too, likewise in front of the gods of kingship
39 undo it, will they cleanse the places of [kin]gship
40 and the thrones, [and] will His Majesty
41 cleanse (himself) from the curse of the *tawannana*?
42 Now, if you, o god, have thus approved,
43 will the affair of the *tawannana* be solved through that deed?
44 In future, will the *tawannana* affair
45 not pull back at us the robe in evil
46 anymore? Through the Old Woman,
47 the diviner and the augur: favorable.

---

48 Concerning the Danuḫepa affair, which was ascertained,
49 we continued the inquiry. Because of the curse, (when) alive,
50 she was ascertained, and the deceased was ascertained (as being) in anger.
51 Because of the estate she was ascertained. [Because] her estate
52 (has been) dispersed, because her gods
53 (have been) 'locked up', (and) because the estate
54 (has been) hand[ed] over to others,
55 she [was] a[scertained] later for that as well.

---

56 We continued the inquiry. Concerning the Danu[ḫepa] affair [which]
57 was ascertained [because of] the curse, (when) alive, [jus]t as they have

Reverse iii

1 undone the [Danuḫepa] affair [at an earlier stage]
2 [in] front of the gods of kingship,
3 will they now, too, likewise undo it in front of (the gods of kingship),
4 will they cleanse the places of kingship [and the thrones]
5 and will His Majesty cl[eanse] <himself>
6 etc.? Through the Old Woman, the diviner [and] the a[ugur: favorable.]

---

§12' 7 *A-NA* É-*TI-ma-aš še-er ku-it* SIxSÁ-*a*[*t*]
II.1B 1 nu-uš-ši ku-it [
8 *nu-kán* UN-*an ú-e-ri-an-zi nu-uš-š*[*i-kán*]
9 *an-da ar-nu-an-zi* GIDIM-*i̯a-kán* ŠÀ ⸢É⸣
10 *a-ri-i̯a-zi nu-uš-ši ma-a-an* EZEN$_4$ *ku*[*-iš-ki*]
11 *na-aš-ma* NINDA.GUR$_4$.RA UD.KAM-*MI kar-ša-an-za* x[
12 *ti-i̯a-an-zi* GIŠ.ḪUR *gul-za-at-ta-ra-pát*? [*ú-u̯a-a*]*n-zi*[18]
13 *nu-uš-ši ma-a-an kar-ša-an ku-it-ki*
II.1B 2 ku-it-ma-aš-ši ⸢kar⸣[-ša-an
14 *na-at* 𒑱*za-ap-pa-an-ta-la-an-zi* GAM-*a*[*n*]
II.1B 3 na-at 𒑱za-ap-pa-a[n-] (4) GAM-na
15 *za-an-ki-la-tar* SUM-*an-zi IŠ-TU* 3 $^{GIŠ!}$[TUKUL] SIG$_5$
II.1B 4 za-an-ki-la-tar [[19]

(to be continued below)

Inserted from the comprehensive version: L 5 r.col. (I.1)

x+1 [ ]x[
2 [DINGIR.MEŠ-*ši-kán ku-it* E]GIR-*p*[*a iš-tap-pa-an-te-eš*?
3 [-*m*]*a-aš* GIŠ.ḪUR [
4 [*nu-kán* U]N-*an ú-e-r*[*i-an-zi*
5 ⸢*nu* EZEN$_4$⸣.MEŠ GIM-*an* [*A-BI* ^{d}UTU-*ŠI da-a-iš*?]
6 *nu-*⸢*uš*⸣*-ma-ša-aš QA-*⸢*TAM*⸣[*-MA*
7 *na-aš QA-TAM-MA e*<*-eš*>*-šu-u*[*-u̯a-an ti-an-zi nu* IGI-*zi* SU.MEŠ SIG$_5$-*ru*]
8 EGIR-*ma* NU.SIG$_5$-*du* I[GI-*zi* SU.MEŠ ... EGIR ...]

---

9 *nu ki-i-ma kiš-an* D[Ù-*an-zi*
10 *du-u-u̯a-an pa-ra-a* x[
11 ⸢*nu*⸣*-uš-ma-ša-aš-kán* [*an-da šar-ni-in-kán-zi*
12 [GAM-*n*]*a za-an-ki-la-*[*tar* SUM-*anzi*
13 [ ]x-*aš ku-u-*⸢*un*⸣[
14 [*nu* IGI-*zi-*]⸢*iš*?⸣ MUŠEN *Ḫ*[*UR*?*-RI*
15 [ ]x x[

§13' 16 GIDIM-*ma ku-it A-NA* DINGIR.MEŠ *še-er* ⸢SIxSÁ⸣*-at*
17 DINGIR.MEŠ-*ši-kán ku-it* EGIR-*pa iš-tap-pa-an-te-eš*
II.1B 5 DINGIR.MEŠ-*ŠU*-ma-aš-ši-kán [ku-it (6) E]GIR-pa iš-tap-pa-an-t[e-eš]
18 *nu* GIŠ.ḪUR *gul-za-at-tar ú-u̯a-an-zi*
II.1B 7 [n]u GIŠ.ḪUR.ḪI.A ú-u̯a-an-[(z)i]

[18] So according to the photo but the last two signs are not present in the handcopy. The ZI sign almost touches the obv. ii 48-49.
[19] There is no paragraph line following in XLIX 93 (II.1B).

7 Concerning the fact that she was ascertaine[d] because of the estate,

II.1B 1 Concerning the fact that [was ascertained] for her [...]

8 they will call a man and to he[r(/him$^?$) ...]
9 they will bring in and he will make the deceased at the estate
10 the subject of an oracle investigation. And if from her so[me] festival
11 or daily bread(-offering) has been withheld,
12 will they start g[iving$^?$ (it)] and [will] they [check] the *gulzattar*-tablets?
13 If something has been withheld from her,

II.1B 2 that which (was) with[held] from her [...]

14 will they ... it (and) additionally$^?$

II.1B 4 [will they] ... it and additionally$^?$

15 will they give compensation? By means of three oracle t[ypes]: favorable.

II.1B 4 compensation [...]

(L 5 r.col.:)

1 [...] ... [...]
2 [because her gods (have been)] 'lo[cked up']
3 [they will check the *gulzattar*] tablet [concerning th]em.$^?$
4 [They will] cal[l a m]an,
5 and just as [the father of the Majesty instituted$^?$] festivals
6 for them likewi[se will they ...
7 and [will they] likewise [start] celebra[ting] them? Then let the first exta be favorable,]
8 but let the following (ones) be unfavorable. The f[irst exta ...

---

9 Or will [...] d[o] this as follows: [...]
10 further [
11 and these for them [will they$^?$ compensate
12 and [additional]ly compensation [will they$^?$ give?
13 [...] ... this [
14 [Then let the fir]st *ḫ*[*urri*]-bird [be

16 Concerning the fact that the deceased has been ascertained in connection with the deities,
17 (that is,) because her gods (have been) 'locked up',

II.1B 5 [Because] for her her gods (6) (have been) 'locked up',

18 will they check the *gulzattar*-tablet?

II.1B 7 th[ey will] check the tablets

19 [*n*]*u*-[*u*]*š-ma-aš-kán A-BI* ^{d}UTU-*ŠI ku-it*

II.1B 8 [n]u-uš-ma-aš-kán *A-BI* [(^{d}UTU-*ŠI*)] (9) GIM-an

20 [SISKUR M]E-*iš nu-uš-ma-ša-*⸢*at*⸣ EGIR-*pa*

II.1B 9 SISKUR ME-iš[20] (II.1A ii 4') na-at *QA-TAM-MA*

21 [*pé-eš*]*-ki-u-u̯a-an ti*[*-i̯a*]*-an-zi*

II.1A ii (4') pé-eš-ki-u[21]-an ti-i̯a-an-zi

II.1A ii 5' ša-ku-u̯a-an-ta[22]-ri-i̯a-nu-uš-kán-te-eš-ma-at-kán

6' ku-it na-aš-kán an-da šar-ni-in-kán-zi

7' ma-a-an-ma GIDIM ZI-an DUḪ-ši

8' ⸢*IŠ*⸣*-TU* ^{MUNUS}ŠU.GI ^{LÚ}IGI.MUŠEN-i̯a SIxSÁ-at

9' [(*I*)]*Š-TU* ^{LÚ}ḪAL NU.SIG$_5$

---

§13a 10' [(ki-i)] ku-it *IŠ-TU* ^{LÚ}ḪAL NU.SIG$_5$-ta

11' [(GIDIM-z)]a *A-NA* É*-TI* še-er TUKU.TUKU-u<-an>-za

12' [ ]x? SIxSÁ-at

13' [k(u-i)]š ⸢GIDIM⸣ *A-NA* É*-TI* še-er

14' [TUKU.TUKU-at-ti? SIxSÁ]-⸢at⸣

15' [(-)]⸢É⸣-ir

16' [ ]x ku-it

17' [ ]x

22 [*IŠ-T*]*U* 3 ^{GIŠ}[TUKUL] SIG$_5$

---

§14' 23 [GIDIM*-ma ku-it*] URU.[DI]DLI.ḪI.A *pa-ra-a* SUM*-an-ta-aš*

24 [*še-er* TUKU.TUKU*-t*]*i* SIxSÁ*-at nu* ^{d}UTU-*ŠI ḫu-u-*⸢*uš-ku*⸣*-u-e-ni*

25 [ ]x.MEŠ URU.DIDLI.ḪI.A *ar-kam-ma-an*

26 [ ]x*-an* GIM*-an me-ma-an-zi*

27 [*-u̯a*(-) *u̯a-aš-*]⸢*ku*⸣*-u̯a-na* KAR*-u-en*

28 [ ]x GIM*-an* SIxSÁ*-at*

29 [*IŠ-TU*]⸢3⸣ ^{GIŠ}TUKUL SIG$_5$

---

§15' 30 [*I-NA* ^{URU}*Ḫal-pa*(?) ^{d}UT]U-*ŠI* SISKUR *ma-an-tal-li-i̯a*

31 [BAL*-u-an-zi*(?)] SIxSÁ*-at* ⟨Glossenkeil⟩[23]

---

§16' 32 [INIM ^{m}*Úr-ḫi-*]^{d}U*-ub ku-iš* SIxSÁ*-at a-ri-i̯a-u-en*

33 [*nu* EME]⸢^{m}⸣*Úr-ḫi-*^{d}U*-ub* SIxSÁ*-at* DUMU.MEŠ*-ŠU-ši-kán ku-it*

34 [KASKAL*-ši*] (erasure) *ti-i̯a-an-te-eš ar-ra-aḫ-ḫa-ni-i̯a-aš*

35 [*ti-u̯a-t*]*a-ni-i̯a še-er* SIxSÁ*-at nu-kán A-BI* ^{d}UTU-*ŠI*

36 [o]x?-x *ku-it-ki še-er ar-ḫa pa-it na-at-kán za-a-iš*

37 [*a-pád-*]⸢*da*⸣ SIxSÁ*-at nu A-BI* ^{d}UTU-*ŠI a-pád-da še-er*

38 [*A-NA*] DINGIR*-LIM-ma ku-e-da-ni-ik-ki ku-it-ki me-ma-an ḫar-ta*

[20] II.1A ii 3' *da-i*[*š*?] (collated).

[21] II.1B 10 add. *-u̯a-*.

[22] II.1B 11 *-da-*.

[23] A large Glossenkeil concludes this line and may mark the transition to another topic of the enquiry.

19 And [the ritual] which the father of His Majesty

II.1B 8 and just as the father of His Majesty

20-21 [insti]tuted for them, will they be[g]in to [giv]e it back to them?

II.1B 9 instituted a ritual for them, (II.1A 4') will they thus begin to give it?

II.1A 5' As to the uncelebrated (festivals)

6' will they compensate for them?

7' If then, deceased one, you relieve (your) soul, < ... >

8' Through the 'Old Woman' and the augur it was ascertained;

9' through the diviner: unfavorable.

10' [As to the fact,] that through the diviner it was unfavorable,

11' are you, [deceased one], angry because of the estate?

12' [...] ... it was ascertained.

13'-14' [Con]cerning the deceased who was [establish]ed [to be angry] because of the estate,

15' [...] the estate

16' [...] ... which/because

17' [...] ...

22 [By me]ans of three or[acle types]: favorable.

23-24 [Concerning the fact, that the deceased] was ascertained [(to be) in ange]r [because of] the cities, (which were) handed over, we will wait for His Majesty.

25 [The ...] ..., the cities, the tribute,

26 [...] if they say [thu]s?,

27 [" ... wro]ngdoings we found."

28 [...] ... as it was ascertained

29 [... Through] three oracle types: favorable.

---

30 [To bring] *mantalli*-rituals [in the city of Ḫalpa(?), His Maj]esty

31 was ascertained.

---

32 Concerning the [Urḫi]teššub [affair], which was ascertained, we made an oracle inquiry.

33 [The curse] of Urḫiteššub was ascertained. Since for him his sons

34 (have been) 'put [on the road]', he was ascertained in connection with perjury?

35 (and) [cur]sing. The father of His Majesty

36 had somehow ignored? [...] ... and he had transgressed it.

37 [Tha]t too was ascertained. Or had the father of His Majesty therefore

38 promised something [to] some deity

39 [*na-a*]*t*$^{?}$ *na-u̯i*$_5$ *pé-eš-ta* SIxSÁ-*at zi-la-aš IŠ-TU* 3 ^{GIŠ}TUKUL SIG$_5$

---

§17' 40 [GAM *kiš-an*] ⸢*a*⸣-*ri-i̯a-u-en pa-a-an-zi A-NA* ^{m}*Úr-ḫi*-^{d}U-*ub*
41 [^{LÚ}*ṬE-MÚ u-i-i̯*]*a-an-zi nu ut-tar* GIM-*an*
42 [*na-at Q*]*A-TAM-MA ḫa-at-ra-a-an-zi*
43 [*nu-un-na-a*]*š*[24] *a-pé-ez* INIM-*za* ḪUL-*lu UL ni-ni-in-ku-u-e-ni*
44 [ ]*Ú-UL ḫé-e-šu-u-e-ni*
45 [*IŠ-TU* ^{MUNUS}ŠU.G]I (erasure)^{LÚ}IGI.MUŠEN NU.SIG$_5$ *IŠ-TU* ^{LÚ}ḪAL ⸢SU.$^{?}$ḪI.A⸣ ⸢4$^{?}$-*ŠÚ*$^{?}$⸣[25] NU.SIG$_5$$^{?}$

---

§18' 46 [*A-NA* ^{m}*Ú*]*r*$^{?}$[-*ḫi*-^{d}U-]⸢*ub*$^{?}$⸣-*m*[*a u*]-*i-i̯a-u-an-zi*[26]
47 [*Ú-U*]*L* ⸢SIxSÁ-*at*⸣ *nu* ⸢*kiš*⸣-*a*[*n* D]Ù-*ir*
48 [*I*]*Š-TU* EME ^{m}*Úr-ḫi*-⸢^{d}⸣[U-*ub* DINGI]R.MEŠ LUGAL-*UT-TI*
49 *AŠ-RI*$^{ḪI.A}$ LUGAL-*UT-TI* ^{GIŠ}DAG.ḪI.⸢A⸣ [*pá*]*r-ku-nu-an-zi*
50 ^{d}UTU-*ŠI-i̯a-za pár-ku-nu*-⸢*zi*⸣ [*šar*-]*ni-ik-ze*$^{!}$[27]-*el*^{MEŠ}-*kán*
51 *da-an-zi na-aš-kán IŠ*-⸢*TU*⸣ LUG[AL$^{?}$-*U*]*T*$^{?}$-*TI ar-ḫa*
52 *ar-nu-an-zi* DUMU.MEŠ-*iš-ši* MUNUS.MEŠ-*i̯a ka-ni-iš-ša-an-zi*
53 ⸢*A*⸣-*NA* DUMU.MEŠ-*ma A-NA* ^{d}UTU-*ŠI* IGI-*an-da* SISKUR *ma-an-tal-li-i̯a*
54 *a-ri-i̯a-u-e-ni nu ma-a-an* SIxSÁ-*ri nu-za* BAL-*an-zi*
55 *ma-a-an Ú-UL-ma* SIxSÁ-*ri nu-za Ú*-⸢*UL*⸣[B]AL-*an-zi*
56 *A-NA* ^{m}⸢*Úr*⸣-*ḫi*-^{d}U-*ub-ma* ^{LÚ}*ṬE-MU Ú-UL* ⸢*u-i-i̯a-u-e-ni*⸣[28]
57 *na-an* ⸢^{TÚG}*še-ek*⸣-*nu-un* EGIR-*pa Ú-UL-pát* SÚD-*u-e-ni*
58 *ma-a-an-ma-an-na-aš ŠA* ^{m}*Úr-ḫi*-^{d}U-*ub* ḪUL-*lu a-pé-ez*
59 INIM-*za* DUḪ-*ri* ḪUL-*lu-na-aš-kán* É-*ir-za pa-ra-a*
60 *ta-ru-up-ta-ri zi-la-du-u̯a-an-na-aš ŠA* ^{m}*Úr-ḫi*-^{d}U-*ub*
61 ḪUL-*u-an-za* ^{TÚG}*še-ek-nu-un* EGIR-*pa Ú-UL nam-ma* SUD-*i̯a-z*[*i*]
62 ⸢*IŠ*⸣-*TU* 3 ^{GIŠ}TUKUL SIG$_5$

---

§19' 63 [DUMU.MEŠ ^{m}*Ú*]*r-ḫi*-^{d}U-*ub-za IT-TI* ^{d}UTU-*ŠI* SISKUR *ma-an-tal-li-i̯a*
64 [BAL-*an-zi m*]*a-a-an-ma-kán A-NA* ^{d}UTU-*ŠI* ḪUL-*lu*
65 [*a-pé-ez*$^{?}$ *Ú-U*]*L ku-it-ki pé-e-da-an-zi ŠA* 3 ^{GIŠ}TUKUL S[IG$_5$]

(text breaks off)

[24] After collation.

[25] The tentative reading of the last four signs I owe to G. Beckman.

[26] The left half of this and the following lines is provided by the join pieces XVI 41+7/v.

[27] The tablet shows two Winkelhaken between the signs ZI and EL.

[28] So after collation; at this point the join piece 7/v starts.

39 (and) not yet given [i]t? It was ascertained. Outcome: through three oracle procedures: favorable.

---

40 We [continued] the inquiry [as follows]. They will proceed
41 [to s]end [an envoy] to Urḫiteššub. As the matter (stands),
42 [ac]cordingly they will write [it].
43 Will we not stir up evil [for ourse]lves by that deed,
44 will we not open up [the affair[?]]?
45 [Through the Old Wom]an, the augur: unfavorable; through the diviner: the signs[?] four times[?] unfavorable.[?]

---

46 It was [no]t ascertained to send (word) [to U]r[ḫitešš]ub
47 and they [ac]ted as follo[ws].
48 [F]rom the curse of Urḫi[teššub] they will [cl]eanse [the go]ds of kingship,
49 the places of kingship (and) the thrones,
50 and His Majesty will cleanse himself. Compensations
51 they will take and bring them away from kin[gshi]p.[?]
52 His sons and wives they will show recognition.
53 We will make the *mantalli*-rituals vis-à-vis the sons (and) His Majesty
54 the subject of an oracle inquiry, and if they are ascertained, they will perform them.
55 If, however, they are not ascertained, they will not [per]form them
56 but we will not send an envoy to Urḫiteššub
57 and we will certainly not pull the robe back at him.
58 If the evil of Urḫiteššub through that
59 deed is solved for us, will the evil be (collectively) removed from our house?
60 And will in future the evil of Urḫiteššub not
61 pull back the robe at us anymore?
62 Through three oracle types: favorable.

---

63 [The sons[?] of U]rḫiteššub will [perform] *mantalli*-rituals (together) with His Majesty.
64 [I]f then they will bring His Majesty
65 [n]o [further] evil , (the result) of three oracle types: favorable.

---

e) XVI 58 ii (I.1)

1 [*IŠ-TU* ^{LÚ}IGI.MUŠ]EN IR-*TUM QA-<-TAM>-MA-pát nu* MUŠEN.ḪI.A SIxSÁ-*an-d*[*u*]
2 [ ] *tar-li*$_{12}$*-an NI-MUR na-aš-kán pí-an* ⸢SIG$_5$⸣[*-za*]
3 [*ú-it na-aš*] 2$^?$*-an ar-ḫa pa-it* TI$_8^{\text{MUŠEN}}$*-ma-ká*[*n*]
4 [EGIR UGU SIG$_5$]*-za ú-it nu-za* GAM*-an ḫa-aš-ta-pí-i*[*n*]
5 [GUN*-liš IK-Š*]*U-UD na-at an-da e-ri-ir*[29]
6 [*na-at-kán p*]*í-an ar-ḫa pa-a-ir*
7 [EGIR KASKAL*-NI a-l*]*i-li-iš-kán* EGIR UGU SIG$_5$[*-za*]
8 [*ú-it na-aš-k*]*án pí-an ar-ḫa pa-it*
9 [*UM-MA* ^{m}*Kur-ša-*]⸢^{d}⸣LAMMA SIxSÁ*-at-u̯a*

---

10 [*IŠ-TU* ^{LÚ}ḪAL IR*-T*]*UM QA-TAM-MA-pát nu* IGI*-zi* SU[30].MEŠ
11 [SIG$_5$*-ru* EGIR*-ma* NU.S]IG$_5$*-du* 3*-ŠU ar-ḫa Ú-UL*
12 [ ] (vacat)

---

13 [ ]x x ⸢DINGIR$^?$.MEŠ⸣*-i̯a*
14 [-]⸢*du*⸣$^?$

(break of unknown length)

f) XXII 35 iii (II.1A)
LII 92 iv (II.4)

§20" x+1 [^{m}*Ḫa*]*l-pa-*⸢LÚ⸣
2 [*ti-u̯a-*]*ta-ni-i̯a-za*
3 [ ]x*-i̯a-za pár-ku-nu-u̯a-an-zi*
4 [*AŠ-RI*$^{\text{ḪI.A}}$ LUGAL*-UT-TI* ^{GIŠ}DA]G.ḪI.A*-i̯a*
5 [*pár-ku-nu-u̯a-an-z*]*i* ⸢GIDIM⸣*-i̯a* SUD*-an-zi*
6 [*nu-za* ^{d}]⸢UTU⸣*-ŠI A-NA* GIDIM (erasure) IGI*-an-da*
7 ⸢SISKUR⸣ *ma-an-tal-li-i̯a-an-za* ⸢BAL⸣*-an-ti*
8 *A-BI* ^{d}UTU*-ŠI-i̯a* SUD*-an-zi*
9 *nu-za A-BI* ^{d}UTU*-ŠI* ^{m}*Ḫal-pa-*LÚ*-iš-ša*
II.4 iv 2' [SISK]UR ma-an-ta[l-lii̯a(-) *ABI* ^{d}UTU*-ŠI* (3') [^{m}Ḫal-p]a-LÚ-iš-š[a
10 1*-aš* 1*-e-da-ni* IGI*-an-da*
II.4 iv [3'?] [1-aš 1-edani IGI-anda]
11 SISKUR *ma-an-tal-i̯a*[31] BAL*-an-ti*
II.4 iv [3'?] [BAL-anti]

[29] The RI sign lacks the inner inscribed verticals.
[30] The sign SU is partly written over erasure. The scribe may have started to write SU without word space, then corrected himself, but left the foremost wedge of this sign standing.
[31] Or *ma-an-tal<-li>-i̯a*?

e)

1 [Through the aug]ur the (same) question likewise: le[t] them establish the birds.
2 [A ... -bird] we observed *tar(wiyal)lian*. It [came] in front [out of] favorable (direction),
3 [and it] went through the centre. An eagle then
4 came [above behind] out of [favorable] (direction) and [came GUN-*liš*]
5 down upon a *ḫaštapi*-bird. They entered
6 [and they] passed in [f]ront.
7 [Behind the road: An *al*]*ili*-bird [came] up behind [out of] favorable (direction)
8 [and it] passed in front.
9 [Thus Kurša-]^{d}LAMMA: "It was ascertained."

---

10 [Through the diviner the (same) quest]ion likewise: [let] the first signs
11 [be favorable,] let [the following ones be unfa]vorable. Threefold not
12 [...]

---

13 [...] ... and the gods$^{?}$
14 [...] ... .

f)

x+1 [... Ḫa]lpaziti
2 [... from the c]urse
3 [...] ... they will cleanse,
4 [the places of kingship] and [the thro]nes
5 [the]y [will cleanse] and they will fetch the deceased,
6-7 [in order for] His Majesty to perform the *mantalli*-ritual vis-à-vis the deceased
8 And they will fetch the father of His Majesty,
9 in order for the father of His Majesty and Ḫalpaziti
II.4 iv 2' The *manta*[*lli*-ritual the father of the Majesty] (3') and Ḫalpaziti
10 to perform vis-à-vis each other
II.4 iv [3'] [will perform for each other].
11 the *mantalli*-ritual.

12 *šar-ni-ik-ze-el A-NA* GIDIM SUM-*an-zi*
II.4 iv 4' [ša]r-ni-ik-z[e-el *A-NA* GIDIM
13 *A-NA* DINGIR.MEŠ ^{URU}*Ḫal-pa-i̯a šar-ni-ik-ze-el*
II.4 iv 4' [DINGIR.MEŠ-i̯a(?)]
14 *ša-ak-nu-u̯a-an-da-za pár-ku-u̯a-i̯a-za*
II.4 iv 5' [š]a-ak-nu-an[-da-za parkuu̯ai̯aza
15 SUM-*an-zi* DUMU.MEŠ-*ŠU-i̯a-aš-*[*ši-*]*kán*
II.4 iv [5'] [SUM-anzi] (6') DUMU.MEŠ-*ŠU*-⌈i̯a⌉[-aššikan
16 KASKAL-*ši ti-i̯a-*⌈*an*⌉*-z*[*i I-NA* ^{URU}*Ḫal-pa-i̯*]*a*?
II.4 iv [6'] [KASKAL-ši tii̯anzi] (7') *I-NA* ^{URU}Ḫal[-pa(-)
17 GIM-*an ki-i*[*t-ta-ri*
II.4 iv [7'] [*QATAMMA*(?)]
18 *pí-di-*⌈*iš*⌉[*-ši*?
II.4 iv 8' GAR-ru ma-a-an [
19 ⌈*a-pa*⌉-x[
II.4 iv 9' ma-a-na-aš ⌈*Ú*⌉[*-UL* (?)
______________________ [32]

g) XVI 58 iii (I.1)

x+1 [ ] x [
2 [*Ú-U*]*L*[33] ⌈SIxSÁ⌉-*ri*
3 [ ]x ⌈*ma-a*⌉*-an-ma-aš-ma-aš* ⌈DINGIR.MEŠ⌉
4 [*QA-TAM-MA ma-la-*]⌈*a*⌉*-an ḫar-te-ni a-ši-kán* INIM-*ša*
5 [*a-pé-e-ez me-m*]*i-az la-it-ta-ri* DINGIR-LUM-*na-aš*
6 [*zi-la-ti-i̯*]*a A-NA* INIM ^{m}*Ḫal-pa*-LÚ ^{TÚG}*še-ek-nu-un*
7 [*i-da-l*]*a-u-u̯a-an-ni Ú-UL nam-ma ku-it-ki* [EGIR-*pa*]
8 [SUD-*i̯a-ši n*]*u* KIN SIG$_5$-*ru* LUGAL-*uš-za* ZAG-*tar*
9 [*ŠA* DINGIR.MEŠ *m*]*i-nu-mar*$^{ḪI.A}$ ME-*aš na-aš* DINGIR.MAḪ-*ni pa-iš*
10 [*I-NA* UD.2.KAM] DINGIR-*LUM-za da-pí-an* ZI-*an* TI-*tar-ra* ME-*aš*
11 [DINGIR.MAḪ-*n*]*i pa-iš I-NA* UD.3.KAM DINGIR-*LUM-za*
12 [EGIR-*an ar-ḫ*]*a kar-pí-in* ME-*aš nu-kán an-da*[34]
13 [ ] SIG$_5$-*u-i* SIG$_5$
(end of column)

h) XXII 35 iv: one possible trace of a sign next to iii 9'.

(break of unknown length till KBo II 6+ and its summary VIII 27(+))

[32] Following the paragraph line in LII 92 iv there is a short space of approximately two lines high with possible traces of erased(?) signs but which looks blank otherwise.

[33] For this restoration and its implications see the commentary.

[34] Last sign written over erasure.

12 Compensation will (thus) be given to the deceased
II.4 iv 4' [co]mpensation [to the deceased
13 and to the deities of Ḫalpa compensation
II.4 iv (4') [and the deities (?)]
14 from the unclean and clean
II.4 iv 5' [from the u]nclea[n and clean]
15 will be given. And for him, his sons
II.4 iv (5') [they will do] (6') and [for him,] his sons
16 they will 'pu[t] on the road'. [An]d [in Ḫalpa,]
II.4 iv (6') [they will 'put on the road'.] (7') [And] in Ḫal[pa]
17 as it [was] la[id down, likewise]
II.4 iv (7') [like it was laid down, likewise]
18 on the spot [let it be laid down.]
II.4 iv (7') [on the spot], (8') let [it] be laid down. If he [is ascertained,
19 he [will be ...
II.4 iv 9' if he[is] no[t ascertained, ...]

---

g)

x+1 [...] ...
2 [... If] he is [no]t ascertained.
3 [he will not be ...] ... If you, o gods,
4 have [thus appr]oved (and) that affair
5 will be solved through [that de]ed (and) you, o god,
6 will not [in futu]re [pull back] the robe at us
7 anymore in [ev]il over the Ḫalpaziti affair,
8 [th]en let the *kin*-oracle be favorable. The KING took himself RIGHTNESS
9 [(and) the GODS' F]AVORS and gave them to the MOTHERGODDESS.
10 [On the second day] the DEITY took itself the ENTIRE SOUL and LIFE (and)
11 gave (it) t[o the MOTHERGODDESS]. On the third day the DEITY
12 took itself WRATH [from behind] and (it is) in
13 FAVORABLE (position). Favorable.

I. KBo II 6+XVIII 51
II.5 VIII 27(+)Bo 7787
6 10/v

II. Obverse i

x+1 *a-š*[*a*?-
2 DINGIR.MEŠ[
3 DUḪ-*ḫi*[(-)?
4 *na*-x[
5 *kiš-a*[*n*
6 *da*-[
7 *na*-x[
8 *me*-x[-
9 x x[35] [

---

10 *IŠ-T*[*U*
11 EGIR-*m*[*a*

---

12 *IŠ-T*[*U*

(blank space of four lines)

13 ⸢*mu*⸣?[
14 x x [
15 *e*-x[
16 LUGAL-x[36][
17 *IŠ-T*[*U*

---

18 *A-NA* [
19 *na-aš*-x?[
20 UD.KAM[
21 x[

[35] Although it might have been expected, a reading *IŠ-TU* here does not seem possible.
[36] After collation a reading LUGAL-*i*[*z*- does not seem impossible.

II. Obv. i (no translation feasible)

I. Obverse i

§1' 1 [TUKU.TUKU-]*u*$^{?}$*-an-za*
2 [ ] (vacat)[37]

(break of approximately 30 lines)

§2'' x+1 [*š*]*e-e*[*r*[38]
2' [*nu* IGI-*zi-iš* MU]ŠEN ⌈*ḪUR-RI*[39] SIG$_5$⌉-*ru*
⌈EGIR-*ma*⌉ NU.⌈SIG$_5$⌉-[*du*]
3' [IGI-*zi-iš* MUŠEN *ḪUR-RI* NU.SIG$_5$]⌈EGIR⌉ SIG$_5$

---

§3'' 4' [*IŠ-TU* ^{MUNUS}ŠU.GI IR-*TUM Q*]*A-TAM-MA-pát* *nu* KIN SIG$_5$-*ru*
5' [ ]⌈ME⌉-*an-te-eš na-at A-NA* ^{d}UTU AN-*E* SUM-
an-⌈*te-eš*⌉ NU.SIG$_5$

---

§4'' 6' [*A-N*]*A* EME *ku-it-ki ta-li-i̯a-an*
7' [*ku-it-ma-na-aš* TI-]⌈*an*⌉$^{?}$-*za*[40] *e-eš-ta nu a-pí-i̯a ku-it*
8' [E]ME *e-eš-ši-*⌈*iš*⌉[41]*-ta nu* MUŠEN *ḪUR-RI* NU.SIG$_5$-*du* NU.SIG$_5$

---

§5'' 9' [*I*]*Š-TU* ^{MUNUS}ŠU.GI IR-*TUM QA-TAM-MA-pát nu* KIN NU.SIG$_5$[-
du
10' *ŠA* DINGIR.MEŠ *kar-pí-uš* ME-*an-te-eš* ⌈*na-at* DINGIR.MAḪ-*ni*
SUM-*an-te-eš*⌉ N[U$^{?}$.SIG$_5$]

---

§6'' 11' *ma-a-an* GIDIM[42]*-pát ku-it-ki* TUKU.TUKU-*u-an-za*
DINGIR.MEŠ-*ŠU-i̯a-aš-ši ku-it kat-ta*
12' *iš-ḫu-u-u̯a-an-te-eš* DUMU.DUMU-*ŠU ŠA* ^{md}*SÎN*-^{d}U-*i̯a* EME *e-eš-*
ša-an-zi
13' *A-NA* GIDIM-*i̯a-kán* IGI-*zi A-NA* ⌈EME⌉ *ta-li-i̯a-an*
14' *nu-za ma-a-an* GIDIM *ke-e-da-aš-pát u̯a-aš-ku-u̯a-aš še-er*
TUKU.TUKU-*u-an-za*
15' *nam-ma-ma-za* GIDIM *da-me-e-da-ni me-mi-ni še-er Ú-UL*
16' *ku-e-da-ni-ik-ki* TUKU.TUKU-*u-an-za nu* IGI-*zi* SU.MEŠ SIG$_5$-*ru*

[37] Both these ends of lines are given in the handcopy only next to column ii; they are not taken into account in the line numbering of column i.

[38] See Walther, "Verbesserungen".

[39] See Walther, "Verbesserungen".

[40] The alleged trace of two wedges seen at the very beginning of the line in the handcopy is not discernible on the photo.

[41] See Walther, "Verbesserungen".

[42] For the right form of this sign see Walther, "Verbesserungen".

Obverse i

1 [... angr]y$^{?}$
2 [...]

(break)

1 [... be]cause [of(?)...]
2 [... then] let [the first] *ḫurri*-[bi]rd be favorable, but [let] the following (one) be unfavorable.
3 [The first *ḫurri*-bird (is) unfavorable,] the following (one) favorable.

---

4 That [s]ame [question through the 'Old Woman'; let the *kin* be favorable.
5 [...] (have been) taken and they (have been) given to the SUNGOD OF HEAVEN; unfavorable.

---

6 [If ...] somehow the curse (had been) ignored$^{?}$[43],
7 [while] he was [ali]ve$^{?}$ and because at that moment he
8 uttered [the c]urse? Then let the *ḫurri*-bird be unfavorable; unfavorable.

---

9 That same question [thr]ough the 'Old Woman'; [let] the *kin* be unfavorable. [?]
10 The GODS' WRATHS (have been) taken and they (have been) given to the MOTHER GODDESS; u[nfavorable.]

---

11 If indeed the deceased (is) somehow angry, and his gods (have) somehow (been)
12 dumped(?), and Armatarḫunta's offspring utters$^{!}$ a curse
13 and the deceased, (that is,) at first$^{?}$ (his) curse (has been) ignored,
14 if you, o deceased, (are) angry only because of these wrongdoings,
15 but furthermore, o deceased, because of some other matter you (are) not
16 angry, then let the first exta be favorable

[43] For this translation see the commentary.

17' EGIR-*ma* NU.SIG$_5$-*du* IGI-*zi* SU.MEŠ *ni ši ke*$^{ḪI.A}$-*uš pu-ru-un-du(-)kar-ri-ta*
18' ^{GIŠ}TUKUL *ŠA* ^{d}U ZAG-*aš* GÙB-*za* RA-*IṢ* 12 ŠÀ *DIR* SIG$_5$
19' EGIR SU.MEŠ *ta* UGU *a-uš-ta* NU.SIG$_5$

---

§7' 20' *IŠ-TU* ^{MUNUS}ŠU.GI IR-*TUM QA-TAM-MA-pát nu* KIN SIG$_5$-*ru*
21' ^{d}UTU AN-*E* GUB-*iš ŠA* DINGIR.MEŠ *kar-pí-uš* ME-*an-te-eš*
22' *na-at A-NA* ^{d}UTU AN-*E* SUM-*an-te-eš INA* UD.2.KAM LUGAL-*uš-za* ZAG-*tar*
23' *A-DAM-MA-i̯a* ME-*aš na-at pa-an-ga-u-i pa-iš*
24' *INA* UD.3.KAM ḪUL-*lu* ME-*an nu-kán an-da* SUD-*li*$_{12}$ SIG$_5$

---

§8" 25' *IŠ-TU* ^{LÚ}IGI.MUŠEN IR-*TUM QA-TAM-MA-pát nu* MUŠEN.ḪI.A SIxSÁ-*an-du*

(blank space of four lines)

30' GAM *kiš-an a-ri-i̯a-u-en*
II.6 x+1]x-u-en

---

§9" 31' EME ^{md}*SÎN*-^{d}U *ku-iš* SIxSÁ-*at nu kiš-an* DÙ-*an-zi*
II.6 1' EM[E
32' EME ^{md}*SÎN*-^{d}U *A-NA* DINGIR.MEŠ LUGAL-*UT-TI pí-an ar-ḫa a-ni-i̯a-an-zi*
II.6 2' DING]IR.MEŠ LUGAL-*UT-TI* pí[-an
33' *AŠ-RI*$^{ḪI.A}$ LUGAL-*UT-TI* ^{GIŠ}DAG.ḪI.A-*i̯a pár-ku-nu-u̯a-an-zi*
II.6 3' ^{GIŠ}DAG.Ḫ]I.A-i̯a pár-ku-nu-u̯a-⌈an⌉[-zi
34' ^{d}UTU-*ŠI-i̯a-az pár-ku-nu-*⌈*uz*⌉-*zi šar-ni-*⌈*ik*⌉-*ze-el-la*
II.6 4' šar-ni-]ik-ze-el$^{ḪI.A}$
35' *ŠA* É-*TI* ME-*an-zi nu ku-it dam-me-li pí-di ti-an-zi*
II.6 4' *Š*[*A* (5') ti-an-z]i
36' *ku-it-ma A-NA* GIDIM SUM-*an-zi* DUMU.DUMU-*ŠU-i̯a ta-me-da-za*
II.6 5' ku-it-ma *A-NA* G[IDIM
37' *ka-ni-iš-ša-an-zi* ⌈*ma*⌉-*a-an-ma-za* DINGIR-*LUM QA-TAM-MA ma-la-a-an ḫar-te-ni*
II.6 6' ka-]⌈ni⌉-eš-ša-an-zi
38' INIM ^{md}*SÎN*-^{d}U-*kán ke-e-ez* INIM-*za* DUḪ-*ta-ri* (erasure)
39' DINGIR-*LUM-na-aš A-NA* INIM ^{md}*SÎN*-^{d}U *še-er* ^{TÚG}*še-ek-nu-un* EGIR-*pa Ú-UL*
40' SUD-*i̯a-ši nu* IGI-*zi-iš* MUŠEN *ḪUR-RI* SIG$_5$-*ru* EGIR-*ma* NU.SIG$_5$-*du*

17 but let the following (ones) be unfavorable. First exta: *ni*(*pašuri*), *ši*(*ntaḫi*), *ke*(*ldi*), *purundi*(-)*karrita*(?),
18 the weapon of the Stormgod (is) on the right, on the left (it is) damaged, twelve coils; favorable.
19 Later exta: *ta*(*nani*) he saw above; unfavorable.

---

20 That same question through the 'Old Woman'; let the *kin* be favorable.
21 The SUNGOD OF HEAVEN has risen. The GODS' WRATHS (have been) taken
22 and they (have been) given to the SUNGOD OF HEAVEN. On the second day the KING took himself RIGHTNESS
23 and BLOOD and gave it to the *panku*.
24 On the third day EVIL (has been) taken and (it is) in SUD-*li*; favorable.

---

25 That same question through the augur; let them establish the birds.

30 In the following way we continued the inquiry.
II.6 x+1]we [... -]ed.

---

31 Concerning the curse of Armatarḫunta, which was ascertained, they will do as follows:
II.6 1' [Concerning] the cur[se
32 The curse of Armatarḫunta in front of the gods of kingship they will undo,
II.6 2']in fr[ont of the go]ds of kingship [
33 the places of kingship and the thrones they will cleanse,
II.6 3'] and [the thro]nes they will cleans[e,
34 and the Majesty will cleanse himself. Also, compensation
II.6 4' compen]sation
35 for the house they will take: some they will place in an immaculate spot,
II.6 4' f[or (5') the]y [will place
36 the other they will give to the deceased. And they will show his offspring recognition in some other way.
II.6 5' the other [they will give] to the de[ceased. (6') [And] they will [show ... re]cognition
37 Now, when you (plural!), o god, have thus approved,
38 will the affair of Armatarḫunta be solved by this deed?
39 Will you, o god, not pull back the robe at us over the Armatarḫunta affair?
40 Then, let the first *ḫurri*-bird be favorable but let the following (one) be unfavorable.

41' IGI-*zi-iš* MUŠEN *ḪUR-RI* SIG$_5$ EGIR[44] NU.SIG$_5$

---

§10" 42' IGI-*an-da* SU.MEŠ IR-*u-en nu*[45] SU.MEŠ SIG$_5$-*ru ni ši ke* GÙB-*za* RA-*IṢ*
43' *zi* GAR-*ri* 12 ŠÀ *DIR* SIG$_5$

44' *IŠ-TU* ^{MUNUS}ŠU.GI IR-*TUM QA-TAM-MA-pát nu* KIN SIG$_5$-*ru*
45' DINGIR-*LUM-za* EGIR-*an ar-ḫa kar-pí-in* ME-*aš nu-kán an-da* (erasure) SIG$_5$-*u-i*

(end of column i)

Obverse ii

1 INA UD.2.KAM *ŠA* DINGIR.MEŠ ⌈*mi*⌉-*nu-mar*$^{ḪI.A}$ ME-*an-te-eš na-at* DINGIR.MAḪ-*ni* SUM-*an-te-eš* x$^?$
2 INA UD.3.KAM *pa-an-ku-uš-za* GÙB-*la-tar* ḪUL-*lu-i̯a* ME-*aš nu-kán an-da* SUD-*li*$_{12}$ SI[G$_5$$^?$]

---

§12" 3 [*IŠ-T*]*U* ⌈^{LÚ}IGI.MUŠEN⌉[46] IR-[*TUM QA-TAM-MA-pát nu* MUŠEN.ḪI.A SIxSÁ-*a*]*n-du*
4 [ ] (vacat)
5 [ ] x

(break of approximately 15 lines in KBo II 6+[47])

II.6 6' *IŠ-T*[*U*

§13" 12 [o o o *ša-ku-u̯a-an-ta-r*]*i-i̯*[*a-*
13 [ ]x GAM-*an* ⌈*ḫa*$^?$-*ma*$^?$-*an*⌉-*ká*[*n*
14 [ ]x-*an ti-an-zi* KI.MIN [*nu* IGI-*zi-i*]*š*
15 [MUŠEN *ḪUR-RI* SIG$_5$-*ru* EGIR-*ma* NU.SIG$_5$-*du* IGI-]*zi-iš* MUŠEN *ḪUR-RI* NU.S[IG$_5$ EGIR] SIG$_5$

---

§14" 16 [*a-n*]*i-an-zi* EZEN$_4$.MEŠ-*ma-aš-ma-a*[*š-ká*]*n*$^?$ *ku-it*

[44] Last sign written over erasure.

[45] Last sign written over erasure.

[46] For this reading see Walther, "Verbesserungen".

[47] For the incorrect line count in the handcopy see the introduction to this chapter.

41 First *ḫurri*-bird favorable, following (one) unfavorable.

---

42 We counterchecked the exta. Let the exta be favorable: *ni*(*pašuri*), *ši*(*ntaḫi*), *ke*(*ldi*) damaged on the left,
43 a bladderworm lies, twelve coils; favorable.

---

44 That same question through the 'Old Woman'; let the *kin* be favorable.
45 The GOD took himself WRATH passing behind and (it is) in FAVORABLE (position).

Obverse ii

1 On the second day the GODS' FAVORS (have been) taken and (been) given to the MOTHERGODDESS.
2 On the third day the *panku* took itself LEFTNESS and EVIL; (it is) in SUD-*li*, favo[rable.]

---

3 [That same question throu]gh the augur; let the[m establish the birds.]
4 [...]
5 [...]

(break)

II.6 6' Throu[gh

12 [... unceleb]ra[ted? ...]
13 [... festival(s)] ... assign[- ...]
14 [... to ...] they will begin, etc. [Then let the firs]t
15 [*ḫurri*-bird be favorable but let the following one be unfavorable; the fi]rst *ḫurri*-bird unfav[orable, the following] favorable.

---

16 [...] they will [celebr]ate, because the festivals for them, however,

17 [š]*a-ku-u̯a-an-ta-ri-i̯a-nu-u̯a-*[*a*]*n-te-eš e-še-er*

18 [ ]⸢2?⸣-*ŠU ḫa-pu-uš-ša-an-zi*

19 [ ]x *pí-iš-ki-u-u̯a-an ti-an-zi*

20 [ ]*ša? kiš-an ma-la-a-an ḫar-te-ni* GIDIM x[ ]

21 [S]IG$_5$-⸢*ru* EGIR⸣[-*m*]*a* NU.SIG$_5$-*du* ⸗*la-a*-x[48][?]

22 [S]IG$_5$

---

§15" 23 (traces of erased exta description)

24 (traces of erased exta description)

25 (traces of erased exta description)[49]

26 (traces of erased exta description) IGI-*zi* SU.MEŠ SIG$_5$-*ru*

27 EGIR-*ma* NU.SIG$_5$-*du* IGI-*zi* SU.MEŠ *ni-kán* GÙB-*l*[*a?* o o o]-*i*

28 *ši* KASKAL 12 ŠÀ *DIR* SIG$_5$ EGIR SU.MEŠ *pu-kán*-⸢*ti*⸣[(-) o o *zu-u*]*l-kiš*

29 ^{GIŠ}TUKUL-*i̯a* GÙB-*la-aš* NU.SIG$_5$

---

§16" 30 *IŠ-TU* ^{MUNUS}ŠU.⸢GI IR-*TUM*⸣ [*Q*]*A*-⸢*TAM*⸣-*MA-pát nu* KIN SIG$_5$-*ru*

31 [-]*za* ZAG-*tar* NINDA.GUR$_4$.RA *iš-pa-an-du-uz-zi-i̯a* ME-*aš*

32 [*na-at A-N*]*A* LUGAL ZAG-*za* ME-*iš INA* UD.2.KAM DINGIR.MAḪ GUB-*iš*

33 *nu* GI[G?] x [o?] *nu-kán* DINGIR-*LIM-ni da-pí-i* ZI-*ni*

34 *INA* UD.3.KAM ^{d}[DA]G-*ti-iš* GUB-*iš nu ŠA* LUGAL *A-DAM-MA* MU-*an-na* ME-*aš*

35 *na-an* DINGIR.MAḪ-*ni pa-iš* SIG$_5$

---

§17" 36 (erased: DINGIR-*LUM*)

(blank space of 11 lines)

---

48 Whereas the handcopy of KBo II 6 only shows the beginning of a low horizontal wedge, the copy of this part of KBo II 6 repeated in KUB XVIII gives the traces of three superimposed horizontals. Since no photo of the edge of KBo II 6 was available, this could not be verified through photo collation.

49 The one Winkelhaken and the word *nam-ma* clearly visible in the handcopy near the end of the line were part of the text meant to be erased: the Winkelhaken was the end of a sign (e.g. TI) and *namma* was already on the edge, thus escaping the scribe's erasing hand.

17 [... (have remained) u]ncelebrated,
18 [...] they will make up [for them] twice(?)
19 [...] ... they will begin to give(?)
20 [If you, o gods, ...] ... have thus approved, (and) the deceased ... [...]
21 [... then,] let the [first ...] be [fa]vorable [b]ut let the following (one) be unfavorable. :*lā*... (?)
22 [... (-)fa]vorable.

23-25 (erased)

26 (beginning erased) Let the first exta be favorable
27 but let the following (ones) be unfavorable. First exta: *ni*(*pašuri*), [on/to$^{?}$] the left [...] ...
28 *ši*(*ntaḫi*), the road, twelve coils; favorable. The following exta: *pukanti*[- ... *zu*]*lki*
29 and the weapon left; unfavorable.

---

30 That [s]ame question through the 'Old Woman'; let the *kin* be favorable.
31 [The ...] took himself RIGHTNESS, THICK BREAD and WINE RATION,
32 [and] put [it] on the KING's right. On the second day the MOTHERGODDESS has risen,
33 ILLNESS ... and (it is) in the GOD, in the ENTIRE(?) SOUL.
34 On the third day the THRONE DEITY has risen and has taken the KING'S BLOOD and YEAR
35 and gave it to the MOTHERGODDESS; favorable.

---

36 (erased: god)

(blank)

§18" 37 DINGIR-*LUM ku-it ŠA* ^{fd}*IŠTAR-at-ti ut-tar* EGIR-*pa* SUD-*at*
38 EME *ŠA* ^{fd}*IŠTAR-at-ti-pát* TI-*an-ta-aš ku-it-ma-na-aš* TI-*an-za e-eš-ta*
39 *nu a-pí-i̯a ku-it ar-ra-aḫ-ḫa-ni-iš-ki-it nu* KIN NU.SIG$_5$-*du*
40 DINGIR.MEŠ GUB-*ir mu-kiš-šar šal-li u̯a-aš-túl* IZI-*i̯a* ME-*ir*
41 *nu-kán A-NA* GIG GAL NU.SIG$_5$

---

§19" 42 *IŠ-TU* ^{LÚ}ḪAL IR-*TUM QA-TAM-MA-pát nu* MUŠEN *ḪUR-RI* NU.SIG$_5$-*du* NU.SIG$_5$

---

§20" 43 *ma-a-an* EME *ŠA* ^{fd}*IŠTAR-at-ti-pát* TI-*an-*⌈*da*⌉*-aš-pát*
44 *ku-it-ma-na-aš* TI-*an-za e-eš-ta nu a-pí-i̯a ku-it*
45 *ar-ra-aḫ-ḫa-ni-iš-ki-it nam-ma-ma* KI.MIN *nu* MUŠEN *ḪUR-RI* SIG$_5$-*ru* NU.SIG$_5$

---

§21" 46 *nu-kán* GIDIM-*ma* [*k*]*u*-[*i*]*t-ki* TUKU.TUKU-*nu-an-za nu* KIN NU.SIG$_5$-*du*
47 DINGIR-*LUM-za da-pí*[*-an* Z]I-*an* ḪUL-*lu-i̯a* ME-*aš* (erasure)
48 *na-at pa-an-g*[*a-u-i*] *pa-iš* NU.SIG$_5$

---

§22" 49 *IŠ-TU* ^{LÚ}ḪAL ⌈IR-*TUM*⌉ *QA-TAM-MA-pát nu* MUŠEN *ḪUR-RI* NU.SIG$_5$-*du* NU.SIG$_5$

---

§23" 50 *ma-a-an* EME *ŠA* ^{fd}*IŠTAR-at-ti-pát* TI-*an-da-aš*
51 *ku-it-ma-na-aš* TI-*an-za e-eš-ta nu a-pí-i̯a ku-it*
52 *ar-ra-aḫ-ḫa-ni-iš-ki-it* GIDIM-*i̯a-kán ku-it* TUKU.TUKU-*nu-an-za*
53 *nam-ma-ma-za* GIDIM *ta-me-e-da-ni me-mi-ni še-er Ú-UL*
54 *ku-it-ki* TUKU.TUKU-*u-an-za nu* MUŠEN *ḪUR-RI* SIG$_5$-*ru* NU.SIG$_5$

---

§24" 55 *nu* DUMU.MEŠ-*ŠU-ma* EME *e-eš-ša-an-zi nu* GIDIM *ni-ni-*⌈*in-kiš*⌉*-kán-zi*
56 *nu* KIN NU.SIG$_5$-*du IŠ-TU* MU.ḪI.A GÍD.DA *ŠA* ⌈LUGAL⌉ *A-*⌈*DAM*⌉[*-M*]*A* ⌈ME⌉*-an*[50]
57 *na-at*![51] *pa-an-ga-u-i* SUM-*an INA* UD.2.KAM ḪUL-*l*[*u* ME-*an*]

(end of column ii)

[50] For this reading see Walther, "Verbesserungen".
[51] The tablet has AN; see commentary.

37 Concerning the fact that the deity has revived the Šaušgatti affair:
38 (Is it) the curse of that same Šaušgatti, (when) alive (and) as long as she lived
39 and because at that moment she had cursed? Then let the *kin* be unfavorable.
40 The GODS have risen, they took PRAYER, GREAT SIN?[52] and FIRE
41 and (it is) in the GREAT ILLNESS; unfavorable.

---

42 That same question through the diviner; let the *ḫurri*-bird be unfavorable. Unfavorable.

---

43 If (it is) the curse of that same Šaušgatti, only (when) alive
44 (and) as long as she lived and because at that moment
45 she had cursed, but furthermore etc., then let the *ḫurri*-bird be favorable; unfavorable.

---

46 Or is the deceased somehow angry? Then, let the *kin* be unfavorable.
47 The GOD took himself the ENTI[RE S]OUL and EVIL
48 and gave it to the *pank*[*u*]; unfavorable.

---

49 That same question through the diviner; let the *ḫurri*-bird be unfavorable. Unfavorable.

---

50 If (it is) the curse of that same Šaušgatti, (when) alive
51 (and) as long as she lived and because at that moment
52 she had cursed and because the deceased (is) angry
53 but furthermore, o deceased, you (are) not because of another matter
54 somehow angry, then let the *ḫurri*-bird be favorable; unfavorable.

---

55 Do her children utter curse(s) and stir up the deceased?
56 Then, let the *kin* be unfavorable. From(?) the LONG YEARS the KING'S BLO[O]D (has been) taken
57 and it (has been) given to the *panku*. On the second day EVI[L ... (has been) taken]

[52] On the possibility of this combination referring to a Great King's death see Ch. VI, Commentary.

Reverse iii

1 [*na-a*]*t A-NA* ^{d}UTU AN-*E* ⸢SUM-*an*⸣ *INA* UD.3.KAM ⸢LUGAL-*uš*⸣-*za* ZAG-*tar* TI-*tar-ra* ⸢ME⸣[53]-*aš*

2 ⸢*nu-kán*⸣ DINGIR.MEŠ-*ni da-pí-i* ZI-*ni* <NU.$^{?}$>SIG$_5$

---

§25" 3 *IŠ-TU* ^{LÚ}ḪAL IR-*TUM QA-TAM-MA-pát nu* MUŠEN *ḪUR-RI* NU.SIG$_5$-*du* NU.SIG$_5$

---

§26" 4 *ma-a-an* EME *ŠA* ^{fd}*IŠTAR-at-ti-pát* TI-*an-da-aš ku-it-ma-na-aš*

5 TI-*an-za e-eš-ta nu* ⸢*a*⸣-*pí-i̯a ku-it ar-ra-aḫ-ḫa-ni-iš-ki-it*

6 GIDIM-*i̯a ku-it* TUKU.TUKU-*u-an-za* DUMU.MEŠ-*ŠU-i̯a-aš-ši* EME *e-eš-ša-an-zi*

7 *nu-za ma-a-an* GIDIM *ke-e-da-aš-pát u̯a-aš-ku-u̯a-aš še-er* TUKU.TUKU-*u-an-za*

8 *nam-ma-ma-za* GIDIM *ta-me-e-da-ni me-mi-ni še-er Ú-UL*

9 *ku-it-ki* TUKU.TUKU-*u-an-za nu* IGI-*zi-iš* MUŠEN *ḪUR-RI* SIG$_5$-*ru*

10 EGIR-*ma* NU.SIG$_5$-*du* IGI-*zi-iš* MUŠEN[!54] *ḪUR-RI* SIG$_5$ EGIR NU.SIG$_5$

---

§27" 11 *IŠ-TU* ^{MUNUS}ŠU.GI IR-*TUM QA-TAM-MA-pát nu* KIN SIG$_5$-*ru*

12 DINGIR-*LUM-za da-pí-an* ZI-*an aš-šu-ul-la* ME-*aš*

13 *na-at* DINGIR.MAḪ-*ni pa-iš INA* UD.2.KAM ḪUL-*lu* ME-*an*

14 *nu-kán A-NA* GIG TUR[!55] *INA* UD.3.KAM DINGIR-*LUM-za da-pí-an* ZI-*an*

15 TI-*tar-ra* ME-*aš nu-kán an-da* SIG$_5$-*u-i* SIG$_5$

---

§28" 16 *IŠ-TU* ^{LÚ}IGI.MUŠEN IR-*TUM QA-TAM-MA-pát nu* MUŠEN.ḪI.A *ar-ḫa pé-eš-ši-an-du*

(blank space of four lines)

--- [56]

§29" 17 ^{fd}*IŠTAR-at-ti-iš ku-u̯a-at-ta im-ma ku-u̯a-at-ta*

18 *še-er* TUKU.TUKU-*u-an-za na-an a-ri-i̯a-u-e-ni*

19 *na-an-kán* KASKAL-*ši ti-i̯a-u-e-ni ma-a-an-ma* GIDIM

20 *Ú-UL* SISKUR *ma-an-tal-la-aš-ša-am-mi-iš*[57]

[53] See Walther, "Verbesserungen".

[54] A Winkelhaken seems to be written in the first horizontal of the sign ḪU.

[55] Tablet has I.

[56] In contrast to the handcopy in KBo II the tablet has only one paragraph line; see Walther, "Verbesserungen".

[57] Last three signs are written over erasure.

Reverse iii

1 [and i]t (has been) given to the SUNGOD OF HEAVEN. On the third day the KING has taken himself RIGHTNESS and LIFE
2 and (it is) in the GOD(S?), in the ENTIRE SOUL; <un?>favorable.

---

3 That same question through the diviner; let the *ḫurri*-bird be unfavorable. Unfavorable.

---

4 If (it is) the curse of that same Šaušgatti, (when) alive (and) as long as she
5 lived and because at that moment she had cursed,
6 and because the deceased (is) angry and (because) her children utter curse(s),
7 if, o deceased, only because of these wrongdoings you (are) angry,
8 furthermore, however, you, o deceased, (are) not because of another matter
9 somehow angry, then, let the first *ḫurri*-bird be favorable
10 but let the following (one) be unfavorable. The first *ḫurri*-bird favorable, the following (one) unfavorable.

---

11 That same question through the 'Old Woman'; let the *kin* be favorable.
12 The GOD took himself the ENTIRE SOUL and WELL-BEING
13 and gave it to the MOTHERGODDESS. On the second day EVIL (has been) taken
14 and (it is) in the SMALL ILLNESS. On the third day the god took himself the ENTIRE SOUL
15 and LIFE and (it is) in GOOD (position); favorable.

---

16 That same question through the diviner; let them cast the *ḫurri*-birds away.

(blank)

---

17 For whatever reason Šaušgatti (is)
18 angry, we will investigate her through an oracle
19 and we will 'put her on the road' (i.e. satisfy her). If, now, the deceased
20 (is) not designated for *mantalli*-rituals,

21 SISKUR *ma-an-tal-li-i̯a-za Ú-UL* BAL![58]*-an-ti*
22 *ma-a-an-ma-at* GIDIM *Ú-UL ša-an-aḫ-ti* (erasure)[59]
23 *nu* SU.MEŠ SIG$_5$*-ru* ZAG*-za* RA*-IṢ* NU.SIG$_5$

---

§30" 24 *IŠ-TU* ^{MUNUS}ŠU.GI IR*-TUM QA-TAM-MA-pát nu* KIN SIG$_5$*-ru*
25 *pa-an-ku-uš-za* ZAG*-tar ŠA* LUGAL*-i̯a A-TA-MA* ME*-aš na-at A-NA* LUGAL ⸢ZAG*-za* ME*-iš*⸣[60]
26 *INA* UD.2.KAM DINGIR.MAḪ GUB*-iš aš-šu-ul* ME*-aš* (*nu-kán* in erasure[61])
27 *nu-kán* EGIR*-pa* ^{d}DAG*-ti INA* UD.3.KAM *pa-an-ku-uš-za-kán*
28 ŠÀ*-za pa-aḫ-ḫur u̯a-aš-du-la* ME*-aš*![62]
29 *nu-kán an-da* SUD*-li*$_{12}$ SIG$_5$

---

§31" 30 ^{fd}⸢*IŠTAR-at-ti*⸣*-iš ku-it IT-TI* ^{d}UTU*-ŠI* SISKUR *ma-an-tal-li-i̯a*<<*-aš*>>
31 BAL!*-u-u̯a-an-zi* SIxSÁ*-at nu-za* ^{d}UTU*-ŠI IT-TI* ⸢GIDIM⸣ SISKUR *ma-an-tal-li-i̯a*
32 BAL*-an-ti ma-a-an-ma-za* DINGIR.MEŠ *ŠA* ^{fd}*IŠTAR-at-*⸢*ti*⸣ SISKUR *ma-an-tal-li*![63]*-i̯a*
33 *IT-TI* ^{d}UTU*-ŠI* BAL*-u-u̯a-an-zi ma-la-a-an* ⸢*ḫar*⸣*-te-ni*
34 *nu* IGI*-zi-iš* MUŠEN *ḪUR-RI* SIG$_5$*-ru* EGIR*-ma* NU.SIG$_5$*-du*
35 IGI*-zi-iš* SIG$_5$ EGIR NU.SIG$_5$<<*-du*>>

---

§32" 36 *IŠ-TU* ^{MUNUS}ŠU.GI IR*-TUM QA-TAM-MA-pát nu* KIN SIG$_5$*-ru*
37 LUG[AL-]*uš-za* ZAG*-tar* ME*-aš*![64] *na-at-*⸢*kán*⸣ *A-NA* ^{fd}*IŠTAR-at-ti*
38 ZAG[65]*-za* ME*-iš* (erasure) *INA* UD.2.KAM GIG TUR ME*-an*
39 *nu-kán an-da* SIG$_5$*-u-i INA* UD.3.KAM *ŠA* DINGIR.MEŠ *kar-pí-uš*
40 ME*-an-te-eš na-at A-NA* ^{d}UTU AN*-E* SUM*-an-te-eš* SIG$_5$

---

§33" 41 GAM *kiš-an a-ri-i̯a-u-en*
II.5 iv 1' GAM kiš-an ⸢a⸣[-ri-i̯a-u-en

[58] The BAL-sign does not seem to start with a broken horizontal.

[59] In the erasure one recognizes an AŠ sign. Possibly the scribe initially wanted to continue with *nu* but then decided to start a new line; for the similar phenomenon see below line 26.

[60] See Walther, "Verbesserungen".

[61] See Walther, "Verbesserungen"; cf. also above line 22.

[62] Tablet has NI, see Walther, "Verbesserungen".

[63] According to the handcopy this LI sign has only one vertical wedge at the end. Because on the edge, this could not be verified through photo collation.

[64] Tablet has NI, see Walther, "Verbesserungen".

[65] See Walther, "Verbesserungen"; for the script in the lines 38-40 see above introductory remarks.

21 he (i.e. the king?) will not perform a *mantalli*-ritual.
22 Now, if you, o deceased, do not seek it,
23 then let the exta be favorable. On the right (it is) damaged; unfavorable.

---

24 That same question through the 'Old Woman'; let the *kin* be favorable.
25 The *panku* took itself RIGHTNESS and the KING'S BLOOD and put it to the KING's right.
26 On the second day the MOTHER GODDESS has risen, she took WELL-BEING
27 and (it is) back with? the THRONE DEITY. On the third day the *panku*
28 took itself from? the HEART FIRE (and) SINS
29 and (it is) in SUD-*li*; favorable.

---

30 Concerning the fact that it was ascertained that Šaušgatti will perform *mantalli*-rituals (together) with His Majesty,
31 will His Majesty perform *mantalli*-rituals (together) with the deceased?
32 Now, if, you, o gods, have approved of Šaušgatti's performing *mantalli*-rituals
33 (together) with His Majesty,
34 then let the first *ḫurri*-bird be favorable but let the following (one) be unfavorable.
35 The first favorable, the following (one) unfavorable.

---

36 That same question through the 'Old Woman'; let the *kin* be favorable.
37 The K[IN]G took himself RIGHTNESS and put it on ŠAUŠGATTI's
38 right. On the second day the SMALL ILLNESS (has been) taken
39 and (it is) in GOOD (position). On the third day the GODS' WRATHS
40 (have been) taken and they (have been) given to the SUNGOD OF HEAVEN. Favorable.

---

41 We continued the inquiry as follows:
II.5 iv 1' We continued the in[quiry] as follows:

42 EME ^{fd}*IŠTAR-at-ti ku-it* TI-*an-da-aš* SIxSÁ-*at*

II.5 iv 1' EME ^{f}]⸢^{d}⸣*IŠTAR*-at-ti ku-i[t] (2) ⸢SIxSÁ⸣-at

43 *nu kiš-an* DÙ-*an-zi* EME ^{fd}*IŠTAR-at-ti A-NA* DINGIR.MEŠ [LUGAL-*UT-TI*]

II.5 iv 2' nu ⸢EME⸣[^{fd}*IŠTAR*-at-ti] *A-NA* DINGIR.MEŠ LUGAL-*U*[*T-TI*]

44 *pí-ra-an ar-ḫa a-ni-i̯a-an-zi* GIDIM-*i̯a ša-ra-a*

II.5 iv 3' pí-an ar-ḫa a-ni[-i̯a-an-zi *AŠ-R*]*I*$^{HI.A}$ LUGAL-*UT-TI* [^{GIŠ}DAG.ḪI.A-i̯a]

4' pár-ku-nu-u̯a-an-zi ^{d}[UTU-*ŠI*-i̯a-az] pár-ku-<nu->uz-zi [GIDIM-i̯a]

5' UGU

45 *a-še-ša-nu-u̯a-an-zi šar-ni-ik-ze-el-la* ME-*an-zi*

II.5 iv 5' a-še-ša-[nu-]an-z[i šar-ni-i]k-ze-el-l[a ME-an-zi]

46 *na-at A-NA* GIDIM SUM-*an-zi ma-a-an-ma-za* DINGIR-*LUM* KI.MIN

II.5 iv 6' na-at *A-NA* GIDIM [SUM-an-zi

47 <<*ŠA*>> INIM ^{fd}*IŠTAR-at-ti-na-aš-kán a-pé-e-ez m*[*e*]*-mi-na-*⸢*za*⸣[66]

48 *la-it-ta-ri* DINGIR-*LUM-na-aš A-NA* INIM ^{fd}*IŠTAR-at-ti*

49 ^{TÚG}*še-ek-nu-un* EGIR-*pa Ú-UL ku-it-ki* SUD-*i̯a-ši*

50 *nu* KIN SIG$_5$-*ru* ^{d}UTU AN-*E* GUB-*iš ŠA* LUGAL ZAG-[*t*]*ar* ME[-*aš*]

51 *na-at-ši-kán u̯a-aš-du-li* ME-*iš* NU.SIG$_5$

---

§34'' 52 *IŠ-TU* ^{LÚ}ḪAL IR-*TUM QA-TAM-MA-pát nu* IGI-*zi-iš* MUŠEN *ḪUR-RI* SI[G$_5$-*ru*]

53 EGIR-*ma* NU.SIG$_5$-*du* IGI-*zi-iš* MUŠEN *ḪUR-RI* NU.SIG$_5$ EGIR SI[G$_5$]

---

§35'' 54 *IŠ-TU* ^{LÚ}IGI.MUŠEN IR-*TUM QA-TAM-MA-pát nu* MUŠEN.ḪI.A SIxSÁ-*an-du*

55 TI$_8$^{MUŠEN}-*kán pí-an ku-uš ú-it na-aš-kán pí-an ar-ḫa pa*[*-it* (?)]

56 *ḫu-u-u̯a-aš* GUN-*liš* x x[67]-*i̯a-aš-kán* EGIR GAM *ku-uš ú-it*

57 *na-*⸢*at*⸣ 2-*an ar-*⸢*ḫa*⸣ [*pa-a-ir* E]GIR KASKAL-*NI šu-lu-pí-iš-kán* [(?)]

58 EGIR GAM *ku-uš ú-i*[*t*?[68] *na-aš* 2-*a*]*n ar-ḫa pa-it*

59 *UM-MA* ^{m}*Kur-ša-*^{d}L[AMMA *ar-ḫa*[69]-]*u̯a pé-eš-šir*

--- [70]

§36'' 60 *nu ki-i-ma kiš-an* DÙ-⸢*an-zi*⸣ (erasure)

61 GIDIM-*i̯a ša-ra-a a-še-ša-an-zi* ⸢*šar*⸣[-*ni-*]⸢*ik-ze*⸣[-*el*?[71] ME-*an-zi*]

62 *na-at A-NA* GIDIM SUM-*an-zi A-NA* DUMU[.MEŠ-*ŠU*]

II.5 iv 6']*A-NA* DUMU.MEŠ-⸢*ŠU*⸣[ ]

[66] See Walther, "Verbesserungen".

[67] See Walther, "Verbesserungen".

[68] After collation.

[69] In contrast to the handcopy there is enough space on the tablet to accommodate this restoration.

[70] For the single paragraph line see Walther, "Verbesserungen".

[71] See Walther, "Verbesserungen".

42 Because the curse of Šaušgatti, alive, has been ascertained,
II.5 iv 1' Becau[se curse of] Šaušgatti (2) has been ascertained,
43 they will do as follows: The curse of Šaušgatti in front of the gods [of kingship]
II.5 iv 2' the curse [of Šaušgatti] in front of the gods of kings[hip]
44 they will undo, and (an effigy of the) deceased
II.5 iv 3' they will und[o, the pla]ces of kingship [and the throne]
4' they will cleanse and [His majesty] will cleanse [himself] and [(an effigy of) the deceased]
45 they will set up and they will take the compensation
II.5 iv 5' the[y] will s[e]t up [and comp]ensation [they will take]
46 and give it to the deceased. Now, if you, o god, etc.,
II.5 iv 6' and give it to the deceased.
47 (if) the affair of Šaušgatti is removed from us by that d[e]ed,
48 (and if) you, o god, over the Šaušgatti affair
49 will not pull back the robe at us in any way,
50 then let the *kin* be favorable. The SUNGOD OF HEAVEN has risen, the KING'S RIGHT[N]ESS [he?] took
51 and put it for him on the SIN. Unfavorable.

---

52 That same question through the diviner; [let] the first *ḫurri*-bird be favo[rable]
53 but let the following (one) be unfavorable. The first *ḫurri*-bird unfavorable, the following (one) favor[able].

---

54 That same question through the augur; let them ascertain the birds.
55 An eagle came in front *kuš*(*tayati*) and it we[nt] past in front[...]
56 a *ḫūu̯a*(-bird) GUN-*liš* ... it came down behind *kuš*(*tayati*)
57 and they [went] through the centre. [Be]hind the road: a *šulupi*(-bird) [?]
58 cam[e] down behind *kuš*(*tayati*) [and it] went through [the cent]er.
59 Thus Kurša-^{d}L[AMMA:] "They have cast [away]."

---

60 Or will they do this as follows:
61 They will set up (an effigy of) the deceased, [they will take] co[mp]ensat[ion]
62 and they will give it to the deceased. To [her] children [they will]
II.5 iv 6' To her children [they will]

63 *ma-a-an-ma-za* DINGIR-*LUM QA-TAM-MA ma-la-a-an* [*ḫa*]*r*-⸢*ši*⸣?
64 INIM ^{fd}*IŠTAR-at-ti-na-aš-kán a-pé*-⸢*e*⸣-*ez me-mi-na-za*
65 *la-it-ta-ri* DINGIR-*LUM-na-aš* ⸢*A-NA*⸣ INIM ^{fd}*IŠTAR-at-ti*
66 ^{TÚG}*še-ek-nu-un* EGIR-*pa Ú-UL nam-ma ku-it-ki* SUD-*i̯a-ši*

(end of column iii)

Reverse iv

1 ⸢*nu* IGI⸣-*zi-iš* MUŠEN *ḪUR*-⸢*RI* SIG$_5$⸣-*ru* EGIR-*ma* NU.⸢SIG$_5$-*du*⸣
2 IGI-*zi-iš* MUŠEN *ḪUR-RI* SIG$_5$ EGIR NU.SIG$_5$

---

§37" 3 IGI-*an-da* SU.MEŠ IR-*u-en nu* SU.MEŠ SIG$_5$-*ru ni ši ke* GÙB-*za an-ša-an*
4 10 ŠÀ *DIR* SIG$_5$

---

§38" 5 *IŠ-TU* ^{MUNUS}ŠU.GI IR-*TUM QA-TAM-MA-pát nu* KIN SIG$_5$-*ru*
6 LUGAL-*uš-za* ZAG-*tar ŠA* DINGIR.MEŠ *mi-nu-mar*$^{ḪI.A}$ ME-*aš na-aš* DINGIR.MAḪ-*ni pa-iš*
7 *INA* UD.2.KAM DINGIR-*LUM-za da-pí-an* ZI-*an* TI-*tar-ra* ME-*aš*
8 *na-at* ^{d}U-*ni pa-iš INA* UD.3.KAM *IŠ-TU* MU.ḪI.A GÍD.DA *ŠA* DINGIR.MEŠ
9 *mi-nu*-⸢*mar*^{ḪI}⸣$^{.A}$ ME-*an-te-eš na-at* DINGIR.MAḪ-*ni* SUM-*an-te-eš* SIG$_5$

---

§39" 10 *IŠ-TU* ^{LÚ}IGI.MUŠEN IR-*TUM QA-TAM-MA-pát nu* MUŠEN.ḪI.A SIxSÁ-*an-du*
11 *šu-lu-pí-in tar-li*$_{12}$-*an NI-MUR na-aš-kán pí-an ar-ḫa pa-it*
12 TI$_8^{MUŠEN}$-*ma-kán* EGIR GAM *ku-uš ú-it nu-za* GAM *ḫa-aš-ta-pí-in*
13 GUN-*liš IK-ŠU-UD na-at an-da e-ri-ir na-at* 2-*an*
14 *ar-ḫa pa-a-ir a-al-li-i̯a-aš-ma-kán pí-an ku-uš ú-it*
15 *na-aš-kán pí-an ar-ḫa pa-it* EGIR KASKAL-*NI a-li-li-iš zi-an*
16 *ku-uš ú-it UM-MA* ^{m}*Kur-ša*-^{d}LAMMA *ar-ḫa-u̯a pé-eš-šir*

---

§40" 17 IGI-*an-da* ^{md}GE$_6$-LÚ *a-uš-ta nu* MUŠEN.ḪI.A SIxSÁ-*an-du*
18 TI$_8^{MUŠEN}$ (erasure) *tar-liš pa-an pa-it ḫar-ra-ni-eš-ma-kán pí-an* SIG$_5$-*za ú-it*
19 *na-aš* 2-*an ar-ḫa pa-it ḫa*-⸢*aš-ta*⸣[72]-*pí-iš-ma-kán* EGIR UGU SIG$_5$-*za*

[72] See Walther, "Verbesserungen".

63 If you, o god, [h]ave thus approved,
64 will the Šaušgatti affair be solved for us by that deed?
65 Will you, o god, over the Šaušgatti affair
66 not pull back the robe at us in any way anymore?

Reverse iv

1 Then let the first *ḫurri*-bird be favorable but let the following (one) be unfavorable.
2 The first *ḫurri*-bird favorable, the following (one) unfavorable.

---

3 We counterchecked the exta. Let the exta be favorable. *ni*(*pašuri*), *ši*(*ntaḫi*), *ke*(*ldi*), on the left (it is) smooth,
4 ten coils; favorable.

---

5 That same question through the 'Old Woman'; let the *kin* be favorable.
6 The KING took himself RIGHTNESS, the GODS' FAVORS and gave them to the MOTHER GODDESS.
7 On the second day the GOD took himself the ENTIRE SOUL and LIFE
8 and gave it to the STORMGOD. On the third day from the LONG YEARS the GODS'
9 FAVORS (have been) taken, and they (have been) given to the MOTHERGODDESS. Favorable.

---

10 That same question through the augur; let them ascertain the birds.
11 A *šulupi*(-bird) we saw *tar*(*wiyal*)*lian* and it went past in front
12 while an eagle came down behind *kuš*(*tayati*). Upon a *ḫaštapi*(-bird)
13 it came down GUN-*li*. They came in and went through the center.
14 An *ālliya*(-bird) then came *kuš*(*tayati*) in front
15 and it went past in front. Behind the road: an *alili*(-bird) came *zi*(*law*)*an*,
16 *kuš*(*tayati*). Thus Kurša-^{d}LAMMA: "They have cast away."

---

17 Armaziti performed a counter observation. Let them ascertain the birds.
18 An eagle went across *tar*(*wiyal*)*li* while a *ḫarrani*(-bird) came in front from favorable (direction)
19 and went through the centre. A *ḫaštapi*(-bird), however, came above behind from favorable (direction)

20 *ú-it na-aš-kán pí-an* ⌈*ar-ḫa*⌉[73] *pa-it* EGIR KASKAL-*NI ḫal-u̯a-aš-ši-iš-kán*
21 EGIR UGU SIG$_5$-*za ú-it* ⌈*na-aš-kán*⌉ *pí-an ar-ḫa pa-it*
22 *i-pár-u̯a-aš-ši-iš-ma-kán* TI$_8$^{MUŠEN} ^{d}UTU-*un* GUN-*liš zi-an ú-it*
23 *UM-MA* ^{md}GE$_6$-LÚ SIxSÁ-*at-u̯a*

(blank space of ca. seven lines)

II. iv 7' *IŠ-TU* 3 ^{GIŠ}TUKUL [SIG$_5$]

Colophon

24 *ŠA* ^{md}*SÎN*-^{d}U *Ù ŠA* ^{fd}*IŠTAR-at-ti*
25 *a-ri-i̯a-še-šar*$_x$

(blank space of ca. ten lines)

26 DUB.5.KAM *Ú-UL QA-TI*

(column iv uninscribed until end)

II. iv

§41'' x+8 ^{fd}*IŠTAR-at-ti-iš-za*[74] *ku-*⌈*at*⌉[-*ta im-m*]*a* ⌈*ku*⌉[-*at-ta še-er*]
9 TUKU.TUKU-*u-an-za na-an-kán* KASKAL-*ši* [*ti-i̯a-u-e-ni ma-a-an-ma* GIDIM]
10 *Ú-UL ma-an-tal-la-aš-ša-am*[-*mi-iš*
11 SISKUR *ma-an-tal-li-i̯a Ú-UL* B[AL-*an-ti*
12 *ma-a-an-ma-at* GIDIM *Ú-UL š*[*a-an-aḫ-ti* ... (?)]

(remainder of column iv, as far as preserved, uninscribed)

[73] Reading after the handcopy; according to the photo part of AR and the entire ḪA are flaked off. If the copy was faithful, the surface of the tablet must have suffered some damage between the making of the handcopy and that of the photograph.

[74] This ZA sign is added right between IŠ and KU but much smaller than either of them.

20 and it went past in front. Behind the road: a *ḫalwašši*(-bird)
21 came above behind out of favorable (direction) and it went past in front.
22 An *iparwašši*-eagle then came GUN-*li* toward the sun *zi*(*law*)*an*.
23 Thus Armaziti: "It was/they were ascertained."

II. iv 7 Through three oracle types: [Favorable].

Colophon

24-25 Oracle investigation of Armatarḫunta and Šausgatti.

26 Fifth tablet; not finished.

II. iv

x+8 For what[ever reason] you, Šausgatti,
9 (are) angry, [we will 'put] her on the road' (i.e. satisfy her). [If, then, the deceased]
10 (is) not designat[ed] for *mantalli*-rituals [?]
11 he (i.e. the king?) will not pe[rform] *mantalli*-rituals. [?]
12 Now, if you, o deceased, [do] not s[eek] it, [through ...].

Left edge a

1 [*ḫé-*]⌈*e-uš*⌉ *ki-i-ša-an-ta*
2 [-*z*]*i*? *ut-ne-e ma-a-i*

---

3 [*ut-ne-*]⌈*e*⌉ *ka-ri-iz pé-e-da-i*
4 [ ]x

---

5 [-*z*]*i*

Left edge b

1 *ták-ku* ᵈ*SÎN ú-iz-zi na-aš* GE_6-*iš-z*[*i*
2 ᵈGAŠAN *A-NA* KUR-*TI* ḪUL-*lu i-i̯a-an-n*[*a-i*

---

3 *ták-ku* ᵈ*SÎN* EGIR-*iz-zi ḫa-a-li pu*[*-u-uš-zi*
4 ŠUB-*TI* NÍG.ÚR.LÍMMU![75] ÚŠ-*an ki-i-ša* [?]

[75] Handcopy ḪÉ.

Left edge a

1 [... r]ains will fall,
2 [...] ..., the country will thrive.

---

3 [...] a flood will wash [the lan]d away,
4 [...] ... .

---

5 [...] ... .

Left edge b

1 If the moon appears and become[s] dark [...]
2 the 'Lady' will march to the country in evil[...]

---

3 If in the last 'vigil' the Moon ec[lipses
4 fall of the cattle (and) death will occur [?]

CHAPTER SIX

PHILOLOGICAL COMMENTARY

1. *Tablets one to four*

a) LII 92 (II.4)

5' For the possibility of an illness as one of the events leading up to this and related oracle inquiries see above Ch. III.3 and 4. Note that the illness is not mentioned here as a token or symbol within the technical part of a KIN-oracle but as part of the oracle question.

7' Since E. Laroche's sole attestation for a deity ^{d}Ḫišḫura in his Rech. 81 (IBoT I 33, 29: abs. ^{d}*Ḫi-iš-ḫu-ra*; under the "Divinités Asianiques"), three more occurrences have become known: KBo XXXIV 139 i 10' (abl. ^{d}*Ḫi-iš-ḫu-ra-az*), XLIX 2(+) i 8' (nom./gen.$^{?}$ ^{d}*Ḫi-iš-ḫu-ra-aš*) and the present attestation in LII 92 i 7' (^{d}*Ḫi-iš-ḫu-ra-za*). To these unp. 250/f (rev. 1 [^{d}*Ḫi-i*]*š-ḫu-ra-za*) can be added; for a complete listing see now B. van Gessel, OHP 154-155. Three out of these five occurrences are either MUŠ oracles (CTH 575: IBoT I 33, XLIX 2(+)) or refer to them (KBo XXXIV 139, 250/f). Whereas in IBoT I 33, 29 (ed. E. Laroche, RA 52 (1958) 152, 156: "Se tenant en haut, il s'est caché au dieu Ḫišḫura.") ^{d}Ḫišḫura is one among many deities present in some form in the basin, through which the eel-like creature seeks its way, in XLIX 2(+) i 8' the deity seems to stand at the very beginning of the MUŠ oracle observation:

7' [... *=ašta/ =kan*] x-x-⌈*š/ta*⌉-*aš*[a] DINGIR-*LUM* ḪUL-*u-i*
8' [*an-da-an*] *Ú-UL ne-i̯a-ši nu* ^{d}*Ḫi-iš-ḫu-ra-aš*
9' [ ]x MUŠ *ŠUM* LUGAL-*kán IŠ-TU* MU.KAM.ḪI.A GÍ[D.DA]
10' [ ] *na-aš-kán* GUNNI *pa-it*

[a] So after collation by E. Neu.

[...] ... you, o god, will not turn [towards ...] in evil, then Ḫišḫura [...]. The 'snake' (called) NAME OF THE KING [came] from LO[NG] YEARS and went to the HEARTH.

One almost gets the impression that Ḫišḫura here represents or introduces this type of oracle after which the actual description of the animal's movements begins. An important and possibly similar role is played by this deity in KBo XXXIV 139 as well. At least four oracle types are attested here: KIN in i 3'-5', SU in i 6'-8', clinomancy/*šašt*-oracle in i 10'-15' and

ḪURRI-bird oracle in iv 2' and 3'. The paragraph containing the *šašt*-oracle, for which in general see H.A. Hoffner, FsHallo 116-119, is introduced as follows:

10' [ ]⌈*e*⌉-*ni ku-it* ^{d}*Ḫi-iš-ḫu-ra-az* ⌈MUŠ *ŠA*⌉ [o o]-NI$^{?}$
11' [SIxSÁ-*at ma-a-an* -]*ma ku-it i-ši-i̯a-aḫ-ta ma-a-an*[(-)
12' [*ku-it Ú-UL i-*]*ši-i̯a-aḫ-ta nu* IGI-*zi-iš* UDU-*i*[*š* SIG$_5$-*ru*]
13' [EGIR-*ma* NU.SIG$_5$-*du* IGI-*zi-i*]*š* UDU-*iš* IGI-*zi ḫa-a-li* [?]

[...] concerning the fact that through Ḫišḫura the 'snake' of [...] ... [... was ascertained(?), whether], however, it predicted something [for ...] or whether it did [not p]redict something [for ...], let the first shee[p be favorable but the next one unfavorable! The fir]st sheep in the first pen[...

It is not certain that the NI sign transliterated at the end of line 10' really belongs there: it is written vertically in the intercolumnium and must belong to one of the first lines of this paragraph. However that may be, here too Ḫišḫura is either one of the most prominent elements within the MUŠ-oracle or perhaps even represents it. In all probability related to KBo XXXIV 139 (cf. also obv. 3' *aši* UN-*aš*, 6' *arḫa* GÙB-*laḫzi=pat*) is the one-sidedly preserved fragment 250/f of an oracle summary (see already Ch. I.4) of which the first five lines run as follows:

Rev.*
1 [^{d}*Ḫi-i*]*š-ḫu-ra-za ku-it* MUŠ *ŠA* SAG.DU x [
2 [*ma-*]⌈*a*⌉-*an* DINGIR.MEŠ *še-ek-te-ni a-ši-na-aš* UN-*aš* GÙB-*la-a*[*ḫ-zi*$^{?}$]
3 ⌈*IŠ*⌉-*TU* ^{LÚ}ḪAL ^{MUNUS}ŠU.GI-*i̯a* SIxSÁ-*at*

---

4 *ki-i ku-it* NU.SIG$_5$-*ta nu ma-a-an* DINGIR.MEŠ *še-ek-te-ni a*[-*ši*$^{?}$(-)
5 *nu-un-na-aš-kán a-pé-ez ar-ḫa* GÙB-*la-aḫ-zi nu IŠ-T*[*U*

---

* Kindly communicated to me by E. Neu with the suggestion that at the end of line 1 perhaps ⌈*A*⌉[-*NA* might be read and that there might be room for an additional *nu* in the break before *ma-* in line 2.

Concerning the fact that through [Ḫi]šḫura the 'snake' of the head ... [...]: If you, o gods, know, will that man make (it) unfavorable/unsuccessful for us? Through the diviner and the 'Old Woman' it was ascertained.
Concerning this fact that it was unfavorable: If you, o gods, know, [will] th[at man ...] and will he thereby make (it) completely unfavorable/ unsuccessful for us? Throu[gh ...

On the basis of these two texts it seems likely, that the form ^{d}*Ḫišḫuraza* in LII 92 is an ablative as well and fulfills a similar function, i.e. it refers to a MUŠ-oracle procedure held earlier. The only preserved MUŠ-oracle probably connected with CTH 569 is XLIX 2(+)$^{?}$XVIII 6, one of the accession oracles. Another such oracle may be referred to here in LII 92, 7' and by the remark in (KBo XVI 98(+)$^{?}$)XLIX 49 ii 21' MUŠ-*kán* [*p*]*a-it* "The snake went" (for these texts see above Ch. III.3 and Ch. IV.2 and 3.3 respectively).

c) KBo IX 151 (II.2)

2' For the verb *šakkuri̯a-* see below ad L 6+ ii 52'.

7' Because of the context with the verb *šakkuri̯a-* a restoration at the beginning of the line to É-]*TI* seems called for.

10' For a restoration to *anda a*]*rnuzi* cf. L 6+ iii 8-9.

d) XVI 32 (II.3A)//L 6+ (II.3B)
XXII 35 ii (II.1A)//XLIX 93 (II.1B)

XVI 32 ii 1' Tentative restoration to *p*[*arā* SUM-*anzi* after L 6+ iii 23 [GIDIM=*ma kuit*] URU.[DI]DLI.ḪI.A *parā* SUM-*antaš*.

ii 2' For the dedication of estates or cities to the cult of a deceased individual from the Royal House and his or her gods see G. del Monte, AION 35 (1975) 324ff. and in P. Xella (ed.), Archeologia dell'Inferno 100ff.

ii 3' Whether opting for a sumerographic (]x x.MEŠ) or Hittite reading (]x x(= *re*?)-*eš*), in either case a nominal sentence results ("and to them (there is/are) ... "), which is not easy to fit into the context. With the enclitic pronoun -*an* of the next line probably referring back to URU, it may have been a relative clause as is indicated in the translation. It can, however, not be excluded that at this point L 6+ had a version different from XVI 32. In that case the simple restoration to *danzi* proposed by A. Ünal, THeth. 4, 104-105 ("Von diesen Städten) [nimmt man] für sich eine Stadt und besiedelt man sie") might be possible.

ii 6' Taking (*na*-)*aš* as a nom.sg.c. ("he, she") looks unlikely since there is no singular noun to refer back to. So the enclitic pronoun -*aš* has to be an acc.pl.c. ("them"; contrary to A. Ünal, THeth. 4, 104-105 *na-aš ar-kam-m*[*a-na-al-li-uš* "[sind] tributpflichtig") referring back to URU.= DIDLI.ḪI.A "cities", and one expects a transitive verb to follow. The general sense seems to be that certain cities are made tributary to the cult of Danuḫepa's gods. This would require a denominative verb from the noun *arkamman-*, either *arkammanaḫḫ-* or ⸓*arkammanallai-*; for both see HW^{2} A s.vv. If one wants to "save" the preserved]x-*ti* at the end of the line in L 6+ ii 6' one could envisage a Luwian 3.pl.pres. **arkammanallanti* "they will make tributary", parallel to the attested Glossenkeil word

1.sg.pres. ⸗*arkammanalaui* KBo VI 29+ iii 6 (CTH 85 - Ḫatt. III). Note, however, there is no Glossenkeil present before *arkamm*[*a*-.

ii 7' The supinum form BAL-*eškiuu̯an* is surprising and unique if it is to be read **šipanteškiuu̯an*; one would expect *išpanza*(*š*)*kiuu̯an*/*šipanza*(*š*)-*kiuu̯an*, cf. N. Oettinger, Stammbildung 321-322. An -*ške*-stem ending in °*nteške*- is only attested with -*ešš*-derivatives of -*nt*-adjectives (e.g. *ašiu̯anteške*- "to keep becoming poor" from *ašiu̯ant*- "poor") or with -*ai*-derivatives of stems ending in °*nt*- (e.g. *ḫanteške*- "to fix always/repeatedly" from *ḫandai*- "to fix"). The use of *arkamman* "tribute" as the direct object of this verb is likewise surprising according to the overview of usages of *šipant*- given by A. Goetze, JCS 23 (1970-1971) 77-94. The verb most often encountered with either the acc.sg. or pl. of *arkamman*- is *piddai*- "to bring". These considerations render the form BAL-*eškiuu̯an* both morphologically and semantically suspicious. No obvious solution, however, presents itself except for the unwelcome assumption that this passage would be corrupt.

ii 8' For *uliḫi*-, a cult object which was or could be made of wool, could be attached to a god's statue and was itself treated as divine, see M. Popko, Kultobjekte 106-107, and V. Haas, GHR 505-506.

u[*danzi*: Because the PÍ-sign is written in XVI 32 ii 8'ff. with a strongly protruding lower horizontal, a reading/restoration to *p*[*edanzi* is excluded. The same combination (⸗*kan šer uda*-) with Zawalli-deities as object is used in XVI 46 i 1'-2' (see above Ch. IV.5.2.1).

ii 9' The combination -*za* ... *arḫa šipand*-/BAL "to perform a ritual to the end, complete a ritual/offering" does not occur often, cf. from Muršili's Second Plague Prayer XIV 11 iii 9-10//XXVI 86 iii 13'-15' (ed. A. Goetze, JCS 23 (1970) 81) and the vow XV 1 ii 17 (ed. J. de Roos, Diss. 186, 326). For other references and this passage see L. Zuntz, Ortsadv. 39 and 50 respectively as well as HW^2 277-278.

On the *mantalli*-offering see above Ch. I.1.

ii 10' On the King of Kargamiš and Katapaili see above Ch. II.8 and 9.

ii 11' If the suggestion made above in Ch. II.5 is correct, that the foundation of a priesthood at Ḫalpa is identical to the installation of a king there, we have to assume that the Stormgod of Ḫalpa/Aleppo is meant specifically here by DINGIR-*LUM*. For the archaic *pidi*⸗*šši* "on his/her spot/premises" in oracle texts cf. below XXII 35 iii 18' and XLIX 92 iv 4, ibid. 94 ii 5'; on the occasional use of the Hittite enclitic possessive pronoun in 13th century compositions see E. Neu, FsPuhvel 151 and 152-153.

ii 17' Because of the consistent use of the plural (SISKUR) *mantalliu̯a* elsewhere in these paragraphs one wonders if perhaps the scribe inadvertently left out the final syllable -*i̯a*. Before the initial *a*- of the immediately following *arḫa* the difference could probably not be heard anyway.

ii 24' On GAL-^{d}U see above Ch. II.9.

ii 26' A general meaning for ⸗*taršul*[*aizzi* in the sense of "to venerate" or "to install in veneration" seems required by the context.

ii 29' The city of Neya /Niya is mentioned in connection with tribute and other unnamed cities (URU.DIDLI.ḪI.A) in the text XXVI 92, 5'//VIII 79 rev. 20' (CTH 209.3, ed. A. Hagenbuchner, THeth. 16, 398-405):

5 *ki-nu-un-ma-kán ki-i* INIM URU.DIDLI.ḪI.A INIM ⸗[a] *ar-kam-ma-na-aš* *ŠA* URU*Ni-ia*[b] ⸢*ú-e*⸣?[*-eḫ*?*-ta-ri*][c]

6 INIM *ku-e-nu-ma-aš-ma-ua-kán Ú-UL ú-e-eḫ-ta-ri nu-ua-mu-kán ku-na-an-zi-pát*

7 *Ú-UL-ua-mu-kán da-a-li-ia-an-*⸢*zi*⸣ *a-pa-a-at-ua NI-EŠ* DINGIR-*LIM* *ta-ma-a-i a-pád-da-*⸢*ia*⸣[o o o?? (*-ma-a-i*)]

a VIII 79 rev. 20' om. Glossenkeile. b VIII 79 rev. 20' *Ne-i-ia*.
c Reading possible after collation but restoration is tentative; A. Hagenbuchner, THeth. 16, 400, reads *Ú-U*[*L* but her translation differs from this reading ("Jetzt hat er aber in Bezug auf diese Angelegenheit des Tributes der Stadt Niya ge[schrieben."). Her translation would solve the problem that there is no quotative particle *-ua*(*r-*) at the beginning of this line which can otherwise only be explained as being irregularly missing.

"Now, however, this affair of the cities, the affair of the tribute of the city of Niya ch[anges] but the affair of killing does not change: they will certainly kill me! They will not let go of me! That divine oath (is) one thing, but that [... (is) an]other."

The text, possibly a letter or a deposition, as a whole involves Bentešina, King of Amurru under Muwatalli, Ḫattušili and Tutḫaliya and temporarily deposed during the reign of Urḫiteššub, in, unfortunately, a very unclear manner; see my remarks StBoT 38, 122-123. From VIII 79 obv. it might be deduced that someone is feeling threatened by Bentešina (cf. A. Hagenbuchner, op.cit. 402). On the reverse of VIII 79//XXVI 92 there is repeated mention of cities (URU.DIDLI.ḪI.A) and their tribute while Bentešina again turns up in the paragraph following the one quoted here. H. Klengel, Gesch.Syr. 2, 63-64, suggested that either the king of Kargamiš (cf. also ibid. 221) or the Hittite Great King would have been the author of the text. Since the king of Kargamiš or his representative (Talmiteššub? See above Ch. II.9) seems to have been involved together with Katapaili in assigning cities to descendants of Armatarḫunta and Urḫiteššub, there might be reason to suspect some connection between the contents of VIII 79//XXVI 92 and this subject in CTH 569. It seems impossible, however, to substantiate such a claim.

L 6+ ii 31' For a comparable absolute use of *piran tiia-* "to step forward, present oneself, make oneself known" cf. KBo II 2 iii 5-7 *mān⸗kan edani memiiani* dUTU URUPÚ*-na* DUMU*-annaš⸗pat piran tiiazi* "If in this matter it is indeed the Sungoddess of Arinna of 'Offspring' who is stepping forward (as the angry deity)"; see similarly V 6+ iv 8 and 13. For the participle in the meaning "advanced, (substantivized:) champion" compare I. Singer, Muwatalli's Prayer 53 with literature. Similar to the use of *piran tii̯a-* here might be the expression *parā ar-* as in KBo II 2 ii 48 (see above Ch. IV.4) and V 6+ ii (65-)67' (*nu=ššan mān kēdani ANA* GIG ^{d}UTU-*ŠI* ^{d}*Zau̯allīš* ^{URU}*Ankuu̯a=i̯a parā aranza* "and if in connection with this illness of His Majesty the Zawalli of Ankuwa too has come forward").

ii 32' For the restoration [GAM *arii̯auen*] "we continued the inquiry" and the available room cf. below ii 49'.

ii 36'ff. For this phrase and its variants in CTH 569 see above Ch. I.3.

ii 40' Since one normally finds ^{GIŠ}DAG(*-ti-*) and related designations (^{GIŠ}ŠÚ.A, ^{GIŠ}GU.ZA, *ḫalmašuit-*, *kešḫi*(*ta*)-, *tabri*(*t*)-, cf. J. Siegelová, RlA 8, 331-332 with lit., D. Symington, Furniture 116-121) for "throne, seat (of kingship)" in the singular, the consistently used plural in CTH 569 when referring to this object (contrary to ^{d}DAG-*ti-*) must be taken seriously. Although the plural could be taken to refer to the thrones of both king and queen (cf. A. Archi, SMEA 1 (1966) 77), this is less attractive because it seems to be the purity of kingship and His Majesty alone which is at stake here and not that of the royal couple. Note that there is no mention at all of a queen in the entire text. Was Tutḫaliya perhaps in a very tangible way thinking of the various thrones in palatial buildings throughout the capital and empire? Note the following passage from the royal substitution ritual KBo XV 2+ rev. 27'-29' (with dupl., CTH 421.1; ed. H.M. Kümmel, StBoT 3, 62-63):

27' ... [... (*namma* LUGAL-*uš kueda*)*š* (*kueda*)*š*]
28' [(*AN*)]*A AŠRI*$^{ḪI.A}$ *ašeškittari nu=za apā*[*ša apēdaš ANA AŠRI*$^{ḪI.A}$]
29' [*aš*]*eškittari* ...

Then, on whateve[r] places the (true) king usually seats himself, that o[ne (i.e. the substitute king) s]eats himself [on those places as well].

ii 43' The sumerogram INIM, encountered here for the first time, may refer as much to the words used by the different persons in their curses and intrigues as to their deeds accompanying the latter. More likely it refers to both of these at the same time which is the reason for choosing the translation "affair" here and henceforth.

ii 44' The variant of this part of the standard phrase characteristic of CTH 569 where the affair is subject of the verb *ḫuittii̯a-*/SUD (possibly also in iii 60-61) apparently conveyed the same sense as the one (KBo II 6+ i 39'-40', iii 48-49, and XVI 58 iii 5'-8') where the deity is the subject ("If you, o god, will not pull back the cloak on us anymore over the matter of PN"). Outside of CTH 569 the expression *šeknun appa ḫuittii̯a-* "to pull back the cloak" seems to be attested only in XXVII 29+ (CTH 780) ii 59-60 (*n=an* ^{TÚG}*šeknun* EGIR-*pa* [?] / *ḫūittii̯anniškiddu* "She (who is not his mother) shall pull back the robe on him"; ed. V. Haas - I. Wegner, ChS I/5 no. 19, p. 136, cf. previously V. Haas - H.J. Thiel, AOAT 31, 142-143 with commentary ibid. 162 and 197). The latter passage shows that in this construction the person "on whom the robe is pulled back" (*-an*; *-naš* in

CTH 569) is expressed by way of an accusativus respectus ("concerning ..."). The question in both variants in CTH 569 obviously is whether the deity will not unveil anymore, that is, reopen a certain case (cf. V. Haas, OLZ 77 (1982) 254 "eine Sache wieder ... aufrollen"). Both in the expression with the compound EGIR-*pa ḫuittii̯a-* "to pull back" as well as in the other one with *šarā pippa-* "to turn up/lift" (cf. H.C. Melchert, JCS 35 (1983) 141-145) it is the idea of "unveiling" rather than "veiling, covering" (cf. H. Otten, ZA 54 (1961) 143 "Das 'Werfen' des Gewandes über ... '", H.M. Kümmel, StBoT 3, 145 "Das 'Darüberstülpen' des wohl schleier- oder schleppenartigen ^{TÚG}*šeknu-*") which seems to be called for. The "pulling back" or "turning up/lifting" of a piece of garment symbolizes the uncovering of something bad which was safely hidden or, more negatively, covered up. By unveiling it, the evil becomes manifest. In some cases it may have had a sexual connotation (cf. H.C. Melchert, loc.cit.). The "pulling back" into the light of the absconded object itself seems to be conveyed by the expression *appa ḫuittii̯a-* with a single accusative as in KBo II 6+ ii 37 DINGIR-*LUM kuit ŠA* ^{fd}*IŠTAR-atti uttar* EGIR-*pa* SUD-*at* "Concerning the fact that the deity has revived/reopened the Šaušgatti affair"; cf. also V 24+ ii 14, 19-20 (CTH 577 - ed. Th. van den Hout, StBoT 38, 256-257) and with *ḫaneššar* as subject of the verb in the passive instead of *uttar* in Ḫattušili's 'Apology' iii 14-15 (ed. H. Otten, StBoT 24, 18-19) [GIM(*-an=ma*)] *uit IŠTU* É.LUGAL DI-*eššar ku*[(*itki* EGIR-*pa ḫuitti*)]*i̯attat* "When it happened that the lawsuit was somehow reopened by the palace" (compare the first attempt in i 33ff.). This proposed meaning seems to fit both the literal meaning of the syntagma and its contexts better than the traditional "protract, prolong".

ii 49' The translation follows G. del Monte in P. Xella (ed.), Archeologia dell'Inferno 113: "lingua viva". This was probably the shortest way of rendering what we find more elaborately phrased several times in KBo II 6+ ii 38 (et passim) EME *ŠA* ^{fd}*IŠTAR-atti=pat* TI-*antaš kuitman=aš* TI-*anza ēšta* "The curse of that same Šaušgatti, alive, as long as she lived". This curse "(when) alive" is contrasted with the anger of her death spirit immediately mentioned hereafter. The following §11' deals with the former, §12' with the latter.

ii 52' Mostly countries are attested as object to the verb *šakkurii̯a-*. Besides that we find objects like a house, a city, ornaments (on a copper cup) and human beings. Its general semantic range is indicated in several omina by, for instance, a preceding sentence with the main verb *mauš-* "to fall" (cf. XLIII 2+VIII 24+ iii 14'-15' KUR-*e=kan maušzi nat arḫa šakkurii̯atari* "The land will fall and it will *š.*") or by juxtaposition of a sentence like LÚ-*aš aki* "A man will die (, his country will *š.*)". K.K. Riemschneider, Omentexte 456-457, rendered it with "zugrunde gehen". Moreover, it corresponds in certain omina to Akkadian *sapāḫu* "to scatter, disperse" (cf. CAD s.v.) which is also used for estates (cf. CAD s.v. 4 and 6b "to squander", and 8a "to be scattered, dispersed, broken up"). In the Annals of Ḫattušili I (CTH 4), however, it corresponds to Akkadian *šapāku*, usually meaning "to heap up, pour" but which occasionally seems to have been used in the sense of "to render limp(?), powerless(?)" (cf. CAD s.v.

3), cf. KBo X 2 ii 18-19 *nu* KUR [URU]*Ḫaššuu̯a* U R.MAḪ GIM-*an* [?] GÌR.ḪI.A-*i*[*t a*]*rḫa šakkurii̯anun* "and like a lion I trampled the city of Ḫaššuwa underfoot". To A. Goetze, JCS 22 (1968) 20, the phonological similarity of Akkadian *sapāḫu* and *šapāku* seemed suspicious, though. The meaning "zugrunde gehen" can be taken quite literally where, also in omen texts, it is used to describe falling stars, cf. VIII 24+ ii 5'-6' [*takku=ka*]*n nepiši ištarna* GAL-*iš* MUL *talukišzi* [*n=aš š*]*akkurii̯atari* "If a big star in heaven becomes long and falls down"; compare the use in Akkadian parallels of *rabû*(*m*)/*rabā'u* "untergehen" here (cf. K.K. Riemschneider, Omentexte 474-475, and AHw s.v.). In the Hurrian-Hittite bilingual KBo XXXII 14 ii 56-57 (corresponding to the Hurrian version i 57) a coppersmith expresses his wish that Tešub may "tear off, destroy" (Hitt. *arḫa šakkuried*<*du*> = Hurr. *samm=al=ašt=o=š̄*, cf. E. Neu, Das Hurritische 30-31, 32 "abreissen, gewaltsam zerstören", StBoT 32, 82-83, 157-158) the artful ornaments he made on the cup. Finally, the Mita-text (CTH 146) XXIII 72+ offers the only certain occurrence so far, it seems, where it is used with human beings as object, cf. rev. 55a *nu* KASKAL-*ši* EGIR-*an* DAM LÚ-*LIM* DUMU.MUNUS LÚ-*LIM lē šakkureškit*[*eni n=uš lē da*]*mmišḫiškiteni* "after a campaign y[ou] shall neither *š*. a man's wife (or) a man's daughter [nor shall] you [h]arm them". The context here strongly suggests something like "to violate, rape" (ed. O.R. Gurney, AAA 28 (1948) 38 and 44, where the verb is left untranslated). A possible earlier example of this usage is offered by the Zukraši-text (CTH 15) KBo VIII 14+ obv. 5-6 as restored by H. Otten, MDOG 91 (1958) 82 n. 24: *nu=tta ḫartakkan mān* [*šakkur*]*iškimi* "and I will *š*. you like a bear". Next to XXXIV 22 iv (1-)2 (*parnaš šakkurii̯auu̯ar* "the house's *š*.-ing") and XLIII 8 iii 5b (É *ABI=ŠU=ši šakurii̯adari* "for him his father's house/estate will be *š*.-ed"), cf. also fragmentary XLIII 14, 3'-4' with Riemschneider, Omentexte 250) all instances of this verb in CTH 569 concern the sumerogram É "house, estate". Especially the passage L 6+ ii 48'-55' (§10') makes it clear that not so much the physical destruction of the building(s) may be meant here but rather a dispersion or squandering of the estate formerly belonging to Danuḫepa and her descendants: É-*ir=ši* [*kuit*] *arḫa sakkurii̯an* DINGIR.MEŠ-*aš=ši =k*[*an*] *kuit* EGIR-*pa ištappanteš* É[-*ir=ma*] *kuit tamēdaš parā* SUM[-*an*] "[because] her estate (has been) *š*.-ed, because her gods (have been) 'locked up' [while] (her) estate (has been) handed over to others." The words DINGIR.MEŠ-*aš=ši=kan* etc. may be taken as an explanation of or elaboration upon the preceding É-*ir=ši* ... *arḫa šakkurii̯an*. The proposed remedy follows in ibid. iii 7-15 (§12'): somebody will be sent to make further inquiries and to restore the cult accordingly.

ii 53' "Locking up" (*=kan* ... EGIR-*pa ištapp*-) gods obviously means in this context putting an end to their cult. The clearest and at the same time most literal use of this expression can be found in the Apology iv 26, where Urḫiteššub is said to have been "locked up like a pig in a sty". It is also attested in the deposition LIV 1 i 24 (CTH 297) as well as in the prayer of Puduḫepa to the Sungoddess of Arinna (CTH 384), used both times in a more metaphorical way very similar to the use in CTH 569 with gods each time as subject. In his edition of the latter text D. Sürenhagen, AoF 8 (1981) 112, basically follows earlier restoration proposals by A. Goetze, ANET 393, and R. Lebrun, Hymnes 331 and 338, where not the gods but either festivals (EZEN.MEŠ) or rituals/offerings (SISKUR.ḪI.A), twice restored, are made the subject or object (so Sürenhagen) of *ištappanteš*. With different restorations, however, which I owe to the courtesy of Prof. H.A. Hoffner, we get a construction identical to the one in L 6+ ii 52'-53' and iii 17 with their parallels: XXI 27 ii 3-8 *nu=nnaš šumel ŠA* DINGIR.=MEŠ *išḫiūl* [*ḫazzi*]*u̯i QĀTAMMA katta aūmmeni* [URU-*ri*?]=*ma*=*šmaš*=*kan* DINGIR.MEŠ *kuit* EGIR-*pa ištappanteš* [*ēšte*]*n nu ANA* DINGIR.MEŠ *annalliuš* EZEN.MEŠ [MU.KAM IT]U.KAM=*i̯a ēššanzi nu*=*šmaš*=*kan* DINGIR.MEŠ EN.MEŠ=*i̯a* [URU-*ri*?] *lē namma ištappanteš* "We will check your, o gods, [cul]t regulations, since you, o gods, have been locked up [in the city (i.e. Arinna?)]. They will celebrate for the gods the old yearly and monthly festivals and may you, o gods, my Lords, never be locked up [in the city?] again!". The passage LIV 1+ i 19-24 (ed. A. Archi - H. Klengel, AoF 12 (1985) 53, 58) is, unfortunately, difficult to interpret. It is probably the same Šaušgaziti, speaking elsewhere in the text, who is complaining to the gods : *ištarakki̯iat*=*u̯a*=*mu ku̯u̯api nu*=*u̯a*=*za AN*[*A*] DINGIR.MEŠ *apadda*=*i̯a arkūu̯ar ēššaḫḫun šumeš*=*u̯a* [DIN]GIR.MEŠ *UL uškitteni kiššan*=*u̯a*=*mu kuiš i̯ian ḫarzi nu*=*u̯a*=*šmaš ammuk taraḫḫan ḫarteni* ᵈUTU-*ŠI*=*ma*=*u̯a*=*za UL taraḫteni nu*=*u̯a*=*šmaš apēniššan ašān āššu* EGIR-*pa*=*ma*=(*šm*)*aš*=*kan ku̯u̯api ištappanteš* "When illness befell me, I directed a prayer to the gods for that reason also (saying): 'Don't you gods see, who treated me this way? You have overcome me but you do not overcome His Majesty! (Has it) thus really pleased you to have been locked up somehow?'"

iii 1-4 The tiny fragment FHL 111 recalls these lines (and cf. also above ii 35'ff.) but the match is not exact enough to consider the possibility of a duplicate seriously:

x+1]x? x[
2]*pár-ku-i*[(-)
3 *ki-nu-n*]*a-i̯a-an* ⌈*QA*⌉[*-TAM-MA*
4]x LUGAL-*UT-T*[*I*

iii 8 For the restoration of the particle =*kan* with *anda arnu-* see HW² A 333.

iii 14 ⸗*zappantalanzi*: Compare the same form without the Glossenkeil in XVI 77 ii 63 (see the Appendix) and the Luwian 3.pl.pres. ⸗*za-ap-pa-an-tal-la-en-ti* ibid. iii 38. The specific meaning is unclear (cf. F. Starke, StBoT 31, 518 n. 1916, and H.C. Melchert, CLL 279) but must be sought in the sphere of retribution and remuneration. In L 6+ iii 14 the object is that which was withheld but in XVI 77 human beings are the object. Both times the expression *šarā ašeš*(*anu*)- occurs in the immediate context which is attested in CTH 569 with GIDIM each time. Compare XVI 77 iii 37-38 [...

]x *kuit eni meqqauš* UN.MEŠ-*uš dammešḫan ḫarta* [GIDIM.ḪI.A *š*]*arā ašešanuu̯anzi n≈aš* ... *zappantallaenti* [*nu dammel*]*i pidi* KASKAL-*šiaḫḫanzi* " ... concerning this fact that he had hurt many people: they will set up [(images of) the deceased], they will remunerate? them and 'put them on the road' [at a sacr]ed spot".

Inserted L 5 (I.1)

r.col. 7' The general context seems to warrant the restoration to a supinum of the verb *ešša-* "to do, make, perform" dependent on a 3.pl.pres. *tii̯anzi* "they will begin (to ...)"; cf. in oracle texts XVI 77 ii 34, 40, XXII 40 ii 9', ABoT 14+ iii 11. In all of its forms, however, the verb *ešša-* (*iššа-*) seems to be written consistently with a double *-šš-*: *e-eš-š°/iš-š°/e-iš-š°*. On the other hand, a writing *e-šu-u*[- is until now attested only in the 1.pl.pret. *e-šu-u-en* "we were" (HW^2 E 93b) and in the difficult and isolated lexical entry *e-šu-u-u̯a-ar* (cf. HW^2 E 94b with literature). The enclitic pronoun *-aš* would be very hard hard to reconcile with either so that an emendation to *e-<eš->šu-u*[*-u̯a-an* seems justified in the present context.

XXII 35 ii (II.1A)

3' Although the traces are not unequivocal, a reading *da-*⌈*iš*⌉ seems possible. That a form of *dai-/tii̯a-* is required here, is shown by ME-*iš* in both the parallel L 6+ iii 20 and the duplicate XLIX 93, 9. The reading *da-ḫ*[*i*?- suggested by G. del Monte, AION 35 (1975) 335-336, as a ritual celebrated for the dead can now be abandoned.

7' For ZI-*an* DUḪ-*ši* see A. Kammenhuber, ZA NF 22 (1964) 161-162, and CHD L-N 3a-b.

L 6+ iii 23ff. The meaning of this paragraph may have been that in case any shortcomings in the tribute from the estates and cities were noticed, these would have to be compensated for as established through an oracle inquiry.

iii 23-24 For the restorations in these two lines compare the translation by G. del Monte in P. Xella (ed.), Archeologia dell'Inferno 114 ("Per quanto riguarda il fatto che la morta è stata indicata nell'ira per i villaggi dati via").

iii 25 The Winkelhaken visible in the sign traces at the beginning of the line as drawn in the copy is less secure judging from the photo. An in itself attractive restoration to É.MEŠ does not seem likely, however.

iii 27 The restoration proposed here to *u̯aš*]*kuu̯ana* "sins, wrongdoings" seems the only likely possibility; the same form is attested in XXI 19 iv 14 (CTH 383), cf. J.J.S. Weitenberg, U-Stämme 271.

iii 30-31 Because the next paragraph starts with the Urḫiteššub affair, this one probably refers back to §3' about the *mantalli*-ritual for the city gods of Ḫalpa. The tentative restoration in line 30 is based on that assumption and the limited space available.

iii 32ff. In the following lines there is somewhat more room on the left side than is suggested in the handcopy. For the restorations in lines 32-33 see G. del Monte in P. Xella (ed.), Archeologia dell'Inferno 114 ("[(Per quanto riguarda) la questione di] Urhiteššub che è stata indicata dalla ricerca oracolare: abbiamo interrogato l'oracolo ed esso ha indicato [la lingua di] Urhiteššub") followed by Ph.H.J. Houwink ten Cate, BiOr 51 (1994) 250 ("[The affair of Urhi-]Tessub which ... appeared to consist in a ['Tongue' viz. in a defamatory remark"). The CHD P 39a differs in both lines, not restoring INIM in line 32 and assuming DUMU.MEŠ instead of EME ("We asked the oracle about the Urḫi-Teššub who was ascertained and [the children of] (said) Urḫi-Teššub were ascertained"). For the restoration to [*nu* EME] cf. below iii 48.

iii 34 The restoration to [KASKAL-*ši*] "on the road" gives the best sense and concurs with the presence of the particle *=kan* in the preceding line. Both del Monte in P. Xella (ed.), Archeologia dell'Inferno 114 ("ed il fatto che i figli aggiuntisi a lui ... "), and Houwink ten Cate, BiOr 51 (1994) 250, in his paraphrase ("his sons had chosen his side"), probably thought of the expression [EGIR-*an*] *tii̯a-* "to choose the side of (someone)" which, however, never takes *=kan*. The same problem confronts the CHD P 39a interpretation where DUMU.MEŠ(-) in 33 to SIxSÁ-*at* in 35 is taken as one sentence, although here too *=kan* would not be expected.

iii 35 Given the fact (see above ad iii 32ff.) that there is more room on the left than shown in the handcopy, a restoration to *tiu̯at*]*anii̯a* seems to give the best sense. This means that we have to split off the *-aš* in *arraḫḫanii̯aš* as the nom.sg.c. of the enclitic pronoun, leaving *arraḫḫanii̯a* dependent on *šer* and asyndetically connected to [*tiu̯at*]*anii̯a*. For the combination *arraḫḫani- tiu̯atani-* see H. Otten, Luv. 95, HW^2 A 235, and F. Starke, StBoT 31, 254 and also 147 with n. 467 (for *tiu̯atanii̯-*); *arraḫḫanii̯aš* as a nom.sg.c. (so H.C. Melchert, CLL 24) thus no longer exists. The tentative translation of both terms follows the observation that in this combination *arraḫḫani-* can be seen to interchange with *ḫirutani-* "oath, perjury"; cf. Otten and Starke, ll.cc., Melchert, CLL 230, and C. Watkins, FsRix 470, for *tiu̯atani-*.

iii 36 Contrary to the handcopy, where the first sign after the break is given as MA preceded by some faint traces, the last vertical of this alleged MA looks like a broken one. Including the said traces there seems to be room for two signs in front of it. A restoration to [*nam*]-*ma* (CHD P 39a) seems therefore excluded. In his paraphrase Houwink ten Cate, BiOr 51 (1994) 250, supposes "[a royal order(?)]" which may indeed be the sort of thing one would expect here.

iii 37-38 For the sequence *ABI* ^{d}UTU-*ŠI* .... *kuitki meman ḫarta* see also the oracle fragment LII 49 iii 11'-12' (*m*]*a-a-an A-BI* ^{d}UTU-*ŠI a-p*[*í*$^{?}$- /]*ku-it-ki me-ma-an ḫar-t*[*a*) but it offers nothing otherwise reminiscent of the present text.

iii 44 For *uttar* as a possible object cf. LVII 66 iii 15' *nu* <<ša>> *ud-da-a-ar* (written over erasure) EGIR-*pa ḫa-aš-ta-r*[*u* "and let the matter/case be opened!", see also ibid. iii 20'. A restoration to *nu uttar* or (*nu*) INIM EGIR-*pa* would seem to fit both the available space and the sense; for the latter cf. Ph.H.J. Houwink ten Cate, BiOr 51 (1994) 251, "open up [a problem(?)".

iii 45 Apart from cases like *IŠTU* MUNUSŠU.GI KIN 3-*ŠU* SIG_5 "Through the 'Old Woman' the KIN-oracle three times, favorable" (V 6+ ii 20'), usually nothing is inserted in the summarizing formula between the *IŠTU* LÚ/MUNUS X and the actual outcome of the oracle. Unfortunately, the photo does not help in clearing up the traces.

iii 52 Judging by his translation G. del Monte in P. Xella (ed.), Archeologia dell'Inferno 114 ("e gli onoreranno i figli e le figlie") emends into <DUMU.>MUNUS.MEŠ which is possible but not necessary, it seems (cf. Ph.H.J. Houwink ten Cate, BiOr 51 (1994) 250-251 with n. 57).

The verb *kanešš-* "to recognize, (openly, officially) acknowledge" is likely to have political connotations here as in, for instance, the Bronze Tablet ii 51 *mā(n)=u̯a=mu* DINGIR.MEŠ *kaniššanzi* LUGAL-*izziaḫhari* "If the gods ackowledge me (and) I will become king"; compare also the many occurrences of *kanešš-/kaneššuu̯ar* in the Apology as an indication of Istar's esteem towards Ḫattušili. It is also attested with human subjects, cf. XXVI 58 obv. 6-7 (CTH 224) mGAL-dIM-*aš=ma* DUMU m*Kant*[*uzzili*] *ANA* dUTU-*ŠI* EGIR-*an tii̯at n=an kaniššun* "GAL-dIM, however, the son of Kant[uzzili], chose My majesty's side and I acknowledged him" (followed by an extensive exemption from duties, levies and taxes). In the present context it probably entailed the recognition of Urḫiteššub's descendants as affiliated to the Royal House and of their claims to certain rights depending on that status. This may have implied the granting of territories. If, as J. Mellaart once suggested in Mél.Mansel 514-516, and has been brought to the fore again recently by J.D. Hawkins, FsAlp 270 and StBoT Beih. 3, 64 (see now also I. Singer, SMEA 38 (1996) 70), the Muršili in the genealogy of king Hartapu of the KIZILDAĞ-KARADAĞ and BURUNKAYA inscriptions is indeed Muršili III/Urḫiteššub, then one might find the root of their claims to rule in this paragraph. Problematic, however, may be that the only territory explicitly mentioned as being handed over to them is part of the city of Niya (§7' - XVI 32 ii 28-30) which was located on the Orontes river in Syria, far from the said inscriptions.

iii 58 The interchange between *ŠA* m*Urḫiteššub* ḪUL-*lu* as subject of the intransitive medio-passive *laittari*/DUḪ-*ri* here and *ŠA* m*Urḫiteššub* ḪUL-*uu̯anza* as subject of the transitive active verb *ḫuittii̯azi*/SUD-*i̯azi* is a late and striking example of the Hittites' reluctance to use a neuter noun as subject in a transitive sentence; see E. Laroche, BSL 57 (1962) 23-43, and E. Neu, HS 102 (1989) 1-15.

iii 63 For the restoration [DUMU.MEŠ] see the CHD L-N 178a, followed by Ph.H.J. Houwink ten Cate, BiOr 51 (1994) 251.

iii 65 For the [*apez*] in the break see Houwink ten Cate, BiOr 51 (1994) 251 "[from that 'Affair' n]o evil whatsoever ...".

f) XXII 35 iii (II.1A)
LII 92 iv (II.4)

2' On *tiu̯atani-* see above ad L 6+ iii 35; of course, a restoration to *ḫiru]tanii̯aza* seems equally possible although this composition may have preferred to use *arraḫḫani-* "perjury(?)".

3' It is possible that the]x-*i̯a-za* is an ablative on a par with *tiu̯a]tanii̯aza*.

12' If the subject of SUM-*anzi* "they give" is interpreted as referring to His Majesty and Ḫalpaziti who were the subject of the previous sentence (9'-11'), the identity of the GIDIM "deceased" who is the beneficiary of line 12', is unclear; compare the legitimate question in the CHD L-N 178a: "but who then is the GIDIM ... of line 12?" There can be hardly any doubt as to who the GIDIM in 5' and 6' is: with A. Archi, AoF 6 (1979) 82, we assume that to be Ḫalpaziti mentioned in 1'. Since the city of Ḫalpa recurs in 13' and 16' (= LII 92 iv 7') and the *-ši* in 15' ("*for him* his sons") can refer only, it seems, to that same Ḫalpaziti, also the GIDIM in 12' must be him. This means the 3.pl. SUM-*anzi* here must be taken impersonally and is therefore translated with a passive ("Compensation will be given ... ", similarly in 15' and 16').

14' For the combination *šaknuu̯ant- parkui-* "unclean (and) clean, contaminated (and) pure" compare V 6+ ii 52-55 *nu ANA* DINGIR.MEŠ *Ù ANA* ^{d}UTU-*ŠI aniūr* GIM-*an n=at QATAMMA ani[i̯]anzi namma* ^{d}UTU-*ŠI šaknuu̯antaš ANA* ^{GIŠ}BANŠUR *parkuu̯ai̯ašša ANA* ^{GIŠ}BANŠUR$^{\mathrm{ḪI.A}}$ EGIR-*an ḫinkzi* ^{d}UTU-*ŠI=ma=kan* ^{URU}KÙ.BABBAR-*aš iu̯ar arḫai̯an apašila šippanti* "And just as the ritual for the gods and His Majesty (is laid down), thus they will carry it out. Then His Majesty will pay reverence to the unclean tables and to the clean tables. His Majesty will, however, separately bring offerings himself according to Hittite fashion"; see further ibid. ii 61'-62' and iii 4-5. Such a ritual involving "unclean and clean tables" seems attested in Emar (Msk. 731027+Msk. 74245 with dupls.) also: 4 ^{GIŠ}BANŠUR.MEŠ *ša ana* DINGIR.MEŠ GAR-*nu ina* ŠÀ-*šunu* 2 ^{GIŠ}BANŠUR KÙ.GA 2 ^{GIŠ}BANŠUR *lā* KÙ.GA "Quant aux quatre tables installées pour les dieux, parmi elles deux tables sont propres, deux tables sont non propres", cf. D. Arnaud, Emar VI 3, 329 (text no. 369, 82-83) and 334 (translation), and see V. Haas, GHR 731. Because of these parallels we are probably dealing with a specific ritual and one could interpret the combination in XXII 35 iii 14' ~LII 92 iv 5' as an elliptic expression "from the unclean (and) clean <tables>" as the CHD P 165a seems to suggest; differently, however, H.A. Hoffner, HS 107 (1994) 226 ("and they will give compensation from pure things and impure (things) to the deities of Aleppo").

18' On *pidi=šši* see above ad XVI 32 ii 11'.

18'ff.-XVI 58 iii 1'-3' As already pointed out in Ch. I.3 as well as in Ch. V.2, XXII 35 iii 3'-5' and XVI 58 iii 3'-8' both contain one of the two constituent parts of the phrase characteristic of CTH 569. As happens more often, between these two parts additional promises for compensation can be made (cf. L 6+ iii 50-57, KBo II 6+ i 34'37' and ibid. iii 44-46). The combination *mān* ... *mān* "if ... if" in LII 92 iv 8'-9' recalls the similar sequence in L 6+ iii 54-55 (*nu mān* SIxSÁ-*ri nu=za* BAL-*anzi mān UL=ma* SIxSÁ-*ri nu=za UL* BAL-*anzi* "and if they are ascertained, they will perform them. If, however, they are not ascertained they will not perform them"), also standing between the two parts of the formula. With the trace before SIxSÁ-*ri* in XVI 58 iii 2' compatible with a reading (-)*U*]*L*, it is conceivable to view XVI 58 iii 1'-3' as the direct textual (but not physical) continuation of XXII 35 iii ~ LII 92 iv! Note, however, that there is one case where the second part of the formula was repeated, viz. KBo II 6+ iii 63ff. (see Ch. I.3). The proposed textual continuation must therefore remain speculative.

g) XVI 58

iii 4' Restoration to [*QA-TAM-MA* etc. after KBo II 6+ i 37', iii 63, L 6+ ii 42; *kiš-an* as in KBo II 6+ ii 20 would be equally possible.

iii 6' This restoration to [*zi-la-ti-i̯*]*a* (after L 6+ ii 44 *zi-la-ti-a*(*n-na-aš*)) seems the only one to fill the required space adequately.

iii 7' Only the proposed restoration to *i-da-l*]*a-uu̯anni* seems to fill the required space more or less adequately.

iii 12' For the restoration [EGIR-*an-ar-ḫ*]*a* see e.g. KBo II 6+ i 45'.

2. *Tablets five to six*

KBo II 6+ i 1ff. Seeing that §4" only speaks of *ANA* EME ... *taliịan*, which returns as the third item mentioned in §6", the first two of them about the "scattering" of Armatarḫunta's gods and the subversive activities of his sons may have been the topic of the opening paragraphs of Armatarḫunta's affair. Note that in the preceding preserved paragraphs the outcome did not correspond to the expected result so that §6" may be considered a further modification of what preceded it.

i 6', 13' For the restoration to *A-N*]*A* cf. i 13'; moreover, EME is gen.comm. witness i 31' so that it could not be the subject of *taliịan*. What the expression *ANA* ... *taliịa-* means here remains enigmatic. The construction with the nom.-acc.sg.n. of the participle as the main verb of the sentence can only be taken, it seems, as another example of the impersonal use of a predicative participle as described by Ph.H.J. Houwink ten Cate, FsDe Liagre Böhl 203-206. For *taliịan* this would result in something like "(there is the act of) leaving". Many questions, however, still remain. Are the two noun phrases with *ANA* equally dependent on *taliịan*, and if so, are they the logical subject ("there is leaving to ... " = " ... are left") or the logical object ("somebody leaves ... ")?

i 7' For the restoration to [*kuitman*=*aš* TI-]*anza* see below ii 38, 44, 51, iii 4-5, cf. also G. del Monte, AION 33 (1973) 379 n. 29, and his translation in P. Xella (ed.), Archeologia dell'Inferno 108. The reading of the first two signs after the break is, however, not immediately evident in view of the handcopy and the traces on the photo.

17' For *ke*$^{\text{HI.A}}$-*uš* as a Hittite nom.pl. of the Hurrian stem *keldi-* see St. de Martino, ChS I/7, 149.

30' The first line of the summary fragment 10/v has]x-*u-en* EM[E where the x, although ending in two verticals of which the last one is 'broken' (= A), cannot be read -*ị*]*a*- and thus simply restored to *a-ri-ị*]*a-u-en* "we conducted an oracle investigation" because of the traces before the verticals. One must either emend and read -*ị*]*a*$^{!}$- or K]AR-*u-en* "we found" (cf. L 6+ iii 27 *ụaš*]*kuụana* KAR-*uen* "wrongdoings we found"?).

ii 12 Because of the expression *kattan* (GAM-*an*) *ḫamank-* (cf. HW^{2} Ḫ 119b-120a) in the next line and the fact that the topic of this paragraph is further elaborated upon in the next one (§14") after a denial, the restoration here to *šakuụantar*] *iị*[*a-* seems relatively assured.

ii 14 Perhaps a supinum has to be restored (-*uụ*]*an tianzi*), cf. immediately below ii 19.

Unless it refers to something lost in the break before line 12, KI.MIN might subsume the phrase *mān*=*ma*=*za* DINGIR-*LUM QĀTAMMA malān ḫarteni* INIM ^{md}*SÎN*-^{d}U=*kan kēz* INIM-*za* DUḪ-*tari* DINGIR-*LUM*=*naš ANA* INIM ^{md}*SÎN*-^{d}U *šer* ^{TÚG}*šeknun* EGIR-*pa UL* SUD-*ịaši* "Now, when you, o god, have thus approved, will the matter of Armatarḫunta be solved by this deed? Will you, o god, not pull back the robe at us over the Armatarḫunta affair?" last used in i 37'-40'.

ii 15 For the restoration compare i 2'-3'; the length and amount of signs required fit the gap perfectly.

ii 21 Assuming the oracle technique deployed in this paragraph is extispicy (a ḪURRI-bird oracle would immediately continue with IGI-*ziš* MUŠEN *ḪURRI* etc.), the apparent Glossenkeil word ⸗*la-a*-x[should be the beginning of the priest's observations. An interpretation through the participle *lānt-* "detached", which is attested in SU oracles (cf. CHD L-N 2a, and M. Schuol, AoF 21 (1994) 293-294) meets the requirement of the plene spelling but never opens the sequence of observations nor is it ever written with a preceding Glossenkeil. Moreover, the last sign trace does not favor a reading AN (see the footnote in the transliteration). Another word which conceivably could start the observations is the – as far as oracles are concerned – rarely attested *latti-* "tribal troops" (cf. CHD L-N 48b) which in oracle terminology could mean something like "knot, lump, joint" (cf. M. Schuol, AoF 21 (1994) 284-285). Although it is not attested with a Glossenkeil, Luwian origin is sometimes suspected (cf. M. Schuol loc.cit.). The problem here might be the failing plene writing in the first syllable of *latti-* in all its occurrences (see CHD L-N 47b).

ii 23ff. Why the last question concerning the Armatarḫunta affair was erased while the technical section with the expected oracle result (ii 26-27), the observations on the extispicy (ii 27-29) as well as the check through the KIN-oracle technique (ii 30-35) was left standing and thereby rendered completely useless, remains enigmatic. It does illustrate, however, the relative unimportance of these technical parts: the scribe or his redactor did not even bother to erase them, he just crudely wiped out the question containing the only relevant information.

ii 26 Although there is a clear break after SIG$_5$-*ru* with room for three or four signs, the sequel (27: EGIR-*ma* etc.) makes it unlikely there was anything in the break.

ii 31 Either DINGIR-*LUM* or *pa-an-ku-uš* seems warranted; the latter might be more likely because of the available room.

ii 32 For the restoration to [*n⸗at AN*]*A* cf. iii 25.

ii 36 The scribe originally continued with his text immediately although at this point the topic shifts from Armatarḫunta to Šaušgatti. Having noticed this he corrected his mistake by erasing the signs already written (DINGIR-*LUM*), by skipping some lines, by drawing a double paragraph line and starting all over again (37 DINGIR-*LUM* etc.).

ii 37 For *appa ḫuittii̯a-* "to reopen/revive" see above ad L 6+ ii 44'.

ii 40 Just like *u̯aštai-* in the combination *šalliš u̯aštāiš* in the Hittite Royal death ritual means "(royal) loss" in the sense of "(royal = a Great King's) death"(cf. Th. van den Hout, Hidden Futures 56-57), it cannot be excluded that *šalli u̯aštul* as a token in the KIN-oracle here is used in the same way. That *u̯aštul* too can mean "loss, lack" besides the more current meaning "sin" was already noted by H. Otten, HTR 119 (see also A. Archi, OA 13 (1974) 136 *u̯aštul* "colpa, mancanza", 137 *šalli u̯aštul* "grande sventura", differently R.H. Beal in Context 209 n. 29 "misbehavior"; see also J. Catsanicos, Vocabulaire 56 and 58 "malheur"). Whether the same applies to *u̯aštul* without the attribute *šalli-* in KIN-oracle passages below in KBo II 6 iii 28 and 51 remains unclear. It may imply that Šaušgatti specifically aimed at a Great Kings's (i.e. Ḫattušili's?) death.

ii 45 KI.MIN probably subsumes the standard phrase *namma=ma=za* GIDIM *damēdani memini šer UL kuedanikki/kuitki* TUKU.TUKU-*uanza* (cf. i 15'-16', ii 53-54) "but furthermore, o deceased, you (are) not (somehow) angry because of (some) other matter".

iii 2 The first part of the inquiry into the Šaušgatti affair is already drawing to a close in this paragraph (§24"). In ii 50-54 (§§23") it became clear that it was not only Šaušgatti's curse and her posthumous anger which were causing trouble but that there was something else. Therefore the next paragraph adds the cursing of her children as a new element to the inquiry which seems to be confirmed in iii 3 (§25") and brought to an overall conclusion in iii 4-10 (§26"). The contradictory result given iii 2 as SIG$_5$ "favorable" after a requested NU.SIG$_5$-*du* (ii 56) "let it be unfavorable" seems therefore due to a scribal error. The remainder of the inquiry after iii 17 (§29") concentrates on what should be done about Šaušgatti's anger and the curses of both her and her children.

iii 30 In view of the nom.-acc.pl.n. SISKUR *mantallii̯a* in line 32 which cannot be but dependent upon the inf. BAL-*uu̯anzi* in 33, it seems preferable to expect a (nom.-)acc.pl.n. here as well. In other cases where we have the two combined (XVI 32 ii 14'-15', 17'-18') in a similar construction SISKUR *mantallii̯a* can either be taken as the subject of SIxSÁ-*at* ("The *mantalli*-rituals were ascertained for PN to (be) perform(ed)") or as objects with an impersonal subject for SIxSÁ-*at* ("It was ascertained for PN to perform *mantalli*-rituals"). Although an interpretation of SISKUR *mantallii̯aš* as a dat.-loc.pl. ("regarding *mantalli*-rituals") here cannot be ruled out, it would result in a less easy construction (lit. "Concerning the fact that Šaušgatti was ascertained regarding *mantalli*-rituals to perform together with His Majesty" instead of "... that Šaušgatti was ascertained to perform *mantalli*-rituals together with His Majesty"). Note also that the AŠ sign at the end of the line seems to be drawn shorter than it normally would be written in this position (cf. e.g. iii 12). It might be that the scribe wanted to continue with BAL (see the next line) but then decided to start a new line. The AŠ sign at the end of the line is therefore emended.

iii 35 The imperative NU.SIG$_5$-*du* is out of place because the expected oracle outcome had already been formulated in the previous line so that an emendation to NU.SIG$_5$<<-*du*>> seems necessary.

iii 41ff. On the relation between the comprehensive KBo II 6+ and its summary VIII 27(+) see in detail Ch. I.6.

VIII 27(+)Bo 7787 iv 4' For the emendation to *pár-ku-*<*nu-*>*uz-zi* see CHD P 163b.

KBo II 6+ iii 45 Here and in the summary VIII 27(+) iv 5' as well as below in line 61 the combination *šarā*/UGU *ašeš(anu)-* is used with GIDIM "deceased, death spirit" as its object. The expression in KBo II 6+ is part of additional compensation and remuneration after the initial cleansing of the different items of Kingship. The said compensation is to be given to the deceased, i.e. Šaušgatti. The use of GIDIM "deceased" here and the literal translation "to make sit up" suggest that the text is referring to her image or effigy as is convincingly proposed by the CHD L-N 177b. Apart from conveying the notion of setting *upright*, the use of *šarā* may also imply the idea of availability as in *šarā ar-* "to be present, available, existing" (cf. H.G. Güterbock - Th. van den Hout, AS 24, 46). This would imply that Šaušgatti's effigy was "locked up" as well, and the promise of setting it up again is meant as a way of reinstatement or rehabilitation. The rendering by A. Archi, AoF 6 (1979) 81 n. 2 ("e scongiureranno/ esorcizzeranno lo spirito") does not do justice to the constituting elements of the compound.

The same combination is attested in the oracle XVI 77 ii 62 (*š*]*arā ašešanzi*), iii 10 (U]GU *ašešanuu̯anzi*) and 38 (*š*]*arā ašešanuu̯anzi*) where in all three cases GIDIM may be a plausible restoration in view of the present text. Further attestations are KBo V 1 ii 17 (CTH 476, ed. F. Sommer - H. Ehelolf, Pap. 6*-7* ("heraufholen"), for commentary see ibid. 50-52), where "two *zipinni*-breads" form the object of *šarā ašešanzi*, and KBo XV 37 i 10-11 (CTH 628) where the genitivus quasi gerundivalis *šarā* / *ašešuu̯aš* dependent on SISKUR (cf. E. Neu, GsKronasser 128 with lit.) occurs in the following context:

1 *nam-ma* ᵈIM *Ma-nu-zi* DINGIR.MEŠ-*i̯a*
2 *šur-zi-i̯a-aš pé-e-da-aš kat-ta-an ar-ḫa*
3 *ú-da-an-zi na-aš-ša-an* EGIR-*pa tap-ri-ti*
4 *da-ni-nu-u̯a-an-zi nu ḫa-pu-pu-un*ᴹᵁŠᴱᴺ
5 *da-an-zi nu* DINGIR-*LAM* É.MEŠ DINGIR.MEŠ-*i̯a*
6 *u̯a-aḫ-nu-u̯a-an-*   *zi*

---

7 *nu IŠ-TU* É.GAL *ḫu-uḫ-ḫa-aš* 1 UDU
8 1 ᴺᴵᴺᴰᴬ*i-du-ri-iš* ZÌ.DA *ḫa-az-zi-la-aš*
9 6 NINDA.SIG.MEŠ-*i̯a da-an-zi*
10 *nu A-NA* ᵈIM *Ma-nu-zi ša-ra-a*
11 *a-še-šu-u̯a-aš* SISKUR *ši-pa-an-da-an-zi*

Then they carry (the images of) the Stormgod of Manuzi and the gods passing under the *šurzi*-places and they put them back on the *tapri*-. They take an owl(?) and turn the deity and the gods.
From the palace of the grandfather they take one sheep, one *iduri*-bread of a *ḫazila* of flour and six flat breads and they perform for the Stormgod of Manuzi the ritual of 'setting up'.

This text too, it would seem, speaks of images that were once removed and are now restored (EGIR-*pa daninu-*) to their former place (i 1-4) whereupon a ritual is performed which in the proposed translation finds an appropriate title; for a different interpretation as possibly referring to the "installation du souverain dans le palais royal, peut-être après son intronisation" see M.-C. Trémouille, Eothen 7, 105 with n. 350.

iii 56 That the sequence of signs KU.UŠ within the augury passages in Hittite oracle texts is to be read as an abbreviation for *kuštai̯ati* was first noted by A. Archi in the *Inhaltsübersicht* to KUB L in his comments to the first text of that volume. In his seminal article on the Hittite bird oracle, SMEA 16 (1975) 119-180, he had already established the systematic relation between the technical terms *kuš(tai̯ati)* – at the time still read as a logographic combination KU.UŠ – and *aššuu̯az*/SIG$_5$-*za*. The two almost exclusively occur with the verb *uu̯a-* "to come" in combination with specific adverbs (*piran, zilau̯an*, and EGIR-*an* GAM and EGIR-*an* UGU respectively) and seem to constitute a contrasting pair (op.cit. 151). This parallelism of *kuštai̯ati* and *aššuu̯az* suggests a similar morphological interpretation for both terms. This obviously leads to the possibility of interpreting *kuštai̯ati* as a Luwian ablative. This seems to be supported by the observation that in the very same expressions we encounter *ku-za* and *ku-uš-za* in a few texts instead of *ku-uš*; compare for instance in XVIII 12+XXII 15 (CTH 564):

obv.
19 2 *a-li-li-uš-ma tar-li*$_{12}$*-an NI-MUR na-at-kán pí-an ar-ḫa pa-a-ir*[o o
]x-*ma-kán pí-an ku-za ú-it na-aš-kán pí-an a*[*r-ḫa pa-it*]
20 *šal-u̯i*$_5$*-ni-eš-ma-kán* EGIR GAM *ku-za ú-it na-aš* 2-*an ar-ḫa pa-i*[*t* 2$^?$
T]I$_8$^{MUŠEN}-*kán* EGIR UGU SIG$_5$-*za ú-e-er* 1-*aš* ⌈*zi-an*⌉[
21 1-*aš-ma-za* EGIR-*pa da-a-aš na-aš-kán* EGIR GAM *ku-za ú-it*
(...)
28 *a-li-li-i̯a-an* ^{d}UTU-*i tar-li*$_{12}$*-an NI-MUR na-aš zi-an ku-za* ⌈*ú*⌉*-i*[*t*

Two *alili*-birds, however, we observed *tar(u̯ii̯al)lian* and they passed in front while [such and such a bird] came forward *ku-za* and pa[ssed] in front. A *šalu̯ini*-bird then came down behind *ku-za* and wen[t] through the center. [Two$^?$ ea]gles came up behind from favorable (direction). One [came] *zi(lau̯)an* [...] while the other retreated(?) and came down behind *ku-za*.
(...)
An *alilii̯a*-bird we observed *tar(u̯ii̯al)lian* in the Sun and it came *zi(lau̯)an ku-za*.

Other examples for *ku-za* in the same text are obv. 32 (= XXII 15, 6'), 33 (= ibid. 7'), rev. 3', 18'(?), see further XVI 59 obv. 5. For *ku-uš-za* compare IBoT I 32 (CTH 577):

obv. 8 *na-aš* 2-*an ar-ḫa pa-it* 2 TI$_8$[^{MU}]^{ŠEN}-*ma-kán* EGI[R G]AM *ku-uš-za ú-e-er*

And it went through the center while two eagles came [d]own behi[nd] *kušza*.

Other examples for *ku-uš-za* are provided by AT 454 (CTH 577) i 59, ii 4, 31, 33, 35, 36. Hitherto this *ku-(uš-)za* was interpreted as TUŠ$^{(UŠ)}$-*za*, that is, as either an ablative or nom. of the participle of the sumerogram for the Hittite verb *eš-/aš-* "to sit down" which does occur in other forms in augury passages (cf. A. Archi, SMEA 16 (1975) 162). Attempts to translate TUŠ$^{(UŠ)}$-*za* in combination with the motion verb *u̯a-*, however, resulted in such unsatisfactory renderings as "sitzend(?) fliegen" (A. Ünal, RHA 31 (1973) 39-40) or "(con volo) basso" (Archi, op.cit. 152). This difficulty can be met by assuming with the CHD P 35b that *ku-za* is the Hittite counterpart of Luwian *kuštai̯ati*. The possible implication of Anatolian provenance for the stem **kušt(a)i-* itself need not surprise us, since the bird oracle as a whole is generally assumed to be of Anatolian origin (cf. A. Archi, BBVO 1 (1982) 287-288, Ägypten-Vorderasien-Turfan 89, and M. Schuol, AoF 21 (1994) 92; A. Kammenhuber, THeth. 7, 10 is non-committal, cf. also A.L. Oppenheim, Ancient Mesopotamia 209). As a consequence, the other technical terms in bird oracles (*taru̯ii̯alli-*, *zilau̯an* and what is usually rendered as GUN-*liš*) might be Anatolian in origin as well; for *taru̯ii̯alli-* see J. Tischler, HEG T, D 248-250.

Contrary to most translators *aššuu̯az*/SIG$_5$-*za* cannot according to Archi, SMEA 16 (1975) 151-152, be taken as an abl. separativus indicating the direction the birds come from. He therefore adduces the following passage XVIII 5 ii

40 *nam-ma-za a-*⌈*ap*⌉*-pa da-a-er na-at-kán* ÍD-*an* EGIR-*pa*
41 *ú-e-er na-at-kán* EGIR ÍD EGIR-*an kat-ta ku-uš ú-e-er*
42 *nam-ma-za* EGIR-*pa da-a-er na-at-kán* EGIR ÍD EGIR-*an ša-ra-a*
43 *aš-šu-u̯a-az ú-e-er nam-ma-at ták-ša-an ar-ḫa pa-a-er*

Archi maintains, that with EGIR ÍD the provenance of the birds has already been given so that another distinction "da un (luogo) sfavorevole" or "da un (luogo) favorevole" would be impossible. This seems by no means conclusive and one could easily imagine that the high flight from behind the river was seen as "from a favorable direction" as opposed to a low flight from behind the river which was termed "from (or: in) a *kušt(a)i*-direction". That we are dealing in all probability with an abl. separativus or an indication of origin may be inferred from the consistent use of the sentence particle *=kan* in the expression *=kan piran* SIG$_5$-*za*/*kuš u̯a-*. F.A. Tjerkstra, Diss. 47-99, has made it clear that the simplex motion verbs *pai-* and *u̯a-* do not have any sentence particle. In the latter category also fall those cases where there is a local adverb present in the sentence which appears, however, independent of the predicate. So-called derived predicates on the other hand, i.e. combinations of *pai-* and *u̯a-* with an adverb which influences the meaning of the verb and sometimes its construction within the sentence as well, seem especially wont to trigger off the use of sentence particles in combination with an indication of origin. Ablativi modi as a rule behave independently of the predicate in sentences with *pai-* and *u̯a-* whether there is a local adverb present or not. Seen from this perspective *piran uu̯a-* would in all likelihood be such a derived predicate and *aššuu̯az*/SIG$_5$-*az* an indication of origin.

iii 57 Where the movement 2-*an arḫa pai-* is said of two birds, i.e. here and below in iv 13, 2-*an* = *takšan* may also be taken in the sense of "together, both".

The particle -*kan* being attached to the first Hittite word of a sentence or the first akkado- and/or sumerographic combination representing a Hittite word, the phrase EGIR KASKAL-*NI* must be an elliptical phrase by itself ("Behind the road (the following can be observed):") because of *šulupiš=kan*. The same applies below iv 20 (EGIR KASKAL-*NI* *ḫalu̯aššiš=kan* etc.). Although there is no particle present in iv 15 (EGIR KASKAL-*NI* *aliliš zi-an kuš uit*), the combination EGIR KASKAL-*NI* is therefore taken as a separate sentence there too.

iii 58 Although one would expect in the break something like *na-aš-kán pí-a*]*n* (cf. iii 55 or iv 15) this is definitely too long. A simple *na-aš-ká*]*n* would certainly fit but *arḫa pai-* by itself does not require the particle *=kan*. For the present restoration (*na-aš* 2-*a*]*n*) compare below iv 19.

iv 15 For EGIR KASKAL-*NI* as a separate syntactic unit, see immediately above ad KBo II 6+ iii 57.

iv 25 For the reading *šar*$_x$ of the ŠIR sign see HZL 5 and compare KBo II 8 iii 9' UZU*ḫa-pé-eš*-ŠIR "joint, limb" (the writing UZU*ḫa-pé-eš*-⌈KIR⌉ ibid. 18' was perhaps influenced by the twice preceding *pé-eš-kir* "they gave" ibid. 7', 15').

VIII 27(+)
left edge a

1 Assuming the restoration is correct, the case form of *ḫēuš* remains problematical: the verb *kīšanta* presupposes a nom.pl. which, however, is only known as *ḫēau̯eš* (*ḫēi̯au̯eš*) or *ḫēu̯eš*; for an overview and discussion of *ḫeu-* "rain" with literature see J.J.S. Weitenberg, U-Stämme 29-31. Among the possible explanations mentioned by Weitenberg, either a *constructio ad sententiam* or *ḫēuš* as an acc.pl. in subject function, the former may be the most probable.

left edge b

2 ḪUL-*lu* can only be taken as a nom.-acc.sg.n., used adverbially.

APPENDIX

XVI 77 AND LX 52

Introductory remarks

G.C. Moore, JNES 40 (1981) 49 n. 7, first proposed to bring XVI 77 under the heading of CTH 569. H. Klengel, KUB LX Inhaltsübersicht v, linked LX 52 to XVI 32 because of the place names Alal[ḫa and Kiuta; Th. van den Hout, BiOr 51 (1994) 123, suggested the possibility of an indirect join of LX 52 to XVI 77 as part of its first column because of the "[son of] Arnuwanta" mentioned there. For the many similarities they share with CTH 569 and for the reasons not to include them in CTH 569 or its preceding inquiries in spite of all that see above Chapters I.12 and III.2.

The tablet XVI 77 (Bo 1960+4808) is preserved in its entire length, measuring 26.7 cm near the middle where it is broken off lengthwise, and 25.5 cm at the edge. Column ii contains 72 lines. Approximately two-thirds of the columns ii and iii are preserved, the original column width will have been ca. 8.5 cm.

Whether LX 52 (Bo 1347) was once part of the same tablet is difficult to ascertain. The widest line (3) measures 5.0 cm; it is not clear how much is missing on either side. The fragment is 4.5 cm high including the upper edge, the lines 1-10 occupy 4.0 cm. Because XVI 77 has 12 lines per 4.0 cm at the average, this could plead against an indirect join. They will therefore be kept apart here. Both pieces are written in regular 13th century New Script.

LX 52

Obverse

1 [DUMU ^{m}*Ar-nu-*]*u̯a-an-ta ku-iš* ⌜SIxSÁ⌝[*-at*
2 [DUMU ^{m}*A*]*r-nu-u̯a-an-ta ku-it* KUR^{UR}[^{U}
3 [ ]x *e-eš-ta ki-nu-un-ma-aš-ši* [
4 [ ]ḪUL-*lu a-pé-e-el* UD.KAM-*a*[*š*
5 [S]UD-*iš-ki-ši nu-u-u̯a-at ni*-x[[1]

[1] If the sign rest at the end of this line were IK (for the resulting older form compare the older IK-sign in L 6+ iii 38, cf. Chapter I.10), one could read Ì.G[ÁL "Is it still th[ere?".

6 [-]⌈*e*⌉ *ku-it-ki* TUKU.TUKU-*u-an-za n*[*u*
7 [^{UR}]^{U}*Ki-ú-ta* ^{URU}*A-la-al-*[*ḫa*
8 [TUKU.TUKU-*at-*$^{?}$*t*]*i* SIxSÁ-*at A-NA* É-*TI-m*[*a-aš še-er*[2]
9 [TUKU.TUKU-*u-an-za*]x *ša-ak-ku-ri-i̯a-*⌈*an*⌉[
10 [T]UKU.TUKU-*at-ti* SIxSÁ-*t*[*a-at*]

Obv. i

1 Concerning[... the son of Arnu]wanta who [was] ascertained[...]
2 [....] since [the son of A]rnuwanta [...] the city of [...]
3 [....] .... was but now to him [...]
4 [....] evil of his/that day[...]
5 [....] you will [p]ull [...]. They/Them/It still ... [...]
6 [....] in any way angry [...]
7 [....] the cities of Kiuta (and) Alal[ḫa
8 [....] was ascertained [(to be) in ange]r$^{?}$. [Because$^{?}$] of the house [...]
9 [....] ... dispersed[3] [...]
10 [....] in [a]nger [is/was?] ascertaine[d].

XVI 77

Obv. ii

1 [DINGIR-*L*]*UM-na-aš A-NA* INIM DUMU ^{m}*Ar-nu-u̯a-an-ta*
2 [EZEN$_4$.MEŠ *še-e*]*r* ^{TÚG}*še-ek-nu-un* EGIR-*pa Ú-UL nam-*⌈*ma*⌉ *ku-it-ki*
3 [SUD-*i̯a-ši*$^{?}$ *nu* IGI-*z*]*i-iš* MUŠEN *ḪUR-RI* SIG$_5$-*ru* EGIR-*ma* NU.SIG$_5$-*du*
4 [IGI-*zi-iš* MUŠEN *ḪUR-RI*] SIG$_5$ EGIR NU.SIG$_5$

---

5 [IGI-*an-da* SU.ME]Š$^{?}$[4] IR-*u-en nu* IGI-*zi* SU.MEŠ SIG$_5$-*ru* EGIR-*ma* NU.SIG$_5$-*du*
6 [ZAG-*z*]*a*[5] GÙB-*za ar-ḫa-i̯a-an še-er-ma-aš-ši* SAG.UŠ$^{?}$
7 [SI]G$_5$ EGIR SU.MEŠ GÙB-*li-kán* RA-*eš-ni*
8 [ ] NU.SIG$_5$

---

9 [*IŠ-TU* ^{LÚ}IGI.MUŠEN IR-*TUM Q*]*A-TAM-MA-pát nu* MUŠEN.ḪI.A SIxSÁ-*an-du*
10 [*NI-M*]*UR*[6] *na-aš-kán pí-an* SIG$_5$-*za ú-it na-aš* 2-*an*

2 For this tentative restoration cf. L 6+ iii 7 and XXII 35 ii 11'.
3 For *šakkurii̯a-* see Chapter V ad L 6+ ii 52'.
4 For this restoration cf. KBo II 6+ i 42'.
5 After collation; for the restoration cf. below ii 28.
6 After collation.

ii

1 [Will you, o go]d, over the matter [of the festivals$^{?}$] of the son of Arnuwanta
2 not anymore somehow [pull] back the robe at us?
3 [Then] let [fir]st *ḫurri*-bird be favorable but let the following (one) be unfavorable.
4 [The first *ḫurri*-bird] favorable, the following (one) unfavorable.

---

5 We [counter]checked [the ext]a. Let the first exta be favorable but the following (one) be unfavorable.
6 [... on the righ]t (and$^{?}$) on the left sideways, while on top of it fixed
7 [... fav]orable. The following exta: at the left in damage
8 [...] unfavorable.

---

9 That [s]ame [question by the augur]. Let the birds be established.
10 [A ... (-bird) we obs]erved and it came in front from favorable (direction) and through the center it

11 [*ar-ḫa pa-it* -*i̯*]*a-an* GUN-*li*$_{12}$-*an NI-MUR na-aš-kán* EGIR UGU
12 [SIG$_5$-*za ú-it na-aš-kán*] *pí-an ar-ḫa pa-it* EGIR KASKAL-*NI ḫu-u-u̯a-aš tar*-⸢*liš*⸣
13 [*ú-it na-aš-kán* EGIR]⸢UGU⸣ SIG$_5$-*za ú-it na-aš-kán pí-an* ⸢*ar-ḫa*⸣
14 [*pa-it UM-MA* ^{m}*Ar-tu*$_4$-]*um-ma-an-na* SIxSÁ-*at-u̯a*

---

15 [*IŠ-TU* ^{MUNUS}ŠU.GI IR-*TUM QA-TA*]*M-MA-pát*

(blank space of three lines)

---

16 [ ] *ti-i̯a-an-zi ma-a-an-ma* DINGIR.MEŠ
17 [ ]x DUMU ^{m}*Ar-nu-u̯a-an-ta*
18 [ḪU]L[7]-*u-an-ni pí-an Ú-UL ku-it-ki*
19 [*nu* IGI-*zi-iš* MU]ŠEN ⸢*ḪUR-RI*⸣ SIG$_5$-*ru* EGIR-*ma* NU.SIG$_5$-*du*
20 [ ] (vacat)

---

21 [ ]*ku-it* TUKU.⸢TUKU⸣-*a*[*t-ti* SIxS]Á-⸢*at*⸣
22 [EZEN$_4$.ME]Š GAM-*an ḫa-ma-an-ká*[*n-t*]*e-eš nu-uš-ma-aš* DINGIR.MEŠ
23 [DUMU ^{m}*Ar-nu-u̯a-an-t*]*a A-NA* EZEN$_4$.MEŠ *še*-⸢*er*⸣ TUKU.TUKU-*u-an-te-eš*
24 [(NU.)S]IG$_5$

---

25 [*nu-uš-ma-aš* DINGIR.MEŠ DU]MU ^{m}*Ar-nu-u̯a-an-ta A-NA* EZEN$_4$.MEŠ-*pát še-er*
26 [TUKU.TUKU-*u-an-te-eš nam-ma-*]*ma* KI.MIN *nu* IGI-*zi-iš* MUŠEN *ḪUR-RI* SIG$_5$-*ru*
27 [EGIR-*ma* NU.SIG$_5$-*du* IGI-*z*]*i-iš* MUŠEN *ḪUR-RI* SIG$_5$ EGIR NU.SIG$_5$

---

28 [IGI-*an-da* SU.ME]Š[8] IR-*u-en nu* SU.MEŠ SIG$_5$-*ru ni* ZAG-*za* ⸢GÙB⸣-*za*
29 [ ]x *šal-li-iš ši ta* ŠU-*TI* ZAG-*na-aš*
30 [-]x[9]-*ki-iz-zi* 10 ŠÀ *DIR* SIG$_5$

---

31 [*nu* DINGIR.MEŠ DUMU ^{m}*Ar*-]*nu-u̯a-an-ta ku-it A-NA* EZEN$_4$.MEŠ
32 [*še-er* TUKU.TUKU-*at-ti* S]IxSÁ-*at nu-kán* UN-*an pa-ra-a ne-i̯a-an-zi*
33 [*nu-uš-ma-aš ma-a-an* E]ZEN$_4$ *na-aš-ma* 𒑱*ḫa-az-zi-u̯i*$_5$
34 [*ku-it-ki kar-ša-a*]*n nu-uš-ma-ša-at e-eš-šu-u-u̯a-an*

[7] After collation.

[8] For this restoration cf. above ad ii 5.

[9] A reading (-)*u*]*š*-(*ki-iz-zi*) does not seem likely if we compare the UŠ sign in, for instance, ii 22. Moreover, the alleged trace of a horizontal is not visible on the photo. There may have been an extra Winkelhaken.

11 [went off. A ...] (-bird) GUN-*lian* we observed and above behind it
12 [from favorable (direction) it came and it] passed in front. Behind the road: a *ḫūu̯a*(-bird) *tarwiyalli*
13 [came and behind] above from favorable (direction) it came and in front it
14 [passed. Thus Art]ummanna: “They have been established.”

---

15 That [sa]me [question by the ...].

(blank space of three lines)

---

16 [....] they put (or: they will begin [to ...])/step. If (you, o?) gods
17 [....] the son of Arnuwanta
18 [....] in [evi]l nothing
19 [.... then let the [first] *ḫurri*-[bi]rd be favorable but let the following (one) be unfavorable.
20 [...] (vacat)

---

21 Because [....] was/were [ascert]ained (as being) in ang[er],
22 [for ...] [festivals] (were) assigned and (are) you, o gods,
23 angry [with the son of Arnuwant]a because of the festivals?
24 [.... (un)fa]vorable.

---

25 [(Are) you, o gods, angry] with [the so]n of Arnuwanta only because of (those) festivals,
26 [furthermore,] however, etc., then let the first *ḫurri*-bird be favorable
27 [but let the following (one) be unfavorable. The fir]st *ḫurri*-bird favorable, the following one unfavorable.

---

28 We [counter]checked [the ext]a. Let the exta be favorable. *ni*(*pašuri*) on the right, on the left
29 [....] large *ši*(*ntaḫi*), *ta*(*nani*) of the right hand
30 [....] he will repeatedly [....] , ten coils; favorable.

---

31 Since [the gods have b]een ascertained [(as being) in anger]
32 [because] of the festivals [of the son of Ar]nuwanta, they will send out a man.
33 [If for them a f]estival or a ritual
34 [(has been) neglecte]d, for them [they will begin to] perform them

35 [*ti-an-zi nu-uš-ma-aš z*]*a-an-ki-la-tar* SUM-*an-zi ma-a-an-ma A-NA* DINGIR.MEŠ
36 [ZI-*an-za a-pé-e-e*]*z me-mi-ia-na-az ua-ar-ši-ia-at-*⸢*ta*⸣*-ri*[10]
37 [*nu* IGI-*zi-iš* MUŠEN *ḪUR-R*]*I* SIG$_5$-*ru* EGIR-*ma* NU.SIG$_5$-*du* IGI-*zi-iš* NU.SIG$_5$ EGIR SIG$_5$

---

38 [*nu-kán* UN-*an pa-r*]*a-a ne-ia-an-zi nu* DINGIR.MEŠ *a-ri-ia-zi*
39 [*ma-a-an A-NA* DINGIR.M]EŠ EZEN$_4$ *na-aš-ma* 𒑱*ḫa-az-zi-ui$_5$ ku-it-ki*
40 [*kar-ša-an na-a*]*t* EGIR-*pa e-eš-šu-u-ua-an ti-an-zi*
41 [*nu za-an-ki-l*]*a-tar* SUM-*an-zi IT-TI* ^{d}UTU-*ŠI-ma-at*
42 [ ]x *ŠA* É.GAL-*LIM máš-kán pé-e-da-an-zi*
43 [*nu* IGI-*zi-iš*] MUŠEN *ḪUR-RI* SIG$_5$-*ru* EGIR-*ma* NU.SIG$_5$-*du*
44 [IGI-*zi-iš* MUŠEN *ḪUR-RI* NU.SI]G$_5$ EGIR SIG$_5$

---

45 [*nu-kán* UN-*an p*]*a-ra-a ne-ia-an-zi nu* DINGIR.MEŠ *a-ri-ia-zi*
46 [*d*]*a-a-i* EZEN$_4$.MEŠ-*ma ku-i-e-eš kar-ša-an-te-eš*
47 [*ḫa-p*]*u*[11]*-uš-ša-an-zi* GAM-*an-na* 𒑱*za*$^{!}$[12]*-an-ki-la-tar* (erasure)
48 [SUM-*an-zi IT-*]*TI*$^{?}$ ^{d}UTU-*ŠI-ma-at ku-it* SIxSÁ-*at*
49 [*ŠA* É.]⸢GAL-*LIM*⸣ *pé-e-da-an-zi* KI.MIN *nu* IGI-*zi-iš*
50 [MUŠEN *ḪUR-RI* SIG$_5$-*ru* E]GIR-*ma* NU.SIG$_5$-*du*
51 [IGI-*zi-iš* MUŠEN *ḪUR-R*]*I* SIG$_5$ EGIR NU.SIG$_5$

---

52 [IGI-*an-da* SU.MEŠ[13] I]R-*u-en nu* SU.MEŠ SIG$_5$-*ru ni ši*
53 [G]ÙB$^{?}$-*aš* EGIR-*pa du-ua-ar-na-an-za* 12 ŠÀ *DIR* SIG$_5$

---

54 [*IŠ-TU* ^{MUNUS}ŠU.GI I]R-*TUM QA-TAM-MA-pát nu* KIN SIG$_5$-*ru*
55 [*ŠA* DINGIR.MEŠ *mi-nu-mar*^{ḪI}]$^{.A}$ ME-*an-te-eš na-at* DINGIR.MAḪ-*ni* SUM-*an-te-eš*
56 [ḪUL-*l*]*u* ME-*an nu-kán an-da* SUD-*liš*
57 [*p*]*í*[14]*-an-za* EGIR-*an ar-ḫa kar-pí-in* ME-*aš*
58 [*nu-kán an-da* SI]G$_5$-*u-i* SIG$_5$

---

59 [^{m}*Pí-iš-ši-li-i*]*n* ^{m}*Ḫa-it-ti-li-in-na* 𒑱*a-ra-an-da-az*
60 [*n*]*u-za* ^{d}UTU-*ŠI IT-TI* ^{m}*Pí-iš-ši-li*
61 [*Ù IT-TI*]⸢^{m}⸣*Ḫa-it-ti-li ar-ha* BAL-*an-ti*
62 [GIDIM-*ia*$^{?}$ *š*]*a-ra-a a-še-ša-an-zi*[15] *nu-uš-ma-aš* ŠU-*TI te-pa-u-ua-az*

[10] Cf. XVI 32 ii 17' and E. Neu, StBoT 5, 191.
[11] After collation.
[12] Tablet: ḪA.
[13] For this restoration see above ad ii 5.
[14] After collation.
[15] For the restoration at the beginning of this line and the resulting expression see Chapter V ad KBo II 6+ iii 45.

35 [and co]mpensation they will give [them]. Now, if for (you), o gods,
36 [(your) soul by tha]t deed he will be pacified,
37 [then let the first *ḫurr*]*i*-bird be favorable but let the following (one) be unfavorable. The first unfavorable, the later (one) favorable.

---

38 [The man] they will send [ou]t and he will question the gods.
39 [If for the god]s a festival or some ritual
40 [(has been) neglected,] will they begin to perform [i]t again
41 [and] will they give [compen]sation, while together with His Majesty it/these
42 [....] (and?) will they bring a propitiatory gift of the palace?
43 [Then let the first] *ḫurri*-bird be favorable but the later (one) unfavorable.
44 [The first *ḫurri*-bird unfavora]ble, the later (one) favorable.

---

45 [The man] they will send [ou]t and he will investigate the gods,
46 [.... he will be]gin?, but which festivals (have been) neglected,
47 they will make up [for them ....] and later compensation
48 [they will give]. Since it was ascertained together with His Majesty,
49 will they bring [.... of the p]alace, etc.? Let the first
50 [*ḫurri*-bird be favorable] but let the [l]ater (one) be unfavorable.
51 [The first *ḫurr*]*i*-[bird] favorable, the later (one) unfavorable.

---

52 We counter[checked the exta]. Let the exta be favorable. *ni*(*pašuri*), *ši*(*ntaḫi*),
53 [.... the l]eft, broken behind, twelve coils; favorable.

---

54 That same [qu]estion [by the 'Old Woman']. Let the *kin* be favorable.
55 [The GODS' FAVOR]S (have been) taken and given to the MOTHERGODDESS.
56 [.... EV]IL (has been) taken and SUD-*liš*
57 [....] .... the WRATH he took away behind
58 [and (it is) in favo]rable (position). Favorable.

---

59 [Piššil]i and Ḫaittili 𒑱*arandaz*[16]
60 [(s)he/they ... a]nd His Majesty together with Piššili
61 [and together with?] Ḫaittili will complete the ritual.[17]
62 [And (an effigy of) the deceased?] they will set up and to them ...[18] in small amount

[16] See HW^2 A 250a, H.C. Melchert, CLL 25.
[17] See above Chapter V ad XVI 32 ii 9'.
[18] Cf. below iii 10-11.

63 [ ]-*zi nam-ma-aš za-ap-pa-an-ta-la-an-zi*
64 [*ma-a-an-k*]*án a-ši* INIM ^{m}*Pí-iš-ši-li Ù* ^{m}*Ḫa-it-ti-li*
65 [*ke-e-e*]*z* INIM-*za la-a-it-ta-ri nu* IGI-*zi-iš* MUŠEN *ḪUR-RI*
66 [SIG$_5$-*ru* EG]IR-*ma* NU.SIG$_5$-*du* IGI-*zi-iš* MUŠEN *ḪUR-RI* NU.SIG$_5$
67 [ ] EGIR SIG$_5$

---

68 [*IŠ-TU* ^{MUNUS}Š]U.GI IR-*TUM QA-TAM-MA-pát nu* KIN SIG$_5$-*ru*
69 [-*i*]*r pa-aḫ-ša-nu-mar* MU-*an-na* ME-*ir*
70 [*na-at pa-a*]*n-ka$_4$-u-i* SUM-*e-er* NU.SIG$_5$

---

71 [*IŠ-TU* ^{LÚ}]IGI.MUŠEN IR-*TUM QA-TAM-MA-pát nu* MUŠEN.ḪI.A SIxSÁ-*an-du*
72 [*t*]*ar-liš a-li-li-iš-ma-kán pí-an* SIG$_5$-*za ú-it*
73 [*na-aš-kán pí-a*]*n ar-ḫa pa-it ḫa-aš-ta-pí-iš tar-liš pa-an pa-it*

(end of column ii)

Rev. iii

1 [ ]x x-*iš-ma-kán ḫa-aš-ta-pí-iš* EGIR UGU SIG$_5$-*za ú-*⸢*it*⸣
2 [*na-aš-ká*]*n pí-an ar-ḫa pa-it* EGIR KASKAL-*NI u-ra-i̯a-an-ni-iš-kán*
3 [EGIR U]GU SIG$_5$-*za ú-it na-aš-kán pí-an ar-ḫa pa-it*
4 [*UM-MA* ^{m}]⸢*Ar*⸣-*tu$_4$-um-ma-an-na* SIxSÁ-*at-u̯a*

---

5 [*ma-a-an Š*]*A* ^{m}*Pí-i̯a-aš-ši-li Ù ŠA* ^{m}*Ḫa-it-ti-li*![19]
6 [*e-eš-ḫar*] *šar-ni-in-ku-u-u̯a-an-zi ša-an-ḫe-eš-ki-ši*
7 [*nu* KIN N]U.SIG$_5$-*du* NU.SIG$_5$

---

8 [*nu* DINGIR-*LU*]*M e-eš-ḫar-pát šar-ni-in-ku-u̯a-an-zi ša-an-ḫe-eš-ki-ši*
9 [*nam-ma-ma* K]I.MIN *nu* IGI-*zi-iš* MUŠEN *ḪUR-RI* NU.SIG$_5$ EGIR SIG$_5$

---

10 [*nu* GIDIM.ḪI.A U]GU *a-še-ša-nu-u̯a-an-zi nu-uš-ma-aš* ŠU-*TUM za*![20]-*az-ki-tal-la-an*
11 [-*z*]*i* ^{d}UTU-*ŠI-ma-za da-pí-aš* GIM-*an* UN.MEŠ-*aš*
12 [*iš-ḫa-a*]*ḫ-ru-u̯a-za pár-ku-nu-zi a-pé-el-la-za QA-TAM-MA*
13 [KI.MIN *nam-ma-*]*ma* EGIR-*an UL-pát ša-an-ḫa-an-zi*
14 [*nu-kán*? INIM-z]*a*? *a-ši* INIM ^{m}*Pí-iš-ši-li* ^{m}![21]*Ḫa-it-ti-li*

[19] Tablet: TI.
[20] Tablet: ḪA.
[21] Tablet: ^{d}.

63 they will [give?], then they will remunerate?[22] them.
64 [If] that affair of Piššili and Ḫaittili
65 [through thi]s deed will be solved, then let the first *ḫurri*-bird
66 [be favorable] but let the [follo]wing (one) be unfavorable. The first *ḫurri*-bird unfavorable,
67 the following (one) favorable.

---

68 [By the 'O]ld Woman' that same question. Let the *kin* be favorable.
69 [....] .... PROTECTION and the YEAR they took
70 and they gave [it to the *pa*]*nku*. Unfavorable.

---

71 [Through the] augur that same question. Let them ascertain the birds.
72 [... *t*]*ar*(*wiyal*)*liš*, an *alili*-bird, however, came in front from favorable (direction)
73 [and in f]ront it passed. A *ḫaštapi*-bird went across *tar*(*wiyal*)*liš*,

iii

1 [...] ... *ḫaštapi*-bird came above behind from favorable (direction)
2 [and it] passed in front. Behind the road: an *urayanni*-bird came
3 [behind abo]ve from favorable (direction) and it passed in front.
4 [Thus A]rtummanna: "It was established."

---

5 [If] you keep seeking to get compensation for Piyaššili's and Ḫaittili's
6 [blood],
7 then let [the *kin*? be u]nfavorable. Unfavorable.

---

8 Do you, [o go]d, keep seeking to get compensation for the blood only,
9 [furthermore, however, e]tc., the first *ḫurri*-bird unfavorable, the later (one) favorable.

---

10 [(An effigy of) the deceased] they will set [u]p and for them the hand? *zazkitallan*[23]
11 they will [...]. Just as His Majesty, however, will clean himself from all people's
12 [... (and?) tea]rs, himself (from) his (own) likewise
13 [etc.?[24] Furthermore], however, they do not at all seek (anything),
14 will [through that dee]d that affair of Piššili (and) Ḫaittili

[22] For the translation compare above Chapter V ad L 6+ iii 14.
[23] Cf. above ii 62.
[24] I.e. will he clean himself from his own tears?

15 [la-a-it-ta-r]i[25] nu SU.MEŠ SIG$_5$-ru zé-ḫi-li-ip-ši-ma-an NU.SIG$_5$

---

16 [Š]A NUMUN EME e-eš-ša-an-zi nu MUŠEN ḪUR-RI
17 [ ] NU.⸢SIG$_5$⸣

---

18 [a-p]é-el pa-an-ku-na-aš ú-u̯a-da-an-zi
19 [ ]⸢e⸣-eš-ḫa-na-az šar-ni-ik-ze-el te-pa-u-u̯a-az
20 [SUM-an-zi na-]aš-kán EME GAM ap-pa-an-zi ^{d}UTU-ŠI-ma-za a-pé-el-pát-<<za>>?
21 [iš-ḫa-aḫ-ru-u̯]a-za ar-ḫa pár-ku-nu-zi a-pu-u-uš-ša
22 [ ]x-an-zi nu-uš-ma-aš ŠU-TUM za[26]-az-ki-tal-la-an
23 [-a]n-zi na-aš KASKAL-ši-aḫ-ḫa-an-zi ma-a-an-ma-an-na-aš-kán
24 [a-ši INIM ^{m}]Pí-iš-ši-li ^{m}Ḫa-it-ti-li a-pé-ez-za INIM-za DUḪ-ri
25 [nu IGI-zi-i]š MUŠEN ḪUR-RI SIG$_5$-ru EGIR-ma NU.SIG$_5$-du
26 [IGI-zi-iš] MUŠEN ḪUR-RI SIG$_5$ EGIR NU.SIG$_5$

---

27 [IGI-an-da S]U.MEŠ[27] IR-u-en nu SU.MEŠ SIG$_5$-ru ni ši ta
28 [ ]x 10 ŠÀ DIR SIG$_5$

---

29 [IŠ-TU ^{LÚ}IG]I.MUŠEN IR-TUM QA-TAM-MA-pát nu MUŠEN.ḪI.A SIxSÁ-an-du
30 [ ]x a-li-li-iš-ma-kán EGIR UGU SIG$_5$-za ú-it
31 [na-aš tar-liš p]a-an pa-it a-al-li-i̯a-aš-ma-kán pí-an
32 [ar-ḫa pa-i]t na-aš GUN-liš zi-an ú-it
33 [EGIR KASKAL-NI]⸢a⸣-li-li-in ta-pa-aš-ši-in-na tar-li$_{12}$-an NI-MUR
34 [a-li-li-i]š-kán pí-an SIG$_5$-za ú-it na-aš 2-an ar-ḫa pa-it
35 [ta-pa-aš-ši-i]š-ma-aš-ši EGIR-an ḫu-u-u̯a-iš na-aš tar-liš
36 [pa-an pa-i]t UM-MA ^{m}Kur-ša-^{d}LAMMA SIxSÁ-at-u̯a

---

37 [ ]x ku-it e-ni me-ek-ka$_4$-uš UN.MEŠ-uš dam-me-eš-ḫa-an ḫar-ta
38 [GIDIM.ḪI.A š]a-ra-a a-še-ša-nu-u̯a-an-zi na-aš ⁑za-ap-pa-an-tal-la-en-ti
39 [na-aš dam-me-l]i[28] pí-di KASKAL-ši-aḫ-ḫa-an-zi TI-an-da-aš-ma EME
40 [ar-ḫa pár-]ku-nu-u̯a-an-zi ^{d}UTU-ŠI-i̯a-za pár-ku-nu-zi

[25] For the tentative restorations at the beginning of the lines 14 and 15 see above ii 64-65 and below iii 23-24. The particle -kan seems to be required in this construction (cf. also Chapter I.3) so that there is probably no room for a demonstrative kēz/apēz.

[26] Last sign written over erasure.

[27] For the restoration see above ad ii 5.

[28] After collation; for the older LI sign cf. in this text ii 29.

15 [be solv]ed, then let the exta be favorable ... Unfavorable.

---

16 [If? ...] malediction against$^{?}$ the offspring they do/practice, then let the *ḫurri*-bird
17 [be ...] Unfavorable.

---

18 [... of th]at/his$^{?}$ *panku* they bring
19 [...]compensation with blood in a small amount
20 [they will give a]nd they hold$^{?}$ them under the curse, His Majesty, however, from his (own)
21 [tear]s only will clean himself, and those
22 [...] they will, and to/for them the hand$^{?}$ *zazkitallan*
23 they will [...] and they will 'put them on the road.' Now, if for us
24 [that affair] of Piššili (and) Ḫaittili through that deed is solved,
25 [then let the fir]st *ḫurri*-bird be favorable but let the following (one) be unfavorable.
26 [The first] *ḫurri*-bird favorable, the following (one) unfavorable.

---

27 We [counter]checked [the e]xta. Let the exta be favorable. *ni*(*pašuri*), *ši*(*ntaḫi*), *ta*(*nani*),
28 [...] ... ten coils. Favorable.

---

29 [Through the au]gur that same question. Let them ascertain the birds.
30 [...] ... an *alili*-bird came above behind from favorable (direction),
31 [and *tar*(*wiyal*)*liš*$^{?}$]it went [a]cross while an *alliya*-bird [pas]sed in front
32 and came GUN-*liš zi*(*law*)*an*.
33 [Behind the road:] an *alili*- and *tapašši*-bird *tar*(*wiyal*)*lian* we observed.
34 [The *alil*]*i*-bird came in front from favorable (direction) and it went off through the center,
35 while [the *tapašš*]*i*-bird fled after it and *tar*(*wiyal*)*liš* it
36 [wen]t [across]. Thus Kurša-LAMMA: "They were established."

---

37 Concerning the fact that he had hurt many people [...],
38 they will set up [(images of) the deceased$^{?}$] and they will remunerate$^{?}$[29] them.
39 [and] 'put [them] on the road' [at a sacr]ed spot. The malediction of$^{?}$ the living
40 they will [cl]ean [away] and His Majesty will clean himself.

[29] For the translation compare above Chapter V ad L 6+ iii 14.

41 [K]IN SIG$_5$-*ru* DINGIR-*LUM-za* EGIR-*an ar-ḫa kar-pí-in* ME-*aš*
42 [*nu-kán an-da*] SIG$_5$-*u-i I-NA* UD.2.KAM ḪUL-*lu* ME-*an* (erasure)
43 [*na-at A-NA*]⸢^{d}⸣UTU AN SUM-*an I-NA* UD.3.KAM *pa-an-ku-uš-za* ZAG-*tar*
44 [TI-*tar*? *iš-pa-a*]*n-du-zi-i̯a* ME-*aš na-at* DINGIR.MAḪ *pa-iš* SIG$_5$

---

45 [*IŠ-TU* ^{LÚ}IGI.MUŠEN I]R-*TUM QA-TAM-MA-pát nu* MUŠEN.ḪI.A SIxSÁ-*an-du*
46 [ ]*pí-an* SIG$_5$-*za ú-it nu-za* GAM-*an a-ra-an tar-li*$_{12}$-*an*
47 [ ]x *tar-li*$_{12}$-*an pa-an pa-a-ir kal-mu-ši-in-ma*
48 [ ]x-*aš-za e-ša-at* KAxU-*ŠU-ma-za-kán tar-liš*
49 [*na-a-iš* I]R-*TAM* IR-*u-en nu-kán a-li-li-iš pí-an*
50 [SIG$_5$-*za ú-it na-a*]*š* 2-*an ar-ḫa pa-it* EGIR KASKAL-*NI a-aš-šu-ra-aš-šu-ra-aš*
51 [-*i*]*š-ma tar-liš pa-an ú-it i-pár-u̯a-aš-ši-iš-ma*
52 [ ]x-*un* GUN-*liš zi-an ú-it*
53 [*UM-MA* ^{m}*Ar-tu*$_4$-*um-m*]*a-an-na Ù* ^{m}*Kur-ša*-^{d}LAMMA SIxSÁ-*at-u̯a*

---

54 [*IŠ-TU* ^{LÚ}ḪAL IR-*TUM QA-TA*]*M-MA-pát nu* SU.MEŠ SIG$_5$-*ru* IGI-*zi* SU.MEŠ *ni-kán*
55 [-*d*]*a-aš* GÙB-*aš* ⸢*ar-ḫa*⸣-*i̯a-an* IGI KASKAL 12 ŠÀ *DIR*
56 [-]⸢*eš*⸣ NU.SIG$_5$

(blank space of ca. 18 lines till break)

41 [... ?] Let [the *k*]*in* be favorable. The GOD, passing behind, took for himself ANGER

42 [and (it is) in] FAVORABLE (position). On the second day EVIL (was) taken

43 [and it] (was) given [to] the SUNGOD OF HEAVEN. On the third day the *panku* took for itself RIGHTNESS

44 [LIFE$^{?}$] and [WINE R]ATION and gave it to the MOTHERGODDESS.

---

45 [Through the augur] that same [qu]estion. Let them ascertain the birds.

46 [A ... (-bird)] came in front from favorable (direction) and down *aran tar*(*wiyal*)*liyan*

47 [...] ... *tarwalliyan* they went across, a *kalmuši*-bird (obj.), however,

48 [... and$^{?}$] ... it sat down. It [turned] its beak *tar*(*wiyal*)*liš*

49 [...] we asked an(other$^{?}$) [ora]cle question. An *alili*-bird in front

50 [came from favorable (direction) and i]t went off through the center. Behind the road: an *āššuraššura*(-bird)

51 [...] ..., however, came across *tar*(*wiyal*)*liš*. while an *iparu̯ašši*(-bird)

52 [...] ... GUN-*liš zi*(*law*)*an* came.

53 [Thus Artumm]anna and Kurša-^{d}LAMMA: “They have been established.”

---

54 [By the diviner] that [sa]me [question]. Let the exta be favorable. The first exta *ni*(*pašuri*)

55 [...] ... left to the side towards the road, twelve coils;

56 [...] ... Unfavorable.

GLOSSARY

This glossary contains all words preserved and partially preserved in the texts belonging to CTH 569 as given in Ch. V as well as in the related texts of Ch. IV. The two texts given in the Appendix have not been not included. Damages of signs indicated in the transliteration by half brackets (⸢ ⸣) are not repeated here nor are the question marks normally indicating uncertainty in determining the obverse or reverse side of a tablet (obv.$^{?}$, rev.$^{?}$) or the exact column (i$^{?}$, ii$^{?}$ etc.). In references to XVI 32 the indication "ii" referring to the second column is left out because there are no traces preserved of any of the other columns. If not otherwise indicated (dep., MP), all verb forms are active; *-ške-* derivatives are given at the end of the verb they are derived from.

A. *Hittite*

-a-	"he, she, it"	defective pers. pron.	
	-aš	nom.sg.c.	KBo II 2 i 2, 6, 31, ii 13, KBo II 6+ ii 38, 44, 51, iii 4, iv 11, 15, 19, 20, 21, KBo XVI 98 ii 19, 24, iv 5', KBo XXIII 114 rev. 2' (or acc.pl.?), VI 9+ ii 3, VIII 27(+) left edge b 1, XVI 32, 16', 21', XVI 46 i 6' (2x), 7', 11', 12', 13' (2x), 14' (2x), 15', ii 5', 6', 9', iv 2, 3 (2x), 4 (2x), 5, 7, 8, 9 (2x), 10, 11 (2x), 12, 16 (2x), 17 (2x), 18, 19, 20, XVI 58 ii 2, XVIII 6 i 19', ii

		2' (?), 4' (?), 5' (?), 6' (?), 8' (?), iv 2, 3, 4, XXII 12, 2', XLIX 2 i 10', 22', 23', ii 13' (?), 14' (?), 15' (?), 16' (*-a*[*š*; ?), XLIX 49 ii 17', 18', L 6+ ii 32', 49', 55', iii 7, 34, L 87 rev. 7'
-an	acc.sg.c.	KBo II 2 i 7, 11, 20, 45, 50, iii 34, KBo II 6+ ii 35, iii 18, 19, KBo XVI 98 iv 22" (or *-at*?), VIII 27(+) iv 9', XVI 20, 17', XVI 32, 4', 12', 25', XVI 46 iv 7, 13, 14, XVIII 6 i 22', iv 7, 8, 11, XLIX 2 i 18', iii 2', 5', 6', 10', L 6+ ii 38', iii 3, 57
-at	nom.-acc.sg.n.	KBo II 6+ ii 57 (!), iii 1 (*-a*]*t*), 22, 37, 46, 51, 62, KBo XVI 98 iv 22" (or *-an*?), VI 9+ iii 12' (*-a*]*t*; or pl.?), VIII 27(+) iv 6', XVI 16 rev. 20, XXII 35 ii 4' (sg./ pl.?), XLIX 49 ii 8' (or pl.?), XLIX 93, 3, L 6+ iii 14, 20, 36, 39 (*-a*]*t*)
-at	nom.pl.c.	KBo II 6+ i 5', 10', 22', ii 1, iii 40, 57, iv 9, 13

			(2x), KBo XVI 98 ii 20, 22, 25, XVI 16 obv. 26', 27', 29', XVI 46 i 8'(2x), 17', 18', iv 15, XXII 35 ii 5'
	-aš	acc.pl.c.	KBo II 2 iv 8, KBo II 6+ iv 6, KBo XXIII 114 rev. 2' (or nom. sg.?), XVI 16 obv. 13', 17', 23', rev. 11, 18, XVI 32, 6', 15', 16', 20', 21', XVI 58 ii 5, iii 9', XVIII 6 ii 2' (?), 4' (?), 5' (?), 6' (?), 8' (?), XXII 35 ii 6', XLIX 2 ii 8', 13' (?), 14' (?), 15' (?), 16' (*-a*[*š*; ?), XLIX 93, 12, L 5 r.col. 6', 7', 11', L 6+ iii 51
	-at	nom.-acc.pl.n.	KBo II 6+ i 23', 48, iii 13, 25, iv 8, VI 9+ iii 12' (*-a*]*t;* or sg.?), XVI 32, 3', XLIX 49 ii 8' (or sg.?), L 77+ r.col. 11'
-a, *-i̯a*	"and, too"	encl. conj.	
	-CC≈*a*		KBo II 2 i 10, 28, iii 41, iv 1, 4, 9, 10, KBo II 6+ i 34', ii 34, iii 1, 12, 15, 45, iv 7, VI 9+ iii 13', XVI 16 obv. 26', XVI 20, 15', 18', XVI 58 iii 4', 10', XXII 35 iii

			9', XLIX 93, 4, L 5 r.col. 12', L 6+ iii 37
	-CC⸗*a*⸗*i̯a*		XVI 16 obv. 14'
	-V⸗*i̯a*		KBo II 2 i 24, KBo II 6+ ii 2, 31, 47, KBo XXIII 114 obv. 18, 30, XVI 16 obv. 16', XVI 20, 15', XXII 35 iii 13', 16' (-*i̯*]*a*), XLIX 93, 15, L 6+ ii 38, iii 3, LII 92 iv 6'
	abl. (-*z*)*i*-*i̯a*		XVI 20, 14'
	logogram⸗*i̯a*		KBo II 2 i 35, ii 20, iv 2, 11, KBo II 6+ i 11', 12', 13', 23', 33', 34', 36', ii 29, 40, 52, iii 6 (2x), 25, 44, 61, KBo XXIII 114 obv. 15, 27, XVI 16 obv. 18', 19', 25', 28', rev. 14, 19, 26, XVI 32, 12', XVI 58 ii 13, XVIII 36, 18', 22', XXII 12, 5' (-*i̯*[*a*?), XXII 13, 3', 7', XXII 35 ii 8', iii 4', 5', 8', 13', 15', 16' (-*i̯*]*a*), XLIX 49 ii 10', L 6+ ii 34', 40', 47', 50', iii 5, 9, 50, 52, L 77+ r.col. 10', 10/v, 3'
-a	"but, however"		
	(*ki-nu-n*)*a*		XVI 32, 8', L 6+ ii 38', iii 3
aiš/*iš*-, n.	"mouth"	see Sum. KAxU	
ak-	"to die"		

	a-ki	3.sg.pres.	XVI 16 obv. 24' (*=kan*)
alli̯a-, c.	(oracle bird)		
	a-al-li-i̯a-aš	nom.sg.	KBo II 6+ iv 14
alili-, c.	(oracle bird)		
	a-li-li-iš	nom.sg.	KBo II 6+ iv 15, XVI 58 ii 7 (*-l*]*i-*)
ani̯a-	"to do, make, perform"		
	a-ni-an-zi	3.pl.pres.	KBo II 6+ ii 16 (*-n*]*i-*), L 6+ ii 39' (*arḫa*), iii 4 (*arḫa*)
	a-ni-i̯a-an-zi		KBo II 6+ i 32', iii 44 (*arḫa*), L 6+ ii 12' (*-i̯*]*a-*), L 87 rev. 10' (*-i̯*[*a-*)
	a-ni[*-*		VIII 27 (+) iv 3' (*arḫa*)
	a[*-*		XVI 32, 11'
	a-ni-i̯a-nu-un	1.sg.pret.	KBo XVI 98 iv 22"
	an-ni-iš-ki-ir	3.pl.pret. *-ške-*	L 6+ ii 37' (*arḫa*), iii 2 (*arḫa*)
	see also Sum. DÙ, KIN		
anku	"completely"	adv.	
	an-ku		L 87 rev. 9'
anš-	"to wipe"		
	an-ša-an	part. nom.-acc.sg.	KBo II 6+ iv 3, KBo XXIII 114 obv. 24
anda(*n*)	"in, into"	adv., prev.	
	an-da		XVI 46 i 5'
		a. SIG$_5$-*u-i*	KBo II 6+ i 45', iii 15, 39, XVI 58 iii 12'
		a. SUD-*li*$_{12}$	KBo II 6+ i 24', ii 2, iii 29
		a. ar- (act.)	KBo II 6+ iv 13, XVI 58 ii 5
		a. arnu-	L 6+ iii 9
		=kan EGIR-*pa a. peda-*	XVI 32, 5

		⸗kan a. šarnink-	XXII 35 ii 6', XLIX 93, 12 (*an*[-)
		(*⸗kan*) *a. u̯emii̯a-*/KAR	KBo II 2 i 3, 46 (*⸗kan*), 55, XVIII 6 i 26', XLIX 2 i 21'
		a. u̯erii̯a-	XVI 16 obv. 27', 29'
		a. SIxSÁ	L 6+ iii 37 (-]⸢*da*⸣?)
		nominal sentence	KBo XVI 98 iv 24", L 77+ r.col. 3'
	an-da-an	*⸗kan a. nai-*	KBo XVI 98 iii 15' (*-a*]*n-*)
	see also Sum. ŠÀ		
antuḫša-, c.	"man, human being"	see Sum. UN	
apā-	"that, he, she, it"	dem. pron.	
	a-pa-a-aš	nom.sg.c.	KBo II 2 ii 26, XVI 32, 26', XVIII 6 i 10', XLIX 2 ii 3', 11' (*-a*[-)
	a-pu-u-un	acc.sg.c.	XVIII 6 i 9'
	a-pa-a-at	nom.-acc.sg.n.	KBo II 2 ii 33 (*-pa*[-), XVI 46 i 5'
	a-pád-d°		L 6+ iii 37 (?, -]*da*)
	a-pé-el	gen.sg.	XVI 32, 16' (⸢*a*⸣[-), 22', L 6+ ii 17' (-]*el*)
	a-pé-da-ni-i̯a	dat.-loc.sg.	L 6+ ii 55'
	a-pé-ez	abl.	XVI 32, 18', 23', L 6+ ii 43', iii 43, 58
	a-pé-e-ez		KBo II 6+ iii 47, 64
	a-pé-e-ez-za		XVIII 6 iv 2 (<*-pé*>)
	a-pu-u-uš	acc.pl.c.	XVI 16 rev. 6, 7
	a-pé-e-da-aš	dat.-loc.pl.	KBo II 2 i 55
	fragm.		XXII 35 iii 19' (⸢*a-pa*⸣-x[)

appa(n)	"behind, after, later"	see Sum. EGIR(-)	
appašiu̯att-	"future"	see Sum. EGIR.UD.KAM	
apadda(n)	"therefore"	adv.	
	a-pád-da (šer)		L 6+ iii 37, L 87 obv. 8' ([*-pá*]*d-*)
	a-pád-da-an (šer)		KBo II 2 iii 21, 24, iv 4
appezzi-	"last, latest, hindmost"	see Sum. EGIR-*zi-*	
api̯i̯a	"there, then"	adv.	
	a-pí-i̯a		KBo II 2 i 6, 7, 13, 45, ii 9 (*-i̯*[*a*]), KBo II 6+ i 7', ii 39, 44, 51, iii 5, XVI 32, 12 (*a-pí-i̯*[*a*]), XVIII 6 i 22', iv 8, L 77+ r.col. 7' (*-i̯*[*a*])
ar- (act.)	"to reach"		
	a-ar-ḫi	1.sg.pres.	KBo XVI 98 ii 11 (*⸗kan* UGU)
	e-ri-ir	3.pl.pret.	KBo II 6+ iv 13 (*anda*), XVI 58 ii 5 (*anda*)
	a-ra-an-za	part. nom.sg.c.	KBo II 2 ii 48 (*parā*)
ar- (dep.)	"to stand"		
	ar-ḫa-ḫa-ri	1.sg.pres.	KBo XVI 98 ii 16 (EGIR-*an*), XLIX 49 ii 15' (EGIR-*an*)
	see also Sum. GUB		
ara-, c.	"friend, colleague"		
	a-ra-aš	nom./gen.sg.	XLIX 2 i 19'(?)
arra-	"to wash, clean"		
	ar-ra-an-zi	3.pl.pres.	XVI 16 obv. 28' (*⸗kan arha*)
arraḫḫani-, c.	"curse"		
	ar-ra-aḫ-ḫa-ni-i̯a	dat.-loc..sg.	L 6+ iii 34
arraḫḫani̯a-	"to curse"		
	ar-ra-aḫ-ḫa-ni-iš-ki-it	3.sg.pret. *-ške-*	KBo II 6+ ii 39, 45, 52, iii 5

araḫza	"outside"	adv.	
	a-ra-aḫ-za		KBo XVI 98 i 10
arai-	"to rise"		
	a-ra-iš	3.sg.pret.	XVI 46 i 15'
	a-ra-e-er	3.pl.pret.	KBo II 2 i 49
	see also Sum. GUB		
aramnant-, c.	(oracle bird)		
	a-ra-am-na-an-ta-an	acc.sg.	XVI 46 iv 6, 18
	a-ra-am-na-an-du-uš	acc.pl.	XVI 46 i 16'
arḫa	"away, off"	adv., prev.	
	ar-ḫa	*a. anii̯a-*/KIN	KBo XVI 98 iv 22", XVI 32, 23', 28', XVI 46 iv 13, L 87 rev. 10'
		pi(r)an a. anii̯a-/anniške-	KBo II 6+ i 32', iii 44, VIII 27 (+) iv 3', L 6+ ii 37', 39', iii 2
		a. arnu-	L 6+ iii 51
		a. epp-/app-	KBo II 2 i 22, 41, XLIX 2 i 15'
		a. išḫuu̯a-	XVI 16 rev. 12
		GAM-*an a. ki-*/GAR	XVIII 36, 13' (*a*]*r-*)
		=kan pi(r)an a. nai-	XVI 46 i 15'
		a. pai-	KBo II 6+ iii 58, iv 14, KBo XVI 98 ii 22, iv 3' (-*ḫ*]*a*), XVI 46 i 16', iv 3, 9, 16, 19, 20, XVI 58 ii 3, XLIX 49 ii 18' (*ar*[-), 21' (-*ḫ*]*a*)
		=kan pi(r)an a. pai-	KBo II 6+ iii 55, iv 11, 15, 20, 21, KBo XVI 98 ii 20, XVI 46 i 7', 8', 12', 18', iv 10, 12, XVI 58 ii 6, 8
		=kan šer a. pai-	KBo XVI 98 i 16,

			L 6+ iii 36
		a. peššii̯a-	KBo II 6+ iii 16, iv 16, XVI 46 iv 5
		⸗za⸗kan pi(r)an a. peššii̯a-	XVIII 6 i 9'
		a. peda-	XVI 46 iv 8
		a. šakkurii̯a-	KBo IX 151, 2' (*a*]*r*?-), 8' (-*ḫ*]*a*), L 6+ ii 52'
		a. šipand-/BAL	XVI 32, 9', 15', 17, 20'
		⸗kan a. dā-/ME	XVI 32, 24' (-*ḫ*[*a*), XLIX 2 ii 12', L 6+ ii 25' (-*ḫ*]*a*)
		⸗za EGIR-*an a. dā-*/ME	KBo II 6+ i 45', XVI 20, 7', XVI 58 iii 12' (-*ḫ*]*a*)
		ištarna a. uu̯a-	XVI 20, 14'
		a. u̯atkunu-	XVIII 36, 21'
		⸗kan a. zalukiš-	VI 9+ ii 13, L 77+ r.col. 5'
		[verb lost]	KBo II 6+ iii 57, KBo XVI 98 ii 24, VI 9+ iii 4', XVI 58 ii 11
arḫai̯an	"outside, apart"	adv.	
	ar-ḫa-i̯a-an		KBo XXIII 114 obv. 5 (-*ḫ*]*a*-), XVI 46 iii 3 (-*i̯*[*a*-)
arii̯a-	"to investigate by oracle"		
	a-ri-i̯a-zi	3.sg.pres.	L 6+ iii 10 (*⸗kan*)
	a-ri-i̯a-u-e-ni	1.pl.pres.	KBo II 2 ii 32, KBo II 6+ iii 18, L 6+ iii 54
	a-ri-i̯a-u-en	1.pl.pret.	KBo II 6+ i 30', iii 41, KBo IX 151, 5' (-]*u*-), KBo XVI 98 i 2, XXII 13, 9' (-]*u*-), L 6+ ii 32'

			([GAM ... -*e*]*n*), 49’ (GAM), iii 32, 40 ([GAM])
	a-ri-i̯a-u-e-en		KBo II 2 ii 22 (*katta*)
	a-ri-i̯[*a-*		LII 92 i 8’
	a[-		VIII 27 (+) iv 1’
arii̯ašeššar, n.	“oracle investigation”		
	a-ri-i̯a-še-šar$_x$	nom.-acc.sg.	KBo II 6+ iv 25
	a-ri-i̯a-še-eš-na-aš	gen.sg.	VI 9+ iii 10’ (-]*eš*-), XVIII 6 i 23’, iv 11, XLIX 2 i 20’ ([-*eš*]-)
	a-ri-i̯a-še-eš-na-az	abl.	XXII 13, 3’
	a-ri-i̯a-še-eš-na-za		KBo II 2 ii 45, XVIII 6 i 8’, L 87 rev. 7’, 12’
	a-ri-i-x[		XVI 46 i 3’
arkamma(*n*)-, c.	“tribute”		
	ar-kam-ma-an	acc.sg.	XVI 32, 7’, L 6+ iii 25
	ar-kam-ma[-		XVI 32, 6’
arnu-	“to bring”		
	ar-nu-an-zi	3.pl.pres.	L 6+ iii 9 (*anda*), 52 (=*kan arḫa*)
⸗*aršulai-*	“to pacify, soothe”		
	⸗*ar-šu-la-iz-zi*	3.sg.pres.	XVI 32, 26’ (-*l*[*a*-), L 6+ ii 27’ (-]*iz*-)
ašatar, n.	“the act of sitting down”		
	a-ša-tar	nom.-acc.sg.	VI 9+ ii 12 (*a*[-), 25 (-*š*]*a*-)
	a-ša-a-tar		XVIII 36, 12’, 17’, XXII 13, 2’, 4’ (-*a*-[)
	a-ša-an-na-aš	gen.sg.	XVIII 36, 19’, 20’
ašeš-/ašaš-	“to settle”		
	a-še-ša-an-zi	3.pl.pres.	KBo II 6+ iii 61 (*šarā*), XVI 32, 4’

ašešanu-	"to (make) settle"		
	a-še-ša-nu-an-zi	3.pl.pres.	VIII 27(+) iv 5' (-[*nu-*])
	a-še-ša-nu-u̯a-an-zi		KBo II 6+ iii 45
aši	"he, she, it"	defective anaph. pron.	
	a-ši	nom.sg.c.	KBo II 2 ii 26, 35, iii 30, iv 34, KBo XVI 98 i 12, XVI 58 iii 4'
	e-ni	nom.-acc.sg.n.	KBo II 2 ii 9, iv 22, 23, 27, 37, KBo XXIII 114 obv. 30
	e-da-ni	dat.-loc.sg.	KBo II 2 ii 55, iii 5
aššu-	"good, favorable"		
	a-aš-šu	nom.-acc.sg.n.	VI 9+ iii 14'
	see also Sum. SIG_5		
aššul, n.	"well-being"		
	aš-šu-ul	nom.-acc.sg.	KBo II 6+ iii 12, 26
	aš-šu-li	dat.-loc.sg.	KBo XVI 98 iii 15'
adamtaḫiš	"?"	(Hurrian technical term in extispicy)	
	a-dam-ta-ḫi-iš	nom.sg.c.?	KBo II 2 ii 38
auš-/au-/u-	"to see"		
	ú-u̯a-an-zi	3.pl.pres.	XXII 35 ii 2' (-*z*[*i*), XLIX 93, 7 (-*an*[-), L 6+ iii 12 (-*a*]*n*-), 18
	u-uḫ-ḫu-un	1.sg.pret.	KBo XVI 98 i 22 (=*za*=*kan*)
	a-uš-ta	3.sg.pret.	KBo II 6+ i 19' (UGU), iv 17
	a-ú-um-me-en	1.pl.pret.	XVIII 6 i 17' (-*e*[*n*), XLIX 2 ii 6', iii 8' (-*um*[-)
	uš-ki-ši	2.sg.pres. -*ške-*	KBo II 2 i 24, 54, ii 12

	see also Akkad. *AMĀRU(M)*		
eniššan	"thus, in that way"	adv.	
	e-ni-eš-ša-an		KBo XVI 98 ii 10
entiš	"?"	(Hurrian technical term in extispicy)	
	en-tíš		KBo II 2 iv 16
epp-/app-	"to take, seize, hold"		
	e-ep-zi	3.sg.pres.	KBo II 2 ii 31 (*-z*[*i*)
	e-ep-te-ni	2.pl.pres.	KBo XVI 98 i 5 (*-te*[-; *parā*)
	ap-pa-an-zi	3.pl.pres.	XVI 16 obv. 18' (*ap*[- ...*-z*]*i*)
	e-ep-ta	3.sg.pret.	XVI 46 iv 7, XVIII 6 iv 6 (=*kan*), XLIX 2 i 13' (=*kan*), 16' (*-t*]*a*), 18'
	e-ep-pir	3.pl.pret.	XVI 16 obv. 13'
	ap-pa-at-ta-at	3.sg.pret. MP	KBo II 2 ii 42 (*arḫa*)
	ap-pa-an-ta-at	3.pl.pret. MP	KBo II 2 i 22 (*arḫa*)
	see also Sum. DAB		
eš-/aš-	"to be"		
	e-eš-zi	3.sg.pres.	XVI 16 rev. 12, XVI 46 i 2'
	e-eš-ta	3.sg.pret.	KBo II 6+ i 7', ii 38, 44, 51, iii 5, XVI 16 rev. 8
	e-šir	3.pl.pret.	XVI 16 rev. 6
	e-še-er	3.pl.pret.	KBo II 6+ ii 17
eš-/aš- (dep.)	"to sit down"		
	e-eš-ḫa-ḫa-ri	1.sg.pres.	KBo XVI 98 ii 12 ([*-e*]*š-*; =*za*=*kan*)
	e-ša-ri	3.sg.pres.	KBo II 2 i 32 (=*za*=*kan*), VI 9+ ii 15 (=*za* =*kan*), XVI 20, 10' (=*za*=*kan*),

			XVIII 6 i 11' (=*za*=*kan*), XVIII 36, 3' (-*š*]*a*), 11' (-*r*[*i*; =*za*=*kan*), 14' (=*za*=*kan*), L 77+ r.col. 7 (=*za* =*kan*)
	see also *ašatar* and Sum. TUŠ		
ešša-/*išša-*	"to do, make, perform"		
	e-eš-ša-an-zi	3.pl.pres.	KBo II 6+ i 12', ii 55, iii 6
	e-eš-ši-iš-ta	3.sg.pret.	KBo II 6+ i 8'
	e-<*eš-*>*šu-u*[-	supinum?	L 5 r.col. 7'
	see also Sum. DÙ and KIN		
ed-/*ad-*	"to eat"		
	az-zi-ki-ir	3.pl.pret. *-ške-*	XVI 16 obv. 25
	see also Sum. GU_7		
ḫaikal^{i}*ni*	"(the) palace"		
	ḫa-i-kal-li-ta	Hurr. dat.sg.	KBo II 2 iii 3
ḫali-, n.	"vigil, watch"		
	ḫa-a-li	dat.-loc.sg.	VIII 27 (+) left edge b 3
ḫalki-, c.	"grain"		
	ḫal-ki-in	acc.sg.	XVI 16 obv. 18'
ḫalu̯ašši-, c.	(oracle bird)		
	ḫal-u̯a-aš-ši-iš	nom.sg.	KBo II 6+ iv 20
	ḫal-u̯a-aš-ši-in	acc.sg.	XVI 46 i 12', iv 19
ḫamank-/*ḫamenk-*	"to establish, assign (a festival)"		
	ḫa-ma-an-ká[*n*	?	KBo II 6+ ii 13 (GAM-*an*)
ḫandai-	"to ascertain"	see Sum. SIxSÁ	
ḫantezzi-	"first, foremost, chief"	see Sum. IGI-*zi-*	
ḫappir(*i̯*)*a-*, c.	"city, settlement"	see Sum. URU	
ḫapušš-	"to make up for"		
	ḫa-pu-uš-ša-an-zi	3.pl.pres.	KBo II 6+ ii 18

har-/ḫark-	"to have, hold"		
	ḫar-ši	2.sg.pres.	KBo II 6+ iii 63 ([*ḫa*]*r-*⌈*ši*⌉)
	ḫar-ti		KBo XVI 98 iii 7', 9', XVI 16 rev. 2, L 6+ ii 42'
	ḫar-zi	3.sg.pres.	XVI 16 rev. 12
	ḫar-te-ni	2.pl.pres.	KBo II 6+ i 37', ii 20, iii 33 (⌈*ḫar*⌉-), KBo XVI 98 ii 17, XVI 20, 4', 12', XVI 58 iii 4', XLIX 49 ii 16'
	ḫar-kán-zi	3.pl.pres.	XVI 32, 6'
	ḫar-ku-un	1.sg.pret.	KBo II 2 iii 20, 27, iv 3
	ḫar-ta	3.sg.pret.	L 6+ iii 38
	ḫar-kán-t[*e-*	part.	KBo XXIII 114 obv. 31
	*ḫar-*x x x		XVIII 6 i 12'
ḫarrani-, c.	(oracle bird)		
	ḫar-ra-ni-eš	nom.sg.	KBo II 6+ iv 18
ḫark-	"to perish, fall"		
	ḫar-ak-ta	3.sg.pret.	XVIII 6 i 18' (*-a*[*k-*, GAM), iv 9 (GAM)
ḫašš-/ḫešš-	"to open"		
	ḫé-e-šu-u-e-ni	1.pl.pres.	L 6+ iii 44
ḫaštapi-, c.	(oracle bird)		
	ḫa-aš-ta-pí-iš	nom.sg.	KBo II 6+ iv 19
	ḫa-aš-ta-pí-in	acc.sg.	KBo II 6+ iv 12, XVI 46 iv 3, 15 (*-t*[*a-*), XVI 58 ii 4
ḫaššu-, c.	"king"	see Sum. LUGAL	
ḫat-	"to dry"		
	ḫa-da-an-ti	part. dat.-loc.sg.	XLIX 2 ii 9'
ḫatrai-	"to write, send"		
	ḫa-at-ra-a-an-zi	3.pl.pres.	L 6+ iii 42
ḫadduli-	"healthy"		
	ḫa-ad-du-liš	nom.sg.c.	L 77+ r.col. 8'
ḫenkan, n.	"death, destruction"	see Sum. ÚŠ-*an*	
ḫeu-, c.	"rain"		
	ḫé-e-uš	nom.sg./pl.?	VIII 27 (+) left

			edge a 1 (*ḫé*]-)
ḫiriḫiš	"?"	(Hurrian technical term in extispicy)	
	ḫi-ri-ḫi-iš	nom.sg.c.?	XVI 16 obv. 30'
ḫuišu̯ant- /*ḫuišu̯atar*, n.	"alive, living/life"	see Sum. TI(*-tar*)	
ḫuittii̯a-	"to pull"	see Sum. SUD	
ḫulla-	"to fight"		
	ḫu-ul-la-at-te-ni	2.pl.pres.	KBo XVI 98 i 6 (*-u*]*l-*)
ḫuppialla-, c./n.?	"?"		
	ḫup-pí-al-la-aš	gen.sg.	KBo II 2 i 53
	ḫup-pí-al-la-za	abl.	KBo II 2 i 41 (<*-pí*>)
ḫuške-	"to wait (for)"		
	ḫu-u-uš-ku-u-e-ni	1.pl.pres.	L 6+ iii 24
ḫuu̯a-, c.	(oracle bird)		
	ḫu-u-u̯a-aš	nom.sg.	KBo II 6+ iii 56
ii̯a-	"to do, make"		
	i-i̯a-mi	1.sg.pres.	KBo XVI 98 ii 15
	i-i̯a-am-mi		XLIX 49 ii 14' (*-i̯*]*a-*)
	i-i̯a-zi	3.sg.pres.	KBo II 2 ii 19, 26
	i-i̯a-an-te-eš$_{17}$	part. nom.pl.c.	KBo XXIII 114 obv. 27 (*-i̯*[*a-a*]*n-*)
ii̯annai-	"to go, march"		
	i-i̯a-an-na-i	3.sg.pres.	VIII 27 (+) left edge b 2 (*-n*[*a*)
imma	see *ku*(*u̯*)*atta imma ku*(*u̯*)*atta*		
iparu̯ašši-, c.	(oracle bird)		
	i-pár-u̯a-aš-ši-iš	nom.sg.	KBo II 6+ iv 22
irkipelli-	"?"	(Hurrian? technical term in extispicy)	
	(abbr.) *ir-liš*	nom.sg.c.	KBo XVI 98 ii 9, XVI 16 obv. 12', rev. 9, 21
irmanant-, c.	"illness"	see Sum. GIG(*-ant-*)	
išḫiulaḫḫ-	"to enjoin"		
	iš-ḫi-ú-la-aḫ-ḫa-an-zi	3.pl.pres.	KBo II 2 iv 35

išḫuu̯ai-	"to scatter, pour"		
	iš-ḫu-u-u̯a-an	part. nom.-acc.sg.n.	XVI 16 rev. 12
	iš-ḫu-u-u̯a-an-te-eš	part. nom.pl.c.	KBo II 6+ i 12' (*katta*)
iškiš-, n.	"back"		
	iš-ki-ša	all. (used as adverb)	KBo XVI 98 i 8 (-]*ša*)
^{DUG}*išnuri-*, n.	"kneading-bowl"		
	^{DUG}*iš-nu-ri*	nom.-acc.sg./pl.	XVI 16 rev. 14
išpant-/šipant-	"to offer, dedicate"	see Sum. BAL	
išpanduzzi-, n.	"libation vase, wine ration"		
	iš-pa-an-du-zi	nom.-acc.sg.	XVI 20, 6', 15'
	iš-pa-an-du-uz-zi		KBo II 6+ ii 31
ištamaš-	"to hear, listen"		
	iš-dam-ma-aš-ti	2.sg.pres.	KBo II 2 ii 35
	iš-ta-ma-aš-te-ni	2.pl.pres.	KBo XVI 98 i 5 (-*t*]*a*-)
ištanzan(a)-, c.	"soul"	see Sum. ZI	
ištapp-	"to lock up"		
	iš-tap-pa-an-te-eš	part. nom.pl.c.	XXII 35 ii 1' (-*tap*[-), XLIX 93, 6 (-*t*[*e*-), L 6+ ii 53', iii 17 (all ⸗*kan* EGIR-*pa*)
ištarna	"in between"	adv., prev.	
	iš-tar-na	*i. arḫa u̯a-*	XVI 20, 14'
idalau̯atar, n.	"badness, evil"		
	i-da-la-u-u̯a-an-ni	dat.-loc.sg.	XVI 58 iii 7' (-*l*]*a*-)
idalu- and derivatives	"bad, evil"	see Sum. ḪUL(-)	
kā	"here"	adv.	
	ka-a		KBo II 2 i 14, 24
kā-	"this"	dem. pron.	
	ku-u-un	acc.sg.c.	KBo XVI 98 ii 17, L 5 r.col. 13'
	ki-i	nom.-acc.sg.n.	KBo II 2 i 21, iii 18 (*k*]*i*-), KBo II 6+ iii 60, XVI 16 obv. 7', 12', 16', 22', 31', rev. 10, 17, 22, left edge

			3, XLIX 93, 17, L 5 r.col. 9'
	ke-e-da-ni	dat.-loc.sg.	VI 9+ ii 1, XVI 16 obv. 5' (-*e*[-), 10' (*k*[*e-* ... -*n*]*i*), 14', 20', 29', rev. 9, 16, 20, left edge 1, XVIII 36, 7'
	ke-e-ez	abl.	KBo II 6+ i 38'
	ke-e-ez-za		XVIII 6 i 14' (also 25'?)
	ku-u-uš	nom.pl.c.	KBo II 2 i 21
	ku-u-uš	acc.pl.c.	XVI 46 i 1'
	ke-e-da-aš	dat.-loc.pl.	KBo II 6+ i 14', iii 7, XVI 46 i 4'
kallaratar, n.	"unfavorableness"		
	kal-la-ra-an-ni	dat.-loc.sg.	KBo II 2 i 21
kaltarši-, c.	(oracle bird)		
	kal-tar-ši-iš	nom.sg.	KBo XVI 98 ii 21, iv 3' (-*i*[*š*), 4' (-*t*[*ar-*)
-kan	(local particle)		
	-kán	*ak-*	XVI 16 obv. 24'
		parā ar- (act.)	KBo II 2 ii 47
		UGU *ar-* (act.)	KBo XVI 98 ii 11
		arḫa arra-	XVI 16 obv. 28'
		arai-/GUB	KBo II 6+ ii 34
		ari̯a-	L 6+ iii 9
		arḫa arnu-	L 6+ iii 51
		auš-/*au-*/*u-*	KBo II 2 i 53
		epp-/*app-*	XVIII 6 iv 5, XLIX 2 i 13'
		=za EGIR-*pa epp-*/*app-*	KBo II 2 ii 30
		=za eš-/*aš-* (dep.)	KBo II 2 i 31, KBo XVI 98 ii 12, VI 9+ ii 14, XVI 20, 10', XVIII 6 i 10', XVIII 36, 11', 13'
		EGIR-*pa ištapp-*	XLIX 93, 5, L 6+ ii 52' (-*k*[*án*), iii 17

karp-	XVIII 6 i 19', XLIX 49 ii 12'
kartimmii̯anu-/ TUKU.TUKU-*nu-*	KBo II 6+ ii 46, 52
laḫlaḫḫeške-	KBo II 2 i 43, ii 7
lai-/DUḪ	KBo II 2 iv 37, KBo II 6+ i 38', iii 47, 64, XVI 58 iii 4', L 6+ ii 43'
⸗za mald-	KBo II 2 ii 40
nai-	KBo II 2 iv 6, XVI 16 obv. 22', rev. 10, left edge 3
andan aššuli nai-	KBo XVI 98 iii 15' (*-ká*[*n*])
GAM-*an parā nai-*	XVI 32, 10'
pi(*r*)*an arḫa nai-*	XVI 46 i 15'
pai-	KBo II 2 ii 45, XVIII 6 i 23', iv 2, 3, 4, 9, XLIX 2 i 10', 11' (*-ká*]*n*), 23', XLIX 49 ii 21'
parranda pai-	XVI 16 rev. 6, 7
pi(*r*)*an arḫa pai-*	KBo II 6+ iii 55, iv 11, 15, 20, 21, KBo XVI 98 ii 20, XVI 46 i 8', 12', 18', iv 10', XVI 58 ii 8 (*-k*]*án*)
UGU *pai-*	XVI 16 rev. 18
šer arḫa pai-	L 6+ iii 35
piran arḫa peššii̯a-	XVIII 6 i 9'
peda-	XVIII 6 iv 1, 7, L 6+ iii 64
anda peda-	XVI 32, 4'
UGU *peda-*	XVI 32, 8'
šakk-/*sekk-*	KBo II 2 iv 36
šakuu̯antarii̯anu-	KBo II 6+ ii 16 (*-ká*]*n*), XXII 35 ii 5'

parrianta šalik-	KBo II 2 ii 55
šer šalik-	XVI 16 obv. 24’
anda šarnink-	XXII 35 ii 6’, XLIX 93, 12, L 5 r.col. 11’
šeš-/šaš-	XVI 16 rev. 19
šipant-/BAL	KBo II 2 iv 10, 11, 13, KBo XVI 98 ii 5
šunna-	XVI 16 obv. 19’
dā-	KBo II 6+ iii 14, 27, L 6+ iii 50
arḫa da(ške)-	XVI 32, 24’, XLIX 2 ii 11’
dai-	KBo II 6+ iii 19, 37, 51, VIII 27(+) iv 9’, XVI 32, 2’, 12’, XXII 35 iii 15’, XLIX 2 ii 8’, XLIX 93, 8, L 6+ iii 19, 33
dalii̯a-	KBo II 6+ i 13’
parā tarup-	L 6+ iii 59
piran tii̯a-	KBo II 2 iii 5
šer uda-	XVI 46 i 1’
uu̯a-	KBo II 6+ iv 22, XLIX 2 i 9’, 20’
pi(r)an uu̯a-	KBo II 6+ iii 55, iv 14, KBo XVI 98 ii 19, XVI 46 i 6’, 14’, iv 3, 4, 7, 8, 17, XVI 58 ii 2
EGIR GAM *uu̯a-*	KBo II 6+ iii 56, 57(?), iv 12, XVI 46 iv 16
EGIR UGU *uu̯a-*	KBo II 6+ iv 19, 20, KBo XVI 98 i 14, ii 18 (verb left out), XVI 46 i 6’, 8’, 11’, 13’, 17’, iv 9, 11, XVI 58 ii 3 (*-ká*[*n*), 7, XLIX 49 ii 19’ (*-ká*]*n*), 20’
šarā uu̯a-	KBo II 2 i 2
UGU *uu̯a-*	XVI 32, 10’

		u̯alḫ-	KBo II 2 i 41
		anda u̯emii̯a-	KBo II 2 i 45
		u̯erii̯a-	L 6+ iii 8
		zai-	L 6+ iii 36
		arḫa zalukis-	VI 9+ ii 12, L 77+ r.col. 4' (-*ká*]*n*)
		nominal sentence	KBo II 2 i 1, 28, ii 13, iii 17, KBo II 6+ i 24', 45', ii 2, 27, 33, 41, iii 2, 15, 27, 29, 39, KBo XVI 98 iv 24", 25", 26", VI 9+ ii 11 (-*ká*[*n*), 15, XVI 16 rev. 8, XVI 20, 18', XVI 46 i 4', XVI 58 iii 12', XVIII 36, 14', L 77+ r.col. 2' (-*ká*[*n*), 3', 12', 13', L 87 obv. 3', 5' (-*ká*]*n*)
		[verb lost]	KBo XVI 98 i 10, 15, ii 21, iii 11', iv 5', 6', KBo XXIII 114 obv. 1, VI 9+ iii 13', XVI 16 obv. 7, 19, XVI 32, 8', XVI 46 ii 5', 6', iv 2, 17, 18, 19, XVIII 6 i 4', 6', 18', ii 2', 4', 5', 6', 8' (-*k*[*án*), XVIII 36, 19', XXII 12, 1', XLIX 2 i 22', ii 3' (-*k*[*án*), 13', 14', iii 3', 5', L 6+ iii 19, L 87 obv. 9', rev. 9', LII 92 i 4'
kanešš-	"to recognize"		
	ka-ni-iš-ša-an-zi	3.pl.pres.	KBo II 6+ i 37',

			L 6+ iii 52
	ka-]*ni-eš-ša-an-zi*		10/v, 6’
karit-, c.	“flood”		
	ka-ri-iz	nom.sg.	VIII 27 (+) left edge a 3
karp-	“to lift, raise”		
	kar-ap-mi	1.sg.pres.	KBo XVI 98 ii 13 (=*za*=*kan*), XLIX 49 ii 12’ (=*za*=*kan*)
	kar-ap-ta	3.sg.pret.	XVIII 6 i 20’, iv 12 (=*za*=*šan*), XLIX 2 i 12 ([=*za*]), 19’ (=*za*)
karpi-, c.	“anger, wrath”		
	kar-pí-in	acc.sg.	KBo II 2 i 39, KBo II 6+ i 45’, XVI 20, 7’ (-*i*[*n*), XVI 58 iii 12’, L 77+ r.col. 3’ (-*p*[*í*-)
	kar-pí	dat.-loc.sg.	KBo II 2 i 20
	kar-pí-uš	nom.pl.	KBo II 6+ i 10’, 21’, iii 39
karš-	“to cut, neglect, skip”		
	kar-ša-an-za	part. nom.sg.c.	L 6+ iii 11
	kar-ša-an	part. nom.-acc.sg.n.	XVI 16 obv. 10’, rev. 5, XLIX 93, 2 (*kar*[-), L 6+ iii 13
	kar-sa-an-te-eš$_{17}$	part. nom.pl.c.	KBo XXIII 114 obv. 26
kartimmii̯att-, c.	“anger”	see Sum. TUKU.TUKU-(*a*)*tt*-	
kartimmii̯au̯u̯ant-	“angry”		
	kar-dim$_{\mathrm{X}}$*-mi-i̯a-u-an-za*	nom.sg.c.	KBo II 2 ii 25
	kar-dim$_{\mathrm{X}}$*-mi-i̯a-u-u̯a-an-za*		KBo II 2 ii 44, iii 22 (-*d*[*i*]*m*$_{\mathrm{X}}$-), 25
	(abbr.) *kar-u-u̯a-an-za*		KBo II 2 iii 15
	see also Sum. TUKU(.TUKU)-*u̯u̯ant-*		

karū	"formerly, already"	adv.	
	ka-ru-ú		KBo XXIII 114 obv. 22, L 6+ ii 26', 36'
katta(*n*)	"down, under; with"	adv., prev.	
	kat-ta	*k. arii̯a-*	KBo II 2 ii 22
		k. išḫuu̯a-	KBo II 6+ i 11'
	kat-ta-an		KBo II 2 iii 41, iv 1, 9
	see also Sum. GAM(*-an*)		
keldi-, c.	"well-being" (part of liver near bladder?)	(Hurrian technical term in extispicy)	
	(abbr.) *ke*		KBo II 2 ii 53, iii 8, iv 15, KBo II 6+ i 42', iv 3, KBo XXIII 114 obv. 5, 10, 24
	(abbr.) *ke-eš*	nom.sg.	KBo II 2 iv 6, XVI 16 obv. 22', rev. 10, left edge 3
	(abbr.) *ke*$^{ḪI.A}$*-uš*	nom.pl.	KBo II 6+ i 17'
ki-	"to lie, be laid down"		
	ki-i[*t-ta-ri*	3.sg.pres.	XXII 35 iii 17'
	see also Sum. GAR		
kinun	"now"	adv.	
	ki-nu-un		KBo II 2 iv 13, L 87 rev. 5'
	ki-nu-n(*a*)		XVI 32, 8', L 6+ ii 38', iii 3
kiš- (dep.)	"to happen, become"		
	ki-i-ša	3.sg.pres.	VIII 27 (+) left edge b 4
	ki-i-ša-an-ta	3.pl.pres.	VIII 27 (+) left edge a 1
	ki-ša-at	3.sg.pres.	KBo II 2 iii 18
kišan	"thus, as follows"	adv.	
	kiš-an		KBo II 2 iv 35, KBo II 6+ i 30',

			31', ii 20, iii 41, 43, 60, VIII 27 (+) i 5' (-*a*[*n*), iv 1', L 5 r.col. 9', L 6+ iii 47 (-*a*[*n*)
kui-	"who, which"	rel.pron.	
	ku-iš	nom.sg.c.	KBo II 2 i 5, 30, 50, 51, 54, iii 2, 30, 33, 35, KBo II 6+ i 31', KBo XXIII 114 obv. 12, XVI 32, 13', 16', 21', XVI 46 i 10', iv 1, 13, XXII 35 ii 13' (-*i*]*š*), XLIX 2 ii 4', XLIX 93, 20 (*k*]*u-i*[*š*), L 6+ ii 35', 48', iii 32
	ku-in	acc.sg.c.	KBo II 2 iv 28
	ku-it	nom.-acc.sg.n. (also used as conjunction "because, since")	KBo II 2 i 21, ii 21, 29, 32, iii 10, 18, 19, 26, iv 2, 22, 23, KBo II 6+ i 7', 11', 35', 36', ii 16, 37, 39, 44, 51, 52, iii 5, 6, 30, 42, KBo XVI 98 i 27, ii 3, 10, KBo XXIII 114 obv. 25, 30 (*k*]*u-*), VI 9+ ii 12, 25, VIII 27 (+) iv 1' (-*i*[*t*), XVI 16 obv. 7', 10', XVI 20, 9' (-*i*]*t*?), 9' (*ku*[-), XVI 32, 14', 15', 19', 20' (*k*[*u-*), 22', 27', XVIII 36, 12', XXII 13, 2', XXII 35 ii 6', 10', 16', XLIX 93, 1, 2, 12, 17 (-*i*[*t*), L 6+ ii 17', 21' (-]*it*), 22',

			31’, 53’ (*ku*$^{!}$-), 54’, iii 7, 16, 17, 19, 33, 47 (-*i*]*t*), L 77+ r.col. 4’, L 87 obv. 7’, 9’, rev. 5’, 10/v, 5’
	ku-e-da-ni	dat.-loc.sg.	KBo II 2 i 43
	ku-i-e-eš	nom.pl.c.	KBo II 2 iv 7, KBo XXIII 114 obv. 3, 7 (-*i*[-*e*-*e*]*š*), 22, XVI 16 obv. 23’, 26’, rev. 6, XVI 32, 1’, 6’, XVI 46 i 1’
	ku-i-e	nom.-acc.pl.n.	KBo XVI 98 iv 21”
	ku-e-da-aš	dat.-loc.pl.	KBo II 2 i 42
kuiški	“some(one/ -thing)”	indef. pron.	
	ku-iš-ki	nom.sg.c.	KBo II 2 i 46, ii 19, 25, 48, KBo XVI 98 iii 3 (*k*]*u*-), XVI 46 i 4’ ([-*k*]*i*), XVIII 36, 21’, L 6+ iii 10 (*ku*[-),
	ku-in-ki	acc.sg.c.	KBo II 2 ii 12, XVIII 36, 16’
	ku-it-ki	nom.-acc.sg.n.	KBo II 6+ i 6’, 11’, ii 46 ([*k*]*u*-[*i*]*t*-), 54, iii 9, 49, 66, KBo XVI 98 ii 15, iii 3’, VI 9+ ii 17 (-*it*[-), XVI 58 iii 7’, XVIII 36, 5’ (-*k*[*i*), XXII 12, 4’, L 6+ iii 13, 36, 38, 65, L 77+ r.col. 9’, L 87 obv. 3’, 6’ (*k*]*u*-)
	ku-e-da-ni-ik-ki	dat.-loc.sg.	KBo II 6+ i 16’, KBo XVI 98 i 11, XVI 16 obv. 24’, L 6+ iii 38

kuitman	"when, as long as, until"	subordin. conj.	
	ku-it-ma-n(*a-*)		KBo II 2 i 2, 6, ii 13, KBo II 6+ ii 38, 44, 51, iii 4, XXII 12, 2'
	ku-it-ma-an		KBo II 2 i 1, 31, VI 9+ ii 14, 15, XVIII 36, 3' (*-i*[*t-*), 11' (*-i*]*t-*), 13', 14', 19' (*-i*]*t-*), XXII 12, 1', L 77+ r.col. 6', 7', 14', L 87 rev. 6' (*-m*[*a-*), 11'
gulzattar, n.	"tablet, inscription"		
	gul-za-at-tar	nom.-acc.sg.	L 6+ iii 18
	gul-za-at-ta-ra (-)x[	nom.-acc.pl.	L 6+ iii 12
kunna(tar)-	"right(ness)"	see Sum. ZAG	
kurakki-, c.	(part of a building)		
	ku-ra-ak-ki	dat.-loc.sg.	XVIII 6 i 19', ii 2' (*-a*[*k-*), XLIX 2 i 11', 12', 23', 28' (*-r*]*a-*)
kuštayati	"?"	(technical term in augury; Luwian abl.)	
	(abbr.) *ku-uš*		KBo II 6+ iii 56, 58, iv 12, 14, 16, KBo XVI 98 ii 24, 25, iv 2', XVI 46 iv 3, 4, 5, 16, 17
kuu̯api	"when; ever"	conj., adv.	
	ku-u̯a-pí		KBo XVI 98 iii 13'
kuu̯atta	in combination *kuu̯atta imma kuu̯atta* "for whatever reason"	adv.	
	ku-u̯a-at-ta im-ma ku-u̯a-at-ta		KBo II 6+ iii 17

	ku-at-ta im-ma ku-at-ta		VIII 27 (+) iv 8' ([*-ta im-m*]*a ku*[-])
kuu̯attarma-, c.?	"?"		
	ku-u̯a-at-tar-ma-aš	?	KBo XVI 98 ii 27
lā-	"to loosen, free"		
	la-it-ta-ri	3.sg.pres. MP	KBo II 2 iv 37 (⸗*kan*), KBo II 6+ iii 48 (⸗*kan*), 65 (⸗*kan*), XVI 58 iii 5' (⸗*kan*)
	see also Sum. DUḪ		
laḫḫa-, c.	"campaign, trip"		
	la-aḫ-ḫa-az	abl.	XXII 12, 2'
laḫlaḫḫeške-	"to worry constantly"		
	la-aḫ-la-aḫ-ḫe-eš-ga-u-e-ni	1.pl.pres.	KBo II 2 i 44 (⸗*kan*), ii 8 ([*-e*]-, ⸗*kan*)
laḫlaḫḫima-, c.	"worry"		
	la-aḫ-la-ḫi-im-ma-an	acc.sg.	XLIX 2 i 25'
	la-aḫ-la-aḫ-ḫi-ma-aš	gen.sg.	KBo XVI 98 ii 23
lalatta-, c.	(designation of a festival)		
	la-la-at-ta-aš	gen.sg.	XVI 16 obv. 9' ([*-aš*])
lazzi-/*lazzii̯a-*	"good; to become good/favorable"	see Sum. SIG_5	
lulut-, n.	"good fortune, well-being"		
	lu-lu-ti	dat.-loc.sg.	XVIII 6 iv 1
	lu-lu[-		XVIII 6 ii 7'
-ma(-)	"however, then"	encl. conj.	
	-ma(-)		KBo II 2 i 3, 14, 16, 17, 41, 56, ii 7, 10, 32, 34, 47, 54, iii 2, 16, 28, 29, 35, 37, 39, iv 7, 13, 14, 29, 30,

36, KBo II 6+ i 2', 15', 17', 36', 37', 40', ii 16, 21 (-*m*]*a*), 27, 45, 46, 53, 55, iii 8, 10, 19, 22, 32, 34, 46, 53, 58 (-*m*]*a*?), 60, 63, iv 1, 12, 14, 18, 19, 22, KBo XVI 98 i 12, 19, ii 5 (2x), 6, 13, 15 (2x), 17, 19, iii 1', 10' (-*m*[*a*), 10', 16', iv 23", KBo XXIII 114 obv. 3, 9, 17, 19, VI 9+ ii 2, 6, 16, 18, VIII 27 (+) i 11' (-*m*[*a*), iv 12', XVI 16 obv. 12', 17', 22', 27', 28', 31', rev. 5, 7, 8, 10, 17, 20, left edge 3, XVI 32, 6', 10', XVI 46 i 12', 15', iv 3, 6, 11, 14, XVI 58 ii 3, iii 3', XVIII 6 i 3', 10', 11', 23', 25', ii 3', iv 2, 5, 9, XVIII 36, 8', 13', 15', 20', XXII 12, 3', XXII 13, 4' (-*m*]*a*), XXII 35 ii 5', 7', XLIX 2 i 19', 20', ii 10' (-*m*[*a*), XLIX 49 ii 3', 11', 14', 15', 20', XLIX 93, 2, 5, L 5 r.col. 8', 9', L 6+ ii 42', iii 7, 16, 38, 53, 55, 56, 58, 64, L 77+ r.col. 6', 8',

			L 87 rev. 8', LII 92 i 3', 8', 9', 10/v, 5'
maḫḫan	"when, as, how"		
	ma-aḫ-ḫa-an		XVIII 6 i 4'
	see also Sum. GIM-*an*		
mai-	"to grow, prosper"		
	ma-a-i	3.sg.pres.	VIII 27 (+) left edge a 2
malai-	"to approve of"		
	ma-la-a-an	part. nom.-acc.sg.n.	KBo II 6+ i 37' (=*za*), ii 20 ([=*za*]), iii 33 (=*za*), 63 (=*za*), KBo XVI 98 ii 17 (=*za* GAM-*an*), XVI 20, 4' (-*a*]*n*, [=*za*]), 12' ([=*za*]), XVI 58 iii 4' (-]*a*-; =*šmaš*), XVIII 6 i 12' (=*za*), XLIX 49 ii 16' (=*za* GAM-*an*), L 6+ ii 42' (=*za*)
	m[*a*-		KBo II 2 iii 37
mald-[1]	"to make a vow"		
	ma-al-ta-i	3.sg.pres.	KBo II 2 ii 40 (=*za*=*kan*)
mān	"if"	subordin. conj.	
	ma-a-an		KBo II 2 i 3, 12, 52, ii 7, 34, 43, iii 5, 13, 24, 37, iv 14, 27, 36, KBo II 6+ i 11', 14', 37', ii 43, 50, iii 4, 7, 19, 22, 32, 46, 63, KBo XVI 98 i 4, 12, ii 5, iii 7', 9', 14', iv 23",

[1] For the possibility of a 1.sg.pres. *ma-al-t*]*a-aḫ-ḫi* (KBo XVI 98 i 12) see above Ch. IV n. 5.

			VI 9+ ii 2, 16, 26 (*-a*[-), VIII 27 (+) iv 12', XVI 16 obv. 2', 5', 12', 16', 22', 24', 31' (*ma*-]), rev. 10, 17, 22, 28 (*m*]*a*-), left edge 3, XVI 20, 10' (*m*[*a*-), XVI 46 iv 14, XVI 58 iii 3', XVIII 6 i 11', XVIII 36, 2' (*-a*[*n*), 7' (*-a*]*n*), 13', 15', 20' (-]*a*-), 21' (-]*an*), XXII 12, 3', XXII 35 ii 7', XLIX 49 ii 15', L 6+ ii 42', iii 10, 13, 54, 55, 58, 64 (*m*]*a*-), L 77+ r.col. 6', 8', L 87 obv. 5' (*m*]*a*-), rev. 12' (<*-a*>), LII 92 i 4' (*-a*[*n*$^{?}$), iv 8'
	ma-a-n°		LII 92 iv 9'
*ma-ni-in-ku-u̯a-*x x x			XVIII 6 i 15'
mantallaššammi-	"designated for a *mantalli*-offering"		
	ma-an-tal-la-aš-ša-am-mi-iš	Luw. part. nom.sg.c.	KBo II 6+ iii 20, VIII 27 (+) iv 10' (*-am*[-)
mantalli-, n.	"*mantalli*-offering"	(always preceded by SISKUR)	
	ma-an-tal-li	nom.-acc.sg.n.	XVI 32, 17
	ma-an-tal-li-i̯a-an-za	Luw. nom.-acc.sg.n.	XXII 35 iii 7'
	ma-an-tal-li-i̯a	nom.-acc.pl.n.	KBo II 6+ iii 21, 30 (*-i̯a*-<<*aš*>>), 31, 32, VIII 27 (+) iv 11', XVI

			32, 9', 14' (*-ta*[*l-*; w. Glossen-keile 𒑱 preceding SISKUR), 19' (*-l*[*i-*), 23', L 6+ ii 15' (*-i̯*]*a*), 20' (*-i̯*]*a*), iii 30, 53, 63, LII 92 iv 2' (*-ta*[*l-*)
	ma-an-tal-i̯a		XXII 35 iii 11' (or <*-li*>?)
marki̯a-	"to disapprove of"		
	mar-ki-i̯a-an	part. nom.-acc.sg.n.	KBo XVI 98 iii 7' (*⸗za, ma*]*r-*), 9' (*⸗za*)
maršanašši-, c.	(oracle bird)		
	mar-ša-na-aš-ši-iš	nom.sg.	KBo XVI 98 ii 19
maškan, n.	"(propitiatory) gift"		
	máš-kán	nom.-acc.sg.	KBo II 2 ii 39, iv 10
𒑱*matašššu*	"?"		
	𒑱*ma-ta-aš-šu*		KBo II 2 iv 11
meḫur, n.	"time, moment"		
	me-e-ḫu-ni	dat.-loc.sg.	VI 9+ ii 1, XVIII 36, 7' (*-ḫ*[*u-*)
mema-, *memi*(*i̯a*)-	"to speak, say"		
	me-ma-an-zi	3.pl.pres.	L 6+ iii 26
	me-ma-an	part. nom.-acc.sg.n.	L 6+ iii 38
	me-mi-ir	3.pl.pret.	KBo XXIII 114 obv. 30, XVI 16 obv. 13', 17' (*me*[-), 23', rev. 3, 11, 18
	me-mi-iš-ki-mi	1.sg.pres. *-ške-*	KBo XVI 98 i 24 (*me-*])
memi̯a(*n*)-/*memin-*, c.	"word, affair, deed"		
	me-mi-ni	dat.-loc.sg.	KBo II 6+ i 15', ii 53, iii 8, XVI 16 obv. 10', 15', 20', 30', rev. 9,

			16, 20
	me-mi-i̯a-ni		KBo II 2 i 43, ii 55, iii 5, XVI 16 left edge 1
	me-mi-na-za	abl.	KBo II 6+ iii 47 (*m*[*e*]-), 64
	me-mi-az		XVI 58 iii 5' (-*m*]*i*-)
	see also Sum. INIM		
minumar, n.	"kindness, favor"		
	mi-nu-mar	nom.-acc.sg./pl.	KBo II 2 i 28, XVI 20, 18'
	mi-nu-mar$^{\text{ḪI.A}}$	nom.-acc.pl.	KBo II 6+ ii 1, iv 6, 9, KBo XVI 98 iv 24", XVI 58 iii 9' (*m*]*i*-)
-mu	"(to) me"	encl.pers.pron. 1.sg.	
	-mu	dat.-loc., acc.	KBo XVI 98 i 4, 5, XXII 35 ii 7', L 87 rev. 7', 12' (-*m*[*u*)
mukiššar, n.	"prayer, invocation"		
	mu-kiš-šar	nom.-acc.sg.n.	KBo II 6+ ii 40
nai-	"to turn, send"		
	ne-eḫ-ḫi	1.sg.pres.	XLIX 49 ii 9' (=*kan parā*)
	ne-i̯a-ši	2.sg.pres.	XLIX 2 i 8' (=*kan andan*)
	ne-i̯a-an-zi	3.pl.pres.	XVI 32, 11' (=*kan* GAM-*an parā*)
	na-a-iš	3.sg.pret.	XVI 46 i 15'
	ne-i̯a-at-ta-ri	3.sg.pres. MP	KBo XVI 98 iii 15' ([-*ri*)
	ne-i̯a-at-ta-at	3.sg.pret. MP	KBo II 2 iv 6 (=*kan*)
	ne-i̯a-ad-da-at		XVI 16 obv. 22', rev. 10, left edge 3 (all w. =*kan*)
namma	"then, subsequently, finally, again"	adv.	

	nam-ma		KBo II 2 i 56, ii 10, 39 (<-*ma*>), 47, iii 16, 28, iv 29, KBo II 6+ i 15', ii 25, 45, 53, iii 8, 66, KBo XVI 98 ii 12, iii 10', KBo XXIII 114 obv. 3, 9, XVI 16 obv. 12', 13', 16', 17', 22', 23', 31', rev. 10, 11, 17, 18, 22, left edge 3, XVI 46 iv 14, XVI 58 iii 7', XLIX 2 i 17', 27', L 6+ ii 46', iii 61
-*naš*	"us"	encl. pers. pron.1.pl.	
	-*na-aš*	acc., dat.-loc.	KBo II 2 ii 34, 35 (-*na*-x[?), iv 37, KBo II 6+ i 39', iii 47, 48, 64, 65, XVI 58 iii 5', L 6+ ii 44', iii 43 (-*a*]*š*), 58, 59, 60
našma	"or"	conj.	
	na-aš-ma		L 6+ iii 11
nau̯i	"not yet"	adv.	
	na-u̯i$_5$		L 6+ iii 39 (*n*]*a*-)
	na-a-u̯i$_5$		KBo II 2 i 32, ii 46
nininink-/ninik-	"to set in motion, mobilize, stir"		
	ni-ni-in-ku-u-e-ni	1.pl.pres.	L 6+ iii 43
	ni-ni-in-kiš-kán-zi	3.pl.pres. -*ške*-	KBo II 6+ ii 55
nipašuri-, c.	(a part of the liver)	(Hurrian technical term in extispicy)	
	(abbr.) *ni*		KBo II 2 ii 53, iii 8, 17, iv 15, 30, KBo II 6+ i 17',

			42', ii 27, iv 3, KBo XVI 98 ii 7, iii 17', KBo XXIII 114 obv. 10, 19, 24, XVI 16 obv. 6' (*n*[*i*)
	(abbr.) *ni-eš*	nom.sg.	KBo XVI 98 iii 11', KBo XXIII 114 obv. 4
nu	"and, Ø"	conj.	
	nu(-)		KBo II 2 i 4, 8, 10, 15, 19, 24, 27, 28 (-*kán*), 33, 35, 36, 41 (-*kán*), 47, 49, 56, ii 2, 9, 14, 16, 23, 25, 26, 27, 30 (-*za-kán*), 32, 33, 36, 41, 45 (-*ut-ták-kán*), 49, 52, 54, 55 (-*kán*), iii 1, 2, 3, 8, 12, 16, 17 (-*kán*), 21 (-*za*), 22, 28, 32, 36 (-*uš-ši*), 38, 39, 45, iv 4, 5, 7, 15, 25, 29, 38, KBo II 6+ i 4', 7', 8', 9', 14' (-*za*), 16', 20', 24' (-*kán*), 25', 31', 35', 40', 42', 44', 45' (-*kán*), ii 2 (-*kán*), 30, 33, 33 (-*kán*), 34, 39 (2x), 41 (-*kán*), 42, 44, 45, 46 (-*kán*), 46, 49, 51, 54, 55 (2x), 56, iii 2 (-*kán*), 3, 5, 7 (-*za*), 9, 11, 14 (-*kán*), 15 (id.), 16, 23, 24, 27 (-*kán*), 29

(id.), 31 (*-za*), 34, 36, 39 (*-kán*), 43, 50, 52, 54, 60, iv 1, 3, 5, 10, 12 (*-za*), 17, KBo XVI 98 i 2 (2x), 13, ii 4 (*-za*), 6, 11 (*-kán*), 12 (*-za-kán*), 14 (2x), 18, 23, iii 8', 14', 16', iv 1', 8', 23", 24" (*-kán*), 25" (*-kán*), 26" (*-kán*), KBo XXIII 114 obv. 2 (*n*]*u*), 9 (2x), 14, 15 (2x), 17, 22, 26, 28, 29, VI 9+ ii 5, 19 (*n*[*u*), iii 13' (*-kán*), VIII 27 (+) iv 2', XVI 16 obv. 4', 6', 11', 12', 13', 15', 16', 17', 19' (*-kán*), 21', 22', 23', 24' (*-u̯a-kán*), 24' (*-u̯a-aš-ma-aš-kán*), 26' (*-u̯a-ra-at*), 29' (*-u̯a-ra-at*), 30', 31', rev. 1, 2, 3 (*n*]*u*), 3, 6 (*-kán*), 8 (*-u̯a*), 9, 10, 11, 13 (*-u̯a*), 15 (*-u̯a*), 16, 17, 18, 20 (*-u̯a-ra-at*), 21, 22, 24, left edge 1, 3, XVI 20, 5', 6', 9', 10' (*-za-kán*), 13', 18' (*-kán*), XVI 32, 2' (*-kán*), 3' (*-uš-ma-aš*), 4' (*-kán*), 6', 7', 9' (*-uš-ma-aš*), 10'

(*-uš-ši-kán*), 11', 16', 17', 22', 26', 28' (2x), XVI 46 i 5' (2x), 11', ii 3', iv 6 (2x), 7, 14, XVI 58 ii 1, 4 (*-za*), 10, iii 8' (*n*]*u*), 12' (*-kán*), XVIII 6 i 4' (*-kán*), 6' (*-uš-ši-kán*), 7', 9' (*-za-kán*), 16', 18' (*-kán*), 24', ii 1' (*-za*), 19'', 20'', 21'' (*-uš*[), 22'' (*-uš*[), 24'' (*-za*), XXII 13, 9', XXII 35 iii 9' (*-za*), XLIX 2 i 8', 13' (*-kán*), 15', 16', 17', 25', 26' (*-za*), 27', ii 2', 7', 11' (*-kán*), iii 3' (*-kán*), 9' (*-n*[*u*), XLIX 49 ii 7', 16', XLIX 93, 1 (*-uš-ši*), 7 (*n*]*u*), 8 (*n*]*u-uš-ma-aš-kán*), L 5 r.col. 5', 6' (*-uš-ma-ša-aš*), 9', 11' (*-uš-ma-ša-aš-kán*), L 6+ ii 36', 57', iii 8 (*-kán*), 8 (*-uš-ši*), 10 (id.), 13 (id.), 18, 19 (*-uš-ma-aš-kán*), 20 (*-uš-ma-ša-at*), 24, 35 (*-kán*), 37, 41, 47, 54, 54 (*-za*), 55 (*-za*), L 77+ r.col. 2' (*-kán*), 3' (*-kán*), 9', 12' (*-kán*), 13' (*-kán*), 15' (*n*]*u*),

L 87 obv. 6', 8', 8' (*n*[*u*), 9' (*n*]*u-kán*), 11, rev. 1' (*n*[*u*), 6', 9' (-*kán*), 11', LII 92 i 4' (-*kán*)

na-aš(-) KBo II 2 iv 8, KBo II 6+ iii 55 (-*kán*), iv 6, 11 (-*kán*), 15 (id.), 19, 20 (-*kán*), 21 (id.), KBo XVI 98 ii 19, 24, iv 5' (-*kán*), KBo XXIII 114 rev. 2' (-*a*[*š*), VIII 27 (+) left edge b 1, XVI 16 obv. 13', 17', 23', rev. 11, 18, XVI 32, 6', 16', 21', XVI 46 i 6' (-*kán*), (2x), 7' (-*kán*), 11' (-*kán*), 12' (-*kán*), 13' (-*kán*), 14' (-*kán*), 14' (-*za*), 15', 16', ii 5' (-*kán*), 6' (-*kán*), 9', iv 2 (-*kán*), 3 (*n*]*a*-), 3 (-*kán*), 4 (-*kán*), 5, 7 (-*kán*), 8 (-*kán*), 9, 9 (-*kán*), 10 (-*kán*), 11, 11 (-*kán*), 12 (-*kán*), 16 (-*kán*), 16, 17 (-*kán*) (2x), 18 (-*kán*), 19 (*n*]*a*-), 20 (*n*]*a*-), XVI 58 ii 2 (-*kán*), iii 9', XVIII 6 i 19 (-*kán*), iv 3 (-*kán*), 4 (-*kán*), XXII 35 ii 6' (-*kán*), XLIX 2 i

10' (-*kán*), 22' (-*kán*), 23' (-*kán*), XLIX 49 ii 17', 18', XLIX 93, 12 (-*kán*), L 5 r.col. 7', L 6+ ii 32', 49', 55', iii 51 (-*kán*), L 87 rev. 7' (-*mu*), 12' (-*mu*)

na-an(-) KBo II 2 i 7, 11, 20 (-*za-an*<<-*kán*>>), 45 (-*kán*), 50, iii 34, KBo II 6+ ii 35, 57, iii 18, 19 (-*kán*), VIII 27 (+) iv 9' (-*kán*), XVI 20, 17', XVI 32, 4', 12' (-*kán*), 25' (*n*]*a*-), XVI 46 iv 7, 13, XVIII 6 i 22', iv 7 (-*kán*), 8, 11 (-*za-an*), iii 2', 5' (-*kán*), 6', 10', L 6+ iii 57, L 87 rev. 10', 12' (-*a*[*n*)

na-at(-) KBo II 6+ i 5', 10', 22', 23', ii 1, 48, iii 13, 25, 37 (-*kán*), 40, 46, 51 (-*uš-ši-kán*), 62, iv 8, 9, 13 (2x), KBo XVI 98 ii 20 (-*kán*), 22, 25, VI 9+ ii 9, iii 12' (-*a*]*t*), 14', VIII 27 (+) iv 6', XVI 32, 3', XVI 46 i 8' (-*kán*) (2x), 17' (-*kán*), 18' (-*kán*), iv 15, XVI 58 ii 5, XXII 35 ii 4', XLIX 49

			ii 8', XLIX 93, 3, L 6+ iii 14, 36 (-*kán*), L 77+ r.col. 11'
	na[-		XVIII 6 ii 25", 26", iii 6', XLIX 2 iii 1'
nuu̯a	"still"	adv.	
	nu-u-u̯a		XVI 32, 16, 21(*u*[-), L 6+ ii 22'
paḫḫur, n.	"fire"		
	pa-aḫ-ḫur	nom.-acc.sg.	KBo II 6+ iii 28
pai-	"to go"		
	pa-i-mi	1.sg.pres.	KBo XVI 98 ii 14, XLIX 49 ii 13' (*pa*[-)
	pa-a-i-mi		KBo XVI 98 i 10
	pa-iz-zi	3.sg.pres.	KBo II 2 ii 30, KBo XVI 98 ii 3, XVI 46 iii 2
	pa-a-i-u-e-ni	1.pl.pres.	KBo II 2 ii 46 (=*kan*)
	pa-a-an-zi	3.pl.pres.	KBo II 2 iv 34, L 6+ iii 40
	pa-it	3.sg.pret.	KBo II 6+ iii 55 (*pa*[-) (=*kan pian arḫa*), 58 (*arḫa*), iv 11 (=*kan pian arḫa*), 15 (id.), 18 (*pan*), 19 (*arḫa*), 20 (=*kan pian arḫa*), 21 (id.), KBo XVI 98 i 16 (=*kan arḫa*), ii 19 (*pan*), iv 3' (*arḫa*), XVI 16 rev. 18 (=*kan* UGU), XVI 46 i 7' (=*kan pian arḫa*), 12' (=*kan pian arḫa*), 13' (*pan*), 16' (*arḫa*), iv 3

			(*arḫa*), 4 (*pan*), 5, 9 (*arḫa*), 10 (⸗*kan pian arḫa*), 12 (⸗*kan pian arḫa*), 16 (*arḫa*), 19 (*arḫa*), 20 (-*i*[*t*, *arḫa*), XVI 58 ii 3 (*arḫa*), 8 (⸗*kan pian arḫa*), XVIII 6 i 24' (⸗*kan*), iv 3 (⸗*kan*) (2x), 4 (⸗*kan*), 10 (⸗*kan*), XLIX 2 i 10 (⸗*kan*), 11' (⸗*kan*), 22', 24', 27', ii 7', iii 9', XLIX 49 ii 17' (-[*i*]*t*), 18', 21', L 6+ iii 36 (⸗*kan šer arḫa*)
	pa-a-ir	3.pl.pret.	KBo II 6+ iv 14 (*arḫa*), KBo XVI 98 ii 20 (⸗*kan pian arḫa*), 22 (*arḫa*), XVI 16 rev. 7 (2x), XVI 46 i 8' (⸗*kan pian arḫa*), 18' (⸗*kan pian arḫa*), XVI 58 ii 6 (⸗*kan pian arḫa*)
pai-/pii̯a-	"to give"		
	pé-eḫ-ḫi	1.sg.pres.	KBo XVI 98 ii 14, XVI 46 iv 14, XLIX 49 ii 13'
	pa-a-i	3.sg.pres.	KBo II 2 ii 39, XVI 46 ii 2'
	pí-an-zi	3.pl.pres.	XVI 32, 3'
	pa-iš	3.sg.pret.	KBo II 2 i 11, KBo II 6+ i 23', ii 35, 48, iii 13, iv 6, 8, KBo XVI 98 iv 19", VI 9+ ii 9

			(*p*[*a*-]), 22 (*p*]*a*-), iii 12', XVI 20, 17', XVI 58 iii 9', 11', L 77+ r.col. 11' (-[*i*]*š*)
	pé-eš-ta		L 6+ iii 39
	pé-eš-ga-u-e-ni	1.pl.pres. -*ške*-	XVI 16 rev. 13, 15
	pé-eš-ki-it	3.sg.pret. -*ške*-	XVI 16 rev. 8
	pé-eš-ki-ir	3.pl.pret. -*ške*-	XVI 16 rev. 25
	pí-iš-ki-ir		XVI 16 obv. 19'
	pé-eš-ki-u-u̯a-an	supinum -*ške*-	XLIX 93, 10, L 6+ iii 21 (-]*ki*-) (EGIR-*pa*)
	pí-iš-ki-u-u̯a-an		KBo II 6+ ii 19
	pé-eš-ki-u-an		XXII 35 ii 4'
	pé-eš-x[		KBo XVI 98 iii 13'
	see also Sum. SUM		
palša- and **palšiaḫḫ*-	"road"	see Sum. KASKAL(-*aḫḫ*-)	
pan	see *pariu̯an*		
panku-, c.	"assembly"		
	pa-an-ku-uš	nom.sg.	KBo II 6+ ii 2, iii 25, 27, KBo XVI 98 iv 20", L 77+ r.col. 10', L 87 rev. 2'
	pa-an-ga-u-i	dat.-loc.sg.	KBo II 2 i 50, KBo II 6+ i 23', ii 48 (-*g*[*a*-), 57, XLIX 49 ii 8'
	pa-an-ka$_4$*-u-i*		VI 9+ iii 12', XVI 20, 17'
	pa-an-ga-u-u̯i$_5$		KBo II 2 i 11
parā	"forth, out of"	adv., prev., postpos.	
	pa-ra-a		KBo II 2 i 31 (*piran p.*), iii 19 (*duu̯an p.*), 26, (*duu̯an* ... *p.*), iv 2 (*duu̯an p.*), KBo XVI 98 ii 15, VI 9+ ii 2, 13 (*duu̯an p.*), XLIX

			2 i 5', XLIX 49 ii 14', L 77+ r.col. 5' (*duu̯a*[*n* ... -*r*]*a*-)
		ar- (act.)	KBo II 2 ii 48
		epp-/app-	KBo XVI 98 i 5
		nai-	XVI 32, 11' (⸗*kan* GAM-*an*), XLIX 49 ii 9' ([⸗*kan*])
		tarna-	XVI 16 obv. 14'
		tarup-	L 6+ iii 59 (⸗*kan*)
		SUM	XVI 32, 1' (*p*[*a*$^{?!}$-), 30' (-]*a*), L 6+ ii 54', iii 23
		[verb lost]	XVIII 6 i 6', L 5 r.col. 10'
pa(*r*)*randa*	"over, across"	adv.	
	pa-ra-an-da		XVI 16 rev. 6 ([-*a*]*n*)
	pár-ra-an-da		XVI 16 rev. 7
parii̯an	"over, across"	adv.	
	(abbr.) *pa-an*	*p. pai-* ("to go")	KBo II 6+ iv 18, KBo XVI 98 ii 19, XVI 46 i 13', iv 4, XLIX 49 ii 17'
		p. uu̯a-	XVI 46 iv 11
		[verb lost]	XVI 46 ii 9
parrianta	"over, across"	adv.	
	pár-ri-an-ta		KBo II 2 ii 56
parkui-	"clean, pure"		
	pár-ku-u̯a-i̯a-za	abl.	XXII 35 iii 14'
parkunu-	"to cleanse, purify"		
	pár-ku-nu-zi	3.sg.pres.	L 6+ ii 41' (⸗*za*), iii 5 (*pár*-[), 50 (⸗*za*)
	pár-ku-nu-uz-zi		KBo II 6+ i 34' (⸗*za*), VIII 27 (+) iv 4' (<*nu*>)
	pár-ku-nu-an-zi	3.pl.pres.	L 6+ ii 40', iii 5, 49 (*pá*]*r*-)

	pár-ku-nu-u̯a-an-zi		KBo II 6+ i 33', XXII 35 iii 3', 5' (-*z*]*i*), VIII 27 (+) iv 4', 10/v, 3' (-*an*[-)
𒑱*paš-*	"to swallow"		
	𒑱*pa-aš-ta*	3.sg.pret.	XLIX 2 i 14' (GAM), 18' (GAM)
-pat		suffixed emphatic part.	
	-pát		KBo II 2 i 9, 13, 18, 26, 34, 48, 55, ii 15, 43, iii 6, 14, 24, iv 27, KBo II 6+ i 4', 9', 11', 14', 20', 25', 44', ii 30, 38, 42, 43 (2x), 49, 50, iii 3, 4, 7, 11, 16, 24, 36, 52, 54, iv 5, 10, KBo XVI 98 ii 16, iv 8', KBo XXIII 114 obv. 14, 18, 23, VI 9+ ii 19, XVI 16 obv. 12', 22', 24', 31', rev. 10, 14, 17, 19, 22, left edge 3, XVI 58 ii 1, 10, XVIII 6 i 21', XLIX 2 i 14', XLIX 49 ii 7', L 6+ iii 12, 57, L 87 obv. 5', rev. 1'
pattarpalḫi-, c.	(oracle bird)		
	pát-tar-pal-ḫi-in	acc.sg.	XVI 46 i 11'
	pát-tar-pal-ḫi-iš	nom.pl.	XVI 46 i 7'
peššii̯a-	"to throw, cast"		
	pé-eš-ši-i̯a-zi	3.sg.pres.	XVIII 6 i 10' (⸗*za*⸗*kan pian arḫa*), XXII 13, 5' ([*arḫa*]?)
	pé-eš-šir	3.pl.pret.	KBo II 6+ iii 59 ([*arḫa*]), iv 16

			(*arḫa*), KBo XVI 98 iv 7', XVI 46 iv 5, XLIX 49 ii 2' (-*š*]*ir*)
	pé-eš-ši-an-du	3.pl.imp.	KBo II 6+ iii 16 (*arḫa*)
peda-, n.	"place, spot"		
	pí-di	dat.-loc.sg.	KBo II 6+ i 35', XVI 32, 11', XXII 35 iii 18', L 87 rev. 8', 10'
	see also Akk. *AŠRU*(*M*)		
peda-	"to carry, take"		
	pé-e-da-i	3.sg.pres.	VIII 27 (+) left edge a 3
	pé-e-da-an-zi	3.pl.pres.	XVI 32, 5' (=*kan* EGIR-*pa anda*), iii 65
	pé-e-da-aš	3.sg.pret.	XVIII 6 iv 1 (=*kan*), 8 (=*kan*), XVI 46 iv 8 (*arḫa*)
pian	see *piran*		
piḫammi-	"imbued with splendor, lightening"		
	pí-ḫa-am-mi-in	acc.sg.c.	XVIII 6 i 24'
piran	"before, in front of"	adv., prev., postpos.	
	pí-ra-an		KBo II 2 i 31 (*p. parā*), 43, ii 7
		p. arḫa anii̯a-	KBo II 6+ iii 44
		p. tii̯a-	KBo II 2 iii 7 (=*kan*), L 6+ ii 31'
	(abbr.) *pí-an*	*p. arḫa anii̯a-*	KBo II 6+ i 32', VIII 27 (+) iv 3', L 6+ ii 37', 39', iii 2 (*p*]*í*-), 3, 10/v, 2' (*pí*[-)
		=*za*=*kan p. arḫa nai-*	XVI 46 i 15'
		=*kan p. arḫa pai-*	KBo II 6+ iii 55, iv 11, 15, 20, 21, XVI 46 i 7', 8',

			12', 18', iv 10, 12, XVI 58 ii 6 (*p*]*í*-), 8
		=*za*=*kan p. arḫa peššii̯a-*	XVIII 6 i 9'
		p. dai-	L 6+ ii 31'
		=*kan p. tii̯a-*	KBo II 2 iii 7
		=*kan p. uu̯a-*	KBo II 6+ iii 55, iv 14, 18, KBo XVI 98 ii 19, iv 2' (-*a*]*n*), XVI 46 i 6', 14', iv 3, 4, 7, 8, 17, XVI 58 ii 2
		no verb	KBo XVI 98 ii 24
		[verb lost]	KBo XVI 98 ii 26, XVI 46 ii 5'
pukanti-?	"?"		
	pu-kán-⸢*ti*⸣[(-)		KBo II 6+ ii 28
punušš-	"to ask, question"		
	pu-nu-uš-ša-an-zi	3.pl.pres.	KBo II 2 iii 32
	pu-nu-uš-šu-u-en	1.pl.pret.	XVI 16 obv. 13', 17', 23', rev. 3, 11, 18, 24 (-*u*[*š*-)
purundu (-) *karrita*	"?"	(Hurrian technical term in extispicy?)	
	pu-ru-un-du(-)*kar-ri-ta*		KBo II 6+ i 17'
puš-	"to eclipse"		
	pu-u-uš-zi	3.sg.pres.	VIII 27 (+) left edge b 3 (*pu*[-)
-*ša-*/-*ši-*	"his, her"	encl. poss. pron. (only in *pidi*=*ši*)	
	-*ši*	dat.-loc.sg.	XVI 32, 11', XXII 35 iii 18' (°*š*[-*ši*?), L 87 rev. 8', 10'
šai-/*šii̯a-*	"to press"		
	ši-i̯a-an	part. nom.-acc.sg.n.	KBo II 2 iii 29
šakii̯aḫḫ-	"to prophesy, give an omen"		
	ša-ki-i̯a-aḫ-ḫi-ir	3.pl.pret.	XVI 46 i 5'
šaknuu̯ant-	"dirty"		

	ša-ak-nu-u̯a-an-da-za	abl.	XXII 35 iii 14'
	š]a-ak-nu-an[-		LII 92 iv 5'
(𒑱)*šakkuri̯a-*	"to disperse, squander"		
	𒑱*ša-ak-ku-ri-an*	part. nom.-acc.sg.n.	KBo IX 151, 2' (*arḫa*), 8' (*arḫa*)
	ša-ak-ku-ri-an		L 6+ ii 52' (*arḫa*; without 𒑱 ? see note in transliteration)
	-r]i-an ?		XXII 35 i 2'
šaku̯andari̯anu-	"to skip, leave uncelebrated" (said of festivals)		
	ša-ku-u̯a-an-ta-ri-i̯a-nu-u̯a-an-te-eš	part. nom.pl.c.	KBo II 6+ ii 17 (*š]a- ... -[a]n-*; *⸗kan*)
	ša-ku-u̯a-an-ta-ri-i̯a-nu-uš-kán-te-eš		XXII 35 ii 5' (*⸗kan*)
	ša-ku-u̯a-an-da-ri-i̯a-nu-uš-kán-te-eš		XLIX 93, 11 (*-i̯[a-*; *⸗kan*)
	fragmentary		KBo II 6+ ii 12 (*-r]i-i̯[a-?*)
šallakart-	"to offend"		
	šal-la-kar-ta-an	part. nom.-acc.sg.n.	KBo II 2 iii 20 (*š]al-*), 27, iv 3
šalli-	"great, big"		
	šal-li	nom.-acc.sg.n.	KBo II 6+ ii 40
šalik-	"to approach, touch"		
	ša-li-ik-ti	2.sg.pres.	KBo II 2 ii 56 (*⸗kan parrianta*)
	ša-li-kiš-kán-zi	3.pl.pres. *-ške-*	XVI 16 obv. 25' (*⸗kan šer*)
šalu̯aru̯ant-	see MUNUS*u̯u̯aru̯ant-*		
šalu̯ini-, c.	(oracle bird)		
	šal-u̯i₅-ni-eš	nom.sg.	XLIX 49 ii 20' (*šal-*])
-šan	(local particle)		
	(*na-an*)*-za-an* (= *⸗za⸗šan*)	*karp-*	XVIII 6 iv 11

		dai-	KBo II 2 i 20 (*-za-an<<-kán>>*)
šanḫ-	"to seek, search"		
	ša-an-aḫ-ti	2.sg.pres.	KBo II 6+ iii 22, VIII 27 (+) iv 12' (*š[a-*)
šarā	"up, above"	adv., prev.	
	ša-ra-a	*š. ašaš-/ašeš-*	KBo II 6+ iii 61
		š. ašešanu-	KBo II 6+iii 44
		=kan š. uu̯a-	KBo II 2 i 2
	see also Sum. UGU		
(ÉRIN.MEŠ) *šarikuu̯a*	"*šarikuwa*-troops"		
	ša-ri-ku-u̯a	abs.	KBo XVI 98 i 1
šarnikzel, n.	"compensation, penance"		
	šar-ni-ik-ze-el	nom.-acc.sg.	KBo II 6+ i 34', iii 45, 61 (*[-n]i-ik[-*), VIII 27(+) 5' (*-i]k-*), XXII 35 iii 12', 13', LII 92 iv 4' (*ša]r-* ... *-z[e-*)
	šar-ni-ik-ze-el^{MEŠ}	nom.-acc.pl.	L 6+ iii 50 (*[šar-]* ... *-ze*$^{!}$*-*)
	šar-ni-]ik-ze-el$^{\text{ḪI.A}}$		10/v, 4'
šarnink-/šarnik-	"to compensate"		
	šar-ni-in-kán-zi	3.pl.pres.	KBo II 2 iii 34, iv 8, XXII 35 ii 6' (*=kan anda*), XLIX 93, 13 (*=kan anda*)
	šar-ni-in-ku-u̯a-aš	gen. "quasi gerundivalis"	KBo II 2 iii 33
	šar-ni-in-ku-u-u̯a-aš		KBo II 2 iii 40 (*-u̯a[-*)
	šar-ni-in-ku-e-eš	nom.pl.c. based on preceding gen.	KBo II 2 iv 8
	šar-ni-in-ku[-		KBo II 2 iii 46
	šar-ni-in[-		KBo II 2 iii 35
šašt(a)-, *c.*	see ^{GIŠ}NÁ		
šekk-/šakk-	"to know"		

	ša-ak-ti	2.sg.pres.	KBo II 2 iv 36 (=*kan*)
	še-ek-ku-e-ni	1.pl.pres.	KBo XXIII 114 obv. 22
	še-ek-te-ni	2.pl.pres.	VI 9+, 3' (GAM-*an*), XVIII 36, 16' (GAM-*an*)
	še-ek-kán-du-uš	part. acc.pl.c.	KBo XXIII 114 obv. 21, 23, 25
TÚG*šeknu*-, c.	"robe, mantle"		
	TÚG*še-ek-nu-un*	acc.sg.	KBo II 6+ i 39', iii 49, 66, XVI 58 iii 6', L 6+ ii 45', iii 57, 61
šelušḫitašši-	"?"	(Luwianized Hurrian technical term in extispicy)	
	še-lu-uš-ḫi-ta-aš-ši-iš	Luw. nom.sg.c.	KBo XVI 98 ii 8
šer	"up, above"	adv., prev., postpos.	
	še-er		KBo II 2 ii 13, 30, iii 11, 15, 31, iv 30, KBo II 6+ i 1', 14', 15', 39', ii 53, iii 7, 8, 18, KBo IX 151, 1', 7', KBo XXIII 114 obv. 23, 25, 28, 29, XVI 16 obv. 10', 15, 20', 30', rev. 9, 16, 21, left edge 1, XXII 13, 8', XXII 35 ii 11', 13', L 6+ ii 50', 51', iii 7, 16, 35
		apadda š.	L 6+ iii 37, L 87 obv. 8'
		apaddan š.	KBo II 2 iii 21, 24, iv 4
		=*kan š. arḫa pai*-	L 6+ iii 36
		=*kan š. šalik*-	XVI 16 obv. 25'
		=*kan š. uda*-	XVI 46 i 2' (*š*]*e*-)

	see also Sum. UGU		
šeš-/šaš-	"to sleep"		
	še-eš-kiš-ke-eš-kán-zi	3.pl.pres. (double!) *-ške-*	XVI 16 obv. 27'
	še-eš-ki-iš-ki-it	3.sg.pret. (double!) *-ške-*	XVI 16 rev. 19 (=*kan*)
-ši	"for/to him, her, it"	encl. dat. pers. pron. 3.sg.	
	-ši		KBo II 2 iii 36, KBo II 6+ i 11', iii 6, 51, VI 9+ ii 17, XVI 32, 10', XVI 46 iv 14, XVIII 6 i 6', XXII 35 iii 15' (°*š-[ši]*), XLIX 93, 1, 2, 5, L 6+ ii 51', 52', iii 8 (*-š[i]*), 10, 13, 17, 33, 52
-ši-	"his, her"	see *-ša-/-ši-*	
šintaḫi-, c.	"stand, position, presence"	(Hurrian technical term in extispicy)	
	(abbr.) *ši*		KBo II 2 ii 53, iii 8, iv 15, 31, KBo II 6+ i 17', 42', ii 28, iv 3, KBo XVI 98 ii 7, iii 17', KBo XXIII 114 obv. 5, 10, 19, 24
šipant-/išpant-	"to offer, dedicate"	see Sum. BAL	
šiu(n)-	"deity"	see Sum. DINGIR	
-šmaš	"for/to them"	encl. dat. pers. pron. 3.pl.	
	°*š-ma-aš*		KBo II 2 iv 30, KBo II 6+ ii 16 (*-a[š]*), XVI 16 obv. 24', 28' (2x), XVI 32, 3', 9', XVI 58 iii 3',

			XLIX 93, 8, L 6+ iii 19
	°*š-ma-š*°		L 5 r.col. 6', 11', L 6+ iii 20
šulupi-, c.	(oracle bird)		
	šu-lu-pí-iš	nom.sg.	KBo II 6+ iii 57
	šu-lu-pí-in	acc.sg.	KBo II 6+ iv 11
	šu-lu-pé-eš	nom.sg./pl.	KBo XVI 98 ii 26
šunna-	"to fill"		
	šu-un-ni-eš-ki-ir	3.pl.pret. *-ške-*	XVI 16 obv. 20
-ta	"(to) you"	encl.pers.pron. 2.sg.	
	-ta	dat., acc.	KBo II 2 iii 26
	-tá(*k-k*°)		KBo II 2 ii 45, 47
dā-	"to take, seize"		
	da-a-i	3.sg.pres.	XVIII 36, 18' (*d*]*a-*)
	da-a-u-e-ni	1.pl.pres.	XVI 16 rev. 20
	da-an-zi	3.pl.pres.	L 6+ iii 51(=*kan*)
	da-at-ta	2.sg.pret.	KBo XVI 98 iii 14'
	da-a-aš	3.sg.pret.	KBo XVI 98 iv 20" (*-a*[*š*), 25"
	da-a-ir	3.pl.pret.	XLIX 49 ii 8'
	da-an-te-eš	part. nom.pl.c.	KBo XVI 98 iv 24"
	da-aš-ga-u-e-ni	1.pl.pres. *-ške-*	XVI 16 rev. 15
	da-aš-ki[*-*	*-ške-* (prob. supinum)	XVI 32, 2' (=*kan*)
	see also Sum. ME		
dai-/tii̯a-	"to put, place; to begin (w. sup.)"		
	ti-i̯a-u-e-ni	1.pl.pres.	KBo II 6+ iii 19 (=*kan*)
	ti-an-zi	3.pl.pres.	KBo II 2 iv 14, KBo II 6+ i 35', ii 14, 19, 10/v, 5' (*-z*]*i*)
	ti-i̯a-an-zi		XVI 32, 7' (*ti*[-), 12' (=*kan*), XXII 35 ii 4', iii 16' (*-z*[*i*); =*kan*), XLIX 93, 10 (*-i̯*[*a-*), L 6+ ii 2'

			(-]*zi*), 13' (*t*]*i*-), iii 12, 21 (-[*i̯a*-])
	da-i[*š*(?)	3.sg.pret.	XXII 35 ii 3' (⸗*kan*)
	ti-a[*n*-		XLIX 2 ii 8' (⸗*kan*)
	ti-i̯a-an-za	part. nom.sg.c.	XLIX 2 ii 5' (or from *tii̯a*-?)
	ti-i̯a-an-te-eš	part. nom.pl.c.	L 6+ iii 34 (⸗*kan*)
	see also Sum. ME		
takšan	"middle, centre"	see 2-*an*	
takku	"if, when"	subordin. conj.	
	ták-ku		VIII 27 (+) left edge b 1, 3
talii̯a-	"to let go, ignore"		
	ta-li-i̯a-an	part. nom.-acc.sg.n.	KBo II 6+ i 6', 13' (⸗*kan*)
dalin	"?"	(Hurrian technical term in extispicy)	
	da-li-in		XVI 16 obv. 30'
tamai-	"other"		
	ta-ma-a-iš	nom.sg.c.	XVIII 6 iv 5
	dam-ma-iš		KBo II 2 ii 25, 47
	dam-ma-in	acc.sg.c.	KBo II 2 ii 11
	ta-me-e-da-ni	dat.-loc.sg.	KBo II 6+ ii 53, iii 8
	da-me-e-da-ni		KBo II 6+ i 15'
	ta-me-da-za	abl.	KBo II 6+ i 36'
	ta-me-e-da-aš	dat.-loc.pl.	L 6+ ii 54'
^{MUNUS}*dammara*-, c.	"*dammara*-woman"		
	^{MUNUS}*dam-ma-ra-aš*	nom.sg.	XVI 16 rev. 19
	$^{\mathrm{MUNUS.MEŠ}}$*dam-ma-ra-aš*	nom.pl.	XVI 16 obv. 13', 18', 23', 26'
dammeli-	"pure, immaculate"		
	dam-me-li	dat.-loc.sg.	KBo II 6+ i 35'
tanani-, c.	"strengthening, reinforcement"	(Hurrian technical term in extispicy)	

	(abbr.) *ta*		KBo II 2 iii 8, iv 15, 31, KBo II 6+ i 19', KBo XXIII 114 obv. 4 (*t*[*a*), 19, 24
(𒑱)*tapašša-*, c.	(some kind of illness, "fever"?)		
	ta-pa-aš-ša-aš	nom.sg.	KBo II 2 i 5, 7, 30
	𒑱*ta-pa-aš-ša-aš*		KBo II 2 i 3, 12, 45, 54
	𒑱*ta-pa-aš-ša-an*	acc.sg.	KBo II 2 i 23, 52, ii 11, 18
	ta-pa-aš-ša	Luwian *a*-case?	XXII 13, 8' (*t*]*a*-)
tapašši-, c.	(oracle bird)		
	ta-pa-aš-ši-iš	nom.sg.	KBo XVI 98 ii 21
	ta-pa-aš-ši-in	acc.sg.	XVI 46 iv 2, 10, 16 (-*i*[*n*)
	ta-pa-aš-ši-iš	acc.pl.	XVI 46 iv 15
dapi-/dapia-	"all, entire"		
	da-pí-an	acc.sg.c.	KBo II 2 i 19, 27 (-*a*[*n*), KBo II 6+ ii 47 (-*pí*[-), iii 12, 14, iv 7, KBo XVI 98 iv 19", 22" (*d*]*a*-), VI 9+ ii 4, 20, XVI 20, 16', XVI 58 iii 10', XVIII 36, 9'
	da-pí-i	dat.-loc.sg.	KBo II 6+ ii 33, iii 2
	da-pí-za	abl.	VI 9+ ii 4
	da-pí-an-te-eš	nom.pl.c	XVI 16 obv. 23', 24', 26'
	da-pí-an-da	nom.-acc.pl.n.	KBo XVI 98 iv 21", XVI 16 rev. 14
tarna-	"to leave (behind)"		
	tar-nu-um-ma-aš	gen. "quasi gerundivalis"	XVI 16 obv. 14' (*parā*)
taru̯alli/taru̯alli-	"?"	(technical term in augury)	

	(abbr.) *tar-li*$_{12}$*-an*		KBo II 6+ iv 11, XVI 46 i 6’, 14’, iv 2, 6, 8, 16, 18, 19, XVI 58 ii 2
	(abbr.) *tar-liš*		KBo II 6+ iv 18, KBo XVI 98 ii 19, XVI 46 i 13’, iv 4, XLIX 49 ii 17’
tarup-	“to gather”		
	ta-ru-up-ta-ri	3.sg.pres. MP	L 6+ iii 60 (*parā ⸗kan*)
^{MUNUS}*tau̯annana-*, c.	“tawannanna”		
	^{MUNUS}*ta-u̯a-an-na-na*	abs.	L 6+ ii 35’, 36’, 41’, 43’, 44’
tautiš	“?”	(Hurrian technical term in extispicy)	
	ta-ú-ti-iš		KBo XXIII 114 obv. 8, XLIX 49 ii 6’
tepnu-	“to belittle, humiliate”		
	te-pa-nu-u̯a-an	part. nom.-acc.sg.n.	XVI 16 rev. 2 (*⸗za*)
tepu-	“little, few”		
	te-pa-u-u̯a-za	abl.	XVI 16 rev. 8
tešḫanii̯a-	“to appear in a dream”		
	te-eš-ḫa-ni-eš-kit$_9$*-ta-ri*	3.sg.pres. MP	KBo XVI 98 ii 10
tii̯a-	“to step, take a stand”		
	ti-i̯a-zi	3.sg.pres.	KBo II 2 iii 7, XLIX 2 i 3 (*t*]*i* ... *z*[*i*)
	ti-i̯a-an-za	part. nom.sg.c.	XLIX 2 ii 5’ (or from *dai-*?)
	ti-i̯a-an-na	inf. II	L 6+ ii 31’ (*piran*)
tiu̯atani-, c.?	“curse”		
	ti-u̯a-ta-ni-i̯a	dat.-loc.sg.	L 6+ iii 35 (-*t*]*a*-)
	ti-u̯a-ta-ni-i̯a-za	abl.	XXII 35 iii 2’ (-]*ta*-)

dudamitta	"?"	(Hurrian technical term in extispicy)	
	du-da-mi-it-ta		XVI 16 obv. 30'
dudduš	"?"	(Hurrian technical term in extispicy)	
	du-ud-du-uš		XVI 16 rev. 4
duu̯an	"away, far off"	adv.	
	du-u̯a-an	*d. parā*	KBo II 2 iii 9, 26, iv 2
	du-u-u̯a-an	*d. parā*	L 5 r.col. 10'
	du-u̯a-a-an	*d. parā*	L 77+ r.col. 5 (-*a*[*n*)
tuu̯az	"away, far off"	adv.	
	tu-u-u̯[*a-a*]*z*		KBo XVI 98 ii 5
uii̯a-	"to send, dispatch"		
	u-i-i̯a-u-e-ni	1.pl.pres.	L 6+ iii 56 (-*u*[-)
	u-i-i̯a-an-zi	3.pl.pres.	L 6+ iii 41 (-*i̯*]*a*-)
	u-i-i̯a-u-an-zi	inf. I	L 6+ iii 46
ukturi-	"normal, fixed"		
	uk-tu-ri-iš	nom.sg.c.	KBo II 2 iv 31
uliḫi-, c.	"?"		
	ú-li-ḫi-uš	acc.pl.	XVI 32, 8'
uda-	"to bring"		
	ú-da-an-zi	3.pl.pres.	XVI 32, 8' (*ú*[-; *=kan* UGU), L 6+ ii 9' (-*a*]*n*-)
	ú-te-er	3.pl.pret.	XVI 46 i 2' (*=kan šer*)
uttar, n.	"word, affair"		
	ut-tar	nom.-acc.sg.	KBo II 2 ii 9, iv 37, KBo II 6+ ii 37, L 6+ iii 41
	ud-da-ni-i	dat.-loc.sg.	XVIII 6 i 3 (*u*]*d*-)
	see also Sum. INIM		
utne, n.	"land, country"		
	ut-ne-e	nom.-acc.sg.	VIII 27 (+) left edge a 2, 3 (-]*e*)
	see also Sum. KUR		
uu̯a-	"to come"		
	ú-iz-zi	3.sg.pres.	KBo II 2 i 2

			(=*kan šarā*), VIII 27 (+) left edge b 1, XVI 32, 10' (=*kan* UGU)
	ú-it	3.sg.pret.	KBo II 6+ iii 56 (=*kan* EGIR GAM), 58(-*i*[*t*, id.), iv 12 (id.), 14 (=*kan pian*), 16, 20 (=*kan* EGIR UGU), 21 (id.), 22 (=*kan*), KBo XVI 98 i 32, iv 2', 5', XVI 20, 14' (*ú*[-), XVI 46 i 6' (=*kan pian*), 7' (=*kan* EGIR UGU), 12' (id.), 13' (id.), 14' (=*kan pian*), iv 3 (id.), 4 (id.), 7 (id.), 8 (id.), 9 (=*kan* EGIR UGU), 11 (*pan*), 12 (=*kan* EGIR UGU), 16 (=*kan* EGIR GAM), 17 (=*kan pian*), XVI 58 ii 4 (=*kan* EGIR UGU), XLIX 2 i 17' ([=*kan*]), 20' (=*kan*), XLIX 49 ii 17', 18', 19' (=*kan*)
	ú-e-er	3.pl.pret.	KBo XVI 98 ii 20 (=*kan pian*), XVI 46 i 8' (=*kan* EGIR UGU), 17' (id.), ii 8, iv 15
^{MUNUS}*uu̯aru̯a*(*nt*)-?, "*u.*-woman" c.			
	^{MUNUS}*u-u̯a-ar-u̯a-an-z*[*i*	Luw.nom.pl.(?)	L 87 rev. 9'

-u̯a(-)/-u̯ar-		quotative part.	
	-u̯a(-)		KBo II 6+ iii 59, iv 16, 23, KBo XVI 98 i 4, 18, KBo XXIII 114 obv. 30 (*-u̯[a*), XVI 16 obv. 13', 17', 18', 19', 23', 24' (2x), 25', 26', 28' (2x), rev. 8 (2x), 11, 12, 13, 14, 15, 18, 19 (2x), 26 (*-u̯[a*), XVI 46 i 9', 18', iv 5, 12, XVI 58 ii 9, XLIX 49 ii 21'
	-u̯a-r(a)-		XVI 16 obv. 10', 26', 27', 29', rev. 20
u̯aḫnu-	"to (cause to) turn, change"		
	u̯a-aḫ-nu-um-me-en	1.pl.pret.	XVI 20, 1' (*u̯a-*] ... *m[e-*), 9'
u̯akšur, n.	(measure of volume)		
	u̯a-ak-šur	nom.-acc.sg.	XVI 16 rev. 4
u̯alḫ-	"to hit, beat, strike"		
	u̯a-al-aḫ-ḫa-an-zi	3.pl.pres.	KBo II 2 i 42
	see also Sum. GUL		
u̯arp-	"to wash, clean"		
	u̯a-ar-pa-an-zi	3.pl.pres.	XVI 16 obv. 28' (=*šmaš*)
u̯aršii̯a-	"to soothe, pacify"		
	u̯a-ar-ši-i̯a-an-za	part. nom.sg.c.	XVI 32, 17', 22' (*-a[n*), L 6+ ii 23' (*a]n-*)
u̯ašku-, c.	"sin"		
	u̯a-aš-ku-uš	acc.pl.	KBo XXIII 114 obv. 21, 23, 25
	u̯a-aš-ku-u̯a-aš	dat.-loc.pl.	KBo II 6+ i 14', iii 7, KBo XXIII

			114 obv. 28, 29 ([-*a*]*š*)
u̯aškuu̯an-, n.	"sin"		
	u̯a-aš-ku-u̯a-na	nom.-acc.pl.	L 6+ iii 27 (-]*ku-*)
u̯aštanu-	"to cause to sin"		
	u̯a-aš-ta-nu-uz-zi	3.sg.pres.	KBo II 2 ii 36
u̯aštanuu̯ant-	"sinful"		
	u̯a-aš-ta-nu-u̯a-an-da-za	abl.	XVI 16 rev. 15
u̯aštul, n.	"sin, lack, loss"		
	u̯a-aš-túl	nom.-acc.sg.	KBo II 6+ ii 40
	u̯a-aš-du-li	dat.-loc.sg.	KBo II 6+ iii 51
	u̯a-aš-du-la	nom.-acc.pl.	KBo II 6+ iii 28
u̯atarnaḫḫ-	"to command, order"		
	u̯a-tar-na-aḫ-ḫa-an-za	part. nom.sg.c.	XVI 32, 26' (*u̯*]*a-*)
u̯atkunu-	"to dispel, chase"		
	u̯a-at-ku-nu-zi	3.sg.pres.	XVIII 36, 21' (-*z*[*i, arḫa*)
u̯ek-	"to ask, demand"	see Sum. IR	
u̯emii̯a-	"to find, encounter"		
	ú-e-mi-i̯a-zi	3.sg.pres.	KBo II 2 i 4 (*anda*), 8, 14 (ŠÀ), 46 (=*kan anda*)
	see also Sum. KAR and Akkad. *KAŠĀDU*(*M*)		
u̯erii̯a-	"to call"		
	ú-e-ri-an-zi	3.pl.pres.	L 5 r.col. 4' (-*r*[*i-*), L 6+ iii 8 (=*kan*)
	ú-e-ri-i̯a-an-zi		KBo IX 151, 9' (*ú-*] ... -*z*[*i*)
	ú-e-ri-i̯a-an-te-eš	part. nom.pl.c.	XVI 16 obv. 27' (*anda*), 29' (*anda*)
-*z*(*a*)		refl.part.	
	-*z*(*a-an* = =*z*=*šan*)	*karp-*	XVIII 6 iv 12
		dai-	KBo II 2 i 20
	-*za*	*auš-*/*au-*/*u-*	KBo XVI 98 i 22

EGIR-*pa epp-/app-*	KBo II 2 ii 30
eš-/aš- (dep.)	KBo II 2 i 31, KBo XVI 98 ii 12, VI 9+ ii 14 (-*z*]*a*), XVI 20, 10', XVI 46 i 14', XVIII 6 i 10', XVIII 36, 11', 13', L 77+ r.col. 6' (-*z*[*a*)
ii̯a-	KBo XVI 98 ii 12, XLIX 49 ii 11'
karp-	KBo XVI 98 ii 13, XLIX 2 i 19', XLIX 49 ii 12' (-*z*]*a*)
malai- (*ḫar-/ḫark-*)	KBo II 2 iii 37, iv 14[2] KBo II 6+ i 37', iii 32, 46[2], 63, KBo XVI 98 ii 5'[2] 17, iv 23"[2] XVI 46 iv 14[2], XVIII 6 i 11', XLIX 49 ii 15', L 6+ ii 42'
markii̯a-	KBo XVI 98 iii 9'
⸗kan mald-	KBo II 2 ii 40
⸗kan pian arḫa nai-	XVI 46 i 15
parkunu-	KBo II 6+ i 34', L 6+ iii 50
⸗kan pian arḫa peššii̯a-	XVIII 6 i 9'
šipant-/BAL	KBo II 6+ iii 21, 31, XVI 32, 9', XXII 35 iii 9', L 6+ iii 54, 55, 63
dā-/ME	KBo II 2 i 27, 35, KBo II 6+ i 22', 45', ii 2, 31, 47, iii 1, 12, 14, 25,

[2] The expression *malān ḫar*(*k*)- is subsumed by KI.MIN here.

			27, 37, iv 6, 7, KBo XVI 98 ii 29, iii 14’, iv 19”, 20”, 25” (-*z*]*a*), VI 9+ ii 8, 21, iii 11’, XVI 20, 7’, 16’, XVI 58 iii 8’, 10’, 11’, XVIII 6 ii 1’, XLIX 2 i 26’, L 77+ r.col. 10’, L 87 rev. 2’
		tepnu-	XVI 16 rev. 2
		u̯emii̯a-/IKŠUD	KBo II 6+ iv 12, XVI 58 ii 4
		nominal sentence	KBo II 2 ii 43, iii 13, 21, 24, 43, KBo II 6+ 14’, 15’, ii 53, iii 7, 8, KBo XXIII 114 obv. 21, VIII 27(+) iv 8’, XVI 16 obv. 2’, 5’, 10’, 14’, 20’, 29’, rev. 9, 16, 20, 27, left edge 1, XXII 35 ii 11’ (-*z*]*a*), XLIX 93, 18, L 87 obv. 3’, 5’
		[verb lost]	KBo XVI 98 i 10, XVI 46 ii 4’, XVIII 6 ii 24”, L 77+ r.col. 14’
zai-	“to cross, transgress”		
	za-a-iš	3.sg.pret.	L 6+ iii 36 (=*kan*)
zaluganu-	“to postpone”		
	za-lu-ga-nu-um-me-e-ni	1.pl.pres.	XLIX 2 i 6’ ([=*kan*]?)
	za-lu-ka$_4$-nu-me-en	1.pl.pret.	XVIII 36, 12’ ([=*kan*]?)
zalukiš-	“to take long, get postponed”		
	za-lu-ki-iš-ta	3.sg.pret.	VI 9+ ii 13 (=*kan*

			parā arḫa), L 77+ r.col. 5' ([*-ta*, ⸗*kan parā arḫa*)
zalziman	"?"		
	za-al-zi-ma-an	(see note in transliteration)	XLIX 49 ii 4'
zankilatar, n.	"compensation"		
	za-an-ki-la-tar	nom.-acc.sg.	KBo II 2 iii 36 (-*la*[-), iv 1, 9, XLIX 93, 4, L 5 r.col. 12' (-*la*-[), L 6+ iii 15
𒑱*zappantalai-*	"?"		
	𒑱*za-ap-pa-an-ta-la-an-zi*	3.pl.pres.	XLIX 93, 3 (-*a*[*n*-), L 6+ iii 14
zeḫilipšiman	"?"		
	zé-ḫi-li-ip-ši-ma-an	(see note in transliteration)	KBo II 2 ii 27, iv 25, KBo XXIII 114 obv. 20
	zé-ḫi-li-ip-ši-im-ma-an		L 87 obv. 4'
zik	"you"	pers.pron. 2.sg.	
	zi-ik	nom.	KBo II 2 ii 43, 55, iii 14
zila-, c.	"(oracle) result, outcome"		
	zi-la-aš	nom.sg.	KBo II 2 ii 24, iii 18, L 6+ ii 33', iii 39
zilatii̯a	"in future"	adv.	
	zi-la-ti-a°		L 6+ ii 44'
	zi-la-ti-i̯a		XVI 58 iii 6' (-*i̯*]*a*)
ziladuu̯a	"in future"	adv.	
	zi-la-du-u̯a		L 6+ iii 60
zilau̯an	"?"	(technical term in augury)	
	(abbr.) *zi-an*		KBo II 6+ iv 15, 22, KBo XVI 98 iv 2' (-*a*]*n*?), XVI 46 iv 5
zizaḫi-, c.	"bladderworm"		
	(abbr.) *zi*		KBo II 2 iii 9, 29, iv 16, 32, KBo II

			6+ i 43', KBo XVI 98 i 8, ii 8, KBo XXIII 114 obv. 16
zulki-, c.	"depression(?)"	(Hurrian technical term in extispicy)	
	zu-ul-kiš		KBo II 6+ ii 28 (*-u*]*l-*), KBo XXIII 114 obv. 10 (*zu*[-)

Fragmentary and acephalous

]-AḪ-*ḫi*		1.sg.pres.	KBo XVI 98 i 12
]x-*ak*			XLIX 49 iii 10'
-]*am-mi*			XLIX 49 iii 11'
an[-			L 87 obv. 2' (or ^{d}[?)
a[*n*-			XVI 46 i 2' (or ^{d}[?)
-]x-*an*			KBo II 6+ ii 14, KBo XVI 98 iv 4', L 6+ iii 26
-]x-*an*(-)x[			KBo IX 151, 11'
x-*an*			KBo II 6+ iii 57
x-*an-da*			LII 92 i 3'
]x-*an-za*			XVI 16 rev. 22
(-)]*ap-pa-an-zi*		3.pl.pres.	XLIX 49 ii 11'
... *-aš*			XVIII 6 i 20'
-]x-*aš*			L 5 r.col. 13'
a-š[*a*-			VIII 27 (+) i 1'
x-*at*			L 6+ i 1', L 87 obv. 11'
]x-*at-ti*			KBo XVI 98 iv 23"
]-*az*			XXII 13, 1'
e-x[			VIII 27 (+) i 15'
]x-*e*			KBo XVI 98 i 28
]x-*e-aš*			XVI 16 obv. 17'
]*ḫu*[			XLIX 49 iii 1
i-x[			KBo XXIII 114 rev. 3'
-]*i*			KBo II 2 i 36, KBo II 6+ ii 27

]x-*i*		XLIX 49 iii 7
-]x-*i̯*[*a*(-)		KBo II 6+ ii 12
]x-*i̯a* x x		XVIII 6 i 1'
-*i̯*]*a*		XLIX 2 i 5'
x x -*i̯a-aš*(-)	nom.sg.c.	KBo II 6+ iii 56
-]x-*i̯a-za*		XXII 35 iii 3'
-]*i-nu-ut*	3.sg.pret.?	L 77+ left col.
]x-*ir*[		L 77+ r.col. 1'
-]*iš*		XVI 46 iv 1
-*i*]*š*(-*kán*)		KBo XVI 98 iv 6'
[o -] x-*iš*	3.sg.pret.	L 6+ iii 20
-]*it*		XLIX 49 iii 4
ki-x[		XXII 35 iii 17'
x-*ki-ir*	3.pl.pret.	XVI 16 obv. 19'
𒑱*la-a*-x[		KBo II 6+ ii 21
x x-*le-e-eš*		XVI 16 rev. 11
-*m*]*a-aš*		L 5 r.col. 3'
me-x[		VIII 27 (+) i 8'
⌈*mu*⌉?[-		VIII 27(+) i 13'
na-x[		VIII 27 (+) i 4', 7'
na-x?-*an*		KBo II 6+ iii 57
na-aš-x[		VIII 27 (+) i 19'
(-)]*na-aš*[(-)		XVIII 36, 1'
]*ne*?[		VI 9+ iii 3'
(-)]*nu*?		KBo XXIII 114 obv. 30
-*n*]*u-ut*	3.sg.pret.	XLIX 2 i 25'
-]x-*nu-zi*		KBo IX 151, 10'
]x-*ra-an-za*	part. nom.sg.c.?	XLIX 49 iii 8'
-]x-*ri-i̯a-an-z*[*i*		KBo IX 151, 9'
-]*ša*?		KBo II 6+ ii 20
]x-*ša-ni*[		KBo II 2 ii 9
-*š*/*t*]*a-ri*	3.sg.pres. MP	KBo XVI 98 i 13
x x-*š*/*ta-aš*		XLIX 2 i 7'
]x-*ši* (or -*LIM*?)		KBo XVI 98 i 11
da-[		VIII 27 (+) i 6'
da-x[		XXII 35 ii 3'
]x-*da*		KBo II 2 i 37
tar-x[		KBo XXIII 114 rev. 4'
]x-*ta-ri*	3.sg.pres. MP	XLIX 2 i 23'
ti[-		XLIX 2 i 4'
-]x-*ti*		L 6+ ii 6'
-]*ti-ši*		KBo XVI 98 i 23

x-*du*?		XVIII 6 i 16’
-]⸢*du*⸣		XVI 58 ii 14
ú-e-x x[		L 87 obv. 9’
-]x-*u-en*	1.pl.pret.	10/v, 1’
-]*uš*		VI 9+ ii 21
]x-*uš*		KBo XXIII 114 obv. 9
u̯[*a*-		XVI 46 ii 1’
]x-*u̯a*		KBo XXIII 114 obv. 31
]x x x x-*za*		KBo XVI 98 i 10
... x x-*zi*		XVIII 6 i 15’
-*z*]*i*		VIII 27 (+) left edge a 2, 5, XVIII 6 i 4’, 6’, 7’

B. *Glossenkeil words*

For words preceded by one or more Glossenkeile (𒑱/𒑲) see above *aršulai*-, (SISKUR) *mantalli*-, *mataššu*, *paš*-, *šakkuri̯a*-, *tapašša*- and *zappantalai*- as well as *la-a*-x[in the fragmentary and acephalous section.

C. *Sumerograms*[3]

AMA	“mother”		
	AMA		KBo XXIII 114 obv. 15 (A]MA)
AN	“heaven”	Akkad. *ŠAMÛ*	
	AN-*E*	obl.pl.	KBo II 6+ i 5’, 21’, 22’, iii 1, 40, 50 (all in combination with ^{d}UTU)
BA.BA.ZA	“porridge”		
	BA.BA.ZA		XVI 16 rev. 3
BAL	“to offer, dedicate”	Hitt. *išpant*- /*šipant*-	

[3] Unless otherwise indicated (“Sum.”, “Akkad.”) the grammatical determinations concern the Hittite phonetic complements.

	BAL-*i*	3.sg.pres.	KBo XVI 98 ii 4 (=*za*), ii 5 (=*kan*)
	BAL-*an-ti*		KBo II 6+ iii 21 (-*za*), 32 (-*za*), VIII 27 (+) iv 11' (B[AL), XXII 35 iii 7' ([=*za*]?), 11' (-*za*)
	BAL-*an-zi*	3.pl.pres.	KBo II 2 iv 10, KBo XVI 98 iv 23", L 6+ iii 54 (=*za*), 55 (=*za*)
	BAL-*u-an-zi*	inf. I	XVI 32, 15' (*arḫa*), 17' (*arḫa* B[AL-), 20' (*arḫa*), L 6+ ii 18'(-]*an*-)
	BAL-*u-u̯a-an-zi*		KBo II 6+ iii 31, 33
	BAL-*an-za-kir*	3.pl.pret. -*ške*-	KBo II 2 iv 12
	BAL-*an-za-ki-u-u̯a-an*	supinum -*ške*-	KBo II 2 iv 13
	BAL-*eš-ki-u-u̯a-an*		XVI 32, 7' (see comm. on this form)
BAL-*nu*-	"to stir up, make rebellious"	Hitt. *u̯akkarii̯anu*-	
	BAL-*nu-ut*	3.sg.pret.	XLIX 2 i 16'
BÁN	(measure of volume)		
	BÁN		XVI 16 rev. 3 (2x), 4 (3x)
BAPPIR	"wort"		
	BAPPIR		XVI 16 rev. 19
GIŠBÚGIN	"trough"		
	GIŠBÚGIN		XVI 16 rev. 14
DAB	"to take, seize, hold"	Hitt. *epp-/app-*	
	DAB-*an*	part. nom.-acc.sg.n.	XVI 16 obv. 15'
GIŠDAG	"dais, throne"	Hitt. *ḫalmašuitt*(*i*)-	
	GIŠDAG-*ti*	dat.-loc.sg.	KBo XVI 98 iv 26"

	^{GIŠ}DAG.ḪI.A	Sum. pl.	KBo II 6+ i 33', XXII 35 iii 4', L 6+ i 33', ii 40', iii 49, 10/v, 3' (Ḫ]I.A)
	see also ^{d}DAG-*ti*(-)		
DINGIR	"deity"	Hitt. *šiu*(*n*)-, c., Akkad. *ILU*(*M*)	
	DINGIR-*LUM*	Akkad. nom.sg.	KBo II 2 i 19, 27, 52, ii 10, 19, 25, 47, iii 19 (DIN]GIR), 21 (]-*LUM*), 24, 37, 43, iv 2, 14, KBo II 6+ i 37', 39', 45', ii 36, 37, 47, iii 12, 14, 46, 48, 63, 65, iv 7, KBo XVI 98 i 2, ii 5, iii 14', iv 19", 23", KBo XXIII 114 obv. 21, XVI 16 obv. 1' (DI]NGIR-*L*[*UM*), 5', 10', 14', 20', 29', rev. 2 (DING]IR-), 9, 12, 16, 20, 27, left edge 1, XVI 20, 7' (-*LU*]*M*), XVI 32, 11', XVI 46 ii 4', XVI 58 iii 5', 10', 11', XLIX 2 i 7', L 6+ ii 42', L 87 obv. 3' (DI]NGIR-), 5', rev. 5', 8' ([-*LU*]*M*)
	DINGIR-*LIM*	Akkad. gen.sg.	KBo II 2 i 23, iv 11, KBo XVI 98

			ii 14, XVI 16 obv. 4', rev. 12, 13, 15, 20, XVI 46 ii 3', XLIX 49 ii 13', L 6+ iii 38, L 87 rev. 6', 11'
	DINGIR-*LIM*-*ni*	dat.-loc.sg.	KBo II 6+ ii 33
	DINGIR.MEŠ-*ni*		KBo II 6 iii 2
	DINGIR.MEŠ	Sum. pl.	KBo II 2 i 49, KBo II 6+ i 10', 11', 21', 32', ii 1, 40, iii 32, 39, 43, iv 6, 8, KBo XVI 98 i 4, ii 17, iv 24", 25", VI 9+ ii 3 (.M]EŠ), VIII 27 (+) i 2', iv 2', XVI 32, 4', 8', XVI 58 ii 13(?), iii 3', XVIII 36, 8', 15', XXII 35 iii 13', XLIX 49 ii 15', XLIX 93, 5, L 6+ ii 38', iii 1, 16, 17, 48 (DINGI]R.), L 87 obv. 7' (DI]NGIR.), 10', 10/v, 2'
	DINGIR.MEŠ-*aš*	nom.pl.	L 6+ ii 52'
	DINGIR.MEŠ-*aš*	dat.-loc.pl.	KBo XVI 98 iv 25", VI 9+ ii 10 (DINGI]R.), 11, XVI 20, 18' (DINGIR.[), L 77+ r.col. 12', 13' ([-*aš*)
	DINGIR[		VI 9+ iii 14'
DINGIR-*LIM*-*tar*, n.	"divinity, divine statue"	Hitt. **šiunatar*, n.	
	DINGIR-*LIM*-*tar*	nom.-acc.sg.	KBo II 2 ii 21, XXII 13, 8', LII 92 i 9'

DÙ	"to do, make; to become (MP)"	Hitt. (*an*)*iịa*-, *ešša*-, *kiš*- (dep.)	
	DÙ-*mi*	1.sg.pres.	KBo XVI 98 ii 13 (*=za*)
	DÙ-*an-zi*	3.pres.pl.	KBo II 6+ i 31', iii 43, 60, L 5 r.col. 9' (D[Ù-)
	DÙ-*ir*	3.pret.pl.	L 6+ iii 47 (D]Ù)
	DÙ-*ri*	3.sg.pres. MP	KBo XVI 98 i 6
DUB	"tablet"		
	DUB.5.KAM		KBo II 6+ iv 26
DUG	"jar"		
	DUG		XVI 16 obv. 9'
DUḪ	"to loosen, free"	Hitt. *la*(*i*)-	
	DUḪ-*ḫi*[(?)	1.sg.pres.(??)	VIII 27 (+) i 3'
	DUḪ-*ši*	2.sg.pres.	XXII 35 ii 7', XLIX 93, 14
	DUḪ-*ri*	3.sg.pres. MP	L 6+ ii 43' (*=kan*), iii 59
	DUḪ-*ta-ri*		KBo II 6+ i 38'
DUMU	"child, son"		
	DUMU.MEŠ	Sum. pl.	KBo II 6+ ii 55, iii 6, 62 ([MEŠ]), VIII 27 (+) iv 6', XVI 32, 14', 19', XXII 35 iii 15', L 6+ ii 29', iii 33, 53, LII 92 iv 6'
	DUMU.MEŠ-*iš*(-)	acc.pl.c.	L 6+ iii 52
DUMU-*atar*, n.	"progeny"		
	DUMU-*an-na-aš*	gen.sg.	KBo II 2 iii 2, 6, 10, 14, 30
DUMU.DUMU	"grandson"		
	DUMU.DUMU		KBo II 6+ i 12', 36'
DUMU.NITA	"male child, son"		
	DUMU.NITA		XVI 16 obv. 24'
É	"house, estate"	Hitt. *pir*/*parn*-, n., Akkad. *BĪTU*(*M*)	
	É		XVI 16 rev. 13, L 6+ iii 9
	É-*TUM*	Akkad. nom.sg.	XVI 32, 2'

	É-*TI*	Akkad. gen.sg.	KBo II 6+ i 35', KBo IX 151, 7' (É-]), XXII 35 ii 11', 13', L 6+ ii 51', iii 7
	É-*ir*	nom.-acc.sg.n.	XXII 35 ii 15' (?), L 6+ ii 51', 53' (É[-)
	É-*ir-za*	abl.	L 6+ iii 59
	É[		XVI 16 obv. 4'
É.DINGIR-*LIM*	"temple"		
	É.DINGIR-*LIM*	Akkad. gen.sg.	KBo XXIII 114 obv. 12, 30 (2x), XVI 16 obv. 27', 29', rev. 3, 24 (É[.), L 87 obv. 3', 5'
	É.DINGIR-*LIM-aš*	gen.sg.?	KBo XXIII 114 obv. 7
É.GAL	"palace"		
	É.GAL.ḪI.A	Sum.pl.	XVI 16 obv. 18'
É.LUGAL	"palace"		
	É.LUGAL		XVI 46 i 10', XVIII 6 iv 10, XLIX 2 i 24'
É.TU_7	"kitchen"		
	É.TU_7		XVI 16 rev. 12
EGIR(-)	"behind, after, later"	Hitt. *appa(n)*	
	EGIR		KBo II 2 i 16, 17, KBo II 6+ i 2', 3', 17', 19', 40', 41', ii 21, 27, 28, iii 10 (2x), 34, 35, 53 (2x), 57 (E]GIR), 58, iv 1, 2, 15, 20, KBo XVI 98 i 2, 15, 19 (EGI]R), ii 2, 6 (E]GIR), 9, iii 1', 10', 11', 16' (E]GIR), 17' (E]GIR), iv 6', KBo XXIII 114 obv. 10, 19, 20, VI 9+ ii 18,

		iii 13' (EGI[R), VIII 27 (+) i 11, XVI 46 i 7', 16', ii 7', iv 2 (EGI[R), 4, 10, 17, 18, XLIX 2 ii 7', XLIX 49 ii 3', L 5 r.col. 8'
	⸗*kan* E. GAM *uu̯a-*	KBo II 6+ iii 56, 58(?), iv 12, KBo XVI 98 ii 25 (verb left out), XVI 46 iv 16
	⸗*kan* E. UGU *uu̯a-*	KBo II 6+ iv 19, 21, KBo XVI 98 i 14, 17, ii 18, XVI 46 i 6', 8', 11', 13', 17', iv 9, 11, XVI 58 ii 7, XLIX 49 ii 17' (EGI]R), 18' (EGI]R), 19', 20'
EGIR-*pa*		KBo XVI 98 iv 26", XVI 16 obv. 27', XLIX 2 i 16'
	⸗*za*⸗*kan* E. *epp-/app-*	KBo II 2 ii 31
	E. *ḫuittii̯a-*/SUD	KBo II 6+ i 39', ii 37, iii 49, 66, L 6+ ii 45', iii 57, 61
	-*kan* E. *ištapp-*	XLIX 93, 6 (E]GIR-), L 5 r.col. 2' (E]GIR-*p*[*a*), L 6+ ii 53', iii 17
	E. *pai-/pii̯a-*	L 6+ iii 20
	E. *anda peda-*	XVI 32, 5'
	⸗*za* E. ME	XVIII 6 ii 1', XLIX 2 i 26'
	nominal sentence(?)	KBo II 6+ iii 27
	[verb lost]	XVIII 36, 19'
EGIR-*an*	E. *ar-* (dep.)	KBo XVI 98 ii 16, XLIX 49 ii 15'

		E. *arḫa* ME	KBo II 6+ i 45', XVI 20, 7'
		E. SIxSÁ	KBo IX 151, 6' (EGI]R-)
		[verb lost]	L 6+ ii 55'
EGIR-*panda*	"later"	adv. Hitt. *appanda*	
	EGIR-*pa-an-da*		VI 9+ ii 16 (EGI]R-), XVIII 36, 15' (EGI]R-)
EGIR-*izzi-*	"last, latest, hindmost"	Hitt. *appezzi-*	
	EGIR-*iz-zi*	dat.-loc.sg.	VIII 27 (+) left edge b 3
EGIR-*ŠÚ*	"later, behind"	adv.	
	EGIR-*ŠÚ*		KBo II 2 iii 29, KBo XXIII 114 obv. 16
EGIR.UD.KAM	"future"		
	EGIR.UD.KAM		XVIII 6 iv 2
EME	"tongue, curse"		
	EME		KBo II 6+ i 6', 8' (E]ME), 12', 13', 31', 32', ii 38, 43, 50, 55, iii 4, 6, 42, 43, VIII 27 (+) iv 2', L 6+ ii 32', 35', 36', 41', 49', 57', iii 48, 10/v, 1' (EM[E)
^{LÚ}EN.NU.UN	"watchman, guard"		
	$^{\text{LÚ.MEŠ}}$EN.NU.UN	Sum.pl.	XVI 16 rev. 7
^{LÚ}ENGAR	"cultivator"	Akkad. *IKKARUTU*(*M*)	
	$^{\text{LÚ.MEŠ}}$ENGAR. MEŠ-*TIM*	Sum.pl. and Akkad. gen.sg.	XVI 16 rev. 5
^{MUNUS}ENSI	"divination priestess"		
	^{MUNUS}ENSI		L 87 rev. 13'
ÉRIN.MEŠ	"(army) troops"		
	ÉRIN.MEŠ		KBo XVI 98 i 1 (*šarikuu̯a*), i (UKU.ÛŠ)

$EZEN_4$	"festival"		
	$EZEN_4$		XVI 16 obv. 9', 14', XVIII 36, 19', 20', L 6+ iii 10
	$EZEN_4$.MEŠ	Sum. pl.	KBo II 6+ ii 16, KBo XVI 98 ii 12, 13, KBo XXIII 114 obv. 26, 27 (E]ZEN_4), XLIX 49 ii 12', L 5 r.col. 5'
	EZ[EN_4		KBo XXIII 114 obv. 26
GA	"milk"		
	GA		XVI 16 rev. 4
GAL	"great, big"		
	GAL		KBo II 6+ ii 41
GAM(-)	"down, under, with"	Hitt. *katta*(*n*)	
	GAM	G. *ari̯a-*	KBo II 6+ i 30', iii 41, VIII 27 (+) iv 1', L 6+ ii 49', 56', LII 92 i 8'
		G. *ḫark-*	XVIII 6 i 18', iv 9
		G. 𒑱*paš-*	XLIX 2 i 14', 18'
		≈*kan* EGIR G. *u̯u̯a-*	KBo II 6+ iii 56, iv 12, KBo XVI 98 ii 25 (verb left out), XVI 46 iv 16
		≈*za* G. *u̯emii̯a-/IKŠUD*	KBo II 6+ iv 12
		no verb	KBo XVI 98 i 8
		[verb lost]	KBo II 6+ iii 58, KBo XVI 98 iv 6', VI 9+ iii 4', LII 92 i 5'
	GAM-*an*	G. *ḫamank-*	KBo II 6+ ii 13
		G. *arḫa ki-*/GAR	XVIII 36, 13'
		≈*za* G. *malai-*	KBo XVI 98 ii 17
		G. *pai-*/*pii̯a-*/SUM	L 6+ iii 14 (-*a*[*n*)

		⸗*kan* G. *parā nai-*	XVI 32, 11'
		G. *šekk-/šakk-*	XVIII 36, 16'
		⸗*za* G. *u̯emii̯a-/IKŠUD*	XVI 58 ii 4
	GAM-*n*°	G. *pai-/pii̯a-/SUM*	XLIX 93, 4
GAR	"to lie, be laid down"	Hitt. *ki-*	
	GAR-*ri*	3.sg.pres.	KBo II 2 iii 9, iv 16, 32, KBo II 6+ i 43', KBo XVI 98 i 8, ii 8, KBo XXIII 114 obv. 16, XLIX 49 ii 5'
	GAR-*ru*	imp. 3.sg.	XVIII 36, 13' (GAM-*an arḫa*), LII 92 iv 8'
GE_6-*ešš-*	"to become dark"	Hitt. *dankuešš-*	
	GE_6-*iš-zi*	3.sg.pres.	VIII 27 (+) left edge b 1 (-*z*[*i*)
GEŠTIN	"wine"		
	GEŠTIN		XVI 16 obv. 18', rev. 4, 26
GEŠTUG	"ear"	Hitt. *ištaman*(*a*)-, c.	
	GEŠTUG-*an*	acc.sg.	KBo XVI 98 i 5
GÍD.DA	"long"		
	GÍD.DA		KBo II 6+ ii 56, iv 8, XVIII 6 iv 4, XLIX 2 i 9' (GÍ[D.)
GIDIM	"deceased, spirit"		
	GIDIM		KBo II 6+ i 11' 13', 14', 15', 36', ii 20, 46, 52, 53, 55, iii 7, 8, 19, 22, 31, 44, 46, 61, 62, VIII 27 (+) iv 6', 12', XVI 16 obv. 24', 25', XVI 32, 3', 7', 25', 26', XXII

			35 ii 7', 13', iii 5', 6', 12', XLIX 93, 18, L 6+ ii 50', iii 9, 16, 10/v, 5' (G[IDIM)
GIG(*-ant-*, c.)	"disease"	Hitt. *irmanant-*, c.	
	GIG		KBo II 2 i 10, 28, ii 26, 29, KBo II 6+ ii 33 (GI[G), 41, iii 14, 38, VI 9+ ii 23, XVI 20, 8', 13' (G[IG), XVIII 36, 16' (GI]G), XXII 13, 3' (G]IG)
	GIG-*an-za*	nom.sg.	LII 92 i 5'
GIM-*an*	"when, as, how"	subordin. conj., Hitt. *maḫḫan*	
	GIM-*an*		KBo XVI 98 ii 11, 13, KBo XXIII 114 rev. 1' (GIM[-), XVI 32, 8', 10', 11', 28', XVIII 6 i 7', iv 1' (G]IM-), XXII 35 ii 3', iii 17', XLIX 49 ii 12' (G]I[M-), XLIX 93, 9, L 5 r.col. 5', L 6+ ii 36', iii 1 (-]*an*), 26, 28, 41, L 87 rev. 7', 9'
GÍN	"shekel"		
	GÍN		KBo XXIII 114 obv. 27 (2x)
GIR$_4$	"ceramics"		
	GIR$_4$.ḪI.A	Sum.pl.	XVI 16 rev. 14
GISKIM	"sign, omen"		
	GISKIM		KBo II 2 iii 3
GIŠ.ḪUR	"tablet"		
	GIŠ.ḪUR		L 5 r.col. 3', L 6+ iii 12, 18
	GIŠ.ḪUR.ḪI.A	pl.	XLIX 93, 7
GU$_7$	"to eat"	Hitt. *ed-/ad-*	

	GU_7-*na*	inf. II	XVI 16 rev. 13, 15
GUB^1	"to rise"	Hitt. *arai-*	
	GUB-*iš*	3.sg.pret.	KBo II 6+ i 21', ii 32, 34, iii 26, 50, L 87 rev. 3'
	GUB-*ir*	3.pl.pret.	KBo II 6+ ii 40
	GUB-*aš*	part. adverbially used obl.(?) case	KBo XVI 98 iv 25" (or from GUB^2 = Hitt. *ar-* (dep.)?)
GUB^2	"to stand"	Hitt. *ar-* (dep.)	
	GUB-*aš*	part. adverbially used obl.(?) case	KBo XVI 98 iv 25" (or from GUB^1 = Hitt. *arai-*?)
GÙB(-*l*)*a-*	"left"		
	GÙB-*aš*	nom.sg.c.	KBo II 2 iv 16
	GÙB-*la-aš*		KBo II 6+ ii 29
	GÙB-*an*	acc.sg.c.	KBo II 2 ii 14, 37, iii 1, 23, KBo XVI 98 i 9, iii 17'
	GÙB-*la-an*		XVI 16 obv. 21'
	GÙB-*za*	abl.	KBo II 2 iv 30, 32, KBo II 6+ i 18', 42', iv 3, KBo XVI 98 ii 1, 8 (GÙ]B-), KBo XXIII 114 obv. 5, 24 (G]ÙB-), XLIX 49 ii 4'
	GÙB-*la-aš*	nom.pl.?	XVI 16 obv. 11', left edge 2
	GÙB-*l*[*a-*		KBo II 6+ ii 27
	GÙB[-		XVI 16 obv. 3'
	GÙ[B-		KBo XXIII 114 obv. 14
GÙB-*latar*, n.	"leftness, unfavorable condition"		
	GÙB-*la-tar*	nom.-acc.sg.	KBo II 6+ ii 2
GUL	"to hit, beat, strike"	Hitt. *u̯alḫ-*	
	GUL-*ḫi-ir*	3.pl.pret.	XVI 16 obv. 14'

GUN-*liš*	"?"	(technical term in augury[4])	
	GUN-*li*$_{12}$-*an*		XVI 46 i 11', 12' (G]UN-), 14', 17' (G]UN-), iv 3, 4, 7, 9, 10, 11, 15 (2x), 17 (G]UN-)
	GUN-*liš*		KBo II 6+ iv 13, 22, XVI 46 iv 11
	GUN-*l*[*iš* or -*l*[*i*$_{12}$-*an*		XVI 46 i 7', iii 5'
	GUN(-) ?		KBo II 6+ iii 56
GUNNI	"oven, hearth"	Hitt. *ḫašša-*	
	GUNNI		XVIII 6 i 21', iv 5, XLIX 2 i 10', 13', 14', 17', 22'
	GUNNI-*za*	abl.	XLIX 2 i 20'
GUŠKIN	"gold"		
	GUŠKIN		XVI 16 rev. 11
^{DUG}ḪAB.ḪAB	"jug"		
	^{DUG}ḪAB.ḪAB		XVI 16 rev. 4
^{LÚ}ḪAL	"diviner, seer"		
	^{LÚ}ḪAL		KBo II 2 ii 20, KBo II 6+ ii 42, 49, iii 3, 52, XVIII 36, 18', 22', XXII 12, 5', XXII 13, 7', XXII 35 ii 9', 10', XLIX 93, 16 (Ḫ[AL), L 6+ ii 33', 47', iii 6, 45
ḪUL-*aḫḫ-*	"to treat badly"	Hitt. *idalau̯aḫḫ-*	
	ḪUL-*aḫ-ḫu-un*	1.sg.pret.	XVI 32, 21', L 6+ ii 16'
	ḪUL-*aḫ-ta*	3.sg.pret.	XVI 32, 16', 21'
ḪUL-(*a*)*u̯ant-*	"bad, evil"	Hitt. *idalau̯ant-*	
	ḪUL-*u-an-za*	nom.sg.c.	L 6+ iii 61
ḪUL-*a*/*uu̯atar*, n.	"badness, evil"	Hitt. *idala*/*uu̯atar*	

[4] It is by no means certain that GUN is indeed a Sumerogram; the transliteration merely follows what was hitherto customary (see also Chapter VI, commentary ad KBo II 6+ iii 56).

	ḪUL-*u-an-ni*	dat.-loc.sg.	XVI 58 iii 7' (ḪU]L-), L 6+ ii 45'
ḪUL-*lu-*	"bad, evil"	Hitt. *idalu-*	
	ḪUL-*lu*	nom.-acc.sg.n.	KBo II 6+ i 24', ii 2, 47, 57 (-*l*[*u*), iii 13, VIII 27 (+) left edge b 2, L 6+ iii 43, 58, 59, 64
	ḪUL-*u-i*	dat.-loc.sg.	XLIX 2 i 7'
	ḪUL-*u-u̯a-z°*	abl.	XVI 20, 14'
ḪUR.SAG	"mountain"		
	ḪUR.SAG-*i*	dat.-loc.sg.	XVI 16 rev. 7
ḪUŠ	"to fear"	Hitt. *naḫḫ-*	
	ḪUŠ-*u-e-ni*	1.pl.pres.	XXII 12, 4' (-*n*[*i*), L 77+ r.col. 9'
Ì.NUN	"butter"		
	Ì.NUN		XVI 16 rev. 14
IGI-*anda*	"against, opposite, counter-"	adv., Hitt. *menaḫḫanda*	
	IGI-*an-da*		KBo II 6+ i 42', iv 3, 17, KBo XVI 98 ii 23, XVI 32, 9', 15', XXII 35 iii 6', 10', L 6+ iii 53
IGI-*zi-*	"first, foremost, chief"	Hitt. *ḫantezzi-*	
	IGI-*zi-iš*	nom.sg.c.	KBo II 6+ i 40', 41', ii 14 (-*i*]*š*), 15 (-]*zi-*), iii 9, 10, 34, 35, 52, 53, iv 1, 2, VI 9+ ii 5, 6, 18 (-*i*]*š*), L 5 r.col. 14' (-]*iš*)
	IGI-*zi*	nom.-acc.sg./pl.n.	KBo II 2 i 15, 16, KBo II 6+ i 13', 16', 17', ii 26, 27, KBo XVI 98 i 8, ii 1, 6, 7, iii 11', 16' (2x), KBo

			XXIII 114 obv. 4, 9, 10, 19, XVI 58 ii 10, L 5 r.col. 8' (I[GI-), L 87 obv. 11'
^{LÚ}IGI.MUŠEN	"augur"		
	^{LÚ}IGI.MUŠEN		KBo II 6+ i 25', ii 3, iii 16, 54, iv 10, XVI 58 ii 1 (MUŠ]EN), XXII 35 ii 8', XLIX 93, 15, L 6+ ii 34', 47', iii 6 (^{L}[^{Ú}), 45
	$^{\text{LÚ.MEŠ}}$]IGI. MUŠEN	Sum.pl.	KBo XVI 98 i 18
INIM	"word, affair, deed"	Hitt. *memii̯a(n)-* /*memin-*, c. or *uttar*, n.	
	INIM		KBo II 2 ii 26, iv 17, 22, 23, 27, 34, KBo II 6+ i 38', 39', iii 47, 48, 64, 65, XVI 32, 27', XVI 58 iii 6', L 6+ ii 43', 44', 48', 56', 57', L 87 rev. 2'(?)
	INIM-*š*°	nom.sg.c.	XVI 58 iii 4'
	INIM-*za*	abl.	KBo II 6+ i 38', XVIII 6 i 14', L 6+ ii 43', iii 43, 59
IR	"to ask"	Hitt. *u̯ek-*	
	IR-*u-en*	1.pl.pret.	KBo II 6+ i 42', iv 3, XVI 16 rev. 1
IR	"(oracle) question"		
	IR-*TUM*	Akkad. nom.sg.	KBo II 2 i 9, 18, 26, 34, 48, ii 1, 15, KBo II 6+ i 4', 9', 20', 25', 44', ii 30, 42, 49, iii 3, 11, 16, 24,

			36, 52, 54, iv 5, 10, VI 9+ ii 7, 19, XVI 58 ii 1, 10 (-*T*]*UM*), XLIX 49 ii 7' (-*TU*]*M*)
	IR-*TAM*	Akkad. acc.sg.	KBo XVI 98 ii 17
ITU	"month"		
	ITU		XLIX 2 i 2'
	ITU.8.KAM		VI 9+ ii 2
	ITU.12.KAM		XVI 20, 11'
	ITU.KAM.ḪI.A	Sum.pl.	XVIII 6 i 13'
	ITU[		VI 9+ iii 9', XVI 20, 3'
IZI	"fire"		
	IZI		KBo II 6+ ii 40
KAxU	"mouth"	Hitt. *aiš-*/*iš-*, n.	
	KAxU		XVI 46 i 15'
	KAxU-*iš*	nom.-acc.sg.	XLIX 2 i 15'
	KAxU-*i*	dat.-loc.sg.	KBo II 2 iii 17
KA.GAG.A	(type of beer)		
	KA.GAG.A		XVI 16 obv. 9'
… .KAM	see DUB, ITU, MU and UD		
KAR	"to find"	Hitt. *u̯emii̯a-*	
	KAR-*i̯a-zi*	3.sg.pres.	KBo II 2 i 55 (*anda*)
	KAR-*at*	3.sg.pret.	XVIII 6 i 26, XLIX 2 i 21'
	KAR-*u-en*	1.pl.pret.	L 6+ iii 27
KASKAL	"road"	Hitt. *palša-*, Akkad. *ḪARRĀNU*(*M*)	
	KASKAL		KBo II 6+ ii 28, KBo XVI 98 ii 16, iii 17'
	KASKAL-*ši*	dat.-loc.sg.	KBo II 6+ iii 19, VIII 27 (+) iv 9', XVI 32, 12', XXII 35 iii 16'
	KASKAL-*NI*	Akkad. gen.sg.	KBo II 6+ iii 57, iv 15, 20, KBo XVI 98 i 15, XVI 46 i 7', 16', ii 7', iv 4, 10, 18

KASKAL-*šiaḫḫ-*	"to put on the road, dispatch"		
	KASKAL-*ši-aḫ-mi*	1.sg.pres.	XVI 46 iv 14
KAŠ	"beer"		
	KAŠ		XVI 16 obv. 19', 20', 25'
KI.MIN	"etc., ditto"		
	KI.MIN		KBo II 2 i 56, ii 40, iii 16, 28, 43 (KI[.), iv 5, 14, 29, KBo II 6+ ii 14, 45, iii 46, KBo XVI 98 ii 5, iv 23", KBo XXIII 114 obv. 9, 14, 18, 29, XVI 16 obv. 12', 16', 22', 31', rev. 10, 17, 22, left edge 3, XVI 20, 5', 13', XVI 46 iv 14, L 6+ iii 6
KIN	"to do, make, perform"	Hitt. (*an*)*i͡ia-*, *ešša-*/*išša-*	
	KIN-*an-zi*	3.pl.pres.	XVI 32, 28' (*arḫa*), XVI 46 iv 13 (*arḫa*)
	KIN-*u-an-zi*	inf. I	XVI 32, 23' (*arḫa*)
KIN	(oracle type)		
	KIN		KBo II 2 i 10, 19, 27, 35 (KI[N), 49, ii 2, 16, KBo II 6+ i 4', 9', 20', 44', ii 30, 39, 46, 56, iii 11, 24, 36, 50, iv 5, KBo XVI 98 iv 18" (K[IN), 23", XVI 20, 5', 13', XVI 58 iii 8', XLIX 49 ii 7', L 77+ r.col. 9'
KÙ.BABBAR	"silver"		
	KÙ.BABBAR		XVI 16 rev. 11

^{LÚ}KÙ.DÍM	"smith"		
	$^{LÚ.MEŠ}$KÙ.DÍM	Sum.pl.	L 87 obv. 7', 9'
KU_6	"fish"		
	KU_6-*un*	acc.sg.	XVIII 6 iv 6, XLIX 2 i 13', 27' ([-*un*?)
KUR	"land"	Akkad. *MĀTU*(*M*)	
	KUR-*TUM*	Akkad. nom.sg.	KBo II 2 i 10
	KUR-*TI*	Akkad. gen.sg.	VIII 27 (+) left edge b 2
LÀL	"honey"		
	LÀL		XVI 16 rev. 5
LÚ	"man"		
	LÚ.MEŠ	Sum.pl.	KBo XXIII 114 obv. 30 (É.DINGIR-*LIM*), XVI 16 obv. 18' (É.GAL.ḪI.A), 26' (KUR *Arzauu̯a*), rev. 3 (É.DINGIR-*LIM*), 6 (^{URU}*Araūnna*), 24 (É.DINGIR-*LIM*), L 87 obv. 2 (^{d}[)
LUGAL	"king"	Hitt. *ḫaššu-*	
	LUGAL		KBo II 6+ ii 32, 34, 56, iii 25 (2x), 50, XVI 16 obv. 8', XVI 32, 10', XVIII 6 ii 3', iv 9, XLIX 2 i 9', 19', ii 10', L 77+ r.col. 10'
	LUGAL-*uš*	nom.sg.	KBo II 2 i 35 (-]*uš*), KBo II 6+ i 22', iii 1, 37, (LUG[AL), iv 6, KBo XVI 98 ii 29, VI 9+ iii 11', XVI 20, 16', XVI 58 iii 8'
	LUGAL-x[		VIII 27 (+) i 16'

LUGAL-*uiznatar*, n. / LUGAL-*UTTU*(*M*)	"kingship"	Hitt. **ḫaššuiznatar*, Akkad. *ŠARRŪTU*(*M*)	
	LUGAL-*u-iz-na-ni*	dat.-loc.sg.	VI 9+ ii 12, 15 (-*n*]*i*), 24 (-*n*[*a*-), XVI 20, 2' (LUGAL[-), 10'
	LUGAL-*iz-na-ni*		XVI 20, 11', XVIII 36, 11', 12' (LUG]AL-), 14' (-*i*]*z*-), 14' (LU[GAL-), 17' (]-*iz*-), XXII 13, 2', 4', L 77+ r.col. 4', 15' (-*n*[*i*)
	LUGAL-*iz-na-an-ni*		KBo II 2 i 32, KBo XVI 98 ii 12, XLIX 49 iii 12' (LUG]AL-)
	LUGAL-*UT-TI*	Akkad. gen.sg.	KBo II 6+ i 32', 33', VIII 27 (+) iv 2' (-*U*[*T*), 3', XVIII 6 i 5', 17' (-*U*[*T*-), L 6+ ii 38, 39 (LUG]AL-), iii 1 (-*U*[*T*-), 4, 48, 49, 51 (LUG[AL-*U*]*T*-), 10/v, 2'
^{LÚ}MÁŠDA	"pauper, poor man"		
	^{LÚ}MÁŠDA		XVI 16 rev. 13, 14, 19
ME^{1}	"to take"	Hitt. *dā*-	
	ME-*an-zi*	3.pl.pres.	KBo II 6+ i 35', iii 45, L 6+ ii 25'
	ME-*aš*	3.sg.pret.	KBo II 2 i 10, 19, 28 (=*za*), 35 (=*za*), 39 (ME[-), KBo II 6+ i 23' (=*za*), 45'(=*za* EGIR-*an arḫa*), ii 2 (=*za*), 31

			(≈*za*), 47 (≈*za*), iii 1 (≈*za*), 12 (≈*za*), 15 (≈*za*), 25 (≈*za*), 26, 28 (≈*za*), 37 (≈*za*), 50 (ME[-), iv 6 (≈*za*), 7 (≈*za*), XVI 20, 15' (-*a*[*š*), 18', XVI 58 iii 9' (≈*za*), 10' (≈*za*), 12' (≈*za*), XVIII 6 ii 1' (≈*za* EGIR-*pa*), XLIX 2 i 26' (≈*za* EGIR-*pa*), L 77+ r.col. 13'
	ME-*ir*	3.pl.pret.	KBo II 2 i 50, KBo II 6+ ii 40, VI 9+ iii 13', XVI 20, 6'
	ME-*an*	part. nom.-acc.sg.n.	KBo II 6+ i 24', iii 13, 38, VI 9+ iii 14'
	ME-*an-te-eš*	part. nom.pl.c.	KBo II 6+ i 5', 10', 21', ii 1, iii 40, iv 9
	ME[		XLIX 2 ii 12' (≈*kan arḫa*)
ME^2	"to put, place"	Hitt. *dai-/tii̯a-*	
	ME-*iš*	3.sg.pret.	KBo II 2 i 20 (≈*šan*), KBo II 6+ ii 32, iii 25, 38 (≈*kan*), 51 (≈*kan*), XLIX 93, 9, L 6+ iii 20 (M]E-; ≈*kan*)
MU(.KAM)	"year"	Hitt. *u̯et-*, c. and **u̯etantatar*, n.	
	MU		XVI 20, 9', 15'
	MU.KAM		KBo XXIII 114 obv. 26
	MU-*an*	acc.sg.	KBo II 6+ ii 34, VI 9+ ii 21, iii 13'
	MU.KAM-*n*°		KBo II 2 i 10
	MU-*ti*	dat.-loc.sg.	XVI 20, 9'

	MU-*an-ni*		VI 9+ ii 1 (M]U-), XVIII 36, 7' (-*a*]*n*-), XLIX 49 ii 14'
	MU.KAM-*an-ni*		KBo XVI 98 ii 15
	MU.2.KAM		XVI 16 obv. 17'
	MU.6.KAM		KBo XXIII 114 obv. 26
	MU.ḪI.A	Sum.pl.	KBo II 6+ ii 56, iv 8
	MU.KAM.ḪI.A		XVIII 6 iv 4, XLIX 2 i 9'
MUD	"blood(shed)"		
	MUD		XVIII 36, 17'
MUNUS	"woman"		
	MUNUS.MEŠ	Sum. pl.	KBo XXIII 114 obv. 31, L 6+ iii 52
MUNUS.LUGAL	"queen"		
	MUNUS.LUGAL		KBo XVI 98 i 3 (M]UNUS.), ii 5
MUŠ	"(oracle) snake"		
	MUŠ		XVI 16 obv. 13, XVIII 6 i 17', 21', 23', 26', ii 3', 23'', iv 5, 9, 11, XLIX 2 i 9', 20' (MU]Š), ii 2', 4', 10', iii 7', XLIX 49 ii 21'
MUŠEN	"bird"		
	MUŠEN		XVI 46 iv 7
	MUŠEN.ḪI.A	Sum. pl.	KBo II 6+ i 25', iii 16, 54, iv 10, 17, KBo XVI 98 i 13, ii 18, 23, iv 1' (.[ḪI.A), XVI 46 i 5' (2x), 11', iv 2, 6, 14, XVI 58 ii 1, XLIX 49 ii 16'
^{LÚ}MUŠEN.DÙ	"bird catcher, augur"		
	^{LÚ}MUŠEN.DÙ		L 6+ iii 6 (^{L}]^{Ú})
MUŠEN *ḪURRI*	(oracle bird)		
	MUŠEN *ḪURRI*		KBo II 2 i 8, 15,

			16, 21, 33, 47, 56, KBo II 6+ i 2' (MU]ŠEN), 8', 40', 41', ii 15, 42, 45, 49, iii 3, 9, 10, 34, 52, 53, iv 1, 2, L 5 r.col. 14' (*Ḫ*[*UR*-?)
^{GIŠ}NÁ	"bed" ^{GIŠ}NÁ-*aš*	Hitt. *šašt*(*a*)-, c. dat.-loc.pl.	 XVI 16 rev. 18
NÍ.TE	"body, person" NÍ.TE		 KBo XVI 98 iv 22"
NÍG.ÚR.LÍMMU	"cattle" NÍG.ÚR.LÍMMU		 VIII 27 (+) left edge b 4
NINDA	"bread" NINDA		 XVI 16 obv. 25'
NINDA.GUR$_4$.RA	"thick bread" NINDA.GUR$_4$.RA		 KBo II 2 i 35 (<.RA>), KBo II 6+ ii 31, XVI 20, 6 (.R]A), L 6+ iii 11
NU.SIG$_5$	"unfavorable" NU.SIG$_5$		 KBo II 2 i 4, 8, 11, 16, 20, 25, 29, 33, 47, 51, 57, ii 14, 24, 28, 49, iii 1, 4, 12, 17, 23, 38 (.S[IG$_5$), iv 6, 26, 38, KBo II 6+ i 5', 8', 10' (N[U), 19', 41', ii 15 (.S[IG$_5$), 29, 41, 42, 45, 48, 49, 54, iii 2 (<NU.>?), 3, 10, 23, 35 (<<*du*>>), 51, 53, iv 2, KBo XVI 98 i 9, 21 (N]U.), ii 2 (N]U.), 9, iii 17', KBo XXIII 114

			obv. 6, 8, 11, 13, 17 (N[U.), 20, XVI 16 obv. 11', 12', 15', 16', 21', 22', 31', rev. 1, 2, 10, 16, 17, 21, 22, left edge 2, 3 (N[U.), XVI 20, 8', XXII 13, 6' (NU$^?$].), 7', XXII 35 ii 9', XLIX 49 ii 6', L 6+ iii 45 (2x), L 87 obv. 4'
NU.SIG$_5$	"to be unfavorable"		
	NU.SIG$_5$-*du*	imp. 3.sg.	KBo II 2 i 8, 10, 16, 24, 27, 33, 47, 49, ii 27, 52, iii 3, 12, 22, iv 25, KBo II 6+ i 2' (-*d*[*u*), 8', 9' (-[*du*), 17', 40', ii 21, 27, 39, 42, 46, 49, 56, iii 3, 10, 34, 53, iv 1, KBo XVI 98 i 19, ii 6, iii 1 (-[*du*), 5' (N]U.), 6' (?, .S]IG$_5$-), 10', 16', iv 18" (.S]IG$_5$-), KBo XXIII 114 obv. 2 (-*d*[*u*), 4 (-*d*]*u*), 10 (-*d*]*u*), 13, (.SI]G$_5$-), 15, 17, 19, 22, 28, VI 9+ ii 6, 18 (-*d*[*u*), XVI 16 obv. 11', 15', 21', rev. 2, 9, 16, 21, left edge 1, XVI 58 ii 11 (S]IG$_5$-), XLIX 49 ii 3', L 5 r.col. 8'

	NU.SIG$_5$-*ta*	3.sg.pret.	KBo XXIII 114 obv. 15 (.S]IG$_5$-), XXII 35 ii 10'
RA^{IṢ}	"beaten, damaged" (said of exta)	Akkad. *MAḪIṢ*	
	RA^{IṢ}	Akkad. stative	KBo II 2 ii 49, iv 32, 38, KBo II 6+ i 18', 42', iii 23, KBo XVI 98 ii 1, 8, KBo XXIII 114 obv. 17, 22 (RA[), XVI 16 obv. 16', 31', rev. 16
SAG.ME	"?"	(technical term in extispicy)	
	SAG.ME		KBo II 2 iii 12, XVI 16 rev. 17
SAG.DU	"head"		
	SAG.DU		VI 9+ ii 4, 17, XVI 20, 4', 12', XVIII 36, 9'
^{LÚ}SANGA-*UTTU*(*M*)	"priesthood"		
	^{LÚ}SANGA-*UT-TA*	Akkad. acc.sg.	XVI 32, 12'
SIxSÁ	"to ascertain (through an oracle inquiry)"	Hitt. *ḫandai-*	
	SIxSÁ-*ri*	3.sg.pres. MP	XVI 32, 13', XVI 58 iii 2', XVIII 6 i 8', L 6+ iii 54, 55
	SIxSÁ-*ta-ri*		KBo II 2 ii 32 ([-*ta*])
	SIxSÁ-*at*	3.sg.pret. MP	KBo II 2 i 5, 30, ii 20, 21, 23, 30, 50, iii 10, 31, iv 22, KBo II 6+ i 31', iii 31, 42, iv 23, KBo IX 151, 3' (S]Á), 6', KBo XVI 98 i 2 (-]*at*),

			10, 18, KBo XXIII 114 obv. 12, 21, VIII 27 (+) iv 2', XVI 32, 15', 18', 20', 28' ([SI]), XVI 46 i 9', 10', 18', iii 1, iv 13, XVI 58 ii 9, XXII 13, 2', 8' (SI[x), 9' (xS[Á), XXII 35 ii 8', 12', 14 (-]*at*), XLIX 93, 15 (S[I), L 6+ ii 24'(?), 31', 33' (-*a*]*t*), 35', 48,' 50', 51', 55' (S]I), 57', iii 7 (-*a*[*t*), 16, 24, 28, 31, 32, 33, 35, 37, 39, 47, L 87 obv. 8', rev. 7' (xS[Á), 12', 13'
	SIxSÁ-*ta-at*		KBo XXIII 114 obv. 7
	SIxSÁ-*du*	3.sg.imp.	XLIX 2 i 9' (-*d*]*u*?)
	SIxSÁ-*an-du*	imp. 3.pl.	KBo II 6+ i 25', ii 3 (-*a*]*n*-), iii 54, iv 10, 17, KBo XVI 98 i 13, ii 18, XVI 46 i 11', iv 2, 6, XVI 58 ii 1 (-*d*[*u*), 14 (-]*du*?), XLIX 49 ii 16'
	SIxSÁ-kit_9-*ta-ri*	3.sg.pres. MP -*ške*-	XXII 13, 3' (-*r*[*i*)
SIG$_4$	"brick"		
	SIG$_4$		XLIX 49 ii 10'?
SIG$_5$	"favorable, good"	Hitt. *aššu*-, *lazzi*-	
	SIG$_5$		KBo II 2 i 17, 40, ii 53, iii 8, 29, KBo II 6+ i 3', 18', 24', 41', 43',

			ii 2 (SI[G$_5$), 15, 22 (S]IG$_5$), 28, 35, iii 10, 15, 29, 35, 40, 53 (SI[G$_5$), iv 2, 4, 9, KBo IX 151, 4', KBo XVI 98 i 8 (S[IG$_5$), 30 (S]IG$_5$), ii 1 (S[IG$_5$), 8, iii 2', 5', 6', 11' (SI]G$_5$), iv 26'', KBo XXIII 114 obv. 10, 16, 20, 24, VI 9+ ii 11 (S[IG$_5$), iii 15', XVI 58 iii 13', XVIII 6 i 2', 16', iv 12, XXII 13, 1', XLIX 49 ii 5', L 6+ ii 34', 47', iii 15, 22, 28, 39, 62, 65 (S[IG$_5$)
	SIG$_5$-*in*	nom.-acc.sg. n.(?)	VI 9+ ii 5 (-]*in*), XVI 20, 5', 13'
	SIG$_5$-*u-i*	dat.-loc.sg.	KBo II 6+ i 45', iii 15, 39, KBo XVI 98 iv 24'', XVI 58 iii 13', L 77+ r.col. 3' (S[IG$_5$)
	SIG$_5$-*za*	abl.	KBo II 6+ iv 18, 19, 21, KBo XVI 98 i 14, 17, ii 18, 19 (S]IG$_5$-), XVI 46 i 6', 8', 11', 13', 14', 17', iv 7, 8, 9, XVI 58 ii 2 ([-*za*]), 4 (]-*za*), 7 ([-*za*]), XLIX 49 ii 17', 18', 19', 20' (-[*z*]*a*)
SIG$_5$	"to be favorable"	Hitt. *lazzii̯a-*	
	SIG$_5$-*ru*	imp. 3.sg.	KBo II 2 i 4, 15,

19, 56, ii 2, 14, 16, 41, 49, iii 1, 8, 16, 28, 38, iv 5, 15, 29, 38, KBo II 6+ i 2', 4', 16', 20', 40', 42', 44', ii 21 (S]IG$_5$), 26, 30, 45, 54, iii 11, 23, 24, 34, 36, 50, 52 (SI[G$_5$), iv 1, 3, 5, KBo XVI 98 ii 6 ([-*ru*), iii 10' (-*r*]*u*), iv 23" (SI]G$_5$-), KBo XXIII 114 obv. 14, 19, 24 (S]IG$_5$-), 29 (S[IG$_5$-), VI 9+ ii 5, 18, iii 11', XVI 16 obv. 6', 12', 16' (SI]G$_5$-), 22', 31', rev. 1, 10, 17, 22 (SI[G$_5$-), left edge 3, XVI 20, 5', 13', XVI 58 iii 8', XLIX 49 ii 3', 7', L 77+ r.col. 9' (-*r*[*u*)

SISKUR "offering, ritual"

SISKUR KBo II 2 iv 4, KBo II 6+ iii 20, 21, 30, 31, 32, KBo XVI 98 ii 14, iii 13', 14', VIII 27 (+) iv 11', XVI 16 rev. 2, 23, XVI 32, 9', 14' (w. Glossenkeil!), 17', 19', 23', XVI 46 iv 14, XXII 35 ii 3', iii 7', 11', XLIX 49 ii 13', XLIX 93, 9, L 6+ iii 30, 53, 63, L 87 rev.

			6', 11', LII 92 iv 2' (SISK]UR)
	SISKUR-*aš*	gen.sg.	KBo XVI 98 iii 14', XVI 16 rev. 1
SU	"intestines, exta"		
	SU.ḪI.A	Sum. pl.	L 6+ iii 45?
	SU.MEŠ		KBo II 2 i 4, KBo II 6+ i 16', 17', 19', 42' (2x), ii 26, 27, 28, iii 23, iv 3 (2x), KBo XXIII 114 obv. 2, 4, 9 (S[U.), 10 (2x), 15, 17, 19 (.ME]Š), 19, 20, 22, 28, 29, XVI 16 obv. 6', 11', 12', 15', 16', 21', 22', 31', rev. 1 (2x), 2, 9, 10, 16, 17, 21, 22, left edge 1, 3, XVI 58 ii 10, L 87 obv. 6' (.ME[Š)
SUD	"to pull"	Hitt. *ḫuittii̯a-*	
	SUD-*i̯a-ši*	2.sg.pres.	KBo II 6+ i 40', iii 49, 66 (all w. EGIR-*pa*)
	SUD-*i̯a-zi*	3.sg.pres.	L 6+ ii 46' (EGIR-*pa*), iii 61 (-*z*[*i*)
	SUD-*u-e-ni*	1.pl.pres.	L 6+ iii 57 (EGIR-*pa*)
	SUD-*an-zi*	3.pl.pres.	XXII 35 iii 5', 8', XLIX 49 ii 10'
	SUD-*at*	3.sg.pret.	KBo II 6+ ii 37 (EGIR-*pa*)
SUD-*li*	"?"	(Hurrian oracle term)	
	SUD-li_{12}		KBo II 2 i 37, KBo II 6+ i 24', ii 2, iii 29
SUM	"to give"	Hitt. *pai-/pii̯a-*	
	SUM-*an-zi*	3.pl.pres.	KBo II 2 ii 34, iv 1, 4, 9, KBo II 6+

			i 36', iii 46, XVI 32, 25', 30' (*par*]*ā*), iii 62, XXII 35 iii 12', 15', L 6+ ii 1' (-*z*]*i*), iii 15, L 87 rev. 6', 11'
	SUM-*u-en*	1.pl.pret.	XVI 16 rev. 20
	SUM-*ir*	3.pl.pret.	KBo II 2 i 50, XLIX 49 ii 8'
	SUM-*an*	part. nom.-acc.sg.n.	KBo II 6+ ii 57, iii 1, VI 9+ iii 15' (SU]M-), L 6+ ii 54' (-[*an, parā*)
	SUM-*an-te-eš*	part. nom.pl.c.	KBo II 6+ i 5', 10', 22', ii 1, iii 40, iv 9
	SUM-*an-ta-aš*	part. gen.pl.	L 6+ iii 23 (*parā*)
	SUM-*an-na-aš*	verbal noun gen.sg.	KBo II 2 iv 17 (-*a*[*n*-), 22, 23, 27, 34
ŠÀ	"in (the middle of)"	adv., preverb, Hitt. *anda*	
	ŠÀ		KBo II 2 i 53, L 6+ iii 9
		Š. *pai-* "to go"	XVIII 6 iv 10, XLIX 2 i 24' (Š]À)
		Š. *u̯emii̯a-*	KBo II 2 i 13
		nominal sentence	KBo II 2 i 1, 6, L 87 obv. 3', 5'
ŠÀ	"heart"	Hitt. *kir*/*kard*(*i*)-	
	ŠÀ		XVI 16 obv. 15'
	ŠÀ-*za*	abl.	KBo II 6+ iii 28
ŠÀ *DIR*	"coils"		
	ŠÀ *DIR*		KBo II 2 ii 53, iii 9, iv 17, 33, KBo II 6+ i 18', 43', ii 28, iv 4, KBo XVI 98 i 8, ii 8, iii 17' ([*DIR*), KBo XXIII 114 obv. 10, 13, 16, 20 (Š]À), 24, 32 ([*DIR*), XLIX 49

			ii 5’
ŠU	“hand”	Akkad. *QĀTU(M)*	
	ŠU-*TI*	Akkad. obl.pl.(?)	KBo XXIII 114 obv. 28, XVI 16 obv. 11’, left edge 2
^{GIŠ}ŠÚ.A-*ḫi*, n.	“chair”	Hurrian/Hitt. *kišḫi(t)-*	
	^{GIŠ}ŠÚ.A-*ḫi*	nom.-acc.sg.	KBo II 2 ii 14, 37 (<.A>-), iii 1, 23, KBo XVI 98 i 9 (.]A-), iii 17’, KBo XXIII 114 obv. 14, XVI 16 obv. 3’, 21’
^{MUNUS}ŠU.GI	“Old Woman”		
	^{MUNUS}ŠU.GI		KBo II 2 i 9, 18, 26, 48, ii 1, 15, 20, KBo II 6+ i 9’, 20’, 44’, ii 30, iii 11, 24, 36, iv 5, VI 9+ ii 7 (Š[U.), 19 (.G]I), XVIII 36, 10’, 18’, 22’, XXII 12, 5’, XXII 13, 6’ (Š]U.), XXII 35 ii 8’, L 6+ ii 34’ (Š]U), 46’, iii 6, 45 (.G]I), L 87 rev. 1’ (.G[I), LII 92 i 1’ ($^{\text{MU[NUS?}}$), 6’ ($^{\text{MUNUS!}}$Š[U)
ŠUB	“defeat”	Akkad. *MIQTU(M)*	
	ŠUB-*TI*	Akkad. obl.pl.	VIII 27 (+) left edge b 4
TA	“from, by, through”		
	TA		XLIX 2 i 17 (T]A)
TI(*-ant-*)	“living, alive”	Hitt. *ḫuišu̯ant-*	
	TI		KBo IX 151, 7’ (?), L 6+ ii 49’, 57’

	TI-*za*	nom.sg.c.	XVI 32, 16', 22'
	TI-*an-za*		KBo II 6+ i 7' (TI]-), ii 38, 44, 51, iii 5, VI 9+ ii 3
	TI-*an-ta-aš*	gen.sg.	KBo II 6+ ii 38
	TI-*an-da-aš*		KBo II 6+ ii 43, 50, iii 4, 42
TI-*tar*, n.	"life"	Hitt. *ḫuišu̯atar*	
	TI-*tar*	nom.-acc.sg.	KBo II 6+ iii 1, 15, iv 7, KBo XVI 98 iv 25", VI 9+ ii 3, 20 (T[I-), XVI 20, 15', XVI 58 iii 10', XVIII 36, 8' (TI[-)
	TI-*an-ni*	dat.-loc.sg.	XVIII 6 iv 3, XLIX 2 i 15'
TI$_8^{\text{MUŠEN}}$	"eagle"		
	TI$_8^{\text{MUŠEN}}$		KBo II 6+ iii 55, iv 12, 18, 22, KBo XVI 98 i 15, ii 18, XVI 46 i 6', 14', iv 4, 8, 9, XVI 58 ii 3
TÚG	"clothes, clothing"		
	TÚG.ḪI.A	Sum.pl.	XVI 16 obv. 28'
TUKU.TUKU (-*a*)*tt*-, c.	"anger, wrath"	Hitt. *kartimmii̯att-*	
	TUKU.TUKU-*az*	nom.sg.	KBo XVI 98 iii 3'
	TUKU.TUKU-*ti*	dat.-loc.sg.	L 6+ ii 50', iii 24 (-*t*]*i*)
	TUKU.TUKU-*at-ti*		L 87 obv. 8'
TUKU.TUKU-*nu*(*u̯*)*ant-*	"made angry"	Hitt. *kartimmii̯a-nuu̯ant-*	
	TUKU.TUKU-*nu-an-za*	nom.sg.c.	KBo II 6+ ii 46, 52
TUKU(.TUKU)-*u*(*u̯*)*ant-*	"angry"	Hitt. *kartimmii̯a-uu̯ant-*	
	TUKU-*u-an-za*	nom.sg.c.	XVI 16 obv. 30', rev. 9, 16, 21, left edge 1

	TUKU.TUKU-*u-an-za*		KBo II 6+ i 1 (-]*u*-), 11', 14', 16', ii 54, iii 6, 7, 9, 18, KBo IX 151, 1' (-<*an*->), KBo XXIII 114 obv. 23 (.T[UKU-), 28, 29, VIII 27 (+) iv 9', XVI 16 obv. 20', XVI 46 i 5', XXII 35 ii 11' (-<*an*->)
	TUKU.TUKU-*u-u̯a-an-za*		L 87 obv. 3' (-*u*[-), 5' (TU[KU.), 6'
	TUK[U.TUKU ?		XLIX 93, 19
^{GIŠ}TUKUL	"oracle type"		
	^{GIŠ}TUKUL		KBo IX 151, 4', VIII 27 (+) iv 7', L 6+ iii 15 ([TUKUL]), 22, 29 (TU[KUL), 39, 62, 65
	"weapon"		
	^{GIŠ}TUKUL		KBo II 2 iv 31, KBo II 6+ i 18', ii 29, KBo XVI 98 ii 7 (^{GIŠ}[), 7, KBo XXIII 114 obv. 19
	^{GIŠ}TUKUL-*an-za*	Luwian acc.pl.	KBo XVI 98 ii 4
TUR	"small"		
	TUR		KBo II 2 i 10, 28, KBo II 6+ iii 14, 38, VI 9+ ii 23, XVI 20, 8'
TUŠ	"to sit down"	Hitt. *eš-/aš-* (dep.)	
	TUŠ-*at*	3.sg.pret.	XVI 46 i 14' (=*za*)
UD.KAM	"day"	Hitt. *šiu̯att-*, c., Akkad. *ŪMU*(*M*)	

	UD.KAM		KBo II 2 i 53, VIII 27 (+) i 20’
	UD.KAM-*MI*	Akkad. gen.sg.	L 6+ iii 11
	UD.KAM-*aš*	dat.-loc.pl.	KBo II 2 i 55
	UD.KAM.ḪI.A	Sum.pl.	KBo II 2 i 42, XVIII 6 i 13’
UD. ... .KAM	“(on) the ...-th day”		
	UD.2.KAM		KBo II 6+ i 22’, ii 1, 32, 57, iii 13, 26, 38, iv 7, KBo XVI 98 ii 30 (.K[AM), iv 18” (.]KAM), 24”, XVI 20, 16’, L 77+ r.col. 11’ (U[D-), L 87 rev. 2’
	UD.3.KAM		KBo II 6+ i 24’, ii 2, 34, iii 1, 14, 27, 39, iv 8, KBo XVI 98 iv 19” (.]3?.), 25”, VI 9+ ii 10 (.K[AM), 22, iii 14’, XVI 20, 17’, XVI 58 iii 11’, L 77+ r.col. 2’ (.K[AM), L 87 rev. 3’
UDU	“sheep”	(Luwian *ḫau̯i-*, c.?)	
	UDU		XVI 16 obv. 14’
	UDU-*iš*	nom.sg.c.	VI 9+ ii 5, 6, 18
	UDU.ḪI.A	Sum.pl.	XVI 16 obv. 19’
UGU	“up, above”		
	UGU	=*kan* U. *ar-* (act.)	KBo XVI 98 ii 11
		U. *ašešanu-*	VIII 27 (+) iv 5’
		U. *auš-*	KBo II 6+ i 19’
		=*kan* U. *pai-* “to go”	XVI 16 rev. 18
		=*kan* UGU *peda-*	XVI 32, 8’
		=*kan* U. *u̯u̯a-*	XVI 32, 10’,

		⸗*kan* EGIR U. *uu̯a-*	KBo II 6+ iv 19, 21, KBo XVI 98 i 14, 17, ii 18, XVI 46 i 6' (U[GU), 8', 11', 13', 17', iv 9, 11 (UG[U), XVI 58 ii 7, XLIX 49 ii 17', 18', 19', 20'
		[verb lost]	XXII 12, 1 (U[GU)
UKU.UŠ	"heavily armed"		
	(ÉRIN.MEŠ) UKU.UŠ		KBo XVI 98 i 1
UN	"human being, man"	Hitt. *antuḫša-*, c.	
	UN-*aš*	nom.sg.	XVI 32, 16', 21', XVIII 36, 17'
	UN-*an*	acc.sg.	L 5 r.col. 4' (U]N-), L 6+ iii 8
UR.GI$_7$	"dog"		
	UR.GI$_7$-*aš*	nom.sg.c.	XVI 16 rev. 18
URU	"city, settlement"	Hitt. *ḫappir(i̯i̯)a-*, c., Akkad. *ĀLU(M)*	
	URU-*an*	acc.sg.	XVI 32, 24'
	URU-*LUM*	Akkad. nom.sg.	XVI 32, 2', 29' (-*L*[*UM*)
	URU.DIDLI.ḪI.A	Sum.pl.	XVI 32, 1', 6', L 6+ iii 23 (.[DI]DLI), 25
	URU [		XVI 32, 3'
ÚŠ-*an*, n.	"death, destruction"	Hitt. *ḫenkan*	
	ÚŠ-*an*	nom.-acc.sg.	KBo XVI 98 i 6, VIII 27(+) left edge b 4
ZA.ḪUM	(a container)		
	ZA.ḪUM		KBo XXIII 114 obv. 27
ZAG	"right"	Hitt. *kunna-*	
	ZAG-*aš*	nom.sg.	KBo II 6+ i 18', KBo XVI 98 ii 7 (Z]AG-), 7

	ZAG-*na-aš*		KBo II 2 iii 17, KBo XVI 98 iii 12' (-*a*[*š*])
	ZAG-*za*	abl.	KBo II 2 ii 49, iv 30, 31, 38, KBo II 6+ ii 32, iii 23, 25, 38, KBo XVI 98 ii 9 (ZAG[-), KBo XXIII 114 obv. 17, 22, XVI 16 obv. 16', 31', rev. 16
	ZAG-x[		L 87 obv. 3'
	ZAG[		KBo XXIII 114 obv. 19
ZAG-*ešš*-	"to become right, favorable"		
	ZAG-*eš-zi*	3.sg.pres.	XVI 46 iii 4 (-*z*[*i*])
ZAG-*tar*, n.	"rightness"	Hitt. *kunnatar*	
	ZAG-*tar*	nom.-acc.sg.	KBo II 2 i 35, KBo II 6+ i 22', ii 31, iii 1, 25, 37, 50 (-[*t*]*ar*), iv 6, KBo XVI 98 iv 20", 25", VI 9+ ii 8 (-[*tar*]), 21, iii 11' (-*t*[*ar*]), 13' (ZA]G-), XVI 20, 16', XVI 58 iii 8', L 77+ r.col. 10', L 87 obv. 2'
^{GIŠ}ZAG.GAR.RA	"altar"		
	^{GIŠ}ZAG.GAR.RA		KBo II 2 ii 52
ZÁLAG.GA	"light"	Hitt. *lalukkima*- (?), c.	
	ZÁLAG.GA-*an*	acc.sg.	XVI 20, 18'
ZI	"soul, person, seat of life"	Hitt. *ištanza*(*n*)-, c.	
	ZI-*za*	nom.sg.	XVI 32, 17'
	ZI-*an*	acc.sg.	KBo II 2 i 19, 27, KBo II 6+ ii 47 (Z]I), iii 12, 14, iv 7, KBo XVI 98 iv 19" (Z[I-), VI

			9+ ii 20, XVI 58 iii 10', XXII 35 ii 7', XLIX 93, 14, L 87 obv. 10'
	ZI-*ni*	dat.-loc.sg.	KBo II 6+ ii 33, iii 2

Fragmentary and acephalous

x x MEŠ			XVI 32, 3' (?; s. footnote there), XVI 58 ii 13
x MEŠ			L 6+ iii 25

D. *Akkadograms*

ABU(*M*)	"father"		
	A-BI	st.constr.	XVI 16 rev. 5, XVI 32, 27', XXII 35 ii 2' (*-B*]*I*), iii 8', 9', XLIX 93, 8, L 6+ iii 19, 35, 37
ADAMMU(*M*)	"blood"		
	A-DAM-MA	acc.sg.	KBo II 6+ i 23', ii 34, 56 ([*-M*]*A*), L 77+ r.col. 10' (*-D*[*AM-*)
	A-TA-MA		KBo II 6+ iii 25
ĀLU(*M*)	"city"	see Sum. URU	
AMĀRU(*M*)	"to see"		
	NI-MUR	1.pl.pret. G	KBo II 6+ iv 11, XVI 46 i 6', 11', 12', 14', 17', iv 2, 3, 4, 6, 8, 9, 10, 11, 15, 16, 17, 18, XVI 58 ii 2
ANA	"for, to"	prep.	
	A-NA		KBo II 2 i 5, 23, 30, 53, ii 10, 18, 29, 33, iii 11, 15, 31, iv 11, KBo II 6+ i 5', 6'

			(-*N*]*A*), 13’ (2x), 22’, 32’, 36’, 39’, ii 32 (-*N*]*A*), 41, iii 1, 14, 25, 37, 40, 43, 46, 48, 62 (2x), 65, KBo XVI 98 i 3, ii 4, 14, 16, iii 13’, 15’, VI 9+ ii 2’, 4 (-*N*]*A*), 17, 23, VIII 27 (+) i 18’, iv 2’, 6’ (2x), left edge b 2, XVI 16 obv. 4’, 9’, rev. 12, 13, 15, 20, XVI 20, 4’, 9’, 11’, 12’, XVI 32, 3’, 7’, 14’ (2x), 19’ (2x), 24’, 25’, 27’, 28’ (-*N*[*A*), XVI 46 ii 3’, XVI 58 iii 6’, XVIII 6 i 7’, 13’, 21’, ii 4’, 5’, 6’, 8’ (-*N*]*A*), iv 4, 5, 7, XVIII 36, 8’, 9’, 14’, 15’, 16’, 19’, 20’, XXII 12, 3’, XXII 13, 4’, XXII 35 ii 11’, 13’, iii 6’, 12’, 13’, XLIX 2 iii 4’, 6’ (-*N*]*A*), XLIX 49 ii 13’, XLIX 93, 18 (-*N*[*A*), L 6+ ii 29’ (-*N*]*A*), 32’, 38’, 49’, 51’, iii 1, 7, 16, 40, 53 (2x), 56, 64, L 77+ r.col. 4’, 8’, L 87 rev. 6’, 11’, LII 92 i 2’ (-*N*]*A*?), 10/v, 5’
ANNÛ(M)	“this”	dem.pron.	
	AN-NU-Ú-TI	obl.pl.	L 87 obv. 2’

AŠRU(*M*)	"place, spot"		
	AŠ-RI$^{\text{ḪI.A}}$	obl.pl.	KBo II 6+ i 33', VIII 27 (+) iv 3' (-*R*]*I*), XXII 35 iii [4'], L 6+ ii 39', iii 4, 49
AŠŠUM	"because of, for the sake of"	prep.	
	AŠ-ŠUM		XVIII 6 i 5' (-*Š*]*UM* or *Š*]*UM* "name"?)
BIBRÛ	"rhyton"		
	BI-IB-RI$^{\text{ḪI.A}}$	obl.pl.	XVI 16 obv. 19'
ḪARRĀNU(*M*)	"road"	see Sum. KASKAL	
ḪURRI	"*ḪURRI* bird"	see MUŠEN *ḪURRI*	
IDÛ(*M*)	"to know"		
	I-DE	3.sg.pret.m. G	KBo II 2 iv 24, 28
IKRIBU(*M*)	"vow"		
	IK-RI-BU	nom.sg.	KBo II 2 iii 33
	IK-RI-BI$^{\text{ḪI.A}}$	obl.pl.	KBo II 2 iii 11, 15, 31, 39, 42, 45 (-*B*[*I*), iv 7
IKRUB	see *KARĀBU*(*M*)		
IKŠUD	see *KAŠĀDU*(*M*)		
INA	"in(to), to"	prep.	
	I-NA		KBo XVI 98 ii 14, 30, iv 24" ([-*N*]*A*), 25", VI 9+ ii 2 (-*N*]*A*), iii 12', 14' (-*N*]*A*), XVI 16 obv. 17', 27', 29', rev. 6, 7, XVI 20, 3', 11', 16', 17', XVI 32, 29', XVI 58 iii 11', XVIII 6 iv 2, L 87 rev. 8', LII 92 iv 7'

	INA		KBo II 2 ii 13, KBo II 6+ i 22', 24', ii 1, 2, 32, 34, 57, iii 1, 13, 14, 26, 27, 38, 39, iv 7, 8, VI 9+ ii 10, 22, L 77+ r.col. 2', L 87 rev. 2' (*IN*]*A*), 3' (*I*]*NA*)
IŠTU	"out (of), by, with"	prep.	
	IŠ-TU		KBo II 2 i 9, 18, 26, 34, 48, ii 1, 15, 20, KBo II 6+ i 9' ([*I*]*Š*-), 20', 25', 44', ii 3 (-*T*]*U*), 30, 42, 49, 56, iii 3, 11, 16, 24, 36, 52, 54, iv 5, 8, 10, KBo XVI 98 ii 11, 28, VIII 27 (+) i 10' (-*T*[*U*), 12' (-*T*[*U*), 17' (-*T*[*U*), iv 7', XVI 16 obv. 19', 20', rev. 5, 13, XVI 20, 13', XVI 32, 2', XVIII 36, 10' (-*T*]*U*), 17', 18' (2x), XXII 12, 3' (*I*[*Š*-), 5', XXII 13, 7' (*I*]*Š*-*T*[*U*), XXII 35 ii 8', 9' ([*I*]*Š*-), 10', XLIX 2 i 9', XLIX 93, 14 (*I*[*Š*-), 16, L 6+ ii 33', 41', 46', iii 6, 15, 22 (-*T*]*U*), 39, 45, 48 ([*I*]*Š*-), 51, 62, L 87 obv. 7', rev. 13' (*I*]*Š*-), LII 92 i 1' (-]*TU*), 6', 10/v,

			6' (-*T*[*U*])
ITTI	"(together) with"	prep.	
	IT-TI		KBo II 6+ iii 30, 31, 33, XVI 16 obv. 26', L 6+ iii 63
KARĀBU(*M*)	"to (make a) vow"		
	IK-RU-UB	3.sg.pret.m. G	KBo XVI 98 i 4
KAŠĀDU(*M*)	"to find, encounter"		
	IK-ŠU-UD	3.sg.pret.m. G	KBo II 6+ iv 13, KBo XVI 98 iv 4, XVI 58 ii 5 (-*Š*]*U*)
-*MA*	(quotative particle)		
	-*MA*		XVI 16 obv. 8'
MAḪIṢ	"beaten, damaged"	see Sum. RA^{IṢ}	
MAMĪTU(*M*)	"oath"		
	MA-ME-TUM	nom.sg.	XVI 32, 27', 28'
	MA-ME-TE^{MEŠ}	obl.pl.	KBo XVI 98 iv 21"
MIQTU(*M*)	"defeat"	see Sum. ŠUB	
NIMUR	see *AMĀRU*(*M*)		
PARĪSU(*M*)	(measure of volume)		
	(abbr.) *PA*		XVI 16 rev. 3
^{DUG}*PURSĪTU*(*M*)	"bowl"		
	^{DUG}*PUR-SÍ-TUM*	nom.sg.	XVI 16 rev. 5
QĀTAMMA	"so, likewise"	adv.	
	QA-TAM-MA		KBo II 2 i 9, 18, 26, 34, 48, ii 1 ([*T*]*AM*-), 15, KBo II 6+ i 4' (*Q*]*A*-), 9', 20', 25', 37', 44', ii 30 (*Q*]*A*-), 42, 49, iii 3, 11, 16, 24, 36, 52, 54, 63, iv

			5, 10, KBo XVI 98 iv 8' (*-T*]*AM-*), VI 9+ ii 7, 19, XVI 58 ii 1 (<*-TAM*>), 10, XVIII 6 i 11', 12', XXII 35 ii 4', XLIX 2 i 4', XLIX 49 ii 7', L 5 r.col. 6' (*-TAM*[-), 7', L 6+ ii 38', 42', iii 3, 42 (*Q*]*A-*), L 87 rev. 1' (*-T*]*AM-*), 10'
QĀTU(*M*)	see Sum. ŠU		
QATÛ(*M*)	"finished"		
	QA-TI	stative	KBo II 6+ iv 26
ŠA	"of"	prep. marking genitive relation	
	ŠA		KBo II 2 ii 51, 54, KBo II 6+ i 10', 12', 18', 21', 35', ii 1, 34, 37, 38, 43, 50, 56, iii 4, 25, 32, 39, 47, 50, iv 6, 8, 24 (2x), KBo XVI 98 ii 7, iv 22" (*Š*]*A*), KBo XXIII 114 obv. 7, 9, 12 (2x), 14, 15, 17, 18 (2x), 21, 26 (2x), VI 9+ ii 22, XVI 16 obv. 25', rev. 11, 14, 19, XVI 32, 1', 8', XVI 46 i 10', iv 1, 6, 13, L 6+ iii 58, 60, 65, L 77+ r.col. 10' (*Š*]*A*), L 87 rev. 4'
ŠAMÛ(*M*)	"heaven"	see Sum. AN	

ŠANGÛTU(M)	"priesthood"	see Sum. ^{LÚ}SANGA-*UTTU(M)*	
ŠARRŪTU(M)	"kingship"	see Sum. LUGAL-*UTTU(M)*	
-ŠU	"his, her"	encl. poss. pron. 3.sg.	
	-ŠU		KBo II 6+ i 11', 12', 36', ii 55, iii 6, VI 9+ ii 17, VIII 27 (+) iv 6', XVI 46 i 15', XXII 35 iii 15', XLIX 93, 5, L 6+ iii 33, LII 92 iv 6'
	-ŠÚ		see EGIR-*ŠÚ* and 3/4-*ŠÚ*
ŠUMU(M)	"name"		
	ŠUM	st.constr.	XVIII 6 i 5' (*Š*]*UM* or *AŠ-Š*]*UM*?), 17', ii 3', iv 9, XLIX 2 i 9', 19', ii 10', iii 7'
ŠUNU	"they"	pers. pron. 3.pl.m.	
	ŠU-NU		XVI 16 obv. 8
^{LÚ}*ṬĒMU(M)*	"messenger, envoy"		
	^{LÚ}*ṬE-MU*	nom.sg.	L 6+ iii 56
TĪRĀNU(M)	"coils"		
	(abbr.) *TE*^{MEŠ}		KBo XVI 98 i 7 ($^{\text{M[EŠ}}$), ii 1 (*T*[*E*), 2 ($^{\text{M[EŠ}}$), 6, 7, 9, iii 8', 11' (*T*[*E*), 11', 14', 16' (2x), 17', KBo XXIII 114 obv. 14, XLIX 49 ii 3 (*T*]*E*)
	(abbr.) *TE*$^{\text{ME.EŠ}}$		KBo II 2 ii 14, 27, 41, 49, 52, iii 1, 3, 8, 12, 16,

			22, 28, 38, iv 5, 15, 29, 38
Ù	"and"	conj.	
	Ù		KBo II 6+ iv 24
UL	"not, no(ne)"	adv. of negation	
	UL		KBo II 2 i 3, XVI 16 obv. 13', 19', rev. 12, XVI 32, 15' (2x), 17', 18', 20' (2x), 22', 23' (*U*[*L*), L 6+ ii 45', iii 43
	Ú-UL		KBo II 2 i 14, ii 12, 41, 48, iii 35, iv 12, KBo II 6+ i 15', 39', ii 53, iii 8, 20, 22, 49, 66, iv 26, KBo XVI 98 i 6, ii 15, KBo XXIII 114 obv. 27, 31, VI 9+ ii 17, VIII 27 (+) iv 10', 11', 12', XVI 16 obv. 14', 18', 28' (2x), XVI 58 ii 11, iii 7', XVIII 6 i 14' ([-*UL*), XVIII 36, 5', 16', 17' (-*U*[*L*), 21', XXII 12, 4, XXII 13, 5', XLIX 2 i 8', L 6+ iii 44, 47 (-*U*]*L*), 55 (2x), 56, 57, 61, 65 (*U*]*L*), L 87 obv. 6' (-*U*[*L*), LII 92 iv 9' (-[*UL*?)
UMMA	"thus, as follows"	adv.	
	UM-MA		KBo II 6+ iii 59, iv 16, 23, KBo XVI 98 ii 22, XVI 16 obv. 8, XVI 46 i 9', 18' ([-*M*]*A*), ii 10', iv

			5, 12
ŪMU(*M*)	"day"	see Sum. UD.KAM	
UPNU(*M*)	"fist(ful)"		
	UP-NI	gen.sg.	XVI 16 rev. 3

E. *Personal names*

Armatarḫunta	see ^{d}*SÎN*-^{d}U		
Armaziti	see GE$_6$-LÚ		
GAL-^{d}U	^{m}GAL-^{d}U		XVI 32, 24'
GE$_6$-LÚ	^{m}GE$_6$-LÚ		KBo II 6+ iv 17, 23
Ḫalpaziti	^{m}*Ḫal-pa*-LÚ		XXII 35 iii 1' (*Ḫa*]*l*-), XVI 58 iii 6'
	^{m}*Ḫal-pa*-LÚ-*iš*	nom.	XXII 35 iii 9', LII 92 iv 3' (-*p*]*a*-)
^{fd}*IŠTAR-atti*	^{fd}*IŠTAR-ti*	abs.	XVI 46 iv 6, 13
	^{fd}*IŠTAR-at-ti*		KBo II 6+ ii 37, 38, 43, 50, iii 4, 32, 37, 42, 43, 47, 48, 64, 65, iv 24, VIII 27 (+) iv 1' (^{f}]), [2']
	^{fd}*IŠTAR-at-ti-iš*	nom.	KBo II 6+ iii 17, 30, VIII 27 (+) iv 8'
	^{fd}*IŠTAR*[-		L 87 rev. 4'
Katapaili	^{m}*Ka-ta-pa*-DINGIR-*LIM*		KBo II 2 iv 24, 28
	^{m}*Ka-ta-pa*-DINGIR-*LIM-iš*	nom.	XVI 32, 25'
	^{m}*Ka-ta-pa*-DINGIR-*LIM-in*	acc.	XVI 32, 10' (^{m}[), L 6+ ii 11' (-*t*]*a*$^{?}$-)
Kurša-^{d}LAMMA	^{m}*Kur-ša*-^{d}LAMMA		KBo II 6+ iii 59 (L[AMMA), iv 16, XVI 58 ii 9 (-]^{d})
Pii̯ammu	^{m}*Pí-i̯a-am-mu*	abs.	XVI 46 iv 5, 12
Šaušgatti	see ^{d}*IŠTAR-atti*		

^{d}*SÎN*-^{d}U	^{d}*SÎN*-^{d}U		KBo II 6+ i 12', 31', 32', 38', 39', iv 24, XVI 32, 19'
Talmiteššub	see GAL-^{d}U		
^{f}*Danuḫepa*	^{f}*Da-nu-ḫé-pa*	abs.	KBo XXIII 114 obv. 17, 18, XVI 16 rev. 1, L 6+ ii 48', 56' (-*nu*[-), 57' (^{f}[)
	^{f}*Ta-nu-ḫé-pa*	abs.	XVI 32, 1', 4' (-[*pa*)
	^{f}*Da-nu-ḫé-pa-aš*	nom.	KBo IX 151, 5'
	-]*pa-aš* ?		XXII 35 i 4'
^{MUNUS}*tau̯ananna*-	see above in the Hittite section		
Urḫiteššub	^{m}*Úr-ḫi*-^{d}U-*ub*	abs.	KBo XXIII 114 obv. 14, 18, XVI 32, 14', 27' (-[^{d}), 29' (^{m}*Ú*]*r*-), L 6+ ii 28' (]^{d}), iii 32 (*ḫi*]-), 33, 40, 46 (^{m}*Ú*]*r*-[*ḫi*- ...]*up*), 48 (^{d}[U), 56, 58, 60, 63 (*Ú*]*r*-)
	^{m}*Úr-ḫé*-^{d}U-*ub*		KBo XXIII 114 obv. 12 (^{d}[), 21, 23, 25
	^{m}*Úr-ḫi*-^{d}U-*ub-ša-aš*	gen.(?)	XVI 16 rev. 23
^{d}UTU-*ŠI*	^{d}UTU-*ŠI*		KBo II 2 i 1, 3, 5, 12, 23 ([U]TU), 30, 41, 53, 54, ii 10, 18, 29, 30, 39, iii 32, KBo II 6+ i 34', iii 30, 31, 33, KBo XVI 98 ii 3, 11, iii 13', 15', iv 22", KBo XXIII 114 obv. 15, VI 9+ ii 2, 12 (-*Š*]*I*), 14, 16, 24, VIII 27 (+) iv 4' (^{d}[), XVI 16 rev.

			5, XVI 20, 2', 3' (^{d}]), 10', 11', 12' (-*Š*[*I*), XVI 32, 9', 14', 19', 27', XVIII 6 i 7', 13', XVIII 36, 4', 8', 9', 11', 13' (^{d}[), 15', 16' (^{d}[), 20', XXII 12, 1', 3', XXII 13, 4', XXII 35 ii 2', iii 6' (^{d}]), 8', 9', XLIX 49 ii 11', 12', L 6+ ii 16' (-*Š*]*I*), 21', 40', iii 5, 19, 24, 30 (UT]U), 35, 37, 50, 53, 64, L 77+ r.col. 4' (^{d}[), 6' (UTU[), 8', LII 92 i 2'
Zella	^{m}*Ze-el-la*	abs.	XVI 46 i 9', 18', ii 10' (^{m}Z[*e*-)
Fragmentary	^{f}x[		XVI 46 iv 1
	^{m}x[		KBo XVI 98 ii 22

F. *Divine names*

DAG-*ti*	^{d}DAG-*ti*	abs. (*Ḫalmašuitti-*)	KBo II 6+ iii 27, L 77+ r.col. 2' (^{d}])
	^{d}DAG-*ti-iš*	nom.	KBo II 6+ ii 34 ([DA]G)
DINGIR.MAḪ	DINGIR.MAḪ	(*Ḫuu̯aššanna-*)	KBo II 6+ ii 32, iii 26
	DINGIR.MAḪ-*ni*	dat.	KBo II 6+ i 10', ii 1, 35, iii 13, iv 6, 9, KBo XVI 98 iv 19" (MA]Ḫ), VI 9+ ii 9 (DIN]GIR), XVI 58 iii 9', 11' (-*n*]*i*), L 77+ r.col. 11', L 87 rev. 3'

GAŠAN	dGAŠAN		VIII 27 (+) left edge b 2
Ḫepat	d*Ḫé-pát*	abs.	KBo XVI 98 i 3 (URU*Kummanni*), ii 7
Ḫišḫura	d*Ḫi-iš-ḫu-ra-aš*	nom.	XLIX 2 i 8’
	d*Ḫi-iš-ḫu-ra-za*	abl.	LII 92 i 7’
Lelwani	d*Le-el-u̯a-ni*	abs.	KBo XVI 98 i 4 (*Le-*])
Pirwa	d*Pí-ir-u̯a*	abs.	KBo XVI 98 iii 13
Šaumadari	d*Ša-ú*[*-ma-d*]*a-ri*	abs.	KBo XVI 98 ii 4
SÎN	d*SÎN*		VIII 27 (+) left edge b 1, 3
U	dU	(*Tarḫu-/ Tarḫun/nt/nta-*)	KBo II 6+ i 18’, XVIII 6 i 24’ (*piḫammin*), iv 7 (URU*Talmaliu̯a*), XLIX 2 i 21’, iii 4’
	dU*-ni*	dat.	KBo II 6+ iv 8
UTU	dUTU		XVIII 6 i 18’
	dUTU AN*-E*		KBo II 6+ i 5’, 21’, 22’, iii 1, 40, 50
	dUTU URUPÚ*-na*		KBo II 2 ii 23, 29, 31, 33, 34 (d[), 39, 43, 50, 51, 54, iii 2, 6, 10, 13, 30, KBo XVI 98 ii 10, XXII 13, 9’
UTU*-u*	dUTU*-un*	acc.	KBo II 6+ iv 22
Zawalli	d*Za-u̯a-al-li*	abs.	XVI 16 rev. 1
	d*Za-u̯a-al-li-iš*	nom.	KBo XXIII 114 obv. 15, 18 (*-a*]*l-*), 23 (*-a*]*l-*), XVI 46 i 3’, 10’ (2x), iv 1, 13, L 87 rev. 4’
	d*Za-u̯a-al-li-*(*l*)*iš*		KBo XXIII 114 obv. 14 (*-a*]*l-*), XVI 16 rev. 23
	-l]*i-iš*		KBo XXIII 114 obv. 17

	-]*iš*		KBo XXIII 114 obv. 12
	^{d}*Za-u̯a-al-li-i̯a-aš*	dat.pl.	XVI 46 i 4'
	^{d}*Za-u̯a-a*[*l-*		KBo XXIII 114 obv. 1, XVI 46 i 4'
	^{d}*Za-u̯*[*a-*		XVI 46 i 1'
Fragmentary	^{d}x (x x)		XVIII 6 i 16', 18'
	^{d}[		XVI 46 i 2' (or *a*[*n-*?), L 87 obv. 2' (or *an*[-?)

G. *Geographical names*

Araunna	^{URU}*A-ra-u-un-na*	abs.	XVI 16 rev. 6
Arinna	^{URU}PÚ-*na*	abs.	KBo II 2 ii 23, 29, 31, 39, 43, 50, 51 (2x), 54 (<-*na*>), iii 2, 6, 10, 13, 30, KBo XVI 98 ii 10, XXII 13, 9'
Arzawa	KUR *Ar-za-u-u̯a*	abs.	XVI 16 obv. 26'
Ḫalpa	^{URU}*Ḫal-pa*	abs.	XVI 32, 8', XXII 35 iii 13', XLIX 2 i 21' ([*Ḫ*]*al-*), LII 92 iv 7' (*Ḫal*[-)
Ḫatti	^{URU}*Ḫat-ti*	abs.	KBo II 2 ii 13, 54
Išuwa	KU[R $^{U]RU}$*I-šu-u̯*[*a*		XVI 16 obv. 8'
Gaittana	^{URU}*Ga*[*-i*]*t-ta-na*	abs.	KBo XVI 98 ii 3
Kargamiš	KUR *Kar-ga-miš*	abs.	XVI 32, 10'
Kiuta	^{URU}*Ki-i-ú-ta-an*	acc.	XVI 32, 24'
Kummanni	^{URU}*Kum-ma-an-ni*	abs.	KBo XVI 98 i 3
	KUR ^{URU}*Kum-ma-an-ni*		KBo XVI 98 ii 11
Liprašša (?)	^{URU}*Li-i*[*p-*		L 87 rev. 8'
Nerik	^{URU}*Ne-ri-ik-ka*$_4$	abs.	KBo XVI 98 ii 14, 16, XLIX 49 ii 13' (-*i*]*k-*), 15' (-*r*]*i-*)
	KUR ^{URU}*Ne-ri-ik-ka*$_4$		KBo II 2 i 6, 13

	KUR *Ne-ri-ik-ka*$_4$		KBo II 2 i 1
Niya	^{URU}*Ne-i-i̯a*	abs.	XVI 32, 29’
Talmaliya	^{URU}*Tal-ma-li-i̯a*	abs.	XVIII 6 iv 7
Zitḫara	^{URU}*Zi-it-ḫa-ra*	abs.	KBo XXIII 114 obv. 7 ([-*ra*), 9, 12
Fragmentary	-]*ma-na*		KBo XVI 98 iii 13’

H. *Numbers*

$\frac{1}{2}$	$\frac{1}{2}$		KBo XXIII 114 obv. 27, XVI 16 rev. 3, 4 (2x)
1	1		XVI 16 obv. 9’, rev. 3, 4 (2x), XVI 32, 2’ (2x), 3’, 29,
	1-*aš*	nom.	XVI 16 rev. 8, XVI 46 i 4’, XXII 35 iii 10’
	1-*e-da-ni*	dat.-loc.	XXII 35 iii 10’
	1-*EN*	= Akkad. *IŠTĒN*	KBo XXIII 114 obv. 26, 27
2	2		KBo XVI 98 ii 19, 21, XVI 16 rev. 3, 5, XVI 46 i 7’, 16’, ii 7’, iv 15
	2-*ŠU*		KBo II 6+ ii 18
	2-*an*	adv., Hitt. *takšan* “middle; together”	KBo II 6+ iii 57, 58 (-*a*]*n*), iv 13, 19, KBo XVI 98 ii 22, 24, XVI 46 i 16’, iv 3, 7, 9, 16 (2[-), 19, 20, XVI 58 ii 3, XLIX 49 ii 18’
	2-*an*	adv., Hitt. *dān* “twice, a second time”	KBo II 2 ii 46
	see also MU.2.KAM and UD.2.KAM		
3	3		KBo IX 151, 4’, VIII 27 (+) iv 7’,

		L 6+ iii 15, 22, 29, 39, 62, 65
	3-*ŠU*	XVI 58 ii 11
	3-*ŠÚ*	KBo II 2 ii 41
	see also UD.3.KAM	
4	4	XVI 16 rev. 3, 4
	4-*ŠÚ*	L 6+ iii 45?
5	see DUB.5.KAM	KBo II 6+ iv 26
6	see MU.6.KAM	
7	7	XVI 16 rev. 4
8	8	KBo XXIII 114 obv. 13
	see also ITU.8.KAM and MU.8.KAM	
10	10	KBo II 6+ iv 4
11	11	KBo XXIII 114 obv. 16
12	12	KBo II 2 ii 53, iii 9, iv 17, 33, KBo II 6+ i 18', 43', ii 28, KBo XVI 98 ii 8, KBo XXIII 114 obv. 10, 24, XLIX 49 ii 5'
	see also ITU.12.KAM	

INDICES

TEXTS

KUB

TOPICS

PLATES

Plate I: L 6 i–ii 31ff.

Plate II: XVI 32 ii

a

b

Plate III: KUB XXII 35 obverse and reverse.

a

b

c

d

Plate IV: a–b: KUB LII 92 obverse and reverse; c–d: KUB VIII 27 obverse and reverse.

Plate V: KBo II 6 + KUB XVIII 51, upper half of obverse.

Plate VI: KBo II 6, lower half of obverse.

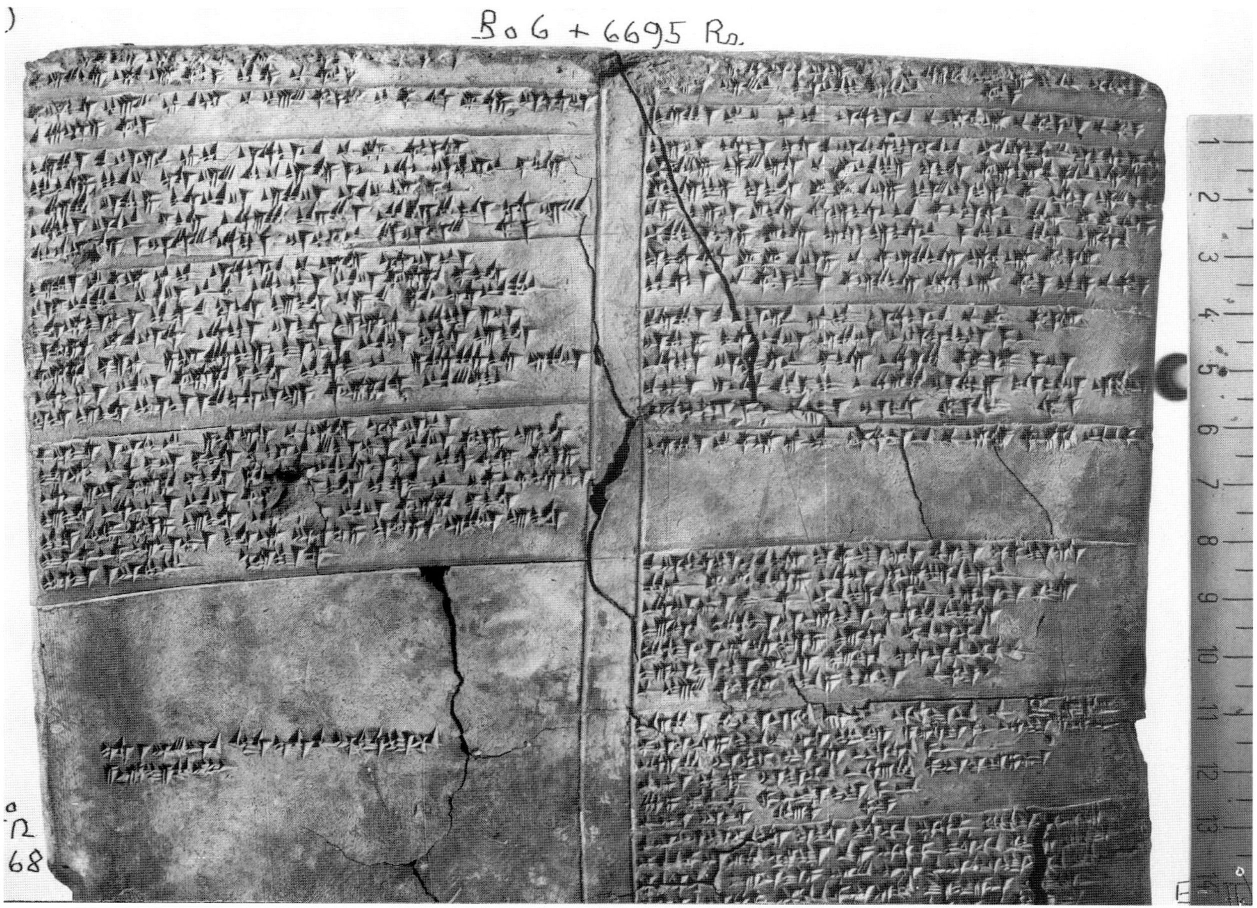

Plate VII: KBo II 6, upper half of reverse.

Plate VIII: KBo II 6, lower half of reverse.